Biotechnology & Biological Frontiers

Biotechnology & Biological Frontiers

Edited by Philip H. Abelson

The American Association for the Advancement of Science

Library of Congress Cataloging in Publication Data
Main entry under title:

Biotechnology & biological frontiers.

Includes index.
1. Biotechnology. 2. Biology—Research. I. Abelson, Philip Hauge. II. Title:
Biotechnology and biological frontiers.
TP248.2.B52   1984   660'.62   84-21655
ISBN 0-87168-308-3
ISBN 0-87168-266-4 (pbk.)

The material in this book has been updated and corrected from the original articles that appeared in *Science*, **219**, 11 February 1983 (Biotechnology) and **222**, 18 November 1983 (Biological Frontiers). *Science* is the official journal of the American Association for the Advancement of Science.

AAAS Publication Number 84-8

Printed in the United States of America.

Copyright 1984 by the
American Association for the Advancement of Science
1515 Massachusetts Avenue, N.W., Washington, D.C. 20005

Contents

I Biotechnology

iv

II Biological Frontiers

Part I
Biotechnology

Biotechnology: An Overview

Philip H. Abelson

Part I of this volume from *Science* is devoted to a broad sampling of the status of a revolution in applied biology. In applications of recombinant DNA and hybridomas, progress has been rapid. As a result, substantial improvements in human and animal health care will occur in the next few years. Human insulin was released for sale in September 1982. Among the other products that have been created, most of which are under clinical or animal test, are a dozen or more subtypes of interferon, human growth hormone, human calcitonin, human albumin, thymosin alpha-1, tissue-type plasminogen activator, porcine and bovine growth hormones, a vaccine for foot and mouth disease, and a bovine leukocyte interferon. Earlier, many of these products, such as interferons, could be obtained only in tiny amounts.

Other areas of applied biology are in earlier phases of development. Protein engineering to produce superior catalysts is doable and is being tackled with vigor. Progress is being made in tissue culture of plants, and ultimately recombinant DNA techniques will be applied in this area. Advances also have been made in industrial fermentations. Microorganisms are being employed to produce antibiotics and an increasing number of specialty chemicals such as amino acids. Ultimately, they will be used in the pro-

duction of large volumes of commodity substances such as oxychemicals.

This potentially rich harvest is the result of wise investments in basic biological research by the National Institutes of Health. Other consequences of NIH support have not been emphasized. Irvine Page has been wont to speak of the chemotactic effect of money. NIH funds combined with the attraction of research opportunities in biomedicine have lured many of the most intelligent and creative scientists into fundamental biology. Many of these people are now key members of the new dynamic bioengineering companies. NIH funds also have created a market for instrumentation and special products used in research. The instrumentation available in this country is superb and is constantly being improved. Companies providing items used in research, such as enzymes, follow trends closely and are quick to supply needed materials, cultures, or animals.

Gene Splicing

A technique that is basic to much of the progress in applied biology is gene splicing. In concept it is simple, but in practice it is complex. A major objective of recombinant DNA techniques is to

1

insert a foreign gene for a desired product into an organism under conditions such that the foreign gene will be expressed more abundantly than the native genes. A favorite organism for this purpose is a mutant of *Escherichia coli* that is unable to synthesize the essential amino acid tryptophan. There are circular forms of DNA (plasmids) that contain a gene for making tryptophan. A foreign gene can be spliced into these plasmids near the tryptophan gene in such a manner that the foreign gene and the tryptophan gene will be expressed simultaneously. Placed in a culture of the mutant *E. coli*, some of these plasmids enter the bacterial cells and, by supplying the needed tryptophan, enable them to survive and multiply. Mechanisms within the *E. coli* are such that a new plasmid may be replicated 20 to 40 times within each bacterial cell. Since tryptophan is in great demand, the gene for it and simultaneously the foreign gene are preferentially expressed.

The tryptophan mutant of *E. coli* is not always the best choice for making recombinant DNA products. Other mutants of the organism may be more convenient, or plasmids of other prokaryotes can be used. But *E. coli* will continue to be used for the synthesis of many proteins. A large body of information and know-how has been accumulated about it, and it has been found to make virtually all the proteins now undergoing clinical tests. Thus, when Genentech decided to seek to prepare a vaccine for rabies, they investigated the possibility of preparing it by recombinant DNA procedures involving *E. coli*. That decision was made despite the fact that the coat protein of the virus contains carbohydrates. *Escherichia coli* could synthesize the protein chain, but not the car-

bohydrates. In chapter 1, Elizabeth Yelverton and her colleagues provide a detailed account of procedures leading to proteins that conform by biochemical and antigenic criteria to rabies glycoprotein.

In addition to its synthetic limitation, *E. coli* has other drawbacks. Mutant forms tend to revert to wild types. The densities to which cultures can be grown are limited. *Escherichia coli* produces an endotoxin. It generally does not secrete proteins into the medium. In contrast, yeasts, which also have plasmids, can be grown to very high densities, are stable with respect to mutation, produce no toxins, and can secrete proteins. In addition, they are eukaryotes and can synthesize glycoproteins. Because of these attractive features, a number of companies have been using yeast for recombinant DNA work. Hitzeman and colleagues have employed *Saccharomyces cerevisiae*. In chapter 2, they describe the procedures that resulted in the secretion of interferon, a desired product.

Discovery of the mechanisms by which genes are turned off or on in higher organisms, such as humans, is one of the major challenges of biology. Liver and skin process the same DNA, but there are controls on its transcription that make the tissues quite different. Delineating these processes would be of transcending importance in fundamental biology. In studying controls on the expression of eukaryote genes, the transcription of simian virus 40 has been used as a model system. Weiher, Konig, and Gruss have identified nucleotide sequences that influence transcriptional activity.

Before recombinant DNA products can be brought to market, they must be subjected to extensive clinical tests. The identity and quality of the product must also be established beyond reasonable doubt. In chapter 4, Johnson describes some of the laboratory procedures employed in providing the chemical information necessary for the Food and Drug Administration to release human insulin for general use.

Monoclonal Antibodies

It is now possible to create long-lived cloned cell lines that produce unique antibodies. The cells have been used to prepare antibodies against many viruses, bacteria, fungi, and parasites. The technique is being employed to produce diagnostic aids, more than a score of which have already been released by the Food and Drug Administration. The cell lines are prepared in vitro by chemically mediated fusion of lymphocytes from immunized mice and a mouse tumor (myeloma) cell line. The hybrid cells have antibody-producing capability from the lymphocyte and ability to grow permanently in culture from the myeloma. Nowinski and colleagues have used the techniques to produce antibodies for diagnosis of some diseases that are sexually transmitted in humans.

Diagnosis and treatment of the various diseases known as cancer is a continuing goal. Monoclonal antibodies have been prepared against forms of cancer. It has been found that some cancer cells are considerably more antigenic than corresponding normal cells—that is, antibodies find more sites to occupy on the cancer cell surfaces than on normal cells. In chapter 6, Vitetta, Uhr, and co-workers describe experiments in which antibodies are used as vehicles to bring a toxic chemical selectively to cancer cells.

Protein Engineering

Given a set of instructions furnished by a gene, organisms can synthesize proteins corresponding to the gene. The template may be obtained from another life form, or it can be an artificial gene. We are now in the beginning phase of exploitation of the ability to engineer proteins. Objectives are to create superior enzymes for use as catalysts in the production of high-value specialty chemicals, to produce biologicals that are superior to natural ones, and to produce enzymes for large-scale use in the chemical industry.

The necessary genes are synthesized by joining nucleotides together. This takes time and effort, but at AMGen a 500-member oligonucleotide for a γ-interferon was made in 2 months by a two-person team. Later it became feasible to modify portions of the interior of this gene, and a variety of artificial γ-interferons were expressed in *E. coli*.

The number of potential proteins approaches infinity. In moving out into the unknown, a good starting point is furnished by natural proteins with known functions. In the future, as new proteins are isolated by the current powerful separative methods, their amino acid sequences will be of fundamental interest. In chapter 7, Hunkapiller and Hood describe the performance of a new modification of the Edman procedure. Automated microsequencing of proteins can be carried out on samples as small as 5 to 10 picomoles. For a given sample, successful runs are limited to 30 to 70 cycles. The sequence of the remainder of a protein can be determined after it is fragmented by chemical or enzymatic methods to generate a set of overlapping peptides. Another way to obtain the amino acid sequence of a protein is to analyze the nucleotide sequence of the gene that codes for the protein. This is very useful when the gene is available.

Sutcliffe, Lerner, and colleagues describe work which extends Lerner's observation that relatively small peptide chains from a protein antigen can elicit an antiserum against the native protein. Using a virus genome sequence as a blueprint, they synthesized peptides which corresponded to different regions of the genome. From immunological tests they established some primitive rules. Peptides that were extremely hydrophobic and those with six or fewer residues were ineffective. Longer, soluble peptides, particularly those containing proline, were effective. This study was extended to other viruses and the results conformed to the rules. Further studies showed that in some, but not all, instances, peptide fragments were capable of serving as effective vaccines.

Ulmer's chapter in Part I is an interesting analysis of the opportunities and techniques available for protein engineering. In nature, specific catalytic functions are served by enzymes of differing properties. For example, enzymes of thermophilic organisms can withstand temperatures approaching 100°C, while those of mesophilic organisms may be destroyed at much lower temperatures. Great differences among organisms exist with respect to turnover rates, pH optima, and other characteristics. The testimony from evolution is that it is possible to select compositions and structures that are superior for particular applications. Through the use of synthetic genes and recombinant DNA techniques, it is now possible to begin to improve on the evolutionary process. In this effort x-ray crystallography and computer capabili-

ties, including graphics, will be important. Such studies will provide solid knowledge about the aspects of protein structure that are crucial to protein functions. Many stable and useful industrial catalysts will be produced.

Agricultural Research

Plant breeders such as Borlaug have worked diligently for about four decades and have been able to obtain varieties in which such characteristics as yield, pest resistance, and nutritive qualities are greatly enhanced. Their techniques will continue to be important, but will be supplemented by new ones now under development.

Tissue culture techniques for growing plant cells have been very successfully developed. Already plants produced in tissue culture are being sold commercially. In chapter 11, Chaleff reviews work on tissue culture and notes that when single cells are allowed to proliferate, the progeny often have a chromosome content that differs from the original. Polyploidy, aneuploidy, and chromosomal rearrangements have been identified. Additional evidence is furnished which makes it clear that tissue culture will facilitate development of many strains of plants, some of which will probably prove superior. Masses of cells respond to herbicides or plant toxins as mature plants would respond.

Another method of creating new plants is to bring together chromosomes from two different plant species. This was done in the 1960's with wheat and rye. The first plants were inferior with respect to yield and other characteristics, but breeding programs have now achieved varieties that in important respects, such as tolerance to poor soils, are superior to wheat. At the Centro Internacional de Mejoramiento de Maiz y Trigo (CIMMYT) crosses of wheat and wild grasses are under study.

Shepard and associates describe work with protoplasts which also yields new forms. The protoplasts are prepared by removing cell walls that are largely cellulosic. When brought together, two protoplasts fuse and the new entity contains nuclear material from both. In this way sexually incompatible pairings can be made. Combinations of unrelated genomes are regularly followed by elimination of chromosomes from either or both of the parental cell lines. However, total elimination of chromosomes from either species does not necessarily occur. Thus, there is a potential for the creation of novel plants. A more immediate possibility is the use of protoplast fusion to create hybrids between related but sexually incompatible species. In this way, a broad spectrum of resistance to disease in a primitive species might be incorporated into a commercial cultivar.

Barton and Brill examine the subject of plant genetic engineering with the hope of using recombinant DNA techniques to improve genomes. Progress will be slow at first because the state of knowledge of plants lags behind that of animals and some microorganisms. Cloned DNA is routinely transferred between microorganisms, but lack of comparable vector systems has inhibited similar experiments in plants. However, progress is now being made in this area. Also lacking has been a transformation marker—a gene present on a vector that permits easy identification of transformed cells. This problem seems solvable, but obstacles remain. Success in plant genetic engineering will rely on a thorough knowledge of the genetics and regulation of the traits to be transferred. At this time, the mechanisms of regulation are not understood. Barton and Brill provide examples which illustrate the problems involved in making a substantial change, such as incorporating nitrogen fixation in plants. As an alternative approach, they emphasize the possibility of improving microorganisms that fix nitrogen and are associated with roots of plants. Other major objectives that seem possible are improvement of photosynthesis and pest and pathogen resistance.

Much of the earth's surface is not suitable for agriculture, but can support growth of trees. Ultimately, forest yields will be substantially increased. In addition to the present product slate, wood will be available for energy and feedstocks to produce food or chemicals. In chapter 14, Farnum, Timmis, and Kulp describe how forest yields are being greatly improved and estimate what can be attained eventually through good forestry practice. They also discuss tissue culture proliferation of superior trees, which shortens the time required to achieve superior forests.

Microbiological Engineering

For several decades, industrial microbiology has been producing antibiotics. Excellent antibiotics have been discovered and, through a laborious process involving mutagens and selection, their yields have been substantially increased. The major pharmaceutical firms have equipment and expertise for effective large-scale production with microorganisms, once the appropriate strains are available. For the production of small-volume, high-value specialty chemicals, small companies will be competitive. One can anticipate that many new products will emerge fairly soon. Many vectors exist for the introduction of genetic material into host microorganisms, and generation times are short. Vournakis and Elander describe some of the methods being employed to increase production of antibiotics and to discover new ones. Current screening methods are more efficient than those employed earlier, and knowledge of detailed synthetic pathways is applied. Protoplast fusion of related and correlated organisms has led to new products. Use of recombinant DNA techniques has begun.

Over the past 30 years, the pharmaceutical industry focused largely on the production of antibiotics through fermentation. Many substances isolated from the fermentation of beer were inactive as antibiotics. However, many were found to have other applications, which Demain surveys in chapter 16. For example, nearly a score have physiological effects in humans that give them medicinal value. Another set of these substances is effective against nematodes. One fermentation product, monensin, is a potent coccidiostat in chickens. In addition, when monensin is incorporated in the feed of ruminants, it suppresses the formation of methane, thereby improving dietary efficiency. A scanning of Demain's compilation of microbiological products must leave the reader with admiration for the microbes' capabilities.

Bacteria, viruses, and fungi grow in a wide variety of circumstances. Some favor insects as a medium, often secreting toxins within them. Miller, Lingg, and Bulla discuss the increasing use of microbiological insecticides. In general, they are ecologically much more benign than the chemicals that have hitherto been employed.

Earlier in this overview, I mentioned the prospects for protein engineering and cited possible applications in the production of superior enzymes to catalyze specific reactions. In practice, it is usually desirable to immobilize either the separated enzymes or the cells containing them. Klibanov describes techniques for doing this and cites the advantages that accrue. For example, the enzymes are not lost and their stability is often improved when they are chemically bound to a support. Immobilized enzymes are being used commercially. Glucose isomerase is being employed on a large scale to convert corn sugar (glucose) into a mixture of glucose and fructose.

It should be evident that, in future, fermentation will have an increasing role. For many products it will become competitive with conventional chemical processing. The decisive consideration will be comparative costs. In biological processing, bioreactors will have a key role, and Cooney discusses design factors for these reactors.

Current annual production of organic chemicals is close to 100 million metric tons, about 99 percent of which is oxychemicals. Many of these could be produced by microbial fermentation with or without chemical processing. These chemicals and their derivatives represent nearly half of the total organic chemical production and their current value is over $15 billion. America's largest chemical company, DuPont, owns abundant reserves of hydrocarbons and coal, but it is conducting substantial research on the conversion of biomass into products. In chapter 20, Ng, Hardy, and colleagues provide an assessment of feedstocks, costs, potential products, and separative processes. They point out that ethyl alcohol produced by fermentation is today cost-competitive with that obtained from ethylene. They mention fermentations resulting in acetic acid, acetone, *n*-butanol, and isopropyl alcohol. One of the handicaps of fermentation is that it is generally conducted in dilute solution. Accordingly, the energy and dollar cost of isolating products is a burden. With time, improvements in bioengineering

are likely to make the picture more favorable.

Many microorganisms have fastidious requirements for carbon and energy sources. But one or more organisms can prosper by using a large number of organic chemicals, CO, CH_3OH, CH_4, $CO_2 + H_2$, and others. This capability can be exploited to produce single-cell proteins that are useful for animal and human food. The subject is reviewed by Litchfield in chapter 21.

1. Rabies Virus Glycoprotein Analogs: Biosynthesis in *Escherichia coli*

Elizabeth Yelverton, Shirley Norton
John F. Obijeski, David V. Goeddel

Rabies, the disease, is caused by a promiscuous neurotropic virus whose hosts include most warm-blooded animals and, of course, humans. Virus particles, normally transmitted by the bite of an infected animal, invade the nerve endings and travel via the spinal cord to the brain, where they multiply and infect efferent neurons, including those supplying the salivary glands. The disease has been greatly feared since antiquity because of associated bizarre behaviors in its victims, including convulsions, raging, drooling, and hydrophobia and also because once symptoms develop the disease nearly always proves fatal for humans (*1*). In 1885, Louis Pasteur developed the first rabies vaccine by emulsifying desiccated spinal cords of rabies-infected rabbits. The victim (patient) received a series of painful abdominal injections extracted from cords which had been air-dried for periods of 15 days decreasing to 5 days. Today, largely as a result of the efforts of workers at the Wistar Institute in Philadelphia, rabies virus can be cultured in vitro, concentrated, and inactivated to produce a more potent and more easily tolerated vaccine. The treatment regimen for ex-posed humans now includes injection with vaccine, the immunoglobulin fraction of antiserum to rabies virus, and sometimes interferon (*2*).

Despite these advances, the incidence of rabies worldwide is still high in hard-to-reach animal reservoirs, and a safe and effective synthetic vaccine is needed. In North America, mandatory vaccination programs have nearly eradicated canine rabies, but the disease is still widespread among the sylvatic population, particularly among skunks. In South America, the death of cattle infected by the bites of rabid vampire bats results in an estimated yearly loss of more than $29 million (*3*). Rabies in foxes is a problem in the northeastern United States and Canada, and an oral vaccine to immunize this species was developed by Baer and colleagues (*4*) in the 1970's. Since the 1940's, the incidence of fox rabies has been increasing in Europe, where a test program to vaccinate foxes orally by means of chicken head baits containing attenuated rabies virus has been instituted (*5*). Because of the possibility that an attenuated virus may revert to virulence, an oral virus-free vaccine would be preferable.

One alternative for virus subunit vaccine design is to use an acquired nucleotide sequence to deduce the amino acid sequence of an immunogenic viral protein, and to select from it short polypeptides which are then chemically synthesized, attached to carrier proteins of known immunogenicity, and injected in an immunopotentiating adjuvant. An important finding, illustrated in the cases of hepatitis virus and foot-and-mouth disease virus (6), is that a given linear array of amino acids can be an effective antigenic domain; the native three-dimensional structure of the intact protein is not required to evoke a spectrum of reactive and neutralizing antibodies in vivo.

Another method for producing subunit vaccines is biosynthesis in which the gene for a protein product is isolated and provided with new regulatory signals appropriate for its expression in a new host organism. The biosynthesis of polypeptide hormones such as insulin, growth hormone, and interferons (7–9) has been well documented, and many biosynthetically produced polypeptides will become commercially available in the next few years (10). Expression of small viral genes has also yielded to techniques of biosynthesis. The gene for the major surface antigen of hepatitis B virus has been directly expressed both in the yeast *Saccharomyces cerevisiae* (11) and in simian cells (12). Also, Kleid and coworkers have reported the synthesis in *Escherichia coli* of an immunogenic fusion protein between an antigen, VP$_3$, of foot-and-mouth disease virus and a protein derived from the *E. coli* pathway for tryptophan biosynthesis (13).

In this chapter we describe the direct expression in *E. coli* of the glycoprotein gene of rabies virus.

The rabies virus itself is an RNA virus of the Lyssavirus genus in the Rhabdoviridae family. Some rabies virus strains, such as CVS, HEP, ERA, and PM, have been developed by cultivation in laboratory. Since conventionally prepared, polyspecifiic antiserum does not differentiate these strains, rabies virus has been considered to consist of a single antigenic species. Correspondingly, all commercially available rabies vaccines now are produced from single strains. However, use of monoclonal antibodies, which provides higher resolution, can reveal some variations among the strains (14). Also, variations in the electrophoretic mobilities of some of the gene products have been observed (15). Five rabies viral proteins have been identified from rabies virus–infected cells and from purified rabies virions: L (large, the viral polymerase), N (nucleocapsid protein), G (glycoprotein), and M$_1$ and M$_2$ (matrix proteins) (16). Of these, the glycoprotein (or G protein) forms the external surface of the virus and is responsible for its immunogenicity; that is, antibodies raised against purified rabies virus glycoprotein can neutralize infectious rabies virus. In fact, Dietzschold et al. (17) showed that 9 nanograms of purified glycoprotein was equivalent to 1630 ng of purified whole virus in a mouse protection test even though the glycoprotein constitutes about 40 percent of the rabies virion protein (16). The amino acid sequences of the glycoproteins of the rabies virus CVS and ERA strains have now been deduced from DNA copies of the respective genes (18, 19). The homology (about 90 percent at the amino acid level) is in conformity with the closely related antigenic characteristics of the two virus strains. We have undertaken the engineering of a rabies subunit vaccine consisting of the glycoprotein gene product from the CVS rabies virus strain to test against many strains of infectious rabies virus.

Structural Features of Rabies

Virus Glycoprotein

From polyadenylated messenger RNA's (mRNA's) of cells infected with the rabies CVS strain, we prepared double-stranded complementary DNA (cDNA) species, introduced single-stranded homopolymeric tails, and annealed them by means of DNA base pairing into the bacterial cloning vehicle pBR322 (20). The heterogeneous hybrid plasmids were then transformed into E. coli to form a colony library. From the library we identified a plasmid, pRab91, which selectively hybridized to rabies virus glycoprotein mRNA (18). Nucleotide sequencing of the cloned DNA, which consisted of > 2000 base pairs (bp) showed that it encoded most of the hydrophobic signal peptide and all of the mature rabies virus glycoprotein, whose NH_2- and COOH-terminus has been established by direct amino acid analysis (21). The amino acid sequence predicted from the cDNA is shown in Fig. 1, where some features of the polypeptide are emphasized.

Although, on the whole, the rabies virus glycoprotein is quite hydrophobic, the signal peptide (denoted S_1-S_{19}) and the 22–amino acid (stippled) region between amino acid positions 439 and 462 are particularly hydrophobic. This latter domain has been postulated by Anilionis et al. (19) to constitute the portion of the protein which would span the viral lipid membrane. In that regard, it is satisfying to note that 9 of these predicted 20 amino acid positions differ between the glycoproteins of the CVS and ERA rabies

strains, but none of the changes alter the hydrophobicity. Hypothetically, the native immunogenic domains of the glycoprotein would occur on the NH_2-terminal side of this transmembrane segment; the carboxyl-terminal portion would be the site of interaction with matrix protein. The many charged residues that follow the hydrophobic segment are indicated in Fig. 1 by underlining. Three sites of possible sugar chain attachment, Asn-X-Thr or Asn-X-Ser (22) which might occur on the virus exterior, are also shown; these are consistent in number with the most highly glycosylated form of the protein (15).

Expression Vectors for the

Rabies Glycoprotein Gene

To effect the expression of the mature rabies virus glycoprotein gene in E. coli, it was necessary to (i) add a translation initiation signal before the codon for the amino-terminal amino acid, (ii) place the gene downstream from an E. coli promoter, or site of initiation of transcription by RNA polymerase, and (iii) make adjustments so that the transcript would be efficiently translated by the host machinery.

The method we used for the first step was similar to that used for the expression of human serum albumin and human fibroblast interferon (23). The synthetic deoxyoligonucleotide (24) primer 5'-dCATGAAGTTCCCCAT was chosen to incorporate an ATG translation initiation codon before the codon for the first amino acid of the mature rabies glycoprotein gene (AAG and Lys). The primer mismatches with the negative strand template in only two positions, and includes a deoxycytidine residue at the 5' position for later assembly to an Eco RI recognition site. The assembly for the mature glycoprotein gene is shown in Fig. 2. A Rsa I restriction fragment (136 bp) containing the coding region for the signal peptide cleavage site was denatured in the presence of the direct expression primer. *Escherichia coli* DNA polymerase I (large fragment) was used to synthesize the revised sense strand, remove the 3′ protruding end, and repair mismatches in the minus strand. A second restriction site within the repair template was used to generate a defined Ava II sticky end for ligation with the 1297 bp Ava II–Pst I fragment containing most of the rabies G coding

```
       S1                                        S10                                  S19
       Met Val Pro Gln Val Leu Leu Phe Val  Leu Leu Leu Gly Phe Ser Leu Cys Phe Gly

Lys Phe Pro Ile  Tyr Thr Ile  Pro Asp Lys Leu Gly Pro Trp Ser Pro Ile  Asp Ile  His His Leu Arg Cys Pro

Asn Asn Leu Val Val Glu Asp Glu Gly Cys Thr|Asn Leu Ser|Gly Phe Ser Tyr Met Glu Leu Lys Val Gly Tyr     (50)

Ile  Ser Ala Ile  Lys Val Asn Gly Phe Thr Cys Thr Gly Val Val Thr Glu Ala Glu Thr Tyr Thr Asn Phe Val

Gly Tyr Val Thr Thr Thr Phe Lys Arg Lys His Phe Arg Pro Thr Pro Asp Ala Cys Arg Ala Ala Tyr Asn Trp     (100)

Lys Met Ala Gly Asp Pro Arg Tyr Glu Glu Ser Leu Gln Asn Pro Tyr Pro Asp Tyr His Trp Val Arg Thr Val

Arg Thr Thr Lys Glu Ser Leu Ile  Ile  Ile  Ser Pro Ser Val Thr Asp Leu Asp Pro Tyr Asp Lys Ser Leu His (150)

Ser Arg Val Phe Pro Ser Gly Lys Cys Ser Gly Ile  Thr Val Ser Ser Thr Tyr Cys Ser Thr Asn His Asp Tyr

Thr Ile  Trp Met Pro Glu Asn Pro Arg Pro Gly Thr Pro Cys Asp Ile  Phe Thr Asn Ser Arg Gly Lys Arg Ala (200)

Ser Asn Gly|Asn Lys Thr|Cys Gly Phe Val Asp Glu Arg Gly Leu Tyr Lys Ser Leu Lys Gly Ala Cys Arg Leu

Lys Leu Cys Gly Val Leu Gly Leu Arg Leu Met Asp Gly Thr Trp Val Ala Met Gln Thr Ser Asp Glu Thr Lys (250)

Trp Cys Ser Pro Asp Gln Leu Val Asn Leu His Asp Phe Arg Ser Asp Glu Ile  Glu His Leu Val Val Glu Glu

Leu Val Lys Lys Arg Glu Glu Cys Leu Asp Thr Leu Glu Ser Ile  Met Thr Thr Lys Ser Val Ser Phe Arg Arg (300)

Leu Ser His Leu Arg Lys Leu Val Pro Gly Phe Gly Lys Ala Tyr Thr Ile  Phe|Asn Lys Thr|Leu Met Glu Ala

Asp Ala His Tyr Lys Ser Val Arg Thr Trp Asn Glu Ile  Ile  Pro Ser Lys Gly Cys Leu Lys Val Gly Gly Arg (350)

Cys His Pro His Val Asn Gly Val Phe Phe Asn Gly Ile  Ile  Leu Gly Pro Asp Asp Arg Val Leu Ile  Pro Glu

Met Gln Ser Ser Leu Leu Arg Gln His Met Glu Leu Leu Glu Ser Ser Val Ile  Pro Leu Met His Pro Leu Ala (400)

Asp Pro Ser Thr Val Phe Lys Glu Gly Asp Glu Ala Glu Asp Phe Val Glu Val His Leu Pro Asp Val Tyr Lys

Gln Ile  Ser Gly Val Asp Leu Gly Leu Pro Asn Trp Gly Lys Tyr Val Leu Met Thr Ala Gly Ala Met Ile  Gly (450)
```

↑
Bgl II   ↑
                                                                              Pst I

```
Leu Val Leu Ile  Phe Ser Leu Met Thr Trp Cys Arg Arg Ala Asn Arg Pro Glu Ser Lys Gln Arg Ser Phe Gly

Gly Thr Gly Gly Asn Val Ser Val Thr Ser Gln Ser Gly Lys Val Ile  Pro Ser Trp Glu Ser Tyr Lys Ser Gly (500)

Gly Glu Ile  Arg Leu End
```

Fig. 1. The deduced amino acid sequence of a rabies virus glycoprotein from the control virus standard (CVS) strain. The first amino acids of the mature protein are indicated as determined by NH₂-terminal analysis of the glycoprotein from another rabies virus strain (*21*). The stippled portion between amino acids 439 and 462 is a hydrophobic domain which may be the site of membrane attachment. Further on in this sequence, charged residues that may interact with capsid proteins are underlined. The amino acid sequence contains four potential glycosylation sites (Asn-X-Ser or Asn-X-Thr). Those three that would hypothetically occur on the external portion of the glycoprotein are indicated by boxes. Two restriction enzyme recognition sites, which occur in the cDNA and were used in the construction of truncated or fused rabies glycoprotein analogs, are shown.

12

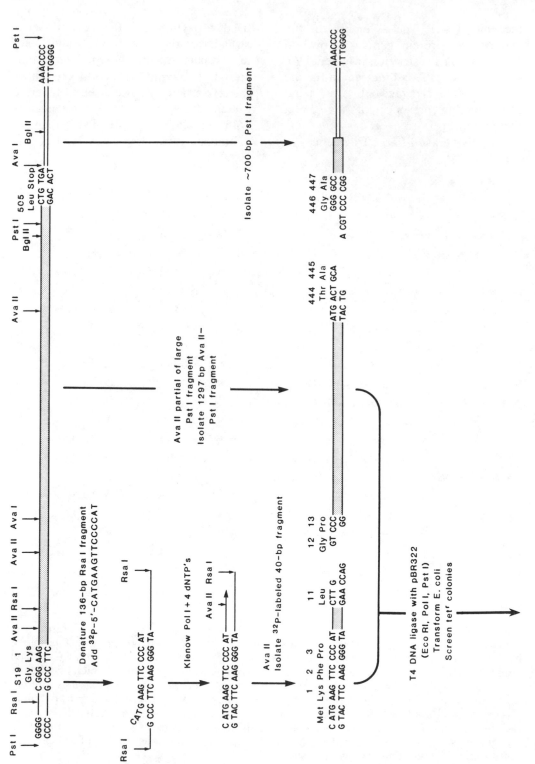

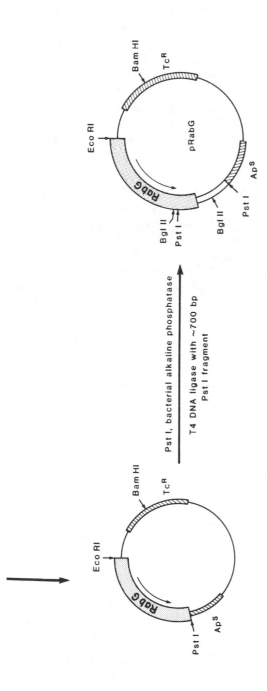

Fig. 2. Construction of a plasmid bearing the gene for mature rabies glycoprotein. The plasmid pRab91, a pBR322 derivative with rabies glycoprotein cDNA introduced by dG/dC pairing at the Pst I site (18) was the source of the template for a DNA polymerase I (Klenow fragment) catalyzed repair reaction. The synthetic deoxynucleotide dCATGAAGTTCCCCAT, synthesized by the modified phosphotriester method (27) was phosphorylated in a reaction containing 500 pmole of primer, ~ 300 μCi of [γ-^{32}P]ATP (2500 Ci/mmole, New England Nuclear) and 2 units of T4 polynucleotide kinase in 60 mM tris-HCl (pH 8), 10 mM MgCl$_2$, 15 mM β-mercaptoethanol. The reaction was allowed to proceed for 20 minutes at 37°C; unlabeled ATP was then added to a final concentration of 200 μM. After 30 minutes the reaction was terminated by extraction with phenol and chloroform, and the aqueous phase was precipitated with ethanol with 3 μg of the 136-bp template Rsa I fragment. The mixture was dissolved in 50 μl of water, boiled for 5 minutes, quenched in dry ice, and diluted at 0°C to 100 μl to contain 100 mM tris-HCl (pH 7.5), 7 mM MgCl$_2$, 60 mM NaCl, and 0.5 mM of each deoxyribonucleotide triphosphate. Ten units of DNA polymerase I (Klenow fragment) (Boehringer-Mannheim) were added, and the reaction was allowed to proceed at room temperature for 4 hours. After phenol extraction and ethanol precipitation, the mixture was treated with 15 μl of Ava II (New England Biolabs) according to the manufacturer's recommended conditions. The reaction mixture was subjected to electrophoresis through a 10 percent polyacrylamide slab gel; the desired 40-bp fragment was located by autoradiography, excised, and electroeluted. Next, plasmid pRab91 was partially digested with Ava II, then digested to completion with Pst I. A 1297-bp fragment was recovered after gel electrophoresis of the restriction products. This fragment was used in a three-part ligation (by means of T4 DNA ligase) with the ^{32}P-labeled 40-bp repaired fragment and a modified pBR322 vector. The ligation mixture was transformed into *E. coli* 294 with selection on LB plates containing tetracycline at 5 μg/ml. Plasmid DNA of the transformants was screened by hybridization in situ with the labeled synthetic oligonucleotide (18) and then by digestion with restriction enzymes. The intermediate plasmid was then cleaved with Pst I, treated with bacterial alkaline phosphatase, and ligated with the ~ 700 bp Pst I fragment containing the remaining complementary DNA.

region. The resultant 1337-bp fragment was propagated in a modified pBR322 plasmid which was prepared by opening at the only Eco RI site, then treating with DNA polymerase I in the presence of deoxyribonucleoside triphosphates to fill in the single-stranded ends, and subsequently treating with Pst I. Tetracycline resistant *E. coli* transformants were first screened by colony hybridization with the same ^{32}P-labeled DNA primer (*18*) to select correct transformation products. The correct intermediate plasmid was then opened at the only Pst I recognition site, treated with bacterial alkaline phosphatase to prevent self-ligation, and ligated in a molar excess of the approximately 700-bp Pst I fragment bearing the remaining coding sequence and nontranslated 3' end. Asymmetric Ava I sites were used to determine the orientation; approximately one-half had the restriction fragment inserted in the orientation to recreate the entire text. The resultant plasmid, pRabG, is shown at the bottom of Fig. 2.

In pRabG, a single Eco RI recognition site directly precedes the structural gene for mature rabies glycoprotein (Fig. 2). The regulatory elements for expression of the rabies G gene were added by means of a 300 bp Eco RI–bounded promoter fragment isolated from the plasmid pLeIFA25 (*5*) which contained the congruent promoter and repressor binding site (operator), and also the ribosome binding site for the *E. coli* tryptophan operon leader peptide (*25*). The plasmid pRabG1 was opened by restriction with Eco RI, treated with bacterial alkaline phosphatase, and ligated with the 300-bp promoter fragment; the ligation reaction

Table 1. Bacterial strains and plasmids used.

Strain or plasmid	Relevant characteristics	Reference or source
E. coli 294	*end*A, *thi*⁻, *hsr*⁻, *hsm*⁺	(*7*)
E. coli W3110	F⁻ K-12 derivative	(*37*)
pBR322	Ap^R Tc^R	(*20*)
pLeIFA25*	Source of 300 bp *trp* promoter fragment	(*8*)
pIFN-γ*trp*48	Control plasmid for protein analysis	(*38*)
pRab91	Rabies virus glycoprotein cDNA introduced at Pst I site of pBR322	(*18*)
pRabG	Contains structural gene for mature rabies glycoprotein	This study; Fig. 2
pRabGT1	For expression of 549 amino acid rabies glycoprotein–β-lactamase fusion protein	This study
pRabG*trp*1	For expression of low level mature rabies glycoprotein, G_{505}	This study
pRabdex1	For expression of truncated rabies glycoprotein, G_{427}	From pRabdex2 by Bgl II restriction
pRabdex2	For expression of mature rabies glycoprotein, G_{505}	From pRabG*trp*1 by Xba I, SI treatment
pRabdex31	For expression of 549 amino acid glycoprotein fusion	From pRabGT1 by Xba I, S1 treatment

*All plasmids confer tetracycline (Tc) but not ampicillin (Ap) resistance (R) unless otherwise noted.

mixture was used to transform competent *E. coli* 294 to tetracycline resistance. An asymmetrically located Xba I site in the Eco RI fragment allowed us to screen for transformant plasmids which had the promoter fragment in the orientation for transcription of the rabies virus G gene. Several plasmid isolates were assembled correctly, and one, pRabG*trp*1, was chosen for study. After the *trp* promoter fragment was added, the nucleotide sequence around the Eco RI junction was determined and showed that incorporation of the new translation initiation codon had occurred as planned (*26–28*). In an alternate order of assembly, the Eco RI promoter fragment was inserted prior to the addition of the ~ 700-bp Pst I fragment bearing the rabies G COOH-terminal coding sequence. In the plasmid pRabGT1, the rabies glycoprotein text is brought into phase at amino acid position 446 with the portion of the β-lactamase gene which extends from the Pst I site of pBR322, an addition of 103 more codons before a translation stop signal is reached.

A preliminary test for expression of the rabies glycoprotein gene in *E. coli* was to examine by gel electrophoresis whole cell extracts of *E. coli* transformed by pRabGT1, pRabG*trp*1, or a control plasmid pIFN-γ*trp*48 (Table 1). A major new protein band, with migration commensurate with a size of about 62,000 daltons, was readily visible by Coomassie-blue staining in the gel lane containing the extract of *E. coli* W3110/pRabGT1 (Fig. 3, lane c). The presence of the protein was correlated with tryptophan depletion in the culture medium; it constituted about 3 percent of the total cell proteins. The protein expressed from pRabG*trp*1 was not as easily detectable. Therefore, one further manipulation was made to the expression vector

to increase production of rabies glycoprotein. Studies with *E. coli lac*Z gene fusion proteins (*29*) and with bacterially synthesized human interferons (*30*) show that expression of a gene can be increased by alterations in the ribosome binding site of the transcript. Specifically, modifying by a few base pairs the distance between the Shine-Dalgarno sequence [the region of mRNA complementary to the 3' end of 16*S* ribosomal RNA (*31*)] and the translation initiation signal, AUG, can result in more than 100-fold difference in the assayed products. The DNA fragment which was introduced to pRabG1 to provide a promoter also supplies a recognition site for Xba I within the presumed ribosome binding site as follows: (5') G̲G̲T̲A̲T̲C̲ T̲A̲G̲A̲ATTCATG (the underlined nucleotides constitute the Xba I site, and the barred nucleotides show the Shine-Dalgarno and translation initiation sequences).

The plasmids pRabGT1 and pRabG*trp*1 were altered by restriction with Xba I, treatment with S1 nuclease, and religation with T4 DNA ligase, as described (*30*). Plasmid DNA from transformants which arose on selective medium were screened for the loss of the Xba I recognition site. Plasmids designated pRabdex31 (derived from pRabGT1) and pRabdex2 (from pRabG*trp*1) were selected for further study. Nucleotide sequencing confirmed that the four nucleotides which form single-stranded ends after Xba I scission had been removed to generate the new ribosome binding site G̅G̅T̅ATAATTCA̅T̅G̅.

Cultures of *E. coli* W3110/pRabdex31 and *E. coli* W3110/pRabdex2 were grown in the absence of tryptophan (Fig. 3). Gel electrophoresis of the whole cell extracts of those strains are shown in Fig. 3, lanes d and f. The full-length bacterially expressed rabies glycoprotein, termed G$_{505}$, comigrates with a major class of *E. coli* proteins, but can be observed as a widening of the stained protein band at about 57,000 daltons. Densitometry scanning of the electrophoretically separated *E. coli* W3110/pRabdex2 proteins, compared to control bacterial extract proteins, showed that G$_{505}$ constituted about 2 percent of the cellular proteins, while the amount of fusion protein expressed from pRabdex31 was slightly less than 5 percent.

The synthesis of highly hydrophobic

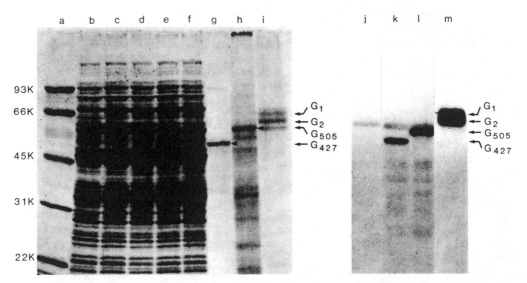

Fig. 3. Discontinuous, 10 percent polyacrylamide slab gel analysis of cellular proteins from *E. coli* bearing rabies virus glycoprotein expression plasmids. (Lane a) Molecular weight standard proteins (Bio-Rad). Lanes b to f are total cell extracts of *E. coli* W3110 transformed with (lane b) a control plasmid, pIFN-γ*trp*48 (*37*); (lane c) pRabGT1, (lane d) pRabdex31, (lane e) pRabdex1, and (lane f) pRabdex2. The inocula were grown overnight in LB plus tetracycline (5 μg/ml), then diluted 1:100 in M9 medium (*40*) containing 0.2 percent glucose, 0.5 percent Casamino acids, and tetracycline. Indole acrylic acid was added to a concentration of 25 μg/ml when A_{550} reached ~ 0.1. Cells were collected by centrifugation when A_{550} reached 1.0. Total cell extracts were prepared by boiling in 2 percent sodium dodecyl sulfate and 0.1M β-mercaptoethanol. (Lanes g and h) Enriched preparations of G$_{427}$ and G$_{505}$, respectively. Cultures (500 ml) of *E. coli* W3110/pRabdex1 and *E. coli* W3110/pRabdex2 were grown in tryptophan-depleted medium as above, harvested by centrifugation at A_{550} = 1.0, and treated with lysozyme, 0.2 percent NP-40, and 1.5M NaCl (*13*). The insoluble pellet was slurried into PBS. Samples to be analyzed by gel electrophoresis were dissolved by boiling in buffer containing 20 percent glycerol, 5 percent β-mercaptoethanol, 0.125M tris-HCl (*p*H 6.8), and 4 percent SDS. (Lane i) A partially purified rabies virus glycoprotein prepared by NP-40 solubilization of rabies virions. Some faster migrating nucleocapsid (N) protein is also present in this preparation. All proteins in lanes a to i are visualized by staining with Coomassie brilliant blue. Lanes j to m show an autoradiogram of a protein blot (*41*) analysis of *E. coli*–derived or authentic rabies glycoprotein. Total cell extracts of *E. coli* W3110 containing plasmids (lane j) pIFN-γ*trp*48, (lane k) pRabdex1, or (lane l) pRabdex2 were placed on electrophoresis gels next to authentic glycoprotein (lane m) and transferred electrophoretically to nitrocellulose filter paper. The filter paper was treated serially with rabbit serum to rabies G and with ^{125}I-labeled protein A from Amersham (*42*). K represents 1000 daltons.

Table 2. Properties of the bacterially derived rabies glycoprotein gene products, G_{427} and G_{505}.

Item	G_{427}	G_{505}
Host or plasmid source	E. coli W3110/pRabdex1	E. coli W3110/pRabdex2
Molecular weight	48,600	56,900
Percent cell protein*	2.5 to 3.0	1.9 to 2.1
Copies/cell†	112,000 to 135,000	73,000 to 81,000
Percent in enriched preparation‡	24.2	21.6
Activity§ in PBS	1.9	2.8
Activity after solubilization in guanidine + urea	68.2	90.0

*Determined from densitometry tracings of electrophoretically separated proteins from three or more cell extracts (39).   †Calculation based on the assumption that 1 liter of E. coli grown to an absorbance of 10 ($A_{550} = 10$) yields 2 g of protein from 5×10^{12} cells (9).   ‡See legend to Fig. 3.   §Reactivity with antibody to glycoprotein compared with an equal amount of authentic glycoprotein.

protein moieties can present problems to the E. coli host. For example, Rose and Shafferman (32) reported that expression of a vesicular stomatitis virus (VSV) glycoprotein-anthranilate synthetase fusion could be obtained only if the coding sequence for the hydrophobic amino terminal signal sequence of the VSV protein were removed. To investigate whether the synthesis of G_{505} was diminished due to the hydrophobic transmembrane amino acids 440 to 461, we undertook a construction in which the translation termination codon (TAG) would be brought into phase immediately preceding the coding sequence for the hydrophobic domain of the rabies virus glycoprotein. In this way analysis of the effect of the hydrophobic domain on expression in E. coli would not be confounded by extra amino acids at the carboxyl terminus. Figure 1 illustrates the position of the Pst I site where the rabies glycoprotein gene is joined to the β-lactamase gene to create the fused protein. In addition, Fig. 1 shows the location of a Bgl II restriction site which was used to design a truncated glycoprotein gene. Inspection of the sequence in the 3'-untranslated portion of the rabies G cDNA (not shown) revealed that excision of an in-

ternal Bgl II fragment from the plasmid pRabdex2 would result in a TAG triplet immediately after the codon for amino acid 427 of the mature rabies glycoprotein. The positions of the two Bgl II sites are indicated in Fig. 2.

The plasmid pRabdex2 was restricted with Bgl II and religated with T_4 DNA ligase. The ligation mix was used to transform E. coli 294 to tetracycline resistance; plasmid DNA from several isolates was screened for the loss of the internal Bgl II fragment. The plasmid pRabdex1 met this criterion and was selected for further characterization. Gel electrophoresis of a whole cell extract of E. coli W3110/pRabdex1 is shown in Fig. 3, lane e. The truncated glycoprotein, termed G_{427}, can be observed readily at a position corresponding to about 49,000 daltons; it constitutes about 2 to 3 percent of the cell proteins. In Table 2, the roughly estimated synthetic levels of G_{505} and G_{427} are shown in relation to the number of protein molecules per bacterium. The per cell synthesis of the more hydrophilic polypeptide, G_{427}, is about one and a half times higher than that of G_{505}, or nearly equal to the level of synthesis of the rabies glycoprotein–β-lactamase fusion protein.

Characterization of Bacterially
Synthesized Rabies Glycoprotein

To demonstrate the antigenic identity of the proteins produced by expression from the plasmids pRabdex1 and pRabdex2, cell extracts were subjected to electrophoresis on polyacrylamide slab gels, transferred to nitrocellulose, and reacted in situ with rabbit antiserum to authentic rabies glycoprotein (33, 34) (Fig. 3, lanes j–m). The antiserum used reacts somewhat with a normal E. coli component (Fig. 3, lane j, a control E. coli extract). The more intensely labeled bands in lanes k and l correspond with the rabies virus specific bands easily visible in stained slab gels. The gel from which this transfer was made is not shown, but is typified by extracts shown in lanes b, e, and f. The rabies glycoprotein–β-lactamase fusion gave a similar reaction (not shown). Polyacrylamide gel analysis of proteins from rabies virions of the CVS strain normally discriminates two electrophoretic glycoprotein species, G_1 and G_2, which differ in their degree of glycosylation (15). The ^{125}I-labeled bands corresponding to the more slowly migrating natural glycoproteins, G_1 and G_2, are shown in Fig. 3, lane m. This procedure showed that at least some of the antigenic determinants survived the denaturing and reducing agents present in the gel-loading buffer. Furthermore, it showed that at least some of the antigenic determinants are independent of post-translational modifications, such as carbohydrate side chain attachment, which are made on the authentic glycoprotein in rabies infected cells, but would not be made in E. coli cells.

Rabies glycoprotein, when removed from intact virions, is quite insoluble. In fact, Lai and Dietzschold (21) reported that in order to dissolve glycoprotein for

amino acid sequence determination it was necessary to boil protein preparations in 1 percent sodium dodecyl sulfate (SDS). The bacterially produced glycoprotein derivatives seem to share this characteristic and behave in E. coli much like other highly expressed, insoluble fusion proteins (13, 34). We obtained an approximately tenfold enrichment of G_{427} and G_{505} from cell extracts of E. coli W3110/pRabdex1 and E. coli W3110/pRabdex2, respectively, by collecting the precipitate of a lysate resulting from treatment with lysozyme in 0.2 percent NP-40 and $1.5M$ NaCl (Fig. 3, lanes g and h). Enriched preparations were then used to better assess the antigenicity of the proteins by comparison with authentic glycoprotein in an enzyme-linked immunosorbent assay (ELISA).

For the ELISA, dilutions of either purified rabies glycoprotein or the test bacterial samples were bound to the surface of a plastic microtiter tray, and were reacted with high-titer rabbit antiserum directed against authentic rabies glycoprotein. Unbound antibody was washed away, and the samples were treated with goat antiserum to rabbit antibody coupled to the enzyme alkaline phosphatase. Cleavage of the alkaline phosphatase substrate resulted in the development of a yellow color, which was monitored spectrophotometrically; conditions were set so that the absorbance was linear in the concentration range of 50 to 500 nanograms of rabies glycoprotein per milliliter (35).

When we assayed the insoluble protein fractions from cultures of E. coli W3110/pRabdex1, and E. coli W3110/pRabdex2, we found that the proteins G_{427} and G_{505} were only about 2 to 3 percent as effective per weight as purified authentic glycoprotein in binding antibodies to glycoprotein. To recover more activity from the bacterially synthesized proteins, a rather vigorous solubilization procedure was used. The enriched preparations were resuspended in 7M guanidine-hydrochloride at room temperature followed by dialysis into 7M urea and 5 mM tris, pH 8.0. (In some experiments, reducing agents were present in the buffers.) Samples were diluted up to 1:2000 in phosphate buffered saline (PBS) just prior to assay. Under these conditions, the proteins dissolved and their apparent activity increased more than 30-fold as indicated by the ELISA. Freshly solubilized preparations of G$_{505}$ reacted with the antibody about 90 percent as effectively as natural glycoprotein, while the activities of solubilized preparations of G$_{427}$ were no higher than 70 percent those of authentic glycoprotein. This reconstitution of activity by solubilization showed that the low reactivities first observed in the ELISA were not inherent properties of the bacterially synthesized glycoprotein analogs, G$_{505}$ and G$_{427}$. Rather, the amount of activity recovered suggests that most antigenic determinants present on the authentic glycoprotein are conserved in the bacterial counterpart, G$_{505}$. We have yet to ascertain whether the incomplete recovery of antigenic activity in the preparations of G$_{505}$ is artifactual or signifies the absence of specific immunogenic domains formed only in the virus-derived, glycosylated molecule.

Further purification of the G$_{427}$ and G$_{505}$ proteins for in vitro competition assays with authentic rabies glycoprotein and for animal inoculation is necessary. Although historical precedent (13) and the in vitro evidence presented here point toward their usefulness as immunogenic agents, these proteins cannot be dubbed subunit vaccines until after successful protection of an animal against lethal challenge with rabies virus. In 1980, reporting on a newly isolated human alpha interferon cDNA, Weissmann (36) mused: "We do not know whether E. coli IF [interferon] has the same specific activity as authentic LeIF [interferon-α] . . . If lack of appropriate glycosylation diminishes the activity of the molecule, we shall have a problem on our hands." In retrospect, glycosylation was not a problem. Today we know that the activities of interferons produced in E. coli are comparable to those of authentic interferon in every biological test to which they have been subjected. Further experimentation is required to determine whether bacterially produced rabies glycoprotein analogs will be as effective as virus-derived rabies glycoprotein in eliciting a protective response against rabies infection.

References and Notes

1. See M. M. Kaplan and H. Koprowski [*Sci. Am.* **242**, 120 (January 1980)] for a lively general article on rabies; J. H. Steele [in *The Natural History of Rabies*, G. M. Baer, Ed. (Academic Press, New York, 1975), p. 1] for a survey of the history of rabies and its prevention; J. F. Bell [*ibid.*, p. 331] for evidence that rabies infections are not necessarily fatal.
2. S. A. Plotkin, *Hosp. Pract.* **15** (No. 6), 65 (1980).
3. J. J. Callis, G. C. Poppensiek, D. H. Ferris, in *Virus Diseases of Food Animals*, E. P. J. Gibbs, Ed. (Academic Press, New York, 1981), p. 55.
4. G. M. Baer, M. K. Abelseth, J. G. Debbie, *Am. J. Epidemiol.* **93**, 487 (1971); J. G. Debbie, M. K. Abelseth, G. M. Baer, *ibid.* **96**, 231 (1972).
5. F. Steck, J. Hafliger, Ch. Stocker, A. Wandeler, in Abstracts from the Swiss Society of Microbiology, *Experientia* **34/12**, 1662 (1978).
6. R. A. Lerner, N. Green, H. Alexander, F.-T. Liu, J. G. Sutcliffe, T. M. Shinnick, *Proc. Natl. Acad. Sci. U.S.A.* **78**, 3403 (1981); J. L. Bittle *et al.*, *Nature (London)* **298**, 30 (1982). For a discussion of advances in this field, see J. G. Sutcliffe, T. M. Shinnick, N. Greene, R. A. Lerner, *Science* **219**, 660 (1983).
7. D. V. Goeddel *et al.*, *Proc. Natl. Acad. Sci. U.S.A.* **76**, 106 (1979); *Nature (London)* **281**, 544 (1979).
8. _____, *Nature (London)* **287**, 411 (1980).
9. M. J. Ross, in *Insulins, Growth Hormone, and Recombinant DNA Technology*, J. L. Gueriguian, Ed. (Raven, New York, 1981), p. 33.

10. See for example the discussion of human insulin (recombinant DNA) [I. S. Johnson, *Science* **219**, 632 (1983)].

11. P. Valenzuela, A. Medina, W. J. Rutter, G. Ammerer, B. D. Hall, *Nature (London)* **298**, 347 (1982); R. Hitzeman, unpublished results.

12. C. C. Liu and A. D. Levinson, in *Eukaryotic Viral Vectors*, Y. Gluzman, Ed. (Cold Spring Harbor Laboratory, Cold Spring Harbor, N.Y., 1982), p. 55.

13. D. G. Kleid *et al.*, *Science* **214**, 1125 (1981).

14. A. Flamand, T. J. Wiktor, H. Koprowski, *J. Gen. Virol.* **48**, 105 (1980).

15. B. Dietzschold, J. H. Cox, L. G. Schneider, *Virology* **98**, 63 (1979).

16. G. D. Coslett, B. P. Holloway, J. F. Obijeski, *J. Gen. Virol.* **49**, 161 (1980).

17. B. Dietzschold, J. H. Cox, L. G. Schneider, *Dev. Biol. Stand.* **40**, 45 (1978).

18. E. Yelverton, J. F. Obijeski, B. Holloway, D. V. Goeddel, in preparation.

19. A. Anilionis, W. H. Wunner, P. J. Curtis, *Nature (London)* **284**, 275 (1981).

20. F. Bolivar *et al.*, *Gene* **2**, 95 (1977).

21. C. Y. Lai and B. Dietzschold, *Biochem. Biophys. Res. Commun.* **103**, 536 (1981).

22. R. J. Winzler, in *Hormonal Proteins and Peptides*, C. H. Li, Ed. (Academic Press, New York, 1973), p. 1.

23. R. M. Lawn *et al.*, *Nucleic Acids Res.* **9**, 6103 (1981); D. V. Goeddel *et al.*, *ibid.* **8**, 4057 (1980).

24. The abbreviations for the bases are A, adenine; C, cytosine; G, guanine; T, thymine; U, uracil. The abbreviations for the amino acid residues are Ala, alanine; Arg, arginine; Asn, asparagine; Asp, aspartic acid; Cys, cysteine; Gln, glutamine; Glu, glutamic acid; Gly, glycine; His, histidine; Ile, isoleucine; Leu, leucine; Lys, lysine; Met, methionine; Phe, phenylalanine; Pro, proline; Ser, serine; Thr, threonine; Trp, tryptophan; Tyr, tyrosine; and Val, valine.

25. C. Yanofsky *et al.*, *Nucleic Acids Res.* **9**, 6647 (1981).

26. The single-stranded deoxyoligonucleotide dTCTGAAATGAGC, which hybridizes to the antisense strand from -50 to -38 bp 5' to the transcription initiation site in the tryptophan operon (*25*), was synthesized by modified solid phase phosphotriester method (*27*) and used as primer for dideoxy chain termination sequencing (*28*) of alkali-denatured supercoiled plasmid. Plasmid DNA to be sequenced was denatured in 0.2M NaOH containing 0.2 mM EDTA for 5 minutes at room temperature, neutralized by addition of 0.13M ammonium acetate (pH 4.5) and precipitated with $2\frac{1}{2}$ volumes of 95 percent ethanol. Primer was hybridized to the plasmid in tenfold molar excess in 6 mM tris-HCl, pH 7.6, 6 mM MgCl$_2$, 50 mM NaCl for 5 minutes at 37°C.

27. R. Crea and T. Horn, *Nucleic Acids Res.* **8**, 2331 (1980).

28. A. J. H. Smith, *Meth. Enzymol.* **65**, 560 (1980).

29. L. Guarente, T. M. Roberts, M. Ptashne, *Science* **209**, 1428 (1980).

30. H. M. Shepard, E. Yelverton, D. V. Goeddel, *DNA* **1**, 125 (1982).

31. J. Shine and L. Dalgarno, *Proc. Natl. Acad. Sci. U.S.A.* **71**, 1342 (1974).

32. J. K. Rose and A. Shafferman, *ibid.* **78**, 6670 (1981).

33. An antibody to rabies glycoprotein was raised against the glycoprotein-containing NP-40 supernatant fraction from purified rabies virions. Rabbits were injected once and then again at 3 weeks; serum titers (all 1:30,000, 3 weeks after the second injection) were determined by immunofluorescent neutralizing antibody assay [J. B. Thomas, in *The Natural History of Rabies*, G. M. Baer, Ed. (Academic Press, New York, 1975), p. 40]. A single crude serum sample from a single rabbit (titer 1:34,800) was diluted 1:300 to 1:1000 for use in ELISA or for filter hybridization. In some experiments, antiserum was first adsorbed to control bacterial extracts to eliminate nonspecific reaction in the ELISA.

34. D. C. Williams, R. M. Van Frank, W. L. Muth, J. P. Burnett, *Science* **215**, 687 (1982).

35. Sample antigens to be assayed were diluted into phosphate-buffered saline (PBS), and 100 μl was pipetted onto the wells of a Falcon flexible assay plate. After a 30-minute incubation period, unbound sample was aspirated away, and 100 μl of PBS plus 0.25 percent gelatin was applied. After 15 minutes, the gelatin solution was removed and the wells were washed three times with PBS plus 0.05 percent Tween. Rabbit antiserum to rabies glycoprotein (100 μl) diluted in PBS-Tween was added and incubated for 30 minutes. After washing three times in PBS-Tween, 100 μl of goat antiserum to rabbit immunoglobulin G–alkaline phosphatase conjugate was added (Zymed Laboratories; diluted 1:1000 in PBS-Tween just prior to use). After 30 to 60 minutes of incubation and washing, 100 μl of substrate (*p*-nitrophenyl phosphate, reconstituted according to Zymed instructions) was added. The absorbance at 405 nm was determined on a Dynatech ELISA reader. The standard plot for each experiment was authentic rabies glycoprotein diluted in duplicate from 5 to 50 ng per well.

36. S. Nagata, H. Taira, A. Hall, L. Johnsrud, M. Streuli, J. Ecsödi, W. Boll, K. Cantell, C. Weissmann, *Nature (London)* **284**, 316 (1980).

37. B. J. Bachmann, *Bacteriol. Rev.* **36**, 525 (1972).

38. P. W. Gray, D. W. Leung, D. Pennica, E. Yelverton, R. Najarian, C. C. Simonsen, R. Derynck, P. J. Sherwood, D. M. Wallace, S. L. Berger, A. D. Levinson, D. V. Goeddel, *Nature (London)* **295**, 503 (1983).

39. Polyacrylamide gel scanning was performed with a Zeineh soft laser scanning densitometer and a Hewlett-Packard 3390A integrator.

40. J. H. Miller, *Experiments in Molecular Genetics* (Cold Spring Harbor Laboratory, Cold Spring Harbor, N.Y., 1972), pp. 431–433.

41. H. Towbin, T. Staehelin, J. Gordon, *Proc. Natl. Acad. Sci. U.S.A.* **76**, 4350 (1979).

42. All antibody binding steps and washings were done in 50 mM tris, pH 7.4, 0.15M NaCl, 5 mM EDTA, 0.25 percent gelatin, and 0.05 percent NP-40 at room temperature for 1 to 2 hours.

43. We thank George Baer and Brian Holloway for developing the antiserum to glycoprotein, Larry Bock for carrying out the protein blot experiment (*41*), Avima Yaffe and Eric Patzer for help in setting up the ELISA, and Jeanne Arch and Alane Gray for help in manuscript preparation. We thank Art Levinson and Ron Wetzel for many helpful discussions. Supported by Genentech, Inc.

2. Secretion of Human Interferons by Yeast

Ronald A. Hitzeman, David W. Leung, L. Jeanne Perry
William J. Kohr, Howard L. Levine, David V. Goeddel

With the advent of recombinant DNA technology, it has been possible to examine the expression and secretion of eukaryotic gene products by the prokaryote *Escherichia coli*. Talmadge *et al.* (*1*) have shown that hybrid gene products containing bacterial–eukaryotic secretion signals (β-lactamase–rat preproinsulin) can be processed to proinsulin, which is then found in the periplasmic space of *E. coli*. They have also shown that for these hybrid proteins the eukaryotic signal (amino-terminal protein sequence) alone is sufficient to obtain secretion and processing in *E. coli* (*2*). Using another *E. coli* expression plasmid, Fraser and Bruce (*3*) have observed expression and secretion of chicken ovalbumin into the periplasmic space of *E. coli*. However, the secretion signal for this protein is thought to be within the protein sequence and there is no cleavage during the process (*4*). These results suggest that secretion signals may be functionally similar for many organisms. In this chapter we examine the secretion and processing of mammalian interferon (IFN) gene products in the lower eukaryote yeast.

The study of protein secretion from *Saccharomyces cerevisiae* (yeast) has focused primarily on the acid phosphatase and invertase enzymes (*5*), which are secreted into the periplasmic space. These enzymes are expressed as precursors having hydrophobic amino-terminal signal sequences (*6*) that are subsequently removed during the secretion process. Schekman and Novick (*5*) have used these enzymes to examine the secretion pathway in temperature-sensitive secretion mutants (*sec*). Characterization of these mutants has led to the recognition of a pathway in yeast that is organelle-dependent (*5*) and similar to that observed for the mammalian exocrine cells (*7*). The yeast pathway appears to start with translation of the pre-protein at the endoplasmic reticulum where the presequence (amino-terminal signal peptide) is removed after passage through the membrane, and then transported to the Golgi where vesicle intermediates are formed. These vesicles then move to the bud of the plasma membrane where fusion occurs with subsequent release of protein from the cell.

Plasmids that allow expression of heterologous (non-yeast) genes in the lower eukaryote yeast have recently been developed. Hitzeman *et al.* (*8*), using the promoter of the highly expressed yeast alcohol dehydrogenase I gene (*9*) to initiate transcription, demonstrated the synthesis of human IFN-α1 in yeast. However, the IFN-α1 used in these experiments was modified so that the NH$_2$-terminal signal peptide coding sequence was replaced by an ATG translational start codon. Therefore the polypeptide produced was mature IFN-α1 (the form found after secretion from human cells); it was not secreted from the yeast cell.

We have recently constructed a different portable yeast promoter (10) from another highly expressed yeast glycolytic gene encoding 3-phosphoglycerate kinase (PGK). This gene was isolated, characterized, and sequenced (11). When the PGK promoter fragment was used in a yeast plasmid, the heterologous complementary DNA (cDNA) genes for both mature (secretion signal absent) and pre-IFN's (secretion signal present) have been expressed in yeast. The pre-IFN genes contain coding sequences for mature IFN's as well as extra amino-terminal protein sequences. These terminal sequences signal the secretion of the proteins from the human cell and are cleaved during the process to give mature IFN's (12). We describe below the expression, processing, and secretion of these pre-IFN gene products by yeast, using the PGK expression system.

Heterologous Gene Expression Plasmid

All the IFN expression plasmids in our study were derived from a single parental plasmid. The plasmid YEp1PT, which contains the PGK promoter fragment and other expression, selection, and maintenance components (Fig. 1), including the large Eco RI to Bam HI fragment of pBR322 (13) containing the ampicillin resistance (Ap^R) gene and replication origin for selection and stable growth in E. coli. Also YEp1PT contains the TRP1 gene on an Eco RI to Pst 1 DNA fragment originating from yeast

chromosome IV (14). This gene permits selection for the plasmid in trp1 mutant yeast cells growing in medium lacking tryptophan. The yeast origin of replication in YEp1PT is contained on a 2.0-kilobase-pair (kbp) fragment (Eco RI to Pst 1) from the endogenous yeast 2 micrometer (circumference) plasmid (15). This origin allows the DNA to replicate autonomously in yeast and be maintained as a plasmid in 90 to 95 percent of yeast cells grown in media depleted of tryptophan (legend to Table 1).

The YEp1PT plasmid system contains the yeast PGK promoter fragment (Hind III to Eco RI). Transcription originates from the PGK promoter near the only Eco RI restriction site in the plasmid [the other Eco RI site was removed (8)] and proceeds in the direction indicated (Fig. 1). The PGK promoter fragment was constructed from the yeast PGK gene based on DNA sequence information (11) and contains about 1600 base pairs (bp) of PGK 5'-flanking DNA sequence. The sequence 5'-TCTA-GAATTC-3' (T, thymine; C, cytosine; G, guanine; A, adenine) which contains Eco RI and Xba I restriction sites for convenient attachment of heterologous genes (12), has been substituted for the 10 bp of PGK sequence preceding the ATG translation initiation codon. A Hind III–Bgl II fragment from the yeast TRP1 gene region (14) was used as a Hind III to Bgl II converter for ligation with the Bam HI site of pBR322. The 2.0-kbp fragment from 2 μm plasmid DNA also contains the transcription termination and polyadenylation signals which are normally the signals for the "Able" (or FLP) gene in the 2 μm plasmid (16). We have recently shown that such a region is essential for heterologous gene expression in yeast (17), which Zaret and Sherman (18) have

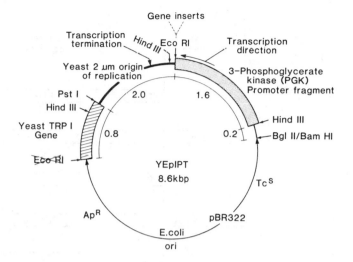

Fig. 1. Yeast expression plasmid. The partial restriction map of YEp1PT is shown. The components required for transcription and translation of a heterologous gene inserted at the single Eco RI site are designated.

shown for homologous gene expression. Each of the IFN genes was inserted as an Eco RI restriction fragment into the only Eco RI site of YEp1PT between the promoter and termination signals. Restriction mapping allowed us to select isolates in which the gene was oriented correctly for transcription from the PGK promoter. Other foreign genes, which have been expressed in yeast when this system was used include the genes for human serum albumin, hepatitis B virus surface antigen, and human growth hormone (10).

Modifications of IFN Complementary DNA's for Expression in Yeast

Some of the Eco RI restriction fragments, containing interferon cDNA's which were constructed for use in the YEp1PT expression plasmid, are illustrated in Fig. 2. The constructions of the DNA fragments for mature IFN-α1 (8), IFN-α2 (19), and IFN-γ (20) are known (21). The mature IFN-α2 construction required a final modification to convert

the Pst I restriction site at the 3' end of the gene to an Eco RI site. A 245-bp Pst I to Eco RI DNA fragment obtained from yeast 2 μm plasmid DNA (16) was used for this purpose. Eco RI sites were placed immediately upstream from the ATG initiation codons of the pre-IFN genes by the primer repair technique (22) or by conversion of convenient restriction sites. The amino-terminal protein sequence of each IFN (21) and the cleavage site recognized during secretion from human cells is shown in Fig. 3. The gene for preD IFN-α1 (construction II) was modified for direct expression by the primer repair method. The preD/A IFN-α2 fragment (construction IV) was then made with a Dde I restriction site common to the signal peptide coding sequences of both the preD IFN-α1 and preA IFN-α2 genes. Amino acids that differ in preA from preD signal sequences are underlined in Fig. 3. The hybrid signal sequence (preD/A) of preD/A IFN-α2 is more like preD than preA, differing only at the −2 residue from preD. Two different preγ IFN-γ cDNA fragments were constructed. The Sau 3a

24

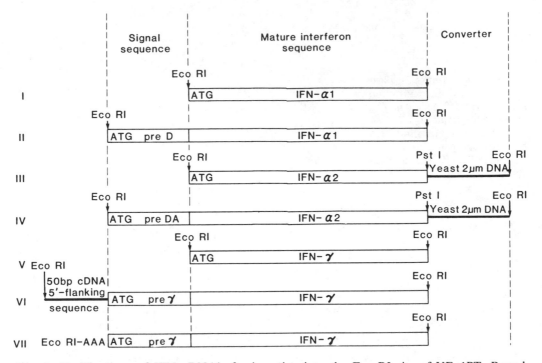

Fig. 2. Modifications of IFN cDNA's for insertion into the Eco RI site of YEp1PT. Boxed regions refer to IFN cDNA sequences and are not drawn to scale. Line sequences show unique characteristics or additional DNA added to the cDNA's. The addition of Eco RI restriction sites and ATG translational starts immediately before the mature IFN sequences have been described for constructions I (8), III (19), and V (20). The Eco RI site in construction II was added by cleavage of the IFN-α1 signal peptide coding region (12) with Hae III and subsequent ligation to the synthetic deoxyoligonucleotide 5' CCATGAATTCATGG 3', which regenerates the rest of the signal sequence and an Eco RI site as in the mature IFN constructions. Hybrid construction IV was made with the use of a Dde I site common to the signal coding regions for preD IFN-α1 and preA IFN-α2 (12) (see Fig. 3). Construction VI was made by conversion of Sau 3A sites in the 3' and 5' flanking regions of IFN-γ cDNA (20) to Eco RI sites by means of converter fragments in plasmid pUC7 (29). The 5' Eco RI site of construction VII was made with synthetic DNA in a primer repair reaction (22). Restriction enzyme cleavage, synthetic DNA synthesis, and ligations were done as described (11). The E. coli K-12 strain 294 (30) was used for all bacterial transformations. Purification of covalently closed circular plasmid DNA's from E. coli, transformation of E. coli, and plasmid miniscreens were done as described (11).

restriction sites on both sides of the structural gene were converted to Eco RI sites in one construction. The resulting fragment (VI) contains 50 bp of 5' untranslated DNA sequence. The other construction (VII) was made with a synthetic DNA converter. The signal sequences (Fig. 3) all have regions of hy-

drophobic residues which are characteristic of other signal sequences (7).

Expression of Interferon Complementary DNA's in Yeast

The genes shown in Fig. 2 were inserted into YEp1PT at the Eco RI site, and

Dde I site in DNA | Cleavage site

	-23	-22	-21	-20	-19	-18	-17	-16	-15	-14	-13	-12	-11	-10	-9	-8	-7	-6	-5	-4	-3	-2	-1	+1	+2
preA	Met	Ala	Leu	Thr	Phe	Ala	Leu	Leu	Val	Ala	Leu	Leu	Val	Leu	Ser	Cys	Lys	Ser	Ser	Cys	Ser	Val	Gly	Cys	Asp
preD	Met	Ala	Ser	Pro	Phe	Ala	Leu	Leu	Met	Ala	Leu	Val	Val	Leu	Ser	Cys	Lys	Ser	Ser	Cys	Ser	Leu	Gly	Cys	Asp
preD/A	Met	Ala	Ser	Pro	Phe	Ala	Leu	Leu	Met	Ala	Leu	Val	Val	Leu	Ser	Cys	Lys	Ser	Ser	Cys	Ser	Val	Gly	Cys	Asp
preγ			Met	Lys	Tyr	Thr	Ser	Tyr	Ile	Leu	Ala	Phe	Gln	Leu	Cys	Ile	Val	Leu	Gly	Ser	Leu	Gly	Cys	Tyr	

Fig. 3. Amino acid sequences of the various secretion signals. A comparison of the amino acid sequences (28) of the signal regions preD, preA, preD/A, and preγ is shown. The amino acids underlined represent differences between the amino acid sequences of preD and preA. The Dde I site indicates the junction shared by these two presequences used to prepare the hybrid (preD/A) presequence. The sites of cleavage used in human cells are also shown.

the *trp*1⁻ yeast strains GM3C-2 (23) and 20B-12 (24) were transformed with these plasmids. Yeast strain 20B-12 was chosen for its diminished protease activity, which might result in more stable secreted IFN molecules. Transformants were assayed for interferon activity by the cytopathic effect test (25). The assays were done on three distinct compartmental locations in the yeast culture (Table 1).

Interferon activity remaining inside the cell after cell wall removal is defined as interferon activity that is not secreted. Interferon activity found in the medium (material completely separate from yeast cell) plus the activity released from the cells after cell wall removal by the enzyme zymolyase (5) together represent the total secreted material. Alternatively, when cell walls were not removed, "inside cell" activity also includes the secreted activity present in the periplasmic space; thus, under these conditions, the "activity secreted" may be an underestimate (Table 1).

Both mature IFN-α1 and IFN-α2 genes (constructions I and III) were expressed in the yeast as 1.0 percent of the total cellular protein based on IFN activity bioassays. This calculated level was confirmed by sodium dodecyl sulfate

(SDS)–polyacrylamide gel protein analysis of whole cell extracts (data not shown). No activity was found when the genes were inserted in the wrong orientation. No secretion of IFN activity was observed with these two mature genes or with the mature IFN-γ gene (construction V). However, IFN activity was found in the media for all of the pre-IFN constructions.

As shown in Table 1, IFN secretion varies from one gene to another with preγ IFN-γ giving the highest percentage of secretion. Depending on yeast strain and the gene construction, secretion into the medium of IFN-γ varies from 10 to 21 percent. However, additional IFN may be in the periplasmic space (not determined). Comparison of the production of preγ IFN-γ directed by constructions VI and VII shows that the presence of 50 bp of 5′ untranslated cDNA sequence reduces but does not destroy expression of the gene. However, this result is not inconsistent with the Kozak hypothesis of translation initiation in eukaryotes (26) since there are no translational start codons in this intervening region. Yeast containing preD IFN-α1 and preD/A IFN-α2 constructions secrete from 3 to 5 percent of IFN activity into the periplasmic space and medium

Table I. Interferon expression.

Gene construction	Eco RI fragments	Yeast	Inside cell*		Released after cell wall removal†		Outside cell (media)		Final‡ A_{660}	Activity secreted§ (%)
			$A_{660} = 1$ (10⁶ U/liter)	Total cell protein (%)	$A_{660} = 1$ (10⁶ U/liter)	Total cell protein (%)	$A_{660} = 1$ (10⁶ U/liter)	Total cell protein (%)		
I	IFN-α1	GM3C-2	130	1.0	0	0	0	0	1.0	0
II	preD IFN-α1	GM3C-2	27	0.3	0.4	0.004	0.8	0.008	1.4	4
III	IFN-α2	20B-12	130	1.0	0	0	0	0	1.0	0
IV	preD/A IFN-α2	20B-12	19	0.2	0.5	0.005	0.5	0.005	1.0	5
IV	preD/A IFN-α2	20B-12	25	0.1			2.0	0.007	3 to 4	8
IV	preD/A IFN-α2	GM3C-2	28	0.3	0.3	0.003	0.5	0.005	1.3	3
V	IFN-γ	20B-12	0.6				0	0	1.0	0
VI	preγ IFN-γ + cDNA 5' flanking sequence	20B-12	0.2				0.03		1.2	15
VI	preγ IFN-γ + cDNA 5' flanking sequence	GM3C-2	0.38				0.06		0.93	16
VII	preγ IFN-γ	20B-12	0.9				0.19		1.0	21
VII	preγ IFN-γ	GM3C-2	1.9				0.19		0.93	10

*Two methods were used for extracts. When cell walls were removed the "inside cell" amount was really inside material; however, when cell walls were not removed, the "inside cell" amount and the "released after cell wall removal" are both part of "inside cell" amount—this type of extract involves glass beading cells without cell wall removal. Glass bead extracts, without cell wall removal, were always made for IFN-γ and preγ IFN-γ and PBS buffer was used instead of 7M guanidine hydrochloride. The specific activities of IFN-α1 and IFN-α2 were both assumed to be 10⁸U per milligram of protein for the calculations. One liter of yeast culture contains about 100 mg of protein at an $A_{660} = 1$. †See procedure for cell wall removal above. ‡Absorbance at 660 nm of culture at each assay done. §The activity secreted is the percent "released after cell wall removal" plus the percent "outside cell". When cell walls were not removed, the "activity secreted" does not include the periplasmic activity.

at an $A_{660} \simeq 1$; however, when preD/A IFN-α2/20B-12 was grown to A_{660} of 3 to 4, secretion into the medium alone was 8 percent. The amount of IFN activity in the periplasmic space was not determined at this higher absorbancy. However, in most instances the IFN activity in the periplasmic space was approximately equal to that found free in the media.

The IFN's produced by two of the yeast strains were further characterized. These were YEp1PT-preD/A IFN-α2/20B-12 and YEp1PT-IFN-α2/20B-12. The former contains construction IV (Fig. 2) in the Eco RI site of YEp1PT and results in IFN-α2 activity inside the cell, in the periplasmic space, and outside the cell (medium). The latter yeast strain contains construction III (Fig. 2) in YEp1PT and produces mature IFN-α2 intracellularly but not in the medium. Growth curves for these two yeast strains in YNB plus Casamino acids

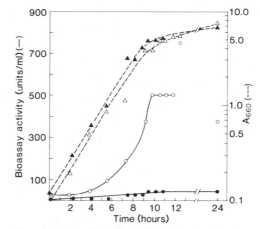

Fig. 4. Growth curves (triangles) showing secretion (circles) of preD/A IFN-α2 into the medium. YEpIPT-IFN-α2/20B-12 (▲, ●) synthesizes mature IFN-α2 which remains within the cell. YEpIPT-preD/A IFN-α2/20B-12 (△, ○) expresses the preD/A IFN-α2 gene and produces IFN activity in the medium. The media were assayed as described in the legend of Table 1.

(Difco) selective medium are shown in Fig. 4. Bioassays of the medium at vari-

Table 1 (facing page) shows interferon expression. Yeast strains 20B-12 (α *trp1 pep4-3*) (*24*) and GM3C-2 (*a leu2-3 leu2-112 trp1-1 his4-519 cyc1-1 cyp3-1*) (*23*) were used for yeast transformations (*33*). Yeast were grown on the following media: (i) YEPD contained 1 percent yeast extract, 2 percent peptone, and 2 percent glucose (used prior to transformation). (ii) YNB+CAA (used for Trp$^+$ selection and plasmid maintenance) contained (per liter) 6.7 g of yeast nitrogen base (without amino acids) (YNB) (Difco), 10 mg of adenine, 10 mg of uracil, 5 g of Difco Casamino acids (CAA), and 20 g of glucose. Solid medium contained 3 percent agar. Stability of plasmids in yeast was determined by replica plating colonies from YEPD (nonselective to YNB+CAA (selective) media. Extracts and media from yeast were assayed for interferon by the cytopathic effect (CPE) inhibition assay and comparison with interferon standards (*25*). Media were assayed directly after cell removal while yeast extracts were prepared as follows: cultures were grown in YNB+CAA and 10-ml samples of cells were collected by centrifugation, resuspended in 3 ml of 1.2M sorbitol, 10 mM KH$_2$PO$_4$ (pH 6.8), and 1 percent zymolyase 60,000, and incubated at 30°C for 30 minutes (about 90 percent of cell wall removed). Spheroplasts were centrifuged, resuspended in 150 μl of 7M guanidine hydrochloride, and diluted in phosphate-buffered saline (PBS) containing bovine serum albumin (BSA) [20 mM NaH$_2$PO$_4$ (pH 7.4), 150 mM NaCl, and 0.5 percent BSA]. Alternatively, 10 ml of cells at the same A_{660} were centrifuged and resuspended in 0.4 ml of 7M guanidine hydrochloride in an Eppendorf (1.5 ml) tube containing about 0.4 ml of glass beads (0.45 to 0.5 mm; B. Braun Melsurgen AG). These tubes were mixed twice for 2 minutes at the highest Vortex setting; they were cooled in ice between the mixings. The extracts were cleared in an Eppendorf centrifuge (0.5 minute) and diluted in PBS/BSA buffer as above. Bioassays were performed with MDBK cells (*25*) for IFN-α1, IFN-α2, and their respective pre-forms, but with HeLa cells (*25*) for IFN-γ and preγ IFN-γ.

Figure 5

——— preD/A secretion signal sequence ——— | ——— mature IFN-α2 sequence

-23- -22- -21- -20- -19- -18- -17- -16- -15- -14- -13- -12- -11- -10- -9- -8- -7- -6- -5- -4- -3- -2- -1 1 2 3 4 5 6 7 8 9 10

Met Ala Ser Pro Phe Ala Leu Leu Met Ala Leu Val Val Leu Ser Cys Lys Ser Ser Cys Ser Val Gly Cys Asp Leu Pro Gln Thr His Ser Leu Gly

Growth medium interferon (10%)
None ——— 36% ——— 64%

Intracellular and periplasmic interferon (90%)
11% ——— 55% ——— 34%

——— preD secretion signal sequence ——— | ——— mature IFN-α1 sequence

Met Ala Ser Pro Phe Ala Leu Leu Met Ala Leu Val Val Leu Ser Cys Lys Ser Ser Cys Ser Leu Gly Cys Asp Leu Pro Glu Thr His Ser Leu Asp

Growth medium interferon (30%)
8% ——— 47% ——— 45%

ous times during cell growth clearly demonstrate that the presequence on IFN-α2 is essential for secretion of IFN activity into the media. When the presequence is absent no activity is released. This has also been confirmed by further analysis of proteins from the two concentrated media. After separation of the proteins on an SDS–polyacrylamide gel and transfer to nitrocellulose paper (27), labeled antibody specific for interferon reacts with a protein the size of mature IFN-α2 only from the preD/A IFN-α2 expressor and not from the mature IFN-α2 expressor (data not shown). It is also evident that the activity in the medium and the percent secreted (Table 1) reach maxima near the stationary phase of cell growth; however, expression in the cell reaches a maximum during the log phase of growth (between $A_{660} = 1$ to 2, data not shown).

One possible explanation for finding IFN in the medium was that the presequence of interferon somehow makes the cells more susceptible to lysis during growth. This possibility was examined by measuring the amounts of protein in the media at stationary phase. The media from both yeast strains (containing constructions III and IV) contained equivalent concentrations of total protein when compared at the same cell density and showed identical patterns upon SDS-gel electrophoresis. Thus, true secretion of IFN must be occurring.

Fig. 5 (facing page) shows processing and distribution of preD/A IFN-α2 and preD IFN-α1 by yeast. The 23 amino acid presequence of preD/A IFN-α2 (consisting of 23 amino acids) is shown as well as the first ten amino acids of mature IFN-α2 sequence. Ten percent of the synthesized IFN activity was found in the medium and 90 percent was cell associated (about 80 percent in the cell and 10 percent in the periplasmic space). The IFN from these two growth fractions (medium and cells) was processed in various forms as shown. The preD IFN-α1 isolated from culture medium was processed as shown with 30 percent in the medium and 70 percent cell associated. Yeast were grown at 30°C to A_{660} of 4. At this time the 5-liter culture was harvested by centrifugation. The medium was concentrated and diafiltered in an Amicon thin channel apparatus or a 2.5-liter stirred cell. The retentate was further purified by ion exchange chromatography on CM-52 and subsequent immunoaffinity column chromatography as described for IFN-α2 (31). Fractions containing IFN were further purified by high-performance liquid chromatography (HPLC) on a Synchropak RP-P column. The column was eluted at a flow rate of 1 milliliter per minute with a linear gradient of 0 to 100 percent acetonitrile containing 0.1 percent trifluoroacetic acid, pH 2.5, in 60 minutes. The protein in the peak fractions containing interferon activity was then sequenced at the amino-terminal end by Edman degradation (32). The cells were disrupted in a Bead Beater (Biospec Products). The lysate was centrifuged, the pellet was washed, and the supernatants were combined. The supernatants were dialyzed, and the IFN was purified as described above for medium material. The protein from fractions containing IFN activity was then sequenced at the amino-terminal end. The protein sequence was interpreted by noting which 3-phenyl-2-thiohydantoin (Pth) amino acid derivatives increased in each Edman cycle and then decreased in the following cycle (32). Pth amino acids that normally give low recoveries (Cys, Ser, Thr, Arg, His) were assumed during a cycle based upon amino acid sequence obtained in previous and following cycles. The percentage of each form was estimated by comparing the areas of the interpreted residue with an area from a standard mixture of Pth amino acids run on the same HPLC run. Most of the forms were sequenced for 21 cycles or 21 amino acids. An internal standard of norleucine was introduced in each chromatogram to ensure that retention times were reproducible.

Nature of Processing of Pre-IFN's

Since yeast cells can secrete preD/A IFN-α2 and since secretory processing of the amino-terminal end might occur as in mammalian cells, it was of interest to purify the protein product from the media and cells separately.

Cell extracts and media were obtained from 5-liter fermentations and the interferon was purified as described (Fig. 5). Cell extracts also contain the IFN from the periplasmic space since the cell wall was not removed prior to extract preparation. The protein sequencing results obtained for this purified preD/A IFN-α2 are shown in Fig. 5. The sequence expected for preD/A IFN-α2 if no processing were to occur and the normal cleavage point of this interferon in mammalian cells (12) are also shown. Two independent sequence runs were performed on two different purified samples from cells and media. Most of the IFN in the medium was properly processed (64 percent), but another form (36 percent) containing three additional amino acids of presequence was also present. The intracellular interferon also contained these two forms, but in slightly different proportions, as well as a third form containing eight amino acids of presequence. Full length presequence was never observed, suggesting that yeast processes all of the pre-IFN in some manner.

It is possible that the processed form containing three amino acids of presequence resulted from the hybrid nature of the preD/A signal sequence. Therefore, the processing of the nonhybrid preD IFN-α1 protein was also examined. PreD is different from preD/A only at amino acid position −2 [Leu versus Val (28)]. When the processing of preD IFN-α1 purified from the medium was examined, both the +1 and −3 forms were

again observed (Fig. 5). However, a minor species was also present in the medium as a −14 form, which was not seen for preD/A IFN-α2. It should be mentioned that preD IFN-α1 was produced from a high cell density yeast fermentation ($A_{550} = 60$) unlike preD/A IFN-α2 ($A_{660} = 4$). This difference in growth conditions may be responsible for the −14 form. Again, even at high cell density, there was no evidence of cell lysis occurring in the culture. Interestingly, at this high cell density, a higher percentage secretion (30 percent) into the medium was obtained for preD IFN-α1. High cell density fermentations of preD/A IFN-α2 expressing yeast also show this higher percentage secretion.

Conclusions and Discussion

To investigate the secretion of heterologous proteins from *S. cerevisiae*, we have constructed plasmids for in vivo transcription of the genes for several mature IFN's and several pre-IFN's. Whenever the coding sequences for hydrophobic signal peptides were present, IFN antiviral activity could be recovered both from the host cells and from the culture medium, while all of the IFN whose synthesis was directed by genes for mature IFN remained inside the cells. We have attempted to characterize the requirements for secretion by undertaking constructions in which the interferon gene would be provided with its own natural signal sequence, as in preD IFN-α1, or would be provided with a hybrid signal sequence designed as a composite of two IFN-α species, as in preD/A IFN-α2. While, in general, the yeast cells which harbored these constructions secreted IFN into the culture medium, the amount of activity differed between strains, and the IFN species purified and sequenced also differed.

Two forms of preD/A IFN-α2, together constituting 10 percent of the total IFN expressed, were purified from the medium of cells harboring the preD/A IFN-α2 gene. The major species was properly processed as in human cells (+1, Fig. 5), while another species had three additional amino acids or presequence (−3, Fig. 4). This second form may indicate a difference between yeast and human cell processing of secreted proteins. Alternatively, the −3 form might be a natural processed form of IFN previously unnoticed in preparations made from human leukocytes. The presence of this species appears not to be caused by the hybrid signal sequence, since interferon species examined from medium of cells harboring the preD IFN-α1 gene are also heterogeneous. In addition to the +1 and −3 forms, that medium contained a minor interferon species which included 14 amino acid residues of signal peptide (−14 in Fig. 5). The presence of this minor form is somewhat surprising because of the preD/A IFN-α2 results and its retention of part of the hydrophobic region of the presequence. The significance of this form requires further investigation.

Three forms of cell-associated IFN-α2, constituting 90 percent of the total interferon expressed, were purified from cells harboring the preD/A IFN-α2 gene. One form (34 percent) was properly processed (+1, Fig. 5), a second form (55 percent) contained three additional amino acids (−3, Fig. 5), and a third form (11 percent) contained eight additional amino acids (−8). The last form was not seen in media, while IFN with a full length presequence (21) was never observed in the cells or media. However, it is possible that this pre-protein could lack IFN activity and would be lost during the purification process. The approximately fivefold lower expression levels observed for leukocyte pre-IFN's compared to mature IFN's are suggestive of this possibility (Table 1). Alternatively, the lower expression levels observed may be the result of pre-protein instability.

Overall, yeast cells appear to process both the secreted and nonsecreted IFN. The amount of activity secreted varies depending on the growth stage of the cells, with maximum percentages occurring at stationary phase in shake flasks and at the end of high cell density fermentations (30 percent of IFN in medium). However, complete secretion of interferon has never been seen even though most of the intracellular IFN is processed as the extracellular IFN. It is possible that IFN may be entering various organelles instead of being released through the plasma membrane. To examine this, we are comparing cellular locations of interferon from both mature and pre-interferon–producing yeast.

Several features make yeast an attractive host microorganism for production of polypeptides. Yeast is capable of withstanding high hydrostatic pressure and does not lyse after death. At no time have we seen evidence of cell lysis in stationary phase cultures, or in cultures grown in fermenters to very high cell densities. Furthermore, the growth medium typically contains only five to eight major protein species of apparent size (probably glycosylated) greater than 50,000 daltons. This relatively "clean" medium (less than 0.5 percent of total yeast protein), combined with the resistance of yeast to lysis by external stresses, provides a good system for secretion studies. We have shown above that secretion of heterologous gene products by yeast can be effected by use of natural or hybrid human signal sequences. Furthermore, we have recently demonstrated that yeast protein signal sequences, such as those for yeast invertase (*34*) and yeast α-factor (*35, 36*), attached to heterologous proteins result in secretion of the heterologous proteins into the culture media and proper processing (*37*).

References and Notes

1. K. Talmadge, S. Stahl, W. Gilbert, *Proc. Natl. Acad. Sci. U.S.A.* **77**, 3369 (1980); K. Talmadge, J. Kaufman, W. Gilbert, *ibid.*, p. 3988.
2. K. Talmadge, J. Brosius, W. Gilbert, *Nature (London)* **294**, 176 (1981).
3. T. H. Fraser and B. J. Bruce, *Proc. Natl. Acad. Sci. U.S.A.* **75**, 5936 (1978).
4. R. D. Palmiter, J. Gagnon, K. A. Walsh, *ibid.*, p. 94.
5. R. Schekman and P. Novick, in *The Molecular Biology of the Yeast Saccharomyces*, J. N. Strathern, E. W. Jones, J. R. Broach, Eds. (Cold Spring Harbor Laboratory, Cold Spring Harbor, N.Y., in press).
6. D. Perlman and H. O. Halvorson, *Cell* **25**, 525 (1981); _____, L. E. Cannon, *Proc. Natl. Acad. Sci. U.S.A.* **79**, 781 (1982); M. Carlson and D. Botstein, *Cell* **28**, 145 (1982).
7. G. Palade, *Science* **189**, 347 (1975); G. Blobel and B. Dobberstein, *J. Cell Biol.* **67**, 835 (1975).
8. R. A. Hitzeman, F. E. Hagie, H. L. Levine, D. V. Goeddel, G. Ammerer, B. D. Hall, *Nature (London)* **293**, 717 (1981).
9. J. L. Bennetzen and B. D. Hall, *J. Biol. Chem.* **257**, 3018 (1982).
10. R. A. Hitzeman *et al.*, *Proceedings of the Berkeley Workshop on Recent Advances in Yeast Molecular Biology: Recombinant DNA* (University of California Press, Berkeley, 1982), p. 173.
11. R. A. Hitzeman, L. Clarke, J. Carbon, *J. Biol. Chem.* **255**, 12073 (1980); R. A. Hitzeman, F. E. Hagie, J. S. Hayflick, C. Y. Chen, P. H. Seeburg, R. Derynck, *Nucleic Acids Res.* **10**, 7791 (1982).
12. D. V. Goeddel *et al.*, *Nature (London)* **290**, 20 (1981).
13. F. Bolivar *et al.*, *Gene* **2**, 95 (1977).
14. D. T. Stinchcomb, K. Struhl, R. W. Davis, *Nature (London)* **282**, 39 (1979); G. Tschumper and J. Carbon, *Gene* **10**, 157 (1980).
15. J. R. Broach, J. N. Strathern, J. B. Hicks, *Gene* **8**, 121 (1979).
16. J. L. Hartley and J. E. Donelson, *Nature (London)* **286**, 860 (1980).
17. C. Chen and R. Hitzeman, unpublished results.
18. K. S. Zaret and F. Sherman, *Cell* **28**, 563 (1982).
19. D. V. Goeddel *et al.*, *Nature (London)* **287**, 411 (1980).
20. P. W. Gray *et al.*, *ibid.* **295**, 503 (1982).
21. Previously, IFN-α1 and IFN-α2 have been called LeIF D and LeIF A, respectively (*12*). Names for presequences (preA, preD, and preD/A) were derived from this previous system of naming.
22. D. V. Goeddel, H. M. Shepard, E. Yelverton, D. Leung, R. Crea, *Nucleic Acids Res.* **8**, 4057 (1980); R. M. Lawn *et al.*, *ibid.* **9**, 6103 (1981).
23. G. Faye, D. W. Leung, K. Tatchell, B. D. Hall, M. Smith, *Proc. Natl. Acad. Sci. U.S.A.* **78**, 2258 (1981).
24. E. Jones, *Genetics* **85**, 23 (1976).
25. W. E. Stewart II, *The Interferon System* (Springer-Verlag, New York, 1979).
26. M. Kozak, *Nucleic Acids Res.* **9**, 5233 (1981).
27. H. A. Erlich, J. R. Levinson, S. N. Cohen, H. O. McDevitt, *J. Biol. Chem.* **254**, 12240 (1979).
28. Abbreviations for amino acid residues are Met, methionine; Ala, alanine; Leu, leucine; Ser, serine; Thr, threonine; Pro, proline; Phe, phenylalanine; Val, valine; Cys, cysteine; Lys, lysine; Gly, glycine; Asp, aspartic acid; Tyr, tyrosine; Ile, isoleucine; Gln, glutamine; Glu, glutamic acid; and His, histidine.
29. Plasmid pUC7 has an Eco RI site on both sides of a Bam HI site and was given to us by Dr. Joachim Messing of the University of Minnesota.
30. K. Backman, M. Ptashne, W. Gilbert, *Proc. Natl. Acad. Sci. U.S.A.* **73**, 4174 (1976).
31. T. Staehelin, D. S. Hobbs, H. Kung, C. Y. Lai, S. Pestka, *J. Biol. Chem.* **256**, 9750 (1981).
32. P. Edman and G. Begg, *Eur. J. Biochem.* **1**, 80 (1967).
33. A. Hinnen, J. B. Hicks, G. R. Fink, *Proc. Natl. Acad. Sci. U.S.A.* **75**, 1929 (1978).
34. M. Carlson and D. Botstein, *Cell* **28**, 145 (1982).
35. J. Kurjan and I. Herskowitz, *Cell* **30**, 933 (1982).
36. A. Singh, E. Y. Chen, J. M. Lugovoy, C. N. Chang, R. A. Hitzeman, P. H. Seeburg, *Nucleic Acids Res.*, in press.
37. A. Singh, C. N. Chang, M. Matteucci, and R. Hitzeman, unpublished results.
38. We thank John Wulf and Dr. James Swartz for yeast fermentations, Mark Vasser for the synthesis of oligonucleotides for restriction site modifications of DNA's, Harvard Morehead and Maurice Woods for high-performance liquid chromatography, Christina Chen and Evelyn Shuster for technical assistance, Dr. Robert Hershberg for advice concerning purification of interferon, and Dr. Rik Derynck for insertion of mature IFN-γ gene into the Eco RI site of YEp1PT.

3. Multiple Point Mutations Affecting the Simian Virus 40 Enhancer

Hans Weiher, Monika König, Peter Gruss

An understanding of the regulatory events controlling gene expression in higher eukaryotes is important in the study of such complex phenomena as differentiation, transformation, and malignancy. The substantial progress made on this subject has been aided by achievements in molecular biology such as molecular cloning and site directed mutagenesis. Much of this information is derived from studies with animal viruses. Because of their limited genetic capacity, the viruses rely on cellular enzymes, and thus provide a useful model system to study the basic mechanisms of cellular gene control.

One of the best studied animal virus systems is simian virus 40 (SV40) (Fig. 1) (*1*). Its genome is a double-stranded covalently closed circular DNA molecule of 5243 nucleotides (*2–4*). In permissive monkey kidney cells, an early and a late phase characterize its life cycle. The early and late coding sequences are situated on opposite halves of the genome and are transcribed in opposite directions (Fig. 1). Early gene expression has been extensively studied, and the controlling elements for transcriptional initiation do not appear to require virally coded gene products.

Several eukaryotic promoters have been examined both by DNA sequencing and by in vitro and in vivo analysis of mutants. These studies have led to the identification of the so-called Goldberg-Hogness or TATA box (T, thymine; A, adenine), a signal that is involved in the precise positioning of 5' RNA ends (*5, 6*). Other sequences upstream of the TATA box, which are absolutely required for promoter activity, have been identified in various promoter sequences (*7*). Recently, a detailed analysis of the promoter of the herpes simplex thymidine kinase (TK) gene (*8*) resulted in an identification of three essential regions within 105 base pairs (bp) upstream of the RNA initiation site.

In SV40 a 72-bp repeated unit located approximately 100 to 175 bp upstream of the early cap (initiation site) position appeared to be essential in *cis* for the expression of the SV40 early genes (*9*). The repeated nature of this element is not essential, as indicated by naturally occurring variants of SV40 containing only a single copy of the 72-bp repeat (*4*). Further analyses revealed some surprising characteristics of this particular controlling element. It was found that the tandem repeats retained their activity when inserted at a different position or in inverse orientation relative to the early

34

Fig. 1. Schematic representation of a functional map of SV40. SV40 has a circular covalently closed double-stranded DNA of 5243 bp (*1–4*). Taking the origin of replication (*ori*) as a start point, the early gene products (small t antigen and large T antigen) are transcribed counterclockwise. After the onset of DNA replication mediated by the origin of replication, abundant late gene products, VP-1,

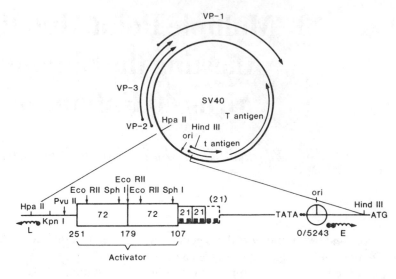

VP-2, and VP-3, are produced. The origin region is enlarged, demonstrating the presence of a 72-bp repeat and a 21-bp repeat. The filled square boxes within the 21-bp repeat represent a CCGCCC unit present at least six times. TATA is representing the Goldberg-Hogness box for early transcripts. The nucleotide numbers used are those of Van Heuverswyn and Fiers (*4*).

coding region (*10, 11*). Earlier studies of Capecchi (*12*) had shown that linkage of SV40 sequences to the herpes TK gene enhanced the frequency of transformation of TK$^-$ to TK$^+$ cells. Similarly, a dramatic increase in rabbit globin gene transcription mediated by the SV40 72-bp repeats was demonstrated (*13*). These experiments showed that this region of the SV40 genome can stimulate transcription from heterologous promoters. The terms "enhancer" (*13*) and "activator" (*14*) have been proposed to describe elements of this kind. Analogous elements have also been found in other animal viruses such as Moloney sarcoma virus (MSV), Rous sarcoma virus (RSV), bovine papilloma virus (BPV), polyoma virus, and in the human genome (*11, 14–16*).

Several of the described activator elements have been tested for their ability

to substitute for one another in functional assays. The MSV (*14*) and the BPV (*11*) enhancers can both replace the SV40 72-bp repeats to some extent as assayed by replication in monkey cells. However, quantitative measurements of gene expression from the SV40 early promoter with either the SV40 or MSV enhancer has indicated that these elements may have different host cell specificity (*17*). In addition, alterations within a region of the polyoma virus genome which contains the enhancer function (*16*) enables the mutated virus to grow in nondifferentiated teratocarcinoma stem cells (*18*). These data not only point to the central role of enhancers as *cis*-acting signal sequences, but also indicate their possible regulatory function. Although activator elements often seem to reside within repeated sequences, very little information is available concerning the critical sequences necessary for enhancer function. Identification of these sequences could help in the elucidation of the mechanism of enhancement. One problem in studying deletion mutants is that the removal of essential sequences brings other sequences into an abnormal juxtaposition. In an effort to define critical nucleotides within the SV40 enhancer region, we have constructed and analyzed mutants containing multiple base pair changes within the 72-bp repeat.

Strategy of Generating Mutants
in the 72-bp Repeat Region

The approach we selected is based on a base-specific chemical treatment in which sodium bisulfite is used in vitro to convert cytosine residues in single-stranded DNA to uracil, without doing significant damage to other bases (19). Thus, the resulting change will eventually be a transition from C (cytosine) to T. This agent has been successfully used to introduce mutations within the SV40 origin of replication (20). Recently, a very efficient modification of this method has been reported (21); its major advantage is the cloning of the desired DNA fragment into a single-stranded bacteriophage, which renders the DNA readily accessible to the chemical agent (Fig. 2). In brief, SV40 fragments were transferred into a suitable single-stranded vector such as fd 106 (22). Single-stranded DNA from two clones (fd-SV40-E_1 and fd-SV40-E_4) carrying SV40 inserts in opposite orientations (23) was treated in vitro with sodium bisulfite. This modified DNA was hybridized with fd-specific fragments, which subsequently served as primers for the repair synthesis of the second strand, creating U · A base pairs (U, uracil) in all positions originally affected by the chemical treatment. After the repair synthesis, the molecules were digested with Sph I and Kpn I, which excised a fragment containing approximately 50 nucleotides of the 5′ end of the 72-bp sequence plus 47 nucleotides of the SV40 late (L) leader (see Fig. 1) (2–4). The excised fragments, which consisted of a mixture of mutagenized DNA segments, were ligated to Sph I and Kpn I digested pSVTR 1-3. This plasmid contains the viable SV40 genome inserted at its only Taq I site into the Cla I site of the plasmid pAd 190 (Fig. 2). The SV40 insert in pSVTR 1-3 is a viable mutant which has been altered at the Hpa II position by insertion of a Bam HI restriction enzyme linker (24), and carries only one copy of the 72-bp repeated in wild-type SV40. The plasmids resulting from this cloning procedure also contain a single copy of the SV40 72-bp repeat and carry base changes exclusively within the Kpn I–Sph I fragment. In order to confirm the physical structure and to determine the individual point mutations, the nucleotide sequence of several mutants in the critical region was determined.

Both strands were sequenced (25) beginning at position 346. A compilation of the resulting nucleotide sequence data of seven cloned mutants compared to the SV40 wild-type sequence is presented in Fig. 3A. It is obvious that all mutants carry the expected nucleotide exchanges only between Kpn I and Sph I. Depending on the orientation of the SV40 insert within the fd vector used for initial mutagenesis (Fig. 2), the expected C → T or G → A (G, guanine) transitions were observed.

Generation of
multiple point
exchanges

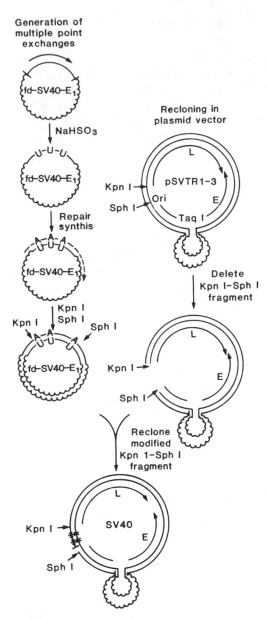

Recloning in
plasmid vector

Delete
Kpn I–Sph I
fragment

Reclone
modified
Kpn 1–Sph I
fragment

Fig. 2. Construction of SV40 point mutants in the enhancer or activator region. *Escherichia coli* C600 and fd recombinant phages (fd-SV40-E$_1$ and fd-SV40-E$_4$) were used (*23*). Phage fd-SV40-E$_4$ contains the entire late strand of SV40; fd-SV40-E$_1$ is the early strand with a 1500-bp deletion within the early region (*42*). Plasmid pSVTR 1-3 consists of a 2.3-kb plasmid (pAd 190) (*43*) conferring an ampicillin resistance marker and the plasmid origin of replication and of a complete SV40 genome. The SV40 is opened at its only Taq I site and fused to the only Cla I site of the plasmid vector. SV40 can be released by Taq I digestion. The SV40 portion of pSVTR 1-3 is different from wild-type SV40 in two regions. It contains only a single 72-bp unit and an additional Bam HI site, which has been introduced at the Hpa II site of SV40 in position 346 (*24*). The point mutants described are derivatives of pSVTR 1-3. For mutagenesis, single-stranded DNA (5 µg and 1 pmole) from phage fd-SV40-E$_4$ or fd-SV40-E$_1$ was dissolved in 17 µl of TE buffer (10 mM tris-HCl, pH 8, 0.1 mM EDTA) and 80 µl of 4M sodium bisulfite reaction mixture (156 mg of NaHSO$_3$, 64 mg of Na$_2$SO$_3$, and 0.43 ml of H$_2$O) and 3 µl of 50 mM hydroquinone were added. After 3 hours at 37°C in the dark, the samples were chromatographed on Sephadex G-100 columns (2 ml) previously equilibrated with 10 mM potassium phosphate buffer, pH 6, to remove bisulfite. The void volume containing the DNA was collected and adjusted to 0.2M tris-HCl, pH 9.2, 50 mM NaCl, 2 mM EDTA. After 12 hours at 37°C, the samples were desalted by filtration through Sephadex G-100 and lyophilized. The treated phage DNA was then hybridized for 10 minutes at 45°C with 0.1 µg of a mixture of fd phage–specific oligonucleotides (*44*) in 20 µl of DS buffer (40 mM tris-HCl, pH 7.2, 10 mM MgCl$_2$, 0.2 mM dithioerythritol, and 100 mM KCl). Subsequently, α-^{32}P-labeled deoxynucleotides dNTP (40 mCi/µmole) were added to a final concentration of 0.2 mM each in a final volume of 30 µl. DNA polymerase I (10 units) was added, and the sample was incubated for 25 minutes at 20°C and 10 minutes at 37°C. The reaction was stopped by ethanol precipitation of the DNA. After cleavage with Sph I and Kpn I, a 94-bp mutagenized DNA fragment was isolated after separation on a 6 percent polyacrylamide gel. This fragment was subsequently recloned after ligation to the Kpn I and Sph I site of pSVTR 1-3. From the mutagenesis of fd-SV40-E$_4$, four mutant clones were further analyzed and from fd-SV40-E$_1$ mutagenesis, three clones were analyzed.

(A)

SV40 Late Leader

```
    Kpn I                    Pvu II
    TTAGGTACCTTCTGAGGCGGAAAGAACCAGCTGTGGAATGTGTGTCAGTTAG

 5              A AA  A                    A A          A
11              A  A            A          A       A
18                    A                    A       A

43                                              T
44             T          T
45
47                   T    T
```

SV40-repeats [72bp]

```
          R II                              Sph I
    [GGTGTGGAAAGTCCCCAGGCTCCCCAGCAGGCAGAAGTATGCAAAGCATGCATCTCAATTAGTCAGCAACCA]

 5 A    A    A              A    A
11      A                   A    A   A   A
18 AA A

43          TTT      TTTT
44          T T                  T            T
45          T TT   T T  T   T    T
47          TTTT   T  T  T       T
```

(B)

Plaque Formation	DNA Replication	CAT Assay (arbitrary units)
+	+	100.0
−	−	5.2
−	−	8.8
+	+	27.0
(+)	+	15.4
+	+	24.7
+	+	75.3
+	+	n.d.

Fig. 3. Sequence analysis of multiple point mutants of SV40. (A) The positions and base changes found in the seven mutants are shown below the wild-type SV40 sequence. (B) A summary of the data obtained with the mutants in three different assays is shown. For plaque formation see Table 1, for DNA replication see Fig. 4, and for CAT assay see Fig. 6. The CAT assay calculation was done with the use of the data from the 30-minute time point in Fig. 6. The amount of acetylated chloramphenicol seen with plasmid 1-3 was assigned 100 arbitrary units.

38

Biological Activity of Point Mutants
in the Activator-Enhancer Region

In an attempt to determine the biological effect of the multiple point mutations in individually cloned mutants, we first tested their ability to form plaques. This analysis was greatly facilitated by the available constructs, since cleavage with Taq I releases a functional SV40 genome (Fig. 2). These data are summarized in Table 1.

We found that two of the seven mutants (5 and 11) were unable to yield plaques, suggesting that these mutants must have nucleotide exchanges at crucial positions. It was further noted that mutants 18, 44, 45, and 47 seemed to produce plaques observable 1 to 2 days

Table 1. Infectious center-plaque assay of SV40 wild-type and point-mutant DNA. A continuous line of African green monkey kidney cells (CV-1) (4×10^4) was transfected with approximately 50 ng of viral specific DNA released from plasmid sequences by cutting each recombinant DNA with Taq I. The assay was performed as an infectious center assay (48). Cells were stained with neutral red 14 days after DNA transfection. Each (+) represents an average of approximately five to ten plaques per dish. The numbers used describe individual mutants (see Fig. 3). Number 1–3 represents a SV40 equivalent carrying a single 72-bp unit as control.

DNA	Plaques after transfection on day				
	14	15	16	18	20
1–3 (wt)	+	+	+	+	+
5	−	−	−	−	−
11	−	−	−	−	−
18	−	+	+	+	+
43	−	−	−	+	+
44	−	+	+	+	+
45	−	+	+	+	+
47	−	−	+	+	+

later than the wild-type control, and that mutant 43 gave rise to very small plaques 3 to 4 days later than did wild-type SV40. Since the region approximately 47 nucleotides toward the late side of the 72-bp repeat was also a target for mutagenesis, it was possible that the defect in mutants 5 and 11 were either in the enhancer element or in some late function (for example, promoter). In order to discern between these possibilities, we attempted to measure directly the amount of early gene product.

Replication of Mutant Viral DNA in
Monkey Kidney Cells

The early gene product T antigen is essential for the replication of the SV40 genome (20, 26). We therefore used an assay in which we indirectly determined the amount of SV40 T antigen by measuring the amount of DNA replication in permissive monkey kidney (CV-1) cells (27, 28). This assay should enable us to determine the relative strength of the early promoter of individual mutants. It has been shown (11) with this assay that sequences to the late side of the Sph I site are not required for efficient early gene expression if an intact enhancer is present elsewhere in the molecule. In our experiments, parallel samples of CV-1 cells were transfected with individually cloned mutant DNA's released from plasmid sequences with the restriction endonuclease Taq I in the presence of DEAE-Dextran. At various times after transfection, cells were harvested and DNA was extracted (29). The appearance of supercoiled DNA was taken as an indication that replication had occurred. The first time point (6 hours after transfection) (Fig. 4), demonstrates that approximately the same amount of linear

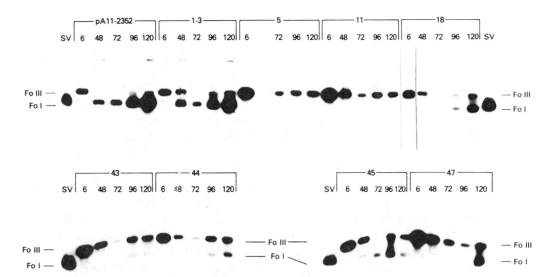

Fig. 4. Replication assay. Parallel dishes (60 mm) of a continuous line of African green monkey kidney cells (CV-1) were incubated for 70 minutes with 0.2 ml of minimal essential medium containing linear mutant DNA (previously cleaved with Taq I) (150 ng/ml) and DEAE-Dextran as facilitating agent. Low molecular weight DNA was isolated as described by Hirt (26), at 6, 48, 72, 96, and 120 hours after DNA transfection. A reflection of the linear input DNA was obtained by harvesting DNA prior to the onset of replication at 6 hours after transfection. Samples of each mutant at each time point were taken and subjected to electrophoresis in a 1.4 percent agarose gel. The DNA was transferred to a nitrocellulose filter (Schleicher and Schuell, 0.45 μm) basically as described (45), except that the gel was treated before denaturing the DNA with 0.25M HCl for 15 minutes. This transferred DNA was hybridized to a nick-translated SV40 DNA with a specific activity of approximately 2×10^8 cpm/μg. ^{32}P-Labeled bands were detected after exposure to an SB-5 x-ray film (Kodak). The numbers in the top lane indicate the mutants used (see Fig. 3). Plasmid 1-3 represents a wild type carrying only a single 72-bp repeat; pAll-2352 represents a 72-bp tandem repeat wild type. The bottom lane indicates the time of DNA harvest. SV stands for SV40 superhelical DNA (FoI), FoIII symbolizes linearized SV40 DNA.

DNA from each mutant DNA preparation was taken up by CV-1 cells.

Subsequent time points (24, 48, 72, and 120 hours) show differences among the mutant DNA preparations. Wild-type controls (pA11-2352 carrying two 72-bp tandem repeats, and pSVTR 1-3, carrying only a single 72-bp copy) and mutants 18, 44, 45, and 47 seem to generate increasing amounts of superhelical DNA, although to various extents. Mutant 43 produces only a minor amount of superhelical DNA and mutants 5 and 11 do not generate detectable circular duplex DNA. These data confirm the results of the plaque analysis. Although these experiments suggest that the mutations affect early gene expression, mutations interfering with the ability of the DNA molecule to replicate for other reasons could lead to spurious conclusions. We therefore wanted to determine directly the relative enhancer strength of each individual mutant independent of viral DNA replication. For this purpose, we have used a sensitive and quantitative assay to measure the effect of the various mutants on gene expression.

Quantitative Assay Measuring
Gene Expression

The assay we selected has been described (*30*). In this assay, a bacterial gene from the transposable element Tn9 was cloned between the SV40 early promoter, and the SV40 small t intron and transcriptional termination signal. With these eukaryotic regulatory signals, this gene can be expressed in eukaryotic cells. It encodes the bacterial enzyme chloramphenicol-3-*O*-acetyltransferase (CAT) (E.C. 2.3.1.28), which can be sensitively and accurately quantified (*30, 31*). The functional analysis of the enzyme is based on the conversion of chloramphenicol to an acetylated form. Since the enzyme is normally absent from eukaryotes, the amount of enzyme produced after transfection of an appropriate plasmid construct into eukaryotic cells reflects the strength of a particular promoter or enhancer. It has also been shown that the extent of CAT activity in cell extracts correlates with gene activity at the level of RNA production. Therefore, the amount of enzyme produced should be proportional to the strength of an enhancer. With the use of this assay, it was recently demonstrated that full enhancer activity is exhibited by a permuted 72-bp repeat (*32*). Thus, in this assay no detectable activity is added by sequences upstream (5') of the 72-bp repeat.

In order to determine the strength of the mutated enhancer elements, we transferred the SV40 Hind III-C fragment of individual mutants (5, 11, 18, 43, 44, 45) and of a control carrying a single copy of the 72-bp repeat into a pSVO

recipient (see Fig. 5). The pSVO plasmid (*17, 30, 33*) effectively lacks all promoter elements, but provides the CAT coding region, the SV40 t intron, and the SV40 transcriptional termination signal. The cloning of the individual Hind III fragments in the sense orientation restores promoter elements, such as the TATA box and the 21-bp repeats in an unaltered form. Thus, a possible defect in the 72-bp repeat will be directly reflected by a reduction of CAT activity. In our experiment, each plasmid was transfected with Ca^{2+} as a facilitating agent onto semiconfluent CV-1 cells. Approximately 44 to 48 hours after transfection, the cells were harvested and the extract was prepared (*30*). A portion (50 microliters) of the extract was used for conversion of ^{14}C-labeled chloramphenicol to [^{14}C]acetylchloramphenicol in the presence of

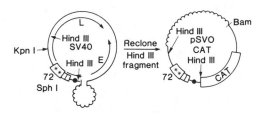

Fig. 5. Construction of mutants with Tn 9 (CAT) as indicator gene. The prokaryotic gene coding for the enzyme CAT has been cloned in a pSV-2 background (*30*) and was utilized for expression in different eukaryotic cells (*17*). A plasmid construct lacking only the eukaryotic promoter element carrying a suitable Hind III cloning site was also reported (*17, 30*). This plasmid (*46*) was used as a recipient for a Hind III fragment isolated from each SV40 point mutant (see also Fig. 2). Each Hind III fragment carried the mutated 72-bp region plus unaltered 21-bp repeats and Goldberg-Hogness box from SV40. After the individual fragments were cloned, their orientation was determined with the use of the restriction enzyme Bgl I, and only the sense orientation relative to the CAT coding region was selected.

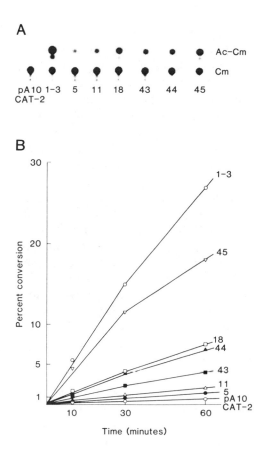

A

B

Percent conversion

Time (minutes)

Fig. 6. Determination of CAT activities of individual point mutants. Each mutant plasmid and plasmid 1-3 carrying a single unmutated 72-bp unit was transfected onto CV-1 cells (70 percent confluent) by a modification of a Ca^{2+} precipitation method (*30, 47*). For each 100 mm dish, 25 μg of plasmid DNA was used. After incubation for 44 to 46 hours, cells were harvested and cell extracts were prepared (*17, 30*). The enzyme reactions were performed with 50 μl out of a total of 180 μl extract per dish and incubated with ^{14}C-labeled chloramphenicol in presence of 4 mM acetyl-coenzyme A in 250 mM tris, pH 7.8. The reactions were terminated by extraction with ethyl acetate either at 60 minutes (A), or portions were taken and extracted at the indicated time (B). The ^{14}C-labeled chloramphenicol was subsequently separated from the acetylated ^{14}C-labeled chloramphenicol by ascending thin-layer chormatography (silica gel 1B, Baker-flex) with a chloroform:methanol solvent (95:5 by volume). (A) An autoradiogram of the amount of CAT present in 50 μl extract, incubated for 60 minutes. In (B), portions of the enzyme reaction mixture were removed at intervals, and the percentage of acetylated chloramphenicol was determined by scraping the spots from the thin-layer plates and measuring the amount of radioactivity by liquid-scintillation counting.

acetyl-coenzyme A as the acetyl donor, and the resulting products were separated by chromatography. In Fig. 6A, the exposed autoradiograms are presented. Depending on the mutant used, varying levels of enzyme activity were detected, as indicated by the amount of acetylchloramphenicol present. In order to ensure that excess substrate was present in the reaction mixture, we subsequently repeated the enzyme assay and removed portions of the reaction mixture at fixed intervals. The percent of ^{14}C-labeled chloramphenicol converted to the acetylated form was determined by scraping the spots from the thin-layer plates and measuring the amount of radioactivity

by liquid scintillation counting (Fig. 6B).

As expected, the positive control (unmutated enhancer) was positive, whereas the negative control, missing 50 nucleotides of the enhancer 5' end (pA10-CAT-2) (*17*) yielded the predicted low conversion rates. It is interesting that neither of the mutants that were negative in plaque and replication assays (5 and 11) convert significantly more chloramphenicol to acetylchloramphenicol than does the repeat minus construct pA10-CAT-2. Thus, we conclude that both mutants have a defect in a vital function, most likely within the SV40 activator. Mutants 18, 43, 44, and 45 all yield CAT activity, although to a variable extent. It should be noted that the low activity of mutant 43 is also reflected in the plaque assay and in the replication assay.

We subsequently compared the data from the replication and the CAT assays. The amount of superhelical DNA present in CV-1 cells 120 hours after transfection with each mutant DNA was quantified by densitometry (see Fig. 4). We assigned 100 arbitrary units to the amount of superhelical DNA (form I, FoI) present in CV-1 cells transfected with the single-repeat control viral DNA and calculated the amount of mutant FoI DNA accordingly.

Similarly, 100 arbitrary units were assigned to the amount of conversion of chloramphenicol to acetylchloramphenicol with the single-repeat plasmid 1-3 (Fig. 5, right), and again the relative CAT conversion rate of each mutant was calculated. We found an excellent correlation between the amount of superhelical DNA and the amount of CAT enzyme (data not presented; Fig. 3B) in these assays.

Identification of Critical Nucleotides

It is of obvious interest to define the role of individual nucleotides that appear to be involved in the function of the SV40 enhancer. Close inspection of the exchanged nucleotides (see Fig. 3) of mutants 43, 44, 45, and 47 indicates that most C → T transitions occurred around the Eco RII site and downstream towards the Sph I site. None of these mutants completely abolished the functional activity of the 72-bp repeat. However, to varying degrees, all mutants showed a decrease in overall gene expression. We therefore conclude that the region containing most of the C → T

transitions seems to contribute to the total activity, although none of the exchanged nucleotides completely eliminates the function. A number of recent studies are significant in relation to this observation. Using the pA10-CAT-2 construct as a control (Fig. 6A), we have shown that the 23 nucleotides at the 3′ terminus of the repeat do not provide enhancer function. Even the 56 nucleotides from the 3′ end of the 72-bp repeat do not mediate functional enhancer activity (13). In contrast, Contreras and co-workers (34) found that deletion mutants (dependent on the mutant) containing only 13 to 26 nucleotides at the 5′ end of the 72-bp repeat still retain viability, although it is greatly reduced. Thus, the region between the Eco RII site and the Sph I site probably does not include an absolutely essential element of the enhancer.

Close inspection, however, of the nucleotide sequence exchanges of the remaining mutants 5, 11, and 18 can help to define essential nucleotides. Mutants 5 and 11 are completely defective in gene expression, indicating that in these cases, the enhancer function is abolished. If the deletion mutants (34, 35) are taken into consideration, only three nucleotides within the 72-bp repeat to the left of the Eco RII site (see Fig. 3A) are exchanged in the case of 5 and only one nucleotide in the case of 11. The G → A transition in mutant 11 is identical to one exchange in mutant 5. As demonstrated by mutant 18, the first three G nucleotides within the 72-bp repeat may add to the overall activity but are not absolutely essential. Therefore, a crucial core element could include the nucleotides T*G*GAAAGT, where the first G (italics) seems to be absolutely required.

In an attempt to find similar sets of nucleotides in known enhancer ele-

DNA	Nucleotide sequences
MSV– repeats 73bp	AACAGAGAG[ACAGCTGAATATGGGCCAAACAGGATATC<u>TGTGGTAAG</u>CAGTTCCTGCCCCGCTCAGGGCCAAGAACAGATGG]₂TCCC
SV40– repeats 72bp	TGTCAGTTAG[<u>GGTGT**G**GAAAG</u>TCCCCAGGCTCCCCAGCAGGCAGAAGTATGAAAGCATGCATCTCAATTAGTCACAACCA]₂TAGT
BK– repeats 68bp	AACATGTCT[GTCATGCACTTTCCTTCCTGAGGAC<u>TGGTTTG</u>GCTGCATTCCAGGGAAGCAGGCTCCTCCCTGTGA]₂GCCTTTTTT
Py(F101) (16,18)	TCCAGAGGG[<u>CGTGTGGTTTT</u>GCAAGAGGAAGCAAAAGCCTCTCCACCCAGGCC<u>TGGAATGT</u>]₂TTCCACCCAATCATTACTATGACA

```
MSV:        T  G  T  G  G  T  A  A  G
SV40:    G  T  G  T  G  G  A  A  A  G
BK:            T  G  G  T  T  T  G
Py:      G  T  G  T  G  G  T  T  T
```

Potential core
nucleotides: (G) T G G ᴬᴬᴬ/ᵀᵀᵀ (G)

Fig. 7. Comparison of nucleotides carrying enhancer activity. Nucleotides with known enhancer or activator function were compared. The crucial core nucleotide in the SV40 is printed in boldface. The sequence in the vicinity of this essential G was compared to MSV, BK, and Py enhancer sequences. We found related sets of nucleotides (underlined and emphasized at the bottom of the figure). References to the sequences are as follows: MSV (*17, 49*); SV40 (*1, 9*); BK (*50*); and Py (F101) (*16, 18*).

ments, we compared this core sequence with other activator sequences (Fig. 7). The comparison revealed that each enhancer element harbors certain nucleotides also characteristic of the SV40 core element (see Fig. 7). The underlined nucleotides demonstrate short stretches of sequences which could potentially be shown to have similar properties. A summary of the related sequences is shown at the bottom of Fig. 7. The fact that no extensive homologies have been detected (*36*) may indicate that the sequence requirements for enhancer function are different in different cells (*11, 17*).

Conclusion

Enhancer or activator sequences are transcriptional controlling elements that exhibit some remarkable features. They seem to be absolutely essential for the expression of some viral genes (*9, 16*) and furthermore drastically increase the transcriptional activity of certain cellular genes (*11–13*). They mediate their activity relatively independent of distance and orientation with respect to a given promoter (*10, 11*) and in a host-specific manner (*17*). These elements provide an extremely active promoter function that can be utilized for the expression of interesting genes in eukaryotes and can help to decipher central questions concerning the control of transcriptional initiation. We constructed a series of multiple point mutants in an attempt to define the core nucleotides required for the functional activity. This led to a spectrum of mutants with nucleotide transitions in different regions of the 72-bp repeat. We were able to correlate the particular functional change with changes of specific nucleotides. From the analysis of seven independently isolated mutants, we arrived at the following conclusions: All mutants carrying either C → T or G → A transitions are, to different degrees, "down mutations." No "up mutation" was isolated when the nonselective mutagenesis procedure was followed (21). Two groups of mutants can be distinguished. The first class has major exchanges around the Eco RII site and toward the Sph I site (see Fig. 3). This group includes only viable mutants, suggesting that an element essential for gene expression does not reside in this region. Interestingly, the second group with major exchanges at the 5' end of the 72-bp repeat completely abolishes enhancer activity. The essential nucleotide (italics) is most likely located within a T*G*GAAAGT sequence. This block of nucleotides is flanked at the 5' end by mostly guanosines (GGTG) and at the 3' end by four cytidines, which can be exchanged without complete elimination of functional activity (Fig. 3). The comparison of this stretch of nucleotide sequences to other known enhancer elements reveals a certain degree of homology (see Fig. 7). In addition, sequences comprising a bovine papilloma enhancer region (37), and a potential enhancer located within the human genome (38) also show homology with these core nucleotides.

Speculation on the process by which the individual mutants decrease functional activity is limited by our lack of understanding of the mechanism of enhancement. However, we recently demonstrated an involvement of host-specific factors in the functional activity of individual enhancers (17). Thus, one possible hypothesis is that the activator provides binding sites for cell specific regulatory proteins (for example, σ-factor-like). If crucial core sequences, such as the ones in mutants 5 and 11, are altered, no binding of this putative protein would occur, whereas interaction to a lesser extent could still be possible if nonessential nucleotides are replaced. Alternatively, specific secondary or tertiary structures could be required for the interaction of the enhancer with cellular factors; this alteration of nucleotides essential for the formation of a particular structure may eliminate both the structure and its function.

It is remarkable that sequences around −60 to −70 in the major late promoter of adenovirus 2 (39) and at −75 to −85 in the promoter of rabbit β-globin (40) show some surprising sequence similarity to the SV40 enhancer core region. In case of rabbit β-globin, it has been shown that certain nucleotide exchanges in this region drastically reduces the in vivo transcriptional activity (41). It remains to be determined whether these critical upstream regions of both genes carry a functional activity similar to the SV40 enhancer sequence.

References and Notes

1. J. Tooze, Ed., *DNA Tumor Viruses* (Cold Spring Harbor Laboratory, Cold Spring Harbor, N.Y., 1980).
2. W. Fiers *et al.*, *Nature (London)* **273**, 113 (1978).
3. V. B. Reddy *et al.*, *Science* **200**, 494 (1978).
4. H. Van Heuverswyn and W. Fiers, *Eur. J. Biochem.* **100**, 51 (1979).
5. T. Shenk, *Curr. Top. Microbiol. Immunol.* **93**, 25 (1981).
6. P. K. Ghosh, P. Lebowitz, R. J. Frisque, Y. Gluzman, *Proc. Natl. Acad. Sci. U.S.A.* **78**, 100 (1981); C. Benoist and P. Chambon, *Nature (London)* **290**, 304 (1981); D. J. Mathis and P. Chambon, *ibid.*, p. 310.
7. R. Grosschedl and M. I. Birnstiel, *Proc. Natl. Acad. Sci. U.S.A.* **77**, 1432 (1980); S. L. McKnight, E. R. Gavis, R. Kingsbury, R. Axel, *Cell* **25**, 385 (1981); D. Benoist and P. Chambon,

Nature (London) **290**, 304 (1981); P. Mellon, V. Parker, Y. Gluzman, T. Maniatis, *Cell* **27**, 279 (1981); J. A. Hassell *et al.*, in *Eucaryotic Viral Vectors* (Cold Spring Harbor Laboratory, Cold Spring Harbor, N.Y., 1982), pp. 71–77; M. Fried and E. Ruley, in *ibid.*, pp. 67–70.

8. S. L. McKnight and R. Kingsbury, *Science* **217**, 316 (1982).
9. P. Gruss, R. Dhar, G. Khoury, *Proc. Natl. Acad. Sci. U.S.A.* **78**, 943 (1981); C. Benoist and P. Chambon, *Nature (London)* **290**, 304 (1981).
10. P. Moreau, R. Hen, R. Everett, M. P. Gaub, P. Chambon, *Nucleic Acids Res.* **9**, 6047 (1981).
11. M. Lusky, L. Berg, M. Botchan, in *Eucaryotic Viral Vectors* (Cold Spring Harbor Laboratory, Cold Spring Harbor, N.Y., 1982), pp. 99–107; S. E. Conrad and M. Botchan, *Mol. Cell. Biol.* **2**, 969 (1982).
12. M. R. Capecchi, *Cell* **22**, 479 (1980).
13. J. Banerji, S. Rusconi, W. Schaffner, *ibid.* **27**, 299 (1981).
14. B. Levinson, G. Khoury, G. Vande Woude, P. Gruss, *Nature (London)* **295**, 568 (1982).
15. E. H. Chang, R. W. Ellis, E. M. Scolnick, D. R. Lowy, *Science* **210**, 1249 (1980); D. G. Blair, M. Oskarsson, T. G. Wood, W. L. McClements, P. J. Fischinger, G. F. Vande Woude, *ibid.* **212**, 941 (1981); W. S. Hayward, B. G. Neel, S. M. Astrin, *Nature (London)* **290**, 475 (1981); G. S. Payne, J. M. Bishop, H. E. Varmus, *ibid.* **295**, 209 (1982).
16. J. deVilliers and W. Schaffner, *Nucleic Acids Res.* **9**, 6251 (1981); C. Tyndall, G. LaMantia, C. M. Thacker, J. Favaloro, R. Kamen, *ibid.*, p. 6231.
17. L. A. Laimins, G. Khoury, C. Gorman, B. Howard, P. Gruss, *Proc. Natl. Acad. Sci. U.S.A.* **79**, 6453 (1982).
18. M. Katinka, M. Yaniv, M. Vasseur, D. Blangy, *Cell* **20**, 393 (1980); M. Katinka, M. Vasseur, N. Montreau, M. Yaniv, D. Blangy, *Nature (London)* **290**, 720 (1981); F. K. Fujimura, P. L. Deininger, T. Friedmann, E. Linney, *Cell* **23**, 809 (1981); K. Sekidawa and A. J. Levine, *Proc. Natl. Acad. Sci. U.S.A.* **77**, 6556 (1980).
19. R. Shapiro, B. Bravermann, J. B. Louis, R. E. Servis, *J. Biol. Chem.* **248**, 4060 (1973); R. Shapiro, B. J. Cohen, R. E. Servis, *Nature (London)* **227**, 1047 (1970); K. Kai, T. Tsuro, H. Hayatsu, *Nucleic Acids Res.* **1**, 889 (1974).
20. D. Shortle and D. Nathans, *Proc. Natl. Acad. Sci. U.S.A.* **75**, 2170 (1978).
21. H. Weiher and H. Schaller, *ibid.* **79**, 1408 (1982).
22. R. Herrmann, K. Neugebauer, E. Pirkl, H. Zentgraf, H. Schaller, *Mol. Gen. Genet.* **177**, 231 (1980).
23. These clones were provided by R. Herrmann.
24. P. Gruss, N. Rosenthal, M. König, R. W. Ellis, T. Y. Shih, E. M. Scolnick, G. Khoury, in *Eucaryotic Viral Vectors* (Cold Spring Harbor Laboratory, Cold Spring Harbor, N.Y., 1982), pp. 13–17.
25. A. M. Maxam and W. Gilbert, *Methods Enzymol.* **65**, 499 (1980).
26. R. Tjian, *Cell* **13**, 165 (1978); D. Shalloway, T. Kleinberger, D. M. Livingston, *ibid.* **20**, 411 (1980); R. McKay and D. DiMaio, *Nature (London)* **289**, 810 (1981); K. W. C. Peden, J. M. Pipas, S. Pearson-White, D. Nathans, *Science* **209**, 1392 (1980).
27. M. Lusky and M. Botchan, *Nature (London)* **293**, 79 (1981).
28. R. M. Myers and R. Tjian, *Proc. Natl. Acad. Sci. U.S.A.* **77**, 6491 (1980).
29. B. Hirt, *J. Mol. Biol.* **26**, 365 (1967).
30. C. Gorman, L. Moffat, B. Howard, *Mol. Cell. Biol.* **2**, 1044 (1982).
31. W. Shaw, *Methods Enzymol.* **53**, 737 (1975); L. Robinson, R. Seligohn, S. Lerner, *Antimicrob. Agents Chemother.* **13**, 25 (1978).
32. L. Laimins and P. Gruss, unpublished data.
33. C. Gorman provided the pSVO plasmid.
34. R. Contreras, D. Gheysen, J. Knowland, A. van de Voorde, W. Fiers, *Nature (London)* **300**, 500 (1982).
35. J. Banerji, S. Rusconi, W. Schaffner, *Cell* **27**, 299 (1981).
36. P. Gruss, R. Dhar, J. Maizel, G. Khoury, in *Genes and Tumor Genes* (Raven, New York, 1982), pp. 39–47.
37. H. Weiher and M. Botchan, personal communication.
38. P. Steele, personal communication.
39. C. Benoist, K. O'Hare, R. Breathnach, P. Chambon, *Nucleic Acids Res.* **8**, 127 (1980).
40. A. Efstratiadis *et al.*, *Cell* **21**, 653 (1980).
41. C. Weissmann, personal communication.
42. R. Herrmann, unpublished observations.
43. B. Zink and H. Schaller, unpublished observations.
44. C. P. Gray, R. Sommer, C. Polke, E. Beck, H. Schaller, *Proc. Natl. Acad. Sci. U.S.A.* **75**, 50 (1978).
45. E. M. Southern, *J. Mol. Biol.* **98**, 503 (1975).
46. This plasmid was provided by C. Gorman.
47. F. Graham and A. van der Eb, *Virology* **52**, 456 (1973).
48. V. W. Brockman and D. Nathans, *Proc. Natl. Acad. Sci. U.S.A.* **71**, 942 (1974).
49. R. Dhar, W. L. McClements, L. W. G. Enquist, G. Vande Woude, *ibid.* **77**, 3937 (1980).
50. I. Seif, G. Khoury, R. Dhar, *Cell* **18**, 963 (1979); N. Rosenthal, personal communication.
51. We thank H. Schaller in whose laboratory the construction of the mutants was done; R. Herrmann for fd SV40 recombinant phages; G. Khoury and C. Liu for helpful comments; and M. Kessel, L. Laimins, R. Muschel, and S. Conrad for discussions. Supported in part by a grant from the Deutsche Forschungsgemeinschaft to H. Schaller (Forschergruppe Genexpression, Heidelberg, F.R.G.).

4. Human Insulin from Recombinant DNA Technology

Irving S. Johnson

During 1982, human insulin of recombinant DNA origin was approved by the appropriate drug regulatory agencies in the United Kingdom, the Netherlands, West Germany, and the United States. This new source guarantees a reliable, expandable, and constant supply of human insulin for diabetics around the world.

The research, development, and production of human insulin by recombinant DNA technology ushers in a new era in pharmaceuticals, agricultural products, and industrial chemicals by establishing the feasibility of commercial production of a gene product initiated at a laboratory level of expression. I shall review how human insulin became the first human health product of this technology. I will also discuss some of the special problems, in terms of regulatory environment and public opinion, that had to be overcome in order to bring it to the current stage of development.

Sources of Insulin

Eli Lilly and Company has been involved in the development and manufacture of insulin and other products for diabetics since 1922. In that year our scientists began working with Frederick G. Banting and his associates at the University of Toronto to develop a standardized and clinically acceptable insulin product. Banting had just begun to extract relatively crude insulin from animals and inject it into his diabetic patients.

In the early 1970's we began to be concerned about a possible shortage of insulin. Until now, the world's insulin needs have been derived almost exclusively from pork and beef pancreas glands, which were collected as by-products from the meat industry. This supply changes with the demand for meat and is not responsive to the needs of the world's diabetics. Indeed, from 1970 to 1975, the supply of pancreas glands in the United States declined sharply (*1*) and remained on a plateau at that lower level in succeeding years. There is no accurate way to predict availability of future supplies of glands, although we predicted that the demand for insulin would continue to increase. Our concern was whether or not there would be a time when the supply of bovine and porcine pancreas glands might not be sufficient to meet the needs of insulin-dependent diabetics. Although it is difficult to obtain substantiated figures for a nonreportable disease, we estimate that there are 60 million diabetics in the world—more than half of them in less developed countries. In the developed countries, some 4

46

million diabetics, 2 million in the United States, are treated with insulin.

Today, the diabetic population is growing more rapidly than the total population. While the U.S. population is increasing at a rate of about 1 percent per year and the world population at slightly more than 2 percent, the annual rate of increase of insulin-using diabetics in this country has been 5 to 6 percent in recent years, and a similar pattern may hold true worldwide (2).

Several factors contribute to this accelerated growth of the insulin-using diabetic population. One factor, of course, is the availability of insulin, which enables diabetics, who often did not survive beyond their teens, to live long, productive—and reproductive—lives. Because of the genetic etiologic component of diabetes, the offspring of diabetics are likely to suffer from the disease as well. Other factors that contribute to growth of the diabetic insulin-using population include improved methods of detection, greater public awareness of the disease and its symptoms, less reliance on oral forms of therapy, and changes in dietary habits.

Because of the uncertainty of the insulin supply and the forecasts of rising insulin requirements, it seemed not only prudent but a responsibility as well for the scientific community and insulin manufacturers to develop alternatives to animal sources for supplying insulin to the world's diabetics. Lilly established several internal committees of scientists to examine various solutions to the problem. They considered augmentation of insulin production from pancreas glands, transplantation of islet of Langerhans cells, chemical synthesis, beta cell culture, directed-cell synthesis, and cell-free biosynthesis, as well as insulin replacements. These discussions touched on the technology called genetic engineering.

The function of DNA in a cell is to serve as a stable repository of coded information that can be replicated at the time of cell division to transmit the genetic information to the progeny cells and to encode the information necessary to synthesize proteins and other cell components. There are several ways of performing genetic engineering, some of which have been practiced for many years by geneticists. The first is mutation. Mutations in DNA can be either spontaneous, due to environmental factors and errors in DNA replication, or they can be induced in the laboratory by physical and chemical agents. Mutations can lead to a change in the structure of the product coded for by the gene in question; sometimes this change in structure is so great that the product is vastly different. Other mutations may affect the regulatory elements that control the expression of the structural gene, leading, in some instances, to increased or decreased production of gene products. A key point is that mutagenesis is an essentially random technique.

A second type of genetic engineering, recombination, has also been used for a long time. Recombination refers to exchange of a section of DNA between two DNA molecules. Recombination of DNA fragments from different organisms can occur by the mating of two organisms—a process called conjugation—where DNA is physically transferred from one organism to another. This is a process occurring in nature, which can be duplicated in the laboratory. Two other natural processes whereby cells exchange DNA in nature are transformation and transduction. Recombination may also occur following the use of a technique known as protoplast fusion, where one literally strips off the outer cell wall of cells of fungi and bacteria. This phenomenon only occurs in the laboratory and allows the remaining protoplasts, which now have just a cell membrane enclosing the components of the cell, to fuse together. The fused protoplasts contain the DNA molecules of both parents, and exchange of sections of DNA can now occur as these cells regenerate and divide. All these recombination processes involve random exchange of DNA sequences, and this exchange is generally, but not always, limited to members of a single species of organism.

In 1972, Jackson, Symons, and Berg (3) described the biochemical methods for cutting DNA molecules from two different organisms, using restriction enzymes, and recombining the fragments to produce biologically functional hybrid DNA molecules. In 1973, Cohen, Chang, and Boyer (4) reported that they could make a hybrid molecule that would express the foreign DNA within it as though it were a part of the original molecule's natural heritage (5). That profoundly significant accomplishment also generated major concern over potential biohazards.

Regulating DNA Research

The Berg Committee was formed, and it responded to concerns about conjectural risk associated with recombinant DNA research in 1974 by calling for a moratorium and deferral of certain types of recombinant DNA research until the scientific community could evaluate the risks and benefits associated with it (6). Work was halted—including work in my own organization—until after the Asilomar Conference in 1975 (7).

The majority of scientists invited to the Asilomar Conference were molecular biologists from government and academia; those with expertise in infectious disease or those from industry with extensive knowledge of large-scale fermentation processes and other techniques that require careful methods of containing potentially harmful materials were underrepresented. As a result, many of us believe that the guidelines defined at Asilomar were unnecessarily restrictive. An example was the establishment of the 10-liter limit. To those of us in industry, this restriction was never considered reasonable. We were accustomed to handling containment problems at much larger volumes. But few of the scientists at Asilomar conceived of performing large-scale fermentation with recombinant organisms; as noted in the British journal *Nature*, "[In 1975] even optimists would have predicted that it would be a decade before genetic engineering would be commercially exploited" (8). This volume limit was established because it was regarded as probably the largest volume that could be conveniently handled in an experimental laboratory by conventional laboratory centrifuges. It was clear that the 10-liter limit excluded industrial-level activity. It was not suggested that increased volume of a culture of a safe organism would result in any increased risk. The conjectural nature of the early concerns soon became clear, and broader participation in research decisions by those expert in infectious diseases, containment, and risk-assessment, as well as more practical experience, led inevitably to revisions and continued relaxation of restrictions around the world.

In June 1976, the National Institutes of Health (NIH) announced guidelines for recombinant DNA work, marking the end of the 2-year moratorium on this type of research. Only research financed by the federal government was subject to the guidelines, for which Lilly, with other companies, NIH, the Pharmaceutical Manufacturers Association (PMA), the Food and Drug Administration (FDA), and the Department of Health, Education and Welfare (HEW), was actively involved in developing compliance procedures.

At Lilly, work on DNA recombination, which had been under way before Jackson, Symons, and Berg (3) published their work, resumed vigorously. We contracted with a new California company, Genentech, Inc., for specific work on human insulin. Genentech subcontracted the synthesis of the human insulin gene to the City of Hope Medical Center, which succeeded in its mission. Scientists at Genentech inserted the genes for both chains of insulin into a K-12 strain of *Escherichia coli* and after isolation and purification, the A and B chains were joined by disulfide bonds to produce human insulin. In the Lilly Research Laboratories, we have also used recombinant DNA technology to produce human proinsulin, the insulin precursor.

Human Insulin

The successful expression of human insulin (recombinant DNA) in *E. coli* was announced on 6 September 1978. This was a first step. Although we had been successful in obtaining expression of the hormone under laboratory conditions and scale, we still faced the equally difficult challenge of achieving satisfactory production of the purified product on a commercial scale. The process we used in accomplishing large-scale pro-

duction has been described (9–11), but it may be useful to touch on some of the methods that we employed to prove that the product produced was indeed human insulin.

High-performance liquid chromatography (HPLC) techniques developed at Lilly can detect proteins that differ by a single amino acid (10), and HPLC tests showed that human insulin (recombinant DNA) is identical to pancreatic human insulin and that it is close to, but not the same as, pork insulin, which differs from the human by one amino acid; beef, which differs by three amino acids; and sheep, which differs at four residue positions (Fig. 1). A chromatogram of human insulin (recombinant DNA), pancreatic human insulin, and a mixture of the two, showed that they were superimposable and identical (Fig. 2). HPLC has become an important analytical tool to determine structure and purity and is now considered to be a more precise measurement of potency than the rabbit assay, although most government regulatory agencies around the world still emphasize the rabbit potency assay.

A measure of the correct tertiary structure and appropriate folding is the circular dichroic spectrum. The spectrum for porcine insulin and for human insulin (recombinant DNA) were found to be identical. X-ray crystallographic studies further revealed the structural integrity of the recombinant molecule (12). We also found the amino acid composition of human insulin (recombinant DNA) and pancreatic human insulin to be identical (Table 1). In addition, we compared polyacrylamide gel electrophoresis for human insulin (recombinant DNA), pancreatic human insulin, and pork insulin, as well as isoelectric focusing gels for these three insulins.

Another technique that we found use-

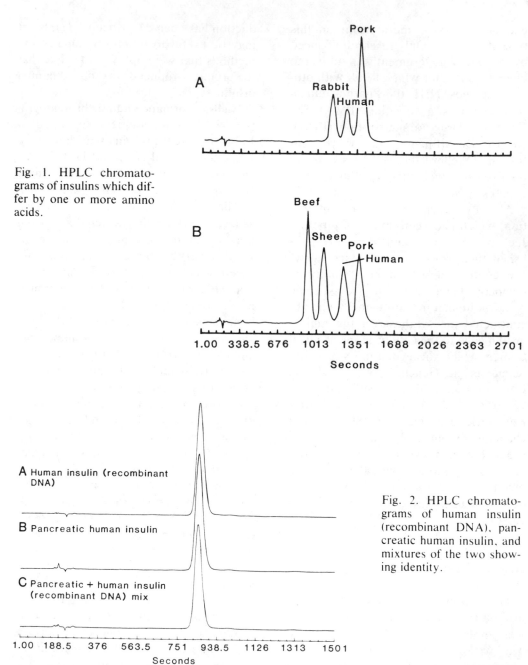

Fig. 1. HPLC chromatograms of insulins which differ by one or more amino acids.

Fig. 2. HPLC chromatograms of human insulin (recombinant DNA), pancreatic human insulin, and mixtures of the two showing identity.

ful for ensuring that we had the appropriate disulfide bonds and lacked other types of protein or peptide contaminants was HPLC of a specifically degraded sample. There is a staphylococcal protease that cleaves insulin in a specific way at five sites—always next to glutamic acid, except for one site between serine and leucine. After treating the insulin with the protease, we looked for and

Table 1. Amino acid compositions of human insulins. Molar amino acid ratios with aspartic acid as unity [actual aspartic acid yields were 160 nanomoles per milligram for human insulin (recombinant DNA) and 156 nanomoles per milligram for pancreatic human insulin (*10*)].

Amino acid	Recombinant DNA	Pancreatic
Aspartic acid	3.00	3.00
Threonine	2.77	2.77
Serine	2.56	2.63
Glutamic acid	7.11	7.10
Proline	1.03	0.99
Glycine	3.98	3.98
Alanine	0.97	0.99
Half-cystine	5.31	5.43
Valine	3.76	3.71
Isoleucine	1.66	1.61
Leucine	6.16	6.14
Tyrosine	3.91	3.90
Phenylalanine	2.99	2.91
Histidine	1.97	1.99
Lysine	0.97	0.97
Ammonia	6.89	6.95
Arginine	1.00	1.00

identified the various peptide fragments by HPLC (Fig. 3) and found none that were not derived from insulin.

In the end, we employed 12 different tests to establish that what we had produced was human insulin. We believe the correlation among three of the tests was particularly important—the radioreceptor assay, the radioimmunoassay, and HPLC. Moreover, the pharmacologic activity of human insulin (recombinant DNA), as demonstrated by a rabbit hypoglycemia test, showed a response essentially identical to pancreatic human insulin.

Another serious question remained to be answered—namely that of the potential contamination of the product with trace amounts of antigenic *E. coli* peptides. Relevant to this question is the difference in starting materials between human insulin of recombinant DNA origin and pancreatic animal insulins. The glandular tissue is collected in slaughter-

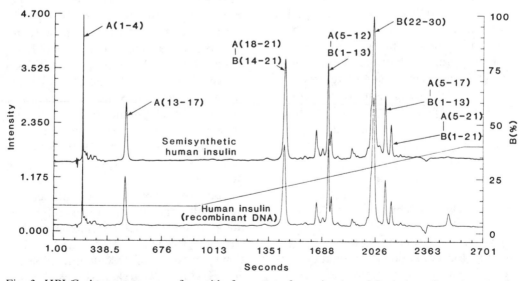

Fig. 3. HPLC chromatograms of peptide fragments from the A and B chains of semisynthetic human insulin and human insulin (recombinant DNA) after treatment with a specific staphylococcal protease. These chromatograms indicate the correctness of the disulfide bridges and the lack of any other major peptide components.

houses, with no control over bacterial contamination. The desired gene product is isolated from a few cells of the islets of Langerhans, which make up less than 1 percent of the glands; thus more than 99 percent of the tissue represents tissue contaminants and undesirable materials. The common protein contaminants of the animal insulins are other pancreatic hormones or proteins, many of which are highly immunogenic.

In contrast, with recombinant DNA production of human insulin, almost 100 percent of the cells (*E. coli*) produce the desired gene product. Because of the method of manufacture, none of the pancreatic contaminants of the animal insulins are found in the human insulin of recombinant origin. The issue of proteinaceous contamination derived from the bacterial host cell was addressed through some experiments that were made possible by running large-scale fermentations of the production strain of *E. coli*, which contains the production plasmid with the code for the insulin chain sequence deleted. The small quantities of peptides isolated after applying the chain purification and disulfide linking process to the "blank" preparation were shown not to be antigenic except in complete Freund's adjuvant (*13*); in addition, no changes in amount of antibody to *E. coli* peptides were detected in serum from patients who had been treated with human insulin for more than a year (*14*).

Commercial Production

As we were scaling up this new technology for commercial production, we recognized that there would be external problems and forces with which to contend. Because this would be the first human health care product resulting from recombinant DNA techniques, we expected that many people would perceive that there were risks associated with this new scientific tool. We also recognized that the existing regulatory systems had not been designed to cope with the new technology. The public's concern reached such levels that some communities, most notably Cambridge, Massachusetts, passed ordinances regulating recombinant DNA research (*15*). In Congress, several bills were introduced to regulate the research. Some of these would have subjected all recombinant DNA research, public or private, to federal regulation (*16*). It was probably fortunate that none of the bills was enacted into law, as former Representative Paul Rogers (D–Fla.) noted: "I think Congress was right [in not regulating rDNA research]. Congress did a good service in airing the issue, but there wasn't a necessity to pass a law" (*17*).

The regulatory system, too, adapted well to this unexpected challenge to its flexibility. On 22 December 1978, the FDA had published in the *Federal Register* a "Notice of Intent to Propose Regulations" governing recombinant DNA work. But, by the time that the FDA's Division of Metabolism and Endocrine Drug Products convened a conference on the development of insulin and growth hormone by recombinant DNA techniques (*11*) in mid-1980, attitudes had changed, and the regulations were never promulgated.

Concerns about the containment of potentially harmful organisms fell under the purview of the Recombinant DNA Advisory Committee (RAC) and the National Institute of Occupational Safety and Health (NIOSH). RAC, established in 1974 by the secretary of HEW, had 11 members, all of whom were scientists. In December 1978, 14 more members were added to RAC; all of the new members were nonscientists. It was apparent that the nonscientists would have to rely heavily on the scientists to develop their understanding of the new technology. Lilly scientists participated actively in all aspects of public discussion, through testimony in both houses of Congress, participation in the open forum of the National Academy of Sciences (*18*), and in meetings of RAC, and by submitting-comments and amendments to NIH for its guidelines.

In June 1979, Lilly made the first application to RAC for an exception to the rule limiting recombinant DNA work to 10-liter volumes. At its meeting in September 1979, RAC recommended that our request to scale up production of bacteria-derived insulin be approved, and a month later the director of the NIH granted us permission to use 150-liter containers. In 1980, permission to expand to 2000-liter containers was granted. This was a major step toward a production type of operation; the submission to RAC contained detailed engineering specifications for equipment and monitoring systems as well as descriptions of the proposed operating procedures. Because of the unprecedented volume increase in the handling of cultures of recombinant organisms, the scale-up request was preceded by a visit to our plant by a group consisting of RAC representatives and NIH officials; they came to see for themselves how we could handle containment problems. With the experience gained at these intermediate levels, we are now routinely using 10,000-gallon fermentors.

Throughout 1980, there were several other positive developments. NIH published in the *Federal Register* draft guidelines on physical containment recommendations for large-scale uses of or-ganisms containing recombinant DNA molecules. This draft was not formally a part of the guidelines, but it did serve as a model for persons preparing submissions to RAC for large-scale fermentations with recombinant organisms. About the same time, the National Institute of Allergy and Infectious Diseases sponsored a workshop on risk assessment. Among the issues discussed were risks associated with pharmacological action of hormones from recombinant organisms populating the human intestinal tract, medical surveillance of workers involved in large-scale fermentation of recombinant organisms, pathogenesis of approved recombinant hosts, and containment practices in commercial-scale fermentation facilities. Most participants indicated that there was little or no risk involved in these practices. A few months later, the industrial practices subcommittee of the Federal Interagency Advisory Committee (FIAC), a working group of representatives from all the cabinet-level departments as well as all federal agencies that are in any way affected by recombinant DNA issues invited Lilly to make a formal statement. Bernard Davis of the Harvard Medical School and I submitted a document on the safety of *E. coli* K-12, the reliability of commercial-scale equipment, operator training, and other topics; this was favorably received. NIOSH also published a favorable report of its on-site inspection of Lilly Research Laboratories' recombinant DNA research facilities and procedures for large-scale fermentations of recombinant organisms.

In July 1980, we began clinical trials of our human insulin in the United Kingdom. Within weeks, similar tests were under way in West Germany and Greece and, finally, in the United States. Plants, specifically designed for the large-scale

Fig. 4. The new production plant in Indianapolis for human insulin produced by recombinant DNA technology.

commercial production of human insulin (recombinant DNA), were built at Indianapolis (Fig. 4) and at Liverpool in the United Kingdom. On 14 May 1982, we filed our new drug application for human insulin with the FDA.

Clinical studies with human insulin (recombinant DNA) indicate its efficacy in hyperglycemic control. It appears to have a slightly quicker onset of action than animal insulins. In double-blind transfer studies with animal insulins, patients previously treated with mixed beef-pork insulin had a 70 percent decrease of bound insulin in comparison with a base line. Species-specific binding of human, pork, and beef insulin at 6 months decreased by 61, 58, and 57 percent, respectively. In patients previously treated with pork insulin, the bound insulin decreased by 30 percent in control subjects treated with pork insulin, and by 51 percent in patients transferred to human insulin. Species-specific

binding of beef and human insulins decreased equally whether patients were maintained on purified pork insulin or switched to human insulin. Species-specific binding for pork insulin, however, remained constant in both groups (19). The clinical importance of these findings remains to be clarified in long-term studies. Occasional patients hypersensitive to animal insulins and semisynthetic human insulin derived from pork insulin tolerated human insulin (recombinant DNA) well. Recombinant technology now permits us to study human proinsulin and mixtures of human proinsulin and insulin much as they are secreted by the beta cell. These studies may provide an improved modality of therapy in diabetes.

The power of recombinant DNA technology resides in its high degree of specificity, as well as the ability it provides to splice together genes from diverse organisms—organisms that will not normally exchange DNA in nature. With this technology, it is now possible to cause cells to produce molecules they would not normally synthesize, as well as to more efficiently produce molecules that they do normally synthesize. The logistic advantages of synthesizing human insulin, growth hormone, or interferon in rapidly dividing bacteria, as opposed to extracting these from the tissues in which they are normally produced, are obvious.

We have shown the practicality of using recombinant technology to produce proteins of pharmacological interest as fermentation products. This was accomplished without adverse environmental impact or increased risk to workers. At this point it seems reasonable to speculate about the future of this new technology.

Impact of the Technology on Industry

A whole growth industry largely dependent on investor interest has developed. Through newsletters, conferences to develop research strategies, market estimates, and so forth, these investors supposedly predict which projects will be brought to fruition through this new biotechnology. It is difficult to estimate the extent to which these prognostications will reflect economic and scientific reality, but there are some items of fact that appear to be supported by fairly simple logic.

In the biomedical area there will certainly be other proteins and peptides of pharmacological interest produced. Some of these are likely to result from new discoveries as additional genes are cloned. As an example, perhaps the most interesting aspect of the cloning of the interferon genes is that they represent a family of genes that code for a large number of interferons, leading to the possibility of producing hybrid molecules that have not been seen in nature. It seems unlikely that interferons should be unique in this respect among cytokines or other biologically interesting messengers.

The technology will probably permit the mapping of the entire human genome during the next decade. Medical geneticists have laboriously mapped human genes by studying electrophoretic variants or phenotypic expression of disease tracked through family trees. It is now possible to isolate individual human chromosomes on a preparative scale, followed by establishment of gene banks or libraries for each chromosome. The work should advance rapidly with an enormous potential impact on new medical research and the understanding of human biology. In addition, it seems likely that eventually we will understand the mechanism of gene control and regulation which, combined with information now being unraveled concerning potent tumor-specific oncogenic DNA sequences, clearly suggests major applications in our understanding of oncology and differentiation. Consider, for example, the recent finding that the point mutation in a normal human gene that leads to the acquisition of transforming properties is due to a single nucleotide change from guanylate to thymidylate. This codon change results in a single amino acid substitution of valine for glycine in the 12th amino acid residue of the T24 oncogene encoded p25 protein; it appears to be sufficient to confer transforming properties on the T24 human bladder oncogene (20).

Assumptions can be made about applications to agriculture as well. It seems incontrovertible that in some areas, for example, the amount of productive land is decreasing because of the fall of water tables and sometimes increasing salinity of ground water. Moreover, the number of people producing crops is decreasing while the population dependent upon them continues to increase. Recombinant technology, in combination with conventional plant breeding, plant cell culture, and regeneration, may well result in the production of new plants. Such plants could increase the productivity of existing farmland as well as permit farming on land currently considered to be nonproductive. Equally important applications are technically feasible in the animal husbandry area, and many other types of applications—in the fermentation industry, industrial chemicals, environmental clean-up—have been suggested.

We can certainly debate how rapidly these further developments will occur and whether or not they will be economically feasible. However, we must all be impressed with the speed with which the technology has progressed since 1974 and can be confident that if we invest wisely, this rate will be maintained or even increased.

References and Notes

1. U.S. Department of Agriculture estimates, *Livestock and Slaughter Reports* (Bulletin of Statistics 522, Economic, Statistic and Cooperative Services, Washington, D.C., 1980).
2. *National Institutes of Health Publ. 78-1588* (April 1978), p. 9.
3. D. A. Jackson, R. H. Symons, P. Berg, *Proc. Natl. Acad. Sci. U.S.A.* **69**, 2904 (1972).
4. S. N. Cohen, A. C. Y. Chang, H. W. Boyer, R. B. Helling, *ibid.* **70**, 3240 (1973).
5. U.S. patent number 4,237,224.
6. P. Berg *et al.*, *Science* **185**, 303 (1974).
7. P. Berg, D. Baltimore, S. Brenner, R. O. Roblin III, M. F. Singer, *ibid.* **188**, 991 (1975).
8. B. Hartley, *Nature (London)* **283**, 122 (1980).
9. R. E. Chance *et al.*, in *Peptides: Synthesis-Structure-Function*, D. H. Rich and E. Gross, Eds. (Proceedings of the Seventh American Peptide Symposium, Pierce Chemical Company, Rockford, Ill., 1981), pp. 721–728.
10. R. E. Chance, E. P. Kroeff, J. A. Hoffmann, B. H. Frank, *Diabetes Care* **4**, 147 (1981).
11. I. S. Johnson, in *Insulins, Growth Hormone, and Recombinant DNA Technology*, J. L. Gueriguian, Ed. (Raven, New York, 1981), p. 183.
12. S. A. Chawdhury, E. J. Dodson, G. G. Dodson, C. D. Reynolds, S. Tolley, A. Cleasby, in *Hormone Drugs: Proceedings of the FDA-USP Workshop on Drugs and Reference Standards for Insulins, Somatotropins, and Thyroid-axis Hormones* (U.S. Pharmacopeia, Inc., Rockville, Md., in press).
13. R. S. Baker, J. M. Ross, J. R. Schmidtke, W. C. Smith, *Lancet* **1981-II**, 1139 (1981).
14. J. W. Ross, R. S. Baker, C. S. Hooker, I. S. Johnson, J. R. Schmidtke, W. C. Smith, in *Hormone Drugs: Proceedings of the FDA-USP Workshop on Drugs and Reference Standards for Insulins, Somatotropins, and Thyroid-axis Hormones* (U.S. Pharmacopeia, Inc., Rockville, Md., in press).
15. *Bull. At. Sci.* **33**, 22 (1977).
16. 95th Congress, 2d sess. amended to S.1217; Calendar No. 334, H. Rep. No. 95359 (1977).
17. A. J. Large, *Wall Street Journal*, 25 January 1982, p. 18.
18. I. S. Johnson, in *Research with Recombinant DNA, an Academy Forum* (National Academy of Sciences, Washington, D.C., 1977), p. 156.
19. I. S. Johnson, *Diabetes Care* **5** (Suppl. 2), 4 (November-December 1982).
20. E. P. Reddy, R. K. Reynolds, E. Santos, M. Barbacid, *Nature (London)* **300**, 149 (1982).
21. Grateful acknowledgment is made to the scores of Lilly associates who have made significant contributions to this project. As in any major technological development of this type, the laboratory, engineering, production, and logistic requirements that had to be met involved the close cooperation of all levels of our administrative and technical staff.

5. Monoclonal Antibodies for Diagnosis of Infectious Diseases in Humans

Robert C. Nowinski, Milton R. Tam
Lynn C. Goldstein, Linda Stong, Cho-Chou Kuo
Lawrence Corey, Walter E. Stamm
H. Hunter Handsfield, Joan S. Knapp, King K. Holmes

Within its unique ecological niche the human organism serves as a biological reservoir for a vast array of microorganisms, ranging from viruses and bacteria to fungi and multicellular parasites (*1*). Most of the host's interactions with these microorganisms are without consequence to health, because physical barriers in the body (such as the gut) or the immune system maintain the microorganisms at a tolerable level. However, in instances of immune nonresponsiveness, or in circumstances involving infection with highly pathogenic organisms, this normal equilibrium is upset and the health of the host is threatened. When this occurs, there is a pressing need to rapidly and specifically identify the overgrowing organisms with a view to designing therapies capable of either restoring the appropriate biological balance or entirely eliminating the pathogens from the body. This need for specific, rapid diagnosis and prompt, targeted therapy has become of paramount importance with (i) the dramatic increase of antibiotic-resistant bacteria in our society, (ii) the growing importance of progressive infections in the immunocompromised host, and (iii) the advent of newer forms of antiviral therapy.

Conventional Diagnosis of Infectious Diseases

Infectious diseases are generally diagnosed by four methods (*2*): (i) microscopic examination of tissue specimens and exudates, with the visual identification of either virus-infected cells (that may show inclusion bodies), bacteria, fungi, or parasites; (ii) culture methods, with the use of selective growth media that allow the amplification of small numbers of organisms that can be tested for susceptibility to potential therapeutic agents; (iii) immunological identification in tissues or body fluids of antigens associated with specific pathogens; or (iv) measurement of specific antibodies produced in the patient as a result of infection with an organism.

Given the complexity of infectious diseases, it is not surprising that no one diagnostic method has proved optimal for all situations. Instead, depending on the particular infection, laboratories commonly use a combination of two or more of the four different diagnostic methods. Thus, while microscopic identification may yield an unequivocal diagnosis of a multicellular parasite, this method is of limited value in identifying viruses. Culture methods, in contrast, provide an unambiguous determination of infectivity and are extremely sensitive; however, these methods also tend to be labor intensive and to involve lengthy incubation periods, and many common pathogens are difficult to grow in culture. Direct identification of pathogens by antibodies, while providing a rapid and specific method for diagnosis, is dependent on the specificity and strength of the antiserums used, which are known to vary considerably. In addition, since many microorganisms are antigenically related to each other, antibodies may demonstrate cross-reactions between pathogenic and nonpathogenic forms.

Monoclonal Antibody Technology

Recently, monoclonal antibody techniques have provided an opportunity to reevaluate the role of immunological methods for the diagnosis of infectious diseases. As a result of the pioneering studies of Kohler and Milstein (3), it is now possible to create immortal cloned cell lines that continuously and reproducibly produce unique antibody molecules. Since these cell lines can be obtained at high frequency (10^{-5} to 10^{-6}) it is relatively easy to scan an enormous repertoire of cells in order to select those that produce antibodies that critically distinguish antigens of different microorganisms.

Immortal cell lines are prepared by the chemically mediated fusion in vitro of lymphocytes from immunized mice and cells from a mouse tumor (myeloma) (3). The resultant hybrid cells acquire both antibody-producing potential (from the normal lymphocyte) and the ability to grow permanently in culture (from the myeloma). Cloned hybrid cells produce individual monoclonal antibodies in a continuous and virtually endless supply. Further, inoculation of the hybrid cells into the peritoneal cavity of compatible mice results in a tumor (referred to as a hybridoma) that secretes high concentrations (1 to 20 milligrams per milliliter) of monoclonal antibody into the tumor ascites fluid. By tapping the ascites fluid and purifying the monoclonal antibody, individual mice can sometimes provide sufficient antibody to perform 10,000 to 50,000 diagnostic assays. As would be expected from their clonal derivation, these antibodies (i) demonstrate extremely precise specificity, (ii) react with uniform avidity, and (iii) can be readily purified to homogeneity, providing reagent-grade materials for analysis.

Monoclonal antibody techniques are now widely practiced and antibodies of diagnostic potential have been prepared in research laboratories against a battery of viruses (4), bacteria (5), and parasites (6). In our laboratories at Genetic Systems Corporation and the University of Washington, we are routinely using monoclonal antibodies for the detection of human sexually transmitted infections. In a joint program with Syva Company (Palo Alto, California) these antibodies will be used to develop a line of rapid, easy-to-perform diagnostic tests. Since the results of our collective studies point to advantages and disadvantages of monoclonal antibody–based diagnostics, we use them in this chapter for further illustration and discussion.

Human Sexually Transmitted Diseases

As changes in sexual attitudes and activities have occurred in our society, sexually transmitted diseases (STD) have become more commonplace. In the United States alone, new infections with three of the most common STD pathogens: *Neisseria gonorrhoeae*, *Chlamydia trachomatis*, and herpes simplex virus (HSV) type 2 are believed to approach 10 million cases annually. In recent years the role of these infections in a wide spectrum of diseases has emerged. These three STD pathogens and their associated diseases are described below.

Neisseria gonorrhoeae. Approximately 1 million new cases of gonorrhoea are reported annually to the Centers for Disease Control in Atlanta (7), and it is estimated that the true incidence of gonorrhoea in the United States exceeds 2 million cases annually. *Neisseria gonorrhoeae* causes urethritis and epididymitis in men; cervicitis, urethritis, endometritis, and salpingitis in women (8); and proctitis and pharyngeal infection in both sexes. Approximately 1 to 3 percent of infected individuals develop disseminated gonococcal infection, with systemic complications including arthritis, dermatitis, endocarditis, and meningitis (8). The bacterium has also been implicated as a cause of morbidity during pregnancy, including chorioamnionitis, premature rupture of membranes, and premature delivery. Neonatal conjunctivitis as a result of infection at birth remains an important cause of blindness in some developing countries.

Detection of the gonococcus is accomplished either by Gram stain and microscopic examination of a patient's specimen, or by culture of the bacterium on a selective medium (8). Results of the culture are confirmed by oxidase reaction, morphology, and sugar utilization tests, or by immunological analysis. In males with urethritis, the Gram stain has a positive predictive value of > 95 percent and requires only 3 to 5 minutes for performance; the same technique in females is considerably less sensitive and at best detects only about 40 to 50 percent of the cervical infections diagnosed by culture. Consequently, cultures with confirmatory tests are the preferred methods for diagnosis in women. These methods, however, require 48 to 72 hours for completion.

Chlamydia trachomatis. Since chlamydial infections are not reported to federal agencies, their incidence can only be estimated. While the prevalence of *C. trachomatis* infection is slightly higher than that of *N. gonorrhoeae* infection in STD clinic populations, the prevalence of chlamydial infection is several times higher than that of gonococcal infection in obstetric, family planning, and student health clinic populations. Thus, the incidence of *C. trachomatis* infections probably is at least 5 to 10 million cases annually in the United States (9).

Like *N. gonorrhoeae*, *C. trachomatis* causes infections of the urethra, cervix, rectum, and conjunctivae, and commonly leads to endometriosis, salpingitis, and epididymitis (10). Thus, chlamydial infections mimic gonococcal infections. In addition, *C. trachomatis* is a common cause of pneumonia in young infants, may be a precipitating factor in Reiter's syndrome, and in developing countries is the cause of lymphogranuloma venereum (10).

The clinical similarities of these two infections are further complicated by the fact that *N. gonorrhoeae* and *C. trachomatis* often are co-transmitted. Approximately 20 percent of heterosexual males and 40 percent of women with gonorrhoea are also infected with chlamydia. Separately, or in combination, chlamydial and gonococcal infections are thought to be responsible for most of the estimated 850,000 annual cases of pelvic inflammatory disease in the United States, resulting in permanent infertility in an estimated 15 to 20 percent of these women (*10*). Approximately 5 to 10 percent of pregnant women previously studied in the United States have been infected with chlamydia, and transmission to the newborn results in ocular, nasopharyngeal, or respiratory infections in about two-thirds of the exposed infants (*10*).

Direct detection of chlamydia infections is not possible at present, except possibly in the diagnosis of neonatal chlamydial conjunctivitis. Since chlamydia are obligate intracellular pathogens, they can be isolated only in chick embryos or mammalian cells. The incubation period for isolation in mammalian cell cultures is 3 days to 1 week (*11*). These cultures are technically difficult and expensive to perform; as a consequence, the inability of most clinicians to conveniently diagnose chlamydia has markedly impaired control of these infections.

Herpesviridae. Herpes simplex virus (HSV) infections are among the most common infections of humans (*12*). Once acquired, these infections demonstrate a life-long pattern of episodic recurrence, such that each infected individual serves as a permanent carrier who is intermittently infectious. The virus can be classified into two subgroups according to genetic and antigenic composition, and by their patterns of infection: HSV type 1 is responsible for recurring orolabial lesions (cold sores), pharyngitis, ocular keratitis, and encephalitis; HSV type 2 is responsible for most genital herpes in adults, and for most neonatal infections. It is now apparent that the "anatomical" mode of classifying these viruses is not truly accurate, as a significant proportion (15 to 50 percent) of primary genital herpes is caused by HSV 1 (*13*). However, the probability of recurrent genital herpes is significantly lower after primary genital HSV 1 infection than after primary genital HSV 2 infection.

Infections with HSV 1 are widespread, particularly in populations of lower socioeconomic status. Infections with HSV 2, although less prevalent than HSV 1 infections, are becoming increasingly common. It has been estimated that approximately 300,000 to 600,000 new cases of genital herpes occur each year, and from 5 to 10 million new or recurrent episodes of genital herpes occur each year in the United States (*14*).

Diagnosis of HSV infection is routinely performed by cell culture. In most cases, cultures yield definitive evidence of virus (that is, cytopathic effect) within 3 to 6 days. After growth of the HSV in culture, detailed typing for HSV 1 or HSV 2 can be accomplished by either immunological analysis (*15*) or by restriction endonuclease analysis of viral DNA (*16*). Classification of HSV's into either of the two subgroups serves several purposes, including (i) prognosis, since the recurrence rate of genital HSV 1 infection is considerably less than that of genital HSV 2 (*13*); (ii) treatment, since certain antiviral drugs demonstrate preferential activity for one of the HSV types [for example, (E)-5-(2-bromorinyl)-2'-deoxyuridine is much more active against HSV 1 than against HSV 2]

(*17*); and (iii) epidemiological, for assessing the association of HSV infection with other disease processes (for example, cervical carcinoma) (*12*).

Preparation of Monoclonal Antibodies

Inherent in the hybridoma technology are difficulties associated with the fusion of somatic cells and the intermingling of two separate sets of genetic information. During early cell divisions after fusion hybrids undergo random loss of chromosomes. As a consequence, the ability to produce antibody may be lost from some of the hybrids. Since hybrids that do not produce antibody grow more rapidly than those that do, overgrowth of the former is certain to occur in mixed cell cultures. The antibody-producing hybrids must therefore be removed and cultured separately. Further, the segregation of chromosomes from the hybrid cells also results in considerable variability in growth properties, making it necessary for investigators to devote individual attention to each cell line. Since the hybridization procedure yields far too many cell lines for individual attention (perhaps 10^4 different hybrids in a good fusion), the initial screening for antibody production is of critical importance.

To obtain maximum information in the early screening, we have adapted replicate-plating techniques from bacterial genetics for the testing of antibody specificities (*18*). To accomplish this, we place hybrid cells in 96-well microtest plates. A small sample of culture fluid is then removed from each well and placed in replicate plates with care being taken to maintain the same physical orientation of the samples. Each of the replicate plates contains a different antigen adsorbed onto the surfaces of the wells. As

many as eight to ten antigen-adsorbed plates can be used, and immune reactions are detected by means of a radioimmunoassay in which ^{125}I-labeled protein A is added to each of the wells which are then examined by autoradiography.

Figure 1 shows an example of a radioimmunoassay of culture fluids containing antibodies against *N. gonorrhoeae*. In this test the culture fluids from a single 96-well plate were replicate-plated onto membrane extracts of three different gonorrhoeal strains (NRL 7122, 8035, and 7929). Four unique antibodies were identified in this test; three of the antibodies (wells A-11, F-10, and D-3) reacted predominantly with only a single bacterial antigen, whereas one of the antibodies (well H-7) reacted with all three of the antigens. In this manner it was possible to rapidly compare individual antibody activities and to select those antibodies desired for continued development.

Selection of Antibodies with Diagnostic Potential

Replicate-plating methods have been used to prepare three independent panels of monoclonal antibodies that distinguish *N. gonorrhoeae*, *C. trachomatis*, and HSV (HSV 1 and HSV 2) from each other and from other common microorganisms (*19–21*). Each antibody in these panels reacts with a single specificity, identifying a particular antigenic determinant of one of these microorganisms.

Examination of more than 1000 monoclonal antibodies against these microorganisms revealed a remarkable diversity in the repertoire of antigens recognized by the mouse (*19–21*). In some instances the monoclonal antibodies identified antigens that were broadly distributed on

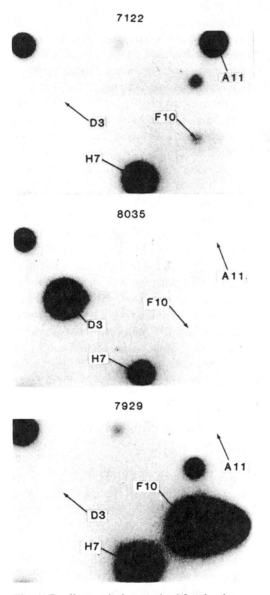

Fig. 1. Replicate-plating method for the detection of monoclonal antibodies against *N. gonorrhoeae*. Culture fluids from a 96-well microtest plate were replicate-plated into microtest plates onto which three different *N. gonorrhoeae* antigen extracts were adsorbed. Immune reactions were detected by the addition of ^{125}I-labeled protein A and subsequent autoradiography.

a variety of bacteria or viruses, while in others, the antibodies identified antigens that were contained within only an extremely small subset of organisms. For the purposes of diagnosis, we attempted to select antibodies that would react with all members of a particular phylogenetic group (for example, *Neisseria gonorrhoeae*), but not with members of other phylogenetically related groups (for example, other *Neisseria* species). To detect such antibodies we used a two-tiered selection system: in the first tier, we identified antibodies that reacted exclusively with organisms within a single phylogenetic group; in the second tier, we selected a subset of these antibodies for their ability to individually identify as many members of the desired phylogenetic grouping as possible.

Figure 2 shows representative results of radioimmunoassays with two panels of monoclonal antibodies prepared against the membrane proteins of *N. gonorrhoeae* and *C. trachomatis*. Antibodies of different specificity could be readily distinguished. In the case of chlamydia, it appeared that a single monoclonal antibody (1-H8) against the 39,000 dalton outer membrane protein (20) could be used to distinguish all members of *C. trachomatis*, without cross-reactions occurring with the closely related *C. psittaci*. With *N. gonorrhoeae*, however, each of the monoclonal antibodies against the principal outer membrane protein (PrI; 34,000 to 37,000 daltons) (19) detected only a subset of the *N. gonorrhoeae* reference strains. Antibodies selected for broader reactivity against *N. gonorrhoeae* were found to cross-react with other *Neisseria* species, decreasing their diagnostic value. This led

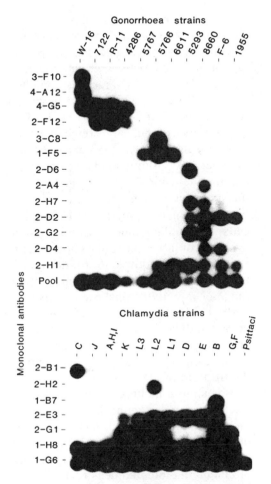

Fig. 2. Binding assays of monoclonal antibodies with different isolates of *N. gonorrhoeae* or *C. trachomatis*. Culture fluids were tested on common serotyping reference strains. Also included were tests with a pool of three culture fluids containing antibodies against *N. gonorrhoeae*. Immune reactions were detected by the addition of ^{125}I-labeled protein A and subsequent autoradiography.

to the concept of pooling several monoclonal antibodies against PrI into a defined polyclonal mixture that would identify the entire spectrum of *N. gonorrhoeae*, without compromising the selective specificity of each antibody.

To select an appropriate antibody mixture, we screened each of 16 different monoclonal antibodies in coagglutination assays (*22*) with 719 different isolates of *N. gonorrhoeae*. Each antibody reacted with a characteristic subset of bacteria, resolving two broad mutually exclusive serological groups (PrIA and PrIB) (*19, 22*). Three of the monoclonal antibodies detected determinants on the PrIA molecule. Antibody 4-G5 reacted most commonly, identifying 99 percent of the PrIA strains. Antibody 2-F12 also reacted with a broad spectrum of PrIA strains, identifying 94 percent of strains, whereas antibody 4-A12 demonstrated a more restricted range of reaction, detecting only 44 percent of the PrIA strains. Six other monoclonal antibodies detected determinants on the PrIB molecule. Antibody 2-H1 reacted most commonly, identifying 93 percent of the PrIB strains. In order of their reactivities, antibodies 3-C8, 2-D6, 1-F5, 2-G2, and 2-D4 reacted with 78, 52, 52, 18, and 17 percent of the PrIB strains, respectively.

On the basis of their patterns of reaction, we pooled three of the monoclonal antibodies (4-G5, 2-H1, and 3-C8) and tested this mixture with the 719 isolates. As could be predicted from the results of tests performed with the individual antibodies, the antibody mixture identified 716 (99.6 percent) of the isolates tested. This same antibody mixture, when tested on 18 different *Neisseria* species, reacted exclusively with *N. gonorrhoeae* (*19*). Thus, in the case of gonorrhoea, the construction of an antibody mixture proved to be a satisfactory method to overcome the limited specificity observed with individual antibodies.

Diagnosis of *Chlamydia trachomatis* with Monoclonal Antibodies

Chlamydia have a life cycle that is reminiscent of viruses (*10, 11*). The infectious form of the organism (referred to as the elementary body) is an extracellular element (300 nanometers in diameter) that is transmissible from one cell to another. Upon entering a cell the organism is contained within an endocytic vacuole. During a 48- to 72-hour cycle the organism replicates to form a large inclusion body that contains several hundred new elementary bodies. Lysis of the cell leads to release of the elementary bodies into the extracellular space and continued rounds of infection in neighboring cells. Because of an accumulation of glycogen in the inclusion body of the infected cell, it is possible to detect intracellular chlamydia 48 to 72 hours after infection by staining with iodine (*11*).

Diagnosis of chlamydia in culture is commonly performed with mammalian cell lines (*11*). To improve sensitivity, duplicate cultures are usually prepared; one is stained with iodine 72 hours after infection, while the other is used for secondary passage onto yet another culture. This secondary culture is stained after another 72 hours after infection, resulting in a total testing period of 6 days. Of all infections detected by culture, approximately 65 to 80 percent are detected in the first passage while 20 to 35 percent are detected in the second passage.

In preliminary studies, the efficacy of a monoclonal antibody against the major membrane protein of *C. trachomatis* was compared to that of iodine for the detection of intracellular chlamydia inclusion bodies (Fig. 3A). At intervals of 18, 24, 48, and 72 hours after infection, the cells were fixed in ethanol, stained with either fluorescein-conjugated antibody or iodine, and then examined by immunofluorescence (IF) or light microscopy. Staining of infected cells with monoclonal antibody revealed characteristic inclusions at 18 hours which could be accurately counted at 24 hours (Fig. 4). The total number of inclusions remained constant throughout the 48- and 72-hour time periods, although at later time periods the inclusions increased in size and the specimen was easier to read. In contrast, staining of a parallel set of infected cells with iodine failed to yield visual evidence of infection until 48 hours, with 72 hours being required for routine quantitation. Throughout a thousandfold range of infectivity, inclusion counts by both the IF and iodine methods were linear, indicative of single-hit kinetics and infection caused by a single chlamydia elementary body. At each point in the titration the IF method detected 8 to 11 times more inclusions than the iodine method. Similar enhanced sensitivity (approximately fourfold) has been demonstrated by comparing the IF monoclonal antibody method to Giemsa staining of chlamydia-infected cells (*23*).

The IF and iodine staining methods have also been compared for the detection of chlamydia in cultures derived directly from patient specimens (Table 1) (*24*). For this purpose, each patient's specimen was inoculated in parallel into four microtiter wells containing cell monolayers. After 72 hours of incubation, one of the wells was tested by the IF method and another by staining with iodine (first passage). The remaining two monolayers were disrupted and passed onto fresh monolayers for another 72-hour incubation period (second passage) and were then stained in the same manner as the first passage specimens. Con-

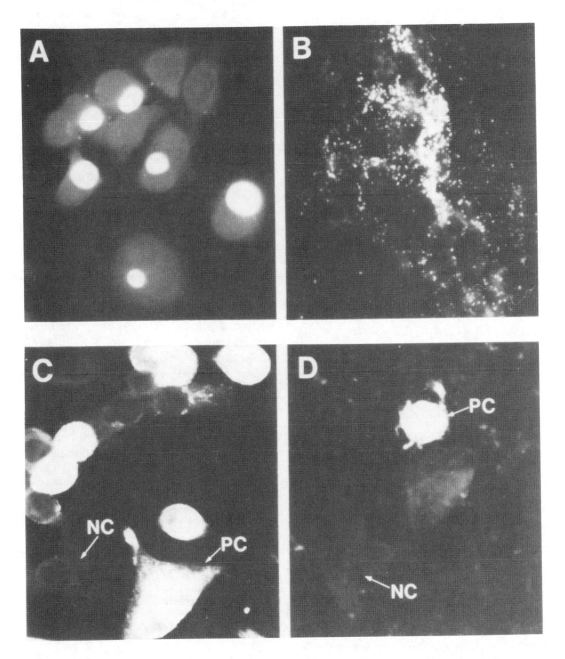

Fig. 3. Diagnosis of chlamydia and herpesvirus-infections with monoclonal antibodies. (A and B) Detection of a chlamydial infection using a monoclonal antibody to stain cells infected in culture (A) and a cervical smear from a patient who tested chlamydia-positive by culture (B). (C and D) Detection of a herpesvirus infection using monoclonal antibodies to stain cells infected in culture (C) and cells scraped from a penile lesion that was culture-positive (D). (NC = negative cell and PC = positive cell). See also color plate I.

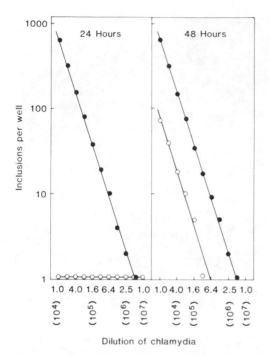

Fig. 4. Comparison of iodine staining and IF tests for the detection of chlamydia inclusion bodies in culture. Cells were infected in duplicate with a serial twofold titration of *C. trachomatis* (serovar I). Twenty-four and 48 hours later the plates were fixed, stained with iodine or fluorescein-conjugated monoclonal antibody, and examined by light or IF microscopy.

cordant results with the two assays were observed in 97 percent of the 2785 specimens tested. Of the 440 specimens that were positive by iodine stain, 417 were also positive in the IF test, indicating a sensitivity of 95 percent. The IF test detected 25 percent more positive specimens on first passage; by second passage, however, the tests showed closer equivalence with the IF test detecting only 5 percent more positive specimens than the iodine stain. With almost all specimens the IF method detected an average of eight times more inclusions per monolayer than the iodine method,

confirming results of the serial titration study.

In an effort to further decrease the time required to diagnose chlamydia infections, IF tests with monoclonal antibodies have also been performed on specimens obtained directly from patients by means of swabs. One swab from the urethra or cervix of each patient was streaked onto a microscope slide for IF testing, while a sample from a duplicate swap was suspended in transport medium for inoculation into cell cultures.

Examination of urethral and cervical smears by IF demonstrated a pattern of staining that was characteristic of chlamydial infection. In approximately 90 percent of the specimens that were positive when stained with iodine in culture, this pattern consisted of large numbers (> 50 per smear) of extracellular elementary bodies which appeared under the microscope as individual small pinpricks

Table 1. Diagnosis of *C. trachomatis* with monoclonal antibodies. Specimens from 2785 patients were inoculated in duplicate into cells cultured in 96-well microtest plates, processed through two culture passages, and then fixed and stained with either iodine or fluorescein-conjugated monoclonal antibody in order to detect intracellular inclusion bodies. Since 417 of the specimens were positive in both tests and 2288 were negative in both tests, the results were concordant in 97 percent of the specimens.

Number of specimens showing positive reaction			
In both tests	With monoclonal antibody only	With iodine only	With neither test
417	57	23	2288

Table 2. Typing of herpes simplex viruses. One hundred and twenty-two different isolates of HSV were typed as HSV 1 or HSV 2 by three different methods: (i) immunoperoxidase stain with rabbit antiserum against HSV 1 or HSV 2. Each antibody was tested on virus-infected cells by twofold serial titration; specimens were scored as HSV 1 or HSV 2 if one of the antiserums demonstrated a fourfold or greater difference in reactivity. (ii) Immunofluorescence tests with monoclonal antibodies against HSV-1 or HSV 2. Antibodies were tested at a single dilution (1/50) of ascites fluid. (iii) DNA restriction endonuclease digestion of ^{32}P-labeled HSV infected cells. Total cellular DNA was subjected to endonuclease digestion with Bam HI and analysis by polyacrylamide gel electrophoresis. Five of the 122 specimens were shown to be mixed HSV 1 and HSV 2 infections by the IF and restriction endonuclease methods; this was confirmed by subsequent plaque purification of HSV 1 and HSV 2 from the mixtures.

Test method	Number of virus isolates scored as			
	HSV 1 alone	HSV 2 alone	Indeterminate	Mixed HSV 1/HSV 2
(i) Rabbit antiserum	11	70	41	Not applicable
(ii) Monoclonal antibodies	34	83	0	5
(iii) Restriction endonuclease	34	83	0	5

of light. In heavily infected specimens the fluorescent elementary bodies produced a delicate "starry sky" pattern that could be observed throughout the sample. A representative example of this IF pattern is presented in Fig. 3B. It was of interest to note that although intracellular inclusions of chlamydia were readily observed in cells infected in vitro, direct clinical specimens rarely contained cells with obvious inclusions.

Since the direct test can be performed in less than 30 minutes, it represents a significant advantage over the culture method. Efforts are now under way to further assess the sensitivity of the IF technique with a larger number of patient specimens.

Identification of HSV with
Monoclonal Antibodies

For typing HSV in culture, we have developed a panel of four monoclonal antibodies that unambiguously distinguish HSV 1 from HSV 2 (Fig. 3C) (21).

Monoclonal antibody 3-G11 reacts with the HSV 1-specific 80,000 to 120,000 dalton glycoprotein (gC) complex, antibody 6-A6 reacts with an HSV 2-specific protein of 140,000 daltons, antibody 6-E12 reacts with an HSV 2-specific protein of 55,000 daltons, and antibody 6-H11 reacts with an HSV 2-specific protein of 38,000 daltons. With this panel, we and our collaborators have now typed over 500 different isolates of HSV (21, 25, 26).

Table 2 shows a comparative analysis in which 122 HSV isolates from 107 patients were typed by three independent methods (immunoperoxidase-labeling with type-specific rabbit antiserums, IF with monoclonal antibodies, and restriction endonuclease analysis of viral DNA) (25). The results obtained with the monoclonal antibody demonstrated 100 percent concordance with restriction endonuclease analysis of viral DNA. In 117 isolates, the HSV was unambiguously typed as either HSV 1 or HSV 2. In five different isolates from three patients, the monoclonal antibodies typed a mixed infection of HSV 1 and HSV 2. The presence of mixed infections in each of these specimens was confirmed by plaque purification of viruses from the mixture and by restriction endonuclease analysis of both the virus mixture and the plaque-purified viruses. In contrast, antiserums prepared in rabbits were capable of typing only 66 percent of the 122 isolates; the remaining 34 percent yielded indeterminate antigen patterns from which a definitive identification could not be made.

In addition to their utility in culture systems, the monoclonal antibodies provided sufficient specificity to enable diagnosis and typing of HSV directly on **primary clinical specimens (Fig. 3D)** *(21)*. For this purpose, cells were obtained from herpes lesions by scraping with swabs and were smeared onto microscope slides for IF tests with monoclonal antibodies against HSV 1 or HSV 2. In each test a duplicate sample of the specimen was inoculated into cell cultures.

Immunofluorescence tests were performed in this way on specimens (of oral, genital, mucocutaneous, and ocular sites) obtained from 59 patients with clinically suspected HSV and 43 control patients with unsuspected HSV infection.

Herpesvirus was isolated in tissue culture from 54 of the specimens obtained from suspected herpes lesions, and in 48 (88 percent) of these, HSV antigens were detected in IF tests. The monoclonal antibodies detected HSV antigens in six clinically suspect specimens from which the culture method did not reveal infectious virus. These latter findings confirmed the results of other investigators showing that IF methods for HSV can demonstrate viral antigens in clinical specimens in the absence of infectious

virus *(27)*. The monoclonal antibodies did not detect HSV antigens in any of the 43 specimens obtained from the control population.

The efficacy of the monoclonal antibodies in typing HSV in clinical specimens was most clearly illustrated when the test predicted types of virus in clinical materials that would be unexpected according to the anatomical site from which they were derived. Thus, we have identified by IF tests with direct specimens (and confirmed by restriction endonuclease analysis and secondary IF tests on culture isolates) examples of genital HSV 1 infection, oral HSV 2 infections, and HSV 2 infections of diverse mucocutaneous sites such as on the tips of fingers, the elbow, and in the axilla.

Advantages, Disadvantages, and the Future of Immunodiagnostics

Until the advent of monoclonal antibodies, immunodiagnostic tests relied exclusively on antibodies obtained from the serum of animals. Although immunization could be used to increase the titer of certain antibodies in antiserums, antibodies per se were always obtained as mixtures of immunoglobulins. Since the precise composition of antiserums could not be controlled, the activity of any particular antiserum (that is, its specificity and affinity) was the sum of the reactions of its multiple constituents. For the most part, "specificity" of a particular antiserum was determined by those antibodies that were in highest concentration (dominant antibodies); the activities of antibodies in lower concentration (minor antibodies) were generally masked by the dominant antibodies.

The ability to control the composition of antibody reactants is of critical importance in the diagnosis of infectious diseases. Since most microorganisms have numerous phylogenetic relatives with common antigens, antiserums prepared in animals cross-react with a spectrum of organisms, including pathogenic and nonpathogenic varieties. In addition, antigen preparations used for immunization are commonly contaminated with unrelated biological materials, resulting in immunization with secondary antigens and the formation of antibodies that cross-react with normal host constituents.

Individual monoclonal antibodies react with only a single antigenic determinant and thus provide a degree of specificity far greater than that of conventionally prepared antibodies. Further, and perhaps most important, since the hybridoma method provides the ability to scan an enormous repertoire of antibodies, it is possible to select individual monoclonal antibodies with highly defined characteristics, for example, specificity, avidity, and isotype. Both minority and dominant antibodies can be studied and used with equal facility. This provides significant opportunity, for, in many instances, minority antibodies are those with preferred specificity for diagnostic tests. For example, antiserums prepared in mice against HSV 1 or HSV 2 demonstrate extensive cross-reaction between the types. In contrast, hybrid cells from these mice can be selected for the production of monoclonal antibodies that react with only one of the types.

Hybrid cell lines also provide a remarkably constant and economic source of antibody. Antibodies of identical chemical structure can be obtained for years and preparations of such antibodies can be easily standardized. Most monoclonal antibodies can be produced on a large scale by passage of hybrido-mas in mice. As much as 1 to 20 milligrams of homogeneous antibody can be purified from each milliliter of tumor ascites fluid. This high level of antibody production, as well as the permanent growth properties of the hybrid cells, allows a virtually unlimited supply of a standardized reagent.

Within the context of these advantages, though, it should be emphasized that the clonal origin of these antibodies also poses certain problems. Each monoclonal antibody has highly defined properties, and it is not uncommon to observe order-of-magnitude differences between individual monoclonal antibodies for properties such as (i) retention of activity after labeling with radioisotopes or fluorochromes, (ii) solubility, as influenced by the ionic strength of pH of buffer, and (iii) stability over long-term storage. Such differences have tended to restrict the routine preparation of monoclonal antibodies to sophisticated laboratories. Other problems include: (i) their high specificity, considered to be too narrow by some critics; (ii) their avidity, which is sometimes lower than antibodies in hyperimmune antiserums; and (iii) the rates at which they are produced by hybridomas, which may vary, and the possibility that their production may cease. Although numerous examples of these problems can be cited, it should also be realized that hybridoma technology is yet in its infancy. Only several years ago it was considered a notable achievement to prepare a single monoclonal antibody against an antigen of choice.

Since monoclonal antibodies represent the individual building blocks of antiserums, there is no a priori reason to consider that the specificity and avidity of the composite antiserum cannot be matched by the individual antibodies themselves. In some instances a single monoclonal antibody may provide the appropriate reactivity to constitute a diagnostic reagent, whereas in others, it may be necessary to mix and match different antibodies to obtain the desired specificity. This latter approach is illustrated by our studies with gonorrhoea, where a mixture of three monoclonal antibodies identified 99.6 percent of isolates tested without cross-reacting with 17 other closely related species of *Neisseria*.

In addressing the issue of stability, two factors need be considered—the stability of the antibody source (that is, the hybrid cell line) and the continued integrity of the antibody molecules produced by a particular cell line. As already mentioned, the stability of antibody production varies from one cell line to another. In our experience approximately 60 percent of hybridomas are sufficiently stable to warrant continued use. Although some lines continue to demonstrate variable antibody production, these can generally be maintained through careful attention, aggressive recloning, and the freezing of adequate samples of cells for future regeneration of stocks. With regard to the stability of the antibody products themselves, there have been recent reports of cellular mutations in hybridomas that affect the antibodies produced by the cells (*28*). In all instances, however, the mutant cells appeared at extremely low frequency (10^{-4} to 10^{-5}). These mutant cells did not show a selective growth advantage over nonmutant cells and they persisted only as a minority population. Thus, with nonselective culture conditions, as are commonly used, it is unlikely that significant drift in the quality of monoclonal antibodies would occur.

These considerations lead us to expect that future areas of development in this field will emphasize (i) the preparation of antibodies with specificities capable of performing novel diagnostic functions, (ii) improved methods of manufacturing antibodies, and (iii) the incorporation of antibody-based reagents into instrumentation.

Antibodies. Not only will the library of monoclonal antibodies necessary for the phylogenetic classification of microorganisms be completed, but new antibodies will be developed to specifically identify pathogenic organisms or the molecular factors responsible for their pathogenesis. The development of monoclonal antibodies against plasmid-encoded proteins responsible for drug resistance will facilitate rapid decisions concerning preferred modalities of treatment.

Manufacturing. Variable chromosome loss, with the concomitant overgrowth of hybrid cells that do not produce antibody, is the most problematic feature of the hybridoma method. As new knowledge is acquired concerning the chromosomal locations of mouse genes, it should be possible to induce mutations in the genes involved with cell metabolism that are closely linked to genes encoding immunoglobulin heavy and light chains. With defined growth media, it should then be possible to select against cells that lose chromosomes encoding either of the immunoglobulin chains.

Instrumentation. The highly defined and reproducible properties of monoclonal antibodies invite their use in instrumentation. For example, they will probably be incorporated into a new generation of instruments for automated blood and tissue typing, detection of specific antibodies in blood, and quantitative determination of microbial antigens in a variety of body fluids and tissues.

Conclusions

Monoclonal antibodies are, in effect, homogeneous immunological reagents of defined specificity, avidity, high specific activity, and selected isotype. Individual antibodies can be selected for their unique reactions with particular microorganisms. In certain instances these antibodies can identify antigenic relations between organisms that are not apparent in tests with conventional antiserums.

We have described the use of monoclonal antibodies for the diagnosis of gonorrhoea, chlamydia, and herpesvirus infections in humans. In each case the monoclonal antibodies showed patterns of specificity and reproducibility that far exceeded those available with conventionally prepared antibodies. Furthermore, direct tests for these organisms required only 15 to 20 minutes to perform, representing a major advancement in the diagnosis of infections that previously required 3 to 6 days of culture to accomplish. In view of these advantages the continued development of techniques for the production and utilization of monoclonal antibodies should lead to great improvements in the quality of microbiological diagnosis.

References and Notes

1. P. D. Hoeprich, Ed., *Infectious Diseases* (Harper & Row, New York, 1978); B. D. Davis, R. Dulbecco, H. N. Eisen, H. S. Ginsberg, W. B. Wood, *Microbiology* (Harper & Row, New York, 1978); K. K. Holmes, P.-A. Mardh, P. F. Sparling, P. J. Wiesner, *Sexually Transmitted Diseases* (McGraw-Hill, New York, in press).
2. E. H. Lennette, A. Balows, W. J. Hausler, Jr., J. P. Truant, *Manual of Clinical Microbiology* (American Society for Microbiology, Washington, D.C., 1980).
3. G. Kohler and C. Milstein, *Nature (London)* **256**, 495 (1975); *Eur. J. Immunol.* **6**, 511 (1975).
4. G. S. David, W. Present, J. Martinis, R. Wang, R. Bartholomew, W. Desmond, E. D. Sevier, *Med. Lab. Sci.* **38**, 341 (1981); R. D. Dix, L.

Pereira, J. R. Baringer, *Infect. Immun.* **34**, 192 (1981); P. C. Doherty and W. Gerhard, *J. Neuroimmunol.* **1**, 227 (1981); M. Robert-Guroff, F. W. Ruscetti, L. E. Posner, B. J. Poiesz, R. C. Gallo, *J. Exp. Med.* **154**, 1957 (1981); M. Imai *et al.*, *J. Immunol.* **128**, 69 (1982); A. L. Schmaljohn, E. D. Johnson, J. M. Dalrymple, G. A. Cole, *Nature (London)* **297**, 70 (1982).
5. E. J. Hansen, S. M. Robertson, P. A. Gulig, C. F. Frisch, E. J. Haanes, *Lancet* **1982-I**, 368 (1982); D. L. Hasty, E. H. Beachey, W. A. Simpson, J. B. Dale, *J. Exp. Med.* **155**, 1010 (1982).
6. K. M. Cruise, G. F. Mitchell, F. P. Tapalaes, E. G. Garcia, S. R. Huant, *Aust. J. Exp. Biol. Med. Sci.* **59**, 503 (1981); D. Snary, M. A. Ferguson, M. T. Scot, A. K. Allen, *Mol. Biochem. Parasitol.* **3**, 343 (1981); N. Yoshida, P. Potocnjak, V. Nussenzweig, R. S. Nussenzweig, *J. Exp. Med.* **154**, 1225 (1981); M. A. Smith, J. A. Clegg, D. Snary, A. J. Trejdosiewicz, *Parasitology* **84**, 83 (1982); J. N. Wood, L. Hudson, T. M. Jessell, M. Yamamoto, *Nature (London)* **296**, 34 (1982).
7. Centers for Disease Control, *Morbidity and Mortality Weekly Report* (Department of Health and Human Services, Washington, D.C., 1982), vol. 31, No. 37.
8. K. K. Holmes and G. A. Stilwell, in *Infectious Diseases*, P. D. Hoeprich, Ed. (Harper & Row, New York, 1978), pp. 491–506.
9. H. H. Handsfield, W. E. Stamm, K. K. Holmes, *Sex. Transm. Dis.* **8**, 325 (1981); K. K. Holmes, *J. Am. Med. Assoc.* **245**, 1718 (1981).
10. J. T Grayston and S. P. Wang, *J. Infect. Dis.* **132**, 87 (1975); M. O. Beem and E. M. Saxon, *N. Engl. J. Med.* **296**, 306 (1977); J. Schachter, *ibid.* **298**, 428 (1978); *ibid.*, p. 490; *ibid.*, p. 540; J. W. Curran, *Am. J. Obstet. Gynecol.* **138**, 848 (1980); J. Schachter and H. D. Caldwell, *Annu. Rev. Microbiol.* **34**, 285 (1980); W. E. Stamm, L. Koutsky, J. Jourden, R. Brunham, K. K. Holmes, *Clin. Res.* **29**, 51A (1981).
11. C. C. Kuo, S. P. Wang, B. B. Wentworth, J. T. Grayston, *J. Infect. Dis.* **125**, 665 (1972); K. T. Ripa and P.-A. Mardh, *J. Clin. Microbiol.* **6**, 328 (1977); R. T. Evans and D. Taylor-Robinson, *ibid.* **10**, 198 (1979); *CDC Laboratory Update: Isolation of* Chlamydia trachomatis *in Cell Culture.* (U.S. Department of Health and Human Services, Centers for Disease Control, Atlanta, 1980); H. Mallinson, S. Sikotra, O. P. Arye, *J. Clin. Pathol.* **34**, 712 (1981); T. F. Smith, S. D. Brown, L. A. Weed, *Lab. Med.* **13**, 92 (1982).
12. A. J. Nahmias and W. Josey, in *Viral Infections of Humans—Epidemiology and Control*, A. Evans, Ed. (Plenum, New York, 1976), pp. 253–271; A. J. Nahmias and S. E. Starr, in *Infectious Diseases*, P. D. Hoeprich, Ed. (Harper & Row, New York, 1978), pp. 726–735.
13. W. C. Reeves, L. Corey, H. G. Adams, L. A. Vontver, K. K. Holmes, *N. Engl. J. Med.* **305**, 315 (1981).
14. NIAAD Study Group, *Sexually Transmitted Diseases, 1980 Status Report* (NIH Publ. No. 81-2213, U.S. Department of Health and Human Services, Bethesda, Md., 1981); W. P. Allen and F. Rapp, *J. Infect. Dis.* **145**, 413 (1982).
15. D. R. Benjamin, *Appl. Microbiol.* **28**, 568 (1974); L. Pereira, D. Dondero, B. Norrild, B. Roizman, *Proc. Natl. Acad. Sci. U.S.A.* **78**, 5202 (1981); N. Balachandran *et al.*, *J. Clin. Microbiol.* **16**, 205 (1982).

16. A. J. Nahmias, W. R. Dowdle, A. M. Naib, A. Highsmith, R. W. Harwell, W. E. Josey, *Proc. Soc. Exp. Biol. Med.* **127**, 1022 (1968); T. G. Buchman, B. Roizman, G. Adam, H. Stover, *J. Infect. Dis.* **138**, 488 (1978); D. M. Lonsdale, *Lancet* **1979-I**, 849 (1979).
17. E. DeClerq, J. Descamps, G. Verhelst, R. T. Walker, A. S. Jones, P. F. Torrence, D. Shugar, *J. Infect. Dis.* **141**, 563 (1980).
18. M. E. Lostrom, M. R. Stone, M. R. Tam, W. N. Burnette, A. Pinter, R. C. Nowinski, *Virology* **98**, 336 (1979).
19. M. R. Tam, T. M. Buchanan, E. G. Sandstrom, K. K. Holmes, J. S. Knapp, A. W. Siadak, R. C. Nowinski, *Infect. Immun.* **36**, 1042 (1982).
20. R. S. Stephens, M. R. Tam, C. Kuo, R. C. Nowinski, *J. Immunol.* **128**, 1083 (1982).
21. L. C. Goldstein, L. Corey, J. K. McDougall, E. Tolentino, R. C. Nowinski, *J. Infect. Dis.*, in press.
22. E. Sandstrom and D. Danielsson, *Acta Pathol. Microbiol. Scand. Sect. B* **88**, 27 (1980); S. D. Bygdeman, D. Danielsson, E. Sandstrom, *Acta Derm. Venercol.* **61**, 423 (1981).
23. R. Stephens, C.-C. Kuo, M. R. Tam, *J. Clin. Microbiol.* **16**, 4 (1982).
24. W. E. Stamm, M. Tam, M. Koester, L. Cles, *J. Clin. Microbiol.*, in press; unpublished data.
25. E. Peterson, G. W. Schmidt, L. C. Goldstein, R. C. Nowinski, L. Corey, *J. Clin. Microbiol.*, in press.
26. D. D. Richman, P. H. Cleveland, M. N. Oxman, *J. Med. Virol.* **9**, 299 (1982).
27. R. C. Mosely, L. Corey, D. Benjamin, C. Winter, M. L. Remington, *J. Clin. Microbiol.* **13**, 913 (1981).
28. S. L. Morrison and M. D. Scharff, *CRC Crit. Rev. Immunol.* **3**, 1 (1981); D. Y. Yelton and M. D. Scharff, *J. Exp. Med.* **156**, 1131 (1982).

6. Immunotoxins: A New Approach to Cancer Therapy

Ellen S. Vitetta, Keith A. Krolick, Muneo Miyama-Inaba
William Cushley, Jonathan W. Uhr

Approximately 75 years ago, Paul Ehrlich discussed the potential use of antibodies as carriers of pharmacologic agents (*1*). During the last decade, there has been considerable progress in the application of this concept to the elimination of cells that are reactive with antibodies coupled to toxic agents. In this chapter, we discuss work by ourselves and others concerning the elimination of normal and neoplastic target cells by conjugates containing antibody and toxin. We also present evidence that conjugates of toxin and antigen can induce specific immunologic unresponsiveness.

The term "immunotoxin" is used here to refer to a cell-binding antibody or antigen covalently bound to a plant or bacterial toxin. The toxin may be the whole molecule or a polypeptide portion carrying the toxic activity. Although much of our understanding of the mechanisms by which these toxins kill cells rests on studies of diphtheria toxin (*2*), the prevalence of diphtheria antitoxin in human populations renders this toxin unsuitable for clinical use. Therefore, most recent investigators have used ricin, a plant toxin. Like most toxic proteins produced by bacteria and plants, ricin has a toxic polypeptide (A chain) attached to a cell-binding polypeptide (B chain) (*3, 4*). The B chain is a lectin that binds to galactose-containing glycoproteins or glycolipids on the cell surface. By mechanisms that are not well understood, ricin A chain gains access to the cell cytoplasm. It is presumed, but has not been proved, that the route of entry is by receptor-mediated endocytosis (*5*) and that the A chain, which has a hydrophobic portion (*6*), penetrates the membrane of an endocytic vesicle or phagolysosome to enter the cytoplasm (*3*). By analogy with other toxins (*7*), it is possible that the B chain has a second function, namely, facilitating the translocation of the A chain through the membrane of the endocytic vesicle (*7–10*) by forming a pore in the membrane. In the cytoplasm, the A chain of ricin inhibits protein synthesis by enzymatically inactivating the EF2-binding portion of the 60S ribosomal subunit (*3*). A postulated model of this process is depicted in Fig. 1. Studies in vitro by Neville and Youle (*8*) and Thorpe and Ross (*9*) have established that different binding moieties (hormones, growth factor, or antibodies) can be substituted for the B chain to yield hybrid molecules in which the binding specificity is changed but the toxicity effected by the A chain is retained. Such

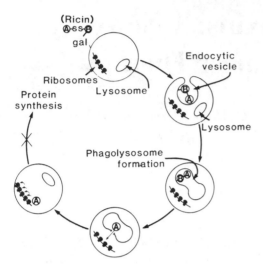

Fig. 1. A model for the cytotoxic action of ricin [based on data from (3–10)].

immunotoxins are not as toxic as intact ricin (possibly because of the absence of the putative second function of the B chain) (7–10) but are nevertheless highly toxic compared to antibody or A chain alone. Since the A chain is nontoxic until it enters the cytoplasm, conjugates of antibody and A chain should be relatively nontoxic to nonphagocytic cells lacking the specific surface molecules to which the antibody is directed. In addition, the release of A chains from killed cells should not pose a significant problem for "bystander cells."

Some of the successful studies conducted in vitro with immunotoxins are summarized in Table 1 (11–28). Several generalizations can be gleaned from these investigations. (i) If antibodies are coupled to whole toxins that are galactose-binding lectins, such as ricin or abrin, then the presence of a high concentration of lactose (or galactose) will prevent lectin binding by the immunotoxin and thereby leave only its antibody specificity (11–14, 23, 24, 27). This approach is restricted to the deletion of target cells in vitro. Immunotoxins containing chemically derived A chains (ricin-A and abrin-A) (15–22, 25, 26) or naturally occurring A chains (gelonin) (28) do not require the use of galactose or lactose since the lectin binding chain is absent. (ii) Immunotoxins containing the antigen binding fragment F(ab)' appear less toxic than those containing the same antibody in its F(ab)'$_2$ form (20). This finding indicates the importance of cross-linking and endocytosis in cell killing. (iii) Immunotoxins prepared with some monoclonal antibodies have poor toxicity (7–9, 29). This could be due to the inability of some antibodies to induce endocytosis because of their low binding affinity or because the target antigen is not readily taken up by endocytosis. Where internalization is slow or incomplete, the A chains in the endocytic vesicle may be below the concentration needed to traverse the membrane of the vesicle prior to degradation by enzymes in the phagolysosome.

These considerations suggest that improved efficacy of immunotoxins may depend on increasing both endocytosis of the conjugate and the ability of the A chain to traverse the membrane of the endocytic vesicle before inactivation by enzymes. Thus, toxicity can, in some cases, be improved by (i) more effectively cross-linking the immunotoxin with a second layer of antibody to facilitate endocytosis (30), (ii) using antibodies of higher affinity (7), (iii) incubating the immunotoxins for longer periods with the target cells (7–8), (iv) adding agents that raise the pH of the phagolysosome (for example, NH_4Cl) (7) and perhaps inactivating enzymes that degrade A chain (17), or (v) adding free B chains to the immunotoxin (8–10).

Preparation of Immunotoxins

The strategy for preparing ricin A chain is to: (i) reduce the interchain disulfide bond (4–6), (ii) purify A chains by chromatography on DEAE-cellulose (4–6), and (iii) remove contaminating B chains (or ricin) by either lectin affinity chromatography (with the use of a galactose-containing solid matrix) or by antibody affinity chromatography (with Sepharose-coupled antibody to B chain in the presence of lactose) (7, 30). The purified A chains should show no evidence of contaminating B chains when analyzed by electrophoresis on sodium dodecyl sulfate gels. However, when tested for toxicity in mice, trace contamination with B chain or ricin can occasionally be detected. Prior to being coupled with antibody, the capacity of purified A chain to inhibit protein synthesis can be assessed in a cell-free translation system (9). Coupling of A chain to antibody can be achieved by any one of several chemical methods (31). The most common strategy is to use the heterobifunctional cross-linking agent N-succinimidyl 3-(2-pyridyldithio)propionate (SPDP), which reacts with free amino groups on the antibody through the succinimide ester portion of the cross-linking agent (7–9). The PDP-derivatized antibody is then mixed at neutral pH with A chains to allow disulfide exchange. The resulting conjugates are separated from both free A chain and uncoupled antibody by a combination of gel filtration (7–9) and affinity chromatography with Sepharose bound to the antigen or Sepharose bound to an antibody to the A chain (30). The immunotoxins can be assayed for antibody activity and active A chain by radioimmunoassay (32) and by killing of the relevant target cells in vitro (4, 7–10, 32).

Testing the Efficacy of Immunotoxins

The murine BCL$_1$ model for studies in vitro. We chose the plant toxin ricin as the toxic agent for our studies because of its potency (one molecule in the cytoplasm of a cell will kill it) (3) and because ricin inhibits protein synthesis and can therefore kill nondividing cells (4). This latter attribute is important for successful therapy of human malignancies in which eradication of small metastatic foci containing nondividing cells may be critical. We have used a murine leukemia involving B cells bearing surface immunoglobulin (Ig) molecules to study in vitro and in vivo the effects of immunotoxins containing antibodies to Ig. Our choice of this model was based on the fact that B cell tumors are monoclonal (33–38) and that each clone synthesizes a distinct $V_H V_L$ Ig (there are 10^6 or more clones of normal B cells in each mouse). The clone-specific antigenic determinants of a particular $V_H V_L$ combination are called, collectively, the idiotype, and antibodies can be raised against them (anti-idiotypic) (33–38). Therefore, the surface Ig of each B cell tumor has a unique idiotype that can be viewed as a tumor-specific antigen. Hence, anti-idiotypic antibody represents an ideal targeting vehicle for guiding toxic agents to neoplastic B cells. The BCL$_1$ tumor arose spontaneously in an elderly BALB/c mouse (39), and healthy mice injected with as few as one to ten cells from this tumor develop severe splenomegaly and leukemia (32, 39). In many respects the BCL$_1$ disease resembles the prolymphocytic variant of chronic lymphocytic leukemia in humans (39–41). Mice bearing the tumor normally survive for 3 to 4 months after receiving 10^5 to 10^6 tumor cells. The BCL$_1$ tumor cells bear Fc receptors, IgMλ, IgDλ, Ia anti-

Table 1. Immunotoxins used to kill target cells in vitro.

| Toxin moiety | Antibody* | | Specificity | Target cell | Reference |
	Heterologous	Monoclonal			
Ricin (R)		+	Mouse T cells (Thy-1.2)	EL-4, WEHI-7	11, 12
		+	Rat T cells (W3/25)	T cells	13
		+	Mouse T cells (Thy-1.1)	T cells (AKR SL3)	14
R-A chain	+		DNP	TNP-HeLA	15
	+		Mouse μ chain	B cells	16, 17
	+		Mouse B cell leukemia (BCL₁) idiotype	BCL₁	16
	F(ab)'		Mouse B cell leukemia	L120	18
	F(ab)', F(ab)'₂		Human Ig	Daudi	19, 20
		+	IgD allotypes	B cells	16
		+	Human colorectal cancer cells	SW1116, SW948	21
		+	Human leukemia (CALLA)	Nalm-1	22
Diphtheria toxin (DT) DT-A chain	+ and F(ab)'₂		Human lymphocytes	Daudi	23, 24
	+		Con A	3T3-ConA	25
	F(ab)'		Mouse B cell leukemia (L1210)	L1210	26
		+	Human colorectal cancer cells	SW1116	21
		+	Mouse T cells (Thy-1.2)	T cells	17
Abrin	+		Human lymphocytes	Daudi	27
Gelonin		+	Mouse T cells (Thy-1.1)	T cells (AKR-A, BW5147)	28

*Plus signs indicate that the antibody is intact.

gens, and H-2 antigens (39). The cells lack complement receptors, suggesting they are analogs of immature B cells (39). This analogy is further supported by the functional properties of the BCL_1 cells (42).

In initial experiments, immunotoxins containing anti-idiotypic antibody were incubated with populations of BCL_1 tumor cells, cells from a different murine B cell tumor (CH1), or normal B cells (16). Protein synthesis was not inhibited in normal splenocytes or in a B cell tumor (CH1) bearing the same surface immunoglobulin isotype (IgMλ) as BCL_1 but a different idiotype. In contrast, anti-idiotype-containing immunotoxins decreased protein synthesis by 70 to 80 percent in spleen cell populations from BCL_1-bearing mice (70 to 80 percent of the cells in these spleens are of tumor origin). Control immunotoxins (containing irrelevant antibodies) had no effect on BCL_1 cells. These results indicate that the exquisite specificity of antibody is reflected in the specificity of killing the cells in vitro by antibody-containing immunotoxins.

Elimination of BCL_1 cells from bone marrow. To test further the precision of immunotoxin-mediated killing, we conducted similar experiments using an adoptive transfer system to assess the number of viable tumor cells remaining in the treated population. We had shown previously that by 12 weeks after the intravenous injection of ten BCL_1 cells, a tumor was detectable in virtually all recipient mice (39–43). About half of the mice injected with one BCL_1 cell had detectable leukemia at this time (32, 43). (This percentage might have been higher if technical maneuvers had ensured that a single cell was actually injected into each mouse.) Thus, experiments in vitro with spleens from BCL_1-bearing animals

were performed as above. Immunotoxin-treated cells were transferred to normal recipient animals (10^4 cells per mouse) and the mice were observed for 12 weeks. Since none of the recipient mice had leukemia at 12 weeks, the results indicate that the immunotoxin could eliminate all tumor cells from a population of cells treated in vitro or, alternatively, that a host antitumor response was transferred with the tumor cell populations and was holding a small number of surviving tumor cells in check.

We performed similar studies on tumor-infiltrated bone marrow because of the clinical implications of removing tumor cells from marrow. Thus, a form of therapy for certain types of leukemias and other forms of cancer is the autologous bone marrow rescue approach (44). In this form of treatment, conventional chemotherapy is used to induce a remission in a patient bearing a tumor. During remission, a portion of the patient's bone marrow is removed and frozen. If the patient relapses, he or she receives supralethal therapy, that is, high doses of irradiation or chemotherapy in order to kill all tumor cells in the body. The result of this therapy, however, is the obliteration of the patient's own bone marrow. The patient is then "rescued" from the lethal effects of the therapy by reinfusion of his or her own bone marrow. Although the supralethal therapy is frequently sufficient to kill all tumor cells remaining in the individual, the reinfused bone marrow may contain small numbers of viable tumor cells that will then cause recurrence of the cancer. Our objective was to use a conjugate of tumor-reactive antibody–ricin A chain to destroy such tumor cells in a preparation of tumor-infiltrated bone marrow (45). Thus, bone marrow containing 15 percent BCL_1 cells was treated in vitro with anti-Ig immunotoxin and the treated cells were adoptively transferred to lethally irradiated animals. It is important to stress that the antibody used in these studies (antibody to Ig) was tumor reactive but not tumor specific. Thus, the only requirement for success in this approach was that the immunotoxin kill all the tumor cells but not the stem cells. The target antigens must be expressed on all the tumor cells but not the stem cells.

As shown in Fig. 2, the results indicate the following. (i) The hematopoietic system of all the animals was reconstituted, because all lethally irradiated mice survived after the administration of bone marrow cells. This finding together with earlier dosage experiments shows that no more than 10 percent of the bone marrow stem cells were damaged by the immunotoxins. (ii) Eighty-five percent of the animals (17 out of 20) treated with tumor-reactive immunotoxin did not develop tumors within 12 weeks although animals in all the control groups became leukemic (45). At 21 weeks after injection with treated cells, another mouse relapsed. At 25 weeks, spleen cells from the remaining mice were examined by analysis on the fluorescence activated cell sorter (FACS) for idiotype-positive cells. Although none were detected, spleen cells from one mouse caused leukemia in a second adoptive recipient. Thus, of the 20 mice receiving treated bone marrow, 5 out of 20 or 25 percent received marrow with at least one viable tumor cell. The one animal with late relapse and the other animal harboring "dormant" BCL_1 cells may have developed immunity to the BCL_1 tumor either from the administration of putative immune cells in the bone marrow itself or as a result of the challenge with the "killed" BCL_1 cells in the bone marrow

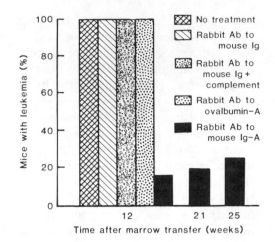

Fig. 2. Adoptive transfer into lethally irradiated recipients of BCL_1-containing bone marrow cells treated with rabbit antibody (Ab) to mouse Ig conjugated with A chain. Bone marrow cells containing 10 to 15 percent tumor cells were injected into groups of 20 mice at 10^6 marrow cells per mouse. Every 2 weeks after adoptive transfer the mice were examined for leukemia. At 25 weeks, all surviving mice were killed and 10^6 spleen cells were adoptively transferred into normal recipients. The spleen cells from one of the mice caused a tumor in these recipients 10 weeks later. Thus, this mouse is scored as "leukemic" at 25 weeks.

inoculum. Of the three animals that relapsed within 12 weeks, all had idiotype positive cells that were susceptible to the lethal effect of Ig antibody-containing immunotoxins in vitro.

The simplest interpretation is that all malignant BCL_1 cells bear surface immunoglobulin (sIg). The use of higher concentrations of immunotoxin or different conditions for treatment might have resulted in complete elimination of tumor cells from the bone marrow. In addition, since many antigens on tumor cells (that are not stem cell malignancies) are not represented on stem cells, it might be possible to make a "cocktail" of monoclonal antibodies reactive with different antigens on the tumor cells to maximize the probability of complete killing. A similar approach in which cells are exposed to antibody-ricin conjugates in the presence of lactose has been used by others to delete tumor cells (13) from rodent bone marrow.

A different strategy for the treatment of cancer patients by means of bone marrow rescue is to transplant allogeneic marrow from which T cells have been eliminated (46–51). Deletion of T cells may avoid the life-threatening syndrome called graft versus host disease. Current methods for eliminating T cells from bone marrow have met with some success, but they are technically limited. Such methods require the use of large amounts of complement; complement batches are difficult to standardize, and killing is frequently incomplete.

Vallera et al. (52) have recently used an anti-T cell–ricin immunotoxin to treat mouse bone marrow. The allogeneic recipients of such bone marrow did not develop graft versus host disease, indicating that the T cells had been efficiently eliminated and that the stem cells remained viable. Should this strategy work in humans it would obviate the necessity of using tumor-infiltrated autologous marrow and would also be applicable to diseases in which the bone marrow fails to generate cells (for example, aplastic anemia).

Therapy of BCL$_1$ in vivo

In these experiments (43) we used mice with massive tumor burdens (20 percent of body weight; approximately 10^{10} tumor cells). The rationale was to use experimental animals that would resemble most closely the clinical situations that would be faced initially with therapy in humans. Our strategy was to reduce the tumor burden by at least 95 percent by using nonspecific cytoreductive methods, and to eliminate remaining tumor cells with immunotoxins directed against either the idiotype or the δ chain of the sIgD on the BCL$_1$ cells. (The anti-idiotype would be the more specific of the two reagents.) The rationale for using antibody to δ is that sIgD is present on BCL$_1$ cells and on more than 50 percent of B cell tumors in humans. Antibody to δ, therefore, would represent a more practical reagent for clinical therapy. It was realized that treatment with anti-δ– A chain would eliminate virtually all virgin B cells, but it was reasoned that stem cells, pre-B cells, or immature IgD$^-$ (IgM$^+$) cells all had the capacity to repopulate the virgin B cell compartment of the animals. Furthermore, since IgD is present in very low concentrations in the serum of both humans and mice, and since cytoreduction of BCL$_1$-bearing mice eliminates most mature B cells, the normal B cells and serum IgD would not represent major sources of competition for the anti-δ immunotoxins.

Nonspecific cytoreduction was accomplished with a combination of fractionated total lymphoid irradiation (TLI) (53) and splenectomy (40, 54). Animals receiving no treatment other than TLI and splenectomy were dead within 7 weeks. The injection of these cytoreduced mice with control immunotoxins did not prolong their survival. In contrast, animals receiving the anti-δ immunotoxin appeared tumor free as judged by the absence of detectable idiotype positive cells 12 to 18 weeks later (three of four such experiments). A successful experiment is depicted in Fig. 3. In one of the three successful experiments, 3×10^6 blood cells were transferred from animals in remission to nor-

80

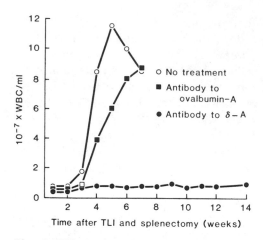

Fig. 3. Effect of total lymphoid irradiation (*TLI*), splenectomy, and administration of immunotoxin on leukemic relapse of BCL_1-bearing mice. After receiving nine doses of TLI and splenectomy, the mice were injected with two doses of 20 micrograms of antibody to δ or control immunotoxin (antibody to ovalbumin-A chain), or they were not injected. There were nine mice per group. Leukemic relapse was monitored by determining the number of white cells in the blood (*WBC*) of the treated mice. The control mice were all dead at 7 weeks after TLI (*43*).

mal animals and leukemia did not develop in the normal animals by 12 weeks, suggesting an absence of tumor cells in the blood of the donor animals. By 14 weeks, mice in remission had normal or above-normal levels of IgD-bearing normal lymphocytes (*43*). These results suggest that either the remaining tumor cells were eradicated in the animals that appeared tumor free, or the tumor cells remained in some organs but were held in check by a host resistance mechanism. However, such cells would have to be present in tissues other than blood, because transfer of blood to normal recipients did not cause tumors.

In ongoing experiments with long-term survivors (25 to 30 weeks after immunotoxin treatment), tissues (liver, lung, kidney, bone marrow, and lymph nodes) adoptively transferred into normal mice did cause tumors 6 to 12 weeks later, suggesting that host resistance had developed. In the one experiment where the treated mice relapsed at 10 weeks, idiotype positive cells were detectable in the blood indicating that remission was prolonged but was incomplete. The partial success of these experiments was probably directly related to the fact that cytoreduction (TLI and splenectomy) was successful in reducing the number of remaining tumor cells to a level that could be effectively killed by a nonlethal dose of the immunotoxin. Moreover, it appears that the immunotoxins need not kill every tumor cell in vivo for prolonged remissions to occur, since a few remaining tumor cells may be permanently held in check by the immune system. Nevertheless, it was clear from preliminary experiments that inadequate cytoreduction (for example, TLI without splenectomy) left too many tumor cells to be effectively handled by such doses of immunotoxin. Thus, in considering the use of immunotoxins for treating human cancer, the tumor burden must be a major consideration—at least until the therapeutic index of immunotoxins can be significantly improved.

Induction of Specific Immunologic Unresponsiveness

A potential problem in the repeated administration of immunotoxins in cancer patients is the generation of an antibody response to the injected immunotoxin (that is, antibody to the antibody or the A chain). The problem could arise in humans from the administration of rodent monoclonal antibodies or even human monoclonal antibodies as carriers of toxins; the latter could stimulate an anti-idiotypic response. Theoretically, an antibody to the immunotoxin should not develop because the B cells bearing antigen-binding determinants reactive with the antibody or A chain should be eliminated after binding the immunotoxin. Nevertheless, it was important to test this possibility directly and to develop a strategy for induction of specific immunological tolerance by means of immunotoxins.

In the first series of experiments along these lines, we attempted to eliminate a subset of B lymphocytes in vitro by a brief exposure to antigen-containing immunotoxin [that is, dinitrophenylated human serum albumin–A chain (DNP-HSA-A chain)]. We then tested the immune responsiveness of this treated cell population by transferring the cells to immunoincompetent irradiated recipients. The recipients were challenged with an immunogen [keyhole limpet hemocyanin (DNP-KLH)] containing the specific hapten to determine if DNP-specific cells had been eliminated from the injected cells and with sheep red blood cells (SRBC) as a control immunogen. Figure 4 shows the results of a representative experiment. The data indicate that the hapten antibody response of mice receiving cells treated with an irrelevant antigen-A chain (HSA-A chain) was unimpaired. However, the specific antigen-A chain (DNP-HSA-A chain) reduced the hapten antibody response by approximately 95 percent but did not effect the response to SRBC. Thus, specific immunologic unresponsiveness can be induced in vitro by such conjugates. The use of hapten as the antigenic determinant in these experiments suggests that B cells were rendered tolerant since it is known that B cells are specific for the hapten in a

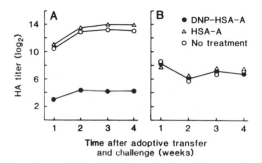

Fig. 4. Serum hemagglutination titer (*HA*) of irradiated mice injected with 10^7 cells and treated as indicated. Spleen cells were obtained from mice previously injected with DNP-keyhole limpet hemocyanin and sheep red blood cells (SRBC). The cells were treated for 15 minutes at 4°C with immunotoxins (50 μg per 10^6 cells), protein, or nothing, and 10^7 washed cells were injected into irradiated mice. These mice were injected with antigen 2 hours later and the hemagglutination titer of the serum was evaluated 1 to 4 weeks later. (A) Antibody to trinitrophenyl, (B) antibody to SRBC. Although not shown in the figure, incubation of cells with antigen alone had no effect on their subsequent responsiveness in vivo.

hapten-carrier conjugate (*55*). However, this tentative conclusion remains to be proved. It will also be important to determine the conditions for inducing unresponsiveness in vivo, the duration of such unresponsiveness, and, if it wanes, the effect of readministration of the specific immunotoxin. Similar studies recently reported by Volkman *et al.* (*56*) suggest that antigen-binding human B cells can be eliminated in vitro by using antigen bound to ricin in the presence of lactose.

These results on the induction of tolerance with soluble antigen-containing immunotoxins have implications at the clinical level. The induction of immunologic unresponsiveness to specific antigens would be useful not only in cancer patients that are to receive immunotoxins containing tumor-reactive antibody but also in treating autoimmune diseases. For example, in the case of an autoimmune disease in which the antigen has been identified, it may be possible to delete the B cells responsive to this autoantigen by injecting autoantigen-A chain.

Other Possibilities for Modulating the Immune Response

There are additional possibilities for using immunotoxins to manipulate the immune response for therapeutic purposes. Immunotoxins directed against T suppressor cells (57), which constitute a minor subpopulation of T lymphocytes, should be effective in stimulating immune responsiveness when desirable, for example, tumor immunity or immune deficiency due to hyperreactivity of the T suppressor system. This maneuver might also be desirable for certain persistent viral infections, such as herpes simplex, in which the objective might be to transiently eliminate suppression in order to stimulate the host antiviral response and thereby bring the viral infection under control. Conversely, immunotoxins directed against various inducer and helper T cells might be desirable for controlling autoimmune diseases in which there is a plethora of autoantibodies, for example, lupus erythematosus. Alternatively, one could delete cytokine-producer cells which sustain the growth of tumor cells or autoreactive cells. The use of this strategy will require a more complete understanding of the target cell specificity of these cytokines and the nature of the cells producing them.

Problems and Future Considerations

Pharmacokinetics. Serum half-life, tissue distribution, and toxicity of immunotoxins have not been investigated in depth. Preliminary studies by ourselves and others (15) indicate that immunotoxins containing normal Ig's have a relatively low toxicity. The organ systems that sustain significant tissue damage appear to be the intestine and the reticuloendothelial system (15), that is, macrophages in the liver and spleen that presumably remove the immunotoxin from the circulation. Since these cells can be replaced by stem cells, it is likely that this type of damage will be reversible. Indeed, past experimental results suggest that it is virtually impossible to exhaust the reticuloendothelial system because of replacement of macrophages from cells in the bone marrow (58). Surprisingly, immunotoxins do not appear to cause major damage in the kidney.

Studies of the metabolic half-life and tissue distribution of immunotoxins are also of a preliminary nature. A relatively short serum half-life for immunotoxins (30 minutes) has been reported (15). This may be due to the hydrophobicity of the A chain. This short half-life might be undesirable in that persistent serum titers of immunotoxin may be critical in permitting its access to tumor cells in sites where there is a blood-tissue barrier that takes time to penetrate. It may be important, therefore, to block uptake of immunotoxins by prior injection of macromolecules that temporarily cause RES blockade, for example, aggregated Ig.

Cross-reactive target antigens on normal tissues. Another major problem in predicting the efficacy of immunotoxins in any type of therapy in vivo is the possible representation of target antigens on normal tissues. For example, it is generally acknowledged that "tumor-specific antigens" are rare, if they exist at all. Most tumor-specific antigens are probably differentiation antigens that are expressed on subsets of cells in normal tissues of the same organ and, possibly, other organs. If such tissues are vital to survival, then it will be crucial to determine whether the unwanted tissue damage is acceptable. At present, there is insufficient information to answer this question.

Solid tumors. Another major issue is whether immunotoxins can gain access to cancer cells that form solid tumors, particularly those with a dense connective tissue component. Two possible approaches are to make the immunotoxin molecule smaller, that is, use an Fv or F(ab)' fragment that contains only the combining site. This fragment might then be attached to an active fragment of the A chain. An alternative approach would be to bind a vasodilator, such as histamine, to the immunotoxin molecule to facilitate its penetration of the blood-tissue barriers.

Tumor cell heterogeneity. The problem of tumor cell heterogeneity, including the emergence of mutants lacking particular surface antigens or resistant to the toxic effects of ricin A chain, represents a major challenge to immunotoxin therapy. Here, the critical issue will be the therapeutic index of immunotoxins. If they have a high index, use of a combinatorial approach, namely, a mixture of immunotoxins directed against a variety of different cell-surface, tumor-associated antigens, might overcome this problem. If it is not possible to eradicate all tumor cells even by this combinatorial approach, a second approach may be to increase the host's immune response to the tumor by using immunotoxins (and other modalities) to provide the host with sufficient immunity to deal with the small number of tumor cells that may remain after administration of tumor antibody-containing immunotoxins.

Antigens in the circulation. Another obstacle to the treatment of cancer or induction of tolerance in autoimmune disease is the presence of tumor-associated antigens or autoantibody, respectively, in the circulation. These might have to be partially removed by plasmaphoresis or the injection of unconjugated antibody (or antigen in the case of autoimmune disease) before injecting the appropriate immunotoxin. However, it is not yet known whether low concentrations of such tumor-associated antigens necessarily represent a major problem. Thus, even under conditions in which immunotoxins exist primarily as serum antigen–antibody complexes, transient binding of a very small number of immunotoxin molecules to surface receptors can occur and may suffice for cell killing.

Conclusions

Immunotoxins represent a new approach to pharmacology. Rather than relying on the innate tissue "specificity" of pharmacologic agents, immunotoxins harness the exquisite specificity of antibodies (or antigens) to direct the pharmacologic agent to cells bearing a particular surface receptor. It is clear that consid-

84

erable additional information of the chemistry, biology, and physiology of immunotoxins is essential to provide a firm foundation for designing regimens of immunotoxin therapy. With regard to treatment of cancer, the use of immunotoxins in vitro to eradicate either tumor cells from bone marrow or T cells from allogeneic marrow probably represents the initial approaches most likely to be helpful. In our judgment, the most rewarding future possibilities lie in the direction of modulation of the immune response. The findings that specific immunologic unresponsiveness can be induced in vitro with antigen-containing immunotoxins and that immunotoxins containing antibody to δ can eliminate sIgD positive lymphocytes in vivo underscores the potential of this approach to manipulate the immune response for therapeutic purposes.

References and Notes

1. F. Himmelweit, in *The Collected Papers of Paul Erlich*, F. Himmelweit, Ed. (Pergamon, New York, 1960), vol. 3.
2. A. M. Pappenheimer, Jr., *Harvey Lect.* **76**, 12 (1980).
3. S. Olsnes and A. Pihl, *Pharmacology of Bacterial Toxins*, J. Drews and F. Dornes, Eds. (Pergamon, New York, in press).
4. _____, *Biochemistry* **12**, 3121 (1973).
5. S. Olsnes, K. Sandvig, K. Refsnes, A. Pihl, *J. Biol. Chem.* **257**, 3985 (1976).
6. G. Funatsu, M. Kimura, M. Funatsu, *Agri. Biol. Chem.* **43**, 2221 (1979).
7. F. K. Jansen *et al.*, *Immunol. Rev.* **62**, 185 (1982).
8. D. M. Neville, Jr., and R. J. Youle, *ibid.*, p. 75.
9. P. E. Thorpe and W. C. J. Ross, *ibid.*, p. 119.
10. L. L. Houston, *J. Biol. Chem.* **257**, 1532 (1982).
11. R. J. Youle and D. M. Neville, Jr., *Proc. Natl. Acad. Sci. U.S.A.* **77**, 5483 (1980).
12. H. E. Blythman, P. Casellas, O. Gros, P. Gros, F. K. Jansen, F. Paulucci, B. Pau, H. Vidal, *Nature (London)* **290**, 145 (1981).
13. P. E. Thorpe, D. W. Mason, A. N. F. Brown, S. J. Simmonds, W. C. J. Ross, A. J. Cumber, J. A. Forrester, *ibid.* **297**, 594 (1982).
14. L. L. Houston and R. C. Nowinski, *Cancer Res.* **41**, 3913 (1981).
15. F. K. Jansen *et al.*, *Immunol. Lett.* **2**, 97 (1980).
16. K. A. Krolick, C. Villemez, P. Isakson, J. W. Uhr, E. S. Vitetta, *Proc. Natl. Acad. Sci. U.S.A.* **77**, 5419 (1980).
17. T. N. Oeltmann and J. T. Forbes, *Arch. Biochem. Biophys.* **209**, 362 (1981).
18. Y. Masuho and T. Hara, *Gann* **71**, 759 (1980).
19. V. Raso and T. Griffin, *J. Immunol.* **125**, 2610 (1980).
20. V. Raso, *Immunol. Rev.* **62**, 93 (1982).
21. D. G. Gilliland, Z. Steplewski, R. J. Collier, K. F. Mitchell, T. H. Chang, H. Koprowski, *Proc. Natl. Acad. Sci. U.S.A.* **77**, 4539 (1980).
22. V. Raso, J. Ritz, M. Basala, S. F. Schlossman, *Cancer Res.* **42**, 457 (1982).
23. P. E. Thorpe, W. C. J. Ross, A. J. Cumber, C. A. Hinson, D. C. Edwards, A. J. S. Davies, *Nature (London)* **271**, 752 (1978).
24. W. C. J. Ross, P. E. Thorpe, A. J. Cumber, D. C. Edwards, C. A. Hinson, A. J. S. Davies, *Eur. J. Biochem.* **104**, 381 (1980).
25. D. G. Gilliland and R. J. Collier, *Cancer Res.* **40**, 3564 (1980).
26. Y. Masuho, T. Hara, T. Noguchi, *Biochem. Biophys. Res. Commun.* **90**, 320 (1979).
27. P. E. Thorpe, A. J. Cumber, N. Williams, D. C. Edwards, W. C. J. Ross, A. J. S. Davies, *Clin. Exp. Immunol.* **43**, 195 (1981).
28. P. E. Thorpe, A. N. F. Brown, W. C. J. Ross, A. J. Cumber, S. I. Detre, D. C. Edwards, A. J. S. Davies, F. S. Stirpe, *Eur. J. Biochem.* **116**, 447 (1981).
29. B. L. Kagen, A. Finkelstein, M. Colombini, *Proc. Natl. Acad. Sci. U.S.A.* **78**, 4950 (1981).
30. E. S. Vitetta, unpublished observations.
31. S. Olsnes and A. Pihl, *Pharmacol. Ther.* **15**, 355 (1982).
32. E. S. Vitetta, K. A. Krolick, J. W. Uhr, *Immunol. Rev.* **62**, 159 (1982).
33. S. M. Fu, R. J. Winchester, H. G. Kunkel, *J. Immunol.* **114**, 250 (1975).
34. D. W. Hough, R. P. Eady, T. J. Hamblin, F. K. Stevenson, G. T. Stevenson, *J. Exp. Med.* **144**, 960 (1977).
35. G. Haughton, L. L. Lanier, G. F. Babcock, M. A. Lynes, *J. Immunol.* **121**, 2358 (1978).
36. J. N. Hurley, S. M. Fu, H. G. Kunkel, G. McKenna, M. D. Scharff, *Proc. Natl. Acad. Sci. U.S.A.* **75**, 5706 (1978).
37. R. Levy, R. Warnke, R. F. Dorman, J. Haimovich, *J. Exp. Med.* **145**, 1014 (1977).
38. K. A. Krolick, P. C. Isakson, J. W. Uhr, E. S. Vitetta, *Immunol. Rev.* **48**, 81 (1979).
39. S. Slavin and S. Strober, *Nature (London)* **272**, 624 (1977).
40. M. J. Muirhead, P. C. Isakson, K. A. Krolick, J. W. Uhr, E. S. Vitetta, *Am. J. Pathol.* **105**, 295 (1981).
41. M. J. Muirhead, J. M. Holbert, J. W. Uhr, E. S. Vitetta, *ibid.*, p. 306.
42. E. Vitetta, E. Puré, P. Isakson, L. Buck, J. Uhr, *Immunol. Rev.* **52**, 211 (1980).
43. K. A. Krolick, J. W. Uhr, S. Slavin, E. S. Vitetta, *J. Exp. Med.* **155**, 1797 (1982).
44. R. P. Gale, *J. Am. Med. Assoc.* **243**, 540 (1980).
45. K. A. Krolick, J. W. Uhr, E. S. Vitetta, *Nature (London)* **295**, 604 (1982).
46. J. H. Kersey, H. J. Meuwissen, R. A. Good, *Hum. Pathol.* **2**, 389 (1971).

47. M. E. Tyan, *Transplantation* **15**, 601 (1973).
48. H. V. Rodt, S. Therfelder, M. Eulitz, *Eur. J. Immunol.* **4**, 25 (1974).
49. R. Korngold and J. Sprent, *J. Exp. Med.* **148**, 1687 (1978).
50. D. A. Vallera, C. Soderling, G. Carlson, J. H. Kersey, *Transplantation* **31**, 218 (1981).
51. H. G. Prentice, H. A. Blacklock, G. Janossy, *Lancet* **1982-I**, 700 (1982).
52. D. A. Vallera, R. J. Youle, D. M. Neville, Jr., J. H. Kersey, *J. Exp. Med.* **155**, 949 (1982).
53. S. Slavin, S. Strober, Z. Fuks, H. S. Kaplan, *Transplant. Proc.* **9**, 1001 (1977).
54. S. Slavin, S. Morecki, L. Weiss, *J. Immunol.* **124**, 586 (1980).
55. N. A. Mitchison, *Eur. J. Immunol.* **1**, 68 (1971).
56. D. J. Volkman, A. Ahmad, A. S. Fauci, D. M. Neville, Jr., *J. Exp. Med.* **156**, 634 (1982).
57. J. S. Goodwin, Ed., *Suppressor Cells in Human Disease* (Dekker, New York, 1981).
58. R. Van Furth and Z. A. Cohn, *J. Exp. Med.* **128**, 415 (1968).

59. We thank M. Bagby-Wyatt, C. Bockhold, Y. Chinn, and L. Trahan for expert technical assistance, D. Marcoulides and G. A. Cheek for helpful secretarial assistance and L. Eidels for reviewing the manuscript. Supported by NIH grants AI-11851 and CA28149. K.A.K. was a postdoctoral fellow in the department of microbiology, University of Texas Southwestern Medical School, Dallas, at the time much of this work was conducted.

7. Protein Sequence Analysis: Automated Microsequencing

Michael W. Hunkapiller and Leroy E. Hood

Since its introduction 25 years ago, the Edman degradation has been the most widely used method for the direct determination of the primary structure of proteins and peptides (*1*). However, the introduction of rapid, simple methods of DNA sequencing, by which protein sequences are obtained indirectly, has raised questions about the utility of protein sequencing. Several years ago in one leading scientific journal, an editorial appeared under the title *The Decline and Fall of Protein Chemistry* (*2*). However, the advent of modern micromethods requiring as little as a few picomoles of proteins and peptides for sequence analysis has firmly established the importance of protein sequencing as a tool for biochemistry and molecular biology.

Chemistry

The Edman chemistry is shown in Fig. 1. One cycle, which results in removal of one amino acid from the amino-terminal end of a peptide and generation of a new peptide that is one amino acid shorter, consists of two separate chemical steps. In the first (coupling), phenyl isothiocyanate is coupled under basic conditions to the amino end of the peptide to form a phenylthiocarbamyl peptide. In the second (cleavage), treatment with a strong, anhydrous acid removes the derivatized amino acid as its anilinothiazolinone. The latter is usually converted in a third reaction (conversion) into the more stable phenylthiohydantoin (Pth) for subsequent analysis.

Repetition of this sequence, in theory, allows one to proceed from the amino-terminal to carboxyl-terminal end of a protein to define its primary structure. In practice, side reactions, incomplete reactions, and loss of sample usually limit successful degradations in a single run to 30 to 70 cycles. The sequence of the remainder of the protein is determined

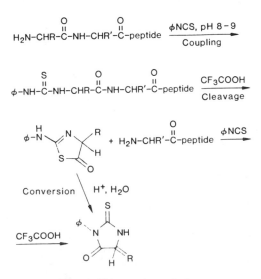

Fig. 1. Edman degradation.

after fragmentation by chemical or enzymic methods (or both) to generate a set of overlapping peptides that are individually analyzed by the Edman chemistry.

Instrumentation

Manual. The Edman degradation was originally developed as a manual method. Despite the subsequent popularity and success of automated methods, there remain many applications where the manual approach is suitable, particularly when there is need for rather limited sequence information and there is no access to automated instruments. Improvements in technique (*3*) and chemistry (*4*) make it particularly attractive for initial screening of a large number of small- to medium-sized peptides to select those most suitable for further, extensive sequence analysis by automated methods. Experienced protein chemists can usually expect five to ten successful degradations with as little as 1 to 10 nanomoles of peptide, and several peptides can be analyzed simultaneously. Manual methods are not routinely used for long amino-terminal sequence analyses of proteins because of the extent of side reactions inherent in the manual manipulations.

Spinning cup (liquid phase) sequenator. The spinning cup sequenator has been the workhorse of protein sequence analysis since its introduction by Edman and Begg (*5*) in 1967. Its design includes (i) an inert gas pressure supply and distribution system, (ii) a series of reagent and solvent reservoirs pressurized by the inert gas, (iii) a reaction vessel consisting of a spinning (1200 to 3600 revolutions per minute) glass cup contained in a sealable chamber, (iv) delivery valves that direct reagents and solvents into and out of the cup, (v) a vacuum system to remove volatile chemicals from the cup, (vi) a fraction collector into which the amino acid anilinothiazolinones cleaved from the peptide are deposited, and (vii) an electronic programmer that controls instrument operation. Some spinning cup sequenators also include a secondary reaction vessel in which the anilinothiazolinones are converted into the Pth amino acids (*6*).

The key feature of the spinning cup design is the cup itself, since it provides the means of immobilizing the peptide during the many cycles of chemical manipulation. A solution of the sample is added to the cup and dried into a thin film on its interior wall. Reagents are added to dissolve the sample and effect the Edman degradation. Excess reagents, by-products, and the anilinothiazolinones are removed first by evacuation and then by extraction with solvents flowing over the dried peptide film.

Since a considerable mass (a few milligrams) is required to form a stable film on the cup wall, the spinning cup sequenator was first used with several hundred nanomoles of protein. Moreover, the large volume of extraction solvents required to clean the cup initially limited its usefulness in sequencing small peptides because many peptides are somewhat soluble in the solvents. The introduction of a nonprotein carrier, Polybrene (see discussion below), has minimized these problems and greatly extended the capabilities of the spinning cup sequenator (*7*).

Solid phase sequenator. Laursen (*8*) sought to eliminate the main problem with the original Edman sequenator, the loss of sample from the cup, by replacing the cup with a column packed with a solid phase support (derivatized glass or polystyrene beads) onto which the peptide is covalently attached prior to initiating the Edman degradation. The column system, owing to its potential miniaturization, efficient flow properties during solvent extractions, and mechanical simplicity, offers substantial theoretical advantages, especially for microsequencing, compared to the spinning cup system. In practice, these advantages have not been realized because of difficulties in coupling many peptides and most proteins in high yield to the solid support. With proper care, reasonable coupling efficiencies can be obtained in certain cases, however, and sequencing in the low nanomole sample range is possible (9).

Gas phase sequenator. Recently, a new type of sequenator, one in which gas rather than liquid phase reagents are used at critical points in the Edman degradation, was described (10) (Fig. 2). This sequenator, which resembles the solid phase instrument in having a cartridge-type reaction chamber, differs from the solid phase instrument in its use of gas phase base and acid for the coupling and cleavage steps, respectively. If these reagents were delivered as liquids, the sample would be dissolved and carried away unless it was covalently attached to the support. The gas phase delivery eliminates the need for covalent attachment and thus the problems associated with this process. The sample solution is applied to the support, a thin disc of glass filter paper coated with Polybrene, in much the same manner as the sample is applied to the spinning cup. The miniaturization possible with this system (Fig. 3) allows use of minimal solvent volumes and makes the gas phase instrument suitable for small peptides as well as proteins.

Pth amino acid analysis. Edman originally used thin-layer chromatography to identify Pth amino acids (5). Others have used a variety of analytical procedures, including gas chromatography (11), mass spectrometry (12), and amino acid analysis after hydrolysis of the Pth amino acids (13). None of these methods alone provided a quantitative analysis of all common Pth amino acids, and their inadequacy hindered sequencing by any of the methods described above, especially at micro levels. The development of high-performance liquid chromatography (HPLC) has provided the analytical resolution, quantitation, speed, and reliability required for microsequencing (14). An example of the quality of HPLC resolution obtainable is shown in Fig. 4, and the sensitivity of this system is such that as little as a few hundred femtomoles (0.1 nanogram) of Pth amino acids can be detected.

Microsequencing

Many interesting biological systems yield very little protein or peptide for study. Hence, the ability to sequence very small amounts of sample (a few micrograms or less) is often crucial. Although the Edman chemistry was originally designed to handle several milligrams of protein (and was at the time of its introduction considered a microsequencing method), the general power of this chemistry is illustrated by the success of efforts to increase the sensitivity of sequencing by several orders of magnitude. The term "microsequencing," although it is arbitrary and changes as technology improves, may now be considered to involve sequencing less than 0.5 nmole of sample. Three microsequencing approaches have been used; two are based on isotopic labeling, primarily to improve sensitivity of the Pth analysis, and the third is based on direct analysis of nonlabeled Pth amino acids.

External label. The first serious attempts at microsequencing involved increasing sensitivity of the phenylhydantoin detection system by introducing an isotopic label via phenylisothiocyanate. The efforts included using [³H]- and [¹⁴C]phenylisothiocyanate and [³⁵S]-phenylisothiocyanate as the coupling reagent in spinning cup sequencing (*15, 16*) and solid phase sequencing (*8, 17*). These external labeling procedures suffered from the use of expensive, unstable, and difficult-to-purify radioactive labeling reagents. Nevertheless, they allowed sequencing at the 0.5- to 10-nmole level. Their usefulness has diminished with the advent of HPLC analysis of Pth amino acids and the excellent sensitivity of this type of analysis.

Internal label. A more successful exploitation of the sensitivity of isotopic labeling methods was the use of internal labeling of the protein itself during its synthesis. This has been achieved by short-term tissue culture procedures that readily incorporate several labeled amino acids into newly synthesized polypeptides (*18*), by longer-term tissue culture techniques in which a mixture of labeled amino acids and Krebs cycle intermediates is used (*19*), and by cell-free translation of messenger RNA (mRNA) with labeled amino acids (*20*). In the former, sequenator analysis of the partially labeled proteins results in partial amino acid sequence data with the unlabeled residues being registered as blanks, while in the latter cases complete sequence information is possible. These techniques have drawbacks as routine microsequencing procedures in that they are expensive and they require a source of cells producing protein or active mRNA. However, they can be used with

any of the sequencing instruments, and they require protein that is only free of other labeled proteins. The presence of nonlabeled protein, such as antibody used in purification of the labeled protein, does not interfere with the sequencing. The in vivo labeling methods allow sequencing with as little as a few picomoles of protein, while the in vitro procedure has been used with as little as 100 fmole of sample. The power of the techniques is illustrated by the structural analysis of the mouse transplantation antigens (*21, 22*).

Microsequencing without isotopic labeling. The development of so-called direct microsequencing, that is with no isotopic labeling, has depended on advances in three areas. The first was the introduction of HPLC analysis of Pth amino acids (*14*). The second was the introduction of a nonprotein carrier to retain the protein in the reaction chamber of the sequenator without the troublesome requirement of covalent attachment to a solid support. The "magic" compound that has revolutionized sequencing is Polybrene, a polymeric quaternary ammonium salt first used by Tarr *et al.* (*7*) to sequence small peptides in the spinning cup sequenator. The Polybrene readily forms a stable film on glass surfaces into which the polypeptide can be embedded and protected from mechanical dislodging by the moving solvent streams. The film is readily penetrated by the Edman reagents, however, and the degradation proceeds smoothly in its presence.

The third area of advancement was in the instrumentation used for performing the Edman degradation—the sequenator. With an HPLC system that can detect less than a picomole of Pth amino acid and with Polybrene to hold picomole quantities of protein in the sequen-

90

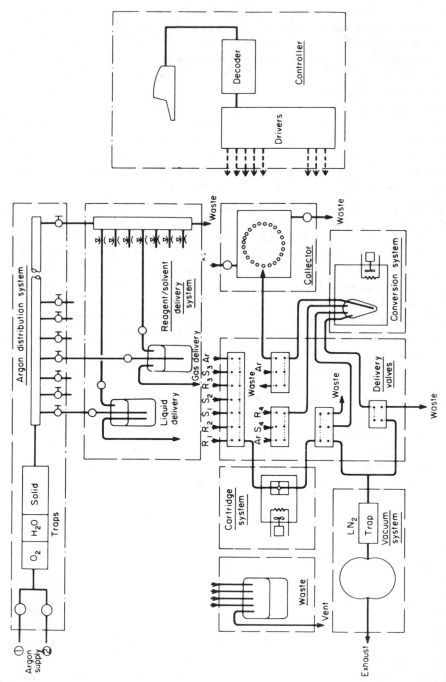

Fig. 2. Schematic diagram of gas phase sequenator. Reprinted by permission of R. M. Hewick, M. W. Hunkapiller, L. E. Hood, W. J. Dreyer, *Journal of Biological Chemistry*, 256, 7990 (1981).

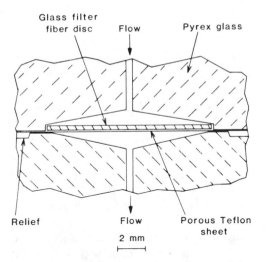

Fig. 3. Enlarged diagram of reaction cartridge for gas phase sequenator. Reprinted by permission of R. M. Hewick, M. W. Hunkapiller, L. E. Hood, W. J. Dreyer, *Journal of Biological Chemistry*, 256, 7990 (1981).

ator, sequencing at the picomole level is possible if the sequenator can produce phenylhydantoins free of significant amounts of ultraviolet-absorbing con-

taminants (primarily side reaction products of the phenylisothiocyanate) that would interfere with the HPLC analysis. Hunkapiller and Hood (*23, 24*), utilizing many design changes originated by Wittmann-Liebold (*25*), were able to sequence both proteins and peptides at the subnanomole level with a spinning cup sequenator. These improvements involved extensive changes in almost all mechanical components of the instrument, including the reagent and solvent delivery valves, spinning cup reaction chamber, vacuum system, inert gas supply, and reagent-solvent storage assemblies, as well as the addition of a secondary reaction vessel for automated Pth conversion (*4*), extensive purification of the reagents and solvents, and use of a versatile microprocessor controller.

Because of problems in purification of some of the reagents required in the spinning cup sequenator, particularly the quadrol (*5*) used as a coupling buffer, and because the large solvent extractions

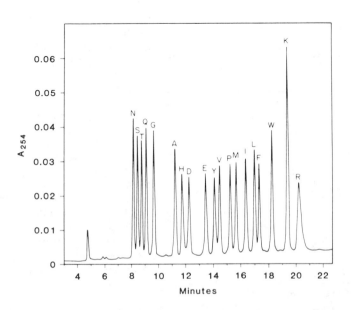

Fig. 4. Separation of Pth amino acids on a cyano column (IBM). The HPLC parameters are 32°C; flow rate, 1 milliliter per minute; column dimensions, 4.6 millimeters (inside diameter) by 25 centimeters in length; guard column, Du Pont Permaphase ETH, 4.6 millimeters (inside diameter) by 5 centimeters in length; aqueous phase 0.015M sodium acetate buffer, pH 5.8; hydrophobic phase (B), acetonitrile and methanol (4:1); gradient, 18 to 35 percent B in 1 minute, 35 to 55 percent B in 10.2 minutes, 55 to 60 percent B in 1.9 minutes, 60 to 18 percent B in 3.7 minutes. Sample: 10 microliters of methanol containing 0.5 nanomole of each of 19 Pth amino acids.

92

tended to dislodge some small samples from the spinning cup, sequencing below 100 pmole in the spinning cup is still very difficult to achieve on a routine basis. These problems have largely been overcome in the gas phase sequenator (*10*). The key to the performance of this sequenator in microsequencing is the combination of miniaturization and a flow path that permits use of less reagent than other sequenators and allows more efficient removal of the reagents and their by-products. The low levels of contaminants appearing in the HPLC analysis of fractions from this instrument are shown in Fig. 5.

The gas phase sequenator has been used to analyze a wide variety of proteins and peptides. These samples include glycoproteins, integral membrane proteins, proteins and peptides purified by one- or two-dimensional polyacrylamide gel electrophoresis (PAGE) and isoelectric focusing, short hydrophobic peptides, large proteins (> 90,000 daltons), and peptides containing numerous prolyl residues. A partial list of the samples analyzed on the Caltech gas phase sequenator is shown in Table 1 and illustrates its versatility. It can provide extended runs (> 70 residues) with a few nanomoles of protein, complete to nearly

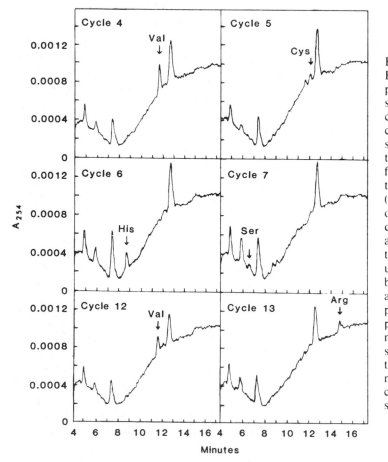

Fig. 5. Representative HPLC traces from gas phase sequenator analysis of 15 pmole of a tridecapeptide. The HPLC conditions were as described (Fig. 4). The traces are not corrected for background from either the HPLC system (the sloping rise and fall of the baseline) or the sequenator (peaks at 4.8 and 5.8 minutes from dithiothreitol, at 6.3 minutes from phenylthiocarbamyl dimethylamine, and 12.4 minutes from diphenylthiourea). The phenylthiocarbamyl dimethylamine came from slight contamination of the particular batch of trimethylamine used as the coupling buffer for this sequenator run.

Table 1. Sample of proteins sequenced on gas phase sequenator.

Protein	Molecular size (daltons)	Residues identified	Amount	
			pmole	μg
Angiotensin II	1,000	8	500	0.5
Angiotensin II	1,000	6	50	0.05
Somatostatin	1,600	14	1,200	2.0
Insulin, B chain	3,400	30	260	1.0
Aplysia neuropeptide B	3,800	31	500	2.0
Dynorphin (1–17)	2,000	14	20	0.04
Dynorphin (1–32)	4,000	32	200	0.6
Calliphora polypeptide	4,000	36	75	0.3
Myoglobin	17,500	90	10,000	175
Myoglobin	17,500	22	5	0.09
Drosophila larval cuticle protein*	18,000	55	850	15
Aplysia membrane phosphoprotein†‡	22,000	23	15	0.3
Human histocompatibility antigen, HLA-DR, α chain‡	32,000	49	700	23
Human histocompatibility antigen, HLA-DR, β chain‡	26,000	39	500	13
Mouse immune response antigen E_β^{k*}†‡	25,000	21	20	0.5
Human erythropoietin§	44,000	40	100	4
Human melanoma cell surface antigen†‡	95,000	13	60	5.5
Eel acetylcholine receptor α subunit†‡	40,000	68	400	16
Calf acetylcholine receptor α subunit†‡	42,000	35	50	2
MOPC-315 heavy chain	55,000	20	20	1
Colony stimulating factor†‡	30,000	25	30	1
Bovine lens gap junction protein, CNBr fragment†‡	14,000	34	120	2
Platelet-derived growth factor subunit†	18,000	20	50	1
Rat transforming growth factor	6,000	42	250	1.5
Transcription regulatory factor, CNBr fragment†	20,000	35	20	0.4
Rat transforming growth factor, lys-C fragment	2,300	20	25	0.06

*Purified by isoelectric focusing in polyacrylamide gels containing urea. Coomassie blue-stained, sodium dodecyl sulfate–polyacrylamide gels. §Sixty percent carbohydrate by weight.

†Electrophoretically eluted from ‡Integral membrane protein.

complete sequencing of small- or medium-sized peptides (< 40 residues) in a single run with a few hundred picomoles or less (Fig. 6), and 15 to 30 residues with as little as 5 to 20 pmole of proteins and many peptides (Fig. 5).

Sample Preparation

Crucial to any microsequencing method is the purification and handling of small quantities of polypeptide without contamination that would interfere with the Edman degradation. The failure of microsequencing efforts can, in fact, be traced most often to loss of sample at the final purification step (for example, by its adherence to the walls of test tubes) or by oxidation reactions that block the amino-terminal residues, or contamination by reagents (or impurities in them) used in the purification.

Two methods of preparation are suitable: (i) HPLC for peptides and small proteins and (ii) PAGE for long peptides and proteins. HPLC is the faster and simpler method, and it causes little damage to the samples. The development of volatile elution systems with the use of trifluoroacetic acid (26) makes handling peptides particularly easy. Using larger pore packings and better ion pairing agents such as $NaClO_4$ (27), one can extend the HPLC method to many large peptides and small proteins. Polyacrylamide gel electrophoresis requires more effort to prevent damage to or loss of the sample, but electroelution of proteins, even after staining with Coomassie blue, can be used to prepare as little as 1 to 2 micrograms of protein for sequence analysis (28). Since many sequencing experiments (for example, those with proteins

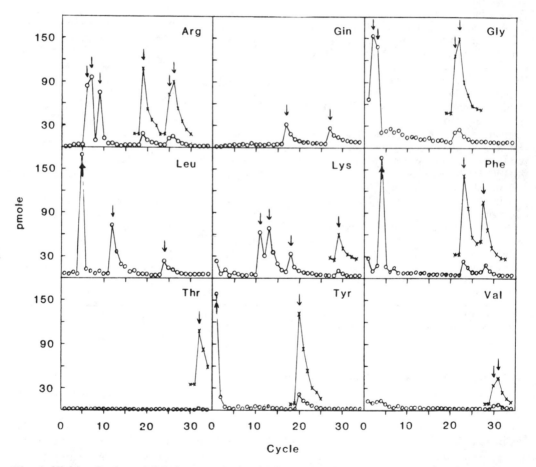

Fig. 6. Yields of selected Pth from analysis of 200 pmole of dynorphin (1–32) on the gas phase sequenator. Portions of the flask extract from each cycle were analyzed by HPLC, peaks were identified and quantified by comparison of peak positions and heights with values for a standard Pth amino acid mixture, and yields were normalized to 100 percent injection. The preparation of the sample and the sequenator analysis were reported by Fischli *et al.* (37). Abbreviations: Arg, arginine; Gln, glutamine; Gly, glycine; Leu, leucine; Lys, lysine; Phe, phenylalanine; Thr, threonine, Tyr, Tyrosine; Val, valine.

containing blocked amino-terminal residues) require generation and separation of peptides, the HPLC and gel techniques may be used several times on a given sample before the desired sequence is obtained. This can increase the amount of starting samples required for analysis by a factor of 10 to 20.

Applications

Complementary DNA cloning. With the advent of rapid DNA sequencing, the role of protein sequencing by Edman degradation has changed. In most cases, complete sequence analysis of large proteins can be obtained much more efficiently by DNA sequence analysis if the DNA encoding the protein can be cloned and identified. With genes that produce small quantities of mRNA (rare-message genes) it is often difficult to obtain complementary DNA (cDNA) probes for subsequent gene cloning by the standard techniques used for frequent-message genes such as antibodies and hemoglobins. An alternative approach is to determine the partial amino acid sequence of a small amount of the desired gene product and then to search through these protein sequence data for stretches of five to seven contiguous amino acids that have minimal ambiguity when translated by the genetic code dictionary into DNA language (*29*). With recent improvements in DNA synthesis (*30, 31*), one can generate mixtures of DNA probes consisting of 14 to 20 bases that cover all possibilities for a five– to seven–amino acid sequence obtained by microsequence analysis. These synthetic DNA probes can then be used as probes to screen cDNA libraries directly or as primers to generate specific probes. Even with a mixture of as many as 32

related oligonucleotides (15 bases in length), one can achieve specific hybridization of the correct oligonucleotide to the desired DNA sequence (*32*). Thus, protein sequencing can provide a powerful approach to the cloning of rare-message genes.

Synthetic polypeptides. An emerging tool of molecular biology is the use of synthetic peptides based on protein or DNA sequences to generate antibodies that recognize the parent protein (*33, 34*). The work of Bittle, Lerner, and their colleagues with peptides from foot and mouth disease virus (*35*) illustrates the power of the technique and points to the potential development of important vaccines. A second use of fundamental importance will be the identification of biologically active polypeptides that must be purified 10^4-fold or more. After sequence analysis, one must always ask whether the sequence is derived from the peptide with appropriate biological activity, or whether it represents a copurifying contaminant. After microsequencing, peptides can be synthesized and used as immunogens, and the resulting antibodies can be used to verify the biological activity of the protein and, if appropriate, to purify larger amounts of the protein.

Other applications. Although DNA sequencing can give the linear peptide sequence of the primary product of translation, it cannot answer questions of post-translation proteolytic processing or side chain modification (that is, removal of signal peptides, carbohydrate attachment, and phosphorylation). Subtle changes in protein structure, such as the attachment of methionine to the amino terminus of a protein produced by recombinant DNA technology, are often almost impossible to detect and quantify by any method other than protein sequence analysis. Direct protein sequencing also can answer questions of stoichiometry of multisubunit protein complexes that cannot be addressed by DNA sequencing. It may be the method of choice for such studies because of the minimum number of assumptions and manipulations required in data analysis (36). Protein sequencing also is becoming an important method for identifying protein or peptide fractions and, perhaps more important, assessing their purity.

The Future

In a variety of ways protein sequencing can provide useful information about the structures of functional proteins and peptides. With only an additional slight increase in the sensitivity of current microsequencing methods to the subpicomole level, one could employ one of the most powerful analytical separation procedures in modern biochemistry, two-dimensional gel electrophoresis, as a single-step preparative method for obtaining proteins available in very small quantities. Direct microsequencing at this subpicomole level would provide even more striking new opportunities to analyze new systems in developmental biology and neurobiology.

References and Notes

1. P. Edman, *Acta Chem. Scand.* **10**, 761 (1956).
2. Anonymous, *Nature (London)* **275**, 90 (1978).
3. G. Tarr, in *Methods in Protein Sequence Analysis*, M. Elzinga, Ed. (Humana Press, Clifton, N.J., 1982), p. 223.
4. J. Y. Chang, D. Brauer, B. Wittmann-Liebold, *FEBS Lett.* **93**, 205 (1978).
5. P. Edman and G. Begg, *Eur. J. Biochem.* **1**, 80 (1967).
6. B. Wittmann-Liebold, H. Graffunder, H. Kohls, *Anal. Biochem.* **75**, 621 (1976).
7. G. E. Tarr, J. F. Beecher, M. Bell, D. J. McKean, *ibid.* **84**, 622 (1978).
8. R. A. Laursen, *Eur. J. Biochem.* **20**, 89 (1971).
9. J. E. Walker *et al.*, *ibid.* **123**, 253 (1982).
10. R. M. Hewick, M. W. Hunkapiller, L. E. Hood, W. J. Dreyer, *J. Biol. Chem.* **256**, 7990 (1981).
11. J. J. Pisano, T. J. Bronzert, H. B. Brewer, Jr., *Anal. Biochem.* **45**, 43 (1972).
12. B. Wittmann-Liebold, A. W. Geissler, E. Marzinzig, *J. Supramol. Struct.* **3**, 426 (1975).
13. O. Smithies, D. M. Gibson, E. M. Fanning, R. M. Goodfliesch, J. G. Gilman, D. L. Ballantyne, *Biochemistry* **10**, 4912 (1971); E. Mendez and C. Y. Lai, *Anal. Biochem.* **68**, 47 (1975).
14. C. L. Zimmerman, E. Appella, J. J. Pisano, *ibid.* **77**, 569 (1977).
15. S. Oroszlan, T. Copeland, M. Summers, G. Smythers, in *Solid Phase Methods in Protein Sequence Analysis*, R. A. Laursen, Ed. (Pierce Chemical Company Press, Rockford, Ill., 1975), p. 179.
16. J. W. Jacobs and H. D. Niall, *J. Biol. Chem.* **250**, 3629 (1975).
17. J. Bridgen, *FEBS Lett.* **50**, 159 (1975).
18. J. Silver and L. Hood, *Contemp. Top. Mol. Immunol.* **5**, 35 (1976).
19. B. Ballou, D. J. McKean, E. F. Freedlender, O. Smithies, *Proc. Natl. Acad. Sci. U.S.A.* **73**, 4487 (1976).
20. Y. Burstein and I. Schecter, *ibid.* **74**, 716 (1977).
21. J. Silver and L. Hood, *ibid.* **73**, 599 (1976).
22. J. E. Coligan, T. J. Kindt, H. Uehara, J. Martinko, S. G. Nathenson, *Nature (London)* **291**, 35 (1981).
23. M. W. Hunkapiller and L. E. Hood, *Biochemistry* **17**, 2124 (1978).
24. _____, *Science* **207**, 523 (1980).
25. B. Wittmann-Liebold, *Hoppe-Seyler's Z. Physiol. Chem.* **354**, 1415 (1973).
26. W. C. Mahoney and M. A. Hermodson, *J. Biol. Chem.* **255**, 1199 (1980).
27. K. J. Wilson, M. W. Berchtold, P. Zumstein, S. Klauser, G. J. Hughes, in *Methods in Protein Sequence Analysis*, M. Elzinga, Ed. (Humana Press, Clifton, N.J., 1982), p. 401.
28. M. W. Hunkapiller, E. Lujan, F. Ostrander, L. E. Hood, *Methods Enzymol.* **91**, 227 (1983).
29. B. Noyes, M. Mevarech, R. Stein, K. Agarwal, *Proc. Natl. Acad. Sci. U.S.A.* **76**, 1770 (1979).
30. M. D. Mattucci and M. H. Caruthers, *J. Am. Chem. Soc.* **103**, 3185 (1981).
31. S. L. Beaucage and M. H. Caruthers, *Tetrahedron Lett.* **22**, 1859 (1981).
32. M. Steinmetz *et al.*, *Nature (London)* **300**, 35 (1982).
33. G. Walter, K.-H. Scheidtmann, A. Carbone, A. P. Laudano, R. F. Doolittle, *Proc. Natl. Acad. Sci. U.S.A.* **77**, 5197 (1980).
34. J. G. Sutcliffe, T. M. Shinnick, N. Green, F.-T. Liu, H. L. Niman, R. A. Lerner, *Nature (London)* **287**, 801 (1980).
35. J. L. Bittle, R. A. Houghten, H. Alexander, T. M. Shinnick, J. G. Sutcliffe, R. A. Lerner, D. J. Rowlands, F. Brown, *ibid.* **298**, 30 (1982).
36. M. A. Raftery, M. W. Hunkapiller, C. D. Strader, L. E. Hood, *Science* **208**, 1454 (1980).
37. W. Fischli, A. Goldstein, M. W. Hunkapiller, L. E. Hood, *Proc. Natl. Acad. Sci. U.S.A.* **79**, 5435 (1982).
38. This work was supported by the Weingart Foundation, National Science Foundation Grant PCM 80-05999, and National Institutes of Health Grant GM 06965.

8. Antibodies That React with Predetermined Sites on Proteins

J. Gregor Sutcliffe, Thomas M. Shinnick
Nicola Green, Richard A. Lerner

Progress in molecular biology and virology has always relied heavily on structural analyses of the components of biological systems. Because of advances in nucleic acid biochemistry during the last decade, culminating with the development of rapid DNA sequencing methods that allow the primary chemical sequences of genes to be read (*1*), we can now often approach a biological problem by identifying and sequencing the responsible genes rather than analyzing the relevant proteins. In fact, nucleotide sequence analysis of a new virus or gene is usually a most rewarding initial step, since it provides the information the virus or gene uses to accomplish its phenotype as well as a record of the evolutionary history of that nucleic acid. No fact is more important about a gene than its primary sequence; however, proteins are responsible for the execution of most biological processes.

Given the ease with which it was possible to generate primary sequence data for genes, what was needed was a way to link gene sequences to proteins, particularly when a protein was known only by the sequence of a gene. The obvious answer was to use an antibody, but the problem was how to make an antigen corresponding to a putative protein de-

duced from a string of nucleotides. One solution was to make a bacterium (or yeast) synthesize the novel protein and then raise antibodies to the bacterially synthesized protein. However, experience showed that although it was possible to make bacteria synthesize specific proteins if the genes for these proteins had been isolated, each new gene had to be handled individually and required many manipulations (*2*). If one were investigating a "gene" whose product was purely hypothetical, a laborious set of experiments might be necessary to achieve its bacterial expression.

An alternative to biological synthesis of antigens is chemical synthesis. However, most biologically interesting proteins whose sequences can be inferred from genes are in the 15,000 to 150,000 dalton range (15K to 150K), whereas chemical synthesis has practical limits in the 4K to 5K range except in exceptional circumstances. Furthermore, most studies of protein immunogenicity (including the work of Landsteiner, Crumpton, Benjamini *et al.*, Atassi and Suplin, Arnon and Sela and their colleagues, and Cebra and others) (*3*) indicated that small portions of a protein would, in general, be unlikely to elicit antiserums reactive against an intact protein [for a recent review, see (4)]. These studies predicted that immunogenic sites in small, intact proteins occurred about once every 5K to 10K and that these few loci relied on complex tertiary interactions between amino acid residues near each other in the protein tertiary structure, but distant in relation to the primary linear amino acid structure (so-called conformational determinants) (see Fig. 1). Therefore, it was generally believed that linear sequences in short peptides would not usually mimic these important sites. Recent experiments have challenged this prediction and have shown that small, chemically synthesized fragments of a protein can, in fact, elicit antibodies reactive with the native protein, thus allowing nucleic acid sequences to be parlayed quickly into biological experiments.

Antibodies to Synthetic Peptides
React with Native Proteins

The belief that most antigenic determinants are conformational was first challenged in experiments with chemically synthesized protein fragments from the amino or carboxyl terminals of viral proteins whose sequences had been determined from nucleic acid studies. Antibodies to synthetic peptides [prepared as described in (5, 6)] corresponding to the COOH-terminus of the envelope polyprotein of Moloney murine leukemia virus (MuLV) and the NH_2- and COOH-terminals of the simian virus 40 (SV40) transforming protein were found to be reactive with the native protein structures (7). That is, each reagent was able to precipitate the corresponding protein

from extracts of virus-infected cells. In addition, the fact that antibodies to peptides are specific for predetermined sequences within the intact protein permitted analysis of the precursor of the MuLV envelope polyprotein that undergoes two stages of proteolytic cleavage necessary to generate mature viral proteins (8).

The first reports that protein-reactive antibodies could be elicited by synthetic peptides corresponding to fragments of proteins whose sequences were known only from nucleic acid studies (7) gave a clear indication that a powerful technology was now available (9). The possibility remained, however, that the utility of the technique would be confined to the terminals of proteins where carrier-coupled peptides might mimic their position in the intact molecule. We needed to know whether the technique would be applicable to all proteins and if it would be necessary to predict the naturally antigenic regions of proteins in order to select suitable synthetic peptides (10). We used the recently derived sequences of the hepatitis B virus surface antigen (HB_sAg) and the hemagglutinin gene of influenza virus type A (HA1) (11) to examine the general utility and expand our understanding of this technology. The two sequences offered different experimental situations. The HB_sAg was known to be a molecule whose immunogenicity is critically dependent on its native tertiary structure (12); furthermore, it is extremely hydrophobic. The crystallographic structure of influenza A hemagglutinin had recently been solved (13) and its dominant antigenic sites were well known (14). In addition, since both molecules are the primary targets of neu-

A

B

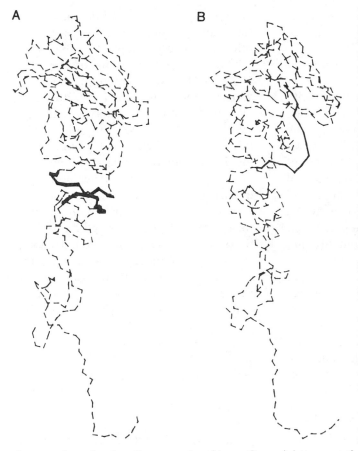

Fig. 1. Simplistic diagrams depicting (A) conformational and (B) sequential (or linear) determinants. The atomic coordinates of the influenza A/Hong Kong HA1 crystallographic structure (13) were rotated until prototypical regions recognized by eye were portrayed with Evans-Sutherland graphics by means of the GRAMPS and GRANNY programs of Donnell and Olson (59) and Connolly (60) to emphasize specific molecular features. The two panels show HA1 at different rotations around its vertical axis. The relevant regions are shown by the solid lines [in bold face in (A)]; the rest of the molecule is shown by dashed lines along the α-carbon backbone. (A) The molecule shows a conformational determinant—two regions of the HA1 polypeptide chain (residues 50 to 55 and 270 to 280) are far apart in the linear protein sequence but intimately related with each other through a disulfide linkage. The chains from the two regions track each other for several residues. One might expect that an antibody response to this region would probably involve contacts with both peptide chains. This appears to be the case during natural infection; this is HA1 site C of (14). However, antiserums to synthetic peptides representing either chain are capable of precipitating HA1 and, in fact, neutralizing the influenza virus. (B) The molecule shows a sequential determinant. The conformation of the peptide chain (residues 255 to 268) in the region shown by the solid line is mostly determined by the particular residues of the chain itself because no other close intramolecular contacts are apparent (nor are there any contacts with HA2 or other HA1 + 2 protomers in the trimeric form of the hemagglutinin). A synthetic peptide might well be expected to antigenically simulate a region such as this. These two extremes are simplifications that help to clarify abstract discussions of protein structure and immunogenicity. In reality, lengthy sequential regions of a protein usually have somewhat extensive contacts with other regions of the protein. However, linear peptides can often mimic the intact protein structure by eliciting a protein-reactive antiserum; therefore, some of the forces that mold global protein structure are already contained in relatively short peptide regions. Clearly, antibody molecules react with a number of spatially related atoms in the antigen molecule, and, in that sense, all determinants are conformational. Recent observations indicate that many peptides from within a protein molecule can act as antigenic determinants; thus many determinants are also sequential. The conformational-sequential nomenclature is probably no longer a useful one.

tralizing antibody during natural infection they are of practical interest in dealing with human disease (*14–16*).

One question we needed to answer concerned the peptide characteristics required to elicit antibodies reactive with the native molecule: Are there restrictions in the chemical makeup or location within the protein structure? The hydrophobic HB_sAg glycoprotein consists of 226 amino acid residues. We synthesized 13 peptides using the HB_sAg amino acid sequence deduced from the hepatitis B genome sequence as a blueprint (*17*). These peptides were distributed throughout the primary sequence, but avoided in those regions that showed significant variability in the different viral isolates. Four were subsets of longer peptides. From the data obtained with these peptides we were able to formulate an elementary set of rules for selecting peptides capable of eliciting antiserums reactive with native proteins. Peptides that were extremely hydrophobic and those of six or fewer residues were ineffective; longer, soluble peptides, especially those containing proline residues, were effective. Antiserums against four of the six HB_sAg peptides in the latter category precipitated the HB_sAg protein in the viral Dane particles. Precipitation also occurred under conditions approximating physiological (saline solutions), indicating that antibodies to these peptides might be expected to bind antigen in vivo. This study showed that linear peptides from more than one region of a protein and, more important, not restricted to its NH_2- or COOH-terminus could elicit protein-reactive antibodies.

We also needed to know the relation between the sites represented by effective peptides and the antigenic determinants selected by the host in the course of a natural immune response against a virus or a protein. For influenza virus, those sites immunogenic during natural infection had been mapped by analysis of variants to four domains of the HA1 chain of the hemagglutinin molecule, whose three-dimensional structure was known from x-ray crystallographic studies (*13–15*). We studied 20 synthetic peptides, many of them overlapping, covering 75 percent of the HA1 primary sequence derived from the nucleotide sequence of a fragment of the influenza genome (*6*). In accordance with the rules formulated in the HB_sAg study (*17*), these peptides ranged in length from 8 to 39 residues, contained enough polar amino acids to render them soluble and, hence, easy to work with, and usually contained one or more proline residues. Some of the peptides fell within the known antigenic domains of HA1; others were clearly outside these domains. The peptides correspond to regions of the protein which in the crystal structure appeared as α-helices, β-sheets, and random coils. Antibodies to 18 of the 20 peptides reacted with HA1 (isolated by bromelain cleavage) or intact virus, demonstrating that sites in proteins accessible to peptide antibodies are more numerous than the few sites recognized in the course of a natural immune response. Furthermore, the information carried within a relatively short linear peptide is sufficient to elicit reactivity against a much larger protein molecule with a complex tertiary and quarternary structure. In more recent studies with peptides selected by the same rules outlined above, 12 of 12 peptides predicted from the MuLV polymerase gene (*18*) and 18 of 18 peptides from the rabies glycoprotein gene (*19*) elicited antibodies that precipitated their putative corresponding proteins. Therefore, it appears that, by following simple rules, one can in general select peptides that will elicit antibodies reactive with intact proteins.

In retrospect, it is easy to understand why, in terms of their chemistry, synthetic peptides have been so successful as immunogens in these and several other recent studies and why it was previously believed that they would be ineffective and were therefore not vigorously studied. All of the effective peptides from the influenza HA1 study (6) could be shown, when matched to the crystallographic structure of the protein, to represent regions exposed to the solvent. This may be due, in part, to the fact that they contain polar residues. Polar residues may also provide components of antigenic determinants capable of forming strong electrostatic interactions with antibody. In addition, proline residues may be important because they occur at bends in the peptide chain, often at "corners" exposed to the solution. Because proline residues have an imide rather than an amide bond, several atoms surrounding a proline residue have a fixed three-dimensional relation to one another, whether in a short peptide or in a complete protein structure, and, as such, will be recognized equally by antibody in either situation. Furthermore, residues on the two sides of a proline tend to be near each other because the peptide chain more or less turns back on itself at cis proline kinks. This produces a two-chain structure which might be thought of as a minor "conformational" determinant, albeit formed by residues not too far from one another in the linear chemical formula of the protein. Although these explanations for the effectiveness of peptides with certain chemical properties are somewhat speculative, it is now clear that, in solution, peptides and proteins are often similar. Peptides in solution probably attain conformations dictated by their chemical makeup which resemble those that occur in native protein structures. Furthermore, proteins are probably not static structures, always closely resembling their crystalline form; in fact, they may exhibit their various linear domains in many conformations. In support of these notions, Niman and Lerner (20) have shown that 50 percent of the monoclonal antibodies selected for reactivity with one of the peptides in the influenza HA1 study also react with HA1 protein.

In contrast, antiserums raised against native HA1 do not react with any of the 20 HA1 peptides (6). Since these peptides span 75 percent of the HA1 primary sequence, including all of the known, mapped determinants, it is clear that most, if not all, of the immune response against native HA1 is directed against determinants not mimicked by short linear peptides. This observation is consistent with the body of data showing that antigenic determinants on intact proteins are largely conformational (3). Earlier investigators reasoned that because the determinants were conformational, only rarely would a linear peptide be an effective antigen; therefore synthetic peptides would not have general utility. The influenza HA1 study shows that pieces of a protein can elicit antibodies reactive with the whole protein which the whole protein itself cannot elicit (6). Moreover, the studies on HB$_s$Ag, influenza HA1, MuLV polymerase, and rabies glycoprotein demonstrate that these peptides are not difficult to select (6, 17–19). On the basis of the rules formulated in the HB$_s$Ag study, one can select one or two peptides from a protein sequence with relatively high confidence of being able to elicit a protein-reactive antiserum, an important economic consideration both in time and research dollars.

Protein-Reactive Peptide Antibodies as Reagents for Molecular Studies

Synthetic peptides that elicit reagents capable of reacting with proteins of known primary sequence can be used to establish identity between a protein sequence and the protein itself. Many sequences are of a hypothetical nature, having been deduced from a gene sequence, and an experiment with a synthetic peptide may be more powerful for demonstrating colinearity between a protein and nucleic acid than a series of successful genetic experiments. Antiserums to peptides have been used to detect the putative products of the MuLV polymerase (*18*) and envelope (*7*) genes as well as the transforming genes of the Moloney sarcoma (*21*), simian sarcoma (*22*), feline sarcoma (*23*), avian myeloblastosis (*24*), SV40 (*7*), and polyoma (*25*) viruses. Such antiserums have also been used in similar studies of six human adenovirus 2 (*26*) transforming genes, the mouse mammary tumor virus long terminal repeat (LTR) (*27*), and several messenger RNA's from rat brain (*28*). Peptides from the NH$_2$- and COOH-terminals as well as from the middle of the adenovirus transforming proteins elicit protein-reactive serums. Antibodies to peptides have been used to track the processing of polyprotein precursors in cells infected with poliovirus (*29*), influenza (Fig. 2), and MuLV (*8, 18*). Because of the predetermined specificity of the antiserums elicited by synthetic peptides, the proteins reacting with them are known to carry the specific peptide sequence. These reagents are particularly powerful when used as sets for tracking simultaneously the fate of various regions of a protein precursor (as shown for influenza HA in Fig. 2 and discussed below for the leukemia virus *pol* prod-

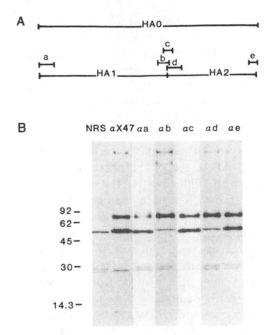

Fig. 2. Illustration of the power of sets of peptide antiserums used to track distinct regions of a protein simultaneously. (A) The influenza hemagglutinin precursor (HA0) and eventual products (HA1 and HA2). The synthetic peptides a to e, located within the HA0 sequence as shown (NH$_2$- and COOH-terminal, flanking and spanning the HA1-HA2 junction), were coupled to a carrier and used to immunize rabbits as described (*5–7*). (B) The resulting antiserums (αa, αb, αc, αd, αe) and a positive control serum (antibody to X47 influenza virus, αX47) and a negative control serum (normal rabbit serum, *NRS*) were used to precipitate extracts of [^{35}S]methionine-labeled influenza X47 virus-infected cells. The five antiserums to the peptides and αX47 precipitated the HA0 molecule (this precursor is not appreciably cleaved during infection of cell lines), whereas the other precipitated proteins were nonspecific (sticky) since they also appeared in the normal control lane.

uct). They are also useful in identifying alternative exon usage [as has been shown with immunoglobulin class D genes (*30*) and the adenovirus 2 E1A transcription unit (*31*)]. With the adenovirus 2 E1B transcription unit synthetic peptides have been used to show that the 53K and 19K protein products are translated in different triplet reading frames (26).

When the existence of a protein has been demonstrated, one wants to know its cellular location. Antiserums to a peptide from the COOH-terminus of the vesicular stomatitis virus (VSV) G protein do not react with intact infected cells, although polyclonal antiserums to the G protein do. When the cells are opened by treatment with detergent, a strong reaction at the inner surface of the membrane is detected with the antiserum to the COOH-terminal peptide (32). These experiments indicate that the VSV G protein spans the plasma membrane with its COOH-terminus protruding into the cytoplasm. In immunofluorescence studies of fixed, transformed fibroblast cells, antiserums to a COOH-terminal peptide from the Rous sarcoma virus (RSV) transforming protein were used (33). Fluorescence was codistributed with vinculin at cell-cell contact sites. Antiserum to an interior RSV src peptide [which cross-reacts with the endogenous cellular src as well as the transforming proteins of Fuginami (fps) and Y73 (yes) viruses] reacted with the focal adhesion plaques of RSV-transformed rat cells (34). Therefore, these reagents, derived by using the sequence of a protein (or gene), are capable of indicating in detail the cellular location of a protein.

Another use for peptide antiserums is the correlation of structure with function. If an antiserum to a peptide perturbs an assayable protein function, a protein containing the peptide sequence is implicated. Antiserum to a peptide present in the middle T sequence of polyoma virus inhibits protein kinase function in vitro (35), and an antiserum

to a peptide present in the feline sarcoma virus fes gene sequence also inhibits protein kinase activity (23). Therefore, each of these proteins must have protein kinase activity: the predetermined specificity of the reagent allows one to rule out the often cited caveats about proteins and enzymatic activities that happen to coincide. Antiserums against several peptides in the NH_2-terminal half of the putative MuLV pol polyprotein inhibit reverse transcriptase activity, whereas some peptides in the COOH-terminal portion inhibit a virion-associated endonuclease activity (18). The two sets of inhibiting antiserums immunoprecipitate two different proteins in infected cells, as well as their common precursor. Therefore, not only do the peptide antiserums establish the colinearity between the pol protein precursor and its nucleic acid sequence, but they identify the products of protein maturation and assign them an enzymatic activity. Antiserum to a COOH-terminal peptide predicted from the poliovirus replicase gene sequence precipitates the core protein p63 and its precursors and inhibits replicase and polyuridylic acid polymerase activities in vitro, indicating that these two activities reside in p63 (36). One can thus imagine a range of experiments in which peptide antiserums will be used to modify specific behaviors of proteins because they bind to a specific predetermined region of that protein.

When neither function nor structure is known, antiserums to peptides can provide a means for purifying the bona fide protein. Walter and his colleagues (37) have coupled to Sepharose the purified immunoglobulin fraction of a peptide antiserum and used this to purify the middle T antigen of polyoma virus. The protein was eluted from the immuno-affinity column by competition with excess peptide. A two-cycle purification scheme in which one uses the immunoglobulin fractions of antiserums against two different peptides from a protein sequence might lead to a quite pure protein preparation (37). Immunoprecipitation and gel electrophoresis have been used to isolate a precursor of the MuLV envelope membrane anchor to a purity such that its NH_2-terminal sequence could be determined by radiochemical sequencing methods (8). It might eventually be possible to use the complement fixation properties of antigen-antibody complexes as an assay for protein purification after various chromatographic steps (38).

Although most work with synthetic peptides has been done with antiserums raised in laboratory animals, some investigators have used clonal populations of peptide-specific lymphocytes for their experiments. The studies of Niman and Lerner (20) on influenza HA1, and those of Gentry et al. (34) on the RSV transforming protein, have shown that a high proportion of hybridomas obtained by fusion of spleen cells from peptide-immunized donors secrete antibody reactive with the native protein. Such doubly specific reagents can be prepared in large quantities and are particularly useful for studies of fixed cells or tissues or for large-scale diagnostic work. Monoclonal populations of B-cell precursors, which can bind peptide but are not yet capable of antibody secretion, have been used to probe the immunological repertoire to determine whether antigen tolerance to host proteins is inherited or acquired (39). In the influenza system, Lamb and his co-workers (40) found that hemagglutin-specific T-cell populations from human donors responded to 12 of 12 HA1 peptides analyzed. One peptide, corresponding to the COOH-terminal 24 amino acids, appeared to be immunodominant in the sense that three of four T-cell clones were specific for determinants within this sequence.

On the technical side, antibody titer is a relevant concern. Some peptides seem highly immunogenic, sometimes even without being coupled to carrier protein, eliciting antiserums of high titer after a 35-day immunization procedure in which three doses, each of 200 micrograms of peptide, are administered (5, 6). Other peptides seem to require several months and several booster injections to achieve a reasonable titer. A second immunization procedure in which the peptide is coupled to a carrier protein different from that used in the initial series of inoculations seems to be very effective for eliciting a peptide-specific rather than a carrier-specific response (28). For many, but not all, peptides we have examined, glutaraldehyde coupling seems to be more effective than coupling through cysteine residues. However, glutaraldehyde modifies lysine NH_2 groups and hence can significantly interfere with key amino acids in some peptides. To increase the activity of antiserums, and to reduce background activities, purified immunoglobulin can be specifically enriched by adsorption to the antigenic peptide coupled to a solid support (25). The immunoglobulin is then released by a chaotropic agent or removed from the column by competition with excess peptide, then dialyzed in the presence of a chaotropic agent.

Synthetic Peptides as Ideal Vaccines

For our studies we have used the immunological targets of infectious pathogens with the goal of eventually applying our findings to the protection of humans and other animals from disease by vaccination with synthetic peptides. Indeed, previous workers have shown that peptides of natural or synthetic origin can elicit antiserums capable of neutralizing or binding to virus or bacteriophage in vitro [for a review, see (41)]. The coat proteins of tobacco mosaic virus (TMV) (42) and more recently bacteriophage MS2 (43) were fragmented with proteases, and fragments that reacted with neutralizing serums to whole virus were identified and isolated biochemically or chemically synthesized. Antiserum to the natural COOH-terminal six residues of TMV had the ability to bind to the virus in vitro and abrogate its infectivity. Antiserums to a synthetic MS2 peptide reduced this bacteriophage's infectivity when a secondary antibody to the antibody or "sandwich" reaction was used (no primary neutralization was demonstrated). Similarly, Audibert *et al.* (44) demonstrated that antiserums against a synthetic peptide from the diphtheria toxin was capable of inhibiting toxin activity in vitro. Our studies on HB_sAg (17) and influenza HA1 (6) showed that it is possible to select, on the basis of simple chemical properties of regions within viral proteins, peptide immunogens that induce virus-specific antibody. However, these studies did not establish the relation between the capacity to bind virus and the capacity to neutralize infection. What was needed was a demonstration of active protection from a virulent disease in an immunized animal.

In terms of neutralization, there seem to be two classes of virus—those that can be neutralized by antiserum to related viruses and those that are quite subtype-specific in their cross-reactivity. Protective peptides from the first class might cluster in regions whose sequences are conserved across related viruses, whereas protective peptides from the second class may reside in the variable regions. Although it is not necessarily the case that the serum of peptide-protected animals will mimic that of animals protected by classical vaccines, we have proceeded with the thought that reproducing the known serology may be important. The most extensive studies to date have been with four viruses: foot-and-mouth, influenza A, hepatitis B, and rabies.

Seven peptides were chosen (45) from the translated nucleic acid sequence of the type O foot-and-mouth disease virus (FMDV) VP1 protein (46). The VP1 was thought to be a target for neutralizing antibodies, because treatment of this picornavirus with trypsin cleaves only VP1 and this is sufficient to cause the virus particle to lose its immunizing activity (47). Rabbits inoculated with each of the seven peptides made strong antipeptide responses, but antiserums to only three of the peptides were capable of neutralizing FMDV in vitro (45). The neutralization was specific to type O virus, as expected from serological considerations. In addition, guinea pigs immunized with a single dose of either of two of the effective peptides (in complete Freund's adjuvant or alum) and challenged with live virus were protected. Thus, a synthetic peptide can elicit a protective immune response. Indeed, one of the peptides that was 20 residues long was as good at protecting the animals from later challenge with 10^4 infectious doses (ID_{50}) of FMDV as inactivated virus particles, the classical vaccine (45). Antiserums raised in rabbits or cattle against peptides from the equivalent region of other FMDV strains neutralize their appropriate strain of virus. These results are particularly encouraging because VP1 itself, whether purified from virus or made by genetically engineered bacteria, is a poor immunogen which thus far has not lent itself to the production of a subunit vaccine.

The antipeptide serums to influenza HA1 peptides (6) have been assayed for virus neutralization. Antibodies to 6 of the 20 peptides described in our original structural study neutralized the cytopathic effect of influenza virus on MDCK (canine kidney) cells (48). Subsequently, six more peptides were synthesized filling in the regions missed in the original study, including the HA1-HA2 junction and the other chain of the site C of Wiley et al. (14). Antiserums to five of these six peptides neutralize the cytopathic effect in vitro (48). In addition, immunizations with several combinations of peptides from the HA1 sequence protect mice from death caused by mouse-adapted influenza virus. However, only two of the five peptides thus far injected individually confer active immunity. Müller et al. (49) report neutralization of the cytopathic effect with antiserum to one influenza peptide and inhibition of virus growth in vivo by immunization with that peptide. Although it is too soon to make generalizations about structure, some statements about broad-range neutralization as measured in vitro by Alexander et al. (48) are possible. Sequences in the site C region (defined by a disulfide bond between residues 52 and 277 in the native HA1) (14), the COOH-terminal region of HA1 and the HA1-HA2 junction are relatively conserved in the several type A influenza hemagglutinins that have been sequenced. Antiserums to peptides from each of these regions neutralize not only viruses of the H_3 subtype (from which the sequence was derived) but also H_1 and B viruses (H_2 has not been tested).

Normally, antiserums against one subtype of influenza virus do not protect against other subtypes. Thus with peptides it may be possible to construct a vaccine with a broad range of specificity not attainable with the intact protein.

The only relevant model for human hepatitis B is the chimpanzee, so direct studies of protection have not been done; however, extensive serological studies have been conducted in vitro. Prince et al. (50) demonstrated that a synthetic peptide corresponding to HB_sAg residues 138 to 149 inhibited the binding of hybridomas against the a and d but not the y subdeterminants of HB_sAg. In apparently conflicting studies carried out in the chimpanzee, Gerin et al. (51) report that a peptide spanning the region 110 to 137 contains the a and y but not the d specificity (d and y are thought to be allelic). This result is consistent with the results of protein chemistry studies of Peterson et al. (52), which show the y/d variation to occur at residues 131 and 134. This is supported by our studies showing that a synthetic peptide corresponding to residues 110 to 137 of the d version elicits d-specific antiserum. Bhatnagar et al. (53) have recently reported that a synthetic peptide covering the region 139 to 147 carries the a but not the y/d determinant. The reason for the discrepancy between the results of Prince et al. (50) and all of the others is not known, but whichever studies are correct, peptides seem to be able to duplicate serologically important antigenic determinants and elicit immune responses in primates corresponding to those seen during infection. No data on neutralization of the virus or active protection against infection are yet available.

In collaboration with colleagues at the Wistar Institute (19), we have investigated the efficacy of synthetic peptides in protecting animals from rabies virus infection. The purified rabies viral glycoprotein is capable of conferring protection from rabies virus, and all neutralizing serums and hybridomas precipitate this protein (54). Eighteen peptides, representing 56 percent of the primary rabies glycoprotein sequence as deduced from the nucleic acid sequence of its gene (55), were originally synthesized and antibodies were raised against these in rabbits and mice (19). All 18 peptides elicited antiserums that bound both rabies glycoprotein and virus as measured in ELISA assays. However, none was capable of neutralizing the virus in vitro or of protecting mice or dogs from challenge from live virus. More recently, it has been shown that the three cyanogen bromide fragments of the glycoprotein capable of eliciting protection were not well covered by the peptide selection (56), hence experiments directed at synthesizing these particular regions are under way. So, while it was easy to pick 18 out of 18 peptides that would elicit binding antibodies, none of these seems capable of protecting against the virus.

Clearly, the studies of FMDV and influenza virus show that one can protect an animal from infection with live virus by injecting synthetic peptides corresponding to parts of the proteins that are the normal targets of neutralizing antibodies. However, the studies with rabies and influenza virus demonstrate that binding antibodies, while easy to elicit, are not necessarily neutralizing antibodies. From the medical-veterinary point of view, one must either resort to synthesizing a series of overlapping peptides covering a complete protein sequence (now a technically feasible, if not particularly elegant, approach) or perform supporting biological experiments to determine which regions of a protein contain its neutralization sites. Although sites capable of interacting with antibody are probably located on the entire surface of the viral protein with frequent representation in its primary linear amino acid sequence, and although such sites can probably be easily mimicked by synthetic peptides, sites susceptible to neutralization seem much less frequent and have not yet been characterized by a set of simple chemical properties. Nonetheless, once the neutralization sites are identified, synthetic peptides seem to be suitable substitutes for whole proteins or viruses (and presumably other infectious agents). For some sites, they may be more effective immunogens than whole protein because they can elicit specificities that whole proteins cannot.

If one projects this technology from prophylaxis to immunological therapy, synthetic peptides from proteins unique to tumor cells may be suitable immunogens for treating neoplasia. The peptides may be from proteins unique to the clonal population of transformed cells or, in tumors of tissues that are dispensable (such as prostate or thyroid), the peptides may be merely tissue-specific cell surface markers.

Conclusions

The desirability of synthetic vaccines of known potency and side effects has been recognized for many years. Some of the drawbacks of currently available inactivated virus vaccines are that they are not stable without refrigeration and sometimes contain incompletely inactivated viruses capable of starting minor epidemics (57). Vaccination with a substance free of any biological contamination introduced in its production (either by virus grown in cell culture or in genetically engineered proteins expressed by *Escherichia coli* protein synthesis factories) and unable to cause any virus-related pathology because of incomplete virus inactivation or imperfect attenuation is the logical goal of protection from infectious disease.

Certainly this technology has not been developed to the level of sophistication that is required for the widespread use of synthetic vaccines in humans and other animals. The adjuvants and carriers used in the studies described in this chapter are in general much too harsh for human use, although alum (used in the FMDV study) is suitable. The work of Chedid, Audibert, and Langbeheim and their colleagues (58) may indicate a possible direction for more suitable and ultimately totally defined vaccines. Suitable doses, the possibility of using modified peptides or combinations or polymers of peptides, and the various routes of injection need to be worked out. But a major theoretical obstacle has been overcome in that solving and then synthesizing complex conformational determinants no longer seems necessary.

Now that it has been shown that protection by synthetic peptides is possible, that such peptides can be at least as effective as biological vaccines, that new protein sequences are rapidly being generated as a result of nucleic acid studies, and that the synthetic approach is economically quite feasible (whether it requires the synthesis, by brute force, of all fragments of a protein or directed biochemical-immunological experiments), research to find the best peptides, the best adjuvants, and the best carriers is likely to become an important priority. As the research progresses, and as synthetic vaccines become commonplace, the somewhat tedious processes used today will become streamlined and consequently much more economical.

References and Notes

1. F. Sanger, *Science* 214, 1205 (1981); W. Gilbert, *ibid.*, p. 1305.
2. E. Yelverton, D. Leung, P. Weck, P. W. Gray, D. V. Goeddel, *Nucleic Acids Res.* 9, 731 (1981); D. G. Kleid, D. Yansura, B. Small, D. Dowbenko, D. M. Moore, M. J. Grubman, P. D. McKercher, D. O. Morgan, B. H. Robertson, H. L. Bachrach, *Science* 214, 1125 (1981); P. Charnay, M. Gervais, A. Louis, F. Galibert, P. Tiollais, *Nature (London)* 286, 893 (1980).
3. K. Landsteiner, *J. Exp. Med.* 75, 269 (1942); M. J. Crumpton, in *The Antigens*, M. Sela, Ed. (Academic Press, New York, 1974), p. 1; E. Benjamini, J. D. Young, M. Shimizu, C. Y. Leung, *Biochemistry* 3, 1115 (1964); M. Z. Atassi and B. J. Suplin, *ibid.* 7, 688 (1968); R. Arnon, E. Maron, M. Sela, C. B. Anfinson, *Proc. Natl. Acad. Sci. U.S.A.* 68, 1450 (1971); J. J. Cebra, *J. Immunol.* 86, 205 (1961).
4. R. A. Lerner, *Nature (London)* 299, 592 (1982).
5. In practice, peptides are synthesized according to the high repetitive yield methods developed by Merrifield and his colleagues [A. Marglin and R. B. Merrifield, *Annu. Rev. Biochem.* 39, 841 (1970)] by generally available automatic synthesizers or by hand. They are usually used without further purification, as possible contaminants are either peptides with trivial sequence variations of that designed or they are multimeric forms. The peptides are coupled to a carrier protein (keyhole limpet hemocyanin, edestin, thyroglobulin, and bovine serum albumin have been used) and injected into animals (usually in complete Freund's adjuvant). Some peptides are immunogenic without being coupled to a carrier. Serum from immunized animals is assayed for its ability to bind peptide antigen, either in solution or in a solid phase [enzyme-linked immunosorbent (ELISA)] assay. Positive serums are then tested against native proteins [see (6)].
6. N. Green, H. Alexander, A. Olson, S. Alexander, T. M. Shinnick, J. G. Sutcliffe, R. A. Lerner, *Cell* 28, 477 (1982).
7. J. G. Sutcliffe, T. M. Shinnick, N. Green, F.-T. Liu, H. L. Niman, R. A. Lerner, *Nature (London)* 287, 801 (1980); G. Walter, K. H. Scheidtmann, A. Carbone, A. P. Laudano, R. F. Doolittle, *Proc. Natl. Acad. Sci. U.S.A.* 77, 5197 (1980).
8. N. Green, T. M. Shinnick, O. Witte, A. Ponticelli, J. G. Sutcliffe, R. A. Lerner, *Proc. Natl. Acad. Sci. U.S.A.* 78, 6023 (1981).
9. R. A. Lerner, J. G. Sutcliffe, T. M. Shinnick, *Cell* 23, 309 (1981).
10. There is nothing intrinsically different between protein sequences derived by translating nucleic acid sequences according to the rules of the genetic code and those empirically determined (except that an empirically determined protein sequence has basis in experiment), but most new protein sequences are determined by nucleic acid sequencing.
11. M. Pasek, T. Goto, W. Gilbert, B. Zink, H. Schaller, P. McKay, G. Leadbetter, K. Murray, *Nature (London)* 282, 575 (1979); W. Minjou, M. Verhoeyen, R. Devos, E. Saman, R. Fang, D. Huylebroeck, W. Fiers, G. Threlfall, C. Barber,

N. Carey, S. Emtage, *Cell* **19**, 683 (1980).

12. G. N. Vyas, K. R. Rao, A. B. Ibrahim, *Science* **178**, 1300 (1972).
13. I. A. Wilson, J. J. Skehel, D. C. Wiley, *Nature (London)* **289**, 366 (1981).
14. D. C. Wiley, I. A. Wilson, J. J. Skehel, *ibid.*, p. 373.
15. W. G. Laver, G. M. Air, T. A. Dopheide, C. W. Ward, *ibid.* **283**, 459 (1980); R. G. Webster and W. G. Laver, *Virology* **104**, 139 (1980).
16. D. L. Peterson, I. M. Roberts, G. N. Vyas, *Proc. Natl. Acad. Sci. U.S.A.* **74**, 1530 (1977).
17. R. A. Lerner, N. Green, H. Alexander, F.-T. Liu, J. G. Sutcliffe, T. M. Shinnick, *ibid.* **78**, 3403 (1981).
18. T. M. Shinnick and J. G. Sutcliffe, unpublished observations.
19. J. G. Sutcliffe, M. Kiel, T. J. Wictor, D. Lopes, H. Koprowski, unpublished observations.
20. H. L. Niman and R. A. Lerner, unpublished observations.
21. J. Papkoff, I. M. Verma, T. Hunter, *Cell* **29**, 417 (1982).
22. K. C. Robbins, S. G. Devare, E. P. Reddy, S. A. Aaronson, *Science* **218**, 1131 (1982).
23. S. Sen, R. Houghten, C. Scherr, A. Sen, personal communication.
24. J. Lukacs and M. Baluda, personal communication.
25. G. Walter, M. A. Hutchinson, T. Hunter, W. Eckhart, *Proc. Natl. Acad. Sci. U.S.A.* **78**, 4882 (1981).
26. M. Green, K. Brackmann, J. Symington, personal communication; P. E. Branton, S. P. Yee, D. T. Rowe, personal communication.
27. N. Fasel, D. Owen, E. Buetti, H. Diggelmann, personal communication.
28. J. G. Sutcliffe, R. J. Milner, T. M. Shinnick, R. A. Houghten, F. E. Bloom, unpublished observation.
29. M. H. Baron and D. Baltimore, *Cell* **28**, 395 (1982); B. L. Semler, C. W. Anderson, R. Hanecak, L. F. Dorner, E. Wimmer, *ibid.*, p. 405.
30. T. M. Shinnick and F. Blattner, unpublished observation.
31. L. Feldman and J. Nevins, personal communication.
32. M. C. Willingham, R. Schlegel, I. Pastan, personal communication.
33. E. A. Nigg, B. M. Sefton, T. Hunter, G. Walter, S. J. Singer, *Proc. Natl. Acad. Sci. U.S.A.* **79**, 5322 (1982).
34. L. E. Gentry, L. R. Rohrschneider, J. E. Casnelli, R. Beer, E. G. Krebs, personal communication.
35. B. Schaffhausen, T. L. Benjamin, L. Pike, J. Casnellie, E. Krebs, *J. Biol. Chem.*, in press.
36. M. H. Baron and D. Baltimore, *J. Virol.* **43**, 969 (1982).
37. G. Walter, M. A. Hutchinson, T. Hunter, W. Eckhart, *Proc. Natl. Acad. Sci. U.S.A.* **79**, 4025 (1982).
38. R. Tijan, *Cold Spring Harbor Symp. Quant. Biol.* **43**, 655 (1979).
39. R. Jemmerson, P. Morrow, N. Klinman, *Fed. Proc. Fed. Am. Soc. Exp. Biol.* **41**, 420 (1982).
40. J. R. Lamb, D. D. Eckols, P. Lake, J. N. Woody, N. Green, *Nature (London)* **300**, 66 (1982).
41. R. Arnon, *Annu. Rev. Microbiol.* **34**, 593 (1980).
42. R. A. Anderer, *Biochim. Biophys. Acta* **71**, 246 (1963).
43. H. Langbeheim, R. Arnon, M. Sela, *Proc. Natl. Acad. Sci. U.S.A.* **73**, 4336 (1976).
44. R. Audibert, M. Jolivet, L. Chedid, J. E. Alout, P. Boguet, P. Rivielle, O. Siffert, *Nature (London)* **289**, 593 (1981).
45. J. L. Bittle, R. A. Houghten, H. Alexander, T. M. Shinnick, J. G. Sutcliffe, R. A. Lerner, D. J. Rowlands, F. Brown, *Nature (London)* **298**, 30 (1982).
46. C. Kurz, S. Forss, H. Kupper, K. Strohmaier, H. Schaller, *Nucleic Acids Res.* **9**, 1919 (1981).
47. K. Strohmaier, R. Franze, K.-H. Adam, *J. Gen. Virol.* **59**, 295 (1982).
48. S. Alexander, H. Alexander, N. Green, R. A. Lerner, personal communication.
49. G. Müller, M. Shapira, R. Arnon, *Proc. Natl. Acad. Sci. U.S.A.* **79**, 569 (1982).
50. A. M. Prince, H. Ikram, T. P. Hopp, *ibid.*, p. 579.
51. J. L. Gerin *et al.*, *ibid.*, in press.
52. D. L. Peterson, N. Natu, F. Gavilanes, *J. Biol. Chem.* **257**, 10414 (1982).
53. P. K. Bhatnagar, E. Papas, H. E. Blum, D. R. Milich, D. Nitecki, M. J. Kareis, G. N. Vyas, *Proc. Natl. Acad. Sci. U.S.A.* **79**, 4400 (1982).
54. J. H. Cox, B. Deitzschold, L. G. Schneider, *Infect. Immun.* **16**, 743 (1977).
55. A. Anilionis, W. H. Wunner, P. J. Curtis, *Nature (London)* **294**, 275 (1981).
56. B. Dietzschold, T. J. Wictor, R. MacFarlan, A. Varrichio, *J. Virol.*, in press.
57. J. Beale, *Nature (London)* **298**, 14 (1982); A. M. Q. King, B. O. Underwood, D. McCahon, J. W. I. Newman, F. Brown, *ibid.* **293**, 479 (1981).
58. L. Chedid, F. Audibert, A. Johnson, *Prog. Allergy* **25**, 63 (1978); H. Langbeheim, R. Arnon, M. Sela, *Immunology* **35**, 573 (1978); F. Audibert, M. Jolivet, L. Chedid, R. Arnon, M. Sela, *Proc. Natl. Acad. Sci. U.S.A.* **79**, 5042 (1982).
59. T. J. O'Donnell and A. J. Olson, *Computer Graphics* **15**, 133 (1981).
60. M. Connolly, unpublished results.
61. We acknowledge the efforts of our co-workers who contributed to designing the experiments and collecting the data to which we refer herein, and thank many of our colleagues for sharing their data in advance of publication. We also thank A. Olson for producing Fig. 1 and R. Ogata for comments on the manuscript. Portions of this work were supported by grants from the American Cancer Society (NP-359) and the National Institutes of Health (R01 AI 18509). This is paper No. 2824 of the Research Institute of Scripps Clinic.

9. Protein Engineering

Kevin M. Ulmer

In the last decade, genetic engineering technology has been developed to the point where we can now clone the gene for essentially any protein found in nature. By precise manipulation of the appropriate regulatory signals we can then produce significant quantities of that protein in bacteria. Recent advances in chemical synthesis of DNA now permit virtually unlimited genetic modification, and offer the prospect for developing protein engineering technology to create novel proteins not found in nature. By starting with the known crystal structure for a protein we would like to directly modify the gene to alter that structure in a predictable fashion, targeted to improve some functional property. At each stage we could verify the structural and functional changes that actually occurred and thereby refine and extend our predictive capability. Step by step, as we gain facility with this technique and learn the detailed rules that relate structure and function, we should be able to create proteins with novel properties which could not be achieved as effectively by any other method.

Rationale

Despite the fact that biochemists have characterized several thousand enzymes, there are only a handful that could be considered enzymes of commerce. Indeed, only a dozen enzymes have worldwide sales in excess of $10 million per year, and together they account for more than 90 percent of the total enzyme market (*1*). Frequently the limiting factor in the industrial use of an enzyme has simply been the high cost of isolating and purifying adequate amounts of the protein. Part of the solution to this problem lies with the ability of genetic engineers to greatly amplify the production of specific enzymes in microorganisms, but beyond cost there are often other limitations to the broader use of enzymes which stem from the fact that the desired industrial application is far removed from the physiological role normally played by the enzyme. In particular, industrial applications require generally robust enzymes with a long half-life under process conditions. Frequently the desired substrate or product is somewhat different from the physiological one, and often the chemical conditions for the reaction are decidedly nonphysiological, ranging to extremes of pH, temperature, and concentration. If enzymes are to be more widely used as industrial catalysts, we must develop methods to tailor their properties to the process of interest. The list of properties of enzymes we would like to be able to control in a predictable fashion would include the following:

1) Kinetic properties including the turnover number of the enzyme and the

Michaelis constant, K_m, for a particular substrate.

2) Thermostability and temperature optimum.

3) Stability and activity in nonaqueous solvents.

4) Substrate and reaction specificity.

5) Cofactor requirements.

6) pH optimum.

7) Protease resistance.

8) Allosteric regulation.

9) Molecular weight and subunit structure.

The solutions to these problems have included extensive searches for the best suited naturally occurring enzyme, mutation and selection programs to enhance the native enzyme's properties, and chemical modification and immobilization to obtain a stable and functional biocatalyst. From such work we know that all of these properties can in general be improved. Specific examples of what has been achieved by these methods and how protein engineering can build on this knowledge to yield still further improvements are cited below.

It is not uncommon to observe wide variations in properties such as turnover number, K_m, molecular weight, temperature optimum, thermostability, pH optimum, and pH stability among enzymes of the same type isolated from different sources. Among the glucose isomerases (E.C. 5.3.1.5) (2), for example, the turnover numbers range from 63 to 2151 glucose molecules converted per enzyme molecule per minute at 60°C and the K_m for glucose can differ by more than an order of magnitude (0.086 to 0.920 molar). Molecular weights vary from 52,000 to 191,000 and temperature optima vary between 50° and 90°C. Some glucose isomerases are so thermolabile that they lose all activity after exposure to 60°C for 10 minutes, while others are thermo-

stable enough that they retain 100 percent activity after exposure to 70°C for 10 minutes. The pH optima differ by as much as 3.5 pH units, and some are stable only in the narrow range of pH 7 to 9 while others can tolerate the range pH 4 to 11. Finding the optimum combination of properties for a particular application is often a difficult task (for instance, the enzyme with the highest activity might not be the most stable) and usually results in compromise. If, instead, we could learn the structural features of each enzyme that confer a specific desirable property, we could perhaps combine these features by protein engineering techniques to create a totally new enzyme that manifests all of the desirable traits. It is difficult to imagine accomplishing this by conventional random mutagenesis techniques, but a directed approach to protein modification guided by adequate structural information should be possible.

It should also be possible to learn general rules for conferring thermostability on a protein. By examining the structures of thermophilic enzymes and comparing them with their mesophilic counterparts it has become clear that salt bridges and other electrostatic interactions confer thermostability, as do specific amino acid modifications that stabilize secondary structures and interactions between secondary structures (3–5). Subtle changes involving many cooperative interactions can impart significant thermostability, but the protein engineer is not necessarily limited to a subtle approach. The most thermostable enzyme may result from a combination of all these modifications, including the creation of additional disulfide bonds.

Mutagenesis and selection can often be used effectively to improve a specific property of an enzyme. For example, it is possible to isolate mutant enzymes affected in allosteric regulation which are released from feedback inhibition. The MTR 2 mutation of *Escherichia coli* anthranilate synthetase, which is insensitive to tryptophan inhibition, is such a mutant (6). In certain cases it has been possible to isolate mutants which have altered substrate specificity or which catalyze a different reaction from the wild-type enzyme. A mutant of xanthine dehydrogenase has been isolated, for example, which oxidizes 2-hydroxypurine at position 6 rather than position 8 (7).

Conventional mutagenesis techniques are generally limited to producing incremental changes in a protein. If several specific amino acid changes distributed throughout the protein are required for an observable improvement in a certain property, it will be exceedingly difficult to detect such an event in the mutant population because of the vanishingly small probability of its occurrence. If, instead, we have some guiding principles for obtaining a desired property, we can directly make whatever modifications are required by gene modification techniques.

One of the major assumptions underlying the belief that protein engineering can be successful is that proteins in general will be forgiving of attempts at modification. This view is supported by the apparent plasticity of proteins. We know from a long history of mutational studies that many amino acid changes in proteins are silent and have little or no effect on the functionality of the protein (8). Indeed, in many cases it is possible to isolate mutant proteins that have amino acid insertions, deletions, and substitutions and still retain normal activity, just as tryptic fragments often retain some degree of function (9). Many protein fusions still exhibit the activity of the two component enzymes, and in fact

fusions to β-lactamase or β-galactosidase have been used as markers for studies of gene expression (10).

There are now enough protein structures available for a detailed comparison of enzymes from closely and distantly related organisms. It is found that there are many variations on the same theme. Proteins appear to have only a limited number of basic architectures with many subtle changes superimposed (11). Very similar patterns of chain folding and domain structure can arise from different amino acid sequences that show little or no homology. The immunoglobulins are a prime example of conservation of structure despite extensive differences in amino acid sequence (12). The natural mechanisms of evolution and gene rearrangement involve recombination of similar sequences, deletions, inversions, and duplications as well as simple point mutations. From an examination of the organization of higher eukaryotic genes it appears that functional domains of proteins may be coded in exons which are separated by introns, facilitating a building-block style of protein evolution. This is supported by recent evidence that intron-exon boundaries map at the surface of proteins (13). It is thus likely that many proteins will be forgiving of our initial attempts to modify their structures. Gradual changes in function and conformation should be the rule for minor changes in sequence. However, this will not always be the case. A single amino acid change (glycine to aspartic acid) in *E. coli* aspartate transcarbamylase, for example, results in loss of activity and alters the binding of catalytic and regulatory subunits (14). The crystals of the mutant enzyme are isomorphous with those of the native enzyme despite these extensive functional modifications. Such sensitivity to modification is likely to arise when we are dealing with critical residues in the active site, but the number of such residues should be small and thus they should be amenable to a more exhaustive analysis of the effects of modifications.

Other evidence for the likelihood of success with protein engineering comes from studies of chemical modification of enzymes. Success with semisynthetic enzymes such as flavopapain (15) encourages a rational approach to enzyme modification starting with crystal structure information. The proteolytic enzyme papain has been modified by specific covalent attachment of flavenoid cofactors to the unique cysteine at position 25 in the active site. From an analysis of the enzyme's structure it was predicted that such a modification would still allow room in the active site for substrate binding and would convert papain into a flavin enzyme. The flavopapain performed as expected.

Many schemes for enzyme immobilization (16) also point to likely success with certain types of modifications. By more or less blindly derivatizing the surface of enzymes through the addition of polymers and other ligands (17), it has been possible to alter the solubility of enzymes, increase their resistance to proteases and thermal denaturation, and alter the local pH at the active site to advantage. All these methods are extremely crude in comparison with what should be possible starting with an accurate crystal structure for the enzyme and an artificial gene that can be specifically changed at will.

Protein Structure Determination

X-ray diffraction methods are the only techniques at present that can provide the detailed structural information at the atomic scale which will be required for protein engineering. Although protein crystallography has traditionally been a very laborious process, recent advances offer the prospect of reducing the time and effort required to solve new protein structures to 1 or 2 years. The most unpredictable aspect of the problem, which is likely to remain the rate-limiting step in the crystallographic process, is obtaining diffraction-quality crystals of the protein. Some progress has been made in recent years (18), but a more systematic approach with simple automated equipment could make the search for appropriate crystallization conditions more efficient. Other possibilities might include the use of zero gravity aboard the space shuttle to eliminate convective effects and improve crystallization and, once the native structure has been solved, the use of protein engineering techniques to modify the protein in order to simplify subsequent crystallizations or obtain better isomorphous derivatives.

Major advances have been made in the collection and analysis of diffraction data for proteins. Synchrotron x-ray sources are now routinely used for protein crystallography in Europe (19), and several facilities will soon be operational in the United States (20). The higher x-ray flux from such sources greatly reduces the data collection time, and the fact that the x-ray wavelength is tunable should permit phase calculation from a single isomorphous derivative by anomalous scattering techniques. The use of position-sensitive x-ray detectors (Fig. 1) in place of photographic film for recording the diffraction patterns, especially when combined with high-brilliance sources, will further reduce data collection time and simplify some of the subsequent processing steps (21). Better algorithms have facilitated the refinement of protein models at higher resolution (22), and techniques such as molecular replace-

Fig. 1. Electronic position-sensitive x-ray detector. [Courtesy of Xentronics Company, Inc., Cambridge, Massachusetts]

ment (23) can significantly reduce the effort required to solve related structures. The latter technique will be particularly useful for structure difference determinations, which will be required to develop protein engineering. If crystals of a modified enzyme are isomorphous with those of the native enzyme, the structural differences can be determined by a simple Fourier difference analysis, as has been done for several temperature-sensitive mutants of T4 lysozyme (4, 5). If the modified protein is not isomorphous, molecular replacement techniques might be used to solve the new structure with much less effort than was required for the initial structure determination. The structural differences that result from each directed modification could thus be analyzed very rapidly. It is this ability to correlate experimentally observed differences in structure with differences in functional properties that will be the key to developing predictive rules for protein engineering.

By collecting diffraction data over a range of temperatures (24) or by using short-pulse x-ray sources it should also be possible to learn something about the dynamic aspects of the protein structure, which are averaged out by traditional methods. It is also possible to obtain experimental data on protein dynamics by nuclear magnetic resonance (NMR) techniques. Recently, two-dimensional proton NMR techniques have been developed which may also provide detailed structural information on proteins in solution rather than in crystals (25). New methods permit the assignment of peaks in high-resolution NMR spectra to specific protons in the protein. A distance matrix can be constructed from such data and can then be converted to a set of three-dimensional coordinates for the molecule. So far the method has been successfully applied only to small peptides and it is not clear whether it can be extended to average-sized proteins.

Protein Modeling

Model building has also been greatly simplified through the use of sophisticated computer graphics. The protein structure can be fitted to the electron density map by simultaneously displaying both with an interactive color graphics program (26). Similar molecular graphics programs eliminate the need for building physical models by providing real-time, three-dimensional color representations that can be manipulated at the turn of a dial (27). Van der Waals surfaces for the protein can be displayed and the interaction between several molecules simulated. Interactive molecular graphics will be the design board for the protein engineer, especially when teamed with programs and superfast array processors (28) capable of calculating, in real time, the perturbations of a known protein structure that would result from specific modifications of the amino acid sequence (Fig. 2).

Most of the theoretical work on protein structure has been concerned with attempting to accurately predict the final three-dimensional conformation of a protein from its amino acid sequence (29). This is a formidable task and, although some progress has been made (30) in calculating the structures of small proteins such as bovine pancreatic trypsin inhibitor by using a combination of conformational energy calculations and distance constraints, the theory is not at the point where it can make significant contributions to the solution of new structures. Ultimately we hope to be able to predict structures on the basis of amino acid sequences alone, thus eliminating the need for experimental methods of structure determination. This capability will be important for the long-term success of protein engineering. Such theoretical work should benefit directly from early attempts at protein engineering, which should provide previously unobtainable experimental data to further refine algorithms or test predictive models.

For the present, however, it would be more useful to develop an accurate perturbation theory for protein structure which would allow us to calculate the effects of small changes in amino acid sequence accurately enough to eliminate the need to perform experiments for each step in the protein engineering process. The present methodology for protein structure refinement and for calculation of the structures of proteins that are homologous to other proteins of known structure would provide a useful starting point for the development of such a perturbation theory (31), and families of monoclonal antibodies that differ only slightly in amino acid sequence may provide a useful natural system for experimental verification of the theory. Initial attempts at protein engineering are likely to be conservative in the selection of modifications to be synthesized, but as we gain confidence in predictive modeling we will want to push the modeling to its limits in order to further extend this approach.

Gene Modification

The technical breakthrough that makes protein engineering feasible is the ability to rapidly and inexpensively synthesize oligonucleotides of defined sequence. In the past several years the chemistry of DNA synthesis has advanced to the point where such oligonucleotides are no longer curiosities but can be considered standard laboratory reagents for the genetic engineer. This is largely due to the development of solid phase synthetic methods used in automated (Fig. 3) or semiautomated procedures (32). There are two general methods of gene modification with synthetic oligonucleotides.

Procedures for oligonucleotide-directed in vitro mutagenesis (33) are used most appropriately for making small insertions, deletions, and substitutions of nucleotides at single specific sites in cloned genes. The method is based on hybridizing a small oligonucleotide primer containing the desired nucleotide modifications to the appropriate site in a cloned gene, and then using DNA polymerase to replicate the rest of the gene, which remains unmodified. Only one modification at a time can be produced with this method, but it requires the least amount of chemically synthesized DNA and will therefore be the method of choice for most initial attempts at protein

116

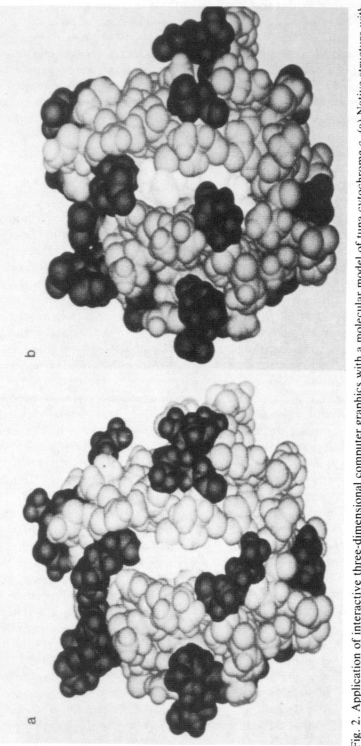

Fig. 2. Application of interactive three-dimensional computer graphics with a molecular model of tuna cytochrome c. (a) Native structure with positively charged lysine residues indicated by dark shading. (b) Lysine residues have been graphically replaced with negatively charged glutamic acid residues to simulate a protein engineering experiment that might reverse the surface charge of the protein. [Courtesy of R. J. Feldmann, National Institutes of Health, Bethesda, Maryland]

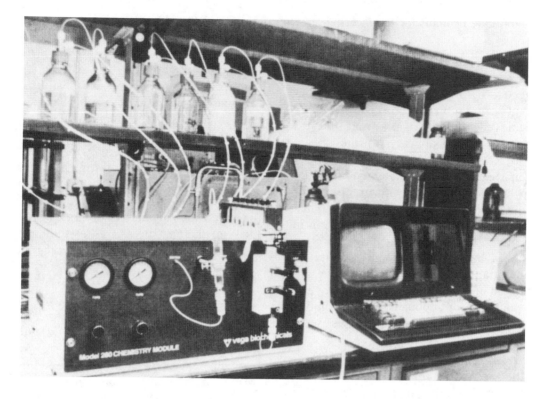

Fig. 3. Automated instrumentation for the synthesis of oligonucleotides.

engineering. Indeed, this approach was recently used to modify the active site of tyrosyl-tRNA synthetase, whose crystal structure was known (*34*). The cysteine at position 35 was converted to serine with the predicted effect of lowering the K_m for adenosine triphosphate. This is a major step toward protein engineering.

The alternative approach is to construct a completely synthetic gene de novo, using chemically synthesized oligomers that are ligated together. This approach requires a chemical DNA synthesis capability beyond that of most laboratories at this time, but offers a number of advantages over the in vitro mutagenesis techniques. The sequence for the synthetic gene can be designed in a modular fashion which places unique restriction enzyme sites at convenient positions within the gene to facilitate subsequent modifications. Since the gene is constructed by ligation of many oligonucleotides, multiple modifications can be created in a single step by incorporating the appropriately modified oligomers into the ligation mixture. This is likely to be the gene modification method of choice when extensive changes in the amino acid sequence of the protein are required during protein engineering. The genes for several small proteins (for instance, somatostatin, insulin, and α-interferon) have now been successfully synthesized de novo by these techniques and expressed at high levels in bacteria, and further improvement is anticipated (*35*).

Candidate Proteins for Engineering

A major investment of effort and resources in protein engineering will be needed before any commercially significant alterations to a protein are achieved. Results of academic interest are starting to appear (*34*) and should lead to the development of a set of general rules for protein modification, which will reduce the effort required for engineering subsequent proteins. To justify the costs of a major undertaking in protein engineering, the target protein should have at least some commercial potential. At present, however, we are limited in our selection of proteins by the availability of adequate structural information (*36*). Several candidates seem promising.

Immunoglobulins have been well characterized structurally (*12*) and a great deal of DNA sequence information is available (*37*). With recent advances in monoclonal antibody production, immunoglobulins have potential applications as reagents for affinity purification or as novel therapeutics, and they seem ideal candidates for protein engineering to specifically adapt them for these purposes. By creating novel gene fusions of antibodies and toxic peptides it may be possible to create targetable, cytotoxic drugs or "magic bullets" (*38*). Some success has already been achieved with the de novo design and synthesis of a toxic peptide with properties similar to those of melittin (*39*).

The α-carbon skeletons for two of the largest volume industrial enzymes, glucose isomerase (*40*) and α-amylase (*41*), have been determined. A number of properties of these enzymes have been identified (*2*) which, if improved, would greatly enhance their performance in the process for conversion of starch to high-fructose corn syrup.

Specific hydroxylation of substituted aromatic compounds is a problem of general interest in the chemical industry. The enzyme *p*-hydroxybenzoate hydroxylase, whose structure is now known (*42*), might serve as the starting point for developing an enzymatic approach to this problem. Protein engineering might be aimed at changing the substrate specificity of the enzyme as well as the position on the ring at which hydroxylation occurs (*7*).

The most abundant protein on the earth, ribulose-1,5-biphosphate carboxylase, is the enzyme responsible for carbon dioxide fixation in photosynthetic organisms. The enzyme can also use molecular oxygen as a substrate, and this results in photorespiration in plants. Approximately 50 percent of the fixed carbon is lost in this process, and there is thus considerable interest in possible methods for eliminating or reducing this activity of the enzyme (*43*). The enzyme's structure is being investigated (*44*) and the gene has been cloned and sequenced. Protein engineering might well be applied to this problem.

The structures of a number of DNA binding proteins including repressors (*45*) and the restriction endonuclease Eco RI (*46*) are receiving a great deal of attention from crystallographers and offer a number of interesting possibilities for protein engineering. It might be possible to alter the recognition specificity (*47*) of these enzymes in a predictable fashion and thus create whole new families of repressors and restriction enzymes.

Future Prospects

The ability to readily produce and analyze directed structural modifications in proteins will be of benefit in helping to solve the long-standing problem of structure-function relations in proteins. The rules learned during this academic exercise can then be applied to create novel proteins with improved properties for commercial applications. The same techniques may also assist in the development of a method for accurately predicting the three-dimensional structure of a protein from its amino acid sequence, paving the way for designing novel enzymes from first principles. Protein engineering thus represents the first major step toward a more general capability for molecular engineering which would allow us to structure matter atom by atom (*48*).

References and Notes

1. Genex Corporation estimate.
2. W. Chen, *Process Biochem.* **15**, 36 (1980).
3. M. F. Perutz, *Science* **201**, 1187 (1978); P. Argos, M. G. Rossmann, U. M. Grau, H. Zuber, G. Prank, J. D. Tratschin, *Biochemistry* **18**, 5698 (1979); M. G. Grutter, K. Rine, B. W. Matthews, *Hoppe-Seyler's Z. Physiol. Chem.* **360**, 1009 (1979); K. Yutani, K. Ogasahara, Y. Sugino, A. Matsushiro, *Nature (London)* **267**, 274 (1977).
4. M. G. Grutter and B. W. Matthews, *J. Mol. Biol.* **154**, 525 (1978).
5. M. G. Grutter, R. B. Hawkes, B. W. Matthews, *Nature (London)* **277**, 667 (1979).
6. M. J. Pabst, J. C. Kuhn, R. L. Somerville, *J. Biol. Chem.* **248**, 901 (1973).
7. C. Scazzocchio and H. M. Sealy-Lewis, *Eur. J. Biochem.* **91**, 99 (1978).
8. J. H. Miller, in *The Operon*, J. H. Miller and W. S. Reznikoff, Eds. (Cold Spring Harbor Laboratory, Cold Spring Harbor, N.Y., 1980), p. 31.
9. D. B. Wetlaufer, *Adv. Protein Chem.* **34**, 61 (1981).
10. L. Guarente, G. Lauer, T. M. Roberts, M. Ptashne, *Cell* **20**, 543 (1980).
11. M. G. Rossmann and P. Argos, *Annu. Rev. Biochem.* **50**, 497 (1981).
12. L. M. Amzel and R. J. Poljak, *ibid.* **48**, 961 (1979).
13. C. S. Craik, S. Sprang, R. Fletterick, W. J. Rutter, *Nature (London)* **299**, 180 (1982).
14. R. Kim, T. Young, H. K. Schachman, S. Kim, *J. Biol. Chem.* **256**, 4691 (1981).
15. J. T. Slama, S. R. Oruganti, E. T. Kaiser, *J. Am. Chem. Soc.* **103**, 6211 (1981); H. L. Levine, Y. Nakagawa, E. T. Kaiser, *Biochem. Biophys. Res. Commun.* **76**, 64 (1977); E. T. Kaiser, H. L. Levine, T. Otuski, H. E. Fried, R. Dupeyre, *Adv. Chem. Ser.* **191**, 35 (1980).
16. K. Mosbach, Ed., *Methods in Enzymology* (Academic Press, New York, 1976), vol. 44.
17. C. H. W. Hirs and N. Tmasheff, Eds., *ibid.* (1972), vol. 25.
18. A. McPherson, *The Preparation and Analysis of Protein Crystals* (Wiley, New York, 1982).
19. DESY at European Molecular Biology Laboratories, Hamburg, West Germany; LURE at the University of Paris-Sud, Orsay, France; DARESBURY at Daresbury, United Kingdom.
20. CHESS (Cornell High Energy Synchrotron Source), Cornell University; SSRL (Stanford Synchrotron Radiation Laboratory), Stanford University; NSLS (National Synchrotron Light Source), Brookhaven National Laboratory.
21. R. P. Phizackerley, C. W. Cork, R. C. Hamlin, C. P. Nielsen, W. Vernon, Ng. H. Xuong, V. Perez-Mendez, *Nucl. Instrum. Methods* **172**, 393 (1980); U. W. Arndt and D. J. Gilmore, *J. Appl. Crystallogr.* **12**, 1 (1979); G. E. Schulz and G. Rosenbaum, *Nucl. Instrum. Methods* **152**, 205 (1978); R. Hamlin, C. Cork, C. Nielsen, W. Vernon, Ng. H. Xuong, *Acta Crystallogr. Sect. A* **34**, 334 (1978); R. Hamlin, C. Cork, A. Howard, C. Nielsen, W. Vernon, D. Matthews, Ng. H. Xuong, *J. Appl. Crystallogr.* **14**, 85 (1981).
22. J. H. Konnert and W. A. Hendrickson, *Acta Crystallogr. Sect. A* **36**, 344 (1980).
23. T. L. Blundell and L. N. Johnson, *Protein Crystallography* (Academic Press, New York, 1976).
24. P. J. Artymuik, C. C. F. Blake, D. E. P. Grace, S. J. Oatley, D. C. Phillips, M. J. E. Sternberg, *Nature (London)* **280**, 563 (1980); H. Frauenfelder, G. A. Petsko, D. Tsernoglou, *ibid.*, p. 558; W. A. Hendrickson and J. H. Konnert, *Biophys. J.* **32**, 645 (1980).
25. K. Wuthrich, G. Wider, W. Braun, *J. Mol. Biol.* **155**, 311 (1982); M. Billeter, W. Braun, K. Wuthrich, *ibid.*, p. 321; G. Wagner and K. Wuthrich, *ibid.*, p. 347; G. Wider, K. H. Lee, K. Wuthrich, *ibid.*, p. 367.
26. J. R. Miller, S. S. Abdel-Meguid, M. G. Rossmann, D. C. Anderson, *J. Appl. Crystallogr.* **14**, 94 (1981).
27. R. Langridge, T. E. Ferrin, I. D. Kuntz, M. L. Connolly, *Science* **211**, 661 (1981).
28. C. Pottle, M. S. Pottle, R. W. Tuttle, R. J. Kinch, H. A. Scheraga, *J. Comput. Chem.* **1**, 46 (1980).
29. R. F. Doolittle, *Abstr. Pap. Am. Chem. Soc.* **1979**, 44 (1979); M. J. E. Sternberg and J. M. Thornton, *Nature (London)* **271**, 15 (1978).
30. H. A. Scheraga, in *Structure and Dynamics of Proteins and Nucleic Acids*, E. Clementi and R. H. Sarma, Eds. (Adenine, Guilderland, N.Y., in press).

31. H. A. Scheraga, *Biopolymers* **20**, 1877 (1981); R. J. Feldmann, personal communication.
32. G. Alvarado-Urbina, G. M. Sathe, W.-C. Liu, M. F. Gillen, P. D. Duck, R. Bender, K. K. Ogilvie, *Science* **214**, 270 (1981); M. W. Hunkapillar and L. E. Hood, *ibid.* **219**, 650 (1983).
33. M. J. Zoller and M. Smith, in *Methods in Enzymology* (Academic Press, New York, in press).
34. G. Winter, A. R. Fersht, A. J. Wilkinson, M. Zoller, M. Smith, *Nature (London)* **299**, 756 (1982).
35. K. Itakura, T. Hirose, R. Crea, A. D. Riggs, H. L. Heyneker, F. Bolivar, H. W. Boyer, *Science* **198**, 1056 (1977); R. Crea, A. Kraszewski, T. Hirose, K. Itakura, *Proc. Natl. Acad. Sci. U.S.A.* **75**, 5765 (1978); D. V. Goeddel *et al.*, *ibid.* **76**, 106 (1979); D. C. Williams, R. M. Van Frank, W. L. Muth, J. P. Burnett, *Science* **215**, 687 (1982); M. D. Edge *et al.*, *Nature (London)* **292**, 756 (1981); J. D. Windass, C. R. Newton, J. De Maeyer-Guignard, V. E. Moore, A. F. Markham, M. D. Edge, *Nucleic Acids Res.* **10**, 6639 (1982).
36. Protein Data Bank, Brookhaven National Laboratory; F. C. Bernstein *et al.*, *J. Mol. Biol.* **112**, 535 (1977).
37. M. O. Dayhoff, R. M. Schwartz, H. R. Chen, L. T. Hunt, W. C. Barker, B. C. Orcutt, Eds., *Nucleic Acid Sequence Database* (National Biomedical Research Council, Washington, D.C., 1981).
38. T. Davies, *Nature (London)* **289**, 12 (1981); S. Olsnes, *ibid.* **290**, 84 (1981).
39. W. F. DeGrado, F. J. Kezdy, E. T. Kaiser, *J. Am. Chem. Soc.* **103**, 679 (1981).
40. H. M. Berman, B. H. Rubin, H. L. Carrell, J. P. Glusker, *J. Biol. Chem.* **249**, 3983 (1974); H. L. Carrell, *Abstr. Am. Crystallogr. Assoc.* **10**, 35 (1982).
41. Y. Matsuura *et al.*, *J. Biochem. (Tokyo)* **87**, 1555 (1980).
42. R. K. Wierenga, R. J. DeJong, K. H. Kalk, W. G. J. Hol, J. Drenth, *J. Mol. Biol.* **131**, 55 (1979).
43. H. W. Siegelman and G. Hind, Eds., *Photosynthetic Carbon Assimilation* (Plenum, New York, 1978); C. R. Somerville and W. L. Ogren, *Trends Biochem. Sci.* **7**, 171 (1982).
44. S. Johal, D. P. Bourque, W. W. Smith, S. W. Suh, D. Eisenberg, *J. Biol. Chem.* **255**, 8873 (1980).
45. C. O. Pabo, W. Krovatin, A. Jeffrey, R. T. Sauer, *Nature (London)* **298**, 441 (1982); C. O. Pabo and M. Lewis, *ibid.* p. 443; D. B. McKay and T. A. Steitz, *ibid.* **290**, 744 (1981); W. F. Anderson, D. H. Ohlendorf, Y. Takeda, B. W. Matthews, *ibid.*, p. 754; D. H. Ohlendorf, W. F. Anderson, R. G. Fisher, Y. Takeda, B. W. Matthews, *ibid.* **298**, 718 (1982).
46. T. Young, P. Modrich, A. Beth, E. Jay, S. Kim, *J. Mol. Biol.* **145**, 607 (1981); J. M. Rosenberg, R. E. Dickerson, P. J. Greene, H. W. Boyer, *ibid.* **122**, 241 (1978).
47. R. T. Sauer, R. R. Yocum, R. F. Doolittle, M. Lewis, C. O. Pabo, *Nature (London)* **298**, 447 (1982).
48. K. E. Drexler, *Proc. Natl. Acad. Sci. U.S.A.* **78**, 5275 (1981); K. M. Ulmer, in *Molecular Electronic Devices*, F. L. Carter, Ed. (Dekker, New York, 1982), p. 213.

10. Prospects in Plant Genetic Engineering

Kenneth A. Barton and Winston J. Brill

Agriculture is both the oldest and the largest of the world's industries. Over a period of thousands of years, a broad spectrum of interacting natural and artificial selective pressures has influenced the evolution of crop plants toward those now found under cultivation. Throughout this evolutionary period efforts have been directed toward increasing crop quality and productivity without understanding the contributing molecular features. While the supply of available nutrients for human consumption worldwide has never been in excess, increases in agricultural productivity within the past few decades have been dramatic. A significant reason for the successes of modern agriculture has been an increased reliance on advanced technology, and a successful integration of new technology with the results of intensive plant breeding programs. However, methods of crop improvement in the past few decades have initiated a series of new problems that are now becoming recognized.

Genetically superior plants derived from modern crop improvement programs typically require a high level of crop management. Included in a management regime may be the input of increasingly expensive nitrogen fertilizer as well as the extensive use of pesticides and herbicides, all of which can result in toxic residue accumulation in the environment. In addition, the high degree of inbreeding and the narrowing of the genetic base of widely cultivated crops cause increasing concern about the susceptibility of crops to major disease outbreaks and imply that important genetic traits may be lost as world germplasm is reduced (*1*). With problems such as these it is not surprising that the advent of recombinant DNA technology is generating excitement. A whole range of very specific plant genetic modifications can now be considered, with the use of methods that may someday generate a genetic diversity not naturally present in cultivated plants.

The molecular genetics of prokaryotic organisms is extremely complex and in many respects poorly understood. The flow of stored genetic information in nucleic acids to the appearance of functional gene products elsewhere in the cell requires completion of an intricate sequence of events, with many points where positive or negative control over expression can be exerted. Genetic regulation present in simple eukaryotes, such as yeast, can be more complex, with the added potential for various interactions between organelles, and with an increasing number of both nuclear and cytoplasmic genes. Higher eukaryotes, among them crop plants, provide the still greater problems of cellular differentiation; for example, thousands of active and interacting genes in a leaf cell may be totally quiescent in a root cell of the same organism (2). The same natural laws that govern the expression of DNA placed in new genetic environments through classical plant breeding apply to the expression, or lack of expression, of DNA placed in plants by recombinant DNA technology. To be successful in plant genetic engineering, we must begin to develop an understanding of the elements that control gene expression. The significance to gene expression of precise DNA constructs is now beginning to be understood in bacterial, yeast, and even mammalian systems, in part because of the development of methods for inducing cell transformation. With transformation methods evolving and useful genes being discussed, genetic transformation of plants can now be considered realistically.

Plant Transformation Vectors

Although the transfer of cloned DNA between microorganisms is routinely carried out in many laboratories, the absence of convenient vector systems has inhibited similar experiments with higher plants. However, rapid progress in this area is being made and a variety of vectors are expected to come into practical use in the near future. One limitation to current vector design is the lack of an ideal transformation marker—a gene present on the vector which enables convenient identification of transformed cells. The ability to provide a dominant selection for plant cells deficient in alcohol dehydrogenase activity and to subsequently identify alcohol dehydrogenase-positive revertants (3) makes the alcohol

dehydrogenase gene an attractive marker for plant host-vector systems. It is also possible that dominant chimeric antibiotic-resistance genes, similar to those now functional in mammalian cells (4), can be constructed for expression in plant cells by using genetic control regions from plant DNA spliced to protein-coding sequences from other organisms. As more convenient markers become available, the development of mechanical gene introduction methods [for example, microinjection or polyethylene glycol–mediated uptake of DNA by protoplasts (5)] will be greatly facilitated. In the absence of conveniently scored markers, many plant transformation experiments have relied on natural routes of entry into plant cells—the routes of plant pathogens. Although a variety of pathogenic organisms may be modified to serve vectorial functions as more becomes known about their mechanisms of infection and replication, efforts to date have centered on the double-strand DNA plant viruses (Caulimoviruses) and *Agrobacterium*.

Only a small number of Caulimoviruses are known, and all are similar in many respects. The most widely studied, cauliflower mosaic virus (CaMV), has a limited natural host range which has been extended only slightly in vitro (6). The transcription and replicative mechanisms of the virus are complex, and the virus is not seed-transmissible. However, the potentially valuable characteristics of CaMV include the capacity of the viruses to infect intact plants, and to then move systemically through the hosts. A vector that would avoid the need for cell culture would be valuable indeed. Unfortunately, experiments directed toward use of CaMV as a gene vector have revealed stringent genome size limitations (7), thereby restricting the amount of foreign DNA that can be transported.

Agrobacterium tumefaciens, a soil bacterium that incites crown gall disease in a wide variety of dicotyledonous plants, has provided greater success than CaMV as a plant vector (8). Virulence is conferred on the bacterium by genetic information carried on large plasmids, the Ti (tumor-inducing) plasmids (9). At the time of infection, a segment of the Ti plasmid, called T-DNA, is inserted into the nuclear DNA of the host plant (10). Genes contained within the T-DNA are functional in transformed cells, and T-DNA gene products are responsible for both hormone independence of crown gall cells in tissue culture (11) and the synthesis of novel metabolites called opines (12). Opines, simple derivatives of amino acids and keto acids, are specifically catabolized by *Agrobacterium* as both carbon and nitrogen sources. The T-DNA insertion into the host plant genome therefore appears as an excellent example of genetic engineering in nature, for it assures a supply of nutrients to the invading bacterium by altering the host plant metabolic pathways.

Tobacco cells containing an intact T-DNA cannot regenerate into normal plants because of hormonal imbalances resulting from the action of T-DNA gene products. However, if the genes responsible for the imbalance are spontaneously deleted from the infected cell, healthy plants containing the remaining T-DNA genes can regenerate (13). It is also possible to "disarm" T-DNA in vitro by experimentally deleting one or more genes of the T-DNA (14). Tobacco cells transformed with disarmed Ti plasmids are fully capable of regenerating into healthy plants, and it seems likely that other plants that adapt well to tissue culture can be similarly transformed. Eu-karyotic DNA placed in the T-DNA of a disarmed Ti plasmid is transported into the plant cell, and the DNA is structurally stable in passage through meiosis, into seeds of the regenerated plants (14). The Ti plasmid can therefore be realistically used as a vector for dicotyledenous plants, although refinements over the current experiments can be expected to result in still more convenient Ti-derivative vectors. Ti plasmids can also now be used to facilitate construction and experimental testing of dominant selectable markers, which may soon be available for transformation of both monocots and dicots.

Rapid progress in vector construction has outdistanced two other areas of research which are critical to plant genetic engineering successes. Initial transformation experiments will be carried out at the level of a single cell in culture, but relatively few agronomically significant crops can yet be regenerated routinely from cell culture (15). Until this technology develops further, or until alternative vectors become available which avoid the need for tissue culture, many crops cannot be modified by recombinant DNA methods. The second problem is equally significant—what genes can we transfer into plants that will improve a crop species? Much of the development of present cultivars has relied on selection in classical breeding programs for polygenic characteristics such as increased yield or protein content, without an understanding of the molecular basis for such traits. In contrast, success in plant genetic engineering will rely, to a great degree, on a thorough knowledge of the genetics and regulation of the traits to be transferred. A number of systems exist in plants which are being considered for manipulation through genetic engineering, although a few examples demonstrate the magnitude of problems to be encountered.

Seed Proteins

The seeds of legumes and cereal grains provide humans directly with approximately 70 percent of their dietary protein requirement (16). Throughout seed development, storage proteins are synthesized and accumulated within the seed, apparently to provide a source of amino acid reserves during early seed germination (17). High levels of such protein in seeds provides an enriched amino acid source for both human and animal consumption. However, various deficiencies of seeds in certain essential amino acids do not allow either cereal grains or legumes to provide a balanced diet without supplementation of the limiting amino acids from other sources (18). One widely discussed approach for overcoming the nutritional deficiencies of seeds would be to genetically engineer genes encoding the various storage proteins to include new codons for the deficient amino acids, either by inserting additional amino acids into the protein, or substituting existing amino acids with ones more nutritionally desirable. However, there are a variety of technical problems to resolve before such an engineering project can be successful. Structural conservation of the zein storage proteins of maize (19, 20) and apparent structural conservation of messenger RNA in legumes (21) provide good examples of such problems.

There are a number of zein proteins in maize, each deficient in the essential amino acids lysine and tryptophan (18–20). The zein proteins amount to 50 percent or more of the total corn endosperm protein. Extensive microheterogeneity exists between the different proteins (19, 20), although there is apparently a strong conservation of an unusual, highly ordered protein secondary structure (20). The basis for the complex folding of zein is the presence of a sequence of 20 amino acids, with alternating hydrophobic and hydrophilic regions, which is repeated nine times in the protein chain. A number of zein genes with minor sequence variation comprise a moderately reiterated multigene family in the maize genome, presumably a result of gene amplification (19, 20). Throughout the amplification process and subsequent divergent evolution of the zein genes, there has been a conservation of the secondary folding characteristics of the resulting polypeptides (20). Attempts to alter the genomic coding sequence of zein proteins by genetic engineering must take into consideration the possible effect of amino acid changes on protein secondary structure, since stability and accumulation of the zein proteins during embryogenesis may well be due to protein structural features. To complicate matters further, there is now evidence that a conservation of nucleotide sequence in the vicilin genes of the seeds of various legumes may be significant to aspects of messenger RNA structural stability and metabolism (21). If this proves correct, the genetic engineer must consider the effect of codon substitution not only on protein stability but also on the folding characteristics of the messenger RNA.

Because the storage protein systems now under scrutiny are encoded in multigene families, engineering of a single gene for higher levels of an amino acid would have a relatively small effect on total seed protein composition unless the engineered gene was transcribed very actively or was amplified in the genome.

Alternative approaches toward improvement of seed protein composition, such as introduction of entirely novel proteins that are highly enriched in specific amino acids, can be considered. However, the problems of RNA and protein stability remain, and there is the additional complication of obtaining accurate and high-level developmental expression of the new gene. The transfer of genes encoding known storage proteins to systems now low in protein, or the provision of additional copies of genes to systems already producing storage proteins, are further possibilities for improving seed protein quality or quantity; however, channeling normal amino acid pools into large amounts of a protein not normally present may well create serious metabolic imbalances, not only within the protein-producing cell but within the plant as a whole. Decreases in seed yield or alterations of other important seed characteristics could easily negate improvements in protein content.

Nitrogen Fixation

The growth of agricultural crops is dependent on an enormous supply of usable nitrogen, either mechanically applied as ammonia, urea, or nitrate fertilizer, or naturally produced in the soil through microbial reduction of atmospheric nitrogen. Increasing energy costs have encouraged research into novel approaches to increase the available supply of naturally reduced nitrogen. Although most organisms cannot assimilate atmospheric nitrogen (N_2), a limited number of prokaryotes are able to reduce N_2 directly to ammonia in a process called nitrogen fixation. The complex of enzymes required for nitrogen fixation has been studied in detail in *Klebsiella pneu-*

moniae, which contains a cluster of 17 contiguous *nif* genes organized in seven operons (*22*). Both the enzymatic machinery and the metabolic controls on nitrogen fixation in *K. pneumoniae* are quite intricate. Information gained from study of this bacterium, which fixes N_2 asymbiotically, is helping to decipher the more complex but agronomically important symbiotic processes of *Rhizobium*. Symbiotic nitrogen fixation occurs within highly differentiated root nodules formed by interactions of *Rhizobium* with plants of the family Leguminosae (soybean, alfalfa, peanut, bean, pea, clover, for example), enabling these plants to grow without addition of nitrogenous fertilizer. The possibilities that increased nitrogen fixation will increase current legume yields or that additional plant varieties could be made capable of carrying out nitrogen fixation are being investigated from several approaches.

The formation of nodules that are effective in nitrogen fixation depends on genetic information present in both the bacterial and host plant cells (*23*). Because *Rhizobium* can be easily manipulated in the laboratory, the potential for generating improvements in the bacterial contribution to symbiotic nitrogen fixation seems high. For example, *Rhizobium*-coded nitrogenase, the enzyme directly responsible for N_2 reduction, has a side reaction that hydrolyzes adenosine triphosphate (ATP) and forms H_2 (*24*). The reaction serves no apparent function and expends considerable energy. Some, but not all, nitrogen-fixing bacteria contain a hydrogenase that regenerates ATP by the oxidation of H_2; the ATP is then available for use in further nitrogen fixation. There is now experimental evidence that strains of bacteria containing the hydrogenase may fix nitrogen more efficiently (*25*). Clearly, introduction of the hydrogenase gene to additional strains of *Rhizobium* has the potential to improve nitrogen fixation and perhaps to increase the yield of legume proteins (*26*).

The potential for improving nitrogen fixation through genetic engineering of host plants is not as well defined. Host proteins are involved in the plant-bacterial symbiosis, but except for leghemoglobin (the protein responsible for protection of the oxygen-sensitive nitrogenase), the functions of host proteins specific for the symbiosis have not yet been resolved (*22*). However, there are examples of variable nitrogen-fixing efficiencies among legume cultivars (*27*). This suggests that exchange or alteration of the "symbiosis genes" in plants might result in enhanced nitrogen fixation efficiency. Until the process is better understood and the genes involved have been identified, we can only speculate on the feasibility of such projects.

Extension of symbiotic or asymbiotic nitrogen fixation to plants which do not now benefit from the process, such as the cereals, would be extremely valuable. Evidence now suggests that free-living nitrogen-fixing bacteria can be encouraged to associate with roots of cereals, enabling the plant host to receive some nitrogen through bacterial nitrogen fixation (*28*). It may be possible to genetically alter the nitrogen-fixing bacteria to bind more tightly to the roots of the cereal and thus create a more beneficial association. However, creation of a new cereal symbiosis which results in nodulation will only be possible when more is known about the host genes that contribute to the nodulation process. The possibility that genes from the bacterial *nif* complex can be moved into cereals by genetic engineering is being explored in several laboratories. However, overcoming the obstacles preventing proper regulation of prokaryotic gene expression in eukaryotic cells will be difficult. In addition, it is unlikely that the host cellular metabolism can be easily adapted to the stringent metabolic requirements for efficient nitrogen fixation even if *nif* gene expression is obtained.

Pest and Pathogen Resistance

A significant proportion of the total world crop production is lost each year because of pest or pathogen damage (*29*). Crop protection is afforded by strict quarantines of produce and crops from infected areas, crop rotation, more sanitary seed preparation and storage, and the use of chemical pesticides. However, the cheapest, and historically one of the most effective, means of combating both pests and disease is through the use of resistant plant varieties. The cultivation cost of resistant plants is no greater than that for susceptible varieties, and the adverse side effects sometimes resulting from chemical control measures can be avoided. It is likely that molecular biology will eventually play a major role in crop protection (*30*) by (i) increasing our understanding of the mechanisms of pathogenicity, (ii) permitting early detection of infection (*31*), (iii) providing means of direct control of disease symptoms and pests, and (iv) enabling us to engineer resistant crop varieties. The most significant practical applications should follow rapidly behind research into the molecular basis for the disease or pest attack. A few specific examples demonstrate the potential for future successes in this area.

The phenomenon of "induced resistance" in plants has an intriguing similarity to immunization by vaccination in mammals. When plants are either inoculated with pathogens or treated with chemicals that cause chronic but localized cell damage, they frequently exhibit enhanced and broad-spectrum resistance to subsequent infection (*32*). Such resistance has been observed with respect to bacterial, fungal, viral, and nematode infections, and the resistance occurs in many, if not all, plant species. The response has been elicited by application to some hosts of either attenuated pathogenic strains or various fractions of destroyed pathogens (*32*). Although the mechanisms of induced resistance are not yet understood, it is apparent that the capability to manipulate these systems in a practical direction will have strong impact on agricultural productivity. It seems likely that herbicides or other crop additives which induce pest resistance will be developed; but it may also be possible (when the mechanisms are known) to engineer plant varieties to exhibit higher levels of broad-spectrum resistance. This may be as conceptually simple as directing plants to constantly produce low levels of endogenous elicitors, or as complex as altering the genetic pathways of resistance.

Several approaches may be used to genetically engineer crop plants with greater insect resistance. A variety of plant secondary metabolites naturally discourage predators through various mechanisms, such as accumulating metabolites that mimic insect hormones thereby upsetting maturation of insects (*33*). The transfer to crop plants of genetic pathways required to synthesize such metabolites may provide resistances not now found in cultivated crops. Alternatively, various polypeptide insecticidal toxins are now in use as biological control agents, including a range of toxins produced in strains of the bacteria *Bacillus thuringiensis* (*34*). While such toxins have the practical ecological advantage of being specific for certain insect species, they now have to be applied to crops in costly spraying programs. The production of such proteins within the cells of genetically engineered plants might provide pest resistance at both reduced cost and with improved environmental safety over present control measures.

Photosynthesis

The ultimate value of plants is their ability to convert solar energy into stored chemical reserves through the processes of photosynthesis. Complex reactions that convert atmospheric CO_2 into carbohydrates and release O_2 to the environment are all carried out either within the chloroplasts of higher plants or in reactions proceeding coordinately between cytoplasmic and organelle enzymatic pathways. Although the chloroplast is dependent on the cell nucleus for information contributing toward its functioning and survival, a separate chloroplast genome, present as 40 to 60 copies of a large circular chromosome, is found within each of the organelles (*35*). The presence of as many as 50 chloroplasts per cell results in the presence of thousands of copies of each chloroplast gene per cell.

Although little is known about the regulation of chloroplast gene expression, new techniques are becoming available to study these mechanisms. Recent development of transformation methods for both the cyanobacterium *Anacystis nidulans* (*36*) and the photosynthetic eukaryote *Chlamydomonas* (*37*) portend rapid progress in elucidating the functions of photosynthetic machinery through analysis and complementation of mutant genes.

As more becomes known of photosynthetic pathways, many areas of potential improvement may be envisaged. Because many enzymes function coordinately during photosynthesis, it is likely that species variation will be found at critical reactions. Transfer of more efficient Calvin cycle enzymes (the pathway responsible for CO_2 fixation) between plant varieties may well provide for higher rates of carbon fixation. For example, ribulosebisphosphate carboxylase (the major enzyme of the Calvin cycle) has been shown in vitro to vary with respect to kinetic rate constant, depending on the plant source of the enzyme (38). This suggests that exchange or modification of genes encoding subunits of the carboxylase might result in an enzyme that provides more efficient CO_2 fixation in the engineered plant. The possibility carries an additional scientific intrigue: one type of the enzyme's two different types of subunits is encoded by chloroplast genes, the other by a small number of nuclear genes (39). Exchange or alteration of genetic information for the two types of subunits therefore depends on our gaining an understanding of and developing the technology for both nuclear and plastid transformations.

Additional prospects for improvement of photosynthetic capabilities may be found in the exchange of various photosystem components between different plants to optimize electron transfer. An increased electron flow rate through photosystems I and II might raise the level of light saturation, enabling more efficient light harvesting (40). The number and complexities of photosynthetic reactions will make this area extremely attractive for genetic manipulation. Ironically, the complexity of the process will probably delay many genetic engineering successes until a more complete understanding of photosynthetic interactions is gained.

Stress Tolerance

Despite continuing efforts to improve cultivation practices, crop plants will always be subject to a variety of environmental extremes. In even the most productive agricultural regions, drought and temperature stress can occur throughout the growing season, resulting in injury and reduced plant yield. As more suboptimal lands are brought under cultivation, or as continued use alters the soils of current growing regions of the world, predictable stresses are becoming widespread: heavily irrigated soils are plagued by salt buildup and mineral toxicity; irrigation water supplies are being depleted in some regions that will soon be subjected to chronic drought; continued and expanded use of marginal land results in trace element deficiencies and the need for increased use of remedial fertilization. It is therefore apparent that crop plants that are tolerant of such extremes as drought, high salt, mineral deficiency or toxicity, or radical temperature alteration would be valuable.

When stress resistance characteristics are variable within a crop species, classical breeding programs can be devised to transfer the trait to new cultivars of economic importance (41). However, plant species of questionable economic value (such as weeds) frequently exhibit dramatic stress resistance. While such plants are incompatible for breeding with cultivated species, it is tempting to consider transfer of resistance traits by genetic engineering. Extensive research efforts are being directed toward developing a greater understanding of the physiological, biochemical, and genetic bases for responses of plants to the environment.

Many of the adaptations of plants to such stress as water deficit or high temperatures involve highly specialized plant morphology. For example, a reduction in leaf surface area and the presence of fewer stomatal openings promotes greater plant water retention (42). Unfortunately, such structural features are likely to result from the interaction of many different genes, the molecular controls of which are not yet accessible. Metabolic responses that are directly induced by stress, such as reductions in cell growth rate (42) or the synthesis of new classes of "heat-shock" proteins (43), are more easily studied in the laboratory. Further research into these areas may result in the identification of genes involved in stress responses, and eventually may suggest ways to engineer resistance in new plant varieties.

Alternative Applications

The few systems mentioned above have been widely discussed in recent years because of the tremendous potential economic impact of improvement. The complex functions of most of these systems, involving many genes of unknown identity, make them now difficult to exploit. However, the improbability that we will see rapid successes in such complex areas as improving plant protein levels or in the construction of plants that fix their own nitrogen does not mean that plant genetic engineering is far from reality. Transfer of single gene traits is now technically feasible.

It is likely that herbicide-resistant plants will soon be developed through transformation technology. A single new gene may be all that is required for this trait and direct selection for transformed cells in tissue culture is provided by the herbicide resistance. Some pathogen resistances may be only slightly more difficult to transfer, since direct selection may again be possible for the desired resistance, both in tissue culture and in the intact plant. Whether or not the initial plant varieties resulting from such experiments can be easily integrated into practical breeding programs is, for now, an unanswerable question—we cannot predict how such genetic alterations will affect the metabolism of an organism as complex as a higher plant.

A recurring problem in considering any specific application of genetic engineering in plants is the lack of understanding of the molecular genetics involved. Before practical applications can be routinely expected, basic research is required in almost all areas of plant molecular biology. In particular, novel approaches are needed to aid in the identification of the genetic components of plant characteristics. Model systems such as yeast, algae, or bacteria, which are more conveniently manipulated under laboratory conditions than are higher plants, will be useful for some applications and will perhaps aid in isolation of some single or closely linked genes. More complex traits, those which are not expressed in model systems or which are polygenic in character, will need to be explored in other ways. One promising mechanism may involve the use of transposable elements. Plant transposons, analogous to those in prokaryotes, are genetic elements that are able to move to new locations in the plant genome (44). Upon moving into a specific genetic locus, a transposon may alter an identifiable gene function. With the use of recombinant DNA technology, it is possible to isolate and characterize DNA surrounding the site of transposon insertion, thus identifying genes responsible for a specific trait (45). It may be possible in this way to characterize the major components of some of the more complex plant traits, where genes cannot be identified in other ways.

Conclusions

The potential for improvement of crop plants through genetic engineering seems vast. Although only a few broad areas have been considered in this chapter, it should be apparent that the present limit on application of the many ideas for crop improvement is basic understanding of the genetic components responsible for plant characteristics. Once genes necessary for valuable plant traits have been identified, there will rapidly be a variety of practical applications. Initially it should be possible to develop convenient germplasm screening methods for the plant breeder, reducing the time required to organize and analyze genetic crosses. Certainly the transfer of genes into new plant species beyond the range of classical breeding will be attempted, and as we delve more into plant biochemistry, molecular biology, and physiology, new applications and new approaches will naturally evolve. Plant molecular biologists can be expected to follow the leadership of scientists working on the better developed animal and bacterial systems; however, recent excitement in plant research is certain to stimulate faster progress in plant genetic engineering. Besides the obvious value to food production, advances in plant biotechnology will contribute to health care (novel pharmaceu-

ticals and more efficient pharmaceutical production), to floriculture (new species of decorative plants), to forestry (acceleration of breeding programs), to the fiber industry (improved and increased fiber production), and to generation of usable energy (production of biomass for conversion to ethanol). The future of plant genetic engineering will be exciting, as much because of applications we cannot yet predict as because of those already expected.

References and Notes

1. C. H. Hanson, S. G. Turnipseed, N. T. Powell, J. M. Good, D. L. Klingman, in *Introduction to Crop Protection*, W. B. Ennis, Ed. (American Society of Agronomy and Crop Science, Madison, Wis., 1979), p. 91.
2. R. B. Goldberg, in *Genome Organization and Expression in Plants*, C. J. Leaver, Ed. (Plenum, New York, 1980), p. 117.
3. M. Freeling and D. S. K. Cheng, *Genet. Res.* 31, 107 (1978).
4. F. Colbere-Garapin, F. Horodniceanu, P. Kourilsky, A.-C. Garapin, *J. Mol. Biol.* 150, 1 (1981).
5. F. A. Krens *et al.*, *Nature (London)* 296, 72 (1982).
6. R. J. Shepard, *Annu. Rev. Plant Physiol.* 30, 405 (1979).
7. S. H. Howell, L. L. Walker, R. M. Walden, *Nature (London)* 293, 483 (1981).
8. L. W. Ream and M. P. Gordon, *Science* 218, 854 (1982).
9. I. Zaenen, N. Van Larebeke, H. Teuchy, M. Van Montagu, J. Schell, *J. Mol. Biol.* 86, 109 (1974); B. Watson, T. C. Currier, M. P. Gordon, M.-D. Chilton, E. W. Nester, *J. Bacteriol.* 123, 255 (1975).
10. M.-D. Chilton, M. H. Drummond, D. J. Merlo, D. Sciaky, A. L. Montoya, M. P. Gordon, E. W. Nester, *Cell* 11, 263 (1977).
11. A. C. Braun, *Am. J. Bot.* 34, 234 (1947); M. Van Montagu and J. Schell, *Curr. Top. Microbiol. Immunol.* 96, 237 (1982).
12. A. Petit, S. Delhaye, J. Tempe, G. Morel, *Physiol. Veg.* 8, 205 (1970); P. M. Klapwijk and R. A. Schilperoort, *J. Bacteriol.* 139, 424 (1979); N. Murai and J. D. Kemp, *Proc. Natl. Acad. Sci. U.S.A.* 79, 86 (1982).
13. F.-M. Yang and R. B. Simpson, *Proc. Natl. Acad. Sci. U.S.A.* 78, 4151 (1981); L. Otten, H. DeGreve, J. P. Hernalsteens, M. Van Montagu, O. Scheider, J. Straub, J. Schell, *Mol. Gen. Genet.* 183, 209 (1981); H. DeGreve, J. Leemans, J. P. Hernalsteens, L. Thia-Toong, M. DeBeuckeleer, L. Willmitzer, L. Otten, M. Van Montagu, J. Schell, *Nature (London)* 300, 752 (1982).

14. K. A. Barton, A. Binns, A. J. M. Matzke, M.-D. Chilton, *Cell* **32**, 1033 (1983).
15. R. Chaleff, *Science* **219**, 676 (1983); R. G. Sears and E. L. Deckard, *Crop Sci.* **22**, 546 (1982).
16. R. N. Oram and R. D. Brock, *J. Aust. Inst. Agric. Sci.* **38**, 163 (1972).
17. E. Derbyshire, D. J. Wright, D. Boulter, *Phytochemistry* **15**, 3 (1976).
18. O. E. Nelson, *Adv. Agron.* **21**, 171 (1969).
19. G. Hagen and I. Rubenstein, *Gene* **13**, 239 (1981); E. D. Lewis, G. Hagen, J. I. Mullins, P. N. Mascia, W. D. Park, W. D. Benton, I Rubenstein, *ibid.*, p. 205; M. D. Marks and B. A. Larkins, *J. Biol. Chem.* **257**, 9976 (1982).
20. K. Pedersen, J. Devereux, D. R. Wilson, E. Sheldon, B. Larkins, *Cell* **29**, 1015 (1982); P. Argos *et al.*, *J. Biol. Chem.* **257**, 9984 (1982).
21. M. A. Schuler, B. F. Ladin, J. C. Pollaco, G. Freyer, R. N. Beachy, *Nucleic Acids Res.* **10**, 8245 (1982).
22. G. P. Roberts and W. J. Brill, *Annu. Rev. Microbiol.* **35**, 207 (1981).
23. J. E. Beringer, N. Brewin, A. W. B. Johnston, H. Schulman, D. A. Hopwood, *Proc. R. Soc. London Ser. B* **204**, 219 (1979).
24. R. W. F. Hardy, E. Knight, Jr., A. J. D'Eustachio, *Biochem. Biophys. Res. Commun.* **20**, 539 (1965).
25. R. O. D. Dixon, *Arch. Mikrobiol.* **85**, 193 (1972); K. R. Schubert and H. J. Evans, *Proc. Natl. Acad. Sci. U.S.A.* **73**, 1207 (1976); K. R. Schubert, N. T. Jennings, H. J. Evans, *Plant Physiol.* **61**, 398 (1978).
26. F. J. Hanus, S. L. Albrecht, R. M. Zablotowicz, D. W. Emerich, S. A. Russell, H. J. Evans, *Agron. J.* **73**, 368 (1981).
27. T. J. Wacek and W. J. Brill, *Crop Sci.* **16**, 519 (1976); M. W. Seetin and D. K. Barnes, *ibid.* **17**, 783 (1977).
28. P. van Berkum and B. B. Bohlool, *Microbiol. Rev.* **44**, 491 (1980); S. W. Ela, M. A. Anderson, W. J. Brill, *Plant Physiol.* **70**, 1564 (1982).
29. G. E. Russell, Ed., *Plant Breeding for Pest and Disease Resistance* (Butterworth, London, 1981).
30. R. C. Staples and G. H. Toenniessen, in *Plant Disease Control, Resistance and Susceptibility*, R. C. Staples and G. H. Toenniessen, Eds. (Wiley, New York, 1981), p. 299.
31. R. A. Owens and T. O. Diener, *Science* **213**, 670 (1981).
32. J. Kuc, in *Active Defense Mechanisms in Plants*, R. K. S. Wood, Ed. (Plenum, New York, 1982), p. 157.
33. W. S. Bowers, in *Insect Biology in the Future*, M. Locke and D. S. Smith, Eds. (Academic Press, New York, 1980), p. 613.
34. L. K. Miller, A. J. Lingg, L. A. Bulla, Jr., *Science* **219**, 715 (1983); P. Luthy, *FEMS Microb. Lett.* **8**, 1 (1980).
35. S. A. Boffey and R. M. Leech, *Plant Physiol.* **69**, 1387 (1982).
36. C. J. Kuhlemeier, W. E. Borrias, C. A. M. J. J. Van den Hondel, G. A. Van Arkel, *Mol. Gen. Genet.* **184**, 249 (1982).
37. J.-D. Rochaix and J. Van Dillewijn, *Nature (London)* **296**, 70 (1982).
38. J. R. Seeman and J. A. Berry, *Carnegie Inst. Washington Yearb.* **81**, 78 (1982).
39. J. R. Bedbrook, D. M. Coen, A. R. Beaton, L. Bogorad, A. Rich, *J. Biol. Chem.* **254**, 905 (1979); R. Broglie, G. Bellemare, S. G. Bartlett, N.-H. Chua, A. R. Cashmore, *Proc. Natl. Acad. Sci. U.S.A.* **78**, 7304 (1981).
40. R. M. Gifford and L. T. Evans, *Annu. Rev. Plant Physiol.* **32**, 485 (1981).
41. J. M. Morgan, in *Adaptation of Plants to Water and High Temperature Stress*, N. C. Turner and P. J. Kramer, Eds. (Wiley, New York, 1980), p. 369.
42. J. E. Begg, in *ibid.*, p. 33.
43. J. L. Key, C. Y. Lin, Y. M. Chen, *Proc. Natl. Acad. Sci. U.S.A.* **78**, 3526 (1981).
44. B. McClintock, *Brookhaven Symp. Biol.* **8**, 58 (1956).
45. B. Burr and F. A. Burr, *Cell* **29**, 977 (1982).

11. Isolation of Agronomically Useful Mutants from Plant Cell Cultures

R. S. Chaleff

It was not until the 1930's that several prior decades of research culminated in the successful propagation of plant organs and tissues in culture. Thereafter, progress in plant tissue culture was rapid. The techniques of culture in vitro were extended to many species and, aided by advances in the knowledge of plant hormones that were made in part through use of tissue culture, regeneration of plants from cultured tissues was achieved in the late 1950's. The first application of these developments was to the clonal multiplication of plants. The ability to regenerate large numbers of plants from masses of disorganized tissue (callus) proliferated in vitro and from cultured organs and axillary buds proved more efficient than conventional methods of asexual plant propagation. The lists in recent reviews (*1, 2*) of the hundreds of species that have been propagated through tissue culture document the extent to which this application of plant tissue culture technology has been developed and utilized.

In the 1960's, research in plant cell and tissue culture produced a number of achievements that individually represented significant technical advances and refinements. But when considered collectively these contributions effected a qualitative change in the conceptual view of the field. In 1960 Bergmann (*3*) demonstrated that single cultured cells plated in an agar medium would divide and form calluses. That same year Cocking (*4*) introduced an enzymatic procedure for isolating large numbers of protoplasts from higher plant tissues. In 1965 Vasil and Hildebrandt (*5*) demonstrated the totipotency of single plant cells by accomplishing the development of a complete and fertile plant from a single isolated somatic cell. Shortly thereafter Guha and Maheshwari (*6*) obtained haploid plants from immature pollen (microspores) contained within cultured *Datura* anthers. And in 1971 Nagata and Takebe (*7*) regenerated plants from cultured tobacco protoplasts. However, the turning point was in the realization that these discoveries, by making possible (albeit with only a small number of species) the experimental manipulations summarized in Fig. 1, conferred upon higher plants many of the attributes that had made microbes so amenable to genetic study. With the availability of large populations of physiologically and developmentally uniform haploid cells came the ability to select defined mutants.

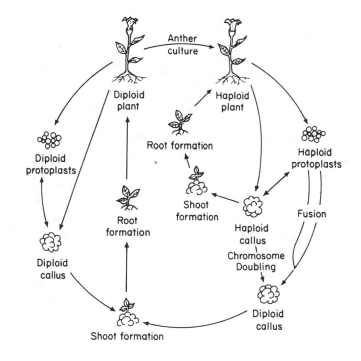

Fig. 1. Summary of experimental manipulations possible with *Nicotiana*, *Datura*, and *Petunia* (*13*). Haploid plants are obtained by culturing anthers or pollen of a diploid plant. Protoplasts capable of wall regeneration and subsequent cell division can be isolated from intact plant tissues and from callus cultures. The formation of shoots and roots from callus tissue is accomplished by altering the hormone composition of the medium.

Genetic analyses could then be performed by conventional methods with regenerated diploid plants. These developments reached fruition in Carlson's (*8*) isolation of auxotrophic mutants from cultured tobacco cells.

Other opportunities for genetic experimentation with higher plants also became evident at this time. The technique of protoplast fusion is reviewed by Shepard and colleagues (*9*) in chapter 12 and the possibility of introducing foreign DNA (genetic transformation) is considered by Barton and Brill (*10*) in chapter 10. Accordingly, this discussion is confined to the application of plant cell culture to mutant isolation.

Genetic Variability in Cell Cultures

The use of tissue culture for clonal propagation is based on the assumption that tissues remain genetically stable when excised from the parent plant and placed into culture. This assumption is largely valid when plant multiplication occurs by development of axillary buds or adventitious shoots directly from explanted organs. However, in cases in which shoot formation is induced from callus tissues, aberrant plants are often produced. Moreover, the frequency of such aberrant types increases with the length of time that the callus is maintained in vitro (*1, 11*).

The phenotypic variability observed among cultured cells and regenerated plants cannot be assumed to result only from genetic events, which include changes of nucleotide sequence and of chromosome number and structure. Physiological responses to the anomalous environment of the culture vessel and epigenetic changes also can contribute to such variability. Epigenetic events reflect altered levels of gene expression (resulting from abnormal operation rather than from mutation of regulatory mechanisms) that are relatively stable in that they persist through mitosis to be expressed by daughter cells. However, in contrast to altered phenotypes having a genetic basis, those resulting from epigenetic changes tend not to be expressed in regenerated plants or their progeny (*12, 13*). For the present, transmission through sexual crosses provides an acceptable criterion by which to distinguish genetic from epigenetic changes. However, this distinction provides us only with an operational definition that should not be applied too rigidly. Certain types of genetic change, such as gene amplification, can be unstable even through mitotic divisions in the absence of selection, and others, such as aneuploidy, often are not gametically transmitted.

Perhaps the earliest and most direct evidence of the genetic variability of cell cultures was furnished by nuclear cytology. Karyotypic variation provides visible proof of genetic heterogeneity within a population of cultured cells. Polyploidy, aneuploidy, and chromosomal rearrangements have been identified in cell cultures derived from a wide variety of plant species (*14*). But because the majority of these studies were conducted with cell cultures derived from tissue explants, they served to establish the fact, rather than the origin, of such variability. In such cases, one cannot determine whether unusual chromosome numbers or structures observed in cultured cell populations arose from the occurrence of mitotic irregularities in vitro or by multiplication of karyotypically abnormal cells present in the initial explant.

One means of resolving this question is by examination of cell cultures initiat-

ed from single cells. If variability is not generated during mitotic division in vitro, all members of the cloned population will be identical: any heterogeneity that is present in that population must have originated in culture. Consequently, the observation of cells of different chromosome numbers (diploid, polyploid, and aneuploid) in callus cultures obtained by cloning single cells of carrot (*15*) and tobacco (*16*) clearly demonstrated the occurrence of genetic variability in vitro. Pollen culture, and certain anther culture systems in which callus formation proceeds from the immature pollen contained within the cultured anther rather than from the surrounding somatic tissue, also provide single cells of a specified ploidy that can be stimulated to divide in vitro. Thus, the recovery of diploid and polyploid plants from pollen-derived callus cultures of *Oryza sativa* furnished additional evidence of abnormal mitoses in cultured cells (*17, 18*).

Another means of illustrating the occurrence of spontaneous genetic changes in cultured cells is by genetic characterization of novel cellular phenotypes. Much to their surprise, Chaleff and Keil (*19*) discovered that more than half of all tobacco cell lines isolated on the basis of resistance to the herbicide picloram were also resistant to hydroxyurea. Crosses with regenerated plants demonstrated that in the three cases analyzed, resistance to hydroxyurea was caused by a single dominant nuclear mutation. In two cases, the mutations conferring resistance to hydroxyurea (*HuR*) and to picloram (*PmR*) were genetically unlinked. Yet the callus culture from which the mutants were derived was sensitive to hydroxyurea and resistance arose only rarely among populations of sensitive cells and could be isolated only by deliberate selection. Moreover, the *HuR* mutations by themselves did not provide any detectable resistance to picloram, nor did they enhance the degree of picloram resistance conferred by the *PmR* mutations. Thus, the *HuR* mutations represented independent genetic events that occurred spontaneously in culture and were recovered in the absence of any known selective pressure, although their appearance seemed related in some way to picloram resistance.

An exceptionally extensive and detailed analysis of the frequency and origin of variability in tobacco cell cultures was reported by Barbier and Dulieu (*20*). By constructing tobacco plants heterozygous at two loci for recessive mutations affecting chlorophyll synthesis, the occurrence of genetic events at either locus could be detected by the appearance of the recessive phenotypes in regenerated plants. The type of event responsible for the altered phenotype was then determined by crossing these plants with individuals homozygous for one or the other mutation. The frequency of genetic changes in populations of plants regenerated directly from explanted cotyledons via induced bud formation represented the amount of variability preexisting in cells of the intact plant (or arising during dedifferentiation and embryogenesis). The frequency of genetically altered plants in populations regenerated from callus cultures provided an estimate of the extent to which variability accumulated during propagation in vitro. Variability among plants regenerated from callus cultures was approximately ten times greater than among plants developed from cotyledonary buds. Interestingly, the greatest amount of variability was generated during the first passage in culture and little increase was observed in subsequent passages.

These several lines of evidence confirm that genetic variability arises spontaneously in plant cell cultures. But as yet we know nothing of the mechanisms by which these changes occur. They may simply be induced by a component of the culture medium. Alternatively, they may result from the breakdown of normal cellular or mitotic processes or from the activation of genetic systems, such as transposable elements, that are normally repressed. Another possibility is that such aberrant events occur at the same frequency in the intact plant, but that some of these mutations or genomic rearrangements either confer a growth advantage in culture that permits their selective proliferation or (as can be imagined for mutations affecting photosynthesis) selection against them is less stringent in vitro than in vivo.

On the one hand, the genetic instability of cultured plant cells can be considered a nuisance. It is more than likely that plants regenerated from cell cultures that have been maintained for a substantial period of time will carry deleterious genetic changes in addition to those of interest. Such excessive variation will confuse analysis of the desired trait and will necessitate outcrossing to incorporate that trait into an agronomically useful form. But on the other hand, the apparently mutagenic effects of cell culture provide a wealth of variability that can be screened for novel characteristics. By treatment with chemical or physical mutagens, the genetic variability of cell cultures can be even further enlarged. The ensuing discussion focuses on the difficulties and successes of attempts to date to isolate mutants of potential agronomic value from this newfound resource of genetic variability.

Screening Regenerated Plants for Desirable Characteristics

The variability present in cell cultures is ultimately visible in populations of regenerated plants. In some of the earliest studies of this type, differences were found in chromosome number, stature, auricle length, pubescence, and isozyme banding patterns among plants regenerated from cultured sugarcane cells (*21*). Because sugarcane plants are mixoploid (that is, not all somatic cells have the same number of chromosomes), some phenotypic variability was to be expected in addition to any variability that might be generated in vitro. Callus cultures established from mixoploid tissues will themselves be composed of cells of different chromosome complements from which plants of a range of chromosome numbers will be regenerated. It was not long before such plant populations were being examined for traits of agronomic significance. Screening for resistance to eyespot disease was performed by treating sugarcane plants regenerated from callus and suspension cultures with the toxin elaborated by *Helminthosporium sacchari*, the causative agent of the disease. An astonishing 15 to 20 percent of the regenerated plants proved resistant. Similarly, resistance to Fiji disease was expressed by 4 of 38 plants that had been regenerated from callus of a susceptible sugarcane variety. Regenerated plants possessing increased sucrose content and downy mildew resistance were also identified. Although no reports have appeared to date on the stability of these traits through sexual crosses, they have been maintained through several generations of vegetative propagation.

Enormous variability has also appeared among populations of potato plants regenerated from leaf mesophyll protoplasts. One study of 65 protoplast-derived clones (vegetatively propagated descendants of single plants) reported significant variation for 26 of the 35 morphological and physiological traits monitored (*22*). As in the case of sugarcane, some of this variability was manifested as resistance to diseases to which the parental cultivar was sensitive. Four clones resistant to early blight were identified by inoculating leaves of 500 regenerated plants with a crude toxin preparation obtained from cultures of *Alternaria solani*. Twenty clones of a population of 800 survived inoculation with the late blight fungus *Phytophthora infestans*. Resistance to both fungal diseases was expressed by subsequent vegetative generations (*23*).

Because the partial or complete infertility of most important sugarcane and potato cultivars makes sexual breeding of these species difficult, it is perhaps not surprising that the first reports of variability among plants regenerated from cultured cells came from studies with these species. Plants regenerated from callus cultures usually vary from the parental cultivar in only one or a few characteristics. This frequency of variation—sufficiently high that most individuals are altered in some way, but not so high that the majority of these individuals possess deleterious alterations— makes screening of regenerated plants a promising alternative to sexual breeding as a means of improving existing cultivars.

But the studies with vegetatively propagated crops leave unanswered two very important questions. First, although we know from the preceding section that genetic changes do occur in cultured cells, we do not know that the specific phenotypic alterations observed in the regenerated sugarcane and potato plants result from mutational events. And second, if these changes do represent genetic events, are they of a type—such as aneuploidy or chromosomal rearrangement—that by causing gametic inviability cannot be maintained in seed-propagated crops?

These questions have been addressed by several investigations on cereal species. A wide range of morphological abnormalities were observed among plants regenerated from oat callus. In many cases inheritance of these traits was followed through several generations of self-fertilization (24). Populations of plants regenerated from callus cultures initiated from rice seeds also displayed phenotypic variability. Differences from the parental variety were found in plant height, morphology, chlorophyll content, heading date, and fertility. Only 28 percent of the regenerated plants were not altered in at least one of these characters. The genetic basis of these phenotypic alterations was established by their expression in two subsequent sexual generations (25).

The genetic diversity of plants emerging from disorganized callus tissues provides the breeder with a means of introducing variability into established cultivars without the use of sexual crosses. But screening for desirable types still must be accomplished by conventional methods, which require large amounts of land and labor. In some cases another application of cell culture may provide a more efficient alternative.

Direct Selection in vitro

One of the major advantages afforded by cell culture for genetic experimentation with higher plants is that it makes possible direct selection for novel phenotypes from large physiologically and developmentally uniform populations of cells grown under defined conditions. Millions of cells, each representing a potential plant, can be cultured in a single petri dish 9 centimeters in diameter. Incorporation of toxic or growth inhibitory compounds in the medium allows growth only of the few resistant cells in the population, and from these isolates plants can ultimately be regenerated (Fig. 2). With recognition of the similarities between cultured plant cells and microorganisms came the expectation that all of the extraordinary feats of genetic experimentation accomplished with microbes would soon be realized with plants. But because of the many ways in which cultured plant cells are unlike microbes, these expectations thus far have not been well fulfilled.

Perhaps it is too often overlooked that, in contrast to microbes, which are autonomous units that have limited capacity for differentiation, plant cells evolved as components of highly complex and differentiated multicellular structures. Doubtless plant cells perform many of the same elemental activities and therefore have many features in common with unicellular organisms. However, as the multicellular plant (metaphyte) is the product of cellular functions and relationships that are unknown to the microbe, the cells of the metaphyte correspondingly must possess some properties and capabilities very different from those of the microbe. Some of these characteristics of cultured plant cells make difficult experimental manipulations that are taken for granted in microbial systems. For example, plant cells tend to grow in culture as aggregates. In addition, single plant cells cannot multiply when placed in an infinite volume of

138

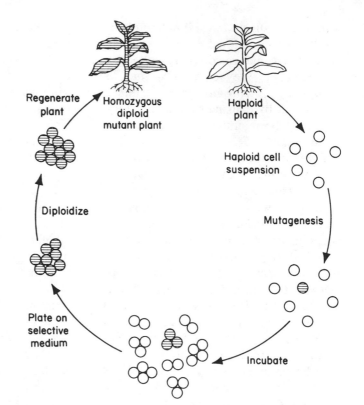

Fig. 2. Schematic representation of a general procedure for positive selection for mutants in plant cell cultures. Selection for recessive, as well as dominant, mutations is made possible by establishing cell cultures from haploid plants. Mutagenesis increases the genetic variability of the cell population, and incubation under nonselective conditions is necessary to allow expression of any newly induced mutant traits. After transfer to a medium that favors growth of mutant (filled circles) over non-mutant (open circles) cells, cultures composed largely or entirely of mutant cells are obtained. Finally, diploidization, occurring either spontaneously or in response to chemical treatment, is required for fertility of the regenerated plants.

Labels in figure: Regenerate plant; Homozygous diploid mutant plant; Haploid plant; Haploid cell suspension; Diploidize; Mutagenesis; Plate on selective medium; Incubate

medium, but require a minimum inoculum density to achieve self-sustaining growth and division. And genetic analysis must await the time-consuming regeneration of plants and the completion of a very lengthy life cycle. But a unique feature of plant cell culture that imposes the most severe restriction on its use for genetic experimentation is that selection for a novel phenotype is conducted at a level of differentiation distinct from that at which phenotypic expression is ultimately desired. This last qualification has several consequences of special significance in selecting at the cellular level for genetic modifications of agronomic traits, which, for the most part, are products of differentiated cells, tissues, and organs present only in the whole plant.

The first constraint imposed by selec-tion in vitro results from the fact that not all traits expressed by the whole plant are expressed by the cultured cell. Of course, one cannot select for modifications of a trait that is not expressed. This point is illustrated by the example of drought tolerance.

If a breeder identified a drought tolerant variety, he or she might look for deeper root penetration, altered control of stomatal closure, or a thicker cuticle as a basis for this phenotype. But these characteristics are functions not only of highly differentiated cells, but of the organization of such cells into complex organs and of interactions between these organs. At present, it is difficult to imagine how the expression of such traits could be elicited from single cells in culture. Accordingly, the somatic cell geneticist must accept that certain traits are exclusively whole plant functions and as such now lie beyond his or her reach. This is not to say that cell culture cannot be used to modify whole plant traits, such as drought tolerance, but only that this technique restricts one to approaches that involve selection for alterations of basic cellular functions. Thus, in applying cell culture to the problem of drought tolerance, one could not expect to select mutants with an altered root architecture. However, it might be possible to select cells capable of regulating their osmotic potential by production of osmotically active solutes. Protoplasts or cells possessing this capability could preferentially survive culture in a hypertonic medium.

Comparative studies on the susceptibility of whole plants and callus cultures to salt suggest that this trait can be effected by several different mechanisms—some acting at the cellular level and others only at the whole plant level. Callus cultures of the halophyte glasswort (*Salicornia*) are as sensitive to NaCl as are callus cultures of cabbage, sweet clover, and sorghum (*26*). But the relative degrees of salt tolerance of callus cultures of two barley species (*Hordeum vulgare* and *H. jubatum*) seem to correspond to those of the whole plants (*27*). These results indicate that one could select in culture for a mechanism of salt tolerance like that in barley, but not for one of the type operating in the halophyte. Salt tolerant cell lines have been selected from cell cultures of several species, but plants have been regenerated only in the case of tobacco. These plants and their progeny survived irrigation with a solution containing a salt concentration lethal to normal plants. However, inheritance of salt tolerance did not fit a conventional pattern and the

possibility remains that tolerance is due to adaptive changes (such as an altered membrane composition) that are transmitted maternally in crosses rather than from a true mutation (*28*).

Other whole plant traits of agronomic importance such as yield, leaf canopy area, grain quality, and many types of pest resistance may prove less accessible by an in vitro approach. Not only are these traits not expressed by cultured cells, but our poor understanding of their molecular and cellular bases prevents identification of correlative cellular functions for which in vitro selection schemes might be devised. Rather ironically, cell culture grants us the general ability to select for mutant types, but precludes selection for many agronomically desirable features that are not expressed by cultured cells.

The second limitation of mutant selection in vitro can be stated as the converse of the first: Not all traits expressed by the cultured cell are expressed by the whole plant. The failure of a regenerated plant to express the novel phenotype of a selected cell line may have any of several causes. As mentioned earlier, phenotypic alterations resulting from epigenetic changes will usually be reversed by the processes of differentiation and meiosis. But expression of genetic alterations also can be developmentally dependent. Function of the mutated gene simply may be restricted to the state of differentiation represented by cultured cells. In some cases developmentally controlled repression of the mutated gene may be accompanied by the activation of distinct genes encoding enzymes with similar catalytic activities (isozymes). The developmental stage in which these nonmutant isozymes are synthesized will appear phenotypically normal, even though the plant harbors a mutant allele of the gene that is predominantly expressed in cultured cells. It is possibly as a consequence of the importance of polyploidization in their evolution that plants possess large numbers of isozymes (29).

To complicate matters further, plants regenerated from mutant cell cultures and in which the altered gene is fully expressed also can appear normal. Such is the case for tobacco mutants that were selected in vitro on the basis of resistance to isonicotinic acid hydrazide (INH), an inhibitor of glycine decarboxylation in the glycolate pathway of photorespiration. The function of the photorespiratory pathway in higher plants is not understood. But because it is a competitor of photosynthetic carbon fixation, elimination of this pathway is considered a possible means of increasing plant productivity.

As a first step toward devising genetic blocks that would decrease photorespiration, mutants resistant to INH were isolated from haploid tobacco cell cultures that had been irradiated with ultraviolet light. The growth of progeny seedlings from plants regenerated from INH-resistant cell lines was as sensitive to INH as was the growth of normal seedlings. However, callus cultures established from plants regenerated from these resistant cell lines and from their progeny were resistant. Thus, INH-resistance has a genetic basis and its expression is restricted to the cellular level (30). By direct biochemical assay glycine decarboxylase activities in both resistant callus cultures and in leaves of mutant plants were shown to be less sensitive to inhibition by INH than were the activities in the corresponding normal tissues. Cosegregation of INH resistance and an altered glycine decarboxylase activity in sexual crosses strongly suggest that the reduced sensitivity of this enzyme complex to INH is the basis for the resistance phenotype (31). But although this biochemical alteration appears in both callus and plant, only callus and not seedling growth displays resistance to INH.

Disease resistance was the first trait of agronomic interest for which selection at the cell level was rewarded by expression by the whole plant. In selecting for disease resistance in vitro, cells are plated on a medium supplemented with a lethal concentration of the disease toxin. Consequently, this procedure is applicable only in cases in which a toxin produced by the microbial pathogen is primarily responsible for the disease symptoms. The wildfire disease of tobacco seemed to provide just such an experimental system. This disease is caused by a bacterial pathogen, *Pseudomonas tabaci*, which elaborates a toxin that produces chlorosis of leaf tissue. Resistant cell lines were selected by exposing populations of mutagenically treated haploid tobacco protoplasts or cells to a growth-inhibitory concentration of methionine sulfoximine, an analog of the wildfire toxin that elicits the same characteristic disease symptoms as does the natural bacterial toxin (32). The chlorosis that normally develops on leaves of the parent plant in response to inoculation with either *P. tabaci* or a solution of methionine sulfoximine did not appear following inoculation of leaves of plants regenerated from three resistant cell lines. Moreover, resistance segregated among progeny of sexual crosses in accordance with conventional Mendelian patterns. But the success of this experiment was only partial. Although inoculation with either methionine sulfoximine or *P. tabaci* did not cause bleaching of mutant leaf tissue, small necrotic spots did develop on leaves of mutant plants at the point of inoculation with the bacterial culture. These lesions resembled those obtained from infection of tobacco with *P. angulata*, a variety of *P. tabaci* that does not produce toxin. Therefore, it is apparent that selection for resistance to methionine sulfoximine yielded plants that were insensitive to the action of the toxin itself but that were still susceptible to other deleterious effects of bacterial infection.

Selection for toxin resistance among cultured cells has also been used to isolate plants resistant to southern corn leaf blight (*33*). *Dreschslera maydis*, the causal agent of the disease, produces a toxin to which both maize plants carrying the Texas male sterile cytoplasm (*cms*-T) and callus cultures derived from such plants are susceptible, but to which plants and callus possessing normal nonsterile cytoplasm are resistant. Because male sterility is of great advantage for hybrid seed production, it is desirable to introduce resistance to the fungal pathogen into the male sterile cytoplasm. To this end *cms*-T callus cultures were transferred to medium supplemented with a crude toxin preparation. Toxin-resistant cell lines were isolated and plants regenerated. All plants regenerated from callus cultures that had been maintained on selective medium for five passages or more were resistant to the toxin. But the majority of these toxin-resistant plants were male-fertile and the sterility of the remainder was due to something other than *cms*-T cytoplasm, since none of these plants could function as either a male or female parent, and in most cases floral organs were deformed. It is probable that the sterility of these plants resulted from random aberrations generated during propagation in vitro. Both the fertility and toxin response of progeny produced by crosses with toxin-resistant regenerated plants always resembled that of the maternal parent. These progeny were also infected with *D. maydis* spores, and in all cases the reactions to the fungus and to the partially purified toxin solution were the same. Thus, in contrast to the results obtained by selection of methionine sulfoximine resistance in tobacco cell cultures, selection for resistance of maize callus to the *D. maydis* toxin produced plants that were also resistant to the causal organism. These experiments were repeated by others with, for the most part, similar results (*34*). However, a curious difference in the latter experiments was the recovery of fertile toxin-resistant plants from control *cms*-T callus cultures that had never been subjected to selection. Nevertheless, in neither set of experiments was the desired product of a male-sterile disease-resistant maize plant obtained.

Perhaps in the immediate future greater practical benefit is to be realized from the application of in vitro selection methods to the isolation of plant mutants altered in the control of amino acid biosynthesis. The nutritional quality of a food crop may be substantially improved by genetic modifications effecting increased production of amino acids that are at present limiting to protein quality.

A means of selecting such mutants is provided by the feedback sensitivities of amino acid biosynthetic enzymes. In maize, the activities of aspartokinase and homoserine dehydrogenase, two enzymes of the pathway for the synthesis of the essential amino acids lysine, methionine, threonine, and isoleucine, are inhibited by lysine and threonine, respectively. Therefore, in the presence of excess lysine and threonine, methionine biosynthesis is interrupted and cell growth is inhibited. However, mutant cells producing an altered enzyme that is insensitive to end-product inhibition will be able to grow under these conditions.

A cell line resistant to growth inhibition by a mixture of lysine and threonine was isolated from maize callus cultures that had been treated with the mutagen sodium azide (35). Fertile plants were regenerated and genetic crosses demonstrated that resistance was inherited as a single semidominant nuclear mutation. Homozygous mutant kernels contained as much as 100-fold more free threonine than did normal kernels. The levels of free methionine, serine, and proline were elevated three- to fourfold and the free pool sizes of the remaining amino acids were essentially unchanged. Although the threonine content of seed protein was not altered, the magnitude of the increase in free threonine resulted in a 50 percent increase in the total amount of threonine present in mutant kernels.

Selection among cultured cells has also been successfully used to enhance the tolerance of a plant for a particular herbicide. The effectiveness of herbicides is based on their ability to discriminate between weed and crop species. Although traditionally it has been left to the chemist to synthesize compounds that display this specificity, differential responses to a herbicide can also be achieved by introducing tolerance into the crop species by genetic means. This genetic approach should broaden the spectrum of applicability of existing herbicides and thereby spare the enormous expense of developing and licensing new herbicides.

Several tobacco mutants resistant to picloram were isolated by plating cultured cells on herbicide-supplemented medium (36). Plants regenerated from five isolates were analyzed genetically. In three cases (*PmR1*, *PmR2*, and *PmR7*) resistance resulted from single dominant nuclear mutations and in two cases (*PmR6* and *PmR85*) from single semidominant nuclear mutations. Additional crosses established genetic linkage between *PmR1* and *PmR7* and assigned *PmR6* and *PmR85* to distinct linkage groups (13). Growth of callus initiated from plants homozygous for the *PmR1* mutation was 100-fold more tolerant of picloram than was growth of normal callus. The expression of increased tolerance by mutant plants is illustrated in Fig. 3.

Conclusion

The genetic variability generated during proliferation of plant cells in culture and that induced by mutagenic treatment can be examined for desirable traits at two levels of differentiation. Regenerated plants can be screened by conventional methods. But even in cases in which visual screens are employed, this procedure is both labor- and land-intensive. Alternatively, novel phenotypes can be selected directly at the cellular level by defining culture conditions that favor growth of the variant and discriminate against growth of normal cells. This is a potentially powerful method that permits enormous numbers of genomes to be scrutinized both rapidly and rigorously within the dimensions of a culture vessel. Unfortunately, however, certain features of selection in vitro preclude its application in many cases and limit one to the more laborious procedure of screening regenerated plants.

One limitation of mutant selection in

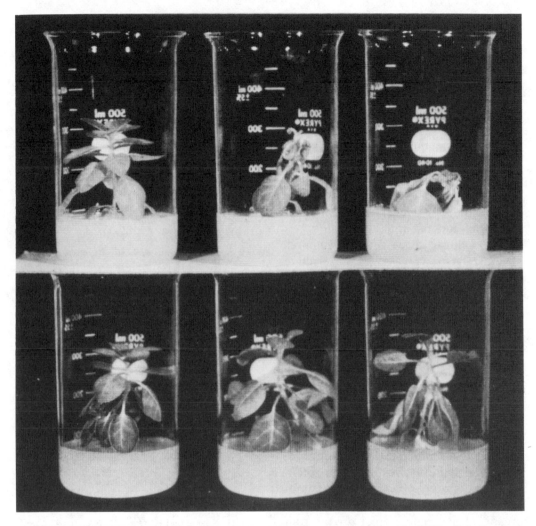

Fig. 3. Effects of picloram on normal (top) and homozygous mutant (*PmR1/PmR1*) (bottom) tobacco plantlets. The plantlets were grown axenically for 8 weeks. Picloram was then added to several of the beakers to the following final concentrations: no picloram (left), 1 μM (center), and 5 μM (right) (*13*).

vitro is that it can only identify modifications of traits that are expressed at the cellular level. The developmental complexity of higher plants makes this restriction rather severe. Many traits of agronomic importance are the products of the organization of highly differentiat-ed cells and, therefore, do not appear in culture. And, because of our rather primitive understanding of their molecular and cellular bases, correlative functions of these traits that may be expressed at the cellular level have not yet been defined. Thus, although certain agronomic traits, such as tolerances for heavy metals, salt, herbicides, and extremes of soil pH, may prove accessible by an in vitro approach, others, such as yield, lodging resistance, and times to flowering and maturity, are, at least for the moment, beyond the reach of the somatic cell geneticist.

Another sine qua non of mutant selection in vitro that greatly limits its application is the ability to regenerate plants from cultured cells. In contrast to the production of regenerated plants for screening, identification of mutant types at the cellular level actually requires several successive passages on selective medium. Therefore, the capacity to regenerate plants must be retained by cells throughout prolonged periods in culture. It is primarily for this reason that most successful selections of mutants from cell cultures have been accomplished with tobacco. Sustained morphogenetic capacity still tends to be the exception rather than the rule among the major crop species. Even in the case of cereals, where significant advances have recently been made (37), morphogenetically competent cell cultures are difficult to obtain and do not grow as dispersed and homogeneous cell populations, but as highly organized aggregates, which are far from ideal for mutant selection.

Notwithstanding the present stage of development of the art of tissue culture, direct selection for mutants from cultured cells is a valuable technique for crop improvement. However, its suitability must be evaluated independently for each application. In some cases, screening of regenerated plants will provide a more efficacious means of identifying desirable phenotypes in the pool of variability produced in cell culture. But as the techniques of cell culture are refined and extended to more species, a corresponding increase can be expected in the contributions of in vitro selection to the genetic improvement of crop plants.

References and Notes

1. T. Murashige, *Annu. Rev. Plant Physiol.* **25**, 135 (1974).
2. B. V. Conger, *Cloning Agricultural Plants Via In Vitro Techniques* (CRC Press, Boca Raton, Fla., 1981).
3. L. Bergmann, *J. Gen. Physiol.* **43**, 841 (1960).
4. E. C. Cocking, *Nature (London)* **187**, 962 (1960).
5. V. Vasil and A. C. Hildebrandt, *Science* **150**, 889 (1965).
6. S. Guha and S. C. Maheshwari, *Phytomorphology* **17**, 454 (1967).
7. T. Nagata and I. Takebe, *Planta* **99**, 12 (1971).
8. P. S. Carlson, *Science* **168**, 487 (1970).
9. J. F. Shepard, D. Bidney, T. Barsby, R. Kemble, *ibid.* **219**, 683 (1983).
10. K. A. Barton and W. J. Brill, *ibid.*, p. 671.
11. R. M. Skirvin and J. Janick, *J. Am. Soc. Hort. Sci.* **101**, 281 (1976).
12. A. Binns and F. Meins, *Proc. Natl. Acad. Sci. U.S.A.* **70**, 2660 (1973).
13. R. S. Chaleff, *Genetics of Higher Plants: Applications of Cell Culture* (Cambridge Univ. Press, New York, 1981).
14. M. W. Bayliss, in *Perspectives in Plant Cell and Tissue Culture, International Review of Cytology Suppl. 11A*, I. K. Vasil, Ed. (Academic Press, New York, 1980).
15. W. H. Muir, in *Proceedings of an International Conference on Plant Tissue Culture*, P. R. White and A. R. Grove, Eds. (McCutchan, Berkeley, Calif., 1965), p. 485.
16. T. Murashige and R. Nakano, *Am. J. Bot.* **54**, 963 (1967).
17. T. Nishi and S. Mitsuoka, *Jpn. J. Genet.* **44**, 341 (1969).
18. H. Niizeki and K. Oono, *Colloq. Int. C.N.R.S.* **193**, 251 (1971).
19. R. S. Chaleff and R. L. Keil, *Mol. Gen. Genet.* **181**, 254 (1981).
20. M. Barbier and H. L. Dulieu, *Ann. Amelior. Plantes* **30**, 321 (1980).
21. D. J. Heinz, M. Krishnamurthi, L. G. Nickell, A. Maretzki, in *Applied and Fundamental Aspects of Plant Cell, Tissue and Organ Culture*, J. Reinert and Y. P. S. Bajaj, Eds. (Springer-Verlag, Berlin, 1977), p. 3.
22. G. A. Secor and J. F. Shepard, *Crop Sci.* **21**, 102 (1981).
23. J. F. Shepard, D. Bidney, E. Shahin, *Science* **208**, 17 (1980).
24. D. P. Cummings, C. E. Green, D. D. Stuthman, *Crop Sci.* **16**, 465 (1976).
25. K. Oono, *Trop. Agric. Res. Ser.* **11**, 109 (1978).
26. B. P. Storgonov, *Structure and Function of Plant Cells in Saline Habitats*. 1973 Israel Program for Scientific Translations [Halsted (Wiley), New York, 1970].
27. T. J. Orton, *Z. Pflanzenphysiol.* **98**, 105 (1980).

28. M. W. Nabors, S. E. Gibbs, C. S. Bernstein, M. E. Meis, *ibid.* **97**, 13 (1980).
29. L. D. Gottlieb, *Science* **216**, 373 (1982).
30. M. B. Berlyn, *Theor. Appl. Genet.* **58**, 19 (1980).
31. I. Zelitch and M. B. Berlyn, *Plant Physiol.* **69**, 198 (1982).
32. P. S. Carlson, *Science* **180**, 1366 (1973).
33. B. G. Gengenbach, C. E. Green, C. M. Donovan, *Proc. Natl. Acad. Sci. U.S.A.* **74**, 5113 (1977).
34. R. I. S. Brettell, E. Thomas, D. S. Ingram, *Theor. Appl. Genet.* **58**, 55 (1980).
35. K. A. Hibberd and C. E. Green, *Proc. Natl. Acad. Sci. U.S.A.* **79**, 559 (1982).
36. R. S. Chaleff and M. F. Parsons, *ibid.* **75**, 5104 (1978).
37. C. E. Green, in *Frontiers of Plant Tissue Culture 1978*, T. A. Thorpe, Ed. (International Association for Plant Tissue Culture, Calgary, 1978), p. 411.
38. The contributions made to this chapter by the critical comments of D. Chaleff, K. Leto, C. Mauvais, and N. Yadav are gratefully acknowledged.

12. Genetic Transfer in Plants Through Interspecific Protoplast Fusion

James F. Shepard, Dennis Bidney
Tina Barsby, Roger Kemble

A living plant cell consists of protoplasm bounded by a unit membrane (the plasmalemma) and encased in a cell wall of complex but largely cellulosic composition. As long ago as 1880 (*1*), the living component of the cell exclusive of the wall (the nucleus and cytoplasm) was termed the "protoplast." In 1910, Kuster (*2*) observed that protoplasts in a calcium salt solution would occasionally make contact and undergo a complete amalgamation of contents, but the process, called protoplast fusion, was infrequent and nonreproducibile.

With the development of efficient enzymatic methods for protoplast isolation in the late 1960's, ample quantities of protoplasts became available for fusion studies. Simultaneously, and beginning with the work of Takebe and his colleagues, isolated protoplasts of some plant species were cultured in defined media and induced to regenerate (from the Latin *regeneratus* meaning to bring into existence once again) complete plants (*3*).

Fusion of Protoplasts

Protoplast fusion begins with firm adhesion between the bounding membranes of adjacent protoplasts (Fig. 1A). As juncture points in the membrane barrier are dissolved, cytoplasmic constituents mix (Fig. 1, B and C). Eventually, the original two protoplasts round up into a sphere containing the nuclei of both parental cells (a dikaryon). A dikaryon is a homokaryocyte if the nuclei are identical and a heterokaryocyte if the nuclei are genetically different. Nuclei in the dikaryon may fuse before, during, or after mitosis and create a mononucleate hybrid cell or synkaryon.

Numerous chemical and physical conditions have been tested to induce protoplast fusion, but a major advance was the discovery of polyethylene glycol (PEG) as an efficient initiator. Polyethylene glycol [$HOCH_2-(CH_2-O-CH_2)_n-CH_2OH$] is highly soluble in water and ranges in molecular weight from less than 1000 to over 20,000. Schenk and Hildebrandt (*4*) first recognized the potential of PEG for stimulating protoplast adhesion, but the molecular weight of the PEG used, about 600, was too low for complete fusion. In 1974, Kao and Michayluk (*5*) and Wallin *et al.* (*6*) independently established the efficacy of PEG, in the molecular weight range of 1540 to 6000, for protoplast fusion. The compound has proved to be effective for protoplasts of all plant species tested and has similarly been applied to animal and bacterial cell fusions. A newer technique, electrofusion (7), also shows considerable promise. By this procedure, protoplast adhesion occurs in a nonuniform electrical field, and fusion of associated protoplasts is then induced by a short pulse of direct current. The technique is highly efficient and, unlike PEG, has relatively little immediate effect on protoplast viability.

Sexual Incompatibility and Chromosome Segregation

Sexual incompatibility precludes natural genetic exchange between distant or unrelated species; even within a single species there may be self- or cross-incompatibility. For related plants, fertilization may fail from cytoplasmic or nuclear factors (prezygotic incompatibility), or fertilized eggs may cease to develop at some early stage (postzygotic

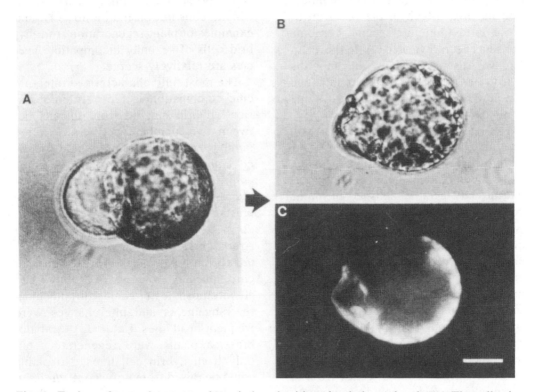

Fig. 1. Fusion of two plant protoplasts induced with polyethylene glycol. (A) The adhesion phase of a mesophyll protoplast from an albino protoclone of 'Russet Burbank' potato (on the left) and a larger leaf cell protoplast of tomato (on the right). (B) Nearly completed fusion between the same two protoplasts after a 15-minute incubation depicted under phase contrast microscopy. (C) The same protoplast pair as in (B) photographed under fluorescence microscopy. The potato protoplast had been stained with fluorescein isothiocyanate before fusion, while the tomato protoplast was left unstained. Transfer of the fluorescent dye to the tomato protoplast has occurred and the remaining juncture between the two protoplasts is clearly evident. Scale bar, 50 μm.

incompatibility). Postzygotic incompatibility can sometimes be overcome by culturing young embryos and stimulating them to develop into plants. Prezygotic incompatibility can occasionally be circumvented by pollinations in vitro (8). Unless otherwise specified, we use the term "sexual incompatibility" to refer only to those interspecific combinations for which no sexual means have yet created hybrid genotypes.

Extensive fusion research has been conducted on protoplasts of species that can either be hybridized sexually or crossed through some form of manipulation in vitro. Much of the research for these intra- and interspecific combinations has been reviewed (9). In this chapter, we discuss sexually incompatible pairings as a possible means of introducing new genetic information into a species.

During early studies, there was considerable hope for new amphiploid plants from fusions between protoplasts of sexually incompatible individuals. But, as had already been established in animal cell research, somatic combinations between distantly related or unrelated genomes was regularly followed by the elimination of parental chromosomes (chromosome segregation) from cell lines. The objectives of interspecific fusion have thus shifted away from synthesis of novel amphiploid plants toward the introduction of small genetic elements from alien species into ones of practical interest. Introgression of genes from diverse alien species could significantly expand germplasm pools for such characters as pest or stress resistance provided that the introduced genes were expressed and were capable of being manipulated by breeding techniques.

Protoplast fusion and mitosis are possible in heterokaryocytes regardless of the extent of relatedness (10), and fusions between protoplasts of distantly related plants do not necessarily result in the total elimination of chromosomes from either species. In a few cases, full chromosome sets are retained, whereas in others, modifications of chromosome structure permit synchronous duplication of alien chromosomes (or segments thereof) in the heterokaryocyte (11). However, developmental processes leading to the formation of embryos or shoot primordia are more sensitive to genetic constitution than mitosis is, and examples of plant regeneration from hybrid cells of sexually incompatible species are relatively scarce.

The most fully characterized interspecific combination is the "Arabidobrassica" hybrid created from fusions between two members of the Cruciferae family: Arabidopsis thaliana and Brassica campestris. Leaf protoplasts of B. campestris have 20 chromosomes ($2n = 2X = 20$) and callus cell protoplasts of A. thaliana are octaploid ($2n = 8X = 40$) (12). After fusion, some Arabidobrassica cell lines had 40 Arabidopsis chromosomes and 20 Brassica chromosomes, whereas two others had 40 chromosomes of each. Chromosomal rearrangements and interchanges were frequent in all lines. Later (13), Arabidobrassica plants were regenerated, but only from hybrid cell lines. No plants could be raised from unfused A. thaliana or B. campestris protoplasts. Plants were categorized as being either symmetric hybrids (true and stable somatic hybrids showing no evidence of chromosomal elimination) or asymmetric hybrids (where portions of either or both parental genomes have been eliminated). Asymmetric plants varied in chromosome number from 35 to 45, but individual karyotypes were stable. Structural modifications were evident in some chromosomes, and recombination was suggested in six of the hybrid plants. None was sexually fertile.

In another pairing between incompatible members of the same family, *Datura innoxia* and *Atropa belladonna*, only calluses with fleshy leaves were regenerated from synkaryons that retained all chromosomes of both parents (*14*). This developmental block was termed "somatic incompatibility," and, unlike Arabidobrassica, complete hybrid plants were only regenerated from hybrid cell lines that had lost one or more *A. belladonna* chromosomes (*15*).

The genus *Petunia* contains compatible and incompatible species. In early studies with sexually compatible individuals (*16*), somatic hybrid plants generally had the predicted amphidiploid chromosome number $(2n = 4X = 32)$. Later (*17*), hybrid plants were obtained from fusions between *Petunia parodii* and *P. parviflora*, which are not sexually compatible. None was a true amphidiploid, but one cell line provided approximately 50 plants with a constant chromosome number of 31. The plants set pollen with a fertility quotient of 36 percent, compared with 98 to 99 percent fertility for parental pollen. Chromosome segregation was not observed in either regenerating cell lines or in hybrid plants.

In more distant interspecific combinations, there has been complete chromosome elimination for one parent. However, in a few examples, some genetic expression from the donor was retained despite total chromosome loss. Hybrid cell lines of *Petunia hybrida* fused with *Parthenocissus* and lacking chromosomes of the latter species expressed peroxidase isozyme patterns of both parents for at least 1 year (*18*). Dudits *et al.* (*19*) fused protoplasts of an albino nuclear mutant of carrot (*Daucus carota*) with those of chlorophyll-containing *Aegopodium podagraria*. Green plants from three callus lines had only carrot chromosomes, but molecular hybridization suggested integration of small *A. podagraria* chromosome segments. If so, the results resemble those in animal somatic cell fusions where, for example, genes from a chick have been incorporated into mouse cells in the absence of complete chick chromosomes (*20*).

It is evident that, except in very distant pairings, the extent or direction of chromosome segregation in interspecific hybrid cell lines is largely unpredictable, and for some combinations virtually any chromosome mix is possible. It is probable, however, that culture conditions more suited to one species than the other or relative stages in the mitotic cycle when protoplasts are isolated and fused might influence the direction or extent of chromosome segregation in proliferating cell lines. It may also prove advantageous to employ techniques such as x-irradiation or bromodeoxyuridine labeling of one parent to induce directional chromosome elimination, as originally described for Chinese hamster cells by Pontecorvo (*21*). Added control of chromosome segregation would be of use for reducing the number of potential genetic combinations that must be analyzed. Total loss of one set of chromosomes has already been achieved in *Nicotiana* fusions by lethal x-irradiation of one parent (*22*), but where chromosomal interchanges between species are desired, it may be advantageous to induce unidirectional chromosome loss over a series of mitotic cycles rather than strictly at the outset.

Gene Expression in
Somatic Hybrid Plants

Proving the hybrid nature of regenerated plants requires a demonstration of genetic contributions from both parents. Morphological characters have often provided suggestive information, but the range of variability observed in plants raised from nonfused protoplasts (23) weakens the value of intermediate morphology as a sole criterion. Results are the most convincing when expression from both parents is in the form of identifiable biochemical markers that are encoded in plastid, mitochondrial, or nuclear DNA. Although relatively few biochemical markers have been analyzed in somatic hybrid plants, considerable differences in expression (or repression) do occur among individual hybrid lines from the same two parental species and even between different plants derived from a single hybrid cell line. Hence, interspecific protoplast fusions do not necessarily yield populations of somatic hybrid plants that manifest a uniform phenotype or that equally express designated molecular markers, even when all possess the predicted amphiploid chromosome number. Both nuclear and extranuclear gene expression may contribute to such differences because fusion produces hybrid cells that at least initially contain mixed organelle as well as mixed nuclear chromosome populations.

Extranuclear genes. Ribulose-1,5-bis-phosphate carboxylase (RUDPcase) constitutes a major percentage of total protein in green plant tissues. The enzyme is composed of a chloroplast DNA–encoded large subunit and a nuclear DNA–encoded small subunit that exhibits Mendelian inheritance. Both subunits are composed of several discrete polypeptide chains. RUDPcase protein has routinely been studied in somatic hybrid plants as a marker for both nuclear and plastid genomes.

The RUDPcase large subunits from one parental species or the other, but not both, have regularly been observed in somatic hybrid plants of *Nicotiana* species (24, 25) and in potato-tomato hybrids (26). Rarely was plastid segregation unidirectional unless there was a genetic lesion in one plastid type or the application of selective pressure. Rather, the consensus is that after protoplast fusion, chloroplasts undergo a random sorting out that results in the survival of a single plastid type per cell (27).

Although intolerance of chloroplast mixtures is a consistent feature of individual cells, multiple plastid types do survive within the tissues of a regenerated plant (28). Iwai *et al.* (29) reported only the large RUDPcase subunit of *N. tabacum* in a *N. tabacum–N. rustica* somatic hybrid plant but later (30) found that in a population of nine androgenetic plants regenerated from anthers of the hybrid, two contained only the large subunit of *N. rustica*. Hence, plastids from both parents must have existed in the original plant.

Since chloroplast segregation predictably follows protoplast fusion, transfer of plastid-determined characters would be aided by techniques favoring the survival of the preferred plastid genome. Potential examples include resistance characters that are encoded in plastid DNA. Medgyesy *et al.* (31), for example, used streptomycin to select colony populations after fusions between mitotically inactivated (with iodoacetate) protoplasts of a streptomycin-resistant *N. tabacum* line and those of *N. sylvestris*. Both cybrid (cytoplasmic hybrid) and nuclear hybrid plants that expressed streptomycin resistance were obtained. Other plastid markers with in vitro selective potential include resistance to tentoxin (liberated by the fungus *Alternaria tenuis*) (*32*) and to triazine herbicides (*33*).

The fate of mitochondrial genomes in synkaryons and ultimately somatic hybrid plants is less clear. Belliard *et al.* (*24, 34*) regenerated hybrid plants from fusions between (sexually compatible) *N. tabacum* and a cytoplasmically male-sterile (cms) *N. debneyi*. Their results suggested retention of the male sterility character, possibly residing in mitochondrial DNA (mtDNA) in some hybrid plants, along with either coexistence of multiple mitochondrial types or recombination of mtDNA (*35*). Both phenomena are recognized in lower eukaryotes (*36*), but neither is proven for higher plants. Even so, additional circumstantial evidence is accumulating. Aviv and Galun (*32*) regenerated six classes of somatic hybrid plants from fusions between *N. sylvestris* and x-irradiated *N. tabacum* protoplasts. Of these, four were cybrid classes containing *N. sylvestris* nuclear genomes, and either (or both) of the chloroplast (tentoxin resistance) and cytoplasmic male fertility characters of *N. tabacum*. The degree of male fertility restoration was independent of plastid origin and hence was possibly correlated with mitochondrial composition. It is significant that in this instance male fertility was restored rather than eliminated through somatic fusions. Further evidence that a heteroplasmic (mixed cytoplasm) state for male sterility may be maintained for a considerable period comes from experiments with *Petunia* species. Izhar and Tabib (*37*) analyzed male-sterile somatic hybrids with the nuclear genome of *P. axillaris* and the cytoplasm of a male-sterile *P. hybrida* line. Two somatic hybrid plants displayed segregation of the sterility-fertility factors in the F_2 or F_3 generations following crosses with a cms tester line. Experiments were sufficient to reject mosaicism or acquisition of fertility-restoring nuclear genes as the explanation for segregation of the cms character in F_2 or subsequent generations.

Nuclear genes. Analysis of nuclear genome expression in putative somatic hybrid plants has essentially relied on morphological characters, isoenzyme distributions in polyacrylamide gels, or translation of specific genes. In the last category, the RUDPcase small subunit has been particularly useful. Small subunit polypeptide patterns produced after isoelectric focusing in a pH gradient are often definitive for a species, and even in the presence of a single plastid type, small subunit polypeptides of both parental species have been demonstrated (*32, 38*).

Somatic Hybrids Between Potato and Tomato

Potato (*Solanum tuberosum* L. spp. *tuberosum*) ($2n = 4X = 48$) and tomato (*Lycopersicon esculentum* Mill) ($2n = 2X = 24$) are members of the Solanaceae family but are not sexually compatible. In 1978, Melchers *et al.* (*39*) provided evidence for a somatic hybrid plant from fusions between protoplasts of a cultured dihaploid potato line and leaf cells of a chlorophyll-deficient tomato. Hybrid plants displayed morphological features of both parents, and analysis of the RUDPcase large subunit revealed that three plants carried the chloroplastic genome of tomato, whereas a fourth had that of potato. Those plants with a tomato plastome were termed "Tomoffeln" or "topatoes" while the ones possessing the plastome of potato were designated "Karmaten" or "pomatoes" (40). Subsequently (26), additional somatic hybrids were recovered; four topatoes and five pomatoes. None possessed the chromosome number of a true amphitetraploid ($2n = 4X = 48$), and it was not determined whether this was a consequence of chromosome segregation or of the use of mixoploid potato cells as protoplast donors. Some hybrid plants formed "tuber-like stolons" (but no tubers), and none set fertile flowers or fruit.

We have produced four somatic hybrid plants from fusions between chlorophyll-deficient protoplasts of a variegating protoclone (protoplast-derived clone) of the potato cultivar 'Russet Burbank' and the 'Rutgers' and 'Nova' cultivars of tomato. The potato protoclone (774) was previously described (41) and has a normal complement of 48 chromosomes. One somatic hybrid was identified from regenerated populations of the 774 potato crossed with 'Rutgers,' and three resulted from fusions of 774 and 'Nova.' The selection scheme developed for somatic hybrid colonies was based on the following observations. First, tomato mesophyll protoplasts divide in very low efficiency when cultured in the light at 24°C, whereas these conditions are optimal for potato mesophyll protoplasts. Second, small protoplast-derived calluses (p-calli) of potato cease growth when abscisic acid (ABA) is included in culture media at concentrations exceeding 0.5 milligram per liter. The growth rate

of tomato p-calli, in contrast, is either unaffected or slightly stimulated at the same ABA levels. Tomato p-calli did not undergo shoot morphogenesis under conditions that were inductive for potato. When green adventitious shoots developed into small plantlets, the final screening characters, which appear when tomato shoots are regenerated from leaf disk callus, were employed; these characters were the formation of lobes and serrations in leaflets and reddish purple pigmentation in stems.

General morphological characters were consistent for all somatic hybrid plants. The basic plant growth habit was that of a potato-like vine; terminal and lateral leaflets were deep green in color and displayed serrations and lobing (Fig. 2, A and B); at 28°C, plants grew vigorously and anthocyanin (red) pigmentation accumulated in stems and on the underside of leaves; at 18° to 21°C, vegetative cuttings accumulated anthocyanins throughout and eventually died; white tubers (2 to 11 centimeters long) were produced that turned reddish purple if exposed to light during development; floral characters were identical to those of parental 'Russet Burbank' potato except for the 774–'Rutgers' hybrid whose petals were light yellow. Sterile fruit up to 2.5 cm in diameter having a yellow color at maturity and liberating a tomato-like odor developed on both 'Rutgers' and 'Nova' hybrids. All hybrids were sensitive to root-invading microorganisms and required initial establishment in sterilized vermiculite. Moreover, under routine greenhouse conditions, somatic hybrid plants were susceptible to the powdery mildew fungus, whereas neither the potato nor the tomato parents were susceptible. When taken together, these characters are found only in our somatic hybrids and were not reported

Fig. 2. (A) Photograph of the 774–'Rutgers' somatic hybrid plant 2 months after transplanting. (B) Leaves of 'Russet Burbank' potato (on the left), 'Rutgers' tomato (middle), and the 774–'Rutgers' somatic hybrid (on the right).

for those previously described by Melchers (26), nor have they been observed in potato protoclonal populations.

Gel electrophoresis of restricted mtDNA and chloroplastic DNA (cpDNA) from 774–'Rutgers' and of 774–'Nova'-1 (42) revealed the extranu-

clear DNA's only of potato (Fig. 3, A and B), suggesting that the plants were true hybrids. If the plants had displayed mtDNA and cpDNA of both parents, they could have been chimeras composed of a mixture of potato and tomato cells rather than hybrids. Analysis of the small RUDPcase subunit from 774–'Rutgers,' 774–'Nova'-1 and 774–'Nova'-3 plants by isoelectric focusing in polyacrylamide gels (43) established the presence of small subunit polypeptides of both tomato and potato (Fig. 4). The 774–'Nova'-2 plant has not yet been examined. Profiles of several isozymes (peroxidase, malate dehydrogenase, esterase, 6-phosphoglucomutase, and polyphenol oxidase) were analyzed from leaf tissue of 774–'Rutgers' and compared with those of parental tomato and potato and with a random population of 15 regenerated protoclones of 'Russet Burbank' potato. For each enzyme, hybrid extracts shared specific bands with both potato and tomato. However, within the protoclonal population, individuals that also shared some tomato-specific bands for each enzyme were identified. No protoclone displayed all of the unique bands of the hybrid.

The potato-tomato somatic hybrid plants were cytologically examined at meiosis and mitosis (44). Observation of root tip cells of the 774–'Rutgers' hybrid shortly after initial transplanting consistently showed 72 chromosomes, the predicted number of a true amphiploid. Over the next 12 months, numerous vegetative cuttings were made from the hybrid, and root tip cells were analyzed for somatic chromosome number. The process was then repeated for each of the 774–'Nova' hybrids. Results from these experiments indicated that root tip cells of 'Nova' and 'Rutgers' somatic hybrid cuttings displayed chromosome numbers

154

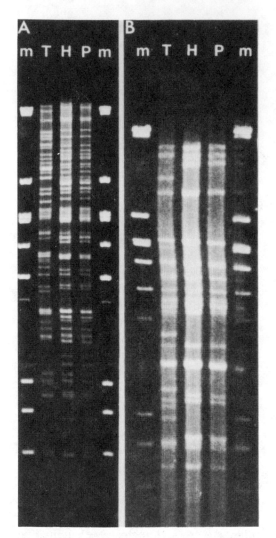

Fig. 3. Electrophoresis of organelle DNA's in 1 percent agarose gels. (A) Mitochondrial DNA's fragmented with the restriction enzyme Xho I. Lane T contains mtDNA from 'Rutgers' tomato, lane H from the 774–'Rutgers' hybrid, and lane P from the 774 potato protoclone. Lanes designated m are size marker fragments produced by independent digestions of lambda DNA by Eco RI and Hae III. (B) Chloroplast DNA's fragmented with Bam HI. Lanes are as in (A).

ranging from 62 to 72 depending on the cutting. The most frequently encountered chromosome number for the

'Rutgers' hybrid was 70, with greater variability observed for the 'Nova' hybrids. These data indicate a degree of mitotic instability and some chromosome segregation in vegetative cuttings, but not wholesale chromosome elimination. Phenotypic variations in the form of misshapen leaflets and color deviations were occasionally observed, particularly among cuttings of the 'Nova'-2 hybrid, but they could not be correlated with a specific change in chromosome number. Each of the hybrid plants flowered profusely but produced no viable pollen. Since parental 'Russet Burbank' potato expresses the same deficiency, it is uncertain whether some measure of fertility would be possible with another potato parent. In meiosis, there was clear evidence of chromosome elimination for 774–'Rutgers' and 774–'Nova'-1 (Fig. 5). The remaining two 'Nova' hybrids have not yet been analyzed.

One objective in our hybrid character-

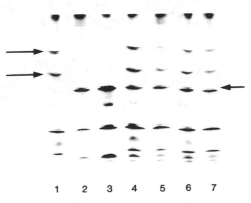

Fig. 4. Isoelectric focusing of small RUDPcase subunits in polyacrylamide gels. RUDPcase small subunit polypeptides from (lane 1) 774 potato protoclone, (lanes 2 and 3) 'Rutgers' tomato, (lane 4) 774–'Rutgers,' (lane 5) 774–'Nova'-1, and (lanes 6 and 7) 774–'Nova'-3. Two prominent potato-specific bands are identified by arrows on the left, and a tomato-specific band is identified by the arrow on the right.

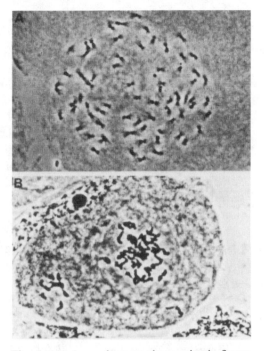

Fig. 5. (A) An early-metaphase mitotic figure in a root tip cell of the 774–'Rutgers' hybrid showing a complement of 72 chromosomes. (B) A pollen mother cell of the 774–'Rutgers' hybrid in metaphase I of meiosis in which chromosome elimination is under way. Estranged chromosomes are seen at lower left and lower middle.

ization is to determine whether karyotype stability can be achieved in populations of vegetative cuttings from hybrid plants. To this end, subpopulations from cuttings displaying chromosome numbers up to 72 are continually being made in order to establish whether any lines will stabilize. Moreover, protoplasts have been cultured from somatic hybrid plants of 774–'Rutgers' to determine whether karyotype stability will prevail in the second somatic (S_2) generation. To date, 50 plants have been regenerated from these protoplasts, and some are now being characterized. One S_2 protoclone displays the leaf morphology of potato, with no evidence of lobing or

anthocyanin pigmentation. Electrophoretic analysis showed the RUDPcase small subunit of both tomato and potato. The predominant chromosome number of root tip cells was 64; hence, although the protoclone had assumed a more potato-like phenotype, it had probably not lost all tomato chromosomes. There are also S_2 protoclones that display a more tomato-like morphology than is seen in their hybrid parent, including more intense red pigmentation, more pointed terminal leaflets, and more extensive leaf serration. These and other S_2 protoclones are being analyzed for chromosome number to ascertain whether protoplast culture has conferred additional karyotypes to some members of the population and whether chromosome substitution or addition occurs. Evidence has accumulated that potato plants regenerated from mesophyll protoplasts display restructured chromosomes and translocations (45). If the same events take place in protoplasts of hybrid plants, translocations between potato and tomato chromosomes might also be anticipated.

Conclusions

In heterokaryocytes from such phylogenetically remote pairings as orange and tobacco protoplasts (46), *Nicotiana glauca* and soybean protoplasts (47), and *Haplopappus* protoplasts and human cells (48), either nuclei failed to fuse or synkaryons lost one set of chromosomes. Sometimes chromosome remnants have remained in cell lines through restructuring events, but there are no examples of modified chromosomes of an otherwise deleted genome persisting in a plant after fusion between members of different families. Such genetic incompatibility currently precludes transfer of whole chromosomes from a widely separated species to the regenerated plant. Despite total and unidirectional chromosome loss, it is still possible that in synkaryons proliferating in culture small chromosomal segments may be integrated into the surviving genome and thus enable genetic transfer.

In contrast to unrelated species, fusions between sexually incompatible members of the same family have produced hybrid plants that retained some chromosomes from both parents. These results are encouraging of potential somatic recombination (in its broadest sense) between formerly intractable species.

Interspecific protoplast fusions are a conceptual extension of interspecific sexual crosses to incompatible species. There is little control over what genetic information is retained and what is eliminated, and fusion lacks the potential precision of recombinant DNA methods. However, until the process of directed transformation with cloned genes reaches a higher level of sophistication, protoplast fusion offers a means for introducing genes from unconventional sources. Somatic hybrid plants such as the pomato are not of immediate value, just as is true of interspecific crosses between most distant sexually compatible species. In the latter, considerable backcrossing is needed to eliminate unwanted portions of the alien genome. Novel somatic hybrid plants are thus only the starting point of a genetic introgression scheme. If the hybrid plants are sexually compatible with either parent, removal of nondesirable material can be straightforward. Where this is not true, protoplast regeneration from interspecific hybrids that undergo continuous chromosome segregation should provide nov-el genomic mixes. Moreover, since evidence is accumulating, at least in potato, that chromosome translocations are frequent in plants regenerated from mesophyll protoplasts, the coexistence of genomic sets may also allow translocation of, for example, tomato chromosome segments into potato chromosomes. Hence, unidirectional chromosome segregation combined with translocation or substitution could allow recovery of one parental phenotype with minor contributions from the other.

In a more immediate sense, protoplast fusion offers the opportunity of creating hybrid plants between related but sexually incompatible species. For example, commerical potato cultivars cannot be crossed with many related *Solanum* species without first passing through a bridging species such as *S. megistacrolobum*. Since many primitive *Solanum* species possess broad-spectrum resistance to disease (for example, *S. etuberosa* for resistance to leaf roll virus), protoplast fusion might allow a rapid introduction of resistance genes into potato germplasm pools.

References and Notes

1. E. C. Cocking, *Annu. Rev. Plant Physiol.* **23**, 29 (1972).
2. E. Kuster, *Arch. Entwicklungsmech. Org.* **30**, 351 (1910).
3. I. Takebe, G. Labib, G. Melchers, *Naturwissenschaften* **58**, 318 (1971); T. Nagata and I. Takebe, *Planta* **99**, 12 (1971).
4. R. U. Schenk and A. C. Hildebrandt, in *Les Cultures de Tissus de Plantes* (Centre National de la Recherche Scientifique, Paris, 1970), pp. 319–331.
5. K. N. Kao and M. R. Michayluk, *Planta* **115**, 355 (1974).
6. A. Wallin, K. Glimelius, T. Eriksson, *Z. Pflanzenphysiol.* **74**, 64 (1974).
7. U. Zimmermann and P. Scheurich, *Planta* **151**, 26 (1981).
8. M. Zenkteler, in *Recent Advances in Plant Cell and Tissue Culture*, I. Vasil, Ed. (Academic Press, New York, 1980), pp. 137–156.

9. O. Schieder and I. K. Vasil, in *Perspectives in Plant Cell and Tissue Culture*, I. K. Vasil, Ed. (Academic Press, New York, 1980), pp. 21–46.

10. F. Constabel, G. Weber, J. W. Kirkpatrick, K. Pahl, *Z. Pflanzenphysiol.* **79**, 1 (1976).

11. K. N. Kao, *Mol. Gen. Genet.* **150**, 225 (1977).

12. Y. Y. Gleba and F. Hoffman, *Naturwissenschaften* **66**, 547 (1979).

13. F. Hoffmann and T. Adachi, *Planta* **153**, 586 (1981).

14. G. Krumbiegel and O. Schieder, *ibid.* **145**, 371 (1979).

15. _____, *ibid.* **153**, 466 (1981).

16. J. B. Power, E. M. Frearson, C. Hayward, D. George, P. K. Evans, S. F. Berry, E. C. Cocking, *Nature (London)* **263**, 500 (1976).

17. J. B. Power, S. F. Berry, J. V. Chapman, E. C. Cocking, *Theor. Appl. Genet.* **57**, 1 (1980).

18. J. B. Power, E. M. Frearson, C. Hayward, E. C. Cocking, *Plant Sci. Lett.* **5**, 197 (1975).

19. D. Dudits, G. Y. Hadlaczky, G. Y. Bajszar, C. S. Knocz, G. Lazar, G. Horvath, *ibid.* **15**, 101 (1979).

20. A. G. Schwartz, P. R. Cook, H. Harris, *Nature (London) New Biol.* **230**, 5 (1971).

21. G. Pontecorvo, *Nature (London)* **230**, 367 (1971).

22. D. Aviv, R. Fluhr, M. Edelman, E. Galun, *Theor. Appl. Genet.* **56**, 145 (1980).

23. J. F. Shepard, D. Bidney, E. Shahin, *Science* **208**, 17 (1980).

24. G. Belliard, G. Pelletier, F. Vedel, F. Quatier, *Mol. Gen. Genet.* **165**, 231 (1978).

25. K. Chen, S. G. Wildman, H. H. Smith, *Proc. Natl. Acad. Sci. U.S.A.* **74**, 5109 (1977); D. A. Evans, L. R. Wetter, O. L. Gamborg, *Physiol. Plant.* **48**, 225 (1980); P. Maliga, F. Nagy, L. T. Xuon, Z. R. Kiss, L. Menczel, G. Lazar, in *Advances in Protoplast Research*, L. Ferenczy and G. L. Farkas, Eds. (Akasemiai Kiado, Budapest, 1980), pp. 341–348.

26. G. Melchers, in *Plant Cell Cultures: Results and Perspectives*, F. Sala *et al.*, Eds. (Elsevier/North-Holland, New York, 1980), pp. 57–58.

27. H. Uchimiya, *Theor. Appl. Genet.* **61**, 69 (1982); W. R. Scowcroft and P. J. Larkin, *ibid.* **60**, 179 (1981).

28. Y. Y. Gleba, N. M. Piven, I. K. Komarnitskii, A. K. M. Sytnik, *Dokl. Akad. Nauk SSSR* **240**, 1223 (1978); K. Glimelius, K. Chen, H. T. Bonnett, *Planta* **153**, 504 (1981).

29. S. Iwai, T. Nagao, K. Nakata, N. Kawashima, S. Matsuyama, *Planta* **147**, 414 (1980).

30. S. Iwai, K. Nakata, T. Nagao, N. Kawashima, S. Matsuyama, *ibid.* **152**, 478 (1981).

31. P. Medgyesy, L. Menczel, P. Maliga, *Mol. Gen. Genet.* **179**, 693 (1980).

32. D. Aviv and E. Galun, *Theor. Appl. Genet.* **58**, 121 (1980).

33. K. E. Steinbeck, S. Darr, C. J. Arntzen, V. S. Machado, *Abstr. Weed Sci. Soc. Am.* (1981), p. 207.

34. G. Belliard, G. Pelletier, M. Ferault, in *Interspecific Hybridization in Plant Breeding*, E. Sanchez-Monge and F. Garcia-Olmedo, Eds. (Escuela Tecnica Superior Ingenieros Agronomos, University of Madrid, 1977), pp. 237–242.

35. G. Belliard, F. Vedel, G. Pelletier, *Nature (London)* **281**, 401 (1979).

36. A. W. Linnane and P. Nagley, *Plasmid* **1**, 324 (1978); C. A. Mannella, T. H. Pittenger, A. M. Lambowitz, *J. Bacteriol.* **137**, 1449 (1979).

37. S. Izhar and Y. Tabib, *Theor. Appl. Genet.* **57**, 241 (1980).

38. G. C. Douglas, L. R. Wetter, W. A. Keller, G. Setterfield, *Can. J. Bot.* **59**, 1509 (1981); D. A. Evans, L. R. Wetter, O. L. Gamborg, *Physiol. Plant.* **48**, 225 (1980).

39. G. Melchers, M. D. Sacristan, A. A. Holder, *Carlsberg Res. Commun.* **43**, 203 (1978).

40. G. Melchers, in *Advances in Protoplast Research*, L. Ferenczy and G. L. Farkas, Eds. (Akasemiai Kiado, Budapest, 1980), pp. 283–286.

41. J. F. Shepard, in *Emergent Techniques for the Genetic Improvement of Crops*, I. Rubenstein, B. Gengenbach, R. L. Phillips, C. E. Green, Eds. (Univ. of Minnesota Press, Minneapolis, 1980), pp. 185–219.

42. Mitochondrial DNA was extracted from leaf mitochondria of tomato cultivars 'Nova' and 'Rutgers,' from yellow and green leaf tissues of the variegating 774 potato protoclone, and from somatic hybrid plants according to the methods of R. Kemble *et al.* [*Genetics* **95**, 451 (1980)]. Chloroplasts were isolated from 3 to 10 grams of leaves from the plants listed above after 65 to 70 hours of incubation in the dark. Leaves were homogenized in 5 volumes of buffer A per gram of tissue (fresh weight) [R. Kolodner and K. K. Tewari, *Biochim. Biophys. Acta* **402**, 372 (1975)] with two 5-second bursts in a blender. The homogenate was filtered through two layers of cheesecloth and four layers of Miracloth before centrifugation at 2000g for 1 minute. Pellets were suspended in buffer A, centrifuged again, and suspended again in buffer A. Magnesium chloride (final concentration of 10 mM) and deoxyribonuclease (final concentration, 10 micrograms per gram of fresh weight) were added and the mixture was incubated at 4°C for 1 hour. Chloroplasts were centrifuged through a layer of buffer B (Kolodner and Tewari, *ibid.*) at 6000g for 20 minutes, washed twice in the same buffer, and lysed in 50 mM tris-HCl (pH 8.0), 10 mM EDTA, 2 percent Sarkosyl and 0.012 percent autodigested pronase at 37°C for 1 hour. Chloroplast DNA was extracted as described for mtDNA. Both mtDNA and cpDNA were fragmented with restriction endonucleases and subjected to electrophoresis in 1 percent agarose gels (according to the methods of Kemble *et al.*, cited above).

43. Analysis of RUDPcase protein in polyacrylamide gels followed the methods of D. Cammaerts and M. Jacobs [*Anal. Biochem.* **109**, 317 (1980)]. Briefly, 500 milligrams of leaf tissue from each parent and somatic hybrid were homogenized in 5 milliliters of extraction buffer [50 mM tris-HCl, 100 mM NaCl, 1 mM Na$_2$EDTA, 10 mM β-mercaptoethanol, and 1 percent (weight to volume) aprotinin (pH 7.5)] and centrifuged at 23,000g for 10 minutes. Precipitates obtained from supernatants at between 30 and 50 percent (NH$_4$)$_2$SO$_4$ saturation were resuspended in 300 microliters of 0.06M trisphosphate (pH 6.9) and 10 percent glycerol. These samples were subjected to electrophoresis in nondenaturing 4.5 percent polyacrylamide gels, RUDPcase bands were identified and cut out, and slices were equilibrated in 8M urea and 4 percent ampholytes [Sepralytes (pH 5 to 8);

Separation Sciences, Inc., Attleboro, Mass.]. Isoelectric focusing to separate small RUDP-case subunits was done by placing equilibrated gel slices near the cathode on slabs, 0.5 millimeter thick, of polyacrylamide consisting of 6.25 percent acrylamide, 0.175 percent N,N'-methylenebisacrylamide, $8M$ urea, 2.6 percent Sepralytes (pH 5 to 8) and 1.4 percent Sepralytes (pH 3 to 10). Electrophoresis time for the gels (11 by 22 centimeters) was 5 hours at 10°C and 15 watts constant power. Gels were fixed for 30 minutes in a solution of 12 percent trichloroacetic acid, 4 percent 5'-sulfosalicylic acid, and 25 percent methanol and then washed for 30 minutes in 25 percent ethanol plus 10 percent acetic acid. Gels were stained for 2 hours in 0.1 percent Coomassie brilliant blue R-250 in 25 percent ethanol and 10 percent acetic acid.

44. Somatic chromosome numbers were established with root tip cells stained with 0.7 percent acetocarmine. Ten vegetative cuttings from each of two 774–'Rutgers' plants and five cuttings each from 774–'Nova'-1, 774–'Nova'-2, and 774–'Nova'-3 were analyzed.
45. J. F. Shepard, *Sci. Am.* **246**, 154 (May 1982); B. S. Gill, L. N. W. Kam, J. F. Shepard, *HortScience* **17**, 103 (Abstr.) (1982).
46. C. T. Harms, J. Kochba, I. Potrykus, in *Advances in Protoplast Research*, L. Ferenczy and G. L. Farkas, Eds. (Akasemiai Kiado, Budapest, 1980), pp. 321–326.
47. L. R. Wetter and K. N. Kao, *Theor. Appl. Genet.* **57**, 273 (1980).
48. A. Lima-De-Faria, T. Eriksson, L. Kjellen, *Hereditas* **87**, 57 (1977).
49. Supported by NSF grant PCM 80-20713. This is Kansas Agricultural Experiment Station Contribution 82-556-J. We thank L. Kam-Morgan and R. J. Singh for performing the chromosome counts.

13. Contributions of Conventional Plant Breeding to Food Production

Norman E. Borlaug

In 1979 world food production of all types reached 3.75 billion metric tons, representing 1.9 billion tons of edible dry matter. Of this dry matter tonnage, 99 percent was produced on land; only slightly more than 1 percent came from oceans and inland waters. Plant products constituted 93 percent of the human diet. The remaining 7 percent of the world's diet, animal products, also came (indirectly) from plants.

Archeological evidence indicates that more than 3000 species of plants have been used by man for food. Currently, the world's people largely depend on about 29 crop species for most of their calories and protein. These include eight species of cereals, which collectively supply 52 percent of the total world food calories, three "root" crops, two sugar crops, seven grain legumes, seven oil seeds, and two so-called tree food crops (bananas and coconuts). These 29 basic food crops are supplemented by about 15 major species of vegetables and a like number of fruit crop species, which supply much of the vitamins and some of the minerals necessary to the human diet.

Origin of Food Crop Species and Early Genetic Improvements

We will never know with certainty when nature first began inducing genetic diversity, making recombinations, and exerting selection pressure on the progenitors of the plant species that would be chosen, much later, by man as his food crop species. But as the Mesolithic Age gave way to the Neolithic there suddenly appeared, in widely dispersed regions, the most highly successful group of plant and animal breeders that the world has ever seen—the Neolithic domesticators. Within a relatively short geological period, apparently only 20 to 30 centuries, Neolithic man, or more probably woman, domesticated all of the major cereals, grain legumes, root crops, and animal species that remain to this day as man's principal sources of food.

Agriculture and animal husbandry spread rapidly from their cradles of origin across vast areas of Asia, Africa, Europe, and the Americas. These migratory diffusions were in large part possible because of the tremendous genetic diversity that existed in the original land races and populations of the domesticated crop plants. This genetic variability permitted—with the aid of continued mutations, natural hybridizations, and recombinations of genes—the spinning off of new genotypes that were suitable for growing in many environments.

Golden Age of Plant Breeding

Until the 19th century, crop improvement was in the hands of farmers who selected the seed from preferred plant types of land races or populations for subsequent sowing. By the early decades of the 1800's, a number of progressive farmers in North America were busy developing and selling superior varieties based on individual plant selections.

The groundwork for genetic improvement of crop plant species by scientific man was laid by Darwin in his writings on the variation of life species (published in 1859) and through Mendel's discovery of the laws of inheritance (reported in 1865). While Darwin's book immediately generated a great deal of interest, discussion, and controversy, Mendel's discovery was largely ignored at first. Nearly 40 years transpired before these two strands of scientific thought were joined by Karl Correns, Erich Tschermak, and Correns De Vries in independent studies. This rediscovery of Mendel's laws in 1900 provoked a tremendous scientific interest in genetics. The fact that Mendel had worked out his principles on a plant (the pea) encouraged many to prepare themselves for a career in applied plant genetics.

Methods Used in Modern Plant Breeding

The three major categories of plant breeding research are divided on the basis of how various species propagate themselves. Species that reproduce sexually and are normally propagated by seeds—including all cereal crops, legumes, and most trees and shrubs—occupy the first two categories. One of these includes species that set seed through self-pollination; the second, species that set seed largely through cross-pollination. The third category includes species that are asexually propagated through the planting of vegetative parts or grafting. In this chapter I mainly discuss plant breeding achievements in wheat, a self-pollinating species, and maize, a cross-pollinating species.

The cornerstones of all plant breeding are (i) the conscious introduction of genetic diversity into populations by intercrossing or mating selected germ plasm with outstanding characters that complement one another and (ii) the selection of superior plants with genes for desired traits until higher levels of improved adaptation (reproductive fitness), genetic uniformity, and agronomic stability are reached. The appropriateness of a breeding methodology is determined mainly by the sexual nature of the crop—inbreeding (self-pollinating) or outbreeding (cross-pollinating)—its genetic structure, and the objectives to be achieved.

Wheat Breeding

As the knowledge of genetics and plant pathology grew during the first and second decades of this century, wheat breeding methods evolved from bulk and pure-line selections of plants from land races to hybridization programs. With this methodology, controlled pollinations are made between two or more superior parent types. In subsequent segregating generations derived from these controlled crosses, the individual plants possessing the best combinations of desirable characteristics are selected and advanced to the next generation. This process is repeated until all progenies from an individual plant row are genotypically and phenotypically uniform. When acceptable uniformity has been attained, the best progenies (lines) are sown in replicated multirow plots and compared with the best commercial varieties for grain yield, agronomic type, disease and insect reaction, and milling and baking quality. The trials are repeated for several years at a number of different locations to obtain reliable information on the interaction of the variety (genotype) with different environments. When a new line or variety has significantly outperformed existing commercial varieties over several years, it is eligible for multiplication and release as a new commercial variety.

As a result of such breeding techniques, a number of major breakthroughs in wheat breeding have occurred during the past four decades. Most significant among these include the progress made in plant pathology research to develop disease-resistant varieties, achievements in raising maximum genetic yield potential, and the benefits derived from broader adaptation in wheat crop cultivars.

Disease resistance. The pioneering work on stem rust by E. C. Stakman in Minnesota during 1913 to 1930 revealed that the rust organism comprises a large number of pathogenic races that differ in their ability to attack wheat varieties. This discovery led to the understanding that, for a wheat variety to maintain its resistance to stem rust, it had to possess resistance to all the races present throughout the region. With this greater understanding of pathogenic organisms, breeders began to develop more stable sources of genetic resistance in different wheat cultivars. Today, many improved wheat varieties have been developed that possess far broader spectrums of polygenic resistance to many of the 30 wheat diseases that can and do cause serious economic losses in different parts of the world.

Yield potential. Until about 1961 there was no significant increase in grain yield directly attributable to the increase in the maximum genetic yield potential of new varieties. The release of the first semidwarf winter wheat variety, Gaines, in Washington State by O. A. Vogel and his colleagues in 1961, followed by the release in Mexico of two semidwarf spring wheat varieties, Pitic 62 and Penjamo 62 in 1962 and Sonora 64, Lerma Rojo 64, Super X, and Siete Cerros in 1964, changed the potential wheat yield situation dramatically. The semidwarf varieties, all with one or two dwarfing genes derived from the Japanese winter wheat variety Norin 10, possessed a 100 percent yield advantage over the best previously available tall commercial varieties. Compared to the taller types, semidwarf varieties have a higher tillering capacity, more grain-filled heads, and shorter stems that make them resistant to lodging under higher levels of fertilization and irrigation. Perhaps even more important, however, was the change in the "harvest index" of semidwarf varieties to partitioning more of the total dry matter production to grain. As such, semidwarf varieties convert a higher percentage of the uptake of fertilizer and soil moisture to grain than do the taller types.

Adaptation. Until the 1950's, the dogma in plant breeding was that the only way to ensure the development of high-yielding, well-adapted varieties was to select them through all the segregating generations in the location where they were to be grown commercially. Faced with the urgent need to develop acceptable stem rust–resistant varieties in Mexico, a decision was made to ignore dogma and use several ecological areas that would permit the growing and selecting of two segregating generations of progeny each year. With two breeding cycles every 12 months, a new variety could be developed in 4 years rather than in the 8 years required with the conventional methods. To accomplish this task in a 12-month period, we at the International Maize and Wheat Improvement Center (CIMMYT) were forced to select two very diverse environments separated from one another by 10° of latitude (with changing day lengths) and differing in elevation by 2600 meters. Segregating populations were shuttled, grown, and selected in these two very different environments. Only lines that withstood the rigors of both environments were advanced in the breeding program.

The results were startling. Not only did these varieties yield well in Mexico, they also performed well in many other environments, from Canada to Argentina, because of their more general insensitivity to differing day lengths. In contrast, U.S. and Canadian varieties performed well only in the areas where they were developed. The development of these broadly adapted spring wheat varieties not only benefited Mexico, but later had a tremendous impact on wheat production in other parts of the world.

Maize Breeding

In the 19th century American farmers made important varietal improvements in the maize species by continuously reselecting the best ears from the best plants in open-pollinated varieties and regrowing them the following year. The introduction of seed from diverse maize-growing areas resulted in natural hybridization with local cultivars. Natural crossing and subsequent mass selection activities gave rise to the open-pollinated dent varieties of the U.S. Corn Belt. These varieties continued in use until the development of hybrids.

Development of F_1 hybrids. It was recognized early that inbreeding in maize leads to reduced vigor in the following generation and that vigor can be restored by crossing. Darwin noted this phenomenon in *The Vegetable Kingdom*, published in 1876. The first organized attempt to exploit hybrid vigor in maize was initiated by W. J. Beal at Michigan State College in 1875. Beal's work and that of others stimulated little interest for 25 years until Edward East and George Schull proved conclusively that although maize lost vigor on inbreeding, when inbred lines were crossed, the progeny of the next generation exhibited an explosive recovery of vigor called heterosis. The problem that remained was how to exploit the heterosis commercially, since the cost of F_1 hybrid seed would be prohibitively expensive. The inbred lines available at that time, when combined in single crosses, produce insufficient seed for an economically viable commercial operation.

The solution was forthcoming from the work of Donald Jones, who had joined East's staff in 1915. In 3 years he found a solution to the high "seed cost" of producing hybrids, and in the process increased yields above those of the original single-cross hybrids. His approach was to mate two single-cross hybrids, formed by intercrossing four inbred lines, to produce what is called a double-cross hybrid. This was a giant step toward solving the problem of reducing the cost of hybrid seed to the farmer.

But there was no stampede to exploit this potential until the mid-1920's, when H. A. Wallace, later to become Secretary of Agriculture and Vice President under Roosevelt, founded Pioneer, Inc., the first private hybrid seed company. Because of the disastrous economic depression of the 1930's, the use of hybrids did not really take off until the early 1940's. But by the mid-1950's hybrids dominated U.S. maize production and the use of open-pollinated varieties virtually disappeared. In the late 1960's, however, F_1 hybrids from single crosses became economically feasible due to the availability of more productive and vigorous inbred lines. Today, more than 90 percent of the F_1 seed in use is from single-cross hybrids.

Since the commercial introduction of the first hybrids in the United States some 40 years ago, many improved elite hybrids with continually higher yields, improved disease and insect resistance, and shorter and stronger stalks suitable for mechanical harvesting have been developed.

Open-pollinated varieties. Efforts to improve maize yields in the developing world have not achieved the spectacular successes characterized by hybrid maize production on the well-watered soils of mid-America. For reasons related to the economic circumstances of farmers and the nascent agricultural infrastructure of most developing countries, the CIM-MYT breeding program has focused on developing superior open-pollinated populations and varieties to serve the special needs of Third World countries. More than 24 populations have been developed that can serve the major envi-

ronmental, maturity, and grain requirements of the developing world. For more than a decade, these populations have been improved by recurrent selection through a multilocational international testing system for yield potential, disease and insect resistance, grain type, and various agronomic characteristics. Some 70 open-pollinated varieties derived from these populations have been released by national breeding programs in over 20 developing countries. These open-pollinated varieties are surpassing traditional Third World varieties in yield potential by 20 to 35 percent and have better agronomic characteristics and earlier maturity.

Certain of these improved populations also maintain their yield superiority (and dependability) over a very wide range of environments. It has now become clear from the dynamic recurrent selection program carried out at multilocational sites that it is possible to breed high-yielding, open-pollinated varieties with a broad spectrum of disease and insect resistance that can, at the same time, have an amazingly broad adaptation across many latitudes and elevations.

Improved nutritional quality. The discovery in 1964 at Purdue University that the mutant opaque-2 gene increases the lysine and tryptophan content of maize by more than 50 percent created considerable excitement among many agricultural scientists and nutritionists. These are the two most limiting essential amino acids in maize for monogastric animals and man. Consequently, it was visualized that it would soon be possible to develop high-yielding maize materials with much-improved nutritional value. However, the difficulty of this task soon became apparent. When the opaque-2 gene was incorporated in maize materials it brought along a host of adverse effects, including a reduction in yield of 15 to 20 percent; a dull, soft, chalky kernel; increased susceptibility to ear diseases and to insects when in storage; and a slower drying rate of grain at physiological maturity.

While many maize breeders soon abandoned their work on opaque-2 maize, CIMMYT persisted in its attempts to develop nutritionally superior maize types with high yield potential and suitable grain and agronomic characteristics. A breakthrough was achieved with the discovery that "normal" maize populations have minor "modifier" genes that can influence the soft texture of the opaque-2 endosperm. A closely coordinated effort to overcome these defects was launched by two CIMMYT scientists and a biochemist. Through the development of a recurrent selection and backcrossing breeding scheme and rapid laboratory screening methods for protein quality, they were able to retain the high levels of lysine and tryptophan associated with the soft-textured opaque-2 endosperm, while pyramiding suitable modifier genes to convert the soft-textured materials to normal maize types with a hard-endosperm.

This conversion was done within the background of the best broadly adapted "normal" CIMMYT populations, so parallel improvements have been carried on for other characteristics simultaneously. The most advanced of the hard-endosperm protein maize materials have been evaluated internationally at a number of locations over the past 2 years. They have been found to be roughly equal in yield, in resistance to disease and insects, and in breadth of adaptation to the best normal varieties included in the yield trials.

Contributions of Plant Breeding to World Food: Wheat and Maize

The contributions of plant breeding research must be seen in the context of total research efforts to improve the effectiveness of agricultural production. Plant breeding, or genetic improvement, is but one element in a research triad that includes improvements through more effective crop husbandry and agronomic practices as well as more productive interactions between particular environments and genotypes.

During the 1940's the research components needed for high-productivity agriculture began to be applied in the United States and yield levels started their take-off, which continues today. The most spectacular increases, however, took place during the 1950's, 1960's, and 1970's with the rapid expansion of the infrastructure for the production and distribution of seed, fertilizers, herbicides, pesticides, and machinery.

Between 1940 and 1980 the combined production of 17 major crops in the United States increased 242 percent, from 252 million to 610 million metric tons (Table 1). This large increase in production was obtained with an increase in the area of cultivated land of only 3 percent. Had 1940 yield levels persisted in 1980, 177 million additional hectares of good U.S. cropland would have been needed to equal the 1980 harvest.

The most impressive change in U.S. crop yields and production during the past 40 years has occurred with maize. Yields have increased 251 percent, due in large part to the introduction of high-yielding hybrids. A conservative estimate is that heterosis in hybrid maize contributed at least 20 percent to the 1980 harvest of 185 million metric tons.

Table 1. Impact of improved technology on land use, crop yield, and production in the United States.

Crop	Area (thousands of hectares)	Yield (tons per hectare)	Production (thousands of tons)
1938 to 1940			
Maize	36,014	1.80	64,104
Wheat	23,635	0.96	22,453
17 major crops*	128,820		252,033
1958 to 1960			
Maize	29,714	3.36	99,891
Wheat	21,419	1.67	35,883
17 major crops	127,436		391,388
1978 to 1980			
Maize	29,338	6.32	185,208
Wheat	25,614	2.22	57,016
17 major crops	132,544		610,293

*Corn, wheat, rice, barley, sorghum, oats, rye, cotton, soybeans, peanuts, beans, flaxseed, potatoes, sugar beets, hay, corn silage, tobacco.

This was an increased production in 1980 of 37 million tons, worth approximately $4.5 billion in additional maize sales over what would have been achieved with the best open-pollinated varieties. As a result of the introduction of the new maize technology, 6.7 million fewer hectares were needed for maize production in 1980 than in 1940. Major yield increases in wheat and many other crops have also been achieved in the United States.

Beginning in the mid-1960's, improved agricultural technology began to reach the developing world as well. The establishment of the 13 international agricultural research centers over the past two decades has been a major factor in stimulating agricultural research on the major food crops and farming systems in the developing world. The most impressive achievements to date have been in wheat and rice. The plant breeding efforts of scientists at the International Rice Research Institute in the Philippines and CIMMYT in Mexico did much to avert the spectre of famine in Asia in the 1960's and 1970's.

In India the introduction of high-yielding wheat and rice varieties, in combination with improved agronomic practices that permitted these varieties to express their high genetic yield potential, has had a major impact on transforming food production.

When high-yielding semidwarf varieties of Mexican wheat were introduced into India during 1966 to 1968, national production stood at roughly 11 million metric tons and average yields were less than 1 ton per hectare (Table 2). The high-yielding wheat varieties quickly took over, and by 1981 wheat production had increased to 36.5 million metric tons, largely as a result of a 100 percent improvement in national wheat yields. The 1981 harvest increase of 25.5 million tons over the 1966 harvest represents sufficient additional grain to provide 186 million people with 65 percent of the carbohydrate portion of a diet containing 2350 kilocalories per day.

Equally impressive wheat production gains have been achieved in Argentina, China, Pakistan, Turkey, and, more recently, in Bangladesh. Total wheat production in developing countries has more than doubled over the past two decades. Although it is difficult to quantify the individual impact of the various components of production because of their interactions, certainly the use of high-yielding varieties developed through conventional plant breeding research, in combination with the increasing use of

Table 2. Wheat production in India before and after the wheat revolution. [Data from the Indian national wheat program. Format adapted from that of B. A. Krantz]

Years	Wheat production (millions of tons)	Gross value of increase* (millions of dollars)	Number of adults provided with carbohydrate needs by increase† (millions)
1966 to 1967	11.39	88	3
1968 to 1969	18.65	1540	50
1970 to 1971	23.83	2576	94
1972 to 1973	24.74	2758	101
1974 to 1975	24.10	2630	96
1976 to 1977	29.08	3626	133
1978 to 1979	35.51	4912	180
1980 to 1981	36.50	5110	186

*The wheat value used is $200 per ton, similar to the landed value imported wheat in India in 1981.   †Calculations are based on the provision of 65 percent of the carbohydrate portion of a diet containing 2350 kilocalories per day, or 375 grams of wheat per person per day.

fertilizers and irrigation, has been a decisive factor in the increasing yields.

More recently, we are seeing the potential for major technological improvements in other vitally important food crops in the developing world. For example, data on maize production over the past two decades in the developing countries reveal that the average annual rate of yield increases in the 1970's was twice the rate achieved in the 1960's. This marked change, I believe, points to the beginning of a technological turning point in Third World maize production in the decade ahead. Given the importance of maize as a food and feed grain, and considering its relatively higher maximum genetic yield potential among the cereals, significant productivity gains will play a pivotal role in future world food production efforts.

The Next Doubling:

Feeding 8 Billion People

World population growth dictates in large measure the increases needed in food production. Since the beginning of agriculture, world population has increased more than 256-fold (eight doublings), and now stands at approximately 4.5 billion. The challenge just to maintain already inadequate per capita food consumption levels is awesome. It took roughly from 12,000 B.C. until about 1850 for world population to reach 1 billion, only 80 years to reach 2 billion, and only 45 years to reach 4 billion. We are now faced with the need to double the world food supply again by the first decades of the 21st century.

The dramatic increases in yield that have occurred in American agriculture since 1940 through the introduction of science-based technology also indicate the long gestation period between the initiation of research programs and the application of results on a large scale. In the case of plant breeding, more than 50 years elapsed between initiation of the original genetic research and the time when the application of research results began to affect production significantly. The magnitude of the food production tasks ahead requires that we find ways to speed up this process of applying and diffusing research results.

The significance of increased crop production in the more marginial agricultural areas is an especially important dimension in feeding future generations. Some 600 million people live in the semiarid tropics and more than 1 billion live in tropical and subtropical areas characterized by serious biological constraints. I must caution that agricultural research alone cannot produce miraculous improvements in many of the more marginal production areas. Some of the biological limitations are simply too overpowering for science to currently overcome. Still, we can put science to work on a number of the problems faced in marginal land areas.

Future Plant Breeding
Research Priorities

In some scientific circles today it is anticipated that major production benefits will soon be forthcoming from the use of genetic engineering. The new techniques in tissue culture, cell fusion, and DNA transfer are all being heralded as the scientific answers to increasing the breadth, level, and stability of disease resistance; eliminating the need for conventional chemical fertilizers; and further raising the genetic yield potential of food crops.

Although great progress has been made by employing genetic engineering techniques with bacteria or yeasts to increase the production of insulin and interferon, there is no firm evidence that similar results will be obtained with higher plants, especially polyploid species such as wheat. It will probably be many years before these techniques can be successfully used to breed superior crop varieties. Furthermore, it is a mistake to assume that the transfer into crop species of disease- and insect-resistant genes through genetic engineering will result in substantially more durable varieties than we have been able to achieve to date. Pathogens and insects, when faced with extinction, mutate into new races capable of attacking the resistant variety. This biological reality will continue to hound mankind in the years ahead.

Although some research funds should be directed toward the development of genetic engineering techniques to improve breeding programs, I believe that most of the research funds for crop improvement should continue to be used for conventional plant breeding research. There is much that remains to be done, and can be done, to further improve disease and insect resistance, enhance tolerance to environmental extremes, and increase genetic yield potential by employing conventional plant breeding methods.

At CIMMYT, increasing attention is being focused on the problems of marginal production areas. Two major breeding approaches are being pursued. One involves conventional breeding procedures in search of genetic variation in a particular crop species for added tolerance or resistance to specific agroclimatic and soil stress conditions. Improved genetic materials—in terms of drought, cold, and heat resistance and tolerance to mineral toxicities such as those found in saline and acidic soils—are emerging from this work. As one example, wheat researchers have identified materials with significantly greater tolerance to acid soils characterized by aluminum toxicity. Aluminum-tolerant wheat lines, developed in cooperation with Brazilian scientists, are showing extraordinarily high yield levels under this soil-stress situation. There are millions of hectares of potential wheat land with acid soils high in soluble aluminum that now can be brought into much higher yielding production.

Wide crosses between plant species are also being explored to transfer useful genes for added environmental stability in major crop species. Triticale—a hybrid of wheat and rye—is an example of research efforts that led to the development of a new crop species. In just two decades, tremendous strides have been made in increasing yield potential and improving agronomic types of triticale. Triticale yields have doubled and now are similar to those of the best bread wheats in optimum production environments. Triticale probably has a higher genetic grain yield potential than bread wheat because of its greater production of dry matter. Its strong production advantage over wheat is most evident in certain marginal areas characterized by cool temperatures, acid or sandy soils, and heavy disease pressure. In such environments triticale has shown a substantially higher yield advantage over wheat.

Research to cross domesticated species with related wild species is another promising research avenue that may lead to the development of varieties with greater yield potential and dependability in a number of important marginal areas. Generally, such wide crosses involve the breaking down of natural barriers between plant species in order to introduce useful genes from alien genera into domesticated crop species. We have identified a number of wild species with greater resistance to certain diseases and insects and tolerance to salinity, temperature, and moisture stresses than we have found to date in the germ plasm of the major crop species. Successful introgression of these desirable genes can lead to crop varieties with greater tolerance to environmental stresses.

I am convinced that the 8 billion people projected to be living 40 to 50 years from now will continue to find most of their sustenance from the same plant species that supply most of our food needs now. Fortunately, we still have large amounts of exploitable yield potential on which to capitalize, especially in the developing world, where eight of every ten new births occur. It is in these areas of the world where it is imperative to close the gap between actual and potential crop yields. We must also continue to work aggressively to raise average yields in the developed nations. Such yield increases will be more difficult to achieve as the maximum genetic yield of each crop species is approached.

New techniques, such as tissue culture and genetic engineering, offer potentially great payoffs and merit research resources in the years ahead. However, we should not neglect the more conventional areas of plant breeding research, since they represent the major line of defense today on the food front.

14. Biotechnology of Forest Yield

Peter Farnum, Roger Timmis, J. Laurence Kulp

In this chapter we review historical levels of productivity in natural forest stands, increases in yield that have resulted from plantation management, and potential productivity from future technologies, in particular genetic manipulation. The estimates of productivity are based on research plot measurements and operational experience (*1*). The discussion is focused on two commercially important temperate coniferous forests: Douglas fir [*Pseudotsuga menziesii* (Mirb.) Franco] in Washington State and loblolly pine (*Pinus taeda* L.) in North Carolina.

There is no single generally accepted measure of forest productivity. In this chapter yield is defined as the live standing phytomass at any point in time. Mean annual yield is yield divided by crop age. Net primary productivity is the total phytomass produced in a given year. Phytomass is the total biomass of the trees in a stand. Productivity is expressed as dry mass per hectare per year for all phytomass produced under stated management practices. Dry mass is expressed in megagrams and is determined by oven drying to a constant weight. Estimates of productivity are made by using growth and yield models along with biomass distribution equations. A range of ±25 percent is indicated for estimated productivity in coniferous for-

ests (*2*). This is a reasonable estimate of uncertainty for the values reported here.

The climatic characteristics for a site of average productivity in the Puget Sound lowlands of Washington State are given in Table 1. Maximum mean annual yield for a natural stand of Douglas fir at this site is about 6 megagrams per hectare per year (*3, 4*).

The loblolly pine site selected for analysis is a pocosin on North Carolina's lower coastal plain. Pocosins are upland

Table 1. Climatic conditions for the selected sites in Washington and North Carolina. Adapted from Gordon *et al.* (*8*).

Variable	Puget Sound lowlands, Washington	Lower coastal plain, North Carolina
Number of frost-free days	200 to 240	240
Temperature (°C)		
Yearly mean	11	15
January mean	4	5
July mean	18	25
Precipitation (mm)		
Yearly mean	1000	1100
Growing season mean	420	770
Yearly mean radiation (cal/cm² day)	290	350

areas with poor natural drainage due to flat topography and impermeable subsoils. Because of the soil conditions and frequent fires, natural pine stands on pocosins are generally understocked, with resultant low levels of productivity. Forests consist of mixed pine stands with dense, shrubby undergrowth and may occupy only 30 percent of the area (5). Data on phytomass productivity for these sites are difficult to obtain, but an estimate of peak mean annual yield for a well-stocked loblolly stand is about 4 Mg/ha per year (6, 7). Typical climatic characteristics for this site are given in Table 1.

As both natural stands and plantations develop, annual net primary productivity is low at first, increases to a broad plateau, and then slowly declines (Fig. 1). The low values for young stands are due to incomplete site occupancy (crowns and roots do not fully utilize the growing space), while declines in vigor and increases in respiration are probably responsible for the lower values at older ages. The best values for comparison are the maximum values of mean annual yield.

Potential Productivity

Potential net primary productivity was estimated with a modification (8) of the model by Loomis and Williams (9). The basic assumption in this model is that solar radiation ultimately limits phytomass productivity. Allowances are made to reduce incident radiation by the amount that is not photosynthetically active, the amount that is reflected, and the amount that is absorbed by the non-photosynthetic parts of the stand.

Potential gross productivity (in moles of CH_2O) is calculated by multiplying the absorbed, photosynthetically active radiation by an assumed quantum efficiency. Allowance is then made for respiration requirements to maintain life processes in the standing crop and to produce new material through growth. The rates of both are adjusted for temperature effects. Gross productivity minus respiration gives the maximum net productivity of carbohydrate. This must be adjusted for inorganic uptake to estimate the maximum net productivity of phytomass. This estimate includes material lost to mortality, to shedding (as of needles and cones), and to consumption by insects and other animals. The coefficients used in the model of potential productivity are given in Table 2. The high values are estimates of the best obtainable from ordinary biological processes, while the standard values are representative of observations in productive stands.

Predicted maximum net productivities for Douglas fir and loblolly pine are given in Table 3. Productivity for loblolly pine is higher than for Douglas fir because of greater annual solar radiation, but the higher temperatures in North Carolina reduce the difference somewhat by increasing respiration. The large range between the high and standard estimates reflects the uncertainties of this kind of analysis.

It should be emphasized that the values predicted by this model are for maximum net primary productivity, whereas the values cited for existing stands are for mean annual yield. Mean annual yield is lower because of poor site occupancy at young ages and because it excludes material lost to mortality, shedding, and so forth. Maximum net primary productivity is about 2.5 times higher than maximum mean annual yield (10, 11).

Loomis and Williams' estimate (9), if

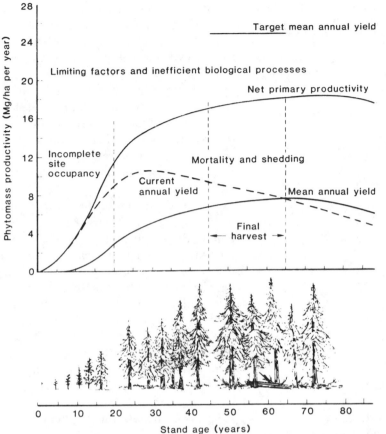

Fig. 1. Components of phytomass production versus age for a plantation of Douglas fir having 1000 trees per hectare at age 17. Mean annual yield falls below the target level because the stand fails to fully utilize the site at young ages, because production is lost to mortality, shedding, and insects, because the soil and climate fail to provide the optimum growing conditions, and because biological processes in the stand are not optimized for growth. Current annual productivity, the change in live standing phytomass during a given year, is equal to net primary productivity minus phytomass lost. Productivity is lower in natural stands because full site occupancy is delayed and because mortality is a greater proportion of yield. Net primary productivity peaks earlier in natural stands, which undergo significant mortality at younger ages. Mortality is delayed in plantations by the uniform size and spacing of the trees. Harvest at the culmination of mean annual yield maximizes the phytomass yield from the forest, although earlier harvests are often economically desirable. Data are derived from a simulation by Curtis et al. (10) and from biomass distribution equations by Gholz et al. (3). The shedding component was estimated as a fixed fraction of foliar biomass by using data from Keyes and Grier (38).

converted to a yearly value, is similar to the maximum reported here. Using a different theoretical approach, Monteith (12) estimated potential net primary productivity at about 55 Mg/ha per year. Maximum productivity for a temperate coniferous forest has been estimated to be at least 45 Mg/ha per year on the basis of a survey of world literature (2).

It appears that 50 Mg/ha per year is a reasonable target for net primary productivity in Douglas fir stands. This value is within the range reported by Gordon et al. (8), close to Monteith's estimate, and near the observed maximum. In Douglas fir plantations the ratio of maximum net primary productivity to maximum mean annual yield is about 2.5. Future technologies should reduce this ratio to about 2. Therefore, the tar-

Table 2. Critical biological coefficients used to calculate potential phytomass productivity as a function of climatic conditions. High values are estimates of the best attainable, while standard values are representative of observations in productive stands. Adapted from Gordon *et al.* (8).

Variable	Value	
	High	Standard
Albedo (fraction)	0.05	0.10
Inactive absorption (fraction)	0.05	0.15
Quantum efficiency (mole/E)	0.10	0.05
Maintenance respiration (g/g day)	0.006	0.016
Growth respiration (g/g)	0.25	0.35
Inorganic uptake (g/g)	0.10	0.05
Relative growth rate (g/g day)	0.33	0.0033

get for maximum mean annual yield is 25 Mg/ha per year. In view of the greater solar radiation in North Carolina, the target for loblolly pine is taken to be 30 Mg/ha per year. The gap between observed mean annual yields in natural Douglas fir and loblolly pine stands (6 and 4 Mg/ha per year, respectively) and these goals is large. Natural production rates at the selected sites are only 23 and 12 percent of the target values.

A sensitivity analysis involving the modified model (8) revealed that changes in quantum efficiency and the intrinsic relative growth rate of tissue per unit mass of live material have the largest impact on productivity, and there is a significant interaction between relative growth rate and the maintenance respiration coefficient. With high relative growth rates only small amounts of live phytomass are required to fully utilize available radiation. In this case total maintenance respiration costs are small even if the maintenance coefficient is large. On the other hand, with low relative growth rates large amounts of live phytomass are required to fully utilize the radiation. In this case total maintenance respiration costs (and therefore potential productivity) are sensitive to the maintenance coefficient. Inactive absorption and albedo reduce absorbed radiation and potential productivity proportionally.

The yield gap can be closed in several ways (Fig. 1): (i) by increasing site occupancy, the number of years of low productivity at young ages can be reduced; (ii) some phytomass lost to mortality may be captured by thinning; (iii) cultural practices, such as fertilization and control of water, may mitigate factors that limit growth; and (iv) certain biological processes may be made more efficient through genetic manipulation.

Progress from Cultural Practices

Douglas fir. Increases in the productivity of Douglas fir since about 1960

Table 3. Theoretical maximum net productivity in a single year for Douglas fir and loblolly pine. High and standard values refer to the settings of the biological coefficients which are input to the model. Values are megagrams per hectare per year. Adapted from Gordon *et al.* (8).

Item	Douglas fir	Loblolly pine
High values		
Entire year	245	300
Growing season	216	236
Standard values		
Entire year	37	46
Growing season	33	36

have been achieved largely through plantation establishment and nitrogen fertilization. Typical silvicultural practices to establish Douglas fir plantations involve clear-cutting, nursery production of 1- to 3-year-old seedlings, site preparation (by fire, mechanical, or chemical means), planting, and tending of the young stand (13). This system offers many opportunities to improve on natural regeneration processes and increase yields. Harvesting and site preparation techniques can be used to control competing vegetation, animal pressure, and the microclimate of the planted seedling. Through nursery practices the physiological vigor and morphological characteristics of the seedlings can be managed. Through proper lifting, packing, and cold-storage techniques, planting can be timed to match the physiological condition of the plant to the climate of the site. Finally, through the planting process itself, uniform stocking in reasonable soil conditions can be achieved. Maximum mean annual yields of phytomass for untreated Douglas fir plantations are about 7 Mg/ha per year (Table 4) (14). Thus harvesting and regeneration practices increase Douglas fir productivity about 30 percent.

Although forest soils in the Douglas fir region often contain large amounts of total nitrogen, low mineralization rates due to low average soil temperatures limit its availability to trees (15). Extensive trials in the region have helped to quantify the response of Douglas fir to single applications of urea (16). Responses to repeated applications are the subject of current research. Maximum mean annual yield may increase 20 percent as a result of applying 200 kilograms of nitrogen per hectare every 5 years starting at age 30. Peak mean annual yield in fertilized plantations would thus be about 9 Mg/ha per year, or 50 percent greater than in unfertilized natural stands (Table 4) (17).

Thinning in Douglas fir stands is primarily regarded as a tool to increase their value (by concentrating the wood produced on fewer but larger stems) rather than their productivity. The situation is by no means simple, however, as the effects of thinning on productivity are related to utilization standards, the timing of the thinnings, and the manner in which removal is carried out (18). Small increases in productivity may result from early thinnings that leave only well-spaced stems on the best microsites.

Loblolly pine. Production of loblolly pine has been increased by site drainage, site preparation, and fertilization with

Table 4. Productivity increases attributable to intensive management of Douglas fir.

Case	Maximum mean annual yield (Mg/ha year)	Cumulative increase (percent)
Natural stands (4)	5.7	
Silvicultural treatments		
Plantation establishment (14)	7.2	30
Nitrogen fertilization (17)	8.8	50
First-generation genetics (56)	9.7	70
Target	25.0	340

Table 5. Productivity increases attributable to intensive plantation management of loblolly pine in North Carolina pocosins.

Case	Maximum mean annual yield (Mg/ha year)	Cumulative increase (percent)
Natural stands (6, 7)	3.6	
Silvicultural treatments		
Drain and plant (24, 25)	7.0	90
Bedding (26)	8.6	140
Preplant phosphorus (30)	10.5	190
Nitrogen fertilization (33)	11.8	230
First- and second-generation genetics (56)	14.3	300
Target	30.0	730

phosphorus and nitrogen. Not only are the interactions between these silvicultural practices important in determining the yield increases, there are important operational interactions between these treatments and basic logging practices.

In undrained pocosins the water table ranges seasonally from about 1 meter below the ground surface to 30 centimeters above. It may be at or above the soil surface during the winter, late spring, and early summer (5). Loblolly pine grows best at a water table depth of 60 to 75 cm (19, 20). With higher water tables both soil aeration and root growth are reduced. In addition, high water tables, particularly when associated with heavier soils, can severely limit mechanical operations on a site. Logging and site preparation may cause significant soil degradation if performed under wet conditions (21, 22).

Early attempts to increase southern pine production by drainage can be traced to the 1930's (19). Current drainage practices include establishing ditches at 200-m intervals before logging and 100-m intervals before planting (22). This practice may lower the water table 30 to 60 cm, although winter rains will still cause the soil to be saturated (5).

Various investigators have estimated the increases in yield that result from drainage. Terry and Hughes (23) gave examples for planted southern pines that range from 133 to 1300 percent. Klawitter (19) indicated that the height of the dominant trees at age 50 will increase by 5 to 8 m as a result of drainage. Maximum mean annual yield in a drained plantation is estimated to be about 7 Mg/ha per year (24, 25). This is an increase of 90 percent over natural levels (Table 5).

Removal of excess moisture makes intensive site preparations more effective. Site preparation is necessary to reduce logging slash, ameliorate soil compaction caused by logging, improve aeration, reduce vegetative competition, and facilitate planting. One operation that provides these benefits is bedding (the forming of ridges in the soil) (23). Drainage facilitates bedding in that it increases the amount of time heavy machinery can operate on the site and allows beds to be formed more easily and to last longer because the soil is not saturated (22, 23).

As stated above, even after drainage pocosin soils are saturated in the winter. Thus, by creating ridges, bedding further increases the effective depth of the water table. Shoulders and Terry (21) reported that 7-year-old loblolly pines were 15 cm taller for every additional 2.5 cm of water table depth in January. Survival of planted seedlings is also likely to increase. Finally, by improving soil aeration and increasing microbial activity, bedding may improve nutrient availability. The estimated maximum mean annual yield in a drained and bedded plantation is about 9 Mg/ha per year (Table 5) (26).

Application of phosphorus before planting interacts with drainage and bedding in several ways. Repeated and prolonged flooding causes anaerobic soil conditions and tends to make phosphorus less available in the soil. Roots subjected to flooding may be less able to absorb phosphorus (27). Application of the fertilizer to the soil to correct this deficiency is facilitated by draining and may be done most effectively in the same operational process as bedding. Finally, significant positive interactions between bedding and phosphorus fertilization have been reported for the pocosin sites (23).

The growth response of pine trees to applications of phosphorus on pocosin-like soils is both large and long-lasting (28). A single application before planting may suffice for an entire rotation (29). Maximum mean annual yield in a drained and bedded plantation with phosphorus is estimated to be 10 to 11 Mg/ha per year (Table 5) (30).

Once drainage has removed excess moisture from the site, bedding has helped further with aeration, and phosphorus fertilization has removed the deficiency for that element, then there may be a strong response to nitrogen fertilization. A well-stocked stand that has been drained and fertilized with phosphorus should grow about 20 percent more in volume as a result of nitrogen fertilization (31, 32). Estimated maximum mean annual yield in a drained, unthinned plantation receiving phosphorus before planting and nitrogen fertilizer at 5-year intervals starting at age 10 is about 12 Mg/ha per year (Table 5) (33).

The effect of thinning on loblolly pine productivity is similar to that on Douglas fir. Overall productivity is not changed substantially (34). Two exceptions should be noted: the growth response to nitrogen fertilizer may be greater in thinned stands (35), and unthinned stands, it not harvested at the right time, will undergo such severe mortality that yield will decline (24).

The discussion of these practices has stressed their interactions on an operational and biological level. One further interaction has to do with increases in value resulting from increases in productivity. The value per unit yield of a tree is proportional to its size. Larger trees are more valuable because they yield more wood and because each unit of that wood is more valuable. For the example given in Table 5, the relative value per unit of yield increased about 50 percent due to these treatments. Thus, while these cultural treatments increased mean annual yield 230 percent, they increased value about 400 percent.

A comparison of the results listed in Tables 4 and 5 to the target mean annual yields shows that, even after gains from present cultural practices, a substantial gap still exists between actual and potential phytomass production. Douglas fir is achieving about 35 percent and loblolly pine about 40 percent of the target yields.

Opportunities for Future Gains from Cultural Practices

Theoretical maximum productivity was defined under the assumption that solar radiation is the only limiting factor. To determine the extent to which controllable site factors limit growth, the exercise must be repeated under other assumptions: for instance, all available growing season water is used to satisfy photosynthesis at the highest water-use efficiencies theoretically attainable (36), or all available nitrogen is supplied and recycled at a rate such that its concentration in all live tissue is maintained at a theoretical minimum level consistent with enzymatic and structural requirements (37). For many sites, the maximum productivity defined in these terms would fall well below the radiation-limited values. The difference would define the benefits possible from treatments alleviating these, and other, deficiencies in the presence of perfectly efficient trees.

Much more needs to be learned about the effects of cultural practices on the allocation of yield between aboveground and belowground structures. Productivity gains will be overestimated by studies that are based only on aboveground measurements when significant reallocation of production from roots to tops occurs. One study of Douglas fir demonstrated that fine root turnover accounts for only 8 percent of total annual production on a good site but for 36 percent on a poor site (38).

The low productivities at young ages (Fig. 1) result from the delay in canopy closure and subsequent maximization of the ratio of leaf to ground area (leaf area index) in even-aged coniferous plantations (39). This period may be shortened by increasing the number of trees planted per unit area. Site occupancy can also be achieved sooner by increasing the rate of crown expansion of established seedlings by controlling noncrop vegetation.

Fertilization. Numerous advances remain to be made in the area of fertilization. Much research has concentrated on determining whether a growth response to a single application will occur and then estimating its size. Recent analysis of the growth of various agronomic crops (40) and young trees in hydroponic culture, however, suggests a more dynamic approach. Ingestad (41) demonstrated that relative growth rate can be maintained as trees increase in size by using micromolar amounts of nitrate, provided that the supply of nitrate is matched to the potential relative growth rate. The constant in this system is the tissue nitrogen concentration, especially in the foliage. The tree apparently has a tendency to maintain this concentration by reducing its relative growth rate when insufficient N is supplied to the roots. Thus productivity can be N-limited even though no deficiency symptoms or lower N concentrations are detectable. The value of this approach in Scots pine plantations was demonstrated in a 6-year study in Sweden (42). Productivity was increased 2.5 times and relatively less of it was allocated to the root system of irrigated and fertilized trees.

Future research must concentrate on defining the optimum frequency and dosage of fertilizer applications to ensure a balanced nutrient supply to tree roots with respect to known limitations at specific sites. Wider application should also be made of existing diagnostic tests for mineral deficiencies (15, 43). In view of the increasing cost of fertilizers and their application, improved encapsulation techniques for controlled-release fertilizers and genetically enhanced microbial sources (*44, 45*) may become prominent.

Control of competing vegetation. Fertilization and other site improvement techniques improve growing conditions for plants that compete with the species of economic interest. Many studies of Douglas fir and loblolly pine have demonstrated that control of competing vegetation during the phase of incomplete site occupancy can lead to substantially increased size and survival of the crop. In one study in which weeds were controlled for loblolly pine during the first 5 years after planting, a 70 percent gain in yield was noted at age 9 (*46*).

An important advance is the development of effective and environmentally safe chemicals to achieve control of competing vegetation. The effectiveness of plant hormone analogs such as 2,4-D and 2,4,5-T is based on their relatively greater absorption by broad-leaved foliage, whose cellular machinery they sabotage. Recent studies of plant hormones, such as that on the role of the cell wall in releasing oligosaccharide fragments with growth-inhibiting effects (*47*), may lead to the development of alternative herbicides.

Exploitation of other interactions. Interactions among cultural treatments play an important role in yield improvement efforts. Studies have been established to determine the effects of site preparation, fertilization, and weed control on loblolly pine survival, growth, and yield (*44*). More such studies are needed, particularly in the Douglas fir region. A key interaction of which there is little quantitative understanding is that between mineral nutrition and water supply. Drip irrigation may become practical in nonremote plantations managed for specific high-value products (*48*). Even in unirrigated plantations, interactions between water and mineral nutri-

ents determine the effectiveness of fertilization and its optimum dosage and timing. These interactions must be understood and represented in models to allow extrapolation from irrigation and fertilizer trials to a wide range of sites.

Maintenance of productivity. One concern for the future deals with the maintenance of productivity over several rotations of intensive management. For example, declines in productivity have been observed in some second-rotation stands in South Australia (*49*).

Declines in productivity due to intensive plantation management could be caused by a number of factors. These include harvesting activities on wet sites, which may cause soil compaction; whole tree utilization, which may deplete nutrient supply on marginal sites; burning, which can remove litter and nutrients; and intensive site preparation, which has the potential to increase erosion.

While mismanagement certainly causes declines in productivity, there is no reason to believe that careful intensive management will do so (*50, 51*). Where productivity losses do occur, they often can be more than offset with fertilizer applications (*52*). In fact, recent results from Australia show that scientifically treated second-rotation stands may significantly outperform first-rotation crops on the same or matched sites (*50*).

Protection efforts have played a vital role in increasing forest yields. Actual yields to date have probably been increased more by protection against fire than the cultural practices discussed. For instance, fire control increased wood volume production 200 percent in one North Carolina pocosin (*5*). Certainly, if increases in productivity are to be realized, fire, insects, disease, and erosion will have to be effectively combated.

Progress from Genetics

Genetic programs for Douglas fir and loblolly pine began in the early 1950's. The programs are designed to cope with a combination of features unique to forest trees: enormous genetic diversity (53); a long juvenile period before flowering; an even longer period before seedling progeny can be confidently evaluated for productivity, self-fertility, and the resulting loss of vigor; and the frequent variation of genotypic expression on the great diversity of sites. Efforts are being made to learn how desired traits are controlled genetically and to tackle the practical and economic problems of working with thousands of large trees.

Growth rate is a complex trait under the control of many genes. The objective of the breeding programs for Douglas fir and loblolly pine is to increase the frequency of desirable genes in the population while maintaining a sufficiently broad genetic base for increases to continue in the future. This is achieved by cycles of selection followed by interbreeding of selects, and by the infusion at each cycle of new parent material from sources outside the breeding population. At present, improved seed is produced operationally in large production orchards relying on the airborne pollen mix. Only the female parent is known and genetic gain is lower than if pollen from selected trees were applied. This is known as half-sib technology. The design and operation of such programs have been reviewed in detail by Faulkner (54). The typical sequence and time scale of operations are illustrated in Fig. 2.

Because of the 10- to 15-year breeding cycle, only recently have the first progeny tests shown stable family rankings for volume production. Current predictions of per hectare yield from them are subject to the uncertainties associated with extrapolating growth curves from individual 10-year-old trees (55). Many such predictions have been made (56). They indicate that, for Douglas fir and loblolly pine, the gain in mean annual yield will be about 12 to 15 percent per generation. Increased value and cost savings may result not only from larger size but also from stem quality characteristics, disease resistance, higher wood density, and greater product uniformity. A 12 percent gain for Douglas fir (Table 4) and a 24 percent gain for two generations of loblolly pine selects (Table 5) brings the estimates of production in intensively managed Douglas fir and loblolly pine plantations to about 10 and 14 Mg/ha per year, respectively. Thus, with current forestry technology, plantations can achieve 40 percent (Douglas fir) or 50 percent (loblolly pine) of the target mean annual yields.

Opportunities for Future Gains from Genetics

Component breeding. Combining parents that have different bases for their superiority (such as a longer growth period in one parent and a greater photosynthetic capacity in the other) will increase the chance of favorable matings over that currently achieved through "blind" selection for stem volume (57, 58). A synergistic gain may be seen in the offspring. To achieve this, however, an understanding of the various biological processes and their interactions is required (Fig. 3). Identifying which processes will have large general effects on growth, site-specific effects, or even mutually antagonistic effects will be aided by further development of mathematical models of growth (59). Many processes in the

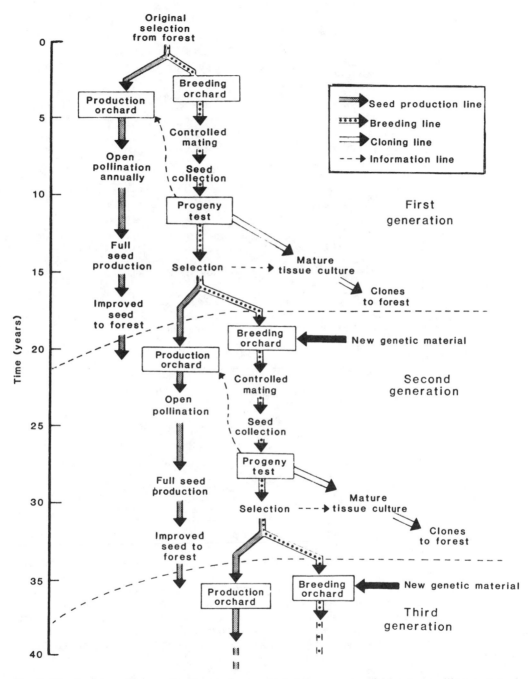

Fig. 2. The tree-breeding cycle. Shoots from selected trees are grafted onto seedling rootstock to establish the orchards. Progeny tests provide shoots for the next generation of breeding and production and information for removing poor parents from the existing production orchards. They will eventually provide material for cloning superior individuals. Breeding and production lines are separated so as to maintain a broad genetic base in the former and specialize for productivity in the latter.

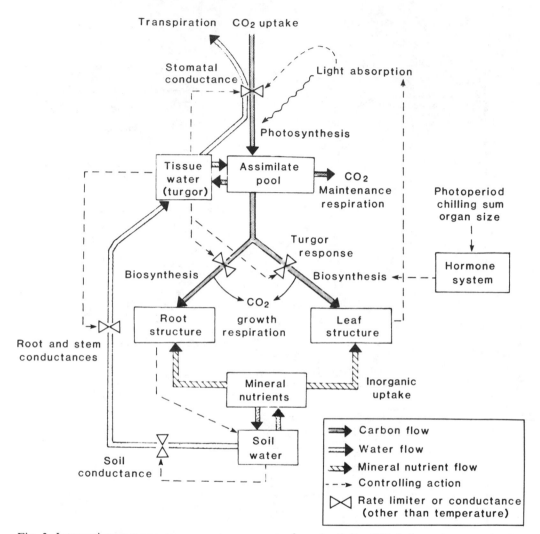

Fig. 3. Interactions among component processes of productivity. The balance between leaves and roots may be the result of competition for carbohydrate from a pool produced by photosynthesis. Competition is dependent on the activities of the respective meristems as a result of organ size or hormonal information. Conductance is the reciprocal of resistance to hydraulic flow along the soil or tissue pathway, or to vapor diffusion in the case of stomata. Water, carbon, and mineral flow processes interact at numerous points. All the indicated plant properties and processes exhibit significant genetic variation, and some contributing to mature-tree superiority can be identified in seedlings. Their separate contributions to growth in given environments must be understood through mathematical modeling for component breeding to be effective.

modified Loomis-Williams model show considerable genetic variation within and among forest populations. Considerable opportunity thus exists for their improvement.

Light absorption by the canopy is one of the few low-level processes consistently showing a direct relation to yield

(*12, 39*). In closed-canopy coniferous forests light absorption is more efficient than in agricultural crops (*39*). Nevertheless, there is still considerable intraspecific variation in components of absorption—such as branch angle and length, leaf clustering, branching frequency, and growth habit—that are considered highly heritable (*57, 60*).

Quantum efficiency is the result of an intricate web of interacting processes, including those controlling the availability of water and mineral nutrients (Fig. 3). Consequently, although many studies have shown significant genetic variation in photosynthesis-related processes in trees (*61*), direct correlation with yield is seldom seen. Ledig (*59*) reviewed some notable exceptions.

Photosynthetic rates of single leaves in trees are only about half of those in agricultural crop species under similar conditions (*62, 63*), and appear to have been less rigorously selected for in nature. Winter photosynthesis is particularly important for annual growth in conifers (*64, 65*), exhibiting considerable genetic change along elevational and other gradients (*66–68*). Genetic variation in the stomatal response to low humidity and water stress has also been observed (*57*). Contrary to experience with agricultural crops (*63*), the prospect is good that improvements in single-leaf processes will contribute to tree crop productivity (*57*).

The rate of conversion of assimilated carbon to new structure ("biosynthesis" in Fig. 3) may limit the productivity of tree crops under field conditions more frequently than photosynthesis. Genetic variation in this conversion rate, or in the accompanying energy use ("growth respiration"), is poorly documented (*57*).

Important genetic variation occurs in the allocation of dry matter to different organs. Some families of loblolly pine, for example, grow faster by reinvesting assimilate in new leaves (*59*), while others (from drier areas) achieve superiority by investing relatively more in roots (*68*). However, allocation differences enabling an isolated tree to capture its surroundings more quickly do not ensure improved productivity per hectare following full site occupancy (*55*).

The date of budbreak in spring, the number of subsequent growth flushes, and the switchover from extension of preformed shoots to building of the new apical dome and leaf primordia are all under some degree of genetic control (*57*). Some of this variation can be exploited by appropriate northward or uphill seed movement (*69*).

Avoidance of water stress by mechanisms of stomatal closure response (*57*), allocation of assimilate to roots (*68, 70*), leaf morphology, osmotic adjustment (*57*), or early dormancy (*71*) are features of genetically superior seedling families or provenances of Douglas fir and loblolly pine. Exploitable genetic differences also occur in the efficiency with which mineral nutrients are utilized (*57, 72, 73*). These and other adaptions to stress need to be emphasized wherever site limitations cannot be alleviated economically through silviculture (*74*).

Little is known of the extent of genetic variation in maintenance respiration with respect to its rate per gram of tissue, its temperature dependence, or the amount of live biomass in the crop. A line of perennial ryegrass with low maintenance respiration has, however, produced yields 12 to 20 percent higher in widely replicated field trials in Britain (*58*). This should lessen concern that low-maintenance selections might show undesirable side effects, like early leaf senescence.

It may be possible to take further advantage of component breeding to shorten the breeding cycle. Parameters of biological processes underlying high annual yields will be identifiable much earlier than the long-term yield trends themselves and are more amenable to rapid screening. In some cases screening may be possible at a cellular level in liquid culture. Recurrent selection of natural or induced mutant cells from a single parent could then be a new source of rapid genetic gain (75). The correlation of fusiform rust resistance in loblolly pine callus with whole-tree resistance (76) and the screening of *Eucalyptus* plantlets for salt tolerance (77) are examples of interest.

Use of in vitro techniques. A portion of genetic variation among individual trees is due to gene interactions that are not normally transmitted intact through sexual reproduction. This "nonadditive" portion can give rise to exceptional individuals within generally superior families. It can be captured by vegetative propagation or the interbreeding of homozygous trees.

Estimates of the magnitude of nonadditive gain are scarce, varying in conifers between 10 and 30 percent (60, 78, 79). The accuracy and comparability of these estimates are uncertain because of the different gains already achieved in the base population, the unspecified selection intensities, and ignorance of clonal effects arising from the particular status of the parent. A clearer example is provided by *Eucalyptus grandis* in Brazil. Record mean annual yields around 60 Mg/ha per year (aboveground stem to a 5-cm top) are anticipated after repeated selection. The best clone had twice the yield of the base crop, which was already enhanced by provenance and family se-

lection (80). From these observations it appears that two generations of breeding and intense clonal selection in Douglas fir and loblolly pine could improve yield nearly 100 percent over that of wild seed.

Vegetative propagation techniques include the use of cuttings and tissue culture. Cuttings are being used successfully to clone a few conifer species and have provided the genetic gain estimates above. However, they suffer from several chronic problems (81, 82), including difficulty of rooting, poor early growth and form, low rates of multiplication, and aging of parents. In vitro culture techniques may eliminate these problems.

Tissue culture consists of the removal of an organ or piece of tissue from the parent, its sterilization to remove surface microorganisms, and its placement in or on a suitable series of chemical media that stimulate its development into whole plants. The media provide energy as sucrose, mineral nutrients, plant hormones, and growth cofactors and are composed and sequenced so as to stimulate and sustain morphogenetic changes along one of several pathways. The current state of this art and its application to forestry have been reviewed in detail (76, 83, 84). As with cuttings, a major difficulty is that tissue in trees old enough to have expressed superiority (in progeny tests) is too old to be easily propagated.

The demonstrated feasibility of propagating plantlets from juvenile (cotyledon) tissue of Douglas fir and loblolly pine (76, 84) is being followed up by several lines of research. Foremost is the effort to make the process economical by multiplying the progeny of full-sib seed from relatively small numbers of controlled crosses in orchards. The second and more profitable step is to rejuvenate older tissue so that it will respond favorably to the juvenile process (84), which could then be used to clone proven individuals. Rejuvenating treatments currently under investigation include serial grafting of buds onto juvenile rootstock, severe pruning of trees to stimulate extension of latent juvenile meristems, spraying of parents with cytokinins, serial subculturing in vitro, and cytokinin-stimulated induction of adventitious buds. While some rejuvenation treatments carry a risk of genetic instability (76, 84), this has not yet been observed in cotyledon-derived plantlets of Douglas fir and loblolly pine. Its evaluation is the objective of extensive field trials.

A third option under study is to store juvenile tissue samples cryogenically for several years until the germ plasm is proven in a progeny test. Organized juvenile tissue of several nonhardy species, such as date palm and carnation, has been successfully recovered after 3 months of storage in liquid nitrogen (85). Whole conifer seedlings can be stored at −1°C for up to 1 year in nonsterile conditions without cryoprotective treatment or nutrient media.

The long-term goal of forest tree tissue culture is to induce single cells or cell aggregates in a liquid medium to associate into embryo-like structures. In this process (somatic embryogenesis) the structures develop a shoot and root simultaneously (86). The technique is applied commercially to some horticultural plants. Feasibility has been demonstrated in a few tree species (83), and partially formed somatic embryos have been induced in Douglas fir (87). Properly controlled, somatic embryogenesis carries low risk of genetic instability, guarantees juvenile plants of normal growth habit, and is amenable to the type of process engineering that results in low production costs in large-scale application (Fig. 4).

Significant additional benefits can accrue from the use of in vitro techniques. Cloning may provide material of reduced variability to aid in the identification of properties and processes correlated with superior performance. Observations of trees flowering during or shortly after in vitro culture (76, 86) may provide clues to better control of the flowering process than is currently achievable (88). This could allow the breeding cycle to be shortened further.

A future alternative to vegetative propagation could be regeneration of haploid plantlets from female gametophytic tissue of conifers (83). Such plantlets offer the possibility of breeding pure lines (in which the members of any gene pair are identical) (75). An open-pollinated orchard containing two such lines developed from superior individuals would allow all their nonadditive genetic gain to be captured through seed.

The use of clones brings into focus the conflict between short-term and long-term objectives of tree breeding (81, 89). What balance should be sought in long-lived crops between specialization for economic yield and maintenance of adaptability? Highly specialized clones cannot accommodate much variation in the environment. They will thus cost more to maintain (90) and are more at risk from climatic extremes and disease than lower-yielding plantations with a broad genetic base. Commercial forests are thus likely to become mosaics of clonal plantations on good sites and improved-seed forests on the poorer and less accessible sites (Fig. 4). The relative proportions will be the outcome of business decisions based on economic gain and risk. Single *Eucalyptus* clones are planted in 50-ha blocks in Brazil because

184

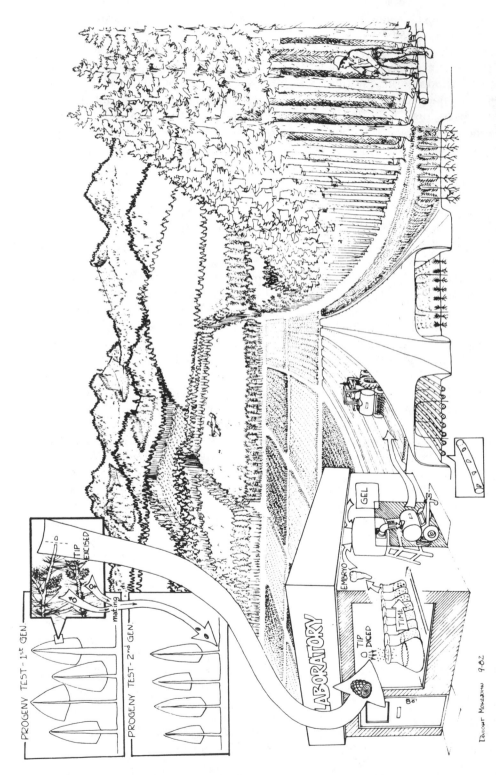

Fig. 4. Management of next century's forests? The scene illustrates the recurrent breeding cycle from first-generation flowers to second-generation progeny test (inset), the cloning of genetically superior trees from buds by embryogenesis in liquid culture, their mechanized sowing in extruded gel in protected nursery beds, intensively managed monoclonal-block plantations containing narrow-crowned, densely packed trees on which advanced fertilization and perhaps trickle irrigation are practiced, and distant mixed-genotype forests managed at lower intensity.

of their superior uniformity of growth over clonal mixtures (*80*). This contrasts with 100-clone mixes of Norway spruce in Germany (*78*).

It is essential, however, to maintain within the breeding population a broad genetic base that includes both productive and adaptive gene complexes. This is best achieved by reducing the genetic overlap among members and the frequency of deleterious genes responsible for inbreeding depression. Component breeding from widely separated parents will enhance the former. Use of pure lines may aid in identifying and eliminating the latter. For some characteristics, such as bole straightness, the genetic base in the breeding population can legitimately be narrowed (*89*).

Germplasm reserves are a necessary insurance against the loss of unrecognized beneficial genes that may befit forests for future changes in climate, atmospheric carbon dioxide concentration, disease and insect pressures, or marketable products (*53, 89*).

Conclusions

Potential productivity and target mean annual yields have been defined by using a theoretical model and observations from existing stands. Target yields for Douglas fir and loblolly pine are 25 and 30 Mg/ha per year, respectively. Even under intensive management with state-of-the-art cultural and genetic practices, both species are currently achieving less than 50 percent of these targets. Increases in yield will result from refinement of fertilizer prescriptions; control of competing vegetation; exploitation of nutrient, fertilizer, and weed control interactions; advanced tree breeding; and tissue culture techniques. In particular,

the diversity of approaches to mature tree cloning and the achievements reported to date suggest that the technology will be successfully developed. Applying it along with advanced cultural techniques on good sites may be sufficient to eliminate the gap between current and target yields for plantations established by the end of the century.

References and Notes

1. D Bruce, *J. For.* **75**, 14 (1977).
2. D. F. Westlake, *Biol. Rev.* **38**, 385, (1963). There are numerous other reports and review articles on phytomass productivity in forest stands. Good access to this literature is provided by J. Padré, *For. Abstr.* **41**, 343 (1980).
3. H. L. Gholz, C. C. Grier, A. G. Campbell, A. T. Brown, *Equations for Estimating Biomass and Leaf Area of Plants in the Pacific Northwest* (Research Paper 41, Oregon State University School of Forestry, Corvallis, 1979), pp. 1–39.
4. C. J. Chambers and F. M. Wilson, *Empirical Yield Tables for the Douglas-Fir Zone* (Rep. 20R, Department of Natural Resources, State of Washington, 1972), pp. 1–16. The estimate is for site index 105 feet and 80 percent normal basal area, corrected to allow for trees under 7 inches in diameter. Maximum mean annual yield occurs at age 50. Site index is the height of the dominant trees at a specified index age. Index age for the selected Douglas fir site is 58 years.
5. R. G. Campbell and J. H. Hughes, in *Pocosin Wetlands*, C. J. Richardson, Ed. (Hutchinson Ross, Stroudsburg, Pa., 1981), p. 199.
6. F. X. Schumacher and T. S. Coile, *Growth and Yields of Natural Stands of the Southern Pines* (Coile, Durham, N.C., 1960), pp. 3–115. The estimate is for site index 60 feet at base age 50 years. This is equivalent to site index 44 feet at base age 25 years. Maximum mean annual yield occurs at age 20.
7. M. A. Taras and A. Clark III, *Tappi* **58**, 103 (1975). Belowground biomass is assumed to be 17 percent of aboveground biomass.
8. J. C. Gordon, P. Farnum, R. Timmis, paper presented at the Seventh North American Forest Biology Workshop, Lexington, Ky. (July 1982). Future refinements of this model will be used to estimate the reduction in productivity associated with subfreezing temperatures.
9. R. S. Loomis and W. A. Williams, *Crop Sci.* **3**, 67 (1963).
10. R. O. Curtis, G. W. Clendenen, D. J. DeMars, *U.S. For. Serv. Gen. Tech. Rep. PNW-128* (1981), pp. 1–79. Biomass estimates are from Gholz *et al.* (*3*).
11. This value was estimated from Curtis *et al.* (*10*) by using a plantation simulation of site index 105 feet, 400 trees per acre (TPA) at age 17. This value of 2.5 is within the range indicated by

186

Westlake (2).

12. J. L. Monteith, *Philos. Trans. R. Soc. London Ser. B.* **281**, 277 (1977).

13. B. D. Cleary, R. D. Greaves, R. K. Hermann, Eds., *Regenerating Oregon's Forests* (Oregon State University Extension Service, Corvallis, 1978), pp. 1–287.

14. This value was estimated from Curtis *et al.* (*10*) by using a plantation simulation of site index 105 feet, 400 TPA at age 17. Maximum mean annual yield occurs at age 66.

15. J. Shumway and W. A. Atkinson, *Commun. Soil Sci. Plant Anal.* **9**, 529 (1978).

16. *Regional Forest Nutrition Research Project Biennial Report 1978–80* (Contribution 39, University of Washington College of Forest Resources, Seattle, 1980), pp. 1–44.

17. This value was estimated from Curtis *et al.* (*10*) by using a plantation simulation of site index 105 feet, 400 TPA at age 17, fertilized from age 30. Maximum mean annual yield occurs at age 69.

18. D. R. M. Scott, in *Regional Silviculture of the United States*, J. W. Barrett, Ed. (Wiley, New York, 1980), p. 447.

19. R. A. Klawitter, in *Proceedings Soil Moisture . . . Site Productivity Symposium*, W. E. Balmer, Ed. (U.S. Department of Agriculture, Atlanta, Ga., 1978), p. 49.

20. C. A. Gresham and T. M. Williams, in *ibid.*, p. 371.

21. E. Shoulders and T. A. Terry, in *Proceedings: A Symposium on Principles of Maintaining Productivity on Prepared Sites*, T. Tippin, Ed. (U.S. Department of Agriculture, New Orleans, 1978), p. 85.

22. T. A. Terry and J. H. Hughes, in *Proceedings Soil Moisture . . . Site Productivity Symposium*, W. E. Balmer, Ed. (U.S. Department of Agriculture, Atlanta, Ga., 1978), p. 148.

23. T. A. Terry and J. H. Hughes, in *Forest Soils and Forest Land Management*, B. Bernier and C. H. Winget, Eds. (Les Presses de l'Université Laval, Quebec, 1975), p. 351.

24. G. W. Smalley and R. L. Bailey, *U.S. For. Serv. Res. Pap. SO-96* (1974), pp. 1–81. Diameters and heights were obtained from these tables by interpolating over site index between the 750 TPA tables. Biomass estimates are from Taras and Clark (*7*).

25. This estimate, from Smalley and Bailey (*24*), assumes that drainage gives a 10-foot site index (base age 25) increase (*23*) to 54 feet. Maximum mean annual yield occurs at age 20.

26. This estimate, from Smalley and Bailey (*24*), is made under the assumption of 12-inch beds and a 6-inch gain in height at age 7 per inch of bed depth (*21*). It is also assumed that there is no response after age 7, so the site index (base age 25) increase is 6 feet to 60 feet. Maximum mean annual yield occurs at age 20.

27. O. G. Langdon and W. H. McKee, Jr., *U.S. For. Serv. Res. Pap. SO-34* (1981), p. 212.

28. *Cooperative Research in Forest Fertilization: Annual Report 1977* (University of Florida, Gainesville, 1977), pp. 1–18.

29. W. L. Pritchett and N. B. Comerford, *Soil Sci. Soc. Am. J.* **46**, 640 (1982).

30. This estimate, from Smalley and Bailey (*24*), is made under the assumption of an 8-foot site index (base age 25) increase (*22*) to 68 feet. Maximum mean annual yield occurs at age 15 to 20.

31. H. W. Duzan, Jr., and H. L. Allen, *U.S. For. Serv. Res. Pap. SO-34* (1981), p. 219.

32. R. Ballard, *South. J. Appl. For.* **5**, 212 (1981).

33. This estimate is made under the assumption that fertilization begins at age 10 and supplies a 21 percent response per year. The response to 100 pounds of N application on site 70 is approximately 16 percent for basal areas greater than 130 square feet per acre (*31*). The optimum biological response occurs to an N application of 200 pounds per acre and is about 33 percent greater than the response to 100 pounds per acre (*32*).

34. Q. V. Cao, H. E. Burkhart, R. C. Lemin, Jr., *Diameter Distributions and Yields of Thinned Loblolly Pine Plantations* (Publ. FWS-1-82, Virginia Polytechnic Institute School of Forestry and Wildlife Resources, Blacksburg, 1982), pp. 1–62.

35. R. Ballard, H. W. Duzan, Jr., M. B. Kane, in *U.S. For. Serv. Res. Pap. SO-34* (1981), p. 100.

36. N. E. Good and D. H. Bell, in *The Biology of Crop Productivity*, P. S. Carlson, Ed. (Academic Press, New York, 1980), p. 3.

37. F. W. T. Penning de Vries, *Neth. J. Agric. Sci.* **22**, 40 (1974).

38. M. R. Keyes and C. C. Grier, *Can. J. For. Res.* **11**, 599 (1981).

39. P. G. Jarvis and J. W. Leverenz, in *Encyclopedia of Plant Physiology* (Springer-Verlag, New York, in press), vol. 12D, chap. 18.

40. A. Wild and V. G. Breeze, in *Physiological Processes Limiting Plant Productivity*, C. B. Johnson, Ed. (Butterworth, London, 1981), p. 331.

41. T. Ingestad, *Ambio* **6**, 146 (1977).

42. S. Linder and B. Axelsson, paper presented at the International Union of Forestry Research Organizations (IUFRO) Conference on High Elevation Forest Ecosystems, Corvallis, Ore. (August 1982).

43. C. G. Wells, D. M. Crutchfield, N. M. Berenyi, C. B. Davey, *U.S. For. Serv. Res. Pap. SE-110* (1973), pp. 1–15.

44. North Carolina State Forest Fertilization Cooperative, *Tenth Annual Report* (School of Forest Resources, North Carolina State University, Raleigh, 1981), pp. 1–52.

45. J. C. Gordon, C. T. Wheeler, D. A. Perry, Eds., *Symbiotic Nitrogen Fixation in the Management of Temperate Forests* (Forest Research Laboratory, Oregon State University, Corvallis, 1979).

46. R. C. Schmidtling, *Can. J. For. Res.* **3**, 565 (1973).

47. A. G. Darvill, P. Albersheim, M. McNeil, J. E. Darvill, J. K. Sharp, M. W. Spellman, M. G. Hahn, W. S. York, paper presented at the 13th International Botanical Conference, Sidney, Australia (1981).

48. E. A. Hansen, H. A. McNeel, D. A. Netzer, H. M. Phipps, P. S. Roberts, T. F. Strong, D. N. Tolsted, J. Zavitkovski, paper presented at the Annual Meeting of the North American Poplar Council, Thompsonville, Mich. (August 1979).

49. A. Keeves, *Aust. For.* **30**, 51 (1966).

50. P. W. Farrell, D. W. Flinn, R. O. Squire, F. G. Craig, in *Seventeenth IUFRO World Congress Proceedings* (Japanese IUFRO Congress Committee, Ibaraki, Japan, 1981), vol. 1, p. 117.

51. C. J. Schutz, *S. Afr. For. J.* **120**, 3 (1982).

52. G. M. Will and R. Ballard, *N. Z. J. For.* **21**, 248 (1976).
53. W. T. Adams, in *Evolution Today, Proceedings of the Second International Congress of Systematic and Evolutionary Biology*, G. G. E. Scudder and J. L. Rezeal, Eds. (Hunt Institute for Botanical Documentation, Carnegie-Mellon University, Pittsburgh, Pa., 1981), p. 401.
54. R. Faulkner, *U.K. For. Comm. Bull. No. 54* (1975).
55. M. G. R. Cannell, in *Proceedings of the Fifth North American Forest Biology Workshop*, C. A. Hollis and A. E. Squillace, Eds. (Univ. of Florida School of Forest Resources, Gainsville, 1979), p. 120.
56. R. W. Stonecypher, *Proc. Soc. Am. For.* (1981), p. 38. The 12 percent gain for Douglas fir is levied on the untreated plantation base. The 24 percent gain for loblolly pine is levied on the preplant phosphorus base. For both species nitrogen response (in megagrams per hectare per year) is assumed to be the same for improved and wild-seed stands.
57. M. G. R. Cannell, R. Faulkner, F. T. Last, J. D. Matthews, in *Tree Physiology and Yield Improvement*, M. G. R. Cannell and F. T. Last, Eds. (Academic Press, New York, 1976), p. 519.
58. D. Wilson, in *Plant Breeding II*, K. J. Frey, Ed. (Iowa State Univ. Press, Ames, 1979), p. 85.
59. F. T. Ledig, in *Tree Physiology and Yield Improvement*, M. G. R. Cannell and F. T. Last, Eds. (Academic Press, New York, 1976), p. 21.
60. C. M. Cahalan, *Silvae Genet.* **30**, 40 (1981).
61. S. Linder, *Stud. For. Suec.* **149**, 1 (1979).
62. P. G. Jarvis, in *Physiological Processes Limiting Plant Productivity*, C. B. Johnson, Ed. (Butterworth, London, 1981), p. 81.
63. J. P. Cooper, in *Genetics in Plant Breeding*, H. Rees, R. Riley, E. L. Breese, C. N. Law, Eds. (University Press, Cambridge, England, 1981), p. 431.
64. W. H. Emmingham and R. H. Waring, *Can. J. For. Res.* **7**, 165 (1977).
65. W. Larcher, in *Physiological Processes Limiting Plant Productivity*, C. B. Johnson, Ed. (Butterworth, London, 1981), p. 253.
66. F. C. Sorensen and W. K. Ferrell, *Can. J. Bot.* **51**, 1689 (1973).
67. J. H. Fryer and F. T. Ledig, *ibid.* **50**, 1231 (1972); R. O. Slatyer, paper presented at the IUFRO conference on High Elevation Forest Ecosystems, Corvallis, Ore. (August 1982).
68. M. G. R. Cannell, F. E. Bridgwater, M. F. Greenwood, *Silvae Genet.* **27**, 217 (1978).
69. R. K. Campbell, *J. Appl. Ecol.* **11**, 1069 (1974); _____ and A. J. Sugano, *Bot. Gaz.* **136**, 290 (1975).
70. E. K. S. Nambiar, P. P. Cotterill, G. D. Bowen, *J. Exp. Bot.* **33**, 170 (1982).
71. A. R. Griffin and K. K. Ching, *Silvae Genet.* **26**, 149 (1977).
72. P. P. Cotterill and E. K. S. Nambiar, *Aust. For. Res.* **11**, 13 (1981).
73. C. C. Lambeth, thesis, North Carolina State University, Raleigh (1979), pp. 1–79.
74. J. S. Boyer, *Science* **218**, 443 (1982).
75. E. C. Cocking and R. Riley, in *Plant Breeding II*, K. J. Frey, Ed. (Iowa State Univ. Press, Ames, 1979), p. 85.
76. R. L. Mott, in *Cloning Agricultural Plants Via In Vitro Techniques*, B. V. Conger, Ed. (CRC Press, Boca Raton, Fla., 1981), p. 217; personal communication.
77. V. Hartney, personal communication.
78. J. Kleinschmit and J. Schmidt, *Silvae Genet.* **26**, 197 (1977).
79. S. D. Ross, *West. For. Conserv. Assoc. Perm. Comm. Proc.* (1974), p. 49.
80. W. T. Gladstone, *Trip Report–Aracruz Cellulose, S.A.* (Tech. Rep. 050-5002/2, Weyerhaeuser Company Research and Development, Tacoma, Wash., 1982); E. Campinhos, Jr., in *Proceedings of the Technical Association of the Pulp and Paper Industry Annual Meeting 1980* (TAPPI, Atlanta, 1980), p. 351.
81. A. Roulund, *For. Abstr.* **42**, 457 (1981).
82. H. Brix and R. van den Driessche, *B. C. For. Serv. Can. For. Serv. Joint Rep. No. 6* (1977).
83. D. F. Karnosky, *BioScience* **31**, 114 (1981).
84. T. A. Thorpe and S. Biondi, preprint from *Applications of Plant Tissue Culture Methods for Crop Improvement*, W. R. Sharp *et al.*, Eds. (Macmillan, New York, 1982), vol. 2.
85. L. A. Withers, in *Frontiers of Plant Tissue Culture*, T. A. Thorpe, Ed. (International Association of Plant Tissue Culture, Calgary, 1978), p. 297; Y.P.S. Bajaj, *Euphytica* **28**, 267 (1979).
86. A. D. Krikorian, *Biol. Rev.* **57**, 151 (1982); personal communication.
87. M. M. Abo El-Nil, U.S. Patent No. 4217730 (1980).
88. S. D. Ross and R. Pharis, *Physiol. Plant.* **36**, 182 (1975).
89. B. Zobel, *For. Ecol. Manage.* **1**, 339 (1978); G. Namkoong, R. D. Barnes, J. Burley, *Commonw. For. Rev.* **59**, 61 (1980).
90. A. D. Hansen and C. E. Nelsen, in *Biology of Crop Productivity*, P. S. Carlson, Ed. (Academic Press, New York, 1980), p. 77.

15. Genetic Manipulation of Antibiotic-Producing Microorganisms

John N. Vournakis and Richard P. Elander

Manipulation of the biosynthetic pathways for antibiotic synthesis in producer microorganisms has generated clinically important antibacterial and antitumor agents during the past 30 years (*1*). There are now approximately 150 antibiotic compounds on the market. Antibiotics that become commercially important are discovered and further developed by research efforts in microbiology and genetics aimed at screening microorganisms for naturally occurring secondary metabolites, by modifying natural substances chemically to produce semisynthetic derivatives having desirable characteristics, and by improvement of techniques for selecting mutants that produce useful antibiotics in large amounts. Compounds must be both cost- and health-effective in order to become marketable.

Approximately 7000 naturally occurring and more than 30,000 semisynthetically derived antibiotics have been discovered since the early part of this century (*1*). In most cases these compounds were obtained or identified by empirical methods (*2*). There have also been great improvements in the techniques used for increasing antibiotic productivity of particular microorganisms, and these have resulted, primarily, from random ap-

proaches. The future of antibiotic screening and strain improvement technology should move away from the empirical, random methods of the past toward the application of scientifically more rigorous approaches. Advances in the understanding of the antibiotic biosynthetic pathways in many organisms (*3*), in the elucidation of regulatory mechanisms related to the induction and repression of genes involved in antibiotic synthesis (*3*), and in the physiology of the relevant microorganisms, make it possible to develop and begin to apply new, nonempirical strategies for both strain improvement and novel antibiotic development. Genetic engineering techniques, including recombinant DNA methods, can facilitate the application of some of these new strategies (*4, 5*). This chapter focuses on the biology of antibiotic-producing microorganisms and has three primary objectives

1) To describe current methods for the genetic improvement of organisms leading to the development of strains that produce large quantities of known antibiotics,

2) To describe methods for altering the genetic structure of antibiotic-producing microorganisms in a controlled, but half-

random, fashion to facilitate the biological synthesis of new, improved antibiotics, and,

3) To describe strategies for the specific alteration of antibiotic synthesis pathways to create new, slightly modified, strains capable of the biological production of known antibiotics currently manufactured by semisynthetic chemical methods.

Selection Techniques: Production of Antibiotics by Mutation and Selection

Historically, the strategies used for the manipulation and screening of microorganisms to generate strains that produce large amounts of antibiotics of commercial importance have included, primarily, random mutation and selection (1, 2). These methods, although successful in some cases (4), are based on empirical experience and have, in general, a moderate probability of success. They are "hit or miss" methods that require brute force effort, persistence, and skill in the art of microbiology. These older technologies were developed at a time when knowledge of the genetics and biochemistry of antibiotic-producer organisms was very limited.

A number of the classical methods have, in recent years, been replaced by more "rational" (that is, directed) selection techniques (6), such as (i) direct colony selection following overlay bioassay, (ii) selection for mutants resistant to toxic precursors or to the toxicity of end product, (iii) use of analog resistant mutants that overproduce rate-limiting biosynthetic intermediates, (iv) selection for mutants resistant to metallic ions that complex antibiotic molecules, (v) selection of auxotrophic strains deficient for biosynthetic intermediates followed by prototrophic reversion, (vi) selection for improved strains after protoplast fusion, and (vii) use of antibiotic selection for the isolation of multiple plasmid-copy strains.

These directed procedures can be much more efficient than random screening for the selection of improved antibiotic-producing strains, since each one is based on studied, known parameters that affect the regulation of the biosynthetic pathway of a particular antibiotic in the producer microorganism. They involve the preliminary screening of mutagenized cells before they are used for laboratory (small-scale) fermentation studies as well as for selection strategies based on known or probable biochemical mechanisms (4), as indicated below.

The work of Elander et al. (7) and of Chang and Elander (6) on the development of methods for selecting strains of Acremonium (Cephalosporium) chrysogenum that produce high yields of the commercially important antibiotic cephalosporin C illustrates the application of the overlay bioassay procedure. Prior to the development of this method, mutagenized A. chrysogenum colonies were picked from agar plates, at random, and were grown in shake flasks for drug assays. In the overlay assay previously mutagenized A. chrysogenum colonies are plated onto agar, and the plates are incubated; the antibiotic activities of the resulting cells were assayed by allowing a second, antibiotic-sensitive organism to grow over the original colonies. Colonies that produce antibiotic can be observed by the appearance of zones of inhibition. An index of potency (PI), defined as the ratio of the diameter of the zone of inhibition to the diameter of the antibiotic-producing colony, can then be determined. Colonies are picked for further analysis based on an arbitrary PI;

for example, all colonies having a PI greater than 4. This procedure can increase the probability of identifying high producer strains. Chang and Elander (6) demonstrate that this method can improve the efficiency of screening methods by a factor of nearly 10. This basic concept can be used to further increase the probability of isolating desirable strains by manipulation of the medium and growth conditions for both the producer and tester strains.

Selection for resistance to toxicity of end product. The β-lactam containing antibiotics include a large number of different compounds that are produced as secondary metabolites (*1*) by both prokaryotic and eukaryotic microorganisms. The range and characteristics of the many β-lactam–producing species have been described (*4*). One of the more novel β-lactam compounds is nocardicin A which is produced by the actinomycete *Nocardia uniformis* (*8*). The substance is the major active component of a series of related secondary metabolites. The compound has in vivo activity in mice infected with strains of *Pseudomonas aeruginosa*. The discovery of this cell wall–active antibiotic from *N. uniformis* was detected with the use of a β-lactam supersensitive mutant of *Escherichia coli* (*8*). The biosynthetic precursors of the compound appear to be L-ρ-hydroxyphenylglycine, L-serine, and L-homoserine; these precursors are not the same as those precursors for the majority of the clinically important β-lactams.

Two major problems were encountered during attempts at selection for improved strains. First, it was found that *N. uniformis* is itself sensitive to a range of β-lactam antibiotics, including nocardicin A. Growth of the microorganisms could be inhibited by the addition, at a concentration of 2 milligrams per milliliter, of the drug at different times in the fermentation, generating fragmented and lysed cells. This problem was addressed by selecting for strains that were mutagenized by either ultraviolet radiation or with nitrosoguanidine and that would survive on agar plates containing varying concentrations of nocardicin A.

The second problem developed as attempts to solve the first proceeded. A number of the mutants resistant to nocardicin A produced significant amounts of β-lactamase that destroyed nocardicin A and other β-lactam antibiotics. The β-lactamase was secreted into the culture medium. It became, therefore, necessary to devise a selection for the subset of mutants resistant to nocardicin A that were β-lactamase negative. Mutagen-treated *N. uniformis* spores were plated onto an agar medium. Soft agar, containing a dilute culture of *Staphylococcus aureus* plus penicillin G (varying concentrations) was overlayed, and the plates were incubated at 37°C for 18 hours. Growth zones of *S. aureus* were observed around colonies that produced β-lactamase, which in turn hydrolyzed the penicillin G in the medium. The β-lactamase negative mutants were selected as colonies showing no growth around them. Stable β-lactamase mutants of *N. utilis* which did not revert to become β-lactamase positive, were then screened for resistance to nocardicin A as described above. The frequency of mutants superior to parent strains in producing nocardicin A was higher when mutagen-treated spores were selected from media containing nocardicin A at concentrations equal to or higher than that which inhibited growth of the parent (Fig. 1).

Thus, selection for two traits, a resistance to toxic levels of end product and the inability to produce an antibiotic

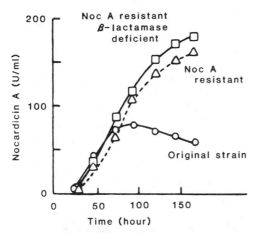

Fig. 1. Improved nocardicin A production by a β-lactamase–deficient and nocardicin A–resistant mutant of *Nocardia uniformis*.

degrading enzyme, greatly improved the productivity of the desired antibiotic, in this case nocardicin A.

Selection for analog resistant mutants. Mutants resistant to amino acid analogs have been used successfully for the overproduction of antibiotics having amino acids as precursors. One example, reported by Elander (9), was the selection of higher pyrrolnitrin-producing strains of *Pseudomonas fluorescens*. Pyrrolnitrin (Fig. 2) is an important antifungal agent for which D-tryptophan is a precursor. Selection methods that included either fluoro- or methyltryptophan in the medium generated a set of mutants that overproduced D-tryptophan, which increased the productivity of pyrrolnitrin more than threefold and, in addition, eliminated the need for adding D-tryptophan to the medium for maximal pyrrolnitrin formation. Other examples where this strategy has proved successful include the selection for mutants of *Penicillium* and *Acremonium* that overproduce the very important β-lactam antibiotics of the penicillin and cephalosporin classes, respectively. The bio-

synthetic pathways for both penicillin and cephalosporin compounds involve the amino acids α-aminoadipic acid, cysteine, and valine as precursors (Fig. 3). A series of analogs of these amino acids (Table 1) was used to select for strains with improved cephalosporin C productivity (9). This approach increased the probability of finding such strains. In addition, methionine analogs were used in separate selection experiments. Although methionine is not a precursor for cephalosporin C biosynthesis, it is a required nutrient for optimal fermentation of the microorganism. Strains were se-

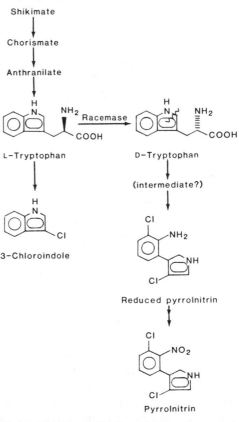

Fig. 2. The biosynthetic pathway of pyrrolnitrin synthesis in *Pseudomonas fluorescens*, illustrating the role of D-tryptophan as precursor.

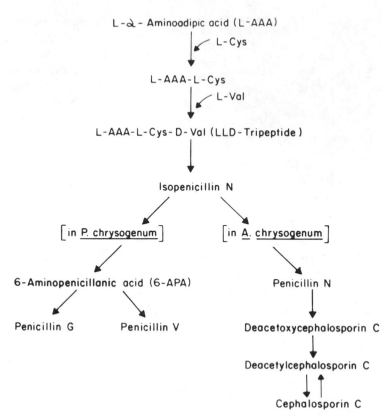

Fig. 3. Biosynthetic pathways for penicillin and cephalosporin production illustrating the various amino acid precursors.

lected that overproduce cephalosporin C, although knowledge of the mechanism remains limited.

Selection for resistance to metal ions. Ions of heavy metals such as mercuric ions (Hg^{2+}), cupric ions (Cu^{2+}), and related organometallic ions are known to form complexes with β-lactam molecules at high concentrations. It is possible that many of the mutants which become resistant to these metallic ions may do so by overproducing β-lactam antibiotics as a means of detoxification, thus preventing metal binding and possible interference with SH-containing compounds that may be substrate intermediates, or binding at active sites of metal ion requiring enzymes. For example, mutants have been isolated for resistance to phenylmercuric acetate (PMA) for improved cephamycin precursor production in *Streptomyces lipmanii* (*10*). Mutants resistant to inhibitory concentrations of Cu^{2+}, PMA, chromate, Mn^{2+}, and Hg^{2+} have been isolated and tested for cephalosporin C production in shake flasks (*11*). The results show that the frequency of superior isolates among mutants resistant to mercuric chloride is higher than for isolates selected at random among survivors of ultraviolet treatment. Isolation of mutants resistant to organometallic compounds has been used for selection of specific types of nutritional mutants. A new class of methionine auxotrophs in *Saccharomyces cerevisiae* has been obtained by isolating methylmercury resistant mutants (*12*).

Table 1. Screening of mutants resistant to various amino acid analogs.

Analog	Antagonized amino acid	Isolates		
		Resistant tested (No.)	Superior retained	
			(No.)	(%)
Selenocysteine	Cysteine	45	0	0
Allylglycine	Cysteine	25	0	0
Norvaline	Valine	27	0	0
DL-α-aminobutyric acid	Valine	151	1	0.66
S-2-aminoethyl-L-cysteine	Lysine	16	1	6.2
Selenomethionine	Methionine	153	8	5.2
Trifluoromethionine	Methionine	55	2	3.6
Selenoethionine	Methionine	87	6	7
α-Methylserine	Serine	25	1	4
Trifluoroleucine	Leucine	35	1	3

Selection of auxotrophs deficient for biosynthetic intermediates followed by prototrophic reversion. The use of auxotrophs for overproduction of amino acids involved as precursors in antibiotic production has been successfully applied (*13*). The operative principle in this approach is to block, by mutation, one part of a branched biosynthetic pathway so that metabolites flow through another branch. Overproduction of a metabolic precursor, and, subsequently, the antibiotic itself, can occur. Work with *S. lipmanii* (*10*) where certain auxotrophs of pyruvate and aspartate metabolism produced increased titers of cephamycin, and by Treichler *et al.* (*14*) where sulfur metabolic auxotrophs resulted in the improved fermentation of cephalosporin C in *A. chrysogenum*, are two well-documented examples illustrating the strength of this approach. Our work has resulted in the isolation of a limited number of *A. chrysogenum* auxotrophs to various nutrients (see Table 2) that are either inferior or normal producers of cephalosporin C. When reverted to prototrophy, a number of these become superior drug producers, having been derived from either high or low producing auxotrophs.

Selection for improved strains after protoplast fusion. Protoplast fusion technology can be used in combination with selection techniques previously described to generate industrial microorganisms having desirable properties. In general, the biochemical mechanisms that result in stable hybrid strains as a result of protoplast fusion and subsequent regeneration are not understood. In spite of this, the technique provides an effective method for the intermixing of genes of two (or more) strains having a set of characteristics that, if combined into a hybrid organism, may improve antibiotic productivity. The work of Okanishi *et al.* (*15*), Ferenczy *et al.* (*16*), and others in protoplast formation, fusion, and regeneration has accelerated the development of the techniques used in gene manipulation in *Streptomyces* and other microorganisms. Complementary auxotrophic strains of a given organism are used in this method. Protoplasts are prepared by treating cells with various lytic enzymes. The presence of an osmotic stabilizer is essential to provide

Table 2. Cephalosporin C production by auxotrophs and some of their revertants.

Strain No.	Nutritional requirement	Cephalosporin C titer (% of control)	Revertants tested (No.)	Superior retained (No.)
A2	Nicotinic acid	10		
A20	Uracil	100		
A47	Serine	110	12	1
A101	Uracil	95		
A103	Thymine	110		
A104	NH_4^+	120	10	1
A114	Riboflavin	90		
A115	Riboflavin	50		
A117	Xanthine	110		
A118	Cysteine or methionine	35	25	2
A119	Cysteine or methionine	10	20	0
A120	Xanthine	10		
A125	Lysine	10	5	0
A127	NH_4^+	65		
A128	NH_4^+	70		
Control	None	100		

osmotic support for the protoplasts, and fusion is enhanced by the addition of polyethylene glycol and Mg^{2+}. The techniques for formation, fusion, and regeneration are well described (17, 18). Both intra- and inter-species fusions have been reported (17).

Significant results in strain improvement have been obtained by means of protoplast fusion. Hamlyn and Ball (19) have, for example, made hybrid strains of nutritional auxotrophs of A. chrysogenum, which produce significantly higher amounts of cephalosporin C, and which can produce cephalosporins efficiently from inorganic sulfate. Protoplast fusion has been applied (17) for the development of fast-growing strains of P. chrysogenum, which produce very little p-hydroxypenicillin V. The development of such strains is economically important because contamination of penicillin V parahydroxylated by-product leads to interference with the chemical ring expansion steps of penicillin to cephalosporin.

An excellent example of combined rational selection and protoplast fusion procedures has been described (20) for improving carbapenem-producing strains of Streptomyces griseus. This organism produces the novel carbapenem antibiotics, C-19393 H_2 and S_2 (carpetimycin A and B) and E_5, as well as epithienamycins and olivanic acids. These compounds are classified into two categories, that is, sulfated (C-19393 S_2, MM-4550, MM-13902, and MM-17880) and unsulfated (C-19393 H_2, E_5, epithienamycins A, B, C, and D) carbapenem antibiotics. Studies on the production of these antibiotics in a chemically defined medium show that the production ratio of these two groups of antibiotics is affected by the sulfate concentration in the medium. Mutants unable to produce sulfated carbapenem antibiotics were successfully derived and were found to be sulfate transport–negative mutants. They were isolated as either auxotrophs requiring thiosulfate or cysteine for growth or mutants resistant to selenate. They produce unsulfated carbapenem antibiotics at almost twice the levels of the parental strain C-19393. Converged accumulation of C-19393 H_2 was achieved by selecting for strains resistant to S-2-aminoethyl-L-cysteine from a sulfate transport–negative mutant. A second mutant produced C-19393 H_2 as the major component and showed a potency ten times greater than that of the original strain C-19393. The sulfate transport system was reintroduced into sulfate transport–negative mutants from the strain C-19393 through protoplast fusion. Stable genetic recombinants were obtained at high frequency by treating the mixed protoplasts with 40 percent polyethylene glycol. High producers of C-19393 S_2 were found among these recombinants. The above examples indicate that the protoplast fusion approach may have a significant impact on the future of antibiotic strain improvement.

Antibiotic selection for plasmid-containing strains. The role of plasmids in the biosynthesis of antibiotics was initially suggested by Okanishi *et al.* (*21*). Genes carried by plasmids are thought to be involved in resistance to antibiotics, formation of morphological characteristics, and many other phenotypic properties of antibiotic-forming microorganisms (*22*).

Streptomyces kasugaensis produces aureothricin, thiolutin, and kasugamycin. The production of all three antibiotics can be eliminated by the so-called plasmid "curing" treatment. Intensive study of aureothricin biosynthesis (*23*) showed that the structural genes for aureothricin biosynthesis seem to be localized on a chromosome, whereas plasmid genes may be involved in determining the properties of the membrane, such as transport mechanisms, and can affect the

cell's ability to accumulate precursors of antibiotic synthesis. Another well-studied model of the interaction of plasmids with antibiotic synthesis is the production of chloramphenicol by *Streptomyces venezuelae* (*24*). It has been found that the structural genes responsible for antibiotic synthesis are usually located on a chromosome, and manipulation of endogenous plasmids may affect the increase in production of chloramphenicol.

The genetics of production of methylenomycin A and actinorhodin by *Streptomyces coelicolor* has been elaborated in detail. For example, the genes for the methylenomycin are carried on the plasmid SCPI (*25*), whereas actinorhodin synthesis is determined by chromosomal genes (*25*). The biosynthesis of the aminoglycosidic antibiotics kanamycin, neomycin, and paromycin is assumed to involve the participation of a plasmid which determines the biosynthesis of deoxystreptamine, a common precursor of these antibiotics (*26*). Results obtained with istamycin indicate that plasmids may participate in catabolite regulation by glucose and in membrane permeability. Plasmids have been studied in other *Streptomyces* strains that produce antibiotics of the neomycin series, particularly in connection with the "modifying" enzymes—glycoside-3'-phosphotransferase and aminoglycoside-acetyltransferase, whose activities cause the inactivation of these substances (*27*). The presence of plasmids in strains that produce the macrolide antibiotics has shown that plasmid genes are involved in the expression of antibiotic resistance and in melanin formation (*22*).

A strain of *Streptomyces kanamyceticus* for industrial use, when propagated on a complex liquid medium and then plated on agar medium, was found to generate a low frequency (0.2 to 1 percent) of small raised colonies having a soft fragmented texture which have lost their capacity to synthesize kanamycin (Km⁻) (28). Growing sonicated mycelia in the presence of acridine orange (AO), ethidium bromide (EB), or acriflavin (Acr) resulted in a higher frequency (10 to 20 percent) of Km⁻ colonies. Incubation of Km⁻ colonies at high temperature (35°C) in the presence of Km⁺ colonies also resulted in a high incidence (90 percent) of the Km⁻ phenotype. The Km⁻ phenotype also developed when conidia from streak cultures were grown on oatmeal agar containing AO, Acr, or EB, where frequencies of 70 to 80 percent Km⁻ colonies were routinely obtained. The Km⁺ colonies were found to be more resistant to kanamycin and amikacin (BB-K8) and than Km⁻ colonies, and the addition of kanamycin to oatmeal agar resulted in complete suppression of conidia of the Km⁻ type. The Km⁺ isolate also produced higher amylase activity in fermentation broths than the Km⁻ isolates. Selected Km⁻ isolates produced kanamycin when grown in media supplemented with deoxystreptamine, streptamine, or D-glucosamine, but not with streptidine: 2,6-dideoxystreptamine, 2,5,6-trideoxystreptamine, or 6-aminoglucose. Similar results were obtained with other plasmid-cured strains of *S. kanamyceticus* (24). These data are consistent with the hypothesis that active kanamycin production and other characteristics may be controlled by a plasmid gene (or genes) in *S. kanamyceticus* (29), and that inclusion of kanamycin in growth media appears to maintain the integrity of cells containing plasmids possibly by suppressing the growth of Km⁻ cells. Incorporation of kanamycin in the vegetative inoculum stage also appears to stimulate kanamycin production in laboratory fermentations.

The development of a clearer understanding of the role of plasmid genes in antibiotic production will open possible strategies for improving production in such strains. Manipulation of plasmid copy number, and plasmid gene regulatory elements, such as specific gene promoter DNA sequences, result in positive future results.

Recombination and Recombinant DNA Techniques for Novel Antibiotics

In addition to the manipulation of microorganisms by mutation-rational selection methods to improve antibiotic productivity, genetic recombination techniques can be applied in a directed manner to create desirable genetic alterations in microorganisms that may then synthesize novel hybrid antibiotics. In a general sense, genetic recombination methods include those techniques that produce organisms having stable, expressable, genetic traits obtained by combining genetic elements from two or more parent organisms. This definition includes transformation methods, phage-mediated transduction, plasmid-mediated conjugation, protoplast fusion, parasexual breeding (in fungi), and application of the recombinant DNA method, which overlaps other methods to some extent in that it involves transformation of cells with laboratory engineered specific recombinant DNA molecules via plasmid or phage vectors. It is possible with these (and other) methods to create new antibiotic-producing organisms having permanently altered genomes, with the hope and intent of either improving antibiotic production or generating new, hybrid antibiotic biosynthetic capabilities.

Among the potentially more promising recombinational methods for developing new antibiotics are (i) protoplast fusion to select for intraspecific recombinant strains that produce new antibiotics, (ii) self and shotgun gene cloning to generate new antibiotic synthetic pathways on a semirandom basis, and (iii) directed gene cloning to provide an added step or steps to an antibiotic synthetic pathway in a specific and highly controlled manner.

Protoplast fusion for new antibiotics. Species of *Acremonium chrysogenum* that overproduce cephalosporin C were obtained (*19*) by protoplast fusion methods for the development of genetic (haploid) recombinants by intraspecific fusion. The use of protoplast fusion for developing hybrid drugs is enhanced by the possibility of interspecific genetic recombination. Interspecific hybrid formation via protoplast fusion was achieved between species of *Aspergillus* and *Penicillium* (*30*). Fusions between distantly related species have been achieved, an indication that genetic recombination is possible given that morphological and metabolic properties of the hybrids are derived from both parent strains (*17*). Protoplast fusion hybrids of *P. chrysogenum* and *A. chrysogenum* were obtained, and they showed in some cases *Acremonium* morphology with *Penicillium* outgrowth, suggesting nutritional complementation. Stable isolates were obtained that had *Acremonium* morphology but differed in their response to phenoxyacetic acid as compared to the *Acremonium* parent in shake-flask fermentations. The prototrophy and altered morphology of these stable fusion products suggests that gene recombination between *Acremonium* and *Penicillium* has occurred in the hybrids (*17*).

Protoplasts of two *Streptomyces* strains, *S. griseus* which produces streptomycin, and *S. tenjimariensis* which produces istamycin, were fused and allowed to revert to a natural filamentous state on a selection medium (*31*). A fused hybrid was selected that produced a new antibiotic differing from the metabolites produced by either of the parents.

The development of recombinant DNA technology and techniques for transformation and transfection of protoplasts as well as intact organisms has made possible the exploitation of these methods for gene cloning in actinomycetes and fungi. The rationale for attempting shotgun and self-cloning is that transformants may acquire new genes for enzymatic activities that can modify the chemical structure of secondary metabolites normally produced by the organism to generate new antibiotics.

The basic requirements for utilization of the recombinant DNA method to transfer and express segments of foreign DNA in a host organism include (i) an appropriate vector DNA molecule (plasmid or phage) compatible with the cell and carrying appropriately localized control elements such as promoters and ribosome binding sequences; (ii) a convenient method for preparing the foreign DNA, cleaving it to a reasonable size range, and splicing into the vector DNA molecule such that it will have a good probability of being expressed should it be a gene; (iii) a method for introducing the recombinant DNA molecules into the host cell so that it is transformed to a new phenotype that includes the properties coded for by the recombinant; and (iv) a method for assaying for the expression of the desired gene products.

Shotgun cloning as used here refers to the transformation of a host organism with a gene library prepared with randomly fragmented DNA from a different

198

donor organism. The library is carried in a vector compatible with the host organism and includes, in a random array, the entire genome of the donor organism. Hopwood (5) discusses aspects of genomic library construction with respect to streptomycetes. He shows that the number of clones needed in a library in order for an entire genome to be represented is a function of both the length of the cloned fragment and the genome size. It is best to use large-sized DNA fragments to construct libraries within the size limits imposed by the ability of the vector to form recombinants. Self-cloning is an example of shotgun cloning where the host and donor species are closely related (Fig. 4).

A major concern in the use of shotgun and self-cloning to generate new hybrid antibiotics is related to the magnitude of the screening effort. If a library from a donor organism is of size L (say 10^3 clones) then L (10^3) colonies will have to be screened when the library is used to transform one host. If cloning combinations are made, then all combinations of n strains cloned pairwise into one another would give $n(n-1)L$ clones to be examined for novel antibiotic activities (5). This number can grow rapidly, and hence considerable creativity and effort

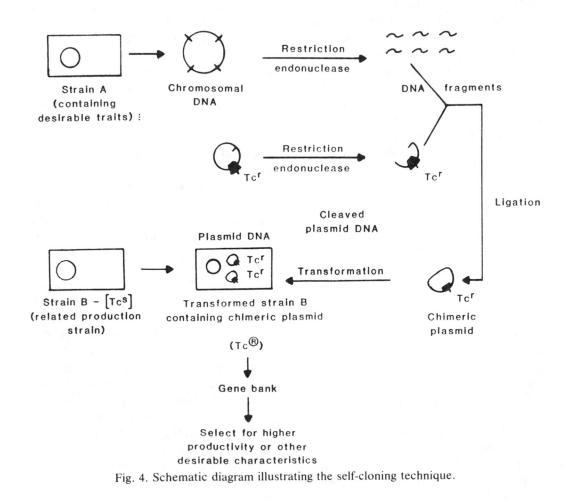

Fig. 4. Schematic diagram illustrating the self-cloning technique.

must be brought to the development of screening methods.

Shotgun and self-cloning techniques have been used to clone antibiotic resistance genes in streptomycetes (9). These experiments demonstrate the potential to mobilize and obtain expression of genes within and between species toward the rapid intermixing of genomes of antibiotic-producing microorganisms, thus increasing the probability and efficiency of new antibiotic discovery.

The use of the recombinant DNA method to isolate specific genes coding for proteins having particular activities has been well established in several biological systems. The potential applications of this method to solve specific problems related to antibiotic production are numerous. Genes coding for enzymes could be cloned into antibiotic-producing organisms to attempt to add one or two steps to existing biosynthetic pathways. Such alterations, although usually minor in terms of the overall physiology of the organism, could be of major economic value leading to large cost reductions of antibiotic production.

The rapidly developing recombinant DNA technology now provides approaches which may result in the successful transfer of acyltransferase genes from *Penicillium* to *Acremonium*, thereby resulting in a strain capable of synthesizing solvent extractable cephalosporins (32). The transfer of hydroxyaminobutyric acid acylase genes from butirosin-producing strains of *Bacillus circulans* to *S. kanamyceticus* could lead to the direct, efficient synthesis of the important semisynthetic aminoglycoside antibiotic, amikacin.

Recombinant DNA technology is also undergoing rapid development in streptomycetes, which produce 60 percent of the known antibiotics (33), therefore, the development of DNA cloning and self-cloning systems (Fig. 4) for *Streptomyces* would facilitate the genetic analysis for specific antibiotic biosynthetic pathways and of molecular mechanisms involved in their differentiation. An effective DNA cloning system for interspecies gene transfer in a number of differing antibiotic-producing species of *Streptomyces* has been reported (34). Thompson *et al.* (35) have described newly constructed cloning vectors from streptomycete plasmid and genomic DNA termed pIJ 101 and pIJ 61 which provide for both replication and transfer functions. pIJ 101 is a multicopy (40 to 300 copies per cell) plasmid with a broad host range occurring in *S. lividans* 5434. Moreover, the plasmid is self-transmissable and can mobilize chromosomal genes (36). Katz *et al.* (37) have used these plasmids to transform protoplasts of *S. lividans* 1326 and obtained expression of the gene coding for the synthesis of the enzyme tyrosinase.

Conclusions

There are many options available for altering the genetics of antibiotic-producing microorganisms to realize particular goals. Rational selection methods based on an enhanced understanding of the biosynthetic pathways for antibiotic synthesis can lead to radical improvements in strain productivity. Protoplast fusion technology can be used to allow genetic recombination to occur among different species of antibiotic producers to generate mixed synthetic pathways that may in turn give rise to hybrid antibiotics. Recombinant DNA methods can be used to clone genes for strain improvement and novel antibiotic synthesis into existing microorganisms in

200

either a semi-random or specific manner. The coming decade promises to be filled with excitement and rewards as many of the ideas discussed here and elsewhere are implemented in the laboratories, pilot plants, and ultimately, production systems of the pharmaceutical industry.

References and Notes

1. A. L. Demain, *Science* **214**, 987 (1981).
2. R. P. Elander and M. Moo-Young, *Adv. Biotech.* **1**, 3 (1981).
3. R. P. Elander and A. L. Demain, in *Biotechnology*, vol. 1, *Microbial Fundamentals*, H. J. Rehm and G. Reed, Eds. (Verlag-Chemie, Weinheim, 1981), p. 235.
4. R. P. Elander and H. Aoki, in *The Chemistry and Biology of β-Lactam Antibiotics*, R. B. Morin and M. Gorman, Eds. (Academic Press, New York, 1982), vol. 3, p. 83.
5. D. A. Hopwood, in *β-Lactam Antibiotics*, M. Salton and G. Shockman, Eds. (Academic Press, New York, 1981), p. 585.
6. L. T. Chang and R. P. Elander, *Dev. Ind. Microbiol.* **20**, 367 (1979).
7. R. P. Elander, J. F. Stauffer, M. P. Backus, *Antimicrob. Agents Annu.* **1**, 91 (1961).
8. H. Aoki *et al.*, *J. Antibiot.* **29**, 492 (1976).
9. R. P. Elander, J. A. Mabe, R. L. Hamill, M. Gorman, *Folia Microbiol.* **16**, 157 (1971); R. P. Elander, in *Trends in Antibiotic Research—Genetics, Biosynthesis, Action and New Substances*. H. Umezawa, A. L. Demain, T. Hata, C. R. Hutchinson, Eds. (Japan Antibiotics Research Association, Tokyo, 1982), p. 16.
10. O. W. Godfrey, *Antimicrob. Agents Chemother.* **4**, 73 (1973).
11. R. P. Elander and L. T. Chang, unpublished data.
12. A. Singh and F. Sherman, *Nature (London)* **274**, 227 (1974).
13. S. Abe, in *The Microbial Production of Amino Acids*, K. Yamudo, Ed. (Halstead, New York, 1972), p. 39.
14. H. J. Treichler, M. Liersch, J. Nuesch, H. Dobeli, in *Proceedings of the Third International Symposium on the Genetics of Industrial Microorganisms*, A. I. Laskin and O. K. Sebek, Eds. (Academic Press, New York, 1979), p. 57.
15. M. Okanishi, K. Suzuki, H. Umezawa, *J. Gen. Microbiol.* **80**, 389 (1974).
16. L. Ferenczy, F. Kevei, J. Zsolt, *Nature (London)* **248**, 793 (1974).
17. L. T. Chang, D. T. Terasaka, R. P. Elander, *Dev. Ind. Microbiol.* **23**, 21 (1982).
18. J. F. Peberdy and R. E. Bradshaw, in *Overproduction of Microbial Products*, V. Krumphamzl, B. Sikyta, Z. Vanek, Eds. (Academic Press, London, 1982), p. 371.
19. P. F. Hamlyn and C. Ball, in *Genetics of Industrial Microorganisms*, O. K. Sebek and A. I. Laskin, Eds. (American Society of Microbiology, Washington, D.C., 1979), p. 185.
20. K. Kitano, Y. Nozaki, A. Imada, *Abstracts of the Fourth International Symposium on the Genetics of Industrial Microorganisms* (Kyoto, 1982), 0-V1-7, p. 66.
21. M. Okanishi, T. Ohta, H. Umezawa, *J. Antibiot.* **23**, 45 (1970).
22. H. Schrempf, *J. Chem. Technol. Biotechnol.* **32**, 292 (1982).
23. M. Okanishi, in *Genetics of Industrial Microorganisms*, O. K. Sebek and A. I. Laskin, Eds. (American Society of Microbiology, Washington, D.C., 1979), p. 134.
24. H. Agawa, M. Okanishi, H. Umezawa, *J. Antibiot.* **32**, 610 (1979).
25. D. A. Hopwood, *J. Nat. Prod.* **42**, 596 (1979).
26. K. Hotta, Y. Okami, H. Umezawa, *J. Antibiot.* **30**, 1146 (1977).
27. J. Davies, K. I. Komatsu, J. Leboul, in *Abstracts of the 6th International Fermentation Symposium, London, Ontario* (American Society of Microbiology, Washington, D.C., 1980), p. 15.
28. L. T. Chang, D. A. Behr, R. P. Elander, *Dev. Indust. Microbiol.* **21**, 233 (1980).
29. R. Knight, unpublished data.
30. J. Anne, *Agricoltura* **25**, 1 (1977); F. Kovei and J. F. Perberdy, *J. Gen. Microbiol.* **102**, 255 (1977). J. F. Perberdy, H. Eyssen, J. Anne, *Mol. Gen. Genet.* **157**, 281 (1977).
31. Y. Okami, personal communication.
32. S. W. Queener and R. H. Baltz, in *Annual Reports on Fermentation Processes*, D. Perlman, Ed. (Academic Press, New York, 1979), vol. 3, p. 5; R. P. Elander, *Biotechnol. Bioeng.* **22**, 49 (Suppl. 1) (1980).
33. J. H. Coats, *Basic Life Sci.* **19**, 133 (1982).
34. M. Bibb, J. L. Schottel, S. N. Cohen, *Nature (London)* **284**, 526 (1980).
35. C. J. Thompson, J. Ward, T. Keiser, E. Katz, D. A. Hopwood, in *Abstracts of the 4th International Symposium on Genetics of Industrial Microorganisms* (GIM-82, Kyoto, 1982), 0-VIII-6, p. 76.
36. T. Keiser, D. J. Lydiate, H. M. Wright, C. J. Thompson, D. A. Hopwood, in *ibid.*, p. 123.
37. E. Katz *et al.*, personal communication.
38. We thank Dr. L. T. Chang for helpful discussions and G. Mareiniss for technical assistance.

16. New Applications of Microbial Products

Arnold L. Demain

The expression "wonder drugs," refers to the selective action that microbial chemicals exert against pathogenic bacteria, fungi, and tumors. The discovery of this selective activity ushered in the "antibiotic era," and for more than 40 years we have been the beneficiaries of this remarkable property of antibiotics. The success rate has been so high that for years the predominant application of microbial secondary metabolites was that of antibacterial, antifungal, and antitumor chemotherapy. Unfortunately, however, such a restricted view of the potential of microbial idiolites (secondary metabolites) has retarded the further development of the fermentation industry. Many industrial microbiologists have felt that antibiotic activity is merely the tip of the iceberg; that is, with regard to the potential application of microbial secondary metabolites for the benefit of humankind, the surface has only been scratched. In this chapter, I point out those cases in which microbial metabolites have surprising applications and also point to some challenges for the future. In this way, I hope to engender further appreciation of Jackson Foster's astute and predictive statement: "Never underestimate the power of the microbe" (*1*).

Antiparasitic Activities

One of the major economic diseases of poultry is coccidiosis, which is caused by species of the parasitic protozoan *Eimeria*. For years, this disease was treated solely by synthetic chemicals, and indeed only synthetic compounds were screened for coccidiostat activity. Although they were generally effective, resistance developed rapidly in the coccidia, and new chemical modifications of the existing coccidiostats had to be made. Then a parenterally toxic and narrow-spectrum antibiotic, monensin, was found by the group at Eli Lilly & Company to have extreme potency against coccidia (*2*). At first there were grave doubts that the fermentation process for this polyether compound could be improved to the point where monensin would become economically feasible. However, industrial genetics and biochemical engineering techniques were applied to this improvement project, and as a result the polyethers (*2a*), especially monensin (produced by *Streptomyces cinnamonensis*) and lasalocid (produced by *Streptomyces lasaliensis*), now dominate the commercial coccidiostat market.

An interesting sidelight of the monensin story is the discovery of its further use as a growth promoter in ruminants. For years, synthetic chemicals had been screened in an effort to supplement cattle and sheep diets with an agent that would eliminate the wasteful methane production and increase volatile fatty acid formation (especially propionate) in the rumen, thus improving feed efficiency. Although the concept was sound, no useful products resulted. Experimentation with monensin showed that polyethers have this beneficial activity, and now these compounds are widely used (3). Polyethers also have cardiovascular effects that are being studied for possible medical application.

Another major agricultural problem has been the infection of farm animals by worms. The predominant screening effort over the years was the testing of synthetic compounds against nematodes, and commercial products did result. Certain antibiotics had also been shown to possess antihelminthic activity (for example, hygromycin, antibiotic G-418, destomycin, paromomycin, antibiotic complex S15-1, antihelvencin, aspiculamycin, anthelmycin, myxin, thaimycin, and axenomycin) against nematodes or cestodes (4), but these failed to compete with the synthetic compounds.

Although the Merck Sharp & Dohme Laboratories had developed a commercially useful synthetic product, thiobenzole, they had enough foresight to also examine microbial broths for antihelminthic activity. They were pleasantly surprised to find a fermentation broth that killed the intestinal nematode, *Nematosporoides dubius*, in mice and was nontoxic, and that it was without antibiotic activity against bacteria or fungi (4). The *Streptomyces avermitilis* broth contained a family of secondary metabolites that they named "avermectins." These are macrocyclic lactones with exceptional activity against parasites; that is, the activity was at least ten times higher than any synthetic antihelminthic agent known. Despite their macrolide structure, avermectins do not inhibit protein synthesis nor are they ionophores; they appear to interfere with neurotransmission in many invertebrates (5). They have activity against both nematode and arthropod parasites in sheep, cattle, dogs, horses, and swine. A semisynthetic derivative, 22,23-dihydroavermectin B_1 ("ivermectin") (6) is 1000 times more active than thiobenzole and is already being used in certain countries. As in the monensin story, these potent molecules have additional activity as insecticides and may be useful in protecting plants (7).

Insecticides and Herbicides

The selective toxicity of the crystal protein (that is, the delta endotoxin) of *Bacillus thuringiensis* against insects of the order Lepidoptera has been exploited commercially for several years (8). Indeed, the selectivity of its toxicity against these insects has limited its commercial success because agricultural practitioners have been spoiled by broad-spectrum chemical insecticides. However, the world is becoming wary of the ecological damage done by many synthetic chemicals and the resistance that is developing in insects (9). In contrast, the insecticidal toxin of *Bacillus thuringiensis* has not disturbed the environment and no resistance has developed. Other intriguing applications that have not yet reached their potential include the activity of certain strains of *B.*

thuringiensis (*8*) and *B. sphaericus* against mosquitoes (*10*) and *B. popilliae* against the Japanese beetle (*11*).

With regard to low-molecular-weight microbial metabolites, there are a number with activity against insects. These include inhibitors of respiration (antimycin A, patulin, and piericidines), of protein synthesis (cycloheximide and tenuazonic acid) and membrane-active agents (destruxin, beauvaricin, and polyene antibiotics). However, their toxicities have restricted their practical application. On the other hand, there is considerable interest in the potential use of nikkomycin against agricultural pests. The nikkomycins are nucleoside analogs, structurally related to the polyoxins which are being used as agricultural antifungal agents. Since these compounds function as inhibitors of chitin synthetase and since chitin is an important structural material for insects (*12*), the nikkomycins have potent insecticidal activity (*13*). Other fermentation products with insecticidal activity include the prasinons (*14*) and the milbemycins (*15*). The macrotetralide tetranactin has been in use since 1974 as a mitocide for plants (*16*).

The current agricultural use of synthetic chemicals as herbicides has worried many environmentalists. Although microbial products have not really been taken seriously as potential herbicides, there are reports of the herbicidal activity of streptomycete secondary metabolites. These include the herbimycins [ansamycins active against mono- and dicotyledonous plants (*17*)] and the herbicidins [nucleoside analogs active against dicotyledons (*18*)]. If economic problems can be solved, this certainly will be a viable commercial area for microbial metabolites in the future.

Plant Growth Regulators

Gibberellins are a group of phytotoxic mycotoxins, produced by *Gibberella fujikuroi*, which is the cause of the "foolish seedling" disease of rice (*19*). In this disease, the infected plant grows abnormally fast and then dies. The gibberellins have been used successfully in regulating the growth of plants. They are used to reduce the time needed for malting of barley, to improve the quality of malt, and to increase the yield of vegetables as well as to allow their earlier marketing. Development of biennial plants can be made so rapid that seed crops may be obtained from lettuce and sugar beets in 1 year instead of the usual 2 years.

Pharmacological Action of Microbial Metabolites

Several investigators (*20*) have pointed out the varied pharmacological activities of microbial secondary metabolites (Table 1). Unfortunately, there has been a reluctance to screen the pharmacological activities of fermentation broths for the following reasons: (i) These activities are normally assayed in living animals, and pharmacologists are reluctant to administer crude broths to their animals. Pharmacologists prefer screening synthetic chemicals since there are fewer side effects and, if activity is observed, they immediately know the structure of the active agent. (ii) There is a bias that microbial metabolites are only useful in solving microbial problems. Although the first reason is quite justifiable, the second reason is not. However, as I describe below, certain microbial metabolites are indeed useful in medicine and it is a source of wonder how their activities

Table 1. Some pharmacological activities of microbial secondary metabolites.

ACTH-like	Diuretic	Hypolipidemic
Anabolic	Edematous	Hypotensive
Anesthetic	Emetic	Hypersensitizing
Analeptic	Erythematous	Immunomodulating
Anorectic	Estrogenic	Leukemogenic
Anticoagulant	Fertility enhancing	Parasympathomimetic
Antidepressive	Hallucinogenic	Photosensitizing
Anti-inflammatory	Hemolytic	Relaxant (smooth muscle)
Antispasmodic	Hemostatic	Sedative
Carcinogenesis inhibition	Herbicidal	Serotin antagonist
Coagulative (blood)	Hormone releasing	Spasmolytic
Complement inhibition	Hypocholesterolemic	Vasodilatory
Dermonecrotic	Hypoglycemic	

were ever detected in view of the above restrictions (i) and (ii).

Some of these metabolites were detected because the products had antibacterial or antifungal activity although they were not suitable for use as antibiotics. Since the products had been purified during the attempt to develop them as antibiotics, there was no reluctance to test such purified materials for pharmacological activities in animals. As a result, cyclosporin A (an antifungal antibiotic produced by *Tolypocladium inflatum*), is used today as an immunosuppressive agent in human organ transplants (*21*). Cyclosporin A has received interest in cases of heart transplantation in that it can block production of white cells that cause rejection but not those fighting infectious microbes. It has also been associated with improvement in the effectiveness of kidney and liver transplants.

A well-known example of the nonantibiotic use of microbial secondary metabolites is that of the ergot alkaloids (*22*). It is remarkable that this group of mycotoxins, responsible for widespread and fatal poisoning of people eating bread from contaminated grain or animals feeding on contaminated grain or infected grass throughout the ages, has also been used for the benefit of humankind. Ergot alkaloids are used for uterocontractant activity in obstetrics, to treat migraine headaches, hypertension, serotonin-related disturbances, to inhibit prolactin release in treating agalactorrhoea, and to disrupt implantation in early pregnancy. They are produced by various species of *Claviceps* in large-scale industrial fermentations. New applications of this large and potent group of fungal products are still being uncovered, especially in the treatment of Parkinsonism and cancer (*23*). Alkaloids are also produced by actinomycetes (*24*) and have antihistaminic, hypotensive, and hypoglycemic activities.

Another mycotoxin whose potent activities have been harnessed is zearelanone, produced by *Gibberella zeae* (*25*). This compound is an estrogen and is used as an anabolic agent in cattle and sheep to improve both growth and feed efficiency.

Some recently discovered pharmacological activities of other microbial metabolites follow.

Anti-inflammatory activity. A number of actinomycete and *Bacillus* products have anti-inflammatory activity as measured by inhibition of rat foot pad edema induced by carrageenin (26–29). One of these is amicomacin A, a *Bacillus pumilus* antibiotic that shows both anti-inflammatory and anti-ulcer activities (28); others are forphenicine and esterastin (29). Other compounds found to show anti-inflammatory activity are the pyrrothine antibiotics produced by *Streptoverticillium* sp. (30).

Hypocholesteremic activity. The ability to inhibit cholesterol formation in the liver of rats has been detected with citrinin, a metabolite of *Pythium ultimum* and with compactin, an antifungal agent produced by *Penicillium brevicompactum* and *Penicillium citrinum*. Compactin has low acute toxicity and shows activity also in hens and dogs (31). More recently discovered metabolites include monacolin K from *Monascus ruber*, a nontoxic metabolite which is structurally similar but four to five times more active than compactin (32). Menivolin, discovered independently as a product of *Aspergillus terreus*, is identical to monacolin K (33). The dihydroderivatives of mevinolin (34) and of compactin (35) have been isolated from *Aspergillus terreus* and *Penicillium citrinum*, respectively, and resemble the activities of their parent compounds.

Hyperlipidemic activity. Hyperlipidemia is one of the causes of coronary heart disease in humans. A synthetic drug, clofibrate, has been used but it has side effects and marginal activity. An antibiotic, ascofuranone, produced by *Ascochyta viciae*, is orally active in rats, reducing serum cholesterol, triglycerides, phospholipids, free fatty acids, and cardiac cholesterol content. Ascofuranone does not induce hepatomegaly, the main side effect of clofibrate, and shows only weak acute toxicity in mice and rats (36).

Hypotensive activity. Dopastin, produced by a *Pseudomonas* strain, shows a hypotensive effect in spontaneously hypertensive rats (37); it is of low toxicity. Another hypotensive agent is oudenone, a product of low toxicity produced by *Oudemansiella radicata* (38). Compound II of *Corynespora cassiicola* is a nontoxic, nonantibacterial agent that is hypotensive. Its structure is 2,3,5-trihydroxy-6-(3-hydroxy-n-butyl)-7-methoxy-1,4-naphthaquinone (39).

Vasodilator activity. Vasodilators WS-1228A and B have been isolated from *Streptomyces aureofaciens* (40). Testing of the B component revealed no antibiotic activity and low acute toxicity. Both compounds contain a N-hydroxytriazene moiety and are thought to be the first natural compounds containing a triazene group.

Enzyme Inhibitors

As stated above, it is extremely difficult for the microbiologist to get adequate pharmacological testing of microbial broths. Yet, it is known that such broths exhibit interesting pharmacological activities. A solution to this dilemma was proposed by Umezawa a number of years ago (41). He suggested that in vitro enzyme assays be used to detect inhibitory compounds in microbial broths. Since known pharmacological agents do inhibit enzymes and since some diseases are associated with excessive or unregulated enzyme activities, it was reasoned that enzyme inhibitors from microbial broths might exhibit valuable pharmacological activities; most important, this was a means of "liberating" the microbiologist from the pharmacologist with respect to the discovery of new, possible nonantibiotic, agents with potential application in medicine.

As a result of the initiative of Umezawa and subsequent extensive studies by his group (41) and others, a large number of extremely potent enzyme inhibitors have been isolated and identified; some 50 inhibitors were found by the Umezawa group alone (42). There is no longer any doubt that given a simple enzymatic assay, extremely potent inhibitors can be found in microbial broths, some of which are orders of magnitude more active than previously known inhibitors, either synthetic or derived from higher animals and plants. Some of these microbial inhibitors are described below.

Inhibitors of 3-hydroxy-3-methylglutaryl-CoA reductase. This rate-limiting enzyme of cholesterol synthesis has been successfully used as an assay to isolate hypocholesterolemic agents. Such agents, for example, monacolin K (mevinolin), which have been described above are extremely active in animals (43) and appear to be headed for clinical use.

Inhibitors of dopamine β-hydroxylase, tyrosine hydroxylase, and catechol-O-methyltransferase. Broths screened for activity in these assays have yielded products showing hypotensive activity in animals (37, 39, 44).

Inhibitors of complement. An inhibitor of the complement activation cascade is known as K-76 monocarboxylic acid, a sesquiterpene derivative that is an oxidation product of the natural compound produced by *Stachybotrys complementi* (45). The action of this compound is rather specific; that is, there is no inhibition of trypsin or plasmin. K-76 monocarboxylic acid acts by inhibiting formation of the chemotactic factor for polymorphonuclear leukocytes in human complement serum. It inhibits nephrotoxic nephritis in rats and may be useful in immune complex diseases, allergic diseases, and inflammation.

Inhibitors of intestinal glycosidases. Agents inhibiting amylase or invertase might be useful for persons who should only consume restricted quantities of carbohydrates to avoid hypoglycemia and increased synthesis of triglycerides in adipose tissue, liver, and the wall of the intestine, that is, patients suffering from carbohydrate-dependent diseases such as diabetes, type IV hyperlipoproteinaemia, and obesity. Such a compound is acarbose (BAYg5421), produced by *Actinoplanes* sp. (46), which is awaiting approval by the German government. Another is product S-AI of *Streptomyces diastaticus* subsp. *amylostaticus* which inhibits α-amylase and glucoamylase but not β-amylase or pullulanase (47).

A specific inhibitor of *Streptococcus mutans*, dextran-sucrase, has been isolated from a streptomycete. Since dextran-sucrase is thought to play a role in the initiation of dental caries, the fungal product (ribocitrin) may have application in preventing cariogenicity. Ribocitrin has no antibiotic activity and appears to have no acute toxicity (48).

Inhibitors of pancreatic esterase. Esterasin, an inhibitor of pancreatic esterase, is produced by *Streptomyces lavendulae*; it is nontoxic and possesses no antibiotic activity (49). It suppresses delayed-type hypersensitivity and antibody formation.

Inhibitors of cholinesterase. A compound (I-6123) inhibiting cholinesterase is produced by *Aspergillus terreus* (50). This is of interest since known synthetic insecticides are cholinesterase inhibitors (51).

Protease inhibitors. The possible role of proteases of polymorphonuclear leukocytes in inflammation and carcinogenesis has been pointed out (52). A large number of potent protease inhibitors have been isolated from streptomycete broths (27); among the best known are leupeptin (53), antipain, chymostatin, elastatinal, bestatin and pepstatin (Table 2). They have been important in studies directed toward assessing the role of proteases in various processes. For example, the inhibition of carcinogenesis in cell culture and animals by leupeptin, pepstatin, chymostatin, elastatinal, and antipain has indicated that protease activity is a necessary step in the tumor-inducing process (53). Elastatinal and antipain are active against chemical mutagenesis in bacteria, apparently inhibiting a protease involved in SOS DNA repair (54). Carboxyprotease inhibitors include pepstatins, pepstanones, and hydroxypepstatins. Pepstatin inhibits focus formation by murine sarcoma virus on YH-7 mouse cells and ascitic accumulation in cancer (55).

Elastase appears to be involved in chronic obstructive lung diseases such as emphysema (56, 57) as well as in pancreatitis, acute arthritis, and various inflammations. Elasnin, a nonantibiotic metabolite of *Streptomyces noboritoensis*, inhibits human granulocyte elastase but is relatively inactive on pancreatic elastase, trypsin, chymotrypsin, thermolysin, and papain (58). Another elastase inhibitor is the peptide, elastatinal, produced by an actinomycete (59). Serine- and thiol-protease inhibitors from microbial broths show anti-inflammatory activity (27, 57).

Pepstatin, a peptide product of several streptomycetes, is an inhibitor of acid protease [especially pepsin (60)] and has a strong diuretic effect, probably due to inhibition of renin (55). Other streptomycete-derived pepsin inhibitors include

SP-I (61) and the pepsinostreptins [isobutyryl-, propionyl-, and acetyl-(valyl-valyl-4-amino-3-hydroxy-6-methylheptanoyl-alanyl-4-amino-3-hydroxy-6-methylheptanoic acid)]. Pepsinostreptin prevents gastric ulceration in rats (62).

A specific inhibitor of the metallic endopeptidase, thermolysin, is phosphoramidon, a nonantibiotic, nontoxic metabolite of *Streptomyces tanashiensis*. Its structure is N-(α-L-rhamnopyranosyloxyhydroxyphosphinyl)-L-leucyl-L-tryptophan (63).

Bestatin [(2S,3R)-3-amino-2-hydroxy-4-phenylbutanoyl]-(S)-leucine is a specific inhibitor of aminopeptidase B and leucine aminopeptidase, and is produced by *Streptomyces olivoreticuli* (64). Since these enzymes are cell surface enzymes in lymphocytes, they could conceivably be involved in the immune response, and compounds binding to such enzymes might be immunomodulators. Bestatin was found to enhance delayed-type hypersensitivity in vivo, activation of peripheral blood lymphocytes by concanavalin A, and the activity of antitumor agents in animals (27). It increased the number of antibody-forming cells in mice and inhibited slow-growing solid tumors such as the Gardner lymphosarcoma and IMC-carcinoma. In clinical studies, bestatin enhanced immunity in cancer patients (29) and showed a number of other beneficial effects (42).

Other surface enzymes are alkaline phosphatase and esterase and microbial inhibitors of these enzymes have immuno-modulation activity (42). Amastatin is an inhibitor of aminopeptidase A and leucine aminopeptidase and is produced by *Streptomyces* sp. Its structure is (2S,3R)-3-amino-2-hydroxy-5-methylhexanoyl-L-valyl-L-valyl-L-aspartic acid. Amastatin is nontoxic and has no antibi-

Table 2. Inhibitory activities of protease inhibitors of microbial origin (27). IC_{50} is the concentration which inhibits the enzyme by 50 percent. [Courtesy of the *Japanese Journal of Antibiotics*]

Enzyme	Substrate	IC_{50} (µg/ml)					
		Leupeptin	Antipain	Chymostatin	Elastatinal	Pepstatin	Bestatin
Trypsin	Casein	2.0	0.26	>250.0	>250.0	>250.0	>250.0
Plasmin	Fibrinogen	8.0	93.0	>250.0	>250.0	>250.0	>250.0
Papain	Casein	0.5	0.16	7.5	>250.0	>250.0	>250.0
Chymotrypsin	Casein	>500.0	>250.0	0.15	>250.0	>250.0	>250.0
Elastase	Elastin–congo red	>250.0	>250.0	>250.0	1.8	>250.0	>250.0
Pepsin	Casein	>500.0	>250.0	>250.0	>250.0	0.01	>250.0
Thermolysin	Casein	>250.0	>250.0	>250.0	>250.0	>250.0	>250.0
Cathepsin A	Z-Glu-Tyr*	>500.0	1.2	62.5	>250.0	>125.0	>250.0
Cathepsin B	BAA†	0.44	0.6	2.6	—	>125.0	>250.0
Cathepsin C	Ser-Tyr-NA‡	>250.0	>250.0	>250.0	>250.0	>250.0	>250.0
Cathepsin D	Hemoglobin	109.0	>250.0	49.0	>250.0	0.01	>250.0
Renin	Peptide§	>250.0	>250.0	>250.0	>250.0	4.5	>250.0
Aminopeptidase B	Arg-NA‖	>250.0	>250.0	>250.0	>250.0	>250.0	0.05
Leucine aminopeptidase	Leu-NA¶	>250.0	>250.0	>250.0	>250.0	>250.0	0.01

*Carbobenzoxy-L-glutamyl-L-tyrosine. †N^α-benzoyl-L-arginine amide hydrochloride. ‡L-Seryl-L-tyrosine β-naphthylamide. §His-Pro-Phe-His-Leu-Leu-(^{3}H-Val)-Tyr-Ser. ‖L-Arginine 2-naphthylamide. ¶L-Leucine 2-naphthylamide.

otic activity (*65*). Forphenicine is an inhibitor of alkaline phosphatase and is produced by *Streptomyces fulvoviridis* var. *acarbodicus* (*66*). Its structure is 4-formyl - 3 - hydroxy - phenylglycine (*67*). Both products increase the number of antibody-forming cells. Forphenicine enhances delayed-type hypersensitivity and shows activity against solid tumors (*42*).

Agents affecting cyclic adenosine monophosphate (AMP) levels. Since cyclic AMP concentrations are altered in cancer, hypertension, asthma, cholera, and diabetes, there has been some interest in identifying agents that bring about these alterations. Of special interest have been cyclic AMP–increasing agents that might increase fat cell lipolysis and bronchodilation. As a result, screening efforts have been directed toward the detection of rabbit brain cyclic AMP phosphodiesterase inhibitors, and several streptomycete products have been isolated. These include 3-carbamoyl-1,2-dihydro - 4 - hydroxy - 5 - methoxy - 3 - [*H*] -pyrrolo [3,2 - *e*]indole - 7 - carboxylic acid and its 3-acetyl derivative from *Streptomyces* sp. (*68*) and reticulol (6,8-dihydroxy-7-methoxy-3-methylisocoumarin) from *Streptomyces mobarensis* (*69*). A useful agar plate assay in which beef brain cyclic AMP phosphodiesterase is used has been described (*70*).

Prolyl-4-hydroxylase inhibitors. Fibrotic collagen accumulation causes fibrotic disease of connective tissue. Lung and liver fibrosis in animal models is prevented by proline analogs. Prolyl-4-hydroxylase is thought to be the target enzyme since there is a hydroxyproline requirement for collagen secretion and thermal stability (*71*). Since there are no known nontoxic inhibitors of collagen synthesis, it is of interest that an inhibitor, P-1894B, has been isolated from

Streptomyces sp. (*72*) and found to be identical to antitumor antibiotic vincomycin A_1 (*73*). P-1894B showed some acute toxicity in rats (LD_{50} = 100 to 200 milligrams per kilogram) when given intraperitoneally but was nontoxic orally.

Ornithine decarboxylase inhibitors. Polyamines such as putrescine, spermine, and spermidine play a mysterious but essential role in cell growth, differentiation, and multiplication. Interfering with their synthesis could be useful in diseases in which abnormally rapid proliferation of cells occurs (*74*). Since L-ornithine decarboxylase is the rate-controlling enzyme of polyamine synthesis in mammalian cells, it is a good target for diseases such as psoriasis, chronic nonsuppurative prostatitis, and cancer. An initial screening of microbial broths led to the isolation from *Streptomyces neyagawaensis* of two known compounds, dihydrosarkomycin and sarkomycin (*75*); the latter is an old antitumor antibiotic (*76*). This successful isolation of an antitumor agent by a simple enzymatic assay suggests further successful application of this system to the discovery of more effective agents.

Other in vitro Tests

Simple means of detecting potentially active pharmacological agents also include in vitro tests that are not based on inhibition of a known enzyme. One such technique involves platelet aggregation induced by various compounds such as adenosine diphosphate or soluble collagen. Inhibitors of aggregation such as the pyrrothine antibiotics appear to have anti-inflammatory activity (*30*). Herquline is an inhibitory alkaloid produced by *Penicillium herquei* (*77*).

Table 3. Enzymes which are potential targets for new drugs.

Enzyme	Target	Reference
Cholinesterase	Myasthenia gravis, insect diseases of plants	50, 51, 83
Monoamine oxidase	Depression	84
Serine protease	Fertility	57
Protease	Inflammation	27, 57
Elastase	Pulmonary emphysema	56–59
Collagenase	Glomerulonephritis	57
Proteinase	Demyelinating diseases	57
Cathepsins B and D	Muscular dystrophy	57
Cyclo-oxygenase of prostaglandin synthetase	Inflammation	85
Viral proteases	Viral disease	86
3-Hydroxy-3-methylglutaryl-CoA-reductase	Hypercholesteremia	43
Dopamine β-hydroxylase, tyrosine hydroxylase, catechol-O-methyltransferase	Hypertension	37–39, 44
Complement activation	Nephritis, immune diseases, allergic disease, inflammation	45
Glycosidase	Hypoglycemia, diabetes, type IV hyperlipoproteinemia, obesity	46, 47
Dextransucrase	Dental caries	48
Esterase	Hypertension	49
Protease	Mutagenesis, carcinogenesis	27, 29, 42, 53–55, 64
Pepsin	Ulcers	62
Cyclic AMP phosphodiesterase	Cancer, hypertension, asthma, cholera, diabetes	68–70
Prolyl-4-hydroxylase	Fibrotic disease	71–73
Ornithine decarboxylase	Psoriasis, chronic nonsuppurative prostatitis, cancer	74, 75
Angiotensin-converting enzyme	Hypertension	78, 79
S-adenosylmethionine decarboxylase	Cancer, psoriasis, chronic nonsuppurative prostatitis	80

Other Enzyme Assays

A number of enzymes appear to be involved in disease processes, yet they have not been seriously used for detection of pharmacological agents in microbial broths. This section highlights such enzymes (Table 3).

Angiotensin-converting enzyme. Blood pressure is normally regulated by the renin-angiotensin system. Angiotensinogen (a plasma protein) is cleaved by trypsin and renin to form an inert peptide angiotensin I. This is cleaved by the angiotensin-converting enzyme, a zinc exopeptidase, to angiotensin II, the most powerful vasoconstrictor known. Overproduction of angiotensin II appears to be a major cause of hypertension. A leading synthetic oral hypotensive drug, captopril (78), and newer compounds (79) act by inhibiting the enzyme. These are small peptide derivatives and it is very possible that improved compounds might be detected in microbial broths.

S-Adenosylmethionine decarboxylase. Polyamine synthesis requires the activity of *S*-adenosylmethionine decarboxylase and for the reasons listed earlier in the ornithine decarboxylase inhibitor section, this enzyme might be a good target for diseases featuring rapidly proliferative and abnormal growth (80). This enzyme assay has not yet been applied to microbial screening.

Final Comments

There is no doubt that microorganisms are capable of producing nonantibiotic secondary metabolites with activities against parasites, insects, weeds, and enzymes, as well as controlling plant growth and exhibiting various pharmacological effects. In addition, microbes can be exploited for their ability to produce new industrially valuable polysaccharides (81), enzymes, and flavor and aroma (82) compounds. In my mind, the only factors limiting the discovery of useful compounds of the future are our own commitment, ingenuity, and ability to devise simple in vitro screening procedures for desirable activities.

References and Notes

1. J. W. Foster, in *Global Impacts of Applied Microbiology*, M. P. Starr, Ed. (Wiley, New York, 1964), p. 61.
2. R. F. Shumard and M. E. Callender, *Antimicrob. Agents Chemother.* **1967**, 369 (1968).
2a. J. W. Westley, *Adv. Appl. Microbiol.* **22**, 177 (1977).
3. M. Chen and M. J. Wolin, *Appl. Environ. Microbiol.* **38**, 72 (1979).
4. R. W. Burg et al., *Antimicrob. Agents Chemother.* **15**, 361 (1979).
5. L. C. Fritz, C. C. Wang, A. Gorio, *Proc. Natl. Acad. Sci. U.S.A.* **76**, 2062 (1979).
6. J. C. Chabala et al., *J. Med. Chem.* **23**, 1134 (1980).
7. E. O. Stapley and H. B. Woodruff, in *Trends in Antibiotic Research*, H. Umezawa, A. L. Demain, T. Hata, C. R. Hutchinson, Eds. (Japan Antibiotic Research Association, Tokyo, in press).
8. L. A. Bulla, Jr., D. B. Bechtel, K. J. Kramer, Y. I. Shethna, A. I. Aronson, P. C. Fitz-James, *CRC Crit. Rev. Microbiol.* **8**, 147 (1980); K. W. Nickerson, *Biotechnol. Bioeng.* **22**, 147 (1980); K. W. Nickerson, *ibid.*, p. 1305; P. Lüthy, *FEMS Microbiol. Lett.* **8**, 1 (1980).
9. T. Boddé, *BioScience* **32**, 308 (1982).
10. P. S. Myers and A. A. Yousten, *Appl. Environ. Microbiol.* **39**, 1205 (1980).
11. L. A. Bulla, Jr., R. N. Costilow, E. S. Sharpe, *Adv. Appl. Microbiol.* **23**, 1 (1978).
12. T. Leighton, E. Marks, F. Leighton, *Science* **213**, 905 (1981).
13. G. U. Brillinger, *Arch. Microbiol.* **121**, 71 (1979).
14. S. J. Box, M. Cole, G. H. Yeoman, *Appl. Microbiol.* **26**, 699 (1973).
15. Y. Takiguchi, H. Mishima, M. Okuda, M. Terao, *J. Antibiot.* **33**, 1120 (1980).
16. K. Ando, T. Sagawa, H. Oishi, K. Suzuki, Y. Nawata, in *Proceedings of the First Intersectional Congress of IAMS* (Science Council of Japan, Tokyo, 1974), vol. 3, p. 630; T. Misato, in *Pesticide Chemistry in the 20th Century*, J. R. Plimmer, Ed. (American Chemical Society, Washington, D.C., 1977), p. 170.
17. S. Ōmura et al., *J. Antibiot.* **32**, 255 (1979).
18. M. Arai, T. Haneishi, N. Kitahara, R. Enokita, K. Kawakubo Y. Kondo, *ibid.* **29**, 863 (1976); Y.

212

Takiguchi, H. Yoshikawa, A. Terahara, A. Torikata, M. Terao, *ibid.* **32**, 857 (1979).
19. E. G. Jefferys, *Adv. Appl. Microbiol.* **13**, 283 (1970).
20. D. Perlman and G. P. Peruzzotti, *ibid.* **12**, 277 (1970); H. W. Matthews and B. F. Wade, *ibid.* **21**, 269 (1977); H. B. Woodruff, *Science* **208**, 1225 (1980); E. D. Weinberg, in *Microorganisms and Minerals*, E. D. Weinberg, Ed. (Dekker, New York, 1977), p. 289; R. L. Hamill, in *Bioactive Microbial Products: Search and Discovery*, J. D. Bu'Lock, L. J. Nisbet, D. J. Winstanley, Eds. (Academic Press, London, 1982), p. 71.
21. D. Weisinger and J. F. Borel, *Immunobiology* **156**, 454 (1979).
22. L. C. Vining and W. A. Taber, in *Economic Microbiology*, vol. 3, *Secondary Products of Metabolism*, A. H. Rose, Ed. (Academic Press, London, 1979), p. 389.
23. J. M. Cassady and H. G. Floss, *Lloydia* **40**, 90 (1977).
24. T. Terashima, Y. Kuroda, Y. Kaneko, *Agr. Biol. Chem.* **34**, 753 (1970); S. Ōmura, Y. Iwai, Y. Suzuki, J. Awaya, Y. Konda, M. Onda, *J. Antibiot.* **29**, 797 (1976).
25. P. H. Hidy, R. S. Baldwin, R. L. Gresham, C. L. Keith, J. R. McMullen, *Adv. Appl. Microbiol.* **22**, 59 (1977).
26. V. Groupe and R. Donovick, *J. Antibiot.* **30**, 1080 (1977).
27. T. Aoyagi, M. Ishizuka, T. Takeuchi, H. Umezawa, *ibid.* (Suppl.), p. S-121.
28. J. Itoh, S. Omoto, T. Shomura, N. Nishizawa, S. Miyado, Y. Yuda, U. Shibata, S. Inouye, *J. Antibiot.* **34**, 611 (1981).
29. T. Aoyagi and H. Umezawa, in *Advances in Biotechnology*, vol. 1, *Scientific and Engineering Principles*, M. Moo-Young, C. W. Robinson, C. Vezina, Eds. (Pergamon, Toronto, 1981), p. 29.
30. Y. T. Ninomiya, Y. Yamada, H. Shirai, M, Onitsuka, Y. Suhara, H. B. Maruyama, *Chem. Pharm. Bull.* **28**, 3157 (1980).
31. A. Endo, M. Kuroda, Y. Tsujita, *J. Antibiot.* **29**, 1346 (1976).
32. A. Endo, *ibid.* **33**, 334 (1980).
33. A. W. Alberts *et al.*, *Proc. Natl. Acad. Sci. U.S.A.* **77**, 3957 (1980).
34. G. Albers-Schönberg *et al.*, *J. Antibiot.* **34**, 507 (1981).
35. Y. K. T. Lam *et al.*, *ibid.*, p. 614.
36. M. Sawada, T. Hosokawa, T. Okutomi, K. Ando, *ibid.* **26**, 681 (1973).
37. H. Iinuma, T. Takeuchi, S. Kondo, M. Matsuzaki, H. Umezawa, M. Ohno, *ibid.* **25**, 497 (1972).
38. H. Umezawa, T. Takeuchi, H. Iinuma, K. Suzuki, M. Ito, M. Matsuzaki, T. Nagatsu, O. Tanabe, *ibid.*, **23**, 514 (1970); M. Ohno, M. Okamoto, N. Kawabe, H. Umezawa, T. Takeuchi, H. Iinuma, S. Takahashi, *J. Am. Chem. Soc.* **93**, 1285 (1971).
39. H. Chimura, T. Sawa, Y. Kumada, F. Nakamura, M. Matsuzaki, T. Takita, T. Takeuchi, H. Umezawa, *J. Antibiot.* **26**, 618 (1973).
40. K. Yoshida, M. Okamoto, K. Umehara, M. Iwami, M. Kohsaka, H. Aoki, H. Imanaka, *ibid.* **35**, 151 (1982); H. Tanaka, K. Yoshida, Y. Itoh and H. Imanaka, *ibid.*, p. 157.
41. H. Umezawa, *Enzyme Inhibitors of Microbial Origin* (Univ. of Tokyo Press, Tokyo, 1972).
42. _____, in *Advances in Biotechnology*, vol. 3, *Fermentation Products*, C. Vezina and K. Singh, Eds. (Pergamon, Toronto, 1981), p. 15.
43. A. Endo, in *Atherosclerosis*, A. M. Gotto, Jr., L. C. Smith, B. Allen, Eds. (Springer-Verlag, New York, 1980), vol. 5, p. 152.
44. H. Umezawa, in *Fermentation Technology Today*, G. Terui, Ed. (Fermentation Technology Society, Osaka, Japan, 1972), p. 401.
45. K. Hong, T. Kinoshita, W. Miyazaki, T. Izawa, K. Inoue, *J. Immunol.* **122**, 2418 (1979).
46. W. Puls, U. Keup, H. P. Krause, G. Thomas, F. Hoffmeister, *Naturwissenschaften* **64**, S.536 (1977); E. Truscheit, W. Frommer, B. Junge, L. Müller, D. D. Schmidt, W. Wingender, *Angew. Chem. Int. Ed. Engl.* **20**, 744 (1981).
47. S. Murao, K. Ohyama, S. Ogura, *Agric. Biol. Chem.* **41**, 919 (1977).
48. Y. Okami, M. Takashio, H. Umezawa, *J. Antibiot.* **34**, 344 (1981).
49. H. Umezawa *et al.*, *ibid.* **31**, 639 (1978).
50. K. Ogata, K. Ueda, T. Nagasawa, Y. Tani, *ibid.* **27**, 343 (1974).
51. B. H. Chin and N. Spangler, *J. Agric. Food Chem.* **28**, 1342 (1980).
52. A. Janoff, *Annu. Rev. Med.* **23**, 177 (1972).
53. K. Suzukake, H. Hayashi, M. Hori, H. Umezawa, *J. Antibiot.* **33**, 857 (1980); M. Hozumi, M. Ogawa, T. Sugimura, T. Takeuchi, H. Umezawa, *Cancer Res.* **32**, 1725 (1972); S. Umezawa, K. Tatsuta, K. Fujimoto, T. Tsuchiya, H. Umezawa, H. Naganawa, *J. Antibiot.* **25**, 267 (1972); T. Kuroki and C. Drevon, *Cancer Res.* **39**, 2755 (1979); A. R. Kinsella and M. Radman, *Proc. Natl. Acad. Sci. U.S.A.* **77**, 3544 (1980).
54. M. S. Meyn, T. Rossman, W. Troll, *Proc. Natl. Acad. Sci. U.S.A.* **74**, 1152 (1977).
55. H. Esumi, S. Sato, T. Sugimura, *J. Antibiot.* **31**, 872 (1978).
56. S. Eriksson, *Acta Med. Scand.* **203**, 449 (1978).
57. A. J. Barrett, in *Enzyme Inhibitors as Drugs*, M. Sandler, Ed. (Macmillan, London, 1980), p. 219.
58. A. Nakagawa, H. Ohno, K. Miyano, S. Ōmura, *J. Org. Chem.* **45**, 3268 (1980).
59. A. Okura, H. Morishima, T. Takita, T. Aoyagi, T. Takeuchi, H. Umezawa, *J. Antibiot.* **28**, 337 (1975).
60. H. Umezawa *et al.*, *ibid.* **26**, 615 (1973).
61. S. Murao and S. Satoi, *Agr. Biol. Chem.* **34**, 1265 (1970).
62. T. Kanamaru *et al.*, *J. Takeda Res. Lab.* **35**, 136 (1976).
63. H. Suda, T. Aoyagi, T. Takeuchi, H. Umezawa, *J. Antibiot.* **26**, 621 (1973).
64. H. Umezawa, T. Aoyagi, H. Suda, M. Hamada, K. Takeuchi, *ibid.* **29**, 97 (1976).
65. T. Aoyagi, H. Tobe, F. Kojima, M. Hamada, K. Takeuchi, H. Umezawa, *ibid.* **31**, 636 (1978).
66. T. Aoyagi *et al.*, *ibid.*, p. 244.
67. T. Yamamoto *et al.*, *ibid.*, p. 483.
68. H. Nakamura, Y. Enomoto, T. Takeuchi, H. Umezawa, Y. Iitaka, *Agr. Biol. Chem.* **42**, 1337 (1978).
69. Y. Furutani, M. Shimada, M. Hamada, T. Takeuchi, H. Umezawa, *ibid.* **41**, 989 (1977).
70. P. J. Somers and C. E. Higgens, *Appl. Environ. Microbiol.* **34**, 604 (1977).
71. G. C. Fuller, *J. Med. Chem.* **24**, 651 (1981).
72. H. Okazaki, K. Ohta, T. Kanamaru, T. Ishi-

maru, T. Kishi, *J. Antibiot.* **34**, 1355 (1981).

73. S. Ōmura, H. Tanaka, R. Ōiwa, J. Awaya, R. Masuma, K. Tanaka, *ibid.* **30**, 908 (1977).

74. J. Koch-Weser *et al.*, in *Polyamines in Biology and Medicine*, D. R. Morris and L. J. Marton, Eds. (Dekker, New York, 1981), p. 437.

75. A. Fujiwara, Y. Shiomi, K. Suzuki, M. Fujiwara, *Agric. Biol. Chem.* **42**, 1435 (1978).

76. H. Umezawa, T. Takeuchi, K. Nitta, Y. Okami, T. Yamamoto, S. Yamaoka, *J. Antibiot. Ser. A* **6**, 101 (1953).

77. A. Furusaki, T. Matsumoto, H. Ogura, H. Takayanagi, A. Hirano, S. Ōmura, *Chem. Soc. Chem. Commun.* **1980**, 698 (1980).

78. M. A. Ondetti and D. W. Cushman, *J. Med. Chem.* **24**, 355 (1981).

79. H. Gavras, B. Waeber, I. Gavias, J. Biollaz, H. R. Brunner, R. O. Davies, *Lancet* **1981-II**, 543 (1981).

80. C. W. Porter, C. Dave, E. Mihich, in *Polyamines in Biology and Medicine*, D. R. Morris and L. J. Marton, Eds. (Dekker, New York, 1981), p. 407.

81. K. S. Kang, G. T. Veeder, P. J. Mirrasoul, T. Kaneko, I. W. Cottrell, *Appl. Environ. Microbiol.* **43**, 1086 (1982).

82. H.-P. Hanssen and E. Sprecher, in *Flavour '81'*, P. Schreier, Ed. (de Gruyter, Berlin, 1981), p. 547.

83. W. N. Aldridge, in *Enzyme Inhibitors as Drugs*, M. Sandler, Ed. (Macmillan, London, 1980), p. 115.

84. J. Knoll, *ibid.*, p. 151.

85. S. Moncada and J. R. Vane, *ibid.*, p. 249.

86. B. D. Korant, J. Langner, J. C. Powers, in *Synthesis and Modification of Cell and Viral Polyproteins*, G. Koch and D. Richter, Eds. (Academic Press, New York, 1980), p. 277.

17. Bacterial, Viral, and Fungal Insecticides

Lois K. Miller, A. J. Lingg, Lee A. Bulla, Jr.

Approximately 1500 naturally occurring microorganisms or microbial by-products have been identified as potentially useful insecticidal agents. The utilization of these microorganisms to regulate insect populations within a defined geographical area constitutes the field of microbial insect control and represents an exciting challenge in applied molecular biology and ecology.

This interest in microbial insecticides is largely a result of the many problems associated with the extensive use of chemical pesticides. Not only do chemical pesticides generally affect beneficial insects as well as pest species, but insects tend to acquire resistance to the chemicals so that new pest problems rapidly develop. Furthermore, chemical residues pose environmental hazards and health concerns. Thus microbial insecticides are seen as an alternative means of pest control that can play an important role in integrated pest management systems and reduce our dependence on chemical pesticides. Microorganisms that are pathogenic to insects (entomopathogens) have relatively narrow host ranges, which makes it possible to reduce specific pest populations while natural predators and beneficial insects are preserved or given the opportunity to become reestablished. Insect resistance to microbial pesticides tends to be less

common or to develop more slowly than resistance to chemical pesticides. As far as is known, entomopathogens now produced commercially do not affect humans or animals other than their target species, and their by-products are biodegradable.

A microbial insecticide is expected to be (i) convenient to apply (as a dust, spray, or bait, alone or in conjunction with chemicals, predators, parasites, or other pathogens), (ii) storable, (iii) economical, (iv) easy to produce, (v) virulent, and (vi) safe and aesthetically acceptable (*1*). Because they must be ingested to cause infection, viruses and bacteria need to be applied at the time the target insect begins feeding, that is, before it has caused any major economic damage. Pathogenic fungi do not necessarily have to be ingested in order to cause infection, but may disable or kill the insect by colonizing its surface. The agents should reach the target insect in sufficient quantity to kill or disable it in a vehicle that does not harm the pathogen. No harmful residues should remain on the commodity treated, especially when diluents or carrier materials are used.

Knowledge of the relation between the particular host insect and the pathogen is important in determining the strategy to be used in controlling the pest. Knowledge of the effect of environmental and physical factors on the host and pathogen is also important. For example, sunlight, temperature, rain, and relative humidity can influence both the behavior of the insect and the ability of the microorganism to infect it; the mode of application of the agent, the carrier material, dose standardization, and scheduling of the application can all determine the effectiveness of short- and long-term insect control. The spores of some bacteria (for example, *Bacillus thuringiensis*) can survive most environmental changes that might be encountered by their insect hosts, whether the spores are applied to field crops or to commodities held in storage. Many other microbial agents, however, particularly viruses, require the use of various techniques to protect them.

Over the past decade, technologies involving fermentation, insect cell culture, and insectaries have been developed for the production of microbial insecticides. Fermentation methods are used for producing bacterial and fungal insecticides, whereas insectaries are used for virus production. Some techniques, such as cell culture for the propagation of obligate parasites or pathogens, have not yet been adapted for large-scale commercial production of microbial agents.

Entomopathogens that are proposed for use as control agents must be scrutinized for their possible effects on the health of humans and other animals, as well as for their effects on the environment. Microbial insecticides that are already being sold commercially have met certain safety, efficacy, and environmental criteria that have been established by the Environmental Protection Agency (EPA). In this chapter we discuss some of the properties of certain bacterial, viral, and fungal pesticides that are already in commercial production or that show promise of being of some use economically (*2, 3*).

Bacterial Insecticides

Most bacteria pathogenic to insects are members of the families Pseudomonadaceae, Enterobacteriaceae, Lactobacillaceae, Micrococcaceae, and Bacillaceae. Except for the Bacillaceae, these families contain nonsporulating microorganisms. Most spore-forming bacteria pathogenic to insects belong to the family Bacillaceae. About 100 bacteria have been reported as entomopathogens, but only four (*Bacillus thuringiensis*, *B. popilliae*, *B. lentimorbus*, and *B. sphaericus*) have been closely examined as insect-control agents. These species are sporeformers; the first two produce, in addition to the spore, discrete crystalline inclusions within the sporulating cell; the last two normally do not. Of these four organisms, *B. thuringiensis* is the only bacterium that has been developed successfully as a commercial insecticide on a very large scale and now is sold in several countries. The EPA has registered it for use on field crops, trees, ornamentals, home vegetable gardens and, more recently, stored products (primarily grain and grain products) to control lepidopteran larvae.

The primary insecticidal activity of *B. thuringiensis* resides in a parasporal glycoprotein crystal that is synthesized and crystallized within the parent cell (*4, 5*). Most studies of *B. thuringiensis* have focused on the field application and efficacy of the organism. However, there has been a recent upsurge of interest in the molecular biology of *B. thuringiensis*, particularly as it relates to toxin synthesis. This organism provides an ideal model for studying the formation and regulation of a protoxin and its subsequent conversion to a toxin.

Bacillus popilliae and *B. lentimorbus* are pathogens of scarabaeid larvae and cause "milky disease" of larvae of the Japanese beetle (6). Characteristics of these pathogens are those of an effective biological control agent. They grow in the hemolymph of the insect larvae and ultimately accumulate billions of spores before the host dies. The spores permit the pathogen to survive in an inert state for long periods in the soil and are the means of disease transmission. To produce spores of *B. popilliae* and *B. lentimorbus* commercially, the bacteria must be grown in living larvae of the Japanese beetle; artificial culture methods are not yet available. *Bacillus sphaericus* apparently synthesizes a toxin (7) that is active against mosquito larvae, but the toxin has not yet been characterized.

The Toxin of *B. thuringiensis*

Subspecies *kurstaki*

The insecticidal activity of *B. thuringiensis* subspecies *kurstaki*, as well as that of other subspecies, is associated with a parasporal glycoprotein crystal that is synthesized within the organism during its sporulation cycle. In its native state, the glycoprotein is a protoxin that is solubilized and activated after ingestion by an insect that is susceptible to the toxic product (8). The protoxin can be activated in vitro by exposure to alkaline buffer. Maximum solubility of the crystal protoxin occurs within several hours after the crystal is titrated with alkali. The protoxin is stable for several hours thereafter, but then begins to degrade into small fragments with a concomitant loss in insecticidal activity. Reaggregation

also occurs, especially after the pH is lowered to near neutrality or near the experimentally determined pI of the protoxin, pH 7 (9). A range of molecular weights has been reported (10) for the protoxin (native subunit), from 0.9×10^5 to 1.3×10^5, depending on the method used for solubilization and for size determination. When material solubilized by a mild titration procedure (9) is examined, all molecular weight determinations give essentially the same result of 1.34×10^5. Also, a single NH_2-terminal residue is detectable in quantitative yield. The crystal protein may be an intact product of translation since methionine is the NH_2-terminal residue.

Upon prolonged incubation of the protoxin at slightly alkaline pH, a glycoprotein toxin (apparent molecular weight, 6.8×10^4) is generated (11). This glycoprotein remains toxic at room temperature for several months at neutral pH. It is the smallest toxic component that has been found by alkali treatment and any further breakdown appears to be detrimental to toxic activity. When compared to the protoxin, the 68,000-dalton polypeptide has very similar toxicity and, like the protoxin, is two to three times more insecticidal than the native crystal.

Figure 1 shows a schematic diagram of the behavior of the protoxin and toxin in solution. The crystal (A_n) is made up of many subunits that are dissociated in native conformation (nA) by mild alkali titration (reaction 1). Reaggregation occurs slowly (reaction 2), especially at pH 12; also, the subunit may break down to smaller fragments (reaction 4). Degradation may be further stimulated by contaminating proteases that cofractionate with the crystals during isolation. Consequently, the subunit must be stabilized by placing it in a denaturing solvent and alkylating the disulfide linkages (SR) (re-

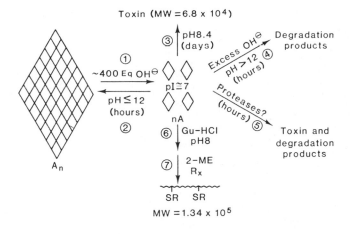

Fig. 1. Schematic diagram of the behavior of the protoxin from *B. thuringiensis* in solution. The reactions are described in the text. Abbreviations: *Eq OH⁻*, equivalent base; *Gu-HCl*, guanidine hydrochloride; *2-ME*, 2-mercaptoethanol; R_x, alkylation reaction; *SR*, alkylated disulfide linkages.

actions 6 and 7). The toxin can be generated by prolonged incubation at slightly alkaline *p*H (reaction 3). Whether this reaction is similar to the mechanism of activation in vivo (reaction 5) is not known.

Insecticidal Proteins from Other Subspecies of *B. thuringiensis*

Bacillus thuringiensis subspecies *kurstaki* is important in agriculture and forestry because it kills leaf-eating Lepidoptera (particularly larval forms of moths). Recently, another potentially useful strain, *B. thuringiensis* subspecies *israelensis*, was isolated. This microorganism produces a toxin effective against Diptera such as mosquitoes and blackflies (*12*). Tyrell *et al.* (*13*) have shown that subspecies *israelensis* produces crystals that are structurally, biochemically, and immunologically different from the protoxin produced by the *kurstaki* subspecies. It appears that the closely related subspecies that are toxic to Lepidoptera, including *kurstaki*, *berliner*, *alesti*, and *tolworthi*, all produce crystals that are similar to each other structurally, bio-

chemically, immunologically, and functionally (Table 1). These four subspecies synthesize bipyramidal crystals, and usually each bacterium contains only one such crystal. Subspecies *israelensis* forms crystals of various shapes and each bacterial cell contains two or three crystals. Electrophoretic profiles of solubilized crystal proteins from the five subspecies reveal a common protein of 1.34×10^5 daltons, similar to the size of the *kurstaki* protoxin (*9*). Presumably, this component is converted to a 68,000-dalton toxin in all of the subspecies. Proteins of approximately this size are the smallest found in electrophoretic profiles of the crystals toxic to Lepidoptera. Crystals of the subspecies *israelensis* have a smaller major component (26,000 daltons) which may also be a product of proteolysis during solubilization and activation of the 134,000-dalton protoxic molecule. However, the 26,000-dalton protein does not appear to be toxic.

All five subspecies have six major tryptic peptides in common, and peptide maps of the subspecies toxic to Lepidoptera are almost identical (Table 1). However, peptide fingerprints of subspecies

Table 1. Characteristics of the subspecies of *B. thuringiensis*.

israelensis	*kurstaki, berliner, alesti, tolworthi*
1. Crystal size and shape varies	1. Crystals are about the same size and have a bipyramidal shape
2. Protoxin subunit has apparent molecular weight of 1.34×10^5	2. Protoxin subunit has apparent molecular weight of 1.34×10^5
3. Major crystal breakdown product has apparent molecular weight of 2.6×10^4	3. Major crystal breakdown product has apparent molecular weight of 6.8×10^4
4. More lysine, threonine, proline, valine, methionine, and isoleucine in crystals	4. More arginine, serine, glutamine, and glycine in crystals; four strains very similar
5. Ineffective against Lepidoptera; toxic to mosquitoes	5. Ineffective against mosquitoes; toxic to Lepidoptera
6. Crystals are immunologically different from other strains	6. Crystals are immunologically related
7. Crystals contain glucose, mannose, fucose, rhamnose, xylose, and galactosamine	7. Crystals contain glucose and mannose
8. Crystal peptide map has major spots not found in maps of other strains	8. Crystal peptide maps are similar in the four strains
9. Crystal protein contained in spore coat along with low molecular weight proteins; the size of the protein differs from that in the other strains	9. Crystal protein contained in spore coats along with low molecular weight proteins; similar sizes in the four strains

israelensis crystals show four major peptides not present in the other four subspecies. Differences also occur in the number and amount of minor peptides, in the amino acid composition, and in the carbohydrate content (Table 1). Crystal protein is a major spore coat component in all of the subspecies, and extracts of the spore coat protein from subspecies *kurstaki* and *israelensis* are insecticidal (*14*).

The Insect Toxin Gene of

B. thuringiensis

To better understand the structure of the insecticidal crystalline protein of *B. thuringiensis* and the regulation of its synthesis, investigators in several laboratories have cloned the gene that codes for the protein in subspecies *kurstaki* (*15–17*). In particular, a recombinant Charon 4A phage, C4K6c, was isolated by Held *et al.* (*16*) and found to produce, when grown in *Escherichia coli*, a protein that reacts with antibodies specific for the crystalline protoxin protein of *B. thuringiensis* subspecies *kurstaki*. Alkali extracts of C4K6c lysates are toxic to insect larvae, and the degree of toxicity is consistent with the quantity of antigen found in lysates of phage-infected cells. Cells of *E. coli* infected with C4K6c produce a polypeptide antigen of the same size as the protoxin molecule obtained by alkali solubilization of *kurstaki* protoxin. Held *et al.* (*16*) identified a 4.6-kilobase-pair (kbp) Eco RI fragment from C4K6c that contains all or part of the toxin gene and subcloned it into two plasmids, pBR328 and pHV33. Both *E. coli* and *Bacillus subtilis* containing these recombinant plasmids produced antigen that cross-reacted with antibody directed against the protoxin. The 4.6-kbp Eco RI

fragment is of chromosomal origin, although a homologous protoxin gene is also present on a 45-kbp plasmid carried by the *kurstaki* subspecies. Several acrystalliferous nontoxic mutants that have been isolated lack the 45-kbp plasmid and, in some mutants, all plasmids are absent. All of the mutants contain the chromosomal gene but do not produce protoxin antigen. The function of the plasmid gene in the expression of insecticidal activity is not known.

Viral Insecticides

Many viruses that belong to the families Baculoviridae, Poxviridae, Reoviridae, Iridoviridae, Parvoviridae, Picornoviridae, and Rhabdoviridae, as well as a number of unclassified viruses, are pathogenic in insects (*17–20*). Some of these viruses cause natural epizootic diseases within insect populations and a few have been commercially developed as pesticides. In the United States, the EPA has registered, or is considering for registration, several baculoviruses including the nuclear polyhedrosis viruses (NPV's) that infect *Heliothis zea* (cotton bollworm), *Orgyia pseudotsugata* (Douglas fir tussock moth), *Lymantria dispar* (gypsy moth), *Autographa californica* (alfalfa looper), and *Neodiprion sertifer* (European pine sawfly) and a granulosis virus (GV) that infects *Cydia pomonella* (codling moth).

The NPV and GV baculovirus subgroups have received the most attention as viral pesticides for several reasons: (i) viruses within the family Baculoviridae are known to cause lethal infections only in invertebrates and, therefore, are thought to be inherently safer than other insect viruses that are more apparently related to vertebrate or plant viruses

(*21*); furthermore, members of the Baculoviridae usually have a relatively narrow host range. (ii) Some baculoviruses are highly pathogenic in insects and can produce sufficient progeny virus per insect [for example, 10^{10} occluded (embedded) virus per larva] to allow commercial production. (iii) The virus particles of NPV's and GV's are occluded in proteinaceous crystals. The viruses are thus more stable in the environment, have a long shelf-life as commercially prepared microbial pesticides, and are compatible with pesticide formulations, other agrochemicals, and pesticide application methods that are currently used in the field.

When used as pesticides, occluded viruses are usually sprayed on foliage; insects that consume virus-contaminated foliage acquire disease. Semiautomated technology has been developed for insect rearing, diet production, and virus preparation (*22*). When the insect hosts are not amenable to mass rearing by the established technology (for example, sawflies) it is sometimes possible to produce NPV's commercially by infecting insects collected in the field (*23*). Some viruses replicate well in insect cell cultures and the feasibility of producing them in such cultures is being considered (*24*). Before field application, viruses are formulated with substances that will protect them from ultraviolet light and with other agents that will optimize the storage, wetting, suspension, flow, and dispersal of the virus during spraying (*25*).

Nonoccluded baculoviruses, such as those infecting the rhinoceros beetle and the citrus red mite, are also used in pest management programs (*26*). Instead of being applied by spraying, nonoccluded viruses are usually introduced within infected insects which then initiate an epizootic disease. For those viruses that spread rapidly in an insect population, horizontally and vertically, such methods can be effective in reducing populations below the economic damage threshold for a number of years. Viruses that are not highly virulent but produce chronic, persistent infection have been used with the idea of stressing the insect population (*27, 28*).

Baculovirus Infections

The important role of baculoviruses in insect control has stimulated interest in their biochemistry and mechanisms of infection [for reviews see (*18, 19, 29–32*)]. Baculoviruses possess large (about 100 to 200 kilobases), double-stranded, circular, covalently closed DNA genomes that are packaged in enveloped, rod-shaped capsids approximately 40 to 140 by 250 to 400 nanometers.

In the occluded forms of baculoviruses, the virions (enveloped nucleocapsids) are embedded in a crystalline protein matrix. Occluded baculoviruses belong to two subgroups based on the morphology of the occlusion; NPV's contain many virions embedded in a single, large (up to 15 micrometers) polyhedral crystal, whereas GV's contain a single virion embedded in a small crystal. The crystalline protein matrix is primarily composed of a single 25,000- to 33,000-dalton polypeptide. The virions are thus protected in the environment during transmission of the virus from insect to insect and in their passage through the foregut of the insect to the midgut where the alkaline pH in the gut lumen solubilizes the crystal, possibly by ionizing tyrosine residues clustered at the NH_2-terminus of the matrix proteins (*33*).

The virions are released from the matrix and begin infection of the midgut columnar cells by fusion with microvillar membranes. Infections with some baculoviruses are confined to these midgut cells. Infections with others may be more extensive, with the virus replicating in the midgut cells and producing nucleocapsids that bud through the basement membrane into the hemolymph of the insect (34). The nonoccluded virions that are released into the hemolymph are responsible for the systemic infection in the insect. Virus replication in the secondary tissues results in both the budding of nonoccluded virus into the insect hemolymph and the formation of occluded virus in the nucleus. Nonoccluded viruses, but not occluded viruses, continue the spread of infection within the insect; occluded viruses require an alkaline *p*H (> 10) to release the virions. Upon death of the insect and disintegration of the integument, the occluded viruses are released and, if consumed by susceptible hosts, spread the infection.

Molecular Biology of a Baculovirus

The most extensively studied baculovirus is the *Autographa californica* nuclear polyhedrosis virus (AcNPV) which has a relatively broad host range: it productively infects over 28 different lepidopteran species. This virus replicates in several lepidopteran cell cultures producing both occluded and nonoccluded forms. With the use of plaque purification in cell culture, a genetic characterization of AcNPV has been initiated with the isolation and characterization of temperature-sensitive (ts) mutants (35). Other mutants, which either have morphologically altered occluded forms (36) or produce only a few occluded viruses per cell (37, 38) have also been isolated and characterized.

Plaque purification and restriction endonuclease analysis of a wild population of AcNPV revealed the presence of many closely related variants differing in the number and size of the DNA fragments produced by restriction endonuclease digestion (39). The use of a virulent, plaque-purified virus for pesticide purposes has been recommended to minimize the presence of defective interfering viruses (40). Restriction endonuclease analysis has been recommended as a means of quality control and detecting genetic variations in commercial virus preparation.

The AcNPV DNA genome (128 kilobases) has been extensively mapped by restriction endonucleases (41–44) (Fig. 2) and is primarily composed of unique nucleotide sequences (41, 43). Correlation of the physical restriction map with specific viral proteins or functions is being approached in several ways (45, 46). A marker rescue technique has been developed which involves gene replacement. The technique can be used to correlate AcNPV mutations with respect to the physical map and also to genetically engineer AcNPV (47, 48). The "hybrid-selection" technique is being used to correlate specific regions of the AcNPV physical map with specific AcNPV proteins (46) (Fig. 2).

The synthesis of virus-induced proteins in AcNPV-infected cells is a temporally controlled process (49–51). Working with a close relative of AcNPV, Kelly and Lescott (51) defined four stages of viral-induced protein synthesis on the basis of function-blocking experiments; an early α phase approximately 2 to 3 hours after infection, an intermediate β phase (6 to 7 hours after infection) requiring functional protein and DNA synthesis, a γ phase (at 10 hours) includ-

222

ing virion structural proteins, and a late δ phase (at 15 hours) associated with occlusion. Infectious nonoccluded progeny of AcNPV are found in the culture medium approximately 10 hours after infection. Immunoperoxidase techniques detected the synthesis of polyhedrin, the major protein of the occlusion matrix, by

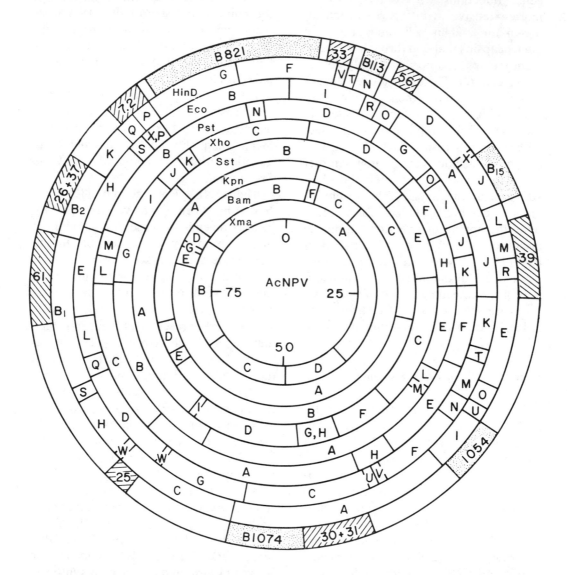

Fig. 2. The physical map and gene organization of the baculovirus AcNPV. The physical map of the restriction endonuclease sites of the 128-kilobase circular, double-stranded DNA genome is presented in the inner eight concentric rings. The outer concentric circle presents information on the gene organization of AcNPV. The stippled areas refer to the position of some of the temperature-sensitive mutations (for example, ts-B113) which have been mapped by marker rescue. The hatched areas refer to the regions encoding various structural and nonstructural proteins of AcNPV as determined by hybrid selection and translation of messenger RNA in vitro. The size of the proteins are given in number of kilodaltons.

12 hours after infection, and this preceded the appearance of occluded virus at 16 or 18 hours after infection (52). Temporal control of transcription is at least in part responsible for the temporal control of AcNPV protein synthesis. The transcription of the polyhedrin gene is first observed at 12 hours after infection and the 1.2-kilobase transcript progressively increases in quantity through 24 hours after infection (48).

Fungal Insecticides

Natural infections by fungi play a major role in the control of many economic insect pests. Occasionally, the resultant disease reaches epizootic levels causing a complete collapse of the pest population. Bassi (53) originally isolated *Beauveria* from a diseased silkworm in 1834, and although many early attempts were made to exploit fungal disease for the control of economic insect pests, they were largely unsuccessful (54). However, in the early 1900's, the introduction of *Aschersonia* species resulted in complete control of citrus white fly in Florida, and control by these species is still effective today.

More than 500 species of fungi are capable of infecting insects (55) and there are susceptible host species in all the major orders of the Insecta. Some fungi can maintain themselves in susceptible populations through many insect generations without requiring repeated introduction. Since most species do not have to be ingested to cause infection, they can be used to control insect populations in nonfeeding stages, often before any economic damage has been done.

In spite of their potential as agents of insect control, however, worldwide use of fungi on a commercial basis is limited. Comparatively little is known about the mode of pathogenesis of many entomopathogenic fungi and many are inhibited by micro- and macroclimate. Technology for the large-scale production of these fungi is difficult and in many cases not yet developed, and the safety of the agents in regard to nontarget insects and other animals has not been adequately established, in part because of a lack of reliable bioassay procedures. The few fungal insecticides that are used on a large scale are as follows. Boverin, prepared from the conidia of *Beauveria bassiana*, is used for control of the Colorado potato beetle (*Leptinotarsa decemlineata*) in the Soviet Union. It is usually applied in combination with reduced dosages of trichlorphon (56) or malathion (57). A preparation of *Metarhizium anisopliae* called Metaquino is produced in Brazil and is used primarily for controlling a spittle bug (*Mahanarva posticata*) in sugarcane (58). Considerable use of *B. bassiana* for control of European corn borer (*Ostrinia nubilalis*) is reported in China (59). In the United States, *Hirsutella thompsonii* is commercially produced and used for control of the citrus rust mite. *Nomurea rileyi* is being used in large-scale field trials as a control for the cabbage looper and the velvet bean caterpillar (60). *Verticillium lecanii* is produced commercially in Great Britain for use against aphids and other pests of glasshouse crops.

Most fungal entomopathogens progress through consistent steps in the infection process (61). Initially the conidium or zoospore attaches to the insect cuticle. If conditions in the microclimate are appropriate the attached spore germinates and penetrates through the cuticle by means of a germ tube or by infection pegs arising from a knoblike structure on the end of a hypha called an appressorium. Once entrance to the haemocoel is gained, yeastlike cells are produced and the host is killed as a result of mechanical disruption or the production of toxic metabolites. After death of the host, a mycelial growth phase usually follows with eventual repenetration of the cuticle of the insect to the exterior where new reproductive units can form.

Beauveria bassiana and *Beauveria brongniartii* cause the disease commonly known as white muscardine. Although their host range is broad, these fungi occur most commonly in populations of hypogean pests or in pests occurring in locations with temperature, moisture, and other physical conditions similar to those in soil. Their pathogenicity and ability to overcome host defense mechanisms (62) is in part due to production of toxins. *Beauveria bassiana* produces the cyclic depsipeptide beauvericin, which is reported to be toxic to mosquito larvae (9) and adult houseflys (57). However, beauvericin was not found to be toxic to lepidopteran larvae (63). Not all isolates of *B. bassiana* produce beauvericin (64). Other cyclodepsipeptides, including the beauverolides (65), bassianolides (66), and isarolides (67), are produced by *B. bassiana* and *B. brongniartii* but, as with beauvericin, broad toxicity screening has not been conducted and conclusive evidence for the role of these metabolites in the pathogenicity of *Beauveria* has not been obtained.

The efficacy of *Beauveria* is affected in part by temperature and humidity in the macroclimate (68); microclimate conditions may also be important (69). Sunlight (70) and possibly biological activity of other organisms (71) affect the ability of *B. bassiana* to survive and to initiate infection. *Beauveria bassiana* (72) and *B. brongniartii* (69) applied with low doses of chemical insecticide can act synergistically to cause mortality in host insect populations. These species are important candidates in integrated pest systems.

Two varieties of *Metarhizium anisopliae*, var. *anisopliae* and var. *major*, cause the syndrome known as green muscardine. *Metarhizium anisopliae* is able to infect the Old World desert locust (*Schistocerca gregaria*) (73) and a weevil, *Hylobius pales* (74), by ingestion. Consequently, bait traps and attractants could be used in conjunction with *M. anisopliae* for some insects.

Common hosts of *Verticillium lecanii* are the Homoptera, but *V. lecanii* also infects Collembola, Diptera, and various mites and spiders. Although seemingly widespread in nature, it only produces epizootics in tropical climates or in greenhouse environments that approximate tropical conditions (75). Virulence of the organism in the absence of a host seems to be remarkably stable (76). Use of *V. lecanii* may be restricted by the inability of its conidia to survive dry conditions (77), making it difficult to produce and store the organism. There is evidence that *V. lecanii* must be applied directly to aphids in wet conditions to be effective (78). It can be grown and distributed on a local basis for immediate use (77) and is being commercially produced in Britain.

In Florida, natural epizootics among populations of the citrus rust mite, *Phyllocoptruta oleivora*, are common during the summer. The epizootics are caused by *Hirsutella thompsonii*, which is one of the few fungal pathogens to be produced commercially in the United States. Mycar, produced by Abbott Laboratories, is registered for use on citrus crops. Generally, experimental applications of *H. thompsonii* have been successful, but this success has depended on the type of preparation, weather conditions, and citrus grove cultural practices. The fungus intially causes large reductions in the mite populations, then maintains the populations at low levels for relatively long periods (6 months) (*79, 80*). *Hirsutella thompsonii* can be applied as a conidial formulation or as mycelial fragments. Growth and sporulation can occur after application on leaf surfaces if the agent is applied with a carrier that can act as a substrate for fungal growth (*80*). This fungus may not be particularly suited for incorporation into integrated pest management programs because it is sensitive to many fungicides and moderately sensitive to many insecticides (*76, 81*).

Nomuraea rileyi produces natural infections in many Lepidoptera. Infection of the host insect is typically through the integument, and toxins may be involved in death of the host (*82*). There are several reports that the application of *N. rileyi* can advance the occurrence of natural epizootics by 2 weeks, thus providing earlier protection (*83*). Conidia, produced on semisolid media, are the usual form of the applied agent (*84*), but it may also be possible to use blastospores or mycelium. Nutrients are required for germination of the conidia and invasion of the host may be through the integument or via the alimentary tract (*85*).

Entomophorales species produce disease in a wide variety of insects, although individual strains or species are often host specific. In spite of their widespread occurrence in nature and ability to produce epizootics, use of these fungi in pest control is virtually nonexistent. Epizootics are influenced a great deal by climate. Conidia of many species are extremely short-lived (*86*) in air at a relative humidity of less than 80 percent. Even culture maintenance was difficult until liquid nitrogen storage systems for the *Entomophorales* were developed (*87*). Resting spores produced by some species are more resistant to temperature, heat, and chemicals than conidia and could be used in control programs, but the spores do not readily germinate, and although they can survive for several years (*88*), they may be less infective after storage. The growth of *Entomophorales* species in artificial media is difficult, but some species can be produced in the form of hyphal bodies and media suitable for production of resting spores have been developed (*89*).

Culicinomyces clavosporus, *Lagenidium giganteum*, and *Coelomomyces* are mosquito pathogens. *Culicinomyces* produces conidia on the surface of artificial media (*90, 91*). Conidia are infective by ingestion and produce mortality in larvae of several major mosquito genera (*90, 92*). *Lagenidium giganteum* grows saprophytically in aquatic environments or parasitically in mosquito larvae (*93*). Infection is by a zoospore which encysts on the larval cuticle and then penetrates by formation of a germ tube. Reproductive structures are produced (*94*) externally and zoospores are liberated in water. *Lagenidium giganteum* can be grown on artificial media and, if supplemented with various sterols, the fungus produces significant quantities of the infective zoospores (*94, 95*). Production of *L. giganteum* zoospores in artificial media and successful laboratory and field trials make it a particularly likely candidate for mosquito control. Species of the genus *Coelomomyces* are often reported as obligate parasites of mosquitoes. Although widespread and capable of producing epizootics, the discovery of a complex life cycle involving intermediate hosts (*96*), as well as the general inability of these fungi to grow well on other than highly complex media (*94*), indicate that more basic information is needed before they may be seriously considered for use in mosquito control programs.

Future Considerations

Currently, microbial pesticides have the greatest potential in intelligently designed and carefully applied pest management programs. Expanded use of these pesticides will depend heavily on the balance between production costs and ecological considerations. Broad-range chemical pesticides disrupt ecosystems (97) and affect natural balances in insect populations. In those cases where disruption of the ecosystem cannot be tolerated (for example, national forests), the increased cost of microbial pesticides may be preferred to the irreparable changes caused by less costly broad-range pesticides. Ironically, the more narrow host range of microorganisms makes them less attractive to industry from a profit perspective.

The genetic engineering of microbial insect pathogens to develop more potent or virulent strains, to improve their physiological tolerance of physical and chemical stresses encountered in nature, and to expand their host spectrum holds great promise. The abundance and variety of extrachromosomal elements in *B. thuringiensis*, for example, should allow their isolation and purification in sufficient quantities for detailed investigation of the structure and biological properties of these molecules. Genetic manipulation of promising plasmids, by simple transformation or recombinant DNA techniques, may ultimately improve the efficacy, pathogenicity, and commercial production of *B. thuringiensis* as well as other entomopathogenic bacteria. As already described, the toxin gene of *B.*

thuringiensis subspecies *kurstaki* has been isolated by means of recombinant DNA technology (*15–17*). New and different toxins may be developed by the genetic manipulation of this toxin gene or by its combination with toxin genes of other subspecies.

Likewise, the genetic manipulation of viruses by both classical selection techniques and recombinant DNA technology may achieve increased efficacy and broadened host range. Thus far, classical genetic selections have been used to increase resistance to ultraviolet light and to increase occluded virus production. Genetic engineering of AcNPV by recombinant DNA techniques is currently under way. Future possibilities include the introduction of an insect-specific toxin (for example, a paralytic neurotoxin) gene into the genome of AcNPV by recombinant DNA technology. Such engineering could hasten the rate at which the virus kills the host and possibly broaden the host range of the virus, thus making these microorganisms more attractive to industrial producers and pest control managers.

Continued expansion of the use of fungal insecticides will require a better understanding of the physiology, genetics, and pathogenicity of these agents. Basic research concerning the production and action of toxic metabolites is needed to establish their role in pathogenesis. Genetic studies should lead to a better understanding of virulence or to the development of strains that are more easily produced in virulent form on artificial culture. Such studies are in their infancy but they are crucial if the role of fungal insecticides is to be enhanced.

In addition to the practical value of investigations of the molecular genetics of entomopathogens, there is considerable potential for answering fundamental biological questions about microorganisms in general. For example, better understanding of the origins and functions of plasmid molecules and the control of their expression in bacilli would enhance substantially our understanding of the molecular basis of bacterial sporulation. An important future use of the *A. californica* nuclear polyhedrosis virus will be as a vector for recombinant DNA research and genetic engineering in invertebrates (*47, 48*). The advantages of the AcNPV vector system include the ability to package large segments of passenger DNA in the rod-shaped viral capsid and the availability of at least one strong promoter (the polyhedrin promoter) which is turned on following the production of infectious nonoccluded viruses. It may be possible to use genetically engineered AcNPV in the production of insect-derived compounds such as pheromones, since all the genes encoding enzymes involved in a biosynthetic pathway can be incorporated into the expandable AcNPV genome.

References and Notes

1. L. A. Bulla, Jr., and A. A. Yousten, in *Economic Microbiology*, A. H. Rose, Ed. (Academic Press, London, 1979), vol. 4, p. 91.
2. For more comprehensive coverage of microbial nsecticides see L. A. Bulla, Jr., *Ann. N.Y. Acad. Sci.* **217**, whole issue (1973); see also (*3*).
3. H. D. Burges, Ed., *Microbial Control of Pests and Plant Diseases 1970–1980* (Academic Press, New York, 1981).
4. D. B. Bechtel and L. A. Bulla, Jr., *J. Bacteriol.* **127**, 1472 (1976).
5. L. A. Bulla, Jr., K. J. Kramer, L. I. Davidson, *ibid.* **130**, 375 (1977).
6. G. St. Julian and L. A. Bulla, Jr., in *Current Topics in Comparative Pathobiology*, T. C. Cheng, Ed. (Academic Press, New York, 1973), p. 57; P. Luthy, *Vischt. Naturf. Ges. Zurich* **120**, 81 (1975); L. A. Bulla, Jr., R. N. Costilow, E. Sharpe, *Adv. Appl. Microbiol.* **231**, 1 (1978); M. G. Klein, in (*3*), p. 183.
7. E. W. Davidson, S. Singer, J. D. Briggs, *J. Invertebr. Pathol.* **25**, 179 (1975); P. Myers and A. Yousten, *Infect. Immun.* **19**, 1047 (1978).
8. L. A. Bulla, Jr., D. B. Bechtel, K. J. Kramer, Y. I. Shethna, A. I. Aronson, P. C. Fitz-James, *CRC Crit. Rev. Microbiol.* **8**, 147 (1980).
9. L. A. Bulla, Jr., K. J. Kramer, D. J. Cox, B. L. Jones, L. I. Davidson, G. L. Lookhart, *J. Biol. Chem.* **256**, 3000 (1981).
10. L. A. Bulla, Jr., K. J. Kramer, D. B. Bechtel, L. I. Davidson, in *Microbiology 1976*, D. Schlessinger, Ed. (American Society for Microbiology, Washington, D.C., 1976), p. 534.
11. L. A. Bulla, Jr., L. A. Davidson, K. J. Kramer, B. L. Jones, *Biochem. Biophys. Res. Commun.* **91**, 1123 (1979).
12. H. deBarjac, *Entomophaga* **23**, 309 (1978); *C.R. Acad. Sci. Ser. D* **286**, 797 (1978); _____ and J. Coz, *Bull. WHO* **57**, 139 (1979); R. Garcia and B. Desrochers, *Mosq. News* **39**, 541 (1979); L. J. Goldberg and J. Margalit, *ibid.* **37**, 355 (1977); A. H. Undeen and W. L. Nagel, *ibid.* **38**,524 (1978); A. H. Undeen and D. Berl, *ibid.* **39**, 742 (1979).
13. D. J. Tyrell, T. A. Davidson, L. A. Bulla, Jr., W. A. Ramoska, *Appl. Environ. Microbiol.* **38**, 656 (1979).
14. J. H. Schesser and L. A. Bulla, Jr., *ibid.* **35**, 121 (1978); D. J. Tyrell, L. A. Bulla, Jr., L. I. Davidson, *Comp. Biochem. Physiol. B* **70**, 535 (1981).
15. H. E. Schnepf and H. R. Whiteley, *Proc. Natl. Acad. Sci. U.S.A.* **78**, 289 (1981).
16. G. A. Held, L. A. Bulla, Jr., E. Ferrari, J. Hoch, A. I. Aronson, S. A. Minnich, *ibid.* **79**, 3000 (1982).
17. A. Klier, F. Fargette, J. Ribier, G. Rapoport, *EMBO J.* **1** (No. 7), 791 (1982).
18. T. W. Tinsley and K. A. Harrap, *Compr. Virol.* **12**, 1 (1978).
19. K. A. Harrap and C. C. Payne, *Adv. Virus Res.* **25**, 273 (1979).
20. C. C. Payne and D. C. Kelly, in (*3*), p. 61.
21. *WHO Tech. Rep. Ser. No. 531* (Geneva, 1973).
22. C. M. Ignoffo and T. L. Couch, in (*3*), p. 329; F. B. Lewis, in (*3*), p. 363.
23. J. C. Cunningham and P. F. Entwistle, in (*3*), p. 379.
24. H. Stockdale and R. A. J. Priston, in (*3*), p. 313.
25. T. L. Couch and C. M. Ignoffo, in (*3*), p. 621.
26. G. O. Bedford, in (*3*), p. 409; D. K. Reed, in (*3*). p. 427.
27. K. Katagiri, in (*3*), p. 433.
28. J. Kalmakoff and J. A. R. Miles, *BioScience* **30**, 344 (1980).
29. K. A. Tweeten, L. A. Bulla, Jr., R. A. Consigli, *Microbiol. Rev.* **45**, 379 (1981); M. D. Summers, R. Engler, L. A. Falcon, P. V. Vail, Eds., *Baculoviruses for Insect Pest Control: Safety Considerations* (American Society for Microbiology, Washington, D.C., 1975); E. A. Steinhaus, Ed., *Insect Pathology: An Advanced Treatise* (Academic Press, New York, 1963), vol. 1; K. M. Smith, *Virus-Insect Relationships* (Longman, New York, 1976); P. Faulkner, in *Pathogenesis of Invertebrate Microbial Diseases*, E. W. Davidson, Ed. (Allanheld, Osmun, Montclair, N.J., 1981), p. 3; E. Carstens, *Trends Biochem. Sci.* **52**, 107 (1980).
30. M. D. Summers, in *The Atlas of Insect and Plant Viruses*, K. Maramorosch, Ed. (Academic Press, New York, 1977), p. 3.
31. R. R. Granados, *Biotechnol. Bioeng.* **22**, 1377 (1980).

228

32. D. C. Kelly, *J. Gen. Virol.* **63**, (1982).
33. G. G. Rohrmann, T. J. Bailey, B. Brimhall, R. R. Becker, G. S. Beaudreau, *Proc. Natl. Acad. Sci. U.S.A.* **76**, 4976 (1979); S. B. Serebryani, T. L. Levitina, M. L. Kautsman, Y. L. Radavski, N. M. Gusak, M. M. Orander, N. V. Sucharenko, F. A. Kozlov. *J. Invertebr. Pathol.* **30**, 442 (1977).
34. K. A. Harrap and J. S. Robertson, *J. Gen. Virol.* **3**, 221 (1968); M. D. Summers, *J. Virol.* **4**, 188 (1969).
35. M. Brown, A. M. Crawford, P. Faulkner, *J. Virol.* **31**, 190 (1979); H. H. Lee and L. K. Miller, *ibid.*, p. 240.
36. M. Brown, P. Faulkner, M. A. Cochran, K. L. Chung, *J. Gen. Virol.* **50**, 309 (1980).
37. E. A. MacKinnon, J. F. Henderson, D. B. Stolz, P. Faulkner, *J. Ultrastruct. Res.* **49**, 419 (1974); W. F. Hink and E. Strauss, *J. Invertebr. Pathol.* **27**, 49 (1976); K. N. Potter, P. Faulkner, E. A. MacKinnon. *J. Virol.* **18**, 1040 (1976).
38. D. W. Miller and L. K. Miller, *Nature (London)* **299**, 562–564 (1982).
39. H. H. Lee and L. K. Miller, *J. Virol.* **27**, 754 (1978).
40. R. E. Andrews, Jr., K. D. Spence, L. K. Miller, *J. Appl. Environ. Microbiol.* **39**, 932 (1980).
41. L. K. Miller and K. P. Dawes, *J. Virol.* **29**, 1044 (1979).
42. G. E. Smith and M. D. Summers, *ibid.* **30**, 828 (1979).
43. M. A. Cochran, E. F. Carstens, B. T. Eaton, P. Faulkner, *ibid.* **41**, 940 (1982).
44. J. M. Vlak and G. E. Smith, *ibid.*, p. 1118.
45. M. D. Summers, G. E. Smith, J. Knell, J. P. Burand, *ibid.* **34**, 693 (1980); L. K. Miller, *ibid.* **39**, 973 (1981).
46. J. M. Vlak, G. E. Smith, M. D. Summers, *ibid.* **40**, 762 (1981); M. J. Adang and L. K. Miller, *J. Virol.* **44**, 782 (1982).
47. L. K. Miller, in *Genetic Engineering in the Plant Sciences*, N. J. Panopoulos, Ed. (Praeger, New York, 1981), p. 203.
48. L. K. Miller, D. W. Miller, M. J. Adang, in *Genetic Engineering in Eukaryotes*, P. F. Lurguin and A. Kleinhofs, Eds. (Plenum, New York, 1983), pp. 89–98.
49. E. B. Carstens, S. T. Tjia, W. Doerfler, *Virology* **99**, 386 (1979).
50. P. Dobos and M. A. Cochran, *ibid.* **103**, 446 (1980); H. A. Wood, *ibid.* **102**, 21 (1980); J. E. Maruniak and M. D. Summers, *ibid.* **109**, 25 (1981).
51. D. G. Kelly and T. Lescott, *Microbiologica* **4**, 35 (1981).
52. M. D. Summers, L. E. Volkman, C. H. Hsieh, *J. Gen. Virol.* **40**, 545 (1978).
53. A. Bassi, *Orcesi Lodi* (1853); G. Balsamo-Crivelli, *Bibli. Ital.* **79**, 125 (1835).
54. E. Metchnikoff, Commission of Odessa Zemstro Office (Odessa, 1879), p. 32; F. H. Snow, 4th Annual Report, Director, University of Kansas (1895), p. 46.
55. C. M. Ignoffo, in *Insect Pathology and Microbial Control* (North Holland, Amsterdam, 1967), pp. 91–117.
56. J. Farques, *Am. Zool. Ecol. Anim.* **7**, 242 (1975); A. I. Sikura, in *Moyens Biologiques de Protections des Vegetaux*, E. M. Chumakova, E. V. Gusev, N. S. Fedornichik, Eds. (Kolos, Moscow, 1974), pp. 299–306.
57. V. F. Drozda and N. V. Lappa, in *Pathologie des Arthropodes en Moyens Biologiques de Lutte* (Kiev, 1974), pp. 64–67.
58. P. Ferron, in (*3*), pp. 465–482.
59. Committee on Scholarly Communicaton with the People's Republic of China, *Report No. 2* (National Academy of Sciences, Washington, D.C., 1977).
60. C. Garcia, personal communication.
61. D. W. Roberts, in (*3*), pp. 441–463.
62. H. Seryczynska and C. Bajan, *Bull. Acad. Pol. Sci. Ser. Biol.* **23**, 267 (1975).
63. M. Kanakoa, A. Isogai, S. Murakoshi, M. Ichinoe, A. Suzuki, S. Tamura, *Agric. Biol. Chem.* **42**, 629 (1978); F. R. Champlin and E. A. Grula, *Appl. Environ. Microbiol.* **37(6)L**, 1122 (1979).
64. F. Frappier, P. Ferron, M. Pals, *Phytochemistry* **14**, 2703 (1975).
65. J. F. Ellsworth and J. F. Grove, *S. Afr. J. Sci.* **70**, 739 (1974).
66. A. Suzuki, M. Kanakoa, A. Isogai, A. Murakoshi, M. Ichinoe, S. Tamura, *Tetrahedron Lett.* **25**, 2167 (1977).
67. L. H. Briggs, B. J. Fargus, J. S. Shannon, *Tetrahedron Suppl.* **8** (No. 1), 269 (1966).
68. P. Ferron, *Entomophaga* **22**, 393 (1977).
69. ———, *Entomol. Exp. Appl.* **14**, 57 (1971).
70. C. M. Ignoffo, D. L. Hostetter, P. P. Sikorowski, G. Sutter, W. M. Brooks, *Environ. Entomol.* **6**, 411 (1977).
71. A. J. Lingg and M. D. Donaldson, *J. Invertebr. Pathol.* **38**, 191 (1981); O. Reisinger, J. Farques, P. Robert, M. F. Arnould, *Ann. Microbiol. (Inst. Paris)* **128B**, 271 (1977).
72. N. A. Telenga, A. I. Sikura, A. I. Smetnik, *Zashch. Rast. (Kiev)* **4**, 3 (1967).
73. K. H. Veen, *Meded. Landbouwhogesch. Wageningen* **68**, 1 (1968).
74. H. G. Schabel, *J. Invertebr. Pathol.* **27**, 377 (1976).
75. A. Samsinakova and S. Kalalova, *Entomophaga* **20**, 361 (1976).
76. C. W. McCoy, R. F. Brooks, J. C. Allen, A. G. Selhime, W. F. Wardowski, *Proc. Fla. State Hortic. Soc.* **89**, 74 (1976).
77. R. A. Hall, in (*3*), pp. 483–498.
78. ———, *Entomophaga* **24**, 191 (1979).
79. C. W. McCoy and A. G. Selhime, *Proceedings of the International Citrus Congress, Murchia 1974*, vol. 2, pp. 521–527; E. W. van Brussel, *Landbouwproefstn. Suriname Bull.* **98**, 30 (1975).
80. C. W. McCoy, in *Microbial Control of Insect Pests: Future Strategies in Pest Management Systems*, G. E. Allen, C. M. Ignoffo, R. P. Jaques, Eds. (NSF-USDA-University of Florida, Gainesville, 1978).
81. M. T. Muttah, thesis, Hebrew University of Jerusalem, Rehvot (1974).
82. S. S. Wasti and G. C. Hartman, *Appl. Entomol. Zool.* **13**, 23 (1978).
83. C. M. Ignoffo, B. Puttler, N. L. Marston, D. L. Hostetter, W. A. Dickerson, *J. Invertebr. Pathol.* **25**, 135 (1975); R. K. Sprenkel, W. M. Brooks, *J. Econ. Entomol.* **68**, 847 (1975); C. M. Ignoffo et al., *ibid.* **71**, 165 (1978).
84. C. M. Ignoffo, in (*3*), pp. 513–538; J. V. Bell, *J. Invertebr. Pathol.* **26**, 129 (1975).
85. L. P. Kish and G. E. Allen, *Fla. Agric. Exp. Stn. Bull.* (1978), p. 795.

86. W. G. Yendol, *J. Invertebr. Pathol.* **10**, 116 (1968).
87. D. Tyrell, S. Soki, M. A. Welton, *Can. J. Microbiol.* **18**, 1967 (1972).
88. R. Krejzova, *Ceska Mykol.* **27**, 107 (1973).
89. R. S. Soper, F. R. Holbrook, I. Majchrowicz, C. C. Gordon, *Technical Bulletin No. 76* (Life Science and Agriculture Experiment Station, University of Maine, Orono, 1975) pp. 1–15; J. P. Latge, R. S. Soper, C. C. Madore, *Biotechnol. Bioeng.* **19**, 1269 (1977).
90. A. W. Sweeney, *Aust. J. Zool.* **26**, 47 (1978).
91. _____, *ibid.*, p. 55.
92. J. N. Couch, S. V. Romney, B. Rao, *Mycologia* **66**, 374 (1974).
93. L. G. Willoughby, *Trans. Br. Mycol. Soc.* **52**, 393 (1969).
94. B. A. Federici, in (*3*), pp. 555–572.
95. A. J. Domnas, J. P. Gehro, B. F. Hicks, *Mycologia* **69**, 875 (1977).
96. H. C. Whisler, S. L. Zebold, J. A. Shemanchuk, *Nature (London)* **251**, 715 (1974); B. A. Federici, *Proc. Pap. Calif. Mosq. Control Assoc.* **43**, 172 (1975).
97. D. Pimentel and C. A. Edwards, *BioScience* **32**, 595 (1982).

18. Immobilized Enzymes and Cells as Practical Catalysts

Alexander M. Klibanov

There has been a great deal of excitement about various practical applications of biotechnology, including the production of chemicals, fuels, foods, and drugs; waste treatment; clinical and chemical analyses; toxicological assays; and uses in medicine. The question arises of which biological entities will serve as bioproducers and bioconverters in those areas. Analysis indicates that there are only two principal candidates for this role: whole cells (microbial, plant, or animal) and isolated enzymes.

Conceptually, it is easy to decide whether to employ growing cells or isolated enzymes as bioproducers and bioconverters in a particular process. Multistep transformations such as the synthesis of interferon or the production of ethanol from cellulose involve a number of different enzymes acting sequentially, and regeneration of cofactors is required; therefore, it is clearly advantageous to use whole cells. For one-step or two-step transformations, however, enzymes are probably superior because their use is free of drawbacks such as competing side reactions, sterility problems, and the cell lysis often associated with fermentations.

Microbe-catalyzed processes constitute industrial microbiology, which today is a diversified, multibillion-dollar industry (*1*). Several other chapters in Part I are devoted to applications of living microbial, plant, and animal cells for the production of useful compounds. Therefore I will focus on practical uses for isolated enzymes and dead (nonviable) cells. The integrity and infrastructure of such dead cells are not required for the processes they catalyze; the main reason for using them is to save the cost and labor involved in isolating and purifying the needed enzymes.

The scope of enzyme technology is indicated by a list of the types of reactions catalyzed by enzymes. These include oxidation, reduction, inter- and intramolecular transfer of groups, hydrolysis, cleavage of covalent bonds by elimination, addition of groups to double bonds, and isomerization (*2*). Hence virtually all organic and many inorganic reactions can be catalyzed by an enzyme or several enzymes acting in sequence. Of course, most of these reactions can also be catalyzed by nonbiological, chemical catalysts (homogeneous or heterogeneous). A great number of such chemical catalysts have been developed, and their importance, power, and versatility are illustrated by the fact that more than 70 percent of all industrial chemical processes involve catalysis (*3*). One may therefore ask why there is a need for enzymes as industrial catalysts. The answer is that enzymes have several remarkable features lacking in most non-biological catalysts: (i) extremely high catalytic activity (which may greatly exceed that of common chemical catalysts); (ii) unique specificity of action (substrate specificity, stereoselectivity, regiospecificity, geometric specificity, and so on); and (iii) ability to function under mild conditions (for instance, at ambient temperature, under normal pressure, and in aqueous solutions).

Despite such striking characteristics, enzymes have not been widely used instead of chemical catalysts. This is because enzymes also suffer from serious drawbacks. From a practical standpoint, the most important drawbacks are that (i) most enzymes are not sufficiently stable under operational conditions and (ii) enzymes are water-soluble molecules, hence difficult to separate from substrates and products and to use repeatedly.

Attempts to circumvent these problems led about 20 years ago to a major breakthrough in applied enzymology, that is, enzyme immobilization.

Immobilization of Enzymes and Cells

Immobilization of isolated enzymes. By definition, immobilization is the conversion of enzymes from a water-soluble, mobile state to a water-insoluble, immobile state. More than 100 immobilization techniques have been elaborated (*4, 5*). They can be divided into the following five groups (Fig. 1).

1) Covalent attachment of enzymes to solid supports (Fig. 1a). A variety of supports have been used, including porous glass and ceramics, stainless steel, sand, charcoal, cellulose, synthetic polymers, and metallic oxides. Enzymes are usually immobilized through their amino

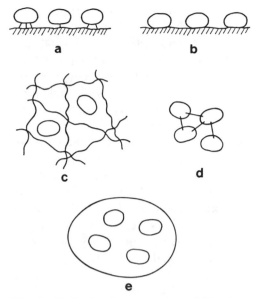

Fig. 1. Methods of enzyme immobilization: (a) covalent attachment to solid supports, (b) adsorption on solid supports, (c) entrapment in polymeric gels, (d) intermolecular cross-linking, and (e) encapsulation.

or carboxyl groups. In most instances, the immobilization procedure consists of at least two steps: activation of the support, and enzyme attachment per se. For example, Corning Glass Works has used porous ceramics for immobilization of industrial enzymes such as glucose isomerase and lactase. The support is first treated with 3-aminopropyltriethoxysilane, $(C_2H_5O)_3Si(CH_2)_3NH_2$. This yields the activated support, ceramic-Si-$(C_2H_5O)_2(CH_2)_3NH_2$. The activation step is completed by reaction of the activated support with glutaraldehyde, $OHC-(CH_2)_3-CHO$, one of whose carbonyl groups forms a Schiff base with an NH_2 group of the support. Then the unreacted glutaraldehyde is washed off and an enzyme solution is added. The second, free carbonyl group of the support-bound dialdehyde reacts with amino groups of the enzyme.

2) Adsorption of enzymes on solid supports (Fig. 1b). Ion-exchangers readily adsorb most proteins, and therefore they have been widely employed for enzyme immobilization. Such supports as the anion-exchangers diethylaminoethyl cellulose (DEAE-cellulose) or Sephadex and the cation-exchanger carboxymethyl cellulose (CM-cellulose) are used industrially for adsorption of enzymes. The appealing feature of adsorption immobilization is its simplicity: an enzyme solution is added to the support, the system is stirred for a few minutes, and then the enzyme remaining in solution is removed by washing.

3) Entrapment of enzymes in polymeric gels (Fig. 1c). In this approach, an enzyme is added to a solution of monomers before the gel is formed. Then gel formation is initiated by either changing the temperature or adding a gel-inducing chemical. As a result, the enzyme becomes trapped in the gel volume. The gels employed for immobilization of enzymes may be covalent (for instance, polyacrylamide cross-linked with N,N'-methylenebisacrylamide) or noncovalent (calcium alginate or kappa-carrageenan); these three gels have been used industrially.

4) Cross-linking of enzymes with bifunctional reagents (Fig. 1d). Among the most popular cross-linkers are glutaraldehyde, dimethyl adipimidate, dimethyl suberimidate, and aliphatic diamines. The first three directly crosslink enzymes through their amino groups. Diamines (for instance, hexamethylene diamine) cross-link enzymes through carboxyl groups following activation of these groups with carbodiimides. Cross-linking may be both intermolecular (forming water-insoluble aggregates) and intramolecular. In the former case, enzyme molecules can be cross-linked either with themselves or with other proteins present in solution. For example, immobilized glucose isomerase manufactured by Novo Industries in Denmark is produced by a glutaraldehyde treatment of pellets of homogenized *Bacillus coagulans* cells containing the glucose isomerase activity.

5) Encapsulation of enzymes (Fig. 1e). In this approach, pioneered by Chang (6), enzymes are enveloped within various forms of membranes that are impermeable for enzymes and other macromolecules but permeable for low molecular weight substrates and products. Typical examples include entrapment of enzymes in microcapsules (produced by interfacial polymerization, liquid drying, or phase separation), in liposomes, and in hollow fibers. The first two methods are intended for medical applications and the third for industrial ones. For instance, the Snamprogetti Company in Italy has used penicillin acylase, lactase, and aminoacylase entrapped in hollow fibers (7).

Comparison of the methods of enzyme immobilization listed above leads to some important conclusions. The advantage of covalent methods 1 and 4 is that they result in strong chemical bonds between the enzyme and the support. The disadvantages are that covalent binding is relatively laborious and expensive and often leads to significant inactivation of enzymes due to attachment through their active centers. The latter problem, however, can be alleviated in many cases if immobilization is carried out in the presence of substrates or other ligands (inhibitors, cofactors, and so on) that selectively protect the active center from the attachment. Methods of immobilization such as adsorption and gel entrapment are very simple and efficient, but since such methods create no strong bonds between the enzyme and the matrix, enzymes often leak from the supports. This problem can be overcome by treatment of adsorbed or entrapped enzymes with a cross-linking reagent such as glutaraldehyde.

Immobilization of whole cells. All five of the methods listed above have been employed for immobilization of both dead and living whole cells (8). By far the most fruitful technique has been entrapment of cells in gels; used with whole cells, gel immobilization is free of its major shortcoming when used with enzymes, that is, leakage from the matrix.

In the case of dead cells, the major reasons for immobilization are the same as for enzymes: to facilitate separation of the biocatalyst from products and to make the biocatalyst more stable. These objectives have often been achieved, and consequently several processes involving immobilized microbial cells have found industrial applications. For instance, polyacrylamide gel–immobilized *Escherichia coli* (possessing aspartase activity) is used for the synthesis of L-aspartic acid and *Brevibacterium ammoniagenes* (possessing fumarase activity) for the production of L-malic acid (8).

From the biotechnological standpoint, a dead cell can be considered a bag filled with enzymes; hence the only objective is to maintain the desired enzymatic activity. In contrast, living cells must have their metabolic machinery substantially intact and also be capable of reproduction. Therefore immobilized living cells represent an alternative to traditional fermentations and have been considered to have certain advantages such as increased cell densities, superior performance in continuous processes, and easier reactor control. Immobilized (gel-entrapped or adsorbed) living cells—microbial (9), plant (10), and animal (11)—have

been successfully used for various biotransformations.

Immobilization techniques have been refined to the point where virtually any enzyme or whole cell can now be immobilized with sufficient retention of enzymatic activity. Immobilization almost always dramatically improves the technological properties of biocatalysts, converting them from water-soluble to water-insoluble molecules and thereby permitting their use in conventional chemical reactors (12). However, with respect to the second major incentive for immobilization of enzymes—their stabilization—the situation is not as straightforward or favorable.

Stabilization of Enzymes by Immobilization

One of the most important biotechnological characteristics of an enzyme is its longevity or stability. Since the environment in chemical reactors is usually much harsher than that in vivo (higher temperature, the absence of a protective milieu, inactivating impurities, aggressive surfaces, and so on), most enzymes are not sufficiently stable under operational conditions. Relatively little is known about mechanisms of enzyme inactivation; therefore stabilization of enzymes is a difficult task.

In a few cases, immobilization assuredly stabilizes enzymes. For instance, the major cause of inactivation of proteases is proteolytic self-degradation (autolysis). Binding proteases to a solid support makes them lose their capacity for intermolecular self-digestion and therefore stabilizes them against autolysis. The same mechanism—mutual spatial fixation of enzyme molecules—affords stabilization against another inter-

234

molecular process, aggregation. Another case in which enzyme stabilization has been achieved involves immobilization of whole cells. Many enzymes are much more stable in their natural cellular environment than in the isolated state—for example, by virtue of stabilization by biological membranes (*13*). Stirring free cells in an aqueous solution eventually results in their rupture, which leads to solubilization and, consequently, destabilization of the enzymes. Entrapment of such cells in a gel makes them mechanically more resistant and hence stabilizes the enzymes by helping to maintain their favorable environment, as shown for *E. coli* aspartase (*14*).

It should be stressed, though, that in general immobilization is not a method of enzyme stabilization, and the latter, when observed, can often be attributed to artifacts (*15*). Statistical analysis indicates (*16*) that immobilization is as likely as any other random treatment to increase, decrease, or have no effect on enzyme stability. However, as illustrated below, if one uses immobilization to realize a rational stabilization strategy, then it should indeed produce more stable enzyme preparations (*15*).

By far the most important cause of enzyme inactivation in industrial reactors is heat, because it is often imperative to operate reactors at elevated temperatures to increase productivity and prevent microbial contamination. Although details of the mechanisms of thermal inactivation of enzymes remain obscure, some aspects are clear. For example, there is no doubt that thermal inactivation involves considerable conformational changes in the protein molecules, that is, partial unfolding (Fig. 2, transition a → b). Imagine now that an enzyme molecule is linked to a solid support by several chemical bonds (Fig. 2c).

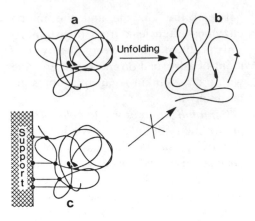

Fig. 2. Schematic representation of thermal unfolding (and consequently inactivation) of an enzyme (a → b). For the enzyme attached by many links to a solid support (c), the unfolding becomes greatly hindered. Filled region depicts the enzyme active center.

The structure of such a molecule is much more rigid than that of its free predecessor; therefore the attached molecule unfolds and is inactivated much less readily. The simplified model shown in Fig. 2 turns out to be realistic. It has been found that multipoint attachment—both covalent and noncovalent—of enzymes to polyacrylic matrices dramatically enhances their resistance to thermal inactivation (*17*). Since unfolding is a common feature of several different modes of enzyme inactivation (for instance, by *p*H, denaturing agents, and organic solvents), making the molecules more rigid through multipoint binding to solid supports appears to be a general approach to enzyme stabilization (*15*).

Another example of stabilization through immobilization concerns oxygen-labile enzymes. While most enzymes are stable in the presence of oxygen, some potentially important ones such as nitrogenase, hydrogenase, and formate dehydrogenase are not. Unless oxygen-labile enzymes are made stable it is not practical to use them in air. An approach to stabilization of oxygen-sensitive enzymes by immobilization has been suggested (*18*) which takes advantage of the fact that oxygen is much less soluble in concentrated salt solutions than in pure water. If an enzyme is placed on the surface of a highly charged support, the effective ionic strength in the microenvironment of the enzyme will be very high and hence the concentration of dissolved oxygen will be much lower than in the bulk solution. This should result in enhanced oxygen stability of the immobilized enzyme. This approach has been used successfully with clostridial hydrogenase; the half-life of the enzyme under air was greatly increased by adsorption on ion-exchangers, being 2 weeks for the hydrogenase immobilized on polyethyleneimine-cellulose compared to 5 minutes for the free enzyme.

It appears that in many other cases, too, rational strategies for enzyme stabilization can be developed (*15*). Stabilization of enzymes remains one of the most challenging areas of biotechnology, and its importance will increase as more and more enzymes are used commercially.

Properties of Immobilized Enzymes and Cells

Immobilization often significantly alters the behavior of biocatalysts. The most important examples and reasons for such changes are briefly considered below.

Partitioning. The properties of immobilized enzymes and their free predecessors differ primarily because the former no longer constitute a homogeneous and isotropic enzymatic system. Instead,

they represent an individual phase separate from the outer solution. The physicochemical properties of that new phase (for instance, an enzyme in a polymeric gel or on an ion-exchanger) are generally different from those of the bulk solution. Therefore, all components of the enzymatic process—hydrogen ions, substrates, products, inhibitors, activators, cofactors, and so on—are partitioned between the immobilized enzyme phase and the aqueous phase. This should significantly affect characteristics of an enzymatic reaction even if the enzyme molecule itself is not altered by immobilization.

A theory of the effect of the microenvironment on the catalytic properties of immobilized enzymes has been developed by Katchalski and co-workers (*19*). Suppose that an enzyme is immobilized in a negatively charged support. Due to electrostatic attraction, the concentration of hydrogen ions in the enzyme's microenvironment will always be higher than in the bulk solution and hence the pH will be lower. This will result in a shift of the profile of enzymatic activity versus pH to a more alkaline pH. The opposite will happen when an enzyme is immobilized in a positively charged support, where there is electrostatic repulsion between protons and the matrix. Quantitatively, the difference in pH between a charged support and the surrounding aqueous solution is determined by the equation $\Delta p\mathrm{H} = 0.43\ e\Psi/RT$, where e is the positive electron charge, Ψ is the electrostatic potential of the immobilized enzyme phase, R is the Boltzmann constant, and T is the absolute temperature. Experimentally observed shifts in activity-pH profiles (or in the pH optima of enzyme action) have been as high as three pH units. In agreement with the electrostatic theory, such changes resulting from immobilization in charged supports greatly decrease when salts are added.

The same approach can be used to describe qualitatively and quantitatively the interaction of enzymes immobilized in charged matrices with charged substrates, inhibitors, and other ligands. For example, the observed binding constants for substrates and inhibitors having a charge opposite to that of the matrix will be lower (that is, the observed affinity will be higher) than those for the free enzyme.

The concept of nonequal distribution of components of enzymatic reactions between the immobilized enzyme and outer solution phases is applicable not only to electrostatic but to other types of interactions as well. For instance, hydrophobic ligands will concentrate around enzymes immobilized in hydrophobic supports, and the opposite will occur in the case of hydrophilic ligands.

Diffusional limitations. Immobilization converts enzymes from homogeneous to heterogeneous catalysts, which results in the appearance of some novel features. In particular, the transport of substrates to catalysts becomes subject to diffusional resistances. The classical consideration of mass transfer in catalytic chemical processes has been successfully applied to immobilized biocatalysts (20, 21). Diffusional resistances can be divided into two categories: (i) external diffusional limitations arising from the fact that substrates must be transported from the bulk solution to the immobilized biocatalyst's surface across a boundary layer of water, and (ii) internal diffusional limitations stemming from the fact that substrates must diffuse inside the immobilized enzyme particle (including the gel, porous support bead, microcapsule, or hollow fiber).

The existence of diffusional limitations reduces the catalytic efficiency of immobilized biocatalysts and therefore should be minimized. This can be achieved by decreasing the size and optimizing the geometry of immobilized biocatalyst particles, increasing the substrate concentration, enhancing the stirring or flow rate, increasing the porosity and optimizing the biocatalyst distribution in the beads, and so on (20). However, diffusional resistances may sometimes have a beneficial effect. For example, in the case of coimmobilized multienzyme systems catalyzing consecutive reactions, such as $A \rightarrow B \rightarrow C \rightarrow \cdots \rightarrow Z$, reduced diffusion of B, C, and other intermediates from the matrix will result in their buildup in the bead and thus increase the overall rate of production of Z.

Steric hindrances. I mentioned earlier that virtually any enzyme can be immobilized with satisfactory retention of its catalytic activity. Although this assertion is valid in the case of low molecular weight substrates, it does not always hold for enzymatic reactions involving high molecular weight substrates. For example, many hydrolases covalently attached to solid supports exhibit markedly lower enzymatic activity toward polymeric substrates (proteins, polysaccharides, and nucleic acids) than expected on the basis of their reactivity to small substrates (21). This effect is due to steric hindrances involving the support's surface, and it can be greatly reduced by attaching enzymes through longer "arms." Similarly, interactions of biocatalysts entrapped in polymeric gels with macromolecules are often severely diminished because of the slow diffusion of the latter in the gel matrices. The ultimate decrease in enzymatic activity upon immobilization occurs when substrates are insoluble in water (for instance, cellulose, starch, and keratin). It appears that such cases call for the use of free enzymes (either native or chemically modified and stabilized) as opposed to their immobilized counterparts.

Applications of Immobilized Biocatalysts

The most significant practical applications of immobilized biocatalysts are discussed briefly in this section in terms of some representative examples that clearly show the scope, possibilities, and limitations of immobilized enzyme technology.

Chemical and pharmaceutical industries. Biotechnology in general and immobilized biocatalysts in particular are unlikely to have an appreciable impact on the production of bulk (commodity) chemicals as long as such conventional feedstocks as oil, natural gas, and coal are used. This conclusion is based on the following facts. (i) Up to 60 to 80 percent of the cost of bulk chemicals is due to the cost of the raw material, so a change in the process technology would have a rather small effect on the economics. (ii) There are excellent chemical catalysts for the synthesis of bulk chemicals and—considering the progress made over the past two decades—the opportunities here appear to be unlimited. (iii) Enormous capital investments have been made in existing chemical plants, and since most of them currently function well below capacity, chances of sizable investments in novel, competing technologies are slim. Only when alternative feedstocks such as biomass and wastes become a major factor can one expect biotechnology to play an important role. And even when that happens, which will probably not be for 30 to 50 years, the

contribution of immobilized biocatalysts is questionable in comparison with conventional fermentations.

Therefore, the chief target for immobilized biocatalysts could only be the production of fine or specialty chemicals, that is, relatively low-volume, high-cost compounds. In such cases enzymes seem to be attractive catalysts because of their specificity of action and ability to function under mild conditions (*22*). Several processes employing immobilized biocatalysts have been or are being commercialized, all of them to produce specialty chemicals.

Immobilized biocatalysts have proved particularly useful for the production of L-amino acids, which are widely used as food additives, as animal feed, and in medicine. The L- (but not D-) amino acids have nutritive value and have traditionally been manufactured by fermentation. Chemical syntheses are simpler, faster, and cheaper than fermentations but almost always result in racemic mixtures of amino acids (*23*). Chibata and co-workers (*5*) developed an enzymatic method for the conversion of such racemic mixtures to pure L-amino acids, and that method is now used industrially in Japan. Chemically synthesized amino acids are first acylated and then passed through a column packed with immobilized aminoacylase, which selectively hydrolyzes (deacylates) the L-isomer. The L-amino acid is then readily separated from the acyl-D-amino acid on the basis of solubility differences. This is followed by racemization of the acyl-D-amino acid by heating and its reuse in the resolution procedure. As in many other immobilized enzyme processes, the major cost savings over the free-enzyme-based batch reactor process come from reductions in labor and enzyme costs.

Other transformations aimed at the

production of L-amino acids and catalyzed by immobilized enzymes and cells include (24) the conversion of ammonium fumarate to L-aspartic acid; synthesis of L-tryptophan from indole and either acetic acid and ammonia or D,L-serine; synthesis of L-tyrosine from phenol, acetic acid, and ammonia; conversion of L-arginine to L-citrulline or L-ornithine; and synthesis of L-glutamic acid from glucose.

Another successful use of immobilized biocatalysts is in the production of 6-aminopenicillanic acid (6-APA)—the starting material for industrial manufacture of the semisynthetic penicillins—from penicillin G, which is readily obtained by fermentation (24, 25). A unique feature of the enzyme penicillin acylase is that (in contrast to OH^- or H^+) it hydrolyzes the more stable of the two amide bonds in penicillin G, which happens to be the desirable reaction. Currently, immobilized penicillin acylase is employed on an industrial scale not only to produce 6-APA but also to acylate 6-APA to form novel penicillins and to deacylate and acylate cephalosporins, which are more potent structural analogs of penicillins (24, 25).

Food industry. Immobilized biocatalysts hold particular promise for use in food processes. Technologically, the food industry is grossly underdeveloped compared with the chemical and pharmaceutical industries. The competitors of enzymes, chemical catalysts, have not played and are not expected to play a significant role in food processing because of their "incompatibility" with food materials and for safety reasons. Enzymes, on the other hand, have been widely used in food technology for many years (26). The introduction of immobilization technology has created several novel applications for biocatalysts (27).

The greatest commercial success of immobilized biocatalyst technology has been in the production of so-called high-fructose corn syrup (HFCS) catalyzed by immobilized glucose isomerase (28). This process converts glucose (produced by enzymatic hydrolysis of starch) to an approximately equimolar mixture of fructose and glucose, HFCS. Because fructose is sweeter than glucose, HFCS is about as sweet as a sucrose syrup of the same solid content, and it has found a wide and growing use in soft drinks (for instance, those manufactured by Coca-Cola and Pepsi-Cola). In 1980 more than 1 million metric tons of HFCS (based on dry weight) was produced in the United States, and by 1985 this figure is expected to double.

The history of the development of HFCS production catalyzed by immobilized glucose isomerase (29) is instructive and indicative of the role of the economic environment in biotechnology. Although the technology was ready by 1970, the price of raw sugar then was less than 10 cents a pound. Since HFCS could not be produced cheaper than that, the process was not commercialized. In November 1974 the price of raw sugar jumped to 50 cents a pound, and the glucose isomerase process suddenly became highly profitable. When the price of sugar plummeted below 10 cents a pound at the end of 1976, industrial HFCS production survived and even expanded, reaching the level stated above and capturing much of the liquid sweetener markets previously held by sucrose.

Another recently commercialized process is the hydrolysis of lactose in whey (a by-product of cheese manufacturing) to a mixture of glucose and galactose, catalyzed by lactase covalently attached to microporous silica beads. The whey glucose-galactose syrup produced is used as a protein-rich sweetener for baked goods, ice creams, candies, and jams. Like glucose isomerase, immobilized lactase converts a nonsweet sugar to sweet ones in a reaction that cannot be readily achieved by conventional chemical means.

Analytical applications of immobilized biocatalysts. Many enzymes exhibit a unique substrate specificity, reacting with only one substrate out of many. This feature (absent in almost all chemical catalysts) is especially valuable in analytical work, where it is commonly wished to measure the concentration of one compound in the presence of many others. The potential of immobilized biocatalysts in chemical and clinical analyses can be best illustrated by "enzyme electrode" technology (*30*).

Determination of particular compounds in complex, multicomponent fluids (such as blood or industrial waste streams) is a difficult task, usually requiring many laborious and time-consuming operations. This is quite different from the ideal determination, which would involve simply placing an electrode in a sample and immediately reading the concentration of the compound of interest. Unfortunately, the electrodes now available are limited to a very narrow range of species—H^+, O_2, NH_4^+, CO_2, and a few others—and cannot be used to directly determine more complex molecules such as amino acids. A revolutionary idea was to couple such an electrode with an immobilized enzyme: an electrode is wrapped with a polymeric film containing an enzyme, which converts the determined compound to a species that can be directly measured by the electrode. For example, the enzyme L-amino acid oxidase produces one ammonium ion per molecule of L-amino acid oxidized. Hence, coupling this enzyme

with an NH_4^+-sensitive electrode creates an "enzyme electrode" that can directly assay L-amino acids. This principle has a general applicability, and it has already been used to assay a wide variety of diagnostically, environmentally, or otherwise important compounds including individual amino acids, glucose and other sugars, phenols, organophosphates, urea, cholesterol, penicillin, and hydrogen peroxide (*30*). In principle, virtually any compound can be assayed by an enzyme electrode composed of a suitable electrochemical probe and an immobilized enzyme or a combination of enzymes acting in sequence (or immobilized whole cells) (*31*).

Medical applications of immobilized enzymes. Most studies of medical uses of immobilized enzymes have focused on removing undesirable compounds from the blood. This can be done either by administering immobilized enzymes into the body or by using various extracorporeal devices (*4, 5*). For instance, microencapsulated (to prevent proteolytic degradation and immunological reactions) asparaginase has been injected intraperitoneally to treat leukemia. Such a treatment is based on the ability of the enzyme to decompose L-asparagine, an amino acid that is required by tumor cells much more than by normal cells.

A promising example of use of immobilized enzymes in extracorporeal therapy comes from a recent study by Langer *et al.* (*32*). Patients' blood that is to be perfused in an artificial kidney or a pump-oxygenator is usually heparinized to keep it from clotting in the device. Before the blood reenters the body, the heparin must be removed to avoid hemorrhagic complications. This problem was solved by using a blood filter containing the immobilized enzyme heparinase, which degrades 99 percent of heparin's anticoagulant activity within minutes (*32*).

Future Developments:

Opportunities and Challenges

As Niels Bohr asserted, "Prediction is very difficult, especially about the future." Therefore, rather than trying to forecast specific events in the area of enzyme technology, I will attempt to identify and rationalize some key trends that may prove important.

Immobilized biocatalysts can be used either to improve existing processes or in novel processes. There are serious practical restrictions in both of these directions: in the former, the immobilized biocatalyst technology must be far superior to the conventional one to be competitive; in the latter, there is uncertainty concerning the market for the new product.

One way to improve a process is to replace a vital component that is expensive or in short supply. For example, Klibanov and Huber (*33*) proposed the use of immobilized microbial hydrogenases in place of platinum compounds as catalysts in the detritiation of aqueous effluents from nuclear power plants and in heavy-water production. Use of a biocatalyst can also make a process more efficient—for example, by making it less labor- and energy-intensive. This approach is illustrated by the use (*34*) of nitrile hydratase to convert acrylonitrile to acrylamide, a monomer used in manufacturing synthetic fibers. The enzyme-based process for acrylamide production has advantages over conventional methods such as the hydration of acrylonitrile catalyzed by copper salts or sulfuric acid, as the latter methods yield several by-products or require high temperatures.

The production of HFCS catalyzed by immobilized glucose isomerase is perhaps the best example of a novel process whose product has found its market. Most developments in the medical and analytical areas will likewise be novel ideas rather than improvements.

An important trend in enzyme technology is the use of nontraditional catalytic properties of enzymes—that is, the ability of many enzymes to catalyze reactions quite different from those they catalyze in vivo (*35*). The enzymatic production of HFCS is a good illustration: in nature the enzyme catalyzing this process isomerizes xylose, not glucose. To identify such unnatural reactions, one must screen known enzymes for unknown catalytic activities; the results of such a search will add to the arsenal of approaches at our disposal.

For several reasons, genetic engineering is expected to contribute significantly to the further development of enzyme technology. Some of the enzymes currently used commercially are from plant and animal sources. To make the supply of such enzymes more stable and abundant, it would be beneficial to clone the genes for them into efficient enzyme-producing microorganisms. The same strategy applies to human enzymes for therapeutic applications and to enzymes needed in a purified state (such as those that are to be covalently attached to solid supports). Finally, it is often desirable to alter the catalytic characteristics of commercial enzymes—for instance, to enhance or reduce thermostability, to shift the pH optimum of the enzymatic activity, or to modify the substrate specificity. Once the genes for such enzymes have been cloned and we know what structural changes in the enzyme molecule will yield the desired result, the genes can be chemically changed correspondingly.

References and Notes

1. A. L. Demain, *Science* **214**, 987 (1981); *Sci. Am.* **245** (No. 3) (1981).
2. M. Dixon and E. C. Webb, *Enzymes* (Academic Press, New York, ed. 3, 1979), chapter 5.
3. H. A. Wittcoff and B. G. Reuben, *Industrial Organic Chemicals in Perspective* (Wiley-Interscience, New York, 1980), part 1, chapter 5.
4. O. R. Zaborsky, *Immobilized Enzymes* (CRC Press, Cleveland, Ohio, 1973); K. Mosbach, Ed., *Methods Enzymol.* **44**, (1976); M. D. Trevan, *Immobilized Enzymes: Introduction and Applications in Biotechnology* (Wiley, New York, 1980).
5. I. Chibata, *Immobilized Enzymes—Research and Development* (Kodansha, Tokyo, 1978).
6. T. M. S. Chang, *Artificial Cells* (Thomas, Springfield, Ill., 1972).
7. W. Marconi and F. Morisi, in *Applied Biochemistry and Bioengineering*, L. B. Wingard, E. Katchalski-Katzir, L. Goldstein, Eds. (Academic Press, New York, 1979), vol. 2, p. 219.
8. T. R. Jack and J. E. Zajic, *Adv. Biochem. Eng.* **5**, 125 (1977); I. Chibata and T. Tosa, *Adv. Appl. Microbiol.* **22**, 1 (1977).
9. F. B. Kolot, *Dev. Ind. Microbiol.* **22**, 1 (1977).
10. P. Brodelius and K. Mosbach, *Adv. Appl. Microbiol.* **28**, 1 (1982).
11. A. L. van Wezel, *Nature (London)* **216**, 64 (1967); W. G. Thilly and D. W. Levine, *Methods Enzymol.* **53**, 184 (1979).
12. M. D. Lilly and P. Dunnill, *Process Biochem.* **6** (No. 8), 29 (1971); W. R. Vieth, K. Venkatasubramanian, A. Constantinides, B. Davidson, in *Applied Biochemistry and Bioengineering*, L. B. Wingard *et al.*, Eds. (Academic Press, New York, 1976), vol. 1, p. 221.
13. A. M. Klibanov, N. O. Kaplan, M. D. Kamen, *Arch. Biochem. Biophys.* **199**, 545 (1980).
14. T. Tosa, T. Sato, Y. Nishida, I. Chibata, *Biochim. Biophys. Acta* **483**, 193 (1977).
15. A. M. Klibanov, *Anal. Biochem.* **93**, 1 (1979).
16. G. J. H. Melrose, *Rev. Pure Appl. Chem.* **21**, 83 (1971).
17. K. Martinek, A. M. Klibanov, V. S. Goldmacher, I. V. Berezin, *Biochim. Biophys. Acta* **485**, 1 (1977); *ibid.* p. 13.
18. A. M. Klibanov, N. O. Kaplan, M. D. Kamen, *Proc. Natl. Acad. Sci. U.S.A.* **75**, 3640 (1978).
19. E. Katchalski, I. Silman, R. Goldman, *Adv. Enzymol.* **34**, 445 (1971); R. Goldman, L. Goldstein, E. Katchalski, in *Biochemical Aspects of Reactions on Solid Supports*, G. R. Stark, Ed. (Academic Press, New York, 1971), p. 1.
20. L. Goldstein, *Methods Enzymol.* **44**, 397 (1976); J.-M. Engasser and C. Horvath, in *Applied Biochemistry and Bioengineering*, L. B. Wingard, E. Katchalski-Katzir, L. Goldstein, Eds. (Academic Press, New York, 1976), vol. 1, p. 127.
21. I. V. Berezin, A. M. Klibanov, K. Martinek, *Russ. Chem. Rev.* **44**, 17 (1975).
22. J. B. Jones, C. J. Sih, D. Perlman, Eds., *Applications of Biochemical Systems in Organic Chemistry* (Wiley, New York, 1976), parts 1 and 2.
23. A spectacular exception to this rule is the Monsanto process for the production of some L-amino acids with chiral Wilkinson-type catalysts [reviewed in R. E. Merrill, *CHEMTECH* **11**, 118 (1981)]. For example, L-phenylalanine (an essential amino acid used in the synthesis of the sweetener aspartame) can be prepared by the condensation of benzaldehyde with *N*-acetylglycine, followed by asymmetric hydrogenation catalyzed by rhodium-phosphine complexes and subsequent hydrolysis of the resulting *N*-acetyl-L-phenylalanine. The major drawback of this process is the high cost and instability of the catalyst.
24. B. J. Abbott, *Adv. Appl. Microbiol.* **20**, 203 (1976).
25. E. J. Vandamme, in *Microbial Enzymes and Bioconversions*, A. H. Rose, Ed. (Academic Press, London, 1980), p. 467.
26. G. Reed, Ed., *Enzymes in Food Processing* (Academic Press, New York, 1975).
27. P. Brodelius, *Adv. Biochem. Eng.* **10**, 75 (1978); A. Kilara and K. M. Shahani, *CRC Crit. Rev. Food Sci. Nutr.* **12**, 161 (1979); M. J. Taylor and T. Richardson, *Adv. Appl. Microbiol.* **25**, 7 (1979).
28. R. L. Antrim, W. Colilla, B. J. Schnyder, in *Applied Biochemistry and Bioengineering*, L. B. Wingard, E. Katchalski-Katzir, L. Goldstein, Eds. (Academic Press, New York, 1979), vol. 2, p. 97; S. H. Hemmingsen, in *ibid.*, p. 157; C. Bucke, in *Enzymes and Food Processing*, G. G. Birch, N. Blakebrough, K. J. Parker, Eds. (Applied Science, London, 1981), p. 51.
29. P. B. Poulsen, *Enzyme Microb. Technol.* **3**, 271 (1981).
30. P. W. Carr and L. D. Bowers, *Immobilized Enzymes in Analytical and Clinical Chemistry* (Wiley, New York, 1980); L. B. Wingard, E. Katchalski-Katzir, L. Goldstein, Eds., *Applied Biochemistry and Bioengineering* (Academic Press, New York, 1981), vol. 3.
31. The biggest problem associated with the use of enzyme electrodes is due to interfering substances, which are often present in "real" samples. Such substances (proteins in the case of biological fluids) interact not with the enzyme (which is indeed specific) but with the surface of the electrode. In principle, this obstacle can be overcome by using semipermeable polymeric membranes to shield the electrode from interfering substances, as was done in the commercial Yellow Springs Instrument Co. glucose analyzer (based on immobilized glucose oxidase coupled with an oxygen-sensitive electrode).
32. R. Langer, R. J. Linhardt, S. Hoffberg, A. K. Larsen, C. L. Cooney, D. Tapper, M. Klein, *Science* **217**, 261 (1982).
33. A. M. Klibanov and J. Huber, *Biotechnol. Bioeng.* **23**, 1537 (1981).
34. Y. Asano, T. Yasuda, Y. Tani, H. Yamada, *Agric. Biol. Chem.* **46**, 1183 (1982).
35. A. M. Klibanov, in *The Biological Basis of New Developments in Biotechnology*, A. Hollaender, A. I. Laskin, P. Rogers, Eds. (Plenum, New York, in press).

19. Bioreactors: Design and Operation

Charles L. Cooney

Biotechnology can be considered to be the integration of several disciplines, including microbiology, biochemistry, molecular biology, and chemical engineering, for the purpose of utilizing biological systems for manufacturing or environmental management. Bioreactors serve a central role in biotechnological processes by providing a link between starting materials and final products, as shown in Fig. 1. It is in this area that multidisciplinary efforts are focused and value is added to a less expensive material through synthesis of a product or rendering of a service. This chapter examines the strategy for selection and design of bioreactors and identify the limits and constraints in their use. A biotechnological process is an integrated set of unit operations involving not only product synthesis and bioconversions but also product recovery. The bioreactor must be designed to meet the specific needs and constraints of a particular process, and its design will affect both cost and quality of the final product or service.

Although the term bioreactor is relatively new, the concept is quite old. Some examples of early bioreactors include the calf stomach, used in ancient times for storage of milk. It was discovered that an active ingredient in the calf stomach transformed the milk into cheese. This active ingredient is rennin,

a protease that catalyzes a specific and limited hydrolysis of milk proteins and promotes their coagulation into cheese. Calf rennin is still used for cheese production. However, the bioreactor has changed from the calf stomach to temperature-controlled vats. In addition, a shortage of calf rennin has led to the use of less expensive microbially derived enzymes in some applications. Another early bioreactor was used in bread making. Bread dough provides a matrix that entraps yeast; this matrix (an early form of immobilized whole cells), placed on a flat, hot pan in an oven, traps carbon dioxide generated from the metabolic action of yeast and rises to form a loaf. With advances in technology we learned to place the dough in a pan and, while not changing the biocatalytic process, change the form and quality of the final product. The use of closed containers to promote anaerobic yeast metabolism in alcohol production is another early example of the evolution of a bioreactor to meet the needs of a particular biocatalytic process. Pasteur demonstrated the importance of oxygen for efficient production of bakers' yeast; this discovery had a considerable impact on the bakers' yeast industry and is an early example of process control. A major development in bioreactor design occurred in the 1940's, when investigators learned how to grow

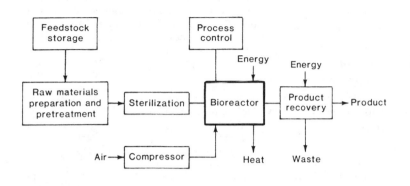

Fig. 1. Schematic overview of a biotechnological process showing the central role of a bioreactor in linking starting materials and the final product. This overview is typical of aerobic fermentation processes and unit operations such as air compression and medium sterilization may not be required in all processes.

molds such as *Penicillium chrysogenum* in submerged culture for the production of antibiotics such as penicillin. Before this, fermentations were carried out on solid substrates, which were difficult to control and keep aseptic (*1*). Thus, the modern bioreactor in the form of a fermentor used in large-scale manufacturing of pharmaceutical products is a relatively new innovation in the fermentation industry.

The fermentation industry has expanded considerably in scope. Today it encompasses much more than fermentation and is more properly called the biochemical process industry, by analogy with the chemical process industry. A discussion of the modern biochemical process industry by Perlman (*2*) gives an overview of a multibillion-dollar industry that involves 145 companies throughout the world and produces more than 250 different products spanning the pharmaceutical, chemical, and agricultural industries. Furthermore, biological processes are used in such diverse applications as waste treatment, the production of detergent enzymes, and the enzyme-catalyzed degradation of the anticoagulant heparin in blood (*3*). Considering the central role

of bioreactors in a diverse industry, it is not surprising that they are emerging in a wide variety of shapes, sizes, and forms. The goals in bioreactor design, however, are common; the purpose of a bioreactor is to minimize the cost of producing a product or a service. The evolution of bioreactors, whether for cheese production or synthesis of antibiotics, is driven by a need to increase the rate of product formation and the quality of the product or service. Bioreactor design has focused on improved biocatalysts; better process control, more recently with computers; better aseptic design and operation; and innovative ways to overcome rate-limiting steps, especially for heat and mass transfer.

Objectives in Bioreactor Design

The primary objective in the design of a bioreactor or any component of a biotechnological process is to minimize the cost of producing a high-quality product or service. Because the bioreactor provides a link between the starting materials and the product, it plays a critical role in the economics of biotechnological processes. To place this in perspective, it is useful to consider the manufacturing costs for different products. These are summarized in Table 1 for a commodity product, ethanol, and a specialty product, penicillin (4, 5). It is apparent that the primary cost is for the raw material and that other major costs include capital investment and utilities, mostly energy. In the case of older plants, where the capital is depreciated, maintenance changes will increase and become more significant. The magnitude of the capital investment is also a strong function of interest rates and method of financing. The cost of energy, since 1978, has risen at an annual rate of 16 percent, while raw materials and labor costs have risen at 6 and 10 percent respectively (6). As a result, the energy cost has become as much as 35 percent of the manufacturing cost for some products (6). For this reason there is increased interest in minimizing energy demands in bioreactor operation and subsequent product recovery.

Processes that require bioreactors and typical products are summarized in Table 2. It is useful to separate these processes into those that are conversion cost-intensive and those that are recovery cost-intensive; although in both cases it is important to minimize the cost of

Table 1. Comparison of manufacturing costs as percent of total for penicillin (4) and ethanol (5) made by fermentation. Ethanol costs are based on corn as the starting material.

Category	Penicillin	Ethanol
Raw materials cost	35	62
Operating cost		26
Utilities	15	
Labor	4	
Maintenance	11	
Plant and overhead	8	
Capital costs	22*	12*

*Includes depreciation, taxes, and insurance.

raw materials for conversion, in conversion cost-intensive processes the volumetric productivity, Q_p (grams of product per liter per hour), is of paramount importance and in recovery cost-intensive processes the product concentration, P (grams per liter), is the dominant criterion for cost minimization.

Biological Reaction Kinetics

Several major differences between biological and chemical reaction kinetics are important in bioreactor design. In most biological systems there is a complex series of reactions that must be

Table 2. Examples of products in different categories in the biochemical process industry.

Category	Example
Cell mass*	Bakers' yeast, single-cell protein
Cell components†	Intracellular proteins
Biosynthetic products†	Antibiotics, vitamins, amino and organic acids
Catabolic products*	Ethanol, methane, lactic acid
Bioconversion*	High-fructose corn syrup, 6-aminopenicillanic acid
Waste treatment	Activated sludge, anaerobic digestion
Service	Heparin degradation, optical isomer resolution

*Typically conversion or feedstock cost-intensive processes.   †Typically recovery cost-intensive processes.

optimized and coordinated. Since the cell is able to facilitate this coordination in an elegant manner, growing cells are often used as a means of synthesizing complex metabolites, proteins, polysaccharides, and other products. Fermentation processes are autocatalytic, and the catalyst concentration as well as the environment changes with time; this leads to some unique process control problems. Furthermore, the reactions are conducted under moderate conditions of pH (near neutrality) and temperature (for instance, 20° to 65°C). While low temperature is often cited as an advantage of biocatalysis, it frequently causes a problem because heat removal is difficult at low temperature (7). Essentially all processing is carried out in an aqueous phase and product streams are relatively dilute (typically 0.2 to 20 percent), making recovery operations expensive.

Despite the apparent complexity of biocatalytic processes, there is usually a single rate-limiting step controlling the reaction as well as a few secondary limitations, and these rate limitations provide a basis for process design. The rate limitation may be biologically imposed, as is often the case in complex reaction sequences for antibiotic, organic acid, or amino acid synthesis, where a single enzyme step may limit metabolic flux. Productivity may be improved either by genetically alleviating the rate-limiting step in the cell or increasing the cell concentration. This is exemplified in Fig. 2, which shows a plot of Q_p versus cell or enzyme concentration, X, in a bioreactor. Productivity increases with increasing catalyst concentration and specific activity or productivity, S_a, which reflects the catalytic capacity of the cell or enzyme. Increasing the catalyst concentration is generally a biochemical engi-

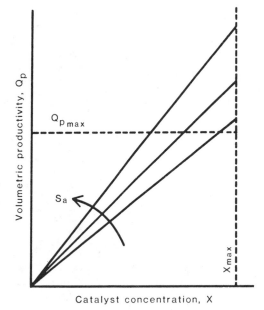

Fig. 2. Volumetric productivity (grams of product per liter per hour) in a bioreactor as a function of catalyst concentration (grams per liter) and specific activity (grams of product divided by grams of catalyst per hour). Physical constraints on productivity are shown by dashed lines and are discussed in the text.

neering problem, while improving specific activity is generally a biological one. Productivity limitations may be externally imposed, either by engineering constraints such as mass or heat transfer or by the need to limit a substrate concentration. With growing cells, limitation of a nutrient such as carbon, nitrogen, or phosphate may be required to overcome catabolite repression problems, in which one of those nutrients, when above a critical concentration, prevents synthesis of enzymes required for product formation (8). With an enzyme, substrate limitation may be required to avoid substrate inhibition.

The goal in bioreactor design is to minimize cost. Maximizing volumetric productivity allows one to minimize cap-

246

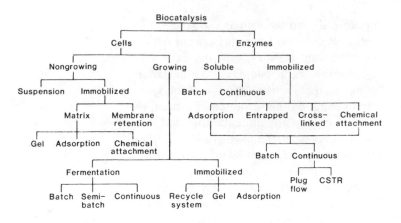

Fig. 3. Decision tree showing the options in selecting biocatalysts and bioreactor configurations.

ital investment. For this reason it is usually desired to operate a reactor at its maximum physical limits, which are often constrained by mass or heat transfer (9). The superposition of this engineering constraint on top of biological capability is shown in Fig. 2 by dotted lines, which represent the operating limits for a bioreactor. The vertical line is the maximum catalyst concentration, which is about 200 grams per liter for cells or cellular organelles that have a moisture content of 80 percent and are packed tightly with little interstitial void volume; for enzymes it is the maximum protein loading times the specific activity. The horizontal line represents a heat or mass transfer limitation that is stoichiometrically related to product formation. When the specific activity or productivity of a microorganism or biocatalyst is improved, less catalyst is required to achieve the maximum productivity, $Q_{p\ max}$, for the reactor. This will be reflected in a reduced catalyst cost. Improvements in engineering design raise the value of $Q_{p\ max}$. Thus, even though engineering constraints limit productivity, improvements in the biological system can have a substantial impact on the cost of bioconversion.

Types of Bioreactors

In view of the importance of engineering constraints and the need to integrate biological and engineering improvements, it is useful to consider the forms of bioreactors that are commonly used today. There are three major types of bioreactors and two forms of biocatalysts. Bioreactors may be batch, semicontinuous (fed-batch), or continuous reactors; furthermore, continuous bioreactors may be continuous stirred tank reactors (CSTR) or plug flow reactors. The biocatalysts may be individual enzymes, used as soluble or immobilized catalysts, or whole cells, and the cells may be in a growing or nongrowing state. Combining these types of reactors and catalysts provides the choice of operating systems summarized in Fig. 3. The literature on novel and alternative bioreactor configurations is quite extensive (10); however, to tap this body of knowledge and design a bioreactor to meet specific needs requires a few simple decisions. The first is the choice between enzymes and whole cells as the biocatalyst. Today, the use of one or a few enzymes in cell-free form is limited to simple and generally degradative—that is, hydrolytic or oxidative—

reactions which do not require energy coupling. Although in vitro biosynthesis, which requires energy coupling, has been demonstrated in the laboratory with cell-free enzymes (*11*), it is generally more practical to use whole cells whenever there are requirements for cofactor regeneration or energy coupling. When using enzymes, one can choose between soluble and immobilized forms that can be employed in a variety of batch and continuous reactors. The design of immobilized enzyme systems has been reviewed (*12*) and a variety of immobilization methods based on physical entrapment, covalent cross-linking, covalent attachment to a matrix, and adsorption have been described (*13*). Immobilized enzyme processes used commercially are summarized in Table 3 (*14*).

When products or services require more complex reaction sequences, it is best to use whole cells. These may be either growing cells, as used in the synthesis of most fermentation products today, or nongrowing cells, which can be used in concentrated suspensions or as immobilized cells for the catalysis of relatively simple reactions. Normally, with nongrowing cells the catalysts are immobilized by incorporation into a matrix or retention by a membrane. Such systems are being used increasingly for industrial applications, as shown by some examples in Table 3. While the biochemical process industry is characterized primarily by the use of growing cells in aqueous systems, some recent work has been done with growing immobilized cells. The apparent contradiction between growth and immobilization is resolved when the latter is considered as a form of cell recycle. Immobilization by entrapment in a gel or adsorption on a support provides a form of internal cell recycle. Alternatively, cell recycle can be achieved by devices external to the bioreactor, such as centrifugal separators, membrane devices, or settling tanks, which collect concentrated cells from a fermentation effluent and return them to the fermentor. It is more common today, however, to use growing cells in batch and semicontinuous or fed-batch fermentors, but this will not necessarily be the case in the future.

Approaches to Bioreactor Design

A bioreactor is a biocatalyst in a container. Its engineering design is based on minimizing process constraints such as heat and mass transfer and allowing optimal control of biocatalytic activity while minimizing total process cost. Since a major cost in most biological processes is that of the raw materials, an important objective in bioreactor design is to maximize the conversion yield of starting materials to final product, $Y_{p/s}$ (grams of product divided by grams of substrate), and this reflects the catalyst selectivity. Selectivity is important not only for maximizing conversion yield but also for minimizing by-product formation, which increases problems of product recovery. While the maximum conversion yield is constrained by thermodynamics (*15*), the actual yield is constrained by bioconversion mechanisms and the requirement for biocatalyst synthesis. The objective function to be maximized is $R_{p/x}$, the ratio of product per unit of biocatalyst,

$$R_{p/x} = Y_{p/s} \int_0^{t_c} S_a(t) \, dt \qquad (1)$$

where $S_a(t)$ is the specific activity as a function of time for the cell or enzyme catalyst (grams of substrate reacted divided by grams of catalyst per unit time)

Table 3. Commercial immobilized enzyme reactors (*14*).

Enzyme	Product	Immobilizing method	Reactor type	Operating mode	Company	Starting date
Aminoacylase	L-Amino acids	Adsorbed	Packed bed	Continuous	Tanabe Seiyaku	1969
Aspartase*	Aspartate	Entrapped	Packed bed	Continuous	Tanabe Seiyaku	1973
Fumarase*	Fumarate	Entrapped	Packed bed	Continuous	Tanabe Seiyaku	1974
Glucose isomerase	HFCS†	Adsorbed	Packed bed	Batch	Clinton Corn	1972
		Covalent	Stirred tank	Batch	Novo	1974
			Packed bed	Continuous	Novo	1975
Lactase	Lactose-free milk	Entrapped	Stirred tank	Batch	Snamprogetti	1977
Penicillin acylase	6-Amino penicillanic acid	Adsorbed	Stirred tank	Batch	Squibb	1966
		Covalent	Stirred tank	Batch	Astra	1973
		Covalent	Stirred tank	Batch	Beecham	1974
		Entrapped	Packed bed	Continuous	Snamprogetti	1975
Steroid dehydrogenase*		Heat-treated			Squibb	1964

*Immobilized cells.   †High-fructose corn syrup.

and t_c is the effective catalyst life (often expressed as a half-life). Values of $R_{p/x}$ can vary greatly for different processes. For enzyme-catalyzed reactions, such as high-fructose corn syrup (HFCS) production with immobilized glucose isomerase, this ratio can be ≥ 2500 g per gram of enzyme preparation. For commodity products, such as single-cell protein and ethanol, $R_{p/x}$ varies from 1 to 10 g of product per gram of cells, respectively. For specialty products, such as penicillin, values of about 1 g per gram of cells are typically observed.

In the case of enzyme-catalyzed reactions, improvements in $R_{p/x}$ are made by using enzymes with high S_a, increasing the enzyme stability (t_c), and increasing the yield of active enzyme per unit mass of organism used for enzyme production. In the biosynthesis of fermentation products, $R_{p/x}$ is improved by controlling the cell's use of raw materials (primarily the carbon source) for the synthesis of cell mass, the desired product, by-products, and cell maintenance in order to maximize $Y_{p/s}$ (9). This can be done genetically, environmentally, or by reusing the biocatalyst as many times as possible as in cell recycle or immobilization systems. Solutions to the problem of maximizing $R_{p/x}$ involve a combination of biological and chemical engineering approaches to increase specific activity, selectivity, and effective catalyst life.

As shown in Fig. 2, bioreactors are designed and operated to achieve a maximum volumetric productivity. The importance of productivity is reflected in the need to minimize capital investment; even if a biological process has attractive overall economics, it is difficult to achieve a high return on investment if the capital investment per unit weight of product is exceptionally high. Volumetric productivity is improved by increasing the specific activity of the enzyme or specific productivity of the growing cell and increasing the concentration of enzyme or cells (or both) in the reactor. The use of immobilized enzymes makes it possible to achieve high catalyst concentrations in the reactor and to reuse the catalyst many times. With soluble enzymes the catalyst capacity of the reactor is often limited by the solubility of the protein catalyst and it is difficult to recover the catalyst after use. With immobilized enzymes it is possible to exceed this solubility limit since the catalyst is coupled to a solid support matrix. Then catalyst loading becomes limited by the specific activity of the immobilized enzyme preparation and the loading capacity of the immobilizing matrix. Immobilized enzyme systems such as packed columns may have protein concentrations of 50 g/liter (16). The specific activity of enzymes can vary (17) from 1 to 10,000 units per milligram of protein (where 1 unit is 1 micromole of substrate reacted per minute under optimal conditions). With highly active enzyme preparations, one could expect to use biocatalysis to achieve product formation rates greater than 100 moles per liter per hour. This is difficult to achieve, however, because of engineering limitations and physical constraints.

The volumetric productivity in fermentation or immobilized whole cell systems is limited by cell density (recall that the moisture content of cells is typically 80 percent) and by the concentration of a rate-limiting enzyme in a metabolic pathway. Bioreactors containing immobilized *Escherichia coli* and the enzyme aspartase can synthesize 3 moles of aspartic acid per liter per hour with 98 percent yield from $1.0M$ ammonium fumarate (18). Immobilized cell reactors containing *Saccharomyces cerevisiae* or

Zymomonas mobilis can produce ethanol at rates greater than 1.5 moles per liter per hour (*19*). By comparison, with fermentations for antibiotics such as penicillin the volumetric productivity is less than 1 millimole per liter per hour (*20*), and the chemical industry often achieves 1 to 10 moles of product per liter per hour.

Once a product is formed, it must be isolated and purified. The cost of recovery is, in general, proportional to the amount of water that must be processed. Thus it is important to maximize the concentration of product leaving the bioreactor in order to minimize both the capital investment and the operating cost of the recovery system. Antibiotics, enzymes, and, more recently, proteins produced by genetically engineered cells are examples of recovery cost-intensive products because they are often formed in dilute solution or coproduced with similar materials from which they must be purified. Recovery of highly purified intracellular protein from bacteria for therapeutic use is an example (*21*).

In a continuous process, the relation between product concentration, P, and operating conditions is

$$P = \frac{S_a VX}{F} \qquad (2)$$

where V is the volume of the reactor and F is the flow rate through the reactor. Product concentration can be maximized by decreasing the flow rate or increasing the activity and concentration of the catalyst. In the traditional fermentation industry—exemplified by antibiotic, amino acid, and organic acid production—batch and fed-batch processes are commonly used, in part because they allow high product concentrations to accumulate by having long residence times. Continuous processes often have

higher volumetric productivities than batch processes, but the product concentration is lower. This limitation can be overcome by using high concentrations of active catalyst; examples are the use of immobilized enzymes in the conversion of penicillin to 6-aminopenicillanic acid, the conversion of glucose to HFCS, and the use of cell recycle in the conversion of sugar to ethanol.

There are other criteria to be considered in bioreactor design. Product quality must be maximized, and this is often achieved by increasing process reproducibility and minimizing by-product formation. Energy costs for air compression, mixing, temperature control, and media steam sterilization have become increasingly important. The major energy cost associated with a bioreactor is that for aeration and mixing. As a consequence, considerable effort over the past 30 years has gone into the design of mass transfer systems for bioreactors that can achieve high mass transfer rates with good energy efficiency. In most biochemical processes the labor cost is relatively low, less than 5 percent of the manufacturing cost. This is achieved by designing equipment that is simple to operate, has minimal maintenance requirements, and has on-line process control. It is a characteristic of many biological processes that the equipment, particularly the bioreactor, is versatile and can be used for many different products. This is generally not true in the chemical industry, but is important in biochemical process development since often a single plant may be used for several different products.

Limitations in Bioreactor Operation and Design

While bioreactors can be loaded with sufficient catalyst to achieve very high rates of product formation, there are physical constraints in the design and operation of the reactors that prevent one from realizing these rates. Catalyst concentration and specific activity is improved by using high cell or enzyme concentrations and catalysts with high specific activity. Ultimately, however, the rate is limited by the problem of mass or heat transfer or both. The problem of mass transfer is particularly important in processes that require oxygen but also occurs when there is a water-insoluble nutrient requirement. Equation 3 illustrates the supply and demand requirements for oxygen by a growing population of microorganisms:

$$\frac{\mu X}{Y_{O_2}} = k_L a \, (C^* - C_L) \qquad (3)$$

where μ is the specific growth rate, X the cell concentration, and Y_{O_2} the oxygen yield for growth and product formation. The rate of oxygen transfer is limited by the liquid film around the air bubble (9). As a consequence, oxygen transfer rates are improved by increasing the bubble surface area, a; maximizing the liquid film mass transfer coefficient, k_L; and maximizing the driving force, $C^* - C_L$, where C^* and C_L are the equilibrium concentration of oxygen in the bubble and the concentration of dissolved oxygen, respectively. Many fermentor configurations have been proposed to improve the rate and efficiency of mass transfer (22). The demand term is controlled by the metabolic rate of the microorganisms as characterized by the specific growth rate, μ; the density of actively growing cells, characterized by X; and the efficiency with which oxygen is coupled to energy generation and biosynthesis, as given by the value of Y_{O_2}. In most aerobic bioreactors oxygen transfer is the rate-limiting step during

part or all of the process. The relation between X and C_L is seen by solving Eq. 3 for X:

$$X = \frac{Y_{O_2}}{\mu} \, k_L a \, (C^* - C_L) \qquad (4)$$

In addition to improvements in equipment design, it is possible to use process control strategies to cope with the oxygen transfer limitation. By reducing μ during periods of high oxygen demand, it is possible to operate at a higher cell density and at the maximum productivity as determined by mass transfer rates, but to continue to accumulate and produce product in the reactor for longer periods of time. This can be done by reducing the temperature of the process or by controlling metabolism by restricting the flow of some essential nutrient such as carbon, nitrogen, or phosphate. The imposition of this restriction is important and allows C_L to be maintained above a critical value to avoid oxygen starvation of the culture, which often leads to decreased product formation and conversion yield. An important aspect of bioreactor design is integration of the design with operating strategy, and this has been a major driving force for investigations into the use of computer control in fermentation processes. In the application of process control, the fermentation industry lags many years behind the chemical process industry (23). This is because it is often difficult or impossible to measure the primary objective parameter—product formation—in a bioreactor and because the use of this information to control the physiology of the culture and achieve process optimization is poorly understood. In addition, biological processes are generally operated in a batch or fed-batch mode, whereas in the chemical industry continuous processes are more common. These factors have slowed the implementation of computer control in biological processes; however, process improvements through modification of microorganisms and better control are likely to provide major improvements in bioreactor operation.

Biological reactions are generally carried out at relatively low temperatures, 20° to 65°C. As a consequence, heat removal is often a problem, particularly for large bioreactors. Heat production increases linearly with volume; however, on scale-up, the surface-to-volume ratio increases by the two-thirds power. Since heat is removed in proportion to the available surface area, there is a maximum reactor size that can be cooled without mechanical refrigeration, and thus heat removal often limits the scale-up of large bioreactors. Improving the conversion efficiency for raw materials to products generally reduces the heat load (24); thus the problem of heat transfer limitation can be attacked by biological as well as mechanical means.

Trends and Future Directions in Bioreactor Development

It will continue to be important to develop catalysts with high specific activity and selectivity. This may be achieved at the molecular level by using genetic engineering techniques to alter the primary structure of enzyme catalysts. An alternative is the use of "artificial enzymes" as recently described by Breslow (25). This problem will also be attacked with better methods of enzyme immobilization, which will lead to higher retention of activity and longer lifetimes. For fermentation or whole cell systems with complex regulated and coordinated pathways, increases in specific activity can be achieved by applying recombinant DNA techniques to increase the

production of rate-limiting enzymes and alter metabolic regulatory schemes in order to maximize the flow of raw materials to desired products and away from undesired by-products. Such efforts, coupled with improved process control of fermentations and improved stability of immobilized cell systems, will result in substantially lower catalyst costs.

However, bioreactor performance is usually ultimately limited by heat and mass transfer capabilities. As a consequence, there is a need to improve methods and equipment for heat and mass transfer in biological reactors. As the ability to increase catalyst loading in the reactor improves, the demands for process technology to remove process heat and transfer nutrients through diffusion barriers will increase.

The processing of large volumes of water after product removal is expensive. To minimize this cost, especially with commodity products such as ethanol and single-cell protein, water recycle is being employed. As a means of minimizing energy use, some processes are being optimized by minimizing water use, and this trend is likely to increase.

In an effort to further minimize capital investment in biotechnological processes, there will be increased emphasis on continuous processes. A major deterrent to the use of continuous bioreactors is the problem of low product concentration. This problem can be minimized by using catalysts with high specific activity. Keeping in mind the limits in carrying out a fermentation, one can envision immobilized whole cell systems providing an opportunity to achieve high productivities and hence high product concentrations. The unit operations in a biological process have a considerable effect on each other, and it is axiomatic that whatever you do upstream will have an impact on downstream processing. For this reason, it is important to carefully integrate bioreactors and all subsequent product recovery operations. Biotechnology holds great promise for the efficient production of pharmaceutical, chemical, and agricultural products. The continued success of biotechnology depends significantly on the development of bioreactors, which represent the focal point for interaction between the life scientist and the process engineer.

References and Notes

1. E. J. Lyons, *AIChE Symp. Ser.* **100**, 31 (1970).
2. D. Perlman, *Am. Soc. Microbiol. News* **43**, 83 (1978).
3. R. Langer, R. J. Linhardt, S. Hoffberg, A. K. Larsen, C. L. Cooney, D. Tapper, M. Klein, *Science* **217**, 261 (1982).
4. R. W. Swartz, *Annu. Rep. Ferment. Processes* **3**, 75 (1979).
5. Mitre Corporation, *Comparative Economic Assessment of Ethanol from Biomass* (NTIS report HCP/ET-2854, National Technical Information Service, Springfield, Va., 1978).
6. T. Murphy and S. Walsh, paper presented at the American Chemical Society meeting, Kansas City, Mo., September 1982.
7. C. L. Cooney *et al.*, *Dev. Ind. Microbiol.* **18**, 255 (1977).
8. J. F. Martin and A. L. Demain, *Microbiol. Rev.* **44**, 230 (1980).
9. D. I. C. Wang, C. L. Cooney, A. L. Demain, P. Dunnill, A. E. Humphrey, M. D. Lilly, *Fermentation and Enzyme Technology* (Wiley, New York, 1979).
10. B. Atkinson, *Biochemical Reactors* (Pion, London, 1974); S. Aiba, A. E. Humphrey, N. F. Millis, *Biochemical Engineering* (Academic Press, New York, ed. 2, 1973).
11. J. G. Stramondo *et al.*, *AIChE Symp. Rev.* **74** (No. 172), 1 (1978).
12. R. A. Messing, *Immobilized Enzymes for Industrial Reactors* (Academic Press, New York, 1975).
13. I. Chibata, *Immobilized Enzymes* (Wiley, New York, 1978); O. R. Zaborsky, *Immobilized Enzymes* (CRC Press, Boca Raton, Fla., 1973); K. Morbach, *Methods Enzymol.* **44** (1976).
14. M. D. Lilly, *DECHEMA-Monogr.* **82**, 1693 (1978).
15. V. K. Eroshin and I. G. Minkevich, *Biotechnol. Bioeng.* **24**, 2263 (1982).
16. K. Buchholz, *DECHEMA-Monogr.* **84**, 1724 (1979).
17. Th. E. Barman, *Enzyme Handbook* (Springer-Verlag, New York, 1969), vols. 1 and 2.
18. M. Fusee, W. E. Swann, G. J. Calton, *Appl. Environ. Microbiol.* **42**, 672 (1981).
19. R. R. Bland *et al.*, *Biotechnol. Lett.* **4**, 323 (1982).
20. C. L. Cooney, *Process Biochem.* **14** (No. 5), 13 (1979).
21. D. V. Goedell *et al.*, *Nature (London)* **287**, 411 (1980); T. Staehelin, D. S. Hobbs, H. Kung, C.-Y. Lai, S. Retska, *J. Biol. Chem.* **256**, 9750 (1981).
22. M. Moo-Young and H. Blanch, *Adv. Biochem. Eng.* **19**, 1 (1981).
23. C. L. Cooney, *Biotechnol. Bioeng. Symp.* **9**, 1 (1979).
24. _____, in *Microbiological Growth on C₁-Compounds*, (Society of Fermentation Technology, Japan, 1975), p. 183.
25. R. Breslow, *Science* **218**, 532 (1982).

20. Production of Feedstock Chemicals

T. K. Ng, R. M. Busche, C. C. McDonald, R. W. F. Hardy

Photosynthetic products accumulated over eons as natural gas, petroleum, coal, and related carbonaceous materials have provided an immense resource for the development of our highly industrialized and energy-intensive civilization. However, we now recognize that this reservoir of fossil carbon is finite and is already limiting industrial growth. We must develop ways to rely more heavily on products of current photosynthesis for the basic feedstocks required by the chemical industry. Conversion of the chemical industry from a fossil carbon base to a renewable carbon base is not likely to be rapid or easy as viewed by one generation. However, it is important for future generations that we give attention and support to initiating and carrying out this conversion.

There are three major approaches to the transformation of biomass to useful feedstock chemicals: chemical, physical, and biological. Hydrogenation, pyrolysis, and fermentation are respective examples. In this chapter we review the current status and potential of fermentative processing of biomass to feedstock chemicals (*1–3*). We discuss the nature, supply, and economics of biomass; the microbial transformation of biomass to desired chemicals by fermentation processes; and the recovery and purification of these materials from the dilute aqueous solutions in which they are produced. We do not deal with fermentation routes to chemicals for energy use, such as ethanol. Ethanol may play a useful role as an octane enhancer in gasoline, but the amount potentially available from biomass would not be a significant replacement for fossil fuel. Fermentation processes for specialty chemicals such as antibiotics and vitamins (*4*) are well established and are not reviewed in this chapter.

Biomass Sources

Biomass consists of collectible plant-derived materials that are abundant, inexpensive, and potentially convertible to feedstock chemicals by fermentation processes. Biomass is found as starch in corn, wheat, potatoes, cassava, the sago palm, and other agricultural products and as monomeric sugars or soluble oligomers in corn syrup, molasses, raw sugar juice, sulfite waste liquors, and so on. It also occurs as lignocellulose in the form of wood chips, crop residues, forest and mill residues, urban refuse, and animal manures.

Biomass supply. The supply of biomass depends on the land dedicated to useful photosynthesis. Of the total 2.3 billion acres of the United States, 380 million acres (17 percent) are devoted to crops, 720 million acres (32 percent) to forest and woodland, and 680 million acres (30 percent) to pasture or grazing land (5). Of all American crops, corn is the primary source of starch because of its ample supply and low cost relative to other sources of starch or sugar and because there is an established commercial system for storing and transporting it cheaply over long distances. The 1981–1982 crop of 8 billion bushels (190 million dry tons) contained enough starch to provide 285 billion pounds of glucose (6).

Lignocellulosic crop residues are also abundant, but commercial collection systems are limited. Lignocellulose is a structural material of plants and is a composite of three polymers: cellulose, a linear polymer of glucose that occurs as crystalline microfibrils; hemicellulose, an amorphous branched copolymer that consists mainly of xylose; and lignin, a cross-linked polymer of substituted phenylpropane units. In wheat straw and hardwoods the proportions of these polymers are 42, 35, and 22 percent, respectively (7, 8). At present, only 8 million dry tons of crop residues such as sugarcane bagasse, cotton gin trash, and rice hulls are collected annually at central processing sites (Table 1). About 105 million dry tons of corn stalks and 180 million dry tons of cereal straw are available annually and could be collected if the demand warranted. Other agricultural residues amount to 500 million dry tons, but they are too diffuse to be collected economically or must be retained on the land to maintain the soil.

The annual growth of American forests could provide an economically collectible supply of 270 million dry tons of lignocellulosic biomass (Table 2). Eastern hardwoods, which are less important to the pulp and paper industry than the stronger fibered conifers, are primary target sources (9, 10).

Solid waste from paper and board products from the 32 largest urban centers might supply another 30 million tons. The supply from each of the centers would exceed the 400,000 dry tons needed annually for a cellulose-based chemicals plant (11–13). However, because of the heterogeneity of these materials, safety and process problems could arise in downstream operations.

The "grassland" cellulose resource—mainly animal manure (Table 3)—is too diffuse, except on a few large feedlots, to be a source of lignocellulose for chemicals (14, 15).

Hence, from a potential annual supply of 1.8 billion dry tons of lignocellulose from U.S. cropland, grassland, and forest, the 550 million dry tons of biomass available as wood chips, cereal straw, and corn stalks and the starch from 190 million tons of corn grain appear to be the most likely basis for a chemicals-from-biomass industry.

Saccharification. Starch or lignocellulose can be converted to chemical products either directly or after hydrolysis to the corresponding monomeric sugar for use as an intermediate feedstock. If technically feasible, direct use of the polysaccharide is preferred (16). However, most fermentations and chemical conversions take place more readily with a monomeric sugar feedstock. Moreover, it may be desirable to have a large common supply of sugar feeding a number of smaller fermentation operations as part of a "biorefinery" complex.

The large corn wet milling industry now provides a supply of hydrolyzed cornstarch (17). We estimate that in 1985 corn syrups could be produced commercially from corn at $3.40 per bushel at a cost of about 12 cents per pound of sugar

(*18*). The price places a competitive cost ceiling on the market value of lignocellulose-based "biosugars."

Cellulosic biomass at $20 to $30 per dry ton is far cheaper than corn at $110 per dry ton (*19, 20*). However, the intractable nature of the cellulose crystallite makes hydrolysis very difficult; hence there is a trade-off between low raw material costs and high investment costs for hydrolysis equipment. In addition, the residues from corn wet milling are high-value oil and protein feeds, while markets for lignin—the residue from cellulose hydrolysis—have yet to be developed. Hence, at present, cellulose hydrolysis is not economically competitive with starch hydrolysis as a source of sugar.

Processes in which concentrated acids are used to catalyze cellulose hydrolysis have been commercially unsuccessful because of the cost of recovering and recycling the acid. Dilute-acid processes have lower acid-associated costs, but they have poorer yields and require rigid control of residence time at high temperature. Consequently, power costs and investment are too high for these processes to compete with corn hydrolysis.

A biological approach to cellulose hydrolysis involves the use of cellulolytic enzymes, such as those produced by the fungus *Trichoderma reesei* (*21*). The enzymes are produced extracellularly in a separate fermentation process and transferred to the hydrolysis process as a

Table 1. U.S. cellulosics potential: cropland resource (1977–1979 crop data). Values are given as million dry tons per year.

Source	Collected supply	Collectible reserve	Potential resource
Corn stover		105	212
Cereal straw		180	180
Soybean residues		25	50
Bagasse, gin trash, and rice hulls	8		8
Other crops			360
Total cropland	8	310	810

Table 2. U.S. cellulosics potential: forest resource (1977–1979 data). Values are given as million dry tons per year.

Source	Collected supply	Collectible reserve	Potential resource
Net annual growth*		270	450
Logging residues		105	145
Process residues and wastes			
Pulp mills	3	38	46
Sawmills (excluding chips)	13	13	26
Paper and board mills		12	13
Fuel wood	3		3
Urban solid wastes	41	12	77
Total forest	60	450	760

*Net after mortality and commercial removals from a commercial inventory of 25 billion tons of standing tree stems.

Table 3. U.S. cellulosics potential: grassland resource (1977 data). Values are given as million dry tons per year.

Source	Collected supply	Collectible reserve	Potential resource
Cattle	5	4	237
Hogs			11
Broilers			6
Chickens		2	4
Sheep			2
Total grass-land	5	6	260

supernatant liquid after the cells have been filtered off. The recent development of hypercellulolytic mutants has increased productivity in this step more than tenfold (22, 23). However, two problems remain: (i) it is necessary to pretreat the lignocellulose to make the substrate more accessible to enzyme attack, and (ii) the enzyme is inhibited by the product glucose and its dimer, cellobiose. Hydrolysis with dilute acid (24) is an effective pretreatment, but we estimate that this step adds 3 cents per pound to the cost of the sugar produced. Steam-explosion pretreatments (25, 26) and a liquid ammonia freeze-explosion technique (27) may prove to be more cost-effective.

Nature of biomass. Chemically, almost all biomass, regardless of the source, contains about 45 percent oxygen on a moisture- and ash-free basis (7, 8) and contains 50 percent moisture as collected. This biomass makes a poor fuel. At 50 percent moisture, materials such as bagasse have a net heating value of only about 6800 Btu's per pound (dry basis), or about half that of bituminous coal (28). Cellulosic biomass is a poor choice as an energy source unless it is a waste material that must be disposed of at least cost. However, biomass as starch or lignocellulose has great potential as a feedstock for oxychemicals that retain the oxygenated nature of the basic CH_2O structure. Fermentative production of oxychemicals and derivatives is discussed in the following section.

Chemical Products

The current annual U.S. production of organic chemicals is approximately 210 billion pounds, 99 percent of which is accounted for by the top 100 chemicals (29, 30). Of the top 100 chemicals, 74 percent are produced from five primary feedstocks: ethylene, propylene, benzene, toluene, and xylene. Many are oxychemicals that have been, are, or could be produced by microbial fermentation with or without chemical processing (Table 4). These oxychemicals from renewable resources could account for 50 billion pounds or 23 percent of the total production of organic chemicals. Their derivatives could amount to another 26 percent, for a total production of half that of the top 100 chemicals (30). The current annual value of these chemicals is over $15 billion (29) (Table 5).

Fermentation. The fermentation of molasses to ethanol by *Saccharomyces cerevisiae* is well documented (31). Fermentation ethanol is now cost-competitive with industrial ethanol. Ethanol concentrations of 10 to 20 percent are obtained in 36 to 48 hours, depending on the yeast strain. Higher rates could be obtained with advanced, experimental process designs. External cooling is necessary to keep the fermentation temperature below 30°C. Recently, researchers have focused on thermophilic microorganisms such as *Thermoanaerobium ethanolicus* or *Clostridium thermohydrosulfuricum* for ethanol production at higher temperatures (32, 33). These microorga-

Table 4. Oxychemicals from renewable resources.

Chemical	1981 U.S. production (million pounds)	Current price (cents per pound)	1981 commercial value (million dollars)	Major use or derivative
Ethanol				
Ethylene	28,867*	25 to 25½†	8,169‡	Polyethylene, ethylene oxides
Butadiene	3,046	34	1,234	Styrene-butadiene rubber, polybutadiene rubber
Industrial	1,157	$1.70 to $1.82 per gallon (27.5 cents per pound)	359	Solvents, ethyl acetate and other esters
Ethylene glycol	4,055	27½ to 28½	1,281	Polyethylene terephthalate, antifreeze
Acetic acid	2,706	26½	511	Vinyl acetate, cellulose acetate
Acetone	2,167	31	483	Solvents, methyl, and other methacrylates
Isopropyl alcohol	1,644	$2.05 per gallon (31 cents per pound)	507	Acetone, solvents
Adipic acid	1,210	57	653	Nylon 66
Butanol	823	33½	251	Solvents, butyl acrylate
Acrylic acid	691	58	276	Polymers
Methyl ethyl ketone	626	37	260	Solvents
Propylene glycol	480	44	208	Unsaturated polyester resin
Glycerol	370	80½	259	Drugs, cosmetics
Citric acid	235	71 to 77½	192	Food, drugs

*Values in this column were collected from the *Chemical Marketing Economics Handbook* and U.S. International Trade Commission data on organic chemicals.   †From *Chemical Marketing Reporter* (20 September 1982); actual prices depend on quality, quantity, and location.   ‡From *Chemical Marketing Economics Handbook*, U.S. Bureau of Census, and U.S. International Trade Commission. Total values do not reflect actual price of transaction or current price.

Table 5. Microbial production of chemicals.

Chemical	Process	Microorganism
Ethanol	$C_6H_{12}O_6 \xrightarrow{M*} C_2H_5OH$	*Saccharomyces cerevisiae* *Zymomonas mobilis*
Ethylene 1,3-Butadiene Ethylene glycol	$C \left\{ \begin{array}{l} CH_2=CH_2 \\ CH_2=CH\text{-}CH=CH_2 \\ CH_2OH\text{-}CH_2OH \end{array} \right.$	
Acetic acid	$CH_6H_{12}O_6 \xrightarrow{M} CH_3COOH$	*Clostridium thermoaceticum* *Acetobacter aceti*
Acetone	$C_5H_5OH \xrightarrow{M} CH_3COOH$ $C_6H_{12}O_6 \xrightarrow{M} CH_3COCH_3$	*Clostridium acetobutylicum*
Butanol Isopropyl alcohol	$C_6H_{12}O_6 \xrightarrow{M} \begin{array}{l} CH_3(CH_2)_2CH_2OH \\ (CH_3)_2CHOH \end{array}$	*Clostridium aurianticum*
Adipic acid Acrylic	$CH_3(CH_2)_nCH_3 \xrightarrow{M} \begin{array}{l} CH_3(CH_2)_2CH_2OH \\ HOOC(CH_2)_4COOH \end{array}$ $C_6H_{12}O_6 \xrightarrow{M_1} CH_3CH(OH)COOH \xrightarrow{M_2/C} CH_2=CHCOOH$ $CH_2OHCH(OH)CH_2OH \xrightarrow{M/C} CH_2=CHCOOH$	*Pseudomonas species* 1. (M₁) *Lactobacillus bulgarius* 2. (M₂/C) *Clostridium propionium* *Klebsiella pneumoniae* (*Aerobacter aerogenes*)
Methyl ethyl ketone	$C_6H_{12}O_6 \xrightarrow{M} CH_3CH(OH)CH(OH)CH_3 \xrightarrow{C} CH_3COCH_2CH_3$	*Klebsiella pneumoniae*
Propylene glycol Glycerol	$CH_2OHCH(OH)CH_2OH \xrightarrow{C} CH_3CH(OH)CH_2OH$ $C_6H_{12}O_6 \xrightarrow{M} CH_2OHCH(OH)CH_2OH$	*Saccharomyces cerevisiae* *Dunaliella sp.*
Citric acid	$H_2O + CO_2 \xrightarrow{M} CH_2OHCH(OH)CH_2OH$ $C_6H_{12}O_6 \xrightarrow{M} CH_2(COOH)(OH)C(COOH)CH_2(COOH)$	*Aspergillus niger*

*M, microbial fermentation (30, 36, 37); C, chemical processing (35).

Fig. 1. Row of 90,000-liter fermentors for acetone/butanol production at National Chemical Products Ltd., Germiston, South Africa. [Courtesy of D. R. Woods, University of Cape Town, Rondebosch, South Africa]

nisms grow at a high temperature (60°C) and they can produce ethanol from starch, xylose, and other carbohydrates, but the concentration of ethanol produced, 4 percent, is too low for economical recovery.

Industrial grade acetic acid, a key feedstock, is now manufactured solely by chemical processes (34), while food grade acetic acid (vinegar) is produced exclusively by oxidation of ethanol with *Acetobacter aceti* (35, 36). The latter reaction is highly exothermic and external cooling is mandatory since the efficiency of the process decreases with increasing temperature. The acetic acid fermentation operates semicontinuously in submerged culture with a 35-hour cycle time. Ethanol is maintained in the

reactor at 1 percent until the acid concentration reaches 12 percent; then 35 percent of the liquid is withdrawn and replaced with fresh medium. A 96 to 98 percent conversion is achieved with a final ethanol concentration of less than 0.2 percent.

Historically, acetone/butanol fermentation has been a highly successful process for the biological production of chemicals (37). Manufacture in the United States lasted from the early 1920's to the late 1950's. Now the acetone/butanol plant in South Africa is probably the only fermentation facility operated for this purpose (Fig. 1), although unconfirmed reports indicate that the People's Republic of China might have a large-scale plant in operation. Fermentation under anaerobic conditions at 30° to 32°C is complete in 40 to 80 hours, depending on the substrate. During this period the pH decreases steadily from 6.0 to 5.0 as butyric acid is produced and then rises to above 6.0 as butyric acid is converted to butanol. Acetone is produced during the latter period. The final broth contains approximately 2 percent total solvents. The solvent yields and ratios vary with different strains. With *Clostridium acetobutylicum* (Fig. 2) the solvent yield is 30 to 33 percent and the acetone : butanol : ethanol ratio is 3 : 6 : 1. Large quantities of hydrogen and carbon dioxide are also produced during the fermentation. Isopropyl alcohol rather than acetone is produced by *Clostridium auorianticum*, with a solvent yield of 30 to 40 percent and an isopropyl alcohol : butanol : ethanol ratio of 2.7 : 1 : 6 (*36*).

The utilization of 2,3-butanediol as a precursor for 1,3-butadiene was investigated thoroughly during World War II, but the project never went beyond the pilot plant stage. The diol can be produced by a number of microorganisms, but *Klebsiella pneumoniae* is generally used. Diol concentrations as high as 10 percent have been reported (*38*). Fermentation efficiency ranges from 80 to 100 percent and the yield from starch is approximately 36 percent.

Traditionally, glycerol has been produced by chemical modification of ethanol-yeast fermentation (*31*). Recently, the production of glycerol through carbon dioxide fixation and sunlight by the alga *Dunaliella* has been suggested and tested at the pilot plant stage (*39*). The algae accumulate 7 molar glycerol intracellularly, an amazing 56 percent solution during growth in 5 molar sodium chloride. Production of glycerol is 8 grams per square meter per day. Besides

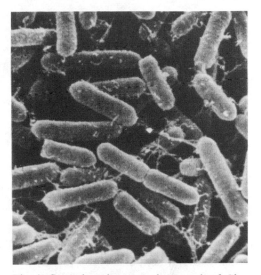

Fig. 2. Scanning electron micrograph of *Clostridium acetobutylicum*, strain NRRL B594 (× 23,500). [Prepared by M. L. Van Kavelaar, E. I. du Pont de Nemours & Co., Wilmington, Delaware]

being an important chemical feedstock, glycerol may be converted to propylene glycol by heating with sodium hydroxide (*34*).

Glucose is fermented to citric acid by *Aspergillus niger* (*35*). The surface culture techniques of the Koji process were used in the past. With better reactor design to increase oxygen transfer, a submerged culture process is employed in newer plants. The fermentation requires 10 to 14 days at 25° to 30°C to convert 20 to 25 percent of the glucose with 80 to 85 percent yield to citric acid, which is recovered as the calcium salt.

The chemicals described here are not exclusive. Other organic acids could be produced microbiologically in high yield and concentration; these include fumaric acid, lactic acid, itaconic acid, and gluconic and oxygluconic acids (*37, 38*). Hitherto, no industrial applications for these compounds have been developed, but with appropriate technology many may be converted to useful feedstocks. Polyhydroxybutyrate produced by *Alcaligenes eutrophus* is being investigated as a possibly useful polymer. Microbial utilization of C_1 compounds (methane, methanol, carbon monoxide, carbon dioxide) was limited in the past to single-cell protein production, but recent developments suggest that chemicals such as acetic acid and butyrate can be derived from syngas through fermentation (*40*). A key advantage in these processes is the high tolerance of the microorganisms to sulfur compounds in syngas, which would otherwise poison the catalysts. However, such a process would have to compete successfully with well-developed syngas and carbonylation chemistry. Another interesting area is the microbial oxidation of hydrocarbons to useful chemicals. Methylotrophs that normally grow on C_1 compounds can convert a wide variety of aliphatic hydrocarbons to oxychemicals (*41*); a process for producing adipic acid from hexanoic acid has been demonstrated (*42*).

Metabolic pathways. Despite the diversity of microorganisms, products, and growth conditions, the metabolic pathways for biosynthesis of various chemicals are quite similar (*43*). With a few exceptions hexoses are metabolized to pyruvate through the Embden-Meyerhof-Parnas (EMP) pathway or the Entner-Doudoroff (ED) pathway (Fig. 3). The main function of these pathways under anaerobic conditions is to generate energy in the form of adenosine triphosphate (ATP). The EMP pathway can provide twice as much energy as the ED pathway. Formation of different products depends on the ability to produce energy and dispose of electrons and the presence or absence of specific enzymes.

Electrons are produced and transferred to biological electron carriers such as nicotinamide-adenine dinucleotide, ferredoxin, or flavin mononucleotide during hexose metabolism. In the absence of oxygen, the disposal of electrons and regeneration of oxidized electron carriers is a major problem for the cells. Some of the electrons are combined with protons to form gaseous hydrogen in the presence of hydrogenases. However, hydrogenases are not universally present, nor are they completely effective in removing electrons. Organic products must serve as electron acceptors. Examples are the reduction of pyruvate to lactate, the reductive decarboxylation of pyruvate to ethanol, and the reduction of acetoacetate to butyrate. If the acceptor consumes more electrons than are produced, as in butanol formation, acetone is produced to provide the extra electrons. Thus, acetone production and butanol production are generally inseparable. For the microorganism, acetate production is more desirable because the transformation of pyruvate to acetate generates an extra ATP, but to dispose of electrons it is necessary to form reduced compounds such as ethanol and lactate.

One group of microorganisms, the acetogens, ferment glucose and in some cases hydrogen and carbon dioxide quantitatively to acetate. Thus, 3 moles of acetate are produced per mole of glucose metabolized. This high conversion is achieved by reducing the product carbon dioxide to a carrier-bound methyl group, which then transcarboxylates pyruvate to provide 2 moles of acetate in addition to another mole formed by a classical route. High-yielding acetogens such as *Clostridium thermoacetium* or *Acetobacter woodii* have great potential for the production of acetic acid.

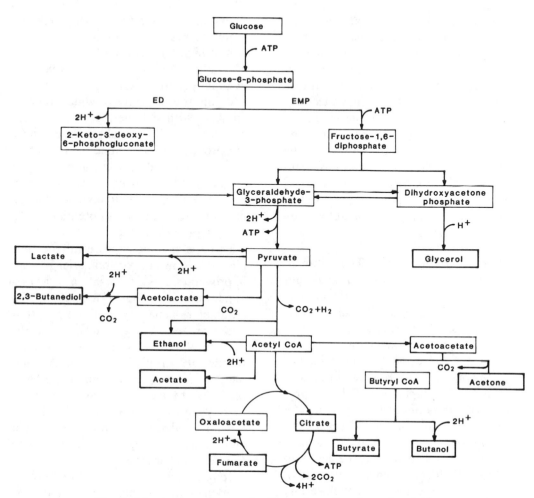

Fig. 3. Metabolic pathways for formation of various chemicals.

Oxygen, which is energetically the most favorable electron acceptor, allows large amounts of ATP to be generated through oxidative phosphorylation. Under aerobic conditions, yeast oxidizes glucose completely to carbon dioxide and water with an 18-fold increase in the ATP yield. In the presence of a small amount of oxygen certain fermentative organisms oxidize the substrate incompletely. Some electrons are used to reduce oxygen to water and some reduce an organic intermediate to a useful product. An example is the reductive decarboxylation of acetolactate to 2,3-butanediol by *Klebsiella pneumoniae* (*Aerobacter aerogenes*).

Product formation is also regulated by the presence of key metabolic enzymes. Selective inhibition of the enzyme for ethanol formation causes yeast to reduce dihydroxyacetone phosphate to glycerol phosphate, forming glycerol as a final product. In citric acid fermentation *Aspergillus niger* can dispose of any electrons formed, but the enzyme for citrate metabolism is inactivated at a low pH. Thus, the acid is accumulated in high concentration only by cells at a stationary phase of growth and at a pH below 2. Microorganisms defective in the tricarboxylic acid (TCA) cycle enzymes have been exploited to produce intermediates, for instance in fumarate production by *Rhizopus nigricans*. In summary, the formation of different products is regulated by the ability to produce energy, the utilization or disposal of excess electrons, and the presence of active key metabolic enzymes.

Process improvement. The ultimate development of an industrial process depends on achieving high productivity, maximum yield, and optimal product concentration. This can be achieved by a number of means, including organism and strain selection, optimization of growth conditions for product formation, and genetic manipulation. Ethanol productivity can be increased by using *Zymomonas mobilis* instead of yeast (*44*). *Clostridium thermocellum* cocultures have been used to ferment cellulose to ethanol at elevated temperatures (*16*). Also, *Trichoderma reesei* cellulase and yeast enable simultaneous saccharification and fermentation of cellulosic materials, and the yeast *Pachysolen tannophilus* ferments pentoses as well as hexoses (*45*). Solvent yields vary considerably between different strains in the acetone/butanol fermentation. Strains that produce mainly acetone/ethanol or butanol/isopropanol have been obtained (*38*). Microorganisms tolerant to higher product concentrations can be found in nature and can be improved by general adaptation.

Processes based on microorganisms derived from extreme environments—for instance, with high temperatures, low pH values, and high salt concentrations—may better fit industrial process requirements. For example, fermentation at high temperature lowers the cost of cooling and facilitates recovery of volatile products such as acetone. In addition, thermophiles provide industrial enzymes with high thermal stability. Acidophilic halophiles could be selected for the production of organic acids such as acetic acid at high concentration. Polyols are accumulated in high concentrations by halophiles. Such unique microorganisms represent a great potential for developing biotechnology.

Perhaps the most powerful tool employed at present for industrial process improvements is optimization of growth conditions for product formation. The parameters generally used are pH, temperature, and oxygen concentration. Butanol production does not commence until the pH drops below 5.5. A slight increase in temperature inhibits ethanol oxidation to acetic acid, and a decrease in oxygen concentration shifts diol to ethanol production. Another key parameter, reactor design, is discussed by Cooney in chapter 19.

Improvement of fermentation processes by genetic manipulation is limited to a few isolated cases, for instance, the development of a hydroxylation plasmid in *Pseudomonas putida* (*42*) or the conversion of fumarate to succinate with *Escherichia coli* containing recombinant plasmids (*46*). Insufficient genetic information about industrial microorganisms, particularly fermentative anaerobes, has limited the applications in this area to date.

Microorganisms clearly have the synthetic capabilities to produce a variety of useful chemical feedstocks (*47*). However, a successful process also depends on the subsequent processing of the broth. In the next section product recovery is examined.

Product Recovery

Recovering a product from a fermentation broth invariably involves separating the product from a dilute (usually under 10 percent and more generally 1 to 5 percent) aqueous solution. The magnitude of this problem and the solution depend on whether the product has a boiling point below or above that of water, occurs as a salt, or is a precipitate. Low-boiling organic solvents are relatively easy to separate from water by distillation, but recovery of a high-boiling solvent from water is excessively energy-consuming. For example, a 1.5 percent (by weight) solution of acetic acid in water requires about 307,000 Btu's per pound of acid recovered.

Low-boiling solvents. Ethanol recovery by distillation is a good example of a method used with a low-boiling solvent. Ethanol forms a minimum-boiling azeotrope with water. In recovering ethanol from fermentation broths, about 18,000 Btu's per gallon are required at the high reflux ratios needed to reach concentrations approaching the 95 percent azeotrope.

Outmoded beverage alcohol plants have reported overall process energy needs of 150,000 Btu's per gallon (*48*). In newer, more energy-efficient fermentation plants, total plant energy demand has been reduced to as little as 40,000 to 50,000 Btu's per gallon—most of which is for the recovery operation (*49*). These newer recovery processes eliminate or recover the heat lost to overhead vapors. They include distillation with vapor recompression and multiple-effect distillation. In addition, azeotropic distillation is in use and vacuum dehydration and extractive distillation have been suggested (*50*) to break the 95 percent azeotrope to produce anhydrous alcohol.

Adsorbents such as molecular sieves and calcium oxide have also been suggested for ethanol dehydration (*48, 51*) but they have not yet been used commercially. In theory, use of grain or cellulosic biomass as the adsorbent would reduce energy demand to zero, provided all the spent adsorbent could be employed, without regeneration, as a feedstock for producing the ethanol (*52*).

In supercritical fluid extraction processes for recovering ethanol from dilute solutions (*53*), carbon dioxide is used at 1000 pounds per square inch and 31°C to extract ethanol, after which the pressure is decreased to form an ethanol phase and a supercritical carbon dioxide phase. The ethanol phase is flashed and recovered, while the carbon dioxide phase is recompressed to extraction conditions and recycled.

Reverse osmosis requires little energy, but its application for recovering organic solvents from dilute solution appears limited (*51*).

High-boiling compounds. The cost of distilling water from a higher boiling product is prohibitive (*54*). In solvent extraction a suitable solvent—one which is more or less immiscible in water but in which the product is preferentially soluble—is used to extract the product (*55*). The extract is subsequently distilled to separate the solvent from the product. Overall, extraction involves lower operating costs than distillation, but requires an added investment for an extractor and a solvent stripper.

Crystallization has several advantages over distillation. Heats of fusion are much lower than heats of vaporization, which can result in large energy savings, and almost pure product can be achieved in a single step. However, refrigeration is frequently required and handling solids is more costly than handling liquids. The development of continuous freeze crystallization equipment may stimulate use of this separation technique (*56*).

Salts of organic acids. When salts of organic acids are produced during fermentation at a neutral *p*H, they cannot be recovered directly by distillation or extraction; hence, other process approaches are used. Evaporation—usually falling film combined with vapor recompression—effectively concentrates dilute salt solutions before the final separation (*57*). The salt is subsequently acidified to recover the free acid by conventional distillation or extraction. Alternatively, salts of organic acids such as acetic acid can be simultaneously acidified and extracted as the free acids by use of carbon dioxide under pressure in the presence of a suitable organic solvent (*58, 59*). Carboxylate salts can be simultaneously acidified and recovered as carboxylic acids from dilute fermentation broths by extraction with supercritical carbon dioxide alone (*60*). Membrane separation methods, including electrodialysis and carrier-mediated transport, show promise for concentrating salts of volatile fatty acids, but improvements in membrane durability and cost will be needed before these methods are acceptable for industrial use (*61, 62*).

In conclusion, the development of efficient processes for recovering products from fermentation broths has lagged behind fermentation programs. However, neither can be effective without the other. For example, in the production of acetic acid from glucose by the bacterium *Clostridium thermoaceticum*, the fermentation operates best at *p*H 7.0. At this *p*H the product concentration reaches 4 to 5 percent by weight (*63*), but the product is substantially all in salt form and is difficult to recover. Attempts have been made to adapt the organism to *p*H 4.5 to 5.5 (*64*), at which about one-third of the product is in the extractable

free-acid form. However, under these adverse conditions the product concentration drops to 0.4 percent by weight. At this low concentration the cost of utilities alone for the recovery operations exceeds 30 cents per pound of acid (*59*). In contrast, utilities would cost about 5 cents per pound of acid for a broth containing 10 percent free acid, such as that produced by *Acetobacter suboxydans* at *p*H 2.8 (*63*). Clearly, more interaction between microbiologists and separation engineers is needed to advance the growth of a fermentation industry.

Concluding Remarks

Fermentation microbiology with renewable resources (starch and cellulose) has the potential to produce a large fraction of the oxychemicals and their derivatives that constitute the bulk of feedstock chemicals. So far, ethanol is the only fermentation oxychemical that is economically competitive with the corresponding industrial compound produced by synthetic means from fossil fuels. Significant advances in research and development are necessary for the potential of fermentation to be realized. For these processes to become useful in the 1990's and beyond, research must be initiated now. Biotechnology will be a key factor in the development of economic processes for the use of lignocellulose and the conversion of the resulting sugars to chemical feedstocks. Engineering for reactor design and recovery of products will also be essential. Economics, of course, will dictate whether biological or synthetic processes, or a combination of the two, will be chosen for new manufacturing plants for specific chemical feedstocks.

References and Notes

1. E. S. Lipinsky, *Science* **212**, 1465 (1981).
2. B. O. Palsson, S. Fathi-Afshar, D. F. Rudd, E. N. Lightfoot, *ibid.* **213**, 513 (1981).
3. D. E. Eveleigh, *Sci. Am.* **245**, 154 (September 1981).
4. A. L. Demain, *Science* **214**, 987 (1981).
5. *Agricultural Statistics—1980* (U.S. Department of Agriculture, Washington, D.C., 1981), p. 419.
6. *1982 Corn Annual* (Corn Refiners Association, Washington, D.C., 1982), p. 15.
7. B. L. Browning, *The Chemistry of Wood* (Interscience, New York, 1963), p. 71.
8. H. F. J. Wenzl, *The Chemical Technology of Wood* (Academic Press, New York, 1970), p. 99.
9. *U.S. For. Serv. For. Resour. Rep. 20* (1974).
10. H. G. Wahlgren and T. H. Ellis, *TAPPI* **61**, 37 (1978).
11. Office of Solid Waste Management, *Research Planning Source Reduction* (Report SW-118, Environmental Protection Agency, Washington, D.C., ed. 3, 1974).
12. N. L. Drobney, H. E. Hall, R. T. Testin, report SW-10c to the U.S. Environmental Protection Agency by Battelle Memorial Institute, Columbus, Ohio (1971).
13. W. R. Niessen and A. F. Alsobrook, in *Proceedings of the National Incineration Conference* (New York, 4 to 7 June 1972), p. 319.
14. C. E. Veirs, *U.S. Environ. Prot. Agency Rep. PB 206-695* (1971).
15. *U.S. Dep. Agric. Rep. LMS-201* (1975).
16. D. I. C. Wang, G. C. Avgerinos, R. Dalal, paper presented at the Third Symposium on Biotechnology in Energy Production and Conservation, Gatlinburg, Tenn., 12 to 15 May 1981.
17. R. A. Janke and F. F. Koppel, *Focus on the 80's* (Corn Products International, Argo, Ill., 1980).
18. Estimated from data of C. R. Keim [*Ind. Eng. Chem. Res. Dev.* **19**, 482 (1980)] and other wet milling industry sources.
19. I. S. Goldstein, D. L. Holley, E. L. Deal, *For. Prod. J.* **28**, 53 (1978).
20. R. A. Arola and E. S. Miyata, *U.S. For. Serv. Gen. Tech. Rep. NC-200* (1981).
21. M. Mandels, "Enzymatic hydrolysis of cellulose to glucose," U.S. Army Natick Research & Development Laboratories, Natick, Mass. (September 1981).
22. A. L. Allen and R. E. Andreotti, paper presented at the Fourth Symposium on Biotechnology in Energy Production and Conservation, Gatlinburg, Tenn., May 1982.
23. B. S. Montenecourt, G. I. Sheir-Neiss, A. Ghosh, T. K. Ghosh, E. M. Frein, D. E. Eveleigh, paper presented at the National Meeting of the American Institute of Chemical Engineers, Orlando, Fla., February 1981.
24. D. Knappert, H. Grethlein, A. Converse, *Biotechnol. Bioeng.* **22**, 1449 (1980).
25. P. Foody, final report on DOE contract DE-AC02-79-ETZ-3050, Iotech Corporation, Ltd., Ottawa, Ontario, Canada (1980).
26. R. Bender, U.S. patent 4,136,207 (23 January 1979).
27. B. E. Dale and M. J. Moreira, paper presented at the Fourth Symposium on Biotechnology in Energy Production and Conservation, Gatlinburg, Tenn., May 1982.
28. J. M. Paturau, *Byproducts of the Cane Sugar Industry* (Elsevier, New York, 1969), p. 31.
29. U.S. International Trade Commission statistics, *Synthetic Organic Chemicals, United States Production and Sales* (Washington, D.C., 1981).
30. R. M. Busche, private communication.
31. A. H. Rose, Ed., *Economic Microbiology*, vol. 1, *Alcoholic Beverages* (Academic Press, London, 1977).
32. T. K. Ng, A. Ben-Bassat, J. G. Zeikus, *Appl. Environ. Microbiol.* **41**, 1337 (1981).
33. L. G. Ljungdahl, U.S. patent 4,292,406 (29 September 1981).
34. *Kirk-Othmer Encyclopedia of Chemical Technology* (Wiley, New York, ed. 3, 1980).
35. A. H. Rose, Ed., *Economic Microbiology*, vol. 2, *Primary Products of Metabolism* (Academic Press, New York, 1978).
36. H. J. Peppler and D. Perlman, *Microbial Technology and Microbial Processes* (Academic Press, New York, 1979), vols. 1 and 2.
37. S. C. Prescott and C. G. Dunn, *Industrial Microbiology* (McGraw-Hill, New York, ed. 3, 1959).
38. L. A. Underkofler and R. J. Hickey, *Industrial Fermentations* (Chemical Publishing Co., New York, 1954), vols. 1 and 2.
39. A. Ben-Amotz and M. Avron, in *Algae Biomass Production and Use*, G. Shelef and C. J. Soeder, Eds. (Elsevier, Amsterdam, 1980), pp. 603–610.
40. J. G. Zeikus, *Adv. Microb. Physiol.*, in press.
41. C. T. Hou, in *Microbial Transformation of Bioactive Compounds*, J. P. Rosazza, Ed. (CRC Press, Boca Raton, Fla., 1982), vol. 1, p. 82.
42. P. A. Harder, L. W. Wagner, D. A. Kunz, paper to be presented at the American Society for Microbiology meeting, New Orleans, La., March 1983.
43. H. W. Doelle, *Bacterial Metabolism* (Academic Press, New York, ed. 2, 1975).
44. P. L. Rogers, K. J. Lee, J. H. Lee, M. L. Skotnicki, R. J. Pagan, D. E. Tribe, in *Proceedings of the First International Alcohol Fuels Conference* (Auckland, N.Z., 1982), vol. 1, p. 253.
45. T. W. Jeffries, *Adv. Biochem. Eng.*, in press.
46. I. Goldberg, K. Lonberg-Holm, B. Stieglitz, *Appl. Environ. Microbiol.*, in press.
47. A. L. Demain and N. A. Solomon, *Sci. Am.* **245**, 66 (September 1981).
48. R. Remirez, *Chem. Eng. (N.Y.)* **87**, 57 (24 March 1980).
49. R. Katzen, *U.S. Dep. Energy HCP/J6639-01* (1978).
50. C. Black, *Chem. Eng. Prog.* **76**, 78 (September 1980).
51. D. E. Eakin, J. M. Donovan, G. R. Cysewki, S. E. Petty, J. V. Maxham (Report PNL-3823, Battelle Memorial Institute, Columbus, Ohio, May 1981).
52. J. Hong, M. Voloch, M. R. Ladisch, G. T. Tsao, *Biotechnol. Bioeng.* **24**, 725 (1982).
53. W. Worthy, *Chem. Eng. News* (3 August 1981), p. 16.
54. E. L. Mongan, Jr., private communication.
55. C. Hanson, *Chem. Eng.* **86**, 83 (7 May 1979).
56. G. J. Sloan, private communication.
57. A. H. Beesley and R. D. Rhinesmith, *Chem. Eng. Prog.* **76**, 37 (August 1980).
58. R. A. Yates, U.S. patent 4,282,323 (4 August 1981).

59. R. M. Busche, E. J. Shimshick, R. A. Yates, paper presented at the Fourth Symposium on Biotechnology in Energy Production and Conservation, Gatlinburg, Tenn., May 1982.
60. E. J. Shimshick, U.S. patent 4,250,331 (10 February 1981).
61. H. P. Gregor, final technical report on SERI subcontract XB-9-8161-1, Solar Energy Research Institute, Golden, Colo. (1980).
62. B. R. Smith, paper presented at the Engineering Foundation Conference on Advances in Fermentation Recovery Process Technology, Alberta, Canada, June 1981.
63. D. I. C. Wang, private communication.
64. R. D. Schwartz and F. A. Keller, Jr., *Appl. Environ. Microbiol.* **43**, 117 (1982).

21. Single-Cell Proteins

John H. Litchfield

The term "single-cell proteins" (SCP) refers to the dried cells of microorganisms such as algae, actinomycetes, bacteria, yeasts, molds, and higher fungi grown in large-scale culture systems for use as protein sources in human foods or animal feeds. Although these microorganisms are grown primarily for their protein contents in SCP production processes, microbial cells contain carbohydrates, lipids, vitamins, minerals, and nonprotein nitrogen materials such as nucleic acids.

The large-scale cultivation of microorganisms for use as a food source for humans and for animal feeds is an example of an early and progressing application of modern biotechnology. Microorganisms have been a component of human foods since ancient times. Examples include yeast as a leavening agent in bread-making; lactic acid bacteria in making fermented milks, cheeses, and sausages; and molds in making a variety of Oriental fermented foods (*1*). Algae of the genus *Spirulina* were harvested from alkaline ponds by the ancient Aztecs in Mexico and consumed as a source of protein. Dried *Spirulina* cells are eaten at the present time by the people in the Lake Chad region of Africa (*2*).

Present-day technology for SCP production began in 1879 in Great Britain with the introduction of aeration of the vats used for producing bakers' yeast. About 1900 in the United States, centrifugation was introduced for separating yeast cells from the growth medium (*1*). The first purposeful SCP production originated in Germany during World War I when bakers' yeast, *Saccharomyces cerevisiae*, was grown—with molasses as the carbon and energy source and ammonium salts as the nitrogen source—for consumption as a protein supplement. Also, incremental feeding of the carbon and nitrogen sources during growth was introduced during this period. In Germany during World War II, *Candida utilis* (Torula yeast) was cultivated on sulfite waste liquor from pulp and paper manufacture and wood sugar derived from the acid hydrolysis of wood and used as a protein source for humans and animals (*3*). During this period, the development of the Waldhof fermentor represented a significant advance in technology for mass cultivation of microbial cells. This fermentor provides both aeration and agitation by use of a wheel-type hollow-bladed impeller (*4*). After World War II, Torula yeast production was introduced into the United States and has continued until the present time. Torula yeast has been produced in many countries including Switzerland, Taiwan, and the U.S.S.R.

In recent years, technological improvements in microbial cell production for food and feed include the introduction of continuous processes, the development of airlift tower fermentors, and

270

Table 1. Selected raw materials used as carbon and energy sources in single-cell protein processes.

Raw material	Process type and scale*	Organism	Producer or developer	Reference
CO_2	Algal, 2 metric tons per day†	*Chlorella* sp.	Taiwan Chlorella Manufacture Co. Ltd., Taipei	28
Cane syrup, molasses (sucrose)	Photosynthetic / Nonphotosynthetic			
CO_2 or $NaHCO_3$-Na_2CO_3	Algal, 320 metric tons per year;‡ photosynthetic	*Spirulina maxima*	Sosa Texcoco, S.A., Mexico City	25
Methanol	Bacterial, 70,000 metric tons per year	*Methylophilus methylotrophus*	Imperial Chemical Industries, Billingham	31
	1000 metric tons per year	*Methylomonas clara*	Hoechst-Uhde, Frankfurt, West Germany	33
Ethanol	Yeast, 7500 short tons per year	*Candida utilis* (Torula)	Pure Culture Products, Hutchinson, Minnesota	19
n-Alkanes, wood hydrolyzates	Yeast (several plants), 20,000 to 40,000 metric tons per year	*Candida* sp.	All-Union Research Institute of Protein Biosynthesis, U.S.S.R.	57
Sulfite waste liquor	Yeast, 15 short tons per day	*Candida utilis*	Rhinelander Paper Corp., Rhinelander, Wisconsin	16
	Mold, 10,000 metric tons per year	*Paecilomyces varioti*	Pekilo Process, Finnish Pulp and Paper Research Institute, Jamsankoski, Finland	17
Glucose	Mold, 50 to 100 metric tons per year	*Fusarium graminearum*	Rank Hovis MacDougall Research Limited, High Wycombe, U.K.	58
Cheese whey (lactose)	Yeast, 5000 short tons per year	*Kluyveromyces fragilis*	Amber Laboratories, Juneau, Wisconsin	13
	Mold, 300 metric tons per year	*Penicillium cyclopium*	Heurty, S. A., France	14

*Plant capacity, metric tons (1000 kilograms), or short tons (2000 pounds) per unit of time indicated. †Total pond area, 83,400 square meters. ‡Pond area, 900 hectares.

the development of novel methods for flocculating microbial cells to reduce centrifugation costs (5).

Raw Materials: Sources and Treatment

Many raw materials have been considered as carbon and energy sources for SCP production (Table 1). In many cases, raw materials must first be treated by physical, chemical, or enzymatic methods before they can be utilized as carbon and energy sources by microorganisms (6).

Sources of cellulose, such as wood and straw, are made up of a lignin-hemicellulose-cellulose (LHC) complex that cannot be readily hydrolyzed by enzymes or acids to liberate fermentable sugars. Lignin is a complex polyphenolic structure that protects cellulose and hemicellulose from acid or enzyme hydrolysis. In addition, the highly crystalline nature of cellulose gives a protective effect. Common physical methods for preliminary treatment of lignocellulosic materials include ball milling, two-roll milling, and grinding (6). Recently, explosive depressurization processes such as the Iotech process developed in Canada have been developed for facilitating the breakdown of the LHC complex and aiding in separating the lignin, hemicellulose, and cellulose components (7). Cellulose produced in this way has not yet been used as a substrate for SCP production. After cellulose is separated from the LHC complex, it is more susceptible to acid or enzyme hydrolysis to yield hexose sugars such as glucose and cellobiose. In the same manner, hemicellulose can be hydrolyzed by acids or enzymes to xylose and arabinose (8, 9).

Microbial cellulases have been investigated extensively for their utility in the hydrolysis of cellulose. *Trichoderma reesei* appears to be the most promising cellulolytic microorganism identified to date (10). The extent of hydrolysis of cellulosic materials such as rice or wheat straw by cellulases varies widely, depending on the raw material and preliminary treatment, enzyme concentration, and time for hydrolysis (11).

Starchy materials, such as potato processing waste, must be converted to mono- and disaccharides to be suitable as substrates for SCP production. The Swedish Sugar Corporation developed the Symba process for treatment of wastes that contain starch, such as those from potato and rice processing. Two organisms used are *Saccharomycopsis fibuligera*, which produces α- and β-amylases for hydrolysis of starch to glucose and maltose, and *C. utilis* for utilizing these sugars as a substrate for growth (12). This process was operated on a pilot plant scale to produce 40 to 100 kilograms of dry yeast per day, but its usefulness is limited by the intermittent availability of the waste stream from potato processing operations. Alternatively, starch can be hydrolyzed by a combination of α-amylase and amyloglucosidase (glucoamylase) as used in converting starchy materials for ethanol production by fermentation.

Only a few microorganisms, such as *Kluyveromyces fragilis* (13) and *Penicillium cyclopium* (14) can use lactose as a carbon and energy source for SCP production. An immobilized enzyme process has been developed by Corning Glass Works and Kroger Company for converting lactose in cheese whey to a glucose-galactose that can be used as a carbon and energy source for growing bakers' yeast (*S. cerevisiae*) (15).

Sulfite waste liquor from paper mill operations contains concentrations of sulfur dioxide or sulfite that inhibit microbial growth. Treatment with lime, which results in the precipitation of calcium sulfite, and steam stripping in a tower are effective methods for reducing inhibitory concentrations of sulfur compounds. These methods have been used successfully in the production of Torula yeast at Rhinelander Paper Company in the United States (16) and in the Pekilo process in Finland (16, 17).

In the development of SCP processes based on hydrocarbons, British Petroleum evaluated both gas oil containing 25 percent C_{15} to C_{30} n-alkanes (boiling range, 300° to 380°C) and purified n-alkanes prepared by a molecular sieve process (97.5 to 99 percent C_{10} to C_{23}, with a boiling range of 175° to 300°C) as substrates for Candida sp. (18). The use of molecular sieves to purify n-alkanes in the British Petroleum process minimized the need for a complicated solvent cleanup of the yeast produced to decrease the amounts of residual hydrocarbons. However, this process was abandoned because it was not economically feasible as a result of increased costs of the hydrocarbon feedstocks (18).

Ethanol has been used for the production of C. utilis by Pure Culture Products, Inc. in the United States (19) and in pilot plant studies in Japan (20) and Czechoslovakia (21). Synthetic ethanol may contain the impurities propanol, 2-methyl-2-propanol, and 2-butanol (crotonaldehyde); these are not present in ethanol produced by yeast fermentation. 2-Butanol inhibits the growth of C. utilis, lengthens the lag phase, decreases cell yield, and decreases the crude protein content of the cells in batch growth systems. However, concentrations in the range of 1 gram per milliliter are tolerated by this organism in continuous culture systems (22).

In most SCP processes, the carbon substrate is present in relatively low concentrations, either because of its solubility or because the amount that can be tolerated by a given microorganism is limited. In algal processes, the amount of carbon dioxide in air (0.03 percent) is inadequate for growth, and additional CO_2 must be supplied from sources such as carbonates or bicarbonates in alkaline waters or from natural deposits of carbonaceous minerals, from combustion gas, or from decomposition of organic matter in sewage or industrial waste. When CO_2 is supplied to algae in the gaseous form, such as in combustion gases, concentrations have ranged from 0.5 percent to 5 percent in air (5).

For nonphotosynthetic microorganisms grown in batch cultures, carbon and energy source concentrations generally range from 1 to 5 percent when soluble carbohydrates are used. Continuous processes are usually used for growing microorganisms on hydrocarbons, methanol, or ethanol. In these processes, concentrations of the carbon and energy source are generally less than 1 percent. The rate of feeding the substrate to the fermentor is adjusted so that the amount supplied will meet the demand of the growing organism, and losses by evaporation will be minimized.

In addition to the carbon and energy source, microorganisms require sources of nitrogen, phosphorus, and mineral nutrients, and may require supplemental nutrients such as vitamins. Suitable nitrogen sources for SCP production are ammonia, ammonium salts, nitrates, urea, and organic nitrogen sources such as protein hydrolyzates. It is important to adjust the supply of the nitrogen source so that a ratio of 10:1 or less for carbon to nitrogen can be maintained in the medium during growth to minimize the accumulation of lipids or storage substances, such as poly-β-hydroxybutyrate, and to favor high protein contents in the cell.

The phosphorus source for SCP production is usually supplied as either phosphoric acid or soluble phosphates; a food- or feed-grade source of phosphorus, which is low in arsenic, fluoride, or heavy metals, should be used. Natural water supplies may provide sufficient quantities of mineral nutrients, such as iron, magnesium, manganese, calcium, sodium, and potassium salts, but in most cases, the water supply must be supplemented to make up for any deficiencies. To avoid corrosion problems in fermentation equipment, mineral salts should be added as sulfates or hydroxides rather than chlorides (5).

It is apparent that large quantities of process water are required for SCP production, including medium preparation, cell washing, cleanup, and steam generation. For example, an estimated water requirement for producing bacterial SCP from methanol is in the range of 45.5 million liters per 100,000 metric tons per year of production (23).

Process Characteristics

The type of process (batch or continuous), growth rate, sterility requirements, type of fermentor or bioreactor, extent of feedstock utilization and yield, temperature, pH, and methods used for product recovery all are important factors in determining the economic viability of SCP process (Table 2). The growth characteristics and protein contents for selective microorganisms for SCP production, including cell yields and crude protein contents, are summarized in Table 3.

Photosynthetic organisms. Both algae and photosynthetic bacteria have been used for SCP production. The photosynthetic production of SCP by *Chlorella* species can be represented by the following typical equation (24):

$$6.14\ CO_2 + 3.65\ H_2O + NH_3 \xrightarrow{\text{light}}$$

$$C_{6.14}H_{10.3}O_{2.24}N + 6.85\ O_2$$

The composition of the cell product will vary with different algal species. Algae can be grown either in batch tanks or semicontinuous ponds operated on a fill and draw principle (Table 2). Algal production is often carried out under nonsterile mixed-culture conditions where the organism that is desired usually predominates over other competing species. *Spirulina maxima* grows best in highly alkaline waters having a pH in the range 9 to 11 as is the case in Lake Texcoco in Mexico (25). In the Indian–West German process, *Scenedesmus acutus* is grown in pure culture at a pH of 7 to 8 (24). Mixed algal cultures develop in the experimental pilot plant systems at the University of California (26) and in Israel (27).

In Japan and Taiwan, *Chlorella* species have been grown either photosynthetically or in nonphotosynthetic heterotrophic systems, with carbon sources such as sugar syrups or molasses at pH 6 to 7 (28). Dried algae and algae tablets are sold as health foods in both of these countries.

Important factors in large-scale photosynthetic algal cultivation systems include lack of cloud cover and minimal diurnal variations in light intensity with temperatures above 20°C for most of the year. Large pond areas must be used because cell densities seldom exceed 1 to 2 grams per liter (dry weight) as com-

Table 2. Operating characteristics of selected single-cell protein processes.

Item	Process			
	Algal *Spirulina maxima*	Bacterial *Methylophilus* *methylotrophus* (methanol)	Yeast *Candida utilis* (ethanol)	Mold *Paecilomyces* *varioti* (sulfite waste liquor)
Type of process	Batch or semicontinuous	Continuous	Continuous or batch	Continuous
Sterility	Nonaseptic	Aseptic	Aseptic	Nonaseptic
Fermentor	Ponds	Airlift	Agitated	Agitated
Feedstock utilization	Partially or fully utilized	Fully utilized	Fully utilized	Partially utilized
Temperature (°C)	Ambient	35 to 42	30 to 40	38 to 39
pH	9 to 11	6.0 to 7.0	4.6	4.5 to 4.7
Product recovery	Filtration	Agglomeration and centrifugation	Centrifugation	Filtration

Table 3. Growth characteristics and protein contents (nitrogen content × 6.25) (percent) of selected microorganisms of interest for single-cell protein production. N.D., no data.

Organism	Carbon and energy source	Specific growth rate $(\mu)^*$ or dilution rate $(D)^\dagger$	Output	Crude protein (%)	Reference
Algae	*Photosynthetic*				
Scenedesmus acutus	CO_2, sunlight	N.D.	20‡	55	24
Spirulina maxima	CO_2, HCO_3, CO_3^{2-}, sunlight	N.D.	15‡	62	25
Bacteria					
Rhodopseudomonas capsulata	Industrial wastes, sunlight	N.D.	1.2 to 2.0§	61	29
	Nonphotosynthetic				
Bacteria					
Cellulomonas sp.	Bagasse	0.20 to 0.29*	0.44 to 0.50‖	87	35
Alcaligenes sp.					
Methylococcus capsulatus	Methane	0.14*	1.00 to 1.03‖	N.D.	59
Methylophilus methylotrophus	Methanol	0.38 to 0.50*	0.50‖	72	31
Yeasts					
Candida lipolytica	*n*-Alkanes	0.16†	0.88‖	65	18
Candida utilis	Ethanol, sulfite waste liquor	0.50*	0.70‖	50 to 55	19
		0.30*	0.50‖		16
Kluyveromyces fragilis	Cheese whey (lactose)	0.66*	0.55‖	45 to 54	13
Saccharomyces cerevisiae	Molasses	0.25*	0.50‖	53	4
Molds and higher fungi					
Cephalosporium eichhorniae	Cassava starch	N.D.	0.45‖	48 to 50	37
Chaetomium cellulolyticum	Agriculture and forestry wastes	0.24*	N.D.	45	39
Paecilomyces varioti	Sulfite waste liquor	0.20*	0.55‖	55	38
Penicillium cyclopium	Cheese whey (lactose)	0.20*	0.68‖	47.5	14
Scytalidium acidophilum	Acid-hydrolyzed waste paper	N.D.	0.43 to 0.46‖	44 to 47	38

*$\mu = dX/X\,dt$, where μ is specific growth rate (hour^{-1}), X is cell concentration (grams per liter), and t is time (hours). †$D = P/X$, where D is dilution rate (in continuous processes) (hour^{-1}), P is productivity (grams per liter per hour), and X is cell concentration (grams per liter). ‡Productivity (area basis) in units of grams per square meter per day. §Cell concentration X in grams per liter. ‖Yield Y in grams per gram substrate utilized; $Y = dX/dS$, where S is the substrate concentration (grams per liter).

pared with 30 to 40 grams per liter with yeasts and some bacteria. Growth occurs in the top 20- to 30-centimeter layer in open ponds. At present, algal productivities of 20 to 25 grams per square meter per day are attained in controlled culture systems. Productivities of 30 to 40 grams per square meter per day are possible under optimum growth conditions (24). The culture system must be agitated either mechanically or by recirculation to prevent settling of the algae and to prevent thermal stratification and depletion of nutrients at the surface. Harvesting algae is a particularly difficult problem in view of the low cell densities and large volumes of water that must be handled. The use of microstrainers and other filtration methods is probably the best approach (25).

Photosynthetic bacteria such as *Rhodopseudomonas capsulata* have been grown in Japan, with sewage or industrial waste as substrates. Generally, these organisms grow in mixed culture with aerobic, heterotrophic, and nitrogen-fixing bacteria. Again, culture densities are low, on the order of 1 to 2 grams per liter (dry weight) (29).

Nonphotosynthetic organisms. Actinomycetes, nonphotosynthetic bacteria, molds, yeasts, and higher fungi all require aerobic conditions for growth in SCP processes. Substrate and oxygen transfer to and across the cell surface are limiting factors in aerobic growth. Since oxygen has a low solubility in water, a fermentor design that gives maximum oxygen transfer rates with minimum power requirements should be selected.

Heat is produced as a result of microbial growth. For yeasts such as *Candida* species, this amounts to approximately 0.46 kilojoule per millimole of oxygen consumed (30) or 14,410 kilojoules per gram of yeast solids if 1 gram of oxygen

is required for each gram of yeast solids produced (4). Consequently, heat removal is a significant factor in SCP production.

Many species of bacteria have been investigated for use in SCP processes because of their short generation times (20 to 30 minutes) and their ability to use a variety of raw materials ranging from carbohydrates to gaseous and liquid hydrocarbons and petrochemicals. Figure 1 shows a schematic diagram for bacterial SCP production from methanol.

An example of a commercial-scale SCP process based on methanol now in operation is that developed by Imperial Chemical Industries, Ltd., in the United Kingdom for growing *Methylophilus methylotrophus*. The conversion of methanol to the SCP product is represented by the equation (31)

$$1.72\ CH_3OH + 0.23\ NH_3 + 1.51\ O_2 \rightarrow$$

$$1.0\ CH_{1.68}O_{0.36}N_{0.22} +$$

$$0.72\ CO_2 + 2.94\ H_2O$$

This process has been operated intermittently over the past year at 6000 metric tons per month. The organism is grown continuously under aseptic conditions (Table 2). A special "pressure cycle" airlift type fermentor is used (30). The process is operated at 35° to 42°C to minimize cooling cost, since the growth of these organisms is highly exothermic. An unusual feature of the process is the initial separation of the cells from the production medium by agglomeration in the aqueous growth medium so that a higher solids slurry can be fed to the centrifuges than is normally practiced in most SCP processes. Purified CO_2 is sold as a by-product. Relatively high specific growth rates of 0.50 hour^{-1} and cell yields exceeding 0.50 gram per gram of substrate (31, 32) (Table 3) are reported for this process.

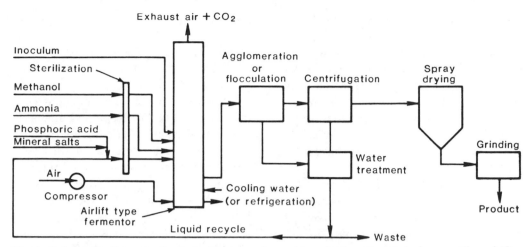

Fig. 1. Schematic diagram of a typical process for making single-cell protein from methanol (5).

Hoechst-Uhde in West Germany has developed a pilot plant process for producing *Methylomonas clara* with methanol as the carbon and energy source (Table 1) (33). Their interest has been on the potential for producing a 90 percent protein concentrate and nucleic acid by-products. Shell Research Ltd. constructed a pilot plant for producing *Methylococcus capsulatus* or a mixed culture of methane-utilizing bacteria from methane (34). However, this process was not developed to a commercial scale for economic reasons. Research was also conducted at Louisiana State University on the use of bagasse, a by-product of sugar mill operations, as a substrate for the growth of cellulolytic bacteria. A mixed culture of *Cellulomonas* and *Alcaligenes* species grew on a medium containing bagasse but the economics of this process were not sufficiently attractive for further development (35).

As mentioned earlier, yeasts were the first microorganisms to be grown on a large scale. At the present time, *C. utilis* (Torula yeast) is being produced from ethanol by Pure Culture Products at Hutchinson, Minnesota (19). This organism can be grown in either continuous or batch culture systems. In the Pure Culture Products process, a conventional baffled, agitated, and aerated fermentor system is used with aseptic conditions. The substrate is fed at a rate adjusted for full utilization by the yeast (Table 2). *Candida utilis* is also produced from sulfite waste liquor from paper mill operations. Operating conditions and growth rates are similar to those in the ethanol-based process (16).

Approximately 14.6×10^9 kilograms of cheese whey are produced in the United States and in Western Europe each year. The yeast *K. fragilis* utilizes lactose readily and has been used to produce an SCP product from whey at Amber Laboratories, Juneau, Wisconsin (Table 1) (13). Again, operating conditions and yields are similar to those obtained with *C. utilis* and bakers' yeast (Table 3). Molds and higher fungi are capable of utilizing diverse carbohydrate materials, including agricultural and food processing wastes. Large-scale systems for producing these microorganisms are similar to those used for yeast SCP production.

The largest mold-SCP process now being operated is the Pekilo process developed in Finland at the Finnish Pulp and Paper Institute (*17*) (Tables 1 and 2). This process is operated continuously. Residual SO_2 is stripped from the sulfite liquor feedstock. Sterile air, ammonia, and feedstock are supplied to two baffled, agitated-aerated fermentors that produce 15 to 16.5 tons (dry weight) of *Paecilomyces varioti* mycelium in 24 hours. The mycelial product has the advantage over bacterial and yeast cells that it can be recovered on drum filters in a process that is less costly than centrifugation. The growth rate is slower than rates observed with yeasts or bacteria, but the yield (grams of dry cell product per gram of substrate) and the protein content (55 percent) are similar to those of yeast (*5*) (Table 3).

In the United Kingdom, Rank Hovis MacDougall has grown *Fusarium graminearum* continuously in 1300-liter fermentors, with glucose as the substrate and ammonia as the nitrogen source. The specific growth rate is approximately 0.18 hour^{-1} and the cells contain 45 percent protein (*36*).

Examples of SCP processes under development are the utilization of cassava starch by *Cephalosporium eichhorniae* (*37*), cheese whey by *Penicillium cyclopium* (*14*), and acid-hydrolyzed waste paper by *Scytalidium acidophilum* (*38*) (Table 3). But, none of these processes have reached even the pilot plant stage.

The so-called "solid substrate" fungal processes are being altered to upgrade the value of agricultural, forestry, and food processing wastes as animal feeds. In these processes, which are analogous to composting, water is removed from the substrate until the moisture content is 50 to 80 percent. Nitrogen and phosphorus are supplied by addition of commercial fertilizer. The waste is inoculated, aerated, and the product is then recovered and dried.

The Waterloo process, developed at the University of Waterloo in Canada, is based on the cellulolytic fungus *Chaetomium cellulyticum* and can be operated either in a conventional aerated fermentation system or in a solid substrate system, depending on the substrate (*39*). In the solid substrate process, materials such as corn stover or Kraft paper mill clarifier sludge are subjected to an initial thermal or chemical treatment, followed by aerobic fermentation, separation of the fungal mycelium, and drying. The final product contains up to 45 percent protein. This process has been operated only on a small pilot plant scale.

Tate and Lyle in the United Kingdom have investigated the use of *Aspergillus niger* in solid substrate systems for recovering fruit and vegetable processing wastes. The yield of the fungal product on carrot wastes was 0.11 gram per gram of substrate, and the crude protein content was increased from 9 percent in the starting material to 29 percent in the finished product (*40*). It is doubtful that this process will be economically feasible for treating fruit and vegetable wastes that are available only during a short growing season.

Economics

Among the factors affecting the economic viability of SCP processes are the capital costs of facilities, including working capital; the site location, taking into account the availability of raw materials and the size and proximity of markets; and manufacturing costs, including costs of raw materials (carbon and energy source, nitrogen source, and mineral nutrients), energy, water supply, waste treatment, labor, and maintenance, as well as depreciation and the desired profit margin.

The highest capital costs for facilities are incurred in processes that must be operated under aseptic conditions to produce a food-grade product. Estimates published for various processes during 1975 and 1976 for producing feed-grade SCP from methanol were in the range of $660 to $1000 per metric ton of annual capacity for 50,000 to 100,000 metric ton capacity plants (5). Current costs for food-grade SCP products would be much higher. Costs of raw materials range from 14 percent of manufacturing costs for agricultural and forestry wastes with solid substrate fermentations (39) to more than 50 percent for processes requiring methanol or ethanol (41). Increasing prices of methanol and ethanol in the future will make SCP processes based on these substrates economically unattractive.

Estimates of energy requirements for SCP processes vary widely. Typical values for total energy inputs are estimated to range from 185 to 190 megajoules per kilogram of protein for *Candida* species grown on ethanol to 30 megajoules per kilogram for *A. niger* grown on agricultural processes wastes, when land and labor requirements are taken into account (42).

Product Quality and Safety

Single-cell protein products can be used as (i) protein supplements in human foods, (ii) functional food ingredients to provide, for example, flavor, fat and water binding, dispersing action, whip-ping and foaming action, and extrusion and spinning characteristics, and (iii) protein supplements for livestock feeding.

Data given in Table 3 on crude protein contents determined by multiplying nitrogen contents by the factor 6.25 do not reflect the true value of these products in human and animal nutrition since amino acid profiles vary widely (42) and nonprotein nitrogen substances such as nucleic acids are included. Nucleic acid contents may range from 5 to 15 percent depending upon the organism and growth conditions used (43). These substances have no nutritional value for nonruminant animals, and intakes by humans must be limited to 2 grams of nucleic acid per day to avoid kidney stone formation or gout. They may be removed by acid, alkali, or enzyme treatment of the cells or by enhancing endogenous nucleases (44). Feeding studies with broiler chickens and swine have shown the importance of supplementing yeast SCP products with methionine or its hydroxy analog and adjusting arginine and lysine ratios (45). Best efficiencies of feed conversion with broiler chickens and swine are obtained when SCP products are used at 7 to 15 percent in the ration, but levels up to 25 percent have been used in broiler chicken rations supplemented with selenium at 0.3 part per million (46).

Currently, in the United States, Food and Drug Administration regulations permit the human food use of dried cells of *S. cerevisiae* (bakers' yeast), *C. utilis* (Torula yeast), *K. fragilis* (fragilis yeast), and bakers' yeast protein concentrate produced by extraction of protein from *S. cerevisiae* (47). In the United Kingdom, the Ministry of Agriculture, Fisheries, and Food has allowed test market studies on the food use of dried mycelium of *F. graminearum* developed by Rank Hovis MacDougall (*36*), and animal feed use of the Imperial Chemical Industries SCP product (dried cells of *M. methylotrophus*) (*31*). However, possible iron and zinc deficiencies in the Rank Hovis MacDougall product may require supplementation with these mineral nutrients. The Protein Advisory Group of the United Nations has developed guidelines for the production and evaluation of SCP products (*48*). In addition to short-term toxicological studies in rats, more extensive assessments of carcinogenicity, teratogenicity, and mutagenicity, including multigenerational feeding studies, may be required by government regulatory agencies.

Market Considerations

Establishing markets or maintaining existing markets for SCP products for animal feed applications depends on their price and feeding performance in broiler chicken, turkey, laying hen, or swine rations as compared with existing protein feedstuffs such as soybean meal and fish meal. The extensive livestock studies conducted by British Petroleum and Imperial Chemical Industries on their SCP products exemplify the demonstration of feeding performance needed to satisfy users and government regulatory agencies (*31, 45, 49*).

In human foods, flavor and texture, in addition to nutritional value of SCP products, are important determinants of acceptability. At the present time, the major market for food-grade SCP products is for functional uses in foods. For example, yeast protein autolyzates and hydrolyzates have been used as food flavoring for many years. Torula yeast products are being sold as functional food additives in processed meats and bakery products in the United States. Typical 1982 selling prices for selected microbial, plant, and animal protein products are presented in Table 4. Food-grade yeast products must provide spe-

Table 4. Typical 1982 selling prices of selected microbial plant and animal protein products. Selling prices were obtained from trade sources.

Product	Protein content (%)	1982 selling price (U.S. dollars per kilogram)
Food-grade products		
Candida utilis (Torula yeast)	50 to 55	1.87 to 2.24
Kluyveromyces fragilis	45 to 50	2.09 to 2.29
Soy protein concentrate	72	0.88 to 1.03
Soy protein isolate	92	2.59 to 2.68
Dried skim milk	37	1.16 to 1.21
Feed-grade products		
Saccharomyces cerevisiae	45 to 50	0.48 to 0.66
Soybean meal	44	0.19 to 0.20
Meat and bone meal	50	0.19 to 0.21
Fish meal	65	0.23 to 0.40

Table 5. Improvements in single-cell protein production.

Item	Example	Reference
Strain improvement	Mutants of *S. cerevisiae* forming enlarged cells for improved recovery	*50*
Genetically engineered cultures	Cloning of genes for higher amino acid contents in methanol-utilizing bacteria	*51*
	Improved NH_3 utilization by transfer of glutamic dehydrogenase gene from *Escherichia coli* to *Methylophilus methylotrophus*	*52*
Enzyme for degrading cell walls for protein concentrate production	*Rhizoctonia solani* 1,3-β-D-glucanase for degrading yeast cell walls	*53*
Extracellular production of proteins	Excretion of protein into medium by *Bacillus brevis*	*54*
Improved harvesting methods	Agglomeration, electrocoagulation	*55*
Automation of production	Computer control of Pekilo process	*56*

cial functional characteristics such as flavoring, in addition to nutrient content, to compete with functional soy protein products. Feed-grade SCP products must be competitive with established feedstuffs, such as soybean meal and fish meal, on price and feeding performance bases. In addition, any new SCP product will have to satisfy government regulatory agency requirements for safety in human or animal feeding.

Prospects

Table 5 summarizes some of the current research and development efforts that may lead to significant improvements in SCP processes. These range from strain improvement (*50–52*), including genetically engineered cultures such as the glutamic dehydrogenase recombinants developed by ICI in the United Kingdom, to improved methods for protein isolation (*53, 54*) and cell harvesting (*55*), process monitoring, and computer control of production (*56*). However, the impact of these developments on the future economic viability of SCP processes remains to be seen.

It is apparent that large-scale processes for manufacturing SCP products are technologically feasible, and selected processes are now being operated to a limited extent on a commercial scale worldwide. However, the introduction of new SCP products will be limited by economic, market, and regulatory factors rather than by technological considerations.

The future prospects for large-scale SCP production for human food appear to be limited to use as protein supplements and functional protein ingredients rather than as primary sources of protein in human diets. For animal-feed applications, SCP production will be limited to those areas where low-cost substrates such as waste carbohydrates are available and conventional protein feedstuffs such as soybean meal and fish meal are in short supply.

282

References and Notes

1. J. H. Litchfield, *Chemtech* **8**, 218 (1978).
2. H. Durand-Chastel, in *Algae Biomass Production and Use*, G. Shelef and C. J. Soeder, Eds. (Elsevier/North-Holland, New York, 1980), pp. 51–64.
3. A. J. Wiley, in *Industrial Fermentations*, L. A. Underkoffler and R. J. Hickey, Eds. (Chemical Publishing Co., New York, 1954), vol. 1, pp. 307–343.
4. G. Reed and H. J. Peppler, *Yeast Technology* (Avi, Westport, Conn., 1973), pp. 68–69 and 328–354.
5. J. H. Litchfield, in *Microbial Technology*, H. J. Peppler and D. Perlman, Eds. (Academic Press, New York, ed. 2, 1979), vol. 1, pp. 93–155; *Bioscience* **30**, 387 (1980).
6. E. S. Lipinsky, in *Hydrolysis of Cellulose: Mechanisms of Enzymatic and Acid Catalysis*, R. D. Brown, Jr., and L. Jurasek, Eds. (American Chemical Society, Washington, D.C., 1979), pp. 1–24; H. R. Bungay, *Science* **218**, 643 (1982).
7. L. Jurasek, *Dev. Ind. Microbiol.* **20**, 177 (1979).
8. M. K. Ladisch, *Process Biochem.* **14** (No. 1), 21 (1979).
9. J. F. Saeman, in *Symposium on Biomass in a Nonfossil Fuel Source*, American Chemical Society and Chemical Society of Japan, Honolulu, 1 to 6 April 1979 (American Chemical Society, Washington, D.C., 1979), p. 472.
10. B. S. Montenecourt and D. E. Eveleigh, *Appl. Environ. Microbiol.* **34**, 777 (1977); S. M. Cuskey, D. H. J. Lohamhart, T. Chase, Jr., B. S. Montenecourt, D. E. Eveleigh, *Dev. Ind. Microbiol.* **21**, 471 (1980).
11. M. Taniguchi *et al.*, *Eur. J. Appl. Microbiol. Biotechnol.* **14**, 35 (1982); Y. W. Han, P. L. Yu, J. K. Smith, *Biotechnol. Bioeng.* **20**, 1015 (1978).
12. H. Skogman, in *Food from Waste*, G. G. Birch, K. J. Parker, J. T. Worgan, Eds. (Applied Science, London, 1976), pp. 167–179.
13. S. Bernstein, C. H. Tzeng, D. Sisson, *Biotechnol. Bioeng. Symp.* (No. 7), 1 (1977).
14. J. H. Kim and J. M. Lebault, *Eur. J. Appl. Microbiol. Biotechnol.* **13**, 151 (1981); J. H. Kim, S. Iibuchi, J. M. Lebault, *ibid.* **13**, 208 (1981).
15. *Food Eng.* **53** (No. 12), 95 (1981).
16. J. M. Holderby and W. A. Moggio, *J. Water Pollution Control Fed.* **2**, 171 (1960); *Lockwood's Directory of the Paper and Allied Trades* (Vance, New York, 1980), p. 162.
17. H. Romantschuk and M. Lehtomaki, *Process Biochem.* **13** (No. 3), 16 (1978).
18. G. H. Evans and J. G. Shennan, U.S. Patent 3,846,238 (1974); *Chem. Eng. News* **56** (No. 38), 12 (1978).
19. J. A. Ridgeway, Jr., T. A. Lappin, B. M. Benjamin, J. B. Corns, C. Akin, U.S. Patent 3,865,691 (1975); *Food Eng.* **49** (No. 6), 95 (1977).
20. Y. Masuda, K. Kato, Y. Takayama, K. Kida, M. Nakanishi, U.S. Patent 3,868,305 (1975).
21. M. Rychtera, J. Barta, A. Flechter, A. A. Einsele, *Process Biochem.* **12** (No. 2), 26 (1977).
22. M. Rychtera, V. Kren, V. Gregr, *Eur. J. Appl. Microbiol. Biotechnol.* **13**, 39 (1981).
23. C. Ratledge, *Chem. Ind. (London)*, No. 21, 918 (1975).
24. L. Enebo, *Chem. Eng. Prog. Symp. Ser.* **65** (No. 93) 80–86 (1969); E. W. Becker and L. V. Venkataraman, in *Algae Biomass Production and Use*, G. Shelef and C. J. Soeder, Eds. (Elsevier/North-Holland, New York, 1980), pp. 35–50; J. C. Goldman, in *ibid.*, pp. 344–359.
25. H. Durand-Chastel and G. Clement, in *Proceedings of the 9th International Congress of Nutrition* (Karger, Basel, Switzerland, 1975), vol. 3, pp. 85–90.
26. W. J. Oswald and C. G. Golueke, in *Single-Cell Protein*, R. I. Mateles and S. R. Tannenbaum, Eds. (MIT Press, Cambridge, Mass., 1968), pp. 271–305; J. Benemann, B. Koopman, J. Weissman, D. Eisenberg, R. Goebel, in *Algae Biomass Production and Use*, G. Shelef and C. J. Soeder, Eds. (Elsevier/North-Holland, New York, 1980), pp. 457–495.
27. J. Berend, E. Simovitch, A. Ollian, in *Algae Biomass Production and Use*, G. Shelef and C. J. Soeder, Eds. (Elsevier/North Holland, New York, 1980), pp. 799–818; Z. Dubinsky, S. Aaronson, T. Berner, in *ibid.*, pp. 819–832.
28. *The Micro-Algae Top Maker in the World* (Taiwan Chlorella Manufacture Co. Ltd., Taipei, Taiwan, undated); P. Soong, in *Algae Biomass Production and Use*, G. Shelef and C. J. Soeder, Eds. (Elsevier/North-Holland, New York, 1980), pp. 92–113; K. Kawaguchi, in *ibid.*, pp. 25–33.
29. M. Kobayashi and S.-I. Kurata, *Process Biochem.* **13** (No. 9), 21 (1981).
30. C. L. Cooney, D. I. C. Wang, R. I. Mateles, *Biotechnol. Bioeng.* **11**, 269 (1969); C. L. Cooney *Science* **219**, 728 (1983).
31. D. C. MacLennan, J. S. Gow, D. A. Stringer, *Process Biochem.* **8** (No. 6), 22 (1973); J. S. Gow, J. D. Littlehailes, S. R. L. Smith, R. B. Walter, in *Single Cell Proteins II*, S. R. Tannenbaum and D. I. C. Wang. Eds. (MIT Press, Cambridge, Mass., 1975), pp. 375–384; *Process Biochem.* **12** (No. 1), 30 (1977); R. J. Margetts and D. A. Stringer, papers presented at International Symposium on Single-Cell Proteins, Paris, 28 to 30 January 1981.
32. J. P. Van Dijken and W. Harder, *Biotechnol. Bioeng.* **17**, 15 (1975).
33. U. Faust, P. Prave, D. A. Lukatsch, *J. Ferment. Technol.* **55**, 609 (1977); W. Sittig, paper presented at International Symposium on Single-Cell Proteins, Paris, France, 28 to 30 January 1981.
34. G. Hamer, in *Economic Microbiology: Microbial Biomass*, A. H. Rose, Ed. (Academic Press, New York, 1979), vol. 4, pp. 315–356.
35. Y. W. Han, C. E. Dunlap, C. D. Callihan, *Food Technol.* **25**, 130 (1970).
36. C. Anderson, J. Longton, C. Maddix, G. W. Scammell, G. L. Solomons, in *Single-Cell Proteins II*, S. R. Tannenbaum and D. I. C. Wang, Eds. (MIT Press, Cambridge, Mass., 1975), pp. 314–329; *Food Eng.* **53** (No. 5), 117 (1981).
37. Y. Mikami, K. F. Gregory, W. F. Levadoux, C. Balagopalan, S. T. Whitwill, *Appl. Environ. Microbiol.* **43**, 403 (1982).
38. K. C. Ivarson and H. Morita, *ibid.*, p. 643.
39. M. Moo-Young, D. S. Chahal, D. Vlach, *Biotechnol. Bioeng.* **20**, 107 (1978); M. Moo-Young, A. J. Douglis, D. S. Chahal, D. G. Macdonald, *Process Biochem.* **14** (No. 13), 38 (1979).

40. C. A. E. Davy, in *Food Industry Wastes: Disposal and Recovery*, A. Herzka and R. G. Booth, Eds. (Applied Science, London, 1981), pp. 219–230.
41. J. H. Litchfield, *Adv. Appl. Microbiol.* **22**, 267 (1977).
42. C. W. Lewis, *J. Appl. Chem. Biotechnol.* **26**, 568 (1976).
43. C. I. Waslien, *Crit. Rev. Food Sci. Nutr.* **6**, 77 (1975).
44. J. H. Litchfield, *Food Technol.* **31** (No. 5), 175 (1977).
45. C. A. Shacklady and E. Gatumel, in *Proteins from Hydrocarbons*, H. Gounelle de Pontanel, Ed. (Academic Press, New York, 1973), pp. 27–52; N. J. Daghir and J. L. Sell, *Poultry Sci.* **61**, 337 (1982).
46. G. Succi, P. Pialorsi, L. DiFiore, G. Cardini, *Poultry Sci.* **59**, 1471 (1980).
47. Code of Federal Regulations, Title 21, 172.325, 172.896 (U.S. Government Printing Office, Washington, D.C., 1981).
48. Protein Advisory Group, Statement No. 4 (FAO/WHO/UNICEF) (United Nations, New York, 1970); Guidelines No. 6 and 7 (1970); *ibid.*, No. 8 (1971); *ibid.*, No. 12 (1972); *ibid.*, No. 15 (1974).
49. B. W. Abbey, K. N. Boorman, D. Lewis, *J. Sci. Food Agric.* **31**, 421 (1980).
50. Y. Miyasaka, C. Rha, A. J. Sinskey, *Biotechnol.*
Bioeng. **22**, 2065 (1980); Y. Miyasaka, A. J. Sinskey, J. Deangelo, C. Rha, *J. Food Sci.* **45**, 558 (1980).
51. F. Gautier, *Abstracts, 6th International Fermentation Symposium, London, Ontario, Canada, 20–25 July 1980* (National Research Council, Ottawa, Canada, 1980), p. 102.
52. J. D. Windass *et al.*, *Nature (London)* **287**, 396 (1980).
53. R. Kobayashi, T. Miwa, S. Yamamoto, S. Nagasaki, *Eur. J. Appl. Microbiol. Biotechnol.* **15**, 14 (1982).
54. S. Udaka, N. Tsukagashi, M. Yamada, S. Miyashiro, in *Advances in Biotechnology*, M. Moo-Young, C. Vezina, K. Singh, Eds. (Pergamon, New York, 1981), vol. 2, pp. 381–386.
55. U. Faust and P. Prave, *Process Biochem.* **14** (No. 11), 28 (1979).
56. A. Halme, *Biotechnol. Bioeng. Symp.* (No. 9), 369 (1979); M. J. Rolf, P. J. Hennigan, R. D. Mohler, W. A. Weigand, H. Lim, *Biotechnol. Bioeng.* **24**, 1191 (1982).
57. *Chem. Eng. News* **52** (No. 33), 30 (1974).
58. C. Anderson, J. Longton, C. Maddix, G. W. Scammel, G. L. Solomons, in *Single-Cell Proteins II*, S. R. Tannenbaum and D. I. C. Wang, Eds. (MIT Press, Cambridge, Mass., 1975), pp. 314–329; *Food Eng.* **53** (No. 5), 117 (1981).
59. J. H. Harwood and S. J. Pirt, *J. Appl. Bacteriol.* **35**, 597 (1972).

Color Plates

Plate I

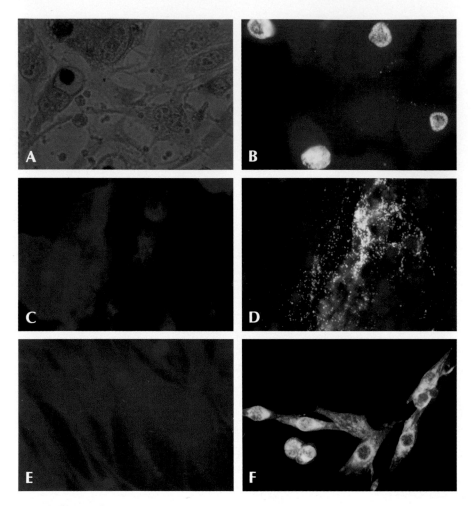

Plate I, Chapter 5

Diagnosis of chlamydia and herpesvirus infections with monoclonal antibodies. (A and B) Detection of chlamydia inclusion bodies in cells infected in culture by (A) iodine stain or (B) IF test with a monoclonal antibody. (C and D) Immunofluorescence tests for chlamydia elementary bodies on (C) a cervical smear from a patient that tested chlamydia-negative by culture, and (D) a cervical smear from a patient that tested chlamydia-positive by culture. (E and F) Immunofluorescence tests for a herpesvirus antigen (IISV 1; gC glycoprotein) on (E) cells infected with HSV 2, and (F) cells infected with HSV 1.

Plate II

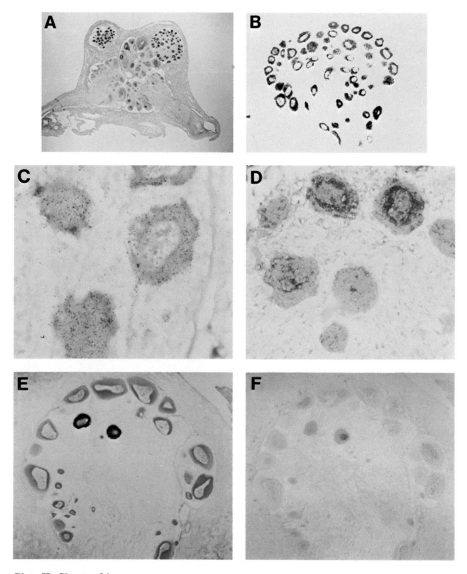

Plate II, Chapter 34

In situ hybridization and immunocytochemical localizations of ELH expressing cells in the central nervous system of *Aplysia*. (A) The abdominal ganglion from an adult animal was dissected, fixed in Bouin's and sectioned as described (*51*). Iodine-125–labeled nick-translated probes were hybridized in situ to tissue sections according to the condition described (*52*). The bag cells comprise the topmost rounded clusters of neurons on both sides of the ganglion. This photomicrograph shows hybridization to cells in both bag cell clusters as well as to a single isolated neuron in the upper left of the ganglion. The staining of the bag cells reflects the intense collection of grains apparent at higher magnification in (C); magnification is ×15. (B) In situ hybridization to a section through a single bag cell cluster. Neurons are stained with methylene blue; magnification is ×58. (C) In situ hybridization to bag cell neurons at high magnification (×368). Grains are observed in the cytoplasm of the cell bodies as well as in the processes. (D) Immunocytochemistry with antibodies in ELH followed by a second antibody coupled to peroxidase (*53*) (generating a green-brown stain in ELH-positive cells) in bag cell

Plate III

cluster (53). Magnification is ×230. (E). In situ hybridization to a section through the pleural ganglia showing a high density of grains in the cytoplasm of two neurons. Magnification is ×92. (F) Immunocytochemistry with the antibody to ELH applied to the section of pleural ganglion contiguous to that shown in (E).

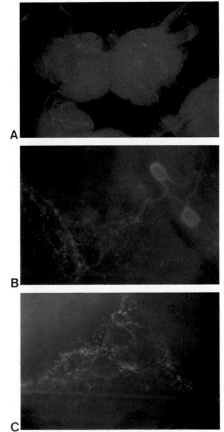

Plate III, Chapter 34
Indirect immunofluorescence in the central nervous system with antibody to ELH. Whole nervous systems were dissected from 45-day postmetamorphic animals, fixed, and reacted with a rabbit antibody to ELH, followed by goat antibody to serum rabbit coupled to rhodamine (54). (A) The buccal ganglia: two large invariant cells that produce ELH lie at the periphery of each ganglion, close to the exit zone of the buccal nerve. In addition, a cluster of four or five smaller cells that produce ELH is always located in the center of the ganglion; magnification is ×95. (B) A pair of invariant bipolar cells producing ELH in the abdominal ganglion; magnification is ×240. (C) The arborization pattern of ELH-containing processes in the abdominal ganglion. The processes of the ELH-containing neurons form a rich arborization pattern that surrounds and appears to make axosomatic contacts with cell bodies in the abdominal ganglion; magnification is ×240.

Plate IV

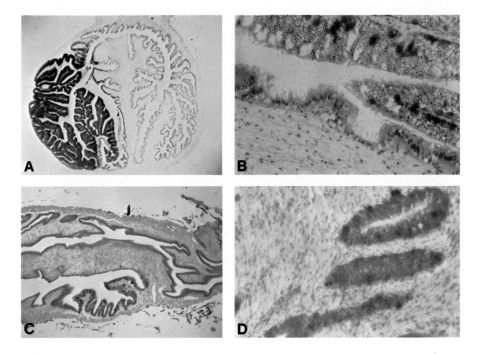

Plate IV, Chapter 34

In situ hybridization and immunocytochemistry to the atrial gland. (A) A section through the large hermaphroditic duct was reacted with antibodies to A peptide followed by a peroxidase-coupled second antibody. The hermaphroditic duct consists of red and white hemiducts on the right and the intensely staining atrial gland on the left; magnification is ×15. (B) In situ hybridization to a magnified section of the atrial and hermaphroditic duct. Grains are evident in the large columnar secretory cells of the atrial gland but diminish at the transitional epithelium bordering the flattened cells of the white hemiduct; magnification is ×370. (C) In situ hybridizations to the developing atrial gland. Sections of tissue from the hermaphroditic ducts of a 67-day postmetamorphic animal. Patchy hybridization with ^{125}I-labeled ELH gene probes is observed in the highly enfolded region destined to become the atrial gland; magnification is ×58. (D) A higher magnification (×230) of in situ hybridization to a developing atrial gland 67 days after metamorphosis.

Plate V

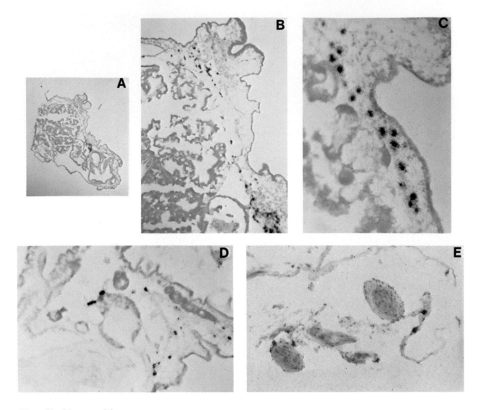

Plate V, Chapter 34
ELH-positive neurons originate in the body wall and migrate to the central ganglia. (A) In situ hybridization to a section through a whole organism 10-days postmetamorphosis. ELH-positive cells are observed along the length of the body wall; magnification is ×15. (B) As in (A), magnification is ×50. (C) As in A, magnification is ×230. (D) In situ hybridization to developing organisms, 35 days, after metamorphosis. ELH-containing neurons appear to migrate from the body wall along connective tissue fibers to their ultimate position in the ganglia. Cells are shown migrating along fibrous threads to a primitive ganglion in the center of the section. Magnification is ×92. (E) In situ hybridization to a transverse section through a developing pleural abdominal connective showing fibers containing ELH-positive cells; magnification is ×92.

Plate VI, Chapter 34 (facing page)
In situ hybridization to developing bag cells. In situ hybridization experiments were performed on sections through the developing pleuroabdominal connective and abdominal ganglion to show the appearance and migration of the cluster of bag cell neurons. (A) A section 49 days after metamorphosis showing a small cluster of cells along the connective. The diameter of one bag cell is about 5 μm, ten times smaller than that of an adult bag cell; magnification is ×92. (B) A section 58 days after metamorphosis showing that the bag cell cluster has increased in size and has moved closer to the ganglion. Magnification is ×92. (C) A section 67 days after metamorphosis in a sexually mature adult capable of egg laying; magnification is ×92. (D) As in A, magnification is ×368. (E) As in B, magnification is ×368. (F) As in C, magnification is ×368.

Plate VI

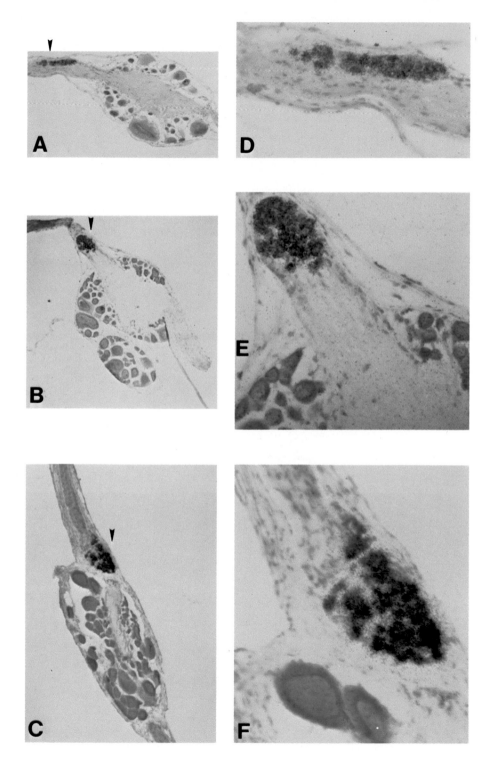

Plate VII

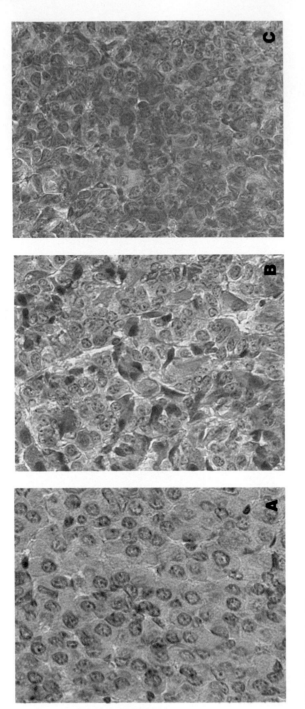

Plate VII, Chapter 35

Histology of pituitaries from normal, transgenic and *lit/lit* (little) mice. Pituitaries were then embedded in paraffin and serial sections (5 μm) were prepared and stained according to Slidders' method (*17*), where acidophilic cells stain yellow. (A) Control male mouse. (B) Transgenic mouse Hyb-184-5 ♂. (C) *Lit/lit* female mouse. Pituitaries were put in Bouin-Hollande fixative (*30*). They were then counted in four random sections of each pituitary. The results, expressed as the number of acidophilic cells per 33 μm² ± s.d. were: control male, 171 ± 16; control female, 132 ±16; *lit/lit* male, 13 ± 8; *lit/lit* female, 10 ± 6; transgenic mouse Hyb-197-5 ♀, 1 ± 1; C57-173-2 ♀, 33 ± 5; Hyb-184-5 ♂, 1 ± 1. In sections from *lit/lit* mice the amount of acidophilic cytoplasm was also greatly reduced compared to controls.

Part II
Biological Frontiers

Biological Frontiers

Frederick R. Blattner

The emphasis of Part II in this volume is fundamental research rather than techniques or practical applications. Philosophers and historians of science will probably regard the current period as a time of explosive advance and refinement of information rather than a true revolution. It has not been necessary, as was the case with quantum theory or relativity, to overturn major paradigms of accepted thought; rather, an enormous increase in the power of experimental techniques is now producing answers to complex long-standing biological questions.

A cornerstone of this advance is the technique of gene cloning, which allows a segment of genetic material to be removed from its normal context in a genome and replicated to high yields for studies in isolation, or to be reintroduced into a variety of cells where it can be studied in new genetic contexts. The basic principle of physically segmenting the genome of interest is an old one. Long before the discovery of restriction enzymes, what amounted to gene cloning (although not called that), the use of transducing phages and sex factors, was a method of choice in the study of bacterial genetics. But the in vitro methods of gene splicing have enormously extended the range of application and the precision of execution of the principle. This has led for the first time to practical methods

for study of eukaryotic genomes, including those of human and important plants and animals, although the techniques have been extraordinarily valuable in the study of prokaryotes as well.

An initial aim of many cloning experiments has been to determine gene structure through DNA sequencing. This purely structural approach has also been remarkably rewarding in providing insight into function. No more striking example can be found than the immune system, in which the first genes to be sequenced were those that code for antibody molecules. Many long-standing issues concerning the mechanisms involved in the generation of diversity, the control of expression, and the path of evolution of these genes have been brought from the level of vague conjecture to one of refined and testable hypotheses built on the discoveries of DNA rearrangement, gene conversion, alternate messenger RNA splicing, and somatic mutation. In chapter 22, Teillaud *et al.* describe one such detailed study focused on the role of somatic mutation in controlling the affinity of antigen for antibody.

Recently, the structural approach, in which DNA sequencing is used, has advanced to the histocompatibility genes that regulate the immune response. The rapid progress in this area and the precise analysis achieved so far (reviewed in chapter 23 by Steinmetz and Hood) exemplify the effectiveness of gene sequencing to unravel the complexities of the most difficult biological problems.

A major line of research toward interpretation of DNA sequence involves the detailed study of "sites" in DNA or RNA that have specific regulatory functions. A site is roughly defined as a small (about 100 base pairs) region that, through its interaction with other cellular components, brings about an effect on the expression of adjacent genetic material. This concept is a very general one, specific examples of which include promoters, operators, terminators, attenuators, cap sites, retroregulators, translational control sites, RNA splice sites, polyadenylation sites, enhancers, origins of replication, ribosome binding sites, site-specific recombination sites, viral encapsidation sites, switch sites, and more. In chapter 24, Rosenberg *et al.* provide a review of the methods developed to study the behavior of transcription initiation and termination sites through the use of specially designed vectors. The key to this type of analysis is the provision of a standard gene whose expression under the control of the particular "site" under investigation can be quantitatively monitored. Recombinant DNA molecules containing regulatory sites are also useful as substrates for in vitro investigation of the cellular factors that are involved in control. Several factors that are involved in the expression by eukaryotes of low molecular weight RNA's (class III genes) are described in the chapter by Lassar *et al.* Recently a new type of site, termed "enhancer," has been described which may turn out to be involved in tissue-specific and developmental regulation of eukaryotic messenger RNA expression—the Holy Grail of molecular biology. The chapter

by Rosenthal *et al.* represents a recent contribution to this burgeoning area of research.

The analysis of nucleic acid structure by hybridization of labeled probes to various types of "blots" has provided a global view that has revealed a remarkable degree of plasticity in both prokaryotic and eukaryotic genomes. The ability of DNA to rearrange is apparently mediated in many cases by specific transposable elements that have evolved the capacity to jump from one point to another in DNA, and at the same time carry neighboring sequences with them. The mechanism by which this takes place in the specific example of the bacterial transposon Tn*903* is the topic of the chapter by Weinert *et al.* DNA rearrangements also take place in eukaryotes. In some instances these are a part of a normal developmental process (for example, gene assembly prior to the expression of antibody genes) but rearrangements may also be involved in neoplastic transformation. The chapters by Leder *et al.* and by Land *et al.* focus on these phenomena whose understanding will be a necessary prerequisite to the conquest of cancer.

Recombinant DNA strategies have been of extraordinary value in the identification and analysis of proteins. In the past few years, more protein sequences have been determined by predictions from DNA than were ever ascertained by direct protein sequence methods. Many proteins that are present in cells in such minute quantities that they would be difficult to identify (much less sequence) by conventional methods have become accessible to analysis. The ease with which genes coding for proteins can now be isolated is illustrated in the chapter by Young and Davis, who developed the technique of antibody screening to isolate clones of a yeast RNA polymerase. Equally important is the capability to express such proteins in large quantities and to high levels of purity for biochemical analysis. The capability to modify precisely the genetic code through site-specific mutagenesis has also been of paramount importance. The study of mutations has always been a cornerstone of genetics but in the past it was necessary to rely on accidents of nature or the haphazard processs of mutagenesis to obtain them. Through strategies based on synthetic oligonucleotide chemistry it is now possible to generate mutations with absolute precision so that the effect of a single amino acid substitution can be evaluated. **The chapter by Villafranca *et al*. provides a beautiful example of the** power of this method in the case of the dihydrofolate reductase gene. Much has been made in the general public press of the role of expression systems in providing medically important products such as insulin. (However, the predominant use of this technique is surely for the acquisition of knowledge of expression of proteins having little potential for commercial exploitation.)

The analysis of genes and proteins, their biochemistry and their regulation, is but a small part of the subject matter of biology. Issues of cell movement, cellular communication, organ formation, and organism behavior are, despite initial skepticism, rapidly becoming part of the frontier to which molecular biology is contributing. The use of monoclonal antibody probes to trace the growth and movement of individual identified leach neurons by McKay and co-workers points to the identification of surface proteins which mediate cell-to-cell interactions guiding the neurons to the cells to which they will make connections. **The chapter by Nirenberg *et al*. provides**

insight into the mechanism of synapse formation itself. McAllister *et al*. deal with a similar theme although in this case the probe method is in situ nucleic acid hybridization. This study demonstrates migration of cells in the marine snail *Aplysia*, which produces an egg-laying hormone. These cells start from an embryonic site in the ectoderm of the body wall and then move to specific locations in the nervous system where they presumably stimulate egg production by secretion of the hormone.

Finally, attention should be drawn to the chapters by Palmiter *et al*. and by Caplan *et al*., which describe the introduction of genetic material into animals and plants, respectively. Methodology of this sort is necessary for the acid test of how a particular gene functions in its normal state (that is, integrated at the gene's normal chromosomal locus). What has been accomplished will need to be refined since current methods do not achieve correct positioning or gene copy number with any reliability. Even so, dramatic results have been obtained in some cases, such as the production of larger than normal mice.

The cross-section of basic research presented in Part II will, I hope, put into perspective the tremendous number of basic research applications that have been opened in all fields of biology, not just molecular biology, by the new technical developments. There is a special need to apply them with vigor in a whole range of fields by scientists who are not trained in molecular biology. In general, molecular biologists have been very good citizens in making techniques and materials available, and the contributions of companies that make restriction enzymes and other tools of quality available commercially should make it possible for more and more scientists to apply these methods in their respective fields. The techniques are basically simple and very well documented. I see no need for the molecular biologists themselves to take over, as some have feared. (Although as a practitioner I have been continually amazed at how expensive it can be to operate a laboratory engaged in gene cloning.) This is to underscore the need to preserve and enhance the money allocated to investigator-initiated basic research from all sources despite the temptation to aim for rapid reduction to practical applications.

To end on a philosophical point, the relative ease of DNA sequencing has had a quantitative effect on the way information is acquired in molecular biology and this had led to a qualitative difference in the way in which it is and will be used. At present the worldwide accomplishment in DNA sequence amounts to 2.3×10^6 base pairs, representing 2500 individual sequences. It is now becoming more or less routine to sequence completely the DNA of whole genetic entities ranging from single genes through multigene families to simple life forms such as viruses and phages. Currently the largest single DNA molecule to have been sequenced is the phage lambda genome (48502 base pairs). We are beginning to recognize that determination of the total genetic specification of more advanced life forms may be a possibility in the relatively near future. Extension of this principle to bacteria (genome size 5×10^6 base pairs)—the simplest free living forms—would require an increase of the worldwide technical effort by only a factor of 2. Some three orders of magnitude more would be needed to progress to the total human genome.

Acquisition of "total" genetic information about a life form adds a new philosophical dimension. In some sense the rest of biology becomes merely a matter of interpretation. One might wonder, given the total DNA sequence of *Escherichia coli* and a big enough computer, could one reconstruct what the organism looks like, what it lives on, what it could be poisoned by and how it behaves? Or will a biological "uncertainty principle" be discovered that would preclude such a development?

Part of our advance depends on whether the information obtained by specific experiments on function can provide general principles. By study of a finite sample of promoters will we be able to derive a rule to tell from a sequence whether it is a promoter and what its characteristics would be. Progress in this area is quite likely and could be extended in principle to all "sites." Progress will also be needed in prediction of secondary and tertiary structures of biological molecules including the proteins and their complexes with substrates. These structural problems have so far seemed beyond the capacity of most computing facilities. However, computer chess programs have already reached the level below the grand master. Perhaps the solution to the protein-folding problem is nearer than we think. Regardless of the particular outcomes of these endeavors, there will surely come some major changes in our perception of ourselves and our place in the universe.

22. Monoclonal Antibodies Reveal the Structural Basis of Antibody Diversity

Jean-Luc Teillaud, Catherine Desaymard, Angela M. Giusti
Barbara Haseltine, Roberta R. Pollock, Dale E. Yelton
Donald J. Zack, Matthew D. Scharff

Immunologists have studied antibodies for two quite different reasons. On the one hand, antibodies are the final products of an immune response that evolved to protect vertebrates from an environment filled with a seemingly infinite number of life-threatening infectious and toxic agents. An essential property of the immune response is its ability to generate enormous sequence diversity in antibody molecules: an individual can produce more than 10^8 different antibodies, each with a different amino acid sequence. To determine the genetic and molecular mechanisms responsible for this diversity, immunologists examine the primary structure of individual antibody molecules and the genes encoding them. On the other hand, scientists in many areas have recognized the usefulness of antibodies as reagents that can be used to identify, locate, and quantitate macromolecules in complex biological mixtures. However, the production of homogeneous antibodies that can be used as reagents for accurate and reproducible immunoassays has proved difficult.

The problem was to some extent solved when it was recognized that the disease multiple myeloma is a malignancy of antibody-forming cells. The large amount of paraprotein in the serum of patients or animals with this malignancy is a monoclonal antibody that is produced by a transformed antibody-forming cell growing in an uncontrolled fashion. Much of what we know about the structure of antibody molecules and the organization and structure of the immunoglobulin genes came from the analysis of myeloma immunoglobulins and cells. However, only a few of these myeloma proteins were found to react with known antigens and it was not possible to use myelomas to precisely dissect the enormous repertoire of antibodies or to harness the disease to produce homogeneous antibodies that would be useful serological reagents. Relatively large amounts of homogeneous antibodies could be produced by immunizing animals with some bacterial polysaccharides (*1*); small amounts of a wider variety of antibodies could be obtained by limiting dilution cloning of antibody-forming cells in the spleens of irradiated animals and subsequent analysis of fragments of such spleens in short-term culture (2). Both approaches provided important information but were limited in their usefulness.

A method for routinely producing large amounts of a wide variety of homogeneous antibodies was discovered in 1975 by Kohler and Milstein (3). These workers were using cultured mouse myeloma cells to study the regulation of immunoglobulin gene expression in somatic cell hybrids. By fusing cultured mouse myeloma cells to normal spleen cells from immunized mice, they were able to introduce individual antibody-forming cells into long-term tissue culture (3). Since immunization selectively increases the number of spleen cells producing antibody reactive with the immunizing antigen, a significant percentage of the hybrids, or hybridomas, were producing the desired antibody. Furthermore, the clonal progeny of each hybridoma synthesized monoclonal antibodies all with the same amino acid sequence. The hybridomas retained the malignant properties of the myeloma parent, causing tumors when injected into mice. The ascites fluid and serum of such tumor-bearing mice contained large amounts of the monoclonal antibody, making it possible to obtain ten to hundreds of milligrams of a desired antibody. The hybridoma cells could also be frozen and recovered at will and the exact same monoclonal antibody could be renewed when needed and was available indefinitely (3). Thus, Kohler and Milstein's discovery simultaneously satisfied the need for large amounts of chemically defined homogeneous antibodies that were easily renewable for immunoassays and allowed the immunologists to repeatedly sample the repertoire of cells making antibody against a particular antigen and to study the protein and nucleic acid structure of representatives of this repertoire. This has led to a better understanding of the genetic and molecular events responsible for antibody diversity.

Molecular Basis of Antibody Diversity and Specificity

Ever since it became obvious that antibodies specific for different antigens differed from each other in the amino acid sequence of their variable (V) region (Fig. 1), there have been debates about whether each individual animal inherited in its germ line all of the genes required to code for the many antibody molecules they would produce during their lifetime, or if they inherited only a few germ line genes which subsequently underwent somatic changes in their base sequence. Early studies by Weigert and Cohn and their colleagues on λ light chains produced by mouse myeloma cells suggested that somatic mutation played a major role in antibody diversity (4). Because very few λ chains are normally produced by mice, it was thought that there might be something peculiar about their genetic control. Even when Tonegawa and his colleagues (5) confirmed the findings of Weigert et al. by showing that there was only one germ line V region gene of λ1 light chains and that its sequence changed in myelomas producing variant λ chains, many immunologists were unwilling to generalize these findings to κ light chains and heavy (H) chains which were much more heterogeneous and abundant. However, evidence soon began to accumulate that somatic mutation also played a role in the generation of the sequence diversity of κ chains (6–9).

The genetic basis for the heterogeneity

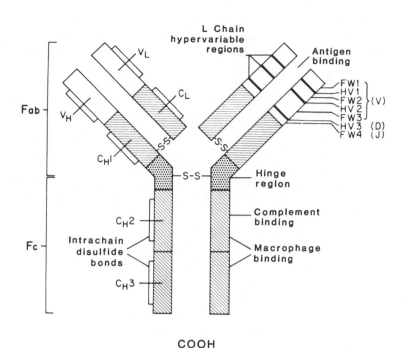

Fig. 1. The structure of an antibody molecule. The different parts of the heavy chain V region are indicated on the right and the segments of the gene which encode them are shown in parentheses.

of both light and heavy chains has now been elucidated by a large number of studies on the immunoglobulin genes. These studies have been recently reviewed (10). Briefly, they reveal that there are 100 to 300 V region genes which, in the case of the light chains, code for the first 95 amino acids of the V region including the first two hypervariable (HV) regions and their surrounding framework (FW) residues (Fig. 1). Each of these germ line V region genes can recombine with any of four functional joining (J) region minigenes to complete the V region of the protein (Fig. 1). In the case of heavy chains, there are also 100 to 300 V region germ line genes, which can associate to any of 12 or more D region minigenes which code for the third HV region, and any of four J minigenes which code for the remaining ami-

no acids in the V region (Fig. 1). These combinatorial rearrangements could generate many different antibody sequences from a limited amount of genetic material. Furthermore, in the course of the VDJ or VJ rearrangement, recombination may occur at different sites and bases are sometimes inserted or deleted, producing even further "junctional" sequence diversity in and around the third HV regions. This sequence diversity generated in the individual chains is further amplified by the fact that a given heavy chain can be expressed with any one of a number of different light chains.

The relative roles of the multiple germ line genes, DNA rearrangements, and junctional diversity in generating antibody diversity have yet to be determined. However, the analysis of even a small number of monoclonal antibodies specific for a few antigens has revealed that all of these events contribute to the specificity of antigen binding. Monoclonal antibodies that bind the hapten phosphocholine (PC) have the same heavy chain V and J but differ from each other in the third HV region which is coded for by D, suggesting that V and J region sequences are crucial for PC binding (*11*). Similarly, many of the antibodies produced by mice of the A/J strain against the hapten *p*-azophenylarsonate (Ars) share the same heavy chain V and J (*12, 13*). Monoclonal antibodies that contain the Ars-binding heavy chain V region but a different J do not bind Ars, indicating that the sequences in both V and J are important for the binding of this hapten. (*14*). Antibodies that bind dextran contain a few different heavy chain V and J regions and a D segment composed of two amino acids. The size of the D seems to be important in forming the dextran binding site and the sequence of the third hypervariable region may determine the fine specificity of antigen binding (*15*). In some cases a particular sort of junctional diversity seems to be required for antigen binding. For example, the light chains of the major family of antibodies to Ars all have an arginine in the first codon of J (*16*). This requires that recombination between V and J occur after the second base of the first triplet of J. A similar restricted recombination is found in the heavy chain of monoclonal antibodies against oxazolone (*17*). Finally, the pairing of certain heavy and light chain V regions determines antigen binding specificity.

Role of Somatic Mutation in

Antibody Diversity

At first it seemed that the availability of multiple germ line genes, gene rearrangements, and junctional diversity could provide all of the sequence diversity that existed. However, detailed analysis of families of PC- and Ars-binding monoclonal antibodies has already revealed that, just as with λ light chains, somatic mutation of both κ light and heavy chains also contributes significantly to the sequence diversity and affinity of antibody molecules. The importance of somatic mutation was established by examining the heavy and light chains of closely related families of PC- and Ars-binding monoclonals, each of which is coded for by a single germ line variable region gene. For example, Gearhart *et al.* have studied 11 immunoglobulin M (IgM) and 9 immunoglobulin G (IgG) monoclonal antibodies from BALB/c mice that react with PC (*11*). The heavy chain V regions of these antibodies are all very similar and are all rearranged to the J_H1 minigene. All of the IgM antibodies were identical in the NH_2-terminal sequence of their V regions. Further, they reflected the exact sequence of one of the four V region genes which form the T15 family of cross-hybridizing germ line genes in BALB/c mice. All of the IgG antibodies were products of the same germ line gene but contained one or at most a few amino acid substitutions in the HV region or FW residues. These changes were best explained by somatic mutation (*11, 18, 19*), although alternative genetic mechanisms such as gene conversion (*20*) have not been completely ruled out. Since IgM heavy chains are made early and IgG heavy chains later in B-cell differentiation, these studies suggested that the mechanism that produces base changes is either turned on during B-cell differentiation or that mutations accumulate during the expansion of B-cell clones.

Although there is considerable debate

about the latter point (*17, 21, 22*), studies on a few other families of monoclonal antibodies, each apparently derived from a single germ line gene, confirm that many antibodies are derived by a few base changes from the germ line sequence. For example, a number of workers have analyzed the CRI family (*23*) of monoclonal antibodies that react with the hapten Ars (*12, 13*). Just as with the T15 family, it has now been shown that many of these Ars-binding antibodies are derived from a single germ line heavy chain V region gene but differ from it by a few amino acid substitutions in the HV or FW parts of the V region. Since no two of the IgG PC-binding monoclonals analyzed by Gearhart *et al.* (*11*) were identical, and there are few repeats in the Ars (*12, 13*) and other systems that have been studied, there must be even more sequence diversity than was previously suspected. This has led to the suggestion that an individual makes 10^8 or more antibodies in a lifetime. Analysis of the types of base changes which occur in monoclonals does not reveal any significant predominance of transitions or transversions or of particular base changes (*6, 7, 11–13, 19*). Gearhart and Bogenhagen (*24*) reported that the base changes occur in clusters and suggest that an error-prone polymerase is involved.

While the ability to sample the repertoire of antibodies through the analysis of monoclonal antibodies can provide important insights, some questions are hard to answer with this approach. The monoclonals obtained are the product not only of B-cell differentiation but also of selection by antigen and by helper and suppressor T cells. It is likely that these immunoregulatory pressures select for variants with higher affinity than the germ line sequence. In fact all of the monoclonal antibodies shown by Gear-hart and Gefter and their colleagues to differ from the germ line sequences have higher affinities for hapten than the germ line antibodies (*25, 26*). Such selective pressures make it difficult to use monoclonal antibodies to determine the exact rate of instability of V region genes in vivo and to recover all of the progeny of the mutational or other processes that are occurring.

Another approach to these questions is to examine the molecular genetics of the immunoglobulin genes in cultured myeloma and hybridoma cells using the methods that have been so effectively exploited in bacterial genetics. This is quite feasible since we and others have developed techniques to identify somatic cell mutants of immunoglobulin-producing cell lines and have shown that such mutants are found in cultures at astonishingly high frequencies of 0.05 to 1 percent (*27*). Such cultured cell lines are clearly different from normal cells in that they carry a variety of viruses, grow continuously in culture, and can form tumors in animals. Information obtained from such cultured cells may or may not be relevant to normal events. However, the high rate of spontaneous mutation appears to be restricted to the immunoglobulin genes since other proteins such as thymidine kinase and hypoxanthine phosphoribosyl transferase undergo mutations at the expected frequencies of 10^{-6} to 10^{-7} (*27, 28*).

Our own studies have concentrated on the T15 heavy chain V region gene as it is expressed in the S107 myeloma cell line and in hybridomas. This is the same PC-binding V region that was studied in hybridomas by Gearhart *et al.* (*11*) and discussed above. It is an extremely well studied antibody because it is produced by many mouse myelomas and is the predominant heavy chain V region expressed in mice immunized with pneumococcal and other bacterial polysaccharides or with PC attached to protein carriers (*29*). The heavy and light chain V regions and the genes that code for the S107 (T15) V region have been completely sequenced (*18, 30, 31*) and the family of closely related germ line heavy chain V regions has also been studied (*18*). In addition, Davies and his colleagues have determined the three-dimensional structure of a related PC-binding antibody and identified the residues that contact the hapten and are essential for the conformation of the hapten binding site (*32*).

When S107 myeloma cells are cloned in soft agar and overlaid with antigen [PC attached to the protein keyhole limpet hemocyanin (PC-KLH)], the antibody secreted by the cells reacts with the antigen in the surrounding agar to form a visible antigen-antibody precipitate around the clones (*33, 34*) (Fig. 2). Clones that are not surrounded by a precipitate are presumptive mutants and are recovered from the agar and characterized. Those presumptive mutants that are producing antibody with a changed ability to bind antigen are considered mutants and are further characterized (*34–36*). The spontaneous frequency of such antigen-binding mutants is 0.05 to 1.0 percent. In the seven mutants analyzed thus far, the defect in antigen binding resides in the heavy chain (*34–36*). Figure 3 shows the amino acid sequences of the heavy chain V region of the parent and two such mutants. Both differ from the parental germ line sequence by only a single amino acid. In U_4, an alanine has replaced the glutamic acid at residue 35 and in U_1 an alanine has replaced the aspartic acid in the fifth residue of the J segment (*35, 36*).

The U_4 mutation is particularly interesting both with respect to the structural basis of antigen binding and the genetic

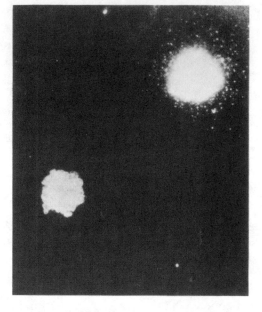

Fig. 2. Identification of antigen-binding mutants. Cells are cloned in soft agar and overlaid with antigen as described in (*34*). The clone on the right is surrounded by an antigen-antibody precipitate. The clone on the left is not surrounded by a visible precipitate and is a presumptive mutant.

expression of the T15 family of V region genes. Since the heavy chain has four residues that make contact with hapten and the light chain has one contact residue (*32*), it was surprising that the glutamic acid to alanine change at residue 35 resulted in an almost complete loss of antigen binding. However, the three-dimensional structure suggests that the hydrogen bond between the glutamic acid and the tyrosine at residue 94 of the light chain is important in stabilizing the conformation of the antigen binding site (*32*). This also explains why only this particular member of the T15 family of crosshybridizing heavy chain V region genes is found in PC-binding antibodies in BALB/c mice; none of the others code for a glutamic acid at residue 35 (*18*).

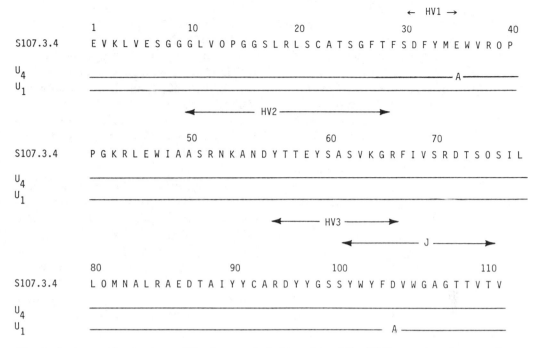

Fig. 3. Amino acid sequence of the heavy chain V region of the S107 parent and two antigen-binding mutants U_1 and U_4. The continuous line indicates sequence homology. The single letter code is used.

Finally, this is a product of the germ line gene which is "degenerate" in that it no longer binds PC. It is not clear whether it will react with another antigen or represents a sort of wastage. In any case, it is a product of the gene that would not be detected in screening for hybridomas that bind PC.

The high spontaneous frequency of antigen-binding mutants suggested a very high rate of base changes in the T15 V region gene in the S107 cultured cell line. In order to examine the exact rate of these events, we conducted a fluctuation analysis (28) to determine the rate at which the U_1 mutant (Fig. 3) reverts to higher antigen binding. The rate was 1.4×10^{-4} per cell per generation (37). A number of independent revertants (34), which bound antigen as well as the parent S107 antibody, are being analyzed and are true revertants in that they have both the amino acid and base sequence of the parent (37). This means that the mutation rate of U_1 is at least 10^{-4} per cell per generation for the fifth residue of J. It is interesting that a survey of myelomas expressing this same J_{H1} revealed a number of somatic mutations at the residue (38), suggesting that it may be unusually unstable. If all the 117 V region residues mutated at the same rate, the rate of mutation for the V region as a whole would be 10^{-2} per cell per generation.

Although the mechanism responsible for the high frequency of base changes both in vivo and in the cultured cells has not been determined, examination of the related V region sequences and of the various monoclonal antibodies suggests that simple recombination is not playing a role and that some sort of hypermutation mechanism is at work (12, 13, 19,

24). Rajewsky and his colleagues have been isolating somatic mutants in culture from a hybridoma that produces antibody against the hapten NP (4-hydroxy-3-nitrophenylacetyl) (39, 40). One of their mutants differs from the presumed germ line sequence by ten closely linked amino acids. This has led to the suggestion that it arose through the interaction of two closely related V region genes and that a gene conversion-like mechanism could play a role in generating antibody diversity (39, 40).

Monoclonal Antibodies to the

Variable Region

In the previous sections we have described how the analysis of closely related families of monoclonal antibodies has provided new insights into the structural basis of antigen binding and the molecular mechanism responsible for antibody diversity. Just as investigators in many areas of biology have used conventional antibodies to identify and quantitate the relatedness of different macromolecules, immunologists generated anti-antibodies that were specific for the variable regions of certain myeloma proteins, monoclonal antibodies, or normally occurring antibodies that reacted with a particular antigen. Such antibodies to the V region, or antibodies to the idiotype, were usually rendered specific by absorbing the antisera with immunoglobulins from unimmunized animals. It was in fact such conventional antibodies to the idiotypic determinants that made it possible to recognize and study the families of PC-, NP-, and Ars-binding antibodies described in the previous sections (41). When the hybridoma technology became available, immunologists wished to exploit the benefits of monoclonal

antibodies and began to generate monoclonal antibodies to the idiotypic determinants. This was usually done by immunizing mice with either monoclonal or myeloma immunoglobulins. The antigenic determinants recognized by monoclonal antibodies to the idiotype are called idiotopes. Some idiotopes are within the antigen binding site while others are located elsewhere on the V region. While it has become increasingly difficult to define the different types of antibodies to the idiotype (41), idiotopes that are coded for by the germ line V region gene are usually found in all mice that express that gene and are called public or cross-reactive. Idiotopes that are coded for by somatic mutations or rare junctional changes occur intermittently in individual mice and on one or a few monoclonals in a family and are said to be private (41).

The specificity of the interactions of monoclonal antibodies to the idiotype and monoclonal antibodies and myeloma proteins of known sequence illustrates both the benefits and complexities of trying to use such reagents to identify chemical relatedness. For example, Clevinger et al. (42) have studied the interaction of monoclonal antibodies with a number of monoclonal and myeloma immunoglobulins that react with $\alpha(1-3)$ dextran. Monoclonal antibodies were found that reacted with the two amino acids that are coded for by the D segment of the heavy chain. However, it is not possible to correlate the various amino acid substitutions that occur with reactivity with monoclonal antibodies to idiotypic determinants (42). Similar observations have been made for idiotype–anti-idiotype interactions in the NP and galactan binding systems (43). Other observations suggest the importance of conformation in forming the idiotopes recognized by some monoclonal antibodies to the idiotype. Morahan *et al.* (*44*) have described a monoclonal which reacts with the T-15 V region only when it is associated with the α constant region, that is, IgM or IgG antibodies with the same V region are not recognized by this monoclonal antibody.

We have studied a similar situation in which a monoclonal antibody only reacts with variants that have different amino acid sequences from the germ line. We have generated mouse monoclonal antibodies that react with the U_1 mutant of S107. As shown in Fig. 3, this mutant differs from the S107 heavy chain sequence by only a single amino acid at the fifth residue of J. These monoclonal antibodies react equally well with the U_4 mutant which has a single amino acid change at residue 35, and U_1 which has an amino acid substitution at residue 105 (Fig. 3), but do not react with the S107 parent (Fig. 4). The substitution at position 35 in U_4 is within the hapten binding site while the change at residue 105 in U_1 is probably at the entrance to the site (*32*). Since the antibodies to the mutant do not interfere with the binding of antigen to U_1, we believe that they are recognizing a conformational change that is distant from both substitutions but shared by both mutants. This idiotope is neither private nor public (see above) and illustrates the difficulty of using such definitions.

In spite of these problems, monoclonal antibodies to idiotypic determinants are being used extensively to study the expression and genetics of V region genes. Since it is impossible to sequence heterogeneous populations of antibodies or very large numbers of monoclonal antibodies, the determination of the frequency of rare antibodies or somatic variants in vivo or among monoclonal

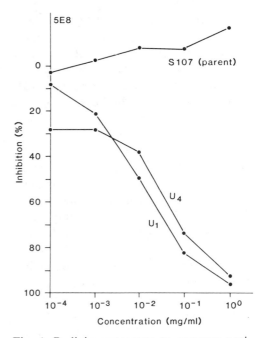

Fig. 4. Radioimmunoassay to compare antigen-binding mutants U_1 and U_4 with the S107 parent. The antimutant monoclonal antibody 5E8 was labeled with [S^{35}]methionine. Mutant immunoglobulin was adsorbed to polyvinyl microtiter wells. Labeled antimutant monoclonal antibody was added to each well in the presence of decreasing amounts of unlabeled mutant and parent proteins. Wells were washed and then counted.

antibodies will require serological analysis. This has been done with collections of monoclonal antibodies to idiotypes that recognize different public idiotopes encoded by the germ line sequence. Monoclonal antibodies that no longer react with one or a few of those antiidiotypic monoclonals are presumptive variants. Monoclonals that react with private idiotopes on somatic variants have been used to determine the frequency with which that variant appears in immunized animals (*41*). Such analyses are complicated by the fact that many of the idiotopes recognized by monoclonal antibodies require the interaction of both heavy and light chain V regions, so changes in either V region could cause the loss of the antigenic determinant (41). We have overcome this problem by immunizing rats with mouse immunoglobulins expressing the T15 germ line sequence and obtaining rat-mouse hybridomas (45). Four out of eight monoclonal antibodies reacted as well with free heavy chains, or heavy chains associated with an irrelevant light chain, as with the intact antibody indicating that they were recognizing heavy chain V region determinants. We have used these to examine a question discussed earlier, that is, do PC-binding IgM antibodies undergo somatic mutations in their V regions? So far, one of 70 IgM monoclonal antibodies does not react with one of the four heavy chain specific monoclonals (45). Preliminary DNA sequencing suggests that the amino acid sequence changes in this somatic variant are not due to changes in D or J (45).

Antibodies to idiotypic determinants have also been used to modulate the expression of antibodies expressing particular V regions in the intact animals. Such experiments were originally carried out with conventional antibodies made in other species with sometimes conflicting results. When mouse monoclonal antibodies to idiotypic determinants became available, they provided more useful reagents both because antibodies that recognized either public or private idiotypes could be used and syngeneic antibodies were being administered to mice. The results of these experiments have been reviewed (41) and there seem to be some generally accepted conclusions. When certain strains of mice are immunized with PC, Ars, NP, and presumably other haptens, the antibody response is usually dominated by a single idiotype which is coded for by a single heavy and light chain germ line gene. If newborn animals are injected with small amounts of antibody to the idiotype and then subsequently immunized with antigen, they no longer express the predominant idiotype but ultimately do make antibodies coded for by other germ line genes. In addition, if adult mice are injected with 10 to 100 nanograms of antibody to idiotype, increasing amounts of idiotype are expressed. However, the injection of 10 micrograms of antibody to the same idiotype suppresses the production of that idiotype in response to antigen, at least for a time (41). The mechanisms of these effects are not fully understood. However, they do provide a means to further analyze both the germ line repertoire and somatic mutation. For example, animals have been suppressed for the expression of a public idiotope and then analyzed for the production of antibodies that bear other idiotopes expressed by the germ line gene (46–48). Monoclonal antibodies generated from such mice can then be analyzed to determine if they are the product of different germ line genes or of somatic mutation of a single germ line gene (48).

Studies of the sort described above were originally complicated by results which suggested that the class of anti-idiotypic antibodies (that is, the structure of the constant region) determined whether suppression or enhancement occurred (41). However, Muller and Rajewsky (49) took an IgG_1 mouse monoclonal antibody to a particular idiotype and in culture derived from it a series of antibodies containing the exact same V region but other C regions of the IgG_{2b} and IgG_{2a} subclasses. These sets of antibodies to idiotypes were used to study suppression and enhancement, and it was shown that the subclass of the antibody was not important and that the earlier results were probably due to different affinities of the antibodies to idio-typic determinants used (*41*).

Generation of Tailor-Made Antibodies

The studies of Muller and Rajewsky (*49*), in which they generated somatic variants of a single monoclonal antibody in order to obtain a better set of serological reagents, point to another benefit of monoclonal antibodies that is beginning to be exploited. We have already discussed the instability of immunoglobulin genes in cultured myeloma and hybridoma cells. We and others had shown some years ago that mutations and recombinations in the constant region arise frequently in such cells (*27*). The changes observed include deletions, point mutations, and class and subclass switching. As it has become obvious that monoclonal antibodies will not only be used as research reagents but also for in vivo diagnosis and therapy, it has also become clear that we do not know enough about the kinds of properties that will make antibodies most effective in passive immunization against infectious agents and toxins, and for targeting radioactive or cytotoxic agents to tumors. The ability to generate mutant monoclonal antibodies with changes in their constant region sequence provides an oppor-tunity not only to learn more about the structural basis of the effector functions of antibodies but also to learn how to tailor-make monoclonal antibodies that will be more effective serological reagents (*27, 50, 51*).

The techniques for isolating such mutants have been reviewed (*27*). In our own studies we use the same immunoplate assay described earlier (Fig. 2), except that the clones are overlaid with antibodies that react with particular parts of the constant region (*51*). Mutants that are not surrounded by a visible antigen-antibody precipitate are screened for the production of antigen-binding antibodies and then characterized to determine the structural changes in the antibody and its impact on effector functions.

We have recently described a set of mutants of an Ars-monoclonal (Ar13.4) with deletions in the C_H2 and C_H3 (see Fig. 1) domains of their constant regions (*51*). Some of these results are summarized in Table 1. These mutants confirm the role of sequences in both the C_H2 and C_H3 domains for binding to the immunoglobulin (Fc) receptors of macrophages, of the C_H2 domain for the fixation of complement, and of the C_H3 domain for the assembly of heavy chains

Table 1. Structural and functional characteristics of Ar13.4 mutant monoclonal antibodies. The size of the heavy chains was measured on unglycosylated proteins synthesized in the presence of tunicamycin. Complement fixation was measured with H_2L_2 molecules of ArM1 and ArM2.

Cell line	H chain size (kd)	Domain predominately affected	Assembly		Binding to Fc receptor	Fixation to complement
			H_2L_2 (%)	HL (%)		
Ar13.4	55		100	0	+	+
ArM1	39	C_H3	27	73	−	+
ArM2	41	C_H3	18	83	−	+
ArM16	39	C_H2	100	0	−	−
ArM20	39	C_H2	100	0	−	−

to form H_2L_2 molecules. It is clear that further refinements of this approach should make it possible to identify the amino acid residues responsible for these functions and to obtain a variety of mutant reagents that can be used to explore the types of structures that should be constructed, probably by the recombinant DNA technology, for in vivo diagnosis and therapy.

References and Notes

1. E. Haber, *Fed. Proc. Fed. Am. Soc. Exp. Biol.* **29**, 66 (1970).
2. N. R. Klinman, *J. Immunol.* **106**, 1345 (1971).
3. G. Kohler and C. Milstein, *Nature (London)* **256**, 495 (1975).
4. M. G. Weigert, I. M. Cesari, S. Yonkovich, M. Cohn, *ibid.* **228**, 1045 (1970).
5. O. Bernard, N. Hozumi, S. Tonegawa, *Cell* **15**, 1133 (1978).
6. E. Selsing and U. Storb, *ibid.* **25**, 47 (1981).
7. M. Pech, J. Hechtl, H. Schnell, H. G. Zachau, *Nature (London)* **291**, 668 (1981).
8. M. Weigert, L. Gatamaitan, E. Loh, J. Schilling, L. Hood, *ibid.* **276**, 785 (1978).
9. D. J. McKean, M. Bell, M. Potter, *Proc. Natl. Acad. Sci. U.S.A.* **75**, 3913 (1978).
10. S. Tonegawa, *Nature (London)* **302**, 575 (1983).
11. P. J. Gearhart, N. D. Johnson, R. Douglas, L. Hood, *ibid.* **291**, 29 (1981).
12. E. C. B. Milner and J. D. Capra, *Mol. Immunol.* **20**, 39 (1983).
13. M. Sieckevitz, S. Y. Huang, M. L. Gefter, *Eur. J. Immunol.* **13**, 123 (1983).
14. M. H. Margolies, L. J. Wysocki, V. L. Sato, *J. Immunol.* **130**, 515 (1983).
15. B. Newman *et al.*, *J. Exp. Med.* **157**, 130 (1983).
16. M. Siegelman and J. D. Capra, *Proc. Natl. Acad. Sci. U.S.A.* **78**, 7679 (1981).
17. M. Kaartinen, G. M. Griffith, A. F. Markam, C. Milstein, *Nature (London)* **304**, 320 (1983).
18. S. Crews, J. Griffin, H. Huang, K. Calame, L. Hood, *Cell* **25**, 59 (1981).
19. S. Kim, M. Davis, E. Sinn, D. Patten, L. Hood, *ibid.* **27**, 573 (1981).
20. D. Baltimore, *ibid.* **24**, 592 (1981).
21. J. A. Owen, N. H. Sigal, N. R. Klinman, *Nature (London)* **295**, 347 (1982).
22. J. Rocca-Serra *et al.*, *J. Immunol.* **129**, 2554 (1982).
23. A. Nisonoff, S.-T. Ju, F. L. Owen, *Immunol. Rev.* **34**, 89 (1977).
24. P. Gearhart and D. F. Bogenhagen, *Proc. Natl. Acad. Sci. U.S.A.* **80**, 3439 (1983).
25. J. D. Rodwell, P. J. Gearhart, F. Karush, *J. Immunol* **130**, 313 (1983).
26. T. L. Rothstein and M. L. Gefter, *Mol. Immunol.* **20**, 161 (1983).
27. S. L. Morrison and M. D. Scharff, *CRC Crit. Rev. Immunol.* **3**, 1 (1981).
28. R. Baumal, B. Birshtein, P. Coffino, M. D. Scharff, *Science* **182**, 164 (1973).
29. H. Kohler, *Transplant. Rev.* **27**, 24 (1975).
30. S. Rudikoff and M. Potter, *Proc. Natl. Acad. Sci. U.S.A.* **73**, 2109 (1976).
31. S. P. Kwan, S. Rudikoff, J. G. Seidman, P. Leder, M. D. Scharff, *J. Exp. Med.* **153**, 1366 (1981).
32. D. R. Davies and H. Metzger, *Annu. Rev. Immunol.* **1**, 87 (1983).
33. P. Coffino, R. Baumal, R. Laskov, M. D. Scharff, *J. Cell. Physiol.* **79**, 429 (1972).
34. W. D. Cook and M. D. Scharff, *Proc. Natl. Acad. Sci. U.S.A.* **74**, 5687 (1977).
35. W. D. Cook, S. Rudikoff, A. Giusti, M. D. Scharff, *ibid.* **79**, 1240 (1982).
36. S. Rudikoff, A. M. Giusti, W. D. Cook, M. D. Scharff, *ibid.*, p. 1979.
37. D. Zack, A. Giusti, M. D. Scharff, in preparation.
38. N. Gough and O. Bernard, *Proc. Natl. Acad. Sci. U.S.A.* **78**, 509 (1981).
39. M. Bruggemann, A. Radbruch, K. Rajewsky, *EMBO J.* **1**, 629 (1982).
40. R. Dildrop, M. Bruggemann, A. Radbruch, K. Rajewsky, K. Beyreuther, *ibid.*, p. 635.
41. K. Rajewsky and T. Takemuri, *Annu. Rev. Immunol.* **1**, 569 (1983).
42. B. Clevinger, J. Thomas, J. M. Davie, J. Schilling, M. Bond, L. Hood, J. Kearney, in *ICN-UCLA Symposia on Cellular and Molecular Biology*, C. Janeway, E. E. Sercarz, H. Wigzell, C. F. Fox, Eds. (Academic Press, New York, 1981), vol. 20, p. 159.
43. M. Pawlita, E. B. Mushinski, R. J. Feldman, M. Potter, *J. Exp. Med.* **154**, 1946 (1981).
44. G. Morahan, C. Berek, J. F. A. P. Miller, *Nature (London)* **301**, 720 (1983).
45. C. Desaymard, A. Giusti, M. D. Scharff, *Mol. Immunol.*, in press.
46. T. L. Rothstein, M. M. Margolies, M. L. Gefter, A. Marshak-rothstein, *J. Exp. Med.* **157**, 795 (1982).
47. J. F. Kearney, R. Barletta, S. Quan, S. Quintans, *Eur. J. Immunol.* **11**, 877 (1981).
48. H. P. Kocher, C. Berek, M. H. Schreer, H. Cosenza, J-C. Jaton, *ibid.* **10**, 258 (1980).
49. C. Muller and K. Rajewsky, *J. Immunol.* **131**, 877 (1983).
50. D. E. Yelton *et al.*, in *From Gene to Protein: Translation into Biotechnology*, F. Ahmad, J. Schultz, E. E. Smith, W. J. Whelan, Eds. (Academic Press, New York, 1982), vol. 20, p. 129.
51. D. E. Yelton and M. D. Scharff, *J. Exp. Med.* **156**, 1131 (1982).
52. Portions of the work described here were supported by grants from the National Institutes of Health (AI05231 and AI10702), National Science Foundation (PCM81-08642), and American Cancer Society (IM-317B). J.-L.T. is supported by a fellowship from the French Minister of Research and Industry, C.D. is a chargé de recherche (INSERM) on leave and supported in part by a Fogarty International Fellowship, A.M.G. is supported by a fellowship from the Golodetz Foundation, R.R.P. was supported by the Damon Runyon Foundation and is currently a fellow of the Arthritis Foundation, and D.E.Y. and D.Z. are medical scientist trainees supported by the NIGMS (5T32GM7288).

23. Genes of the Major Histocompatibility Complex in Mouse and Man

Michael Steinmetz and Leroy E. Hood

In the past 3 years fundamental new insights into the structure, organization, and evolution of the genes of the major histocompatibility complex (MHC) in mouse and man have resulted from the cloning and characterization of these genes. The molecules encoded by the MHC genes play a critical role in the rejection of organ transplants and the control of the immune response. The molecular mechanisms of these functions are being studied by means of DNA-mediated gene transfer into cells and embryos.

Major Histocompatibility
Complex in Mouse and Man

Three families of genes. The MHC appears to be present in all vertebrates. Because there are allelic forms of the genes of the MHC it has been possible to produce alloantisera that identify the gene products of three families of MHC genes in mouse and man (*1*). These three families are denoted class I, class II, and class III. The class I and class II molecules, typified by transplantation antigens and the Ia (I-region associated) antigens, respectively, are integral membrane proteins involved in the recognition reactions that permit the immune system to distinguish between self and nonself. The class III family encodes several components in the activation pathway of complement and will not be discussed further.

Serological analyses of recombinant MHC chromosomes in mice and man have been used to construct genetic maps for the murine and human MHC's (Fig. 1). The MHC, also known as the H-2 complex, is located on chromosome 17 and spans about 2 centimorgans of DNA which corresponds to approximately 4000 kilobase pairs (kbp) of DNA. The complex is divided into six regions called K, I, S, D, Qa, and Tla. The classical H-2 complex comprises the genes of the K through the D regions and encodes the class I transplantation antigens K, D, and L, the class II and the class III molecules. At least three molecules, denoted Qa-1, Qa-2, and TL, which are structurally closely related to the class I transplantation antigens are encoded by genes located to the right of the H-2 complex (*2*). The two categories of class I molecules are distinguished by their tissue distributions in that the transplantation antigens are present on virtually

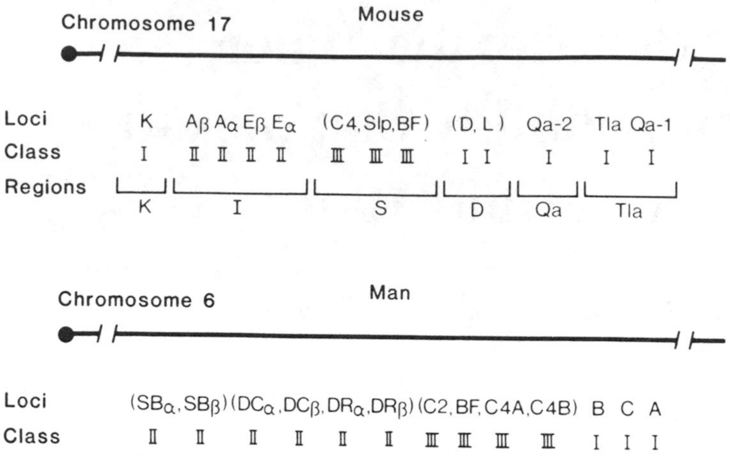

Chromosome 17   Mouse

Loci	K	Aβ Aα Eβ Eα	(C4,Slp,BF)	(D, L)	Qa-2	Tla Qa-1
Class	I	II II II II	III III III	I I	I	I I
Regions	K	I	S	D	Qa	Tla

Chromosome 6   Man

Loci	(SBα, SBβ)	(DCα, DCβ, DRα, DRβ)	(C2, BF, C4A, C4B)	B	C	A
Class	II II	II II II II	II III III III III	I	I	I

Fig. 1. Genetic maps of the mouse and human major histocompatibility complexes. The order of loci given in brackets is not known. The centromere is located to the left. For other explanations see text.

all somatic cells of the mouse, whereas the Qa antigens are preferentially expressed on B cells and T cells and the TL antigen on thymocytes and certain leukemia cells. The two categories are furthermore distinguished by the fact that the genes encoding transplantation antigens are extremely polymorphic with more than 50 different alleles present at the K and at the D loci, whereas the Qa and TL antigens are much less polymorphic. In addition, alleles at the K and D loci are very different from each other, whereas Tla alleles appear to be much more homologous (3). Individual alleles are denoted by a capital letter for the gene and a superscript for the H-2 genotype (also called haplotype) of the inbred strain, for example, the K^d and D^d genes of the BALB/c mouse. Two distinct types of Ia molecules, I-A and I-E, have been identified. The Ia molecules have limited tissue distribution—primarily on B cells, macrophages, and T cells. The Ia molecules also exhibit extensive serological polymorphisms.

The human MHC, also referred to as the HLA complex, is contained on chromosome 6 and encompasses about 3 centimorgans of DNA extending perhaps over 6000 kbp of DNA. The human class I genes differ from their mouse counterparts in genetic organization in that the A, B, and C genes are contiguous to one another, whereas in the mouse the K gene is separated from the other class I genes by the class II and class III gene families (Fig. 1). Possible human homologs to the mouse Qa and TL antigens have been characterized serologically and biochemically but their genes have not yet been mapped (4). Three distinct types of human class II molecules have been described which are designated DR, DC, and SB (5).

Class I and class II molecules. Structures of the class I and class II molecules are similar (Fig. 2) (6, 7). The class I polypeptide contains three external domains, each about 90 residues in length, a transmembrane region, and a cytoplasmic domain. The third external domain is noncovalently associated with β_2-microglobulin, a small polypeptide that shows homology to the constant region domains of immunoglobulins and is not encoded in the MHC. The class II molecules are composed of two noncovalently associated polypeptide chains, denoted α and β, both of which are encoded in

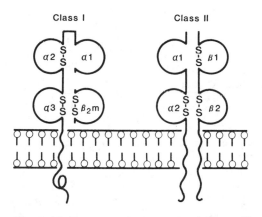

Fig. 2. Structures of class I and class II molecules. These models emphasize the structural homologies between class I and class II molecules. *S-S* indicates disulfide bridges in external domains of class I and class II molecules and β_2-microglobulin (β_2m).

the MHC. Each of these polypeptides has two external domains that are of similar size as for class I molecules, a transmembrane region, and a small cytoplasmic domain.

Functions of class I and class II molecules. Transplantation antigens restrict the recognition of foreign antigens by cytotoxic T cells (8). For example, when cells of mouse or man are infected with a virus, foreign viral antigens often are expressed on the cell surface. In order for cytotoxic T cells to destroy these infected cells, the T-cell receptor must interact with the foreign antigen and with a transplantation antigen. Thus the T cell recognizes the viral antigen in the context of a particular transplantation antigen, a process called H-2 restriction. Cells expressing the same viral antigen but a different transplantation antigen will not be killed by the same cytotoxic T cells. The functions of the Qa and TL antigens are unknown.

The class II molecules also function as restricting elements, but for regulatory T cells, which have the capacity to help or suppress a cellular or humoral immune response against foreign antigens (9). As we shall see subsequently, the isolation of class I and class II genes has given us the tools to begin to dissect the interactions between the restricting element, the foreign antigen, and the T-cell receptor.

Class I Genes

Structure. Class I complementary DNA (cDNA) clones were isolated by hybrid selection, primer extension, and cross-hybridization with cDNA's from a different species (6). The class I cDNA's then were used to screen genomic libraries constructed in lambda and cosmid vectors. The typical structure of a mouse class I gene is given in Fig. 3. All mouse class I genes that have been completely sequenced [K^b (*10*), K^d (*11*), K^k (*12*), L^d (*13*, *14*), and the Qa gene 27.1 (*15*)] are split into eight exons. The exons correlate with the structural domains of the transplantation antigen. The first exon encodes the leader or signal peptide; exons 2, 3, and 4 encode the three external domains; exon 5 encodes the transmembrane region; and exons 6, 7, and 8 encode the cytoplasmic domain. At least three different patterns of RNA splicing occur at the 3' end of mouse class I genes (*6*, *11*). First, for the L^d gene the last intron is 139 base pairs (bp) long and is located between positions 1 and 2 of the last sense codon. Second, for the K^d and K^b genes the acceptor splice site in this intron is located 27 nucleotides upstream from the site used for L^d. Third, a cDNA clone, pH-2II, has been isolated which derives from a class I messenger RNA (mRNA) that has retained this last intron entirely.

306

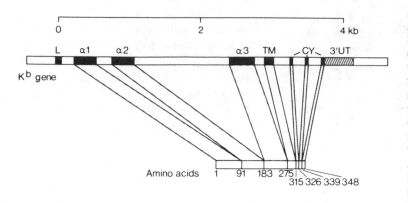

Fig. 3. H-2K^b gene structure (*10*). Exons are shown as closed boxes and labeled *L* (leader or signal peptide), *α1*, *α2*, *α3* (the three external domains), *TM* (transmembrane domain), *CY* (cytoplasmic domain), *3'UT* (3' untranslated region). Amino acid numbers refer to the location of introns in the K^b gene.

The class I proteins encoded by these differentially spliced mRNA's will therefore differ at their carboxyl terminals. It is not known whether a single class I gene can also be spliced in two or more alternative ways. In this regard, it is interesting that the two human class I genes analyzed to date have the same exon-intron organization as the mouse genes but contain only two cytoplasmic exons (*16*).

Organization. Compared to the limited number of class I molecules identified serologically, it was surprising to find that the mouse contains about 40 class I genes. Thirty-six distinct class I genes have been isolated from a cosmid library constructed from DNA of the inbred BALB/c mouse strain (*17*). These genes have been ordered into 12 class I gene clusters which range in size from 40 to 215 kbp of DNA and contain between one and eight class I genes (*18*). A similar screen of a C57Bl/10 cosmid library has yielded seven clusters ranging in size from 40 to 120 kb with a total of about 20 class I genes (*19*). From a comparison of genomes examined by the Southern blotting technique it is unlikely that there is a twofold difference in class I genes between BALB/c and C57Bl/10 mice.

Congenic mice, a series of inbred strains with different MHC's superimposed on the same genetic background, and recombinant congenic mice, obtained from intra-MHC recombinant strains, have permitted the class I gene clusters to be assigned to one of the four MHC regions, K, D, Qa, and Tla, which encode class I molecules (Fig. 4). By using single- or low-copy probes from each of the gene clusters, restriction enzyme site polymorphisms could be identified in various inbred strains and correlated with corresponding serologic polymorphisms for the four regions in recombinant congenic mice (*19, 20*). Four significant observations emerged from this analysis. First, all 36 class I genes isolated from BALB/c DNA map to the MHC of the mouse (*20*). This is surprising because most other multigenic families have pseudogenes that have been translocated to other chromosomal regions. Second, only 5 of the 36 class I genes from BALB/c and only 3 from the 20 class I genes from C57Bl/10 map to the H-2 complex of the MHC (*19, 20*). Indeed, it is likely that only three of the five BALB/c genes and only two of the three C57Bl/10 genes are functional as restricting elements. In contrast, 31 of

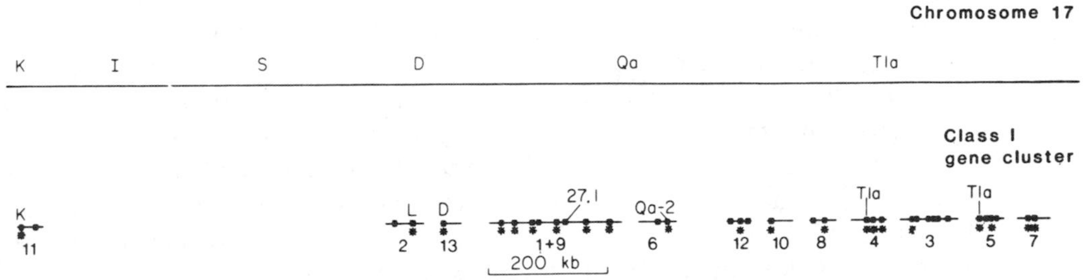

Fig. 4. The location of 36 class I genes in the MHC of the BALB/c mouse (*17, 20*). Regions of the MHC are shown with the class I gene clusters (labeled 1 to 13) that have been mapped to them. Clusters 1 and 9 have recently been shown to overlap (*18*). Clusters 5 and 12 map either to the Qa or Tla region. Class I genes (squares) encoding serologically defined molecules are labeled accordingly; those that encode molecules which associate with β_2-microglobulins at the cell surface are indicated by asterisks. 27.1 is a class I gene that has been sequenced and mapped into the Qa region (*15*).

the 36 BALB/c genes and 17 of the 20 C57Bl/10 genes map to the Qa and Tla regions and hence the vast majority of the class I genes are located distal to the classical H-2 complex.

Third, a great deal of polymorphism in the flanking regions has been noted in the three BALB/c gene clusters contained in the H-2 complex, whereas very little polymorphism has been noted in these sequences in nine BALB/c gene clusters contained in the Qa and Tla regions (*20*). This restriction site polymorphism in the flanking sequences of class I genes correlates with the corresponding sequence diversity and the polymorphism of the genes contained in these respective gene clusters. It also explains why only limited differences are seen when different haplotypes are compared by Southern blot analysis with class I probes. Since most of the class I genes detected map to the Qa and Tla regions which show limited sequence variability, it appears that the restriction enzyme site polymorphism is primarily generated by just the five class I genes mapping to the H-2 complex. Thus, the MHC contains areas that show high sequence divergence and other areas that

are more conserved. This will be an important point in the discussion of the I region genes. Fourth, the single- and low-copy probes from the BALB/c gene clusters have been used to count homologous fragments in the DNA's from various inbred strains of mice (*20*). These types of analyses suggest that the number of fragments detected can vary by approximately 25 percent, thus suggesting that in various inbred strains of mice the corresponding class I genes may expand or contract in number, presumably by unequal crossing-over. Most of the expansion or contraction appears to occur in the Qa and Tla regions.

Although much less information is available about the organization of class I genes in humans, it is generally concluded from Southern blot analyses as well as from cloning studies that humans have 20 to 40 class I genes. Of these, only two genes have been completely sequenced, both of which appear to be pseudogenes (*16*). Well-characterized human recombinants together with their parental haplotypes are not available, but x-ray–induced deletion mutants which have lost various portions of the HLA complex on chromosome 6 have been used for the mapping of the human genes. In fact, a recent analysis of such a deletion mutant with class I DNA probes has shown that some human class I genes map distal to the A locus to a region corresponding to the mouse Qa and Tla regions (21).

Polymorphic restriction fragments analyzed by Southern blots and correlated with certain HLA genes can be used for HLA typing (22). In addition, polymorphic restriction sites will allow us to study the association between HLA type and susceptibility to certain diseases.

Expression. DNA-mediated gene transfer of class I genes into cells of a different genetic background has permitted the identification of most of the serologically defined gene products using specific monoclonal antibodies. Thus, the K^b (23), K^{bm1} (24), K^d (25), K^k (12), D^b (19), D^d (25, 26), L^d (25, 26), Qa-2 (25), and two Tla genes (25) have been identified. Moreover, the observation that the concentrations of endogenously expressed transplantation antigens in mouse L cells remain approximately the same before and after class I gene transfer permitted the use of an assay for cell-surface β_2-microglobulin to determine whether class I gene products for which there are no available serologic reagents were being expressed (25). It appears that at least 15 unidentified class I genes in the BALB/c mouse can be expressed and thus may increase levels of β_2-microglobulin upon transfer into mouse L cells. All 15 of these novel genes are found in the Qa and Tla regions (Fig. 4). Thus, there may be a large number of class I antigens that are perhaps, like the Qa and TL antigens, preferentially expressed on distinct subsets of lymphocytes and indeed in the future these gene products may be useful in identifying functional subsets of lymphocytes. Sev-

eral laboratories are now in the process of preparing specific antisera to the novel gene products in order to determine their patterns of expression. Other class I genes that do not increase levels of β_2-microglobulin on the cell surface might encode secreted (27), cytoplasmic, or pseudo class I molecules.

Human class I genes have also been transfected into mouse L cells and successfully expressed in association with mouse β_2-microglobulin. These analyses have permitted the A2, A3, B7, B40, and CW3 class I genes to be identified (28).

Generation of diversity. Protein and DNA sequence analyses of alleles of the transplantation antigens have demonstrated that most of the sequence variation between alleles occurs in the first and second external domains (6). The variation found within these two polymorphic domains between alleles is up to 20 percent at the amino acid sequence level. Within these domains there appear to be at least three regions (positions 62 to 83, 92 to 121, and 135 to 157) that are "hypervariable" (Fig. 5A). The functional implications of these allelic differences are unknown.

The origin of this diversity is unknown. An ideal system for analyzing mechanisms for generating diversity is that of the mutant transplantation antigens at the K locus of the b haplotype mouse. A series of 12 K^b mutants has been analyzed biochemically with several surprising results (29). First, seven of the mutants exhibit multiple amino acid substitutions rather than the single residue substitutions so characteristic of other mutant proteins such as hemoglobin and cytochrome c. Second, these multiple substitutions are generally tightly clustered in a single location. Third, several independently derived but identical mutants have been observed. Recently, the K^{bm1} mutant gene has been analyzed at the DNA level (24). The striking observation is that the mutant gene is identical to its wild-type counterpart, apart from seven nucleotide substitutions which occur within a span of 13 bases (Fig. 5B). Furthermore, it has been shown that there is a distinct class I gene in the Qa region of the b haplotype that contains the mutant sequence at the same place where it is identical in sequence to K^{bm1} over a stretch of 51 nucleotides (30). Presumably this second gene interacted with the K^b gene through a gene conversion event to generate the bm1 mutant gene. Thus, it is attractive to speculate that a fundamental mechanism for rapidly generating the extensive variability characteristic of class I alleles is gene conversion from one class I gene to a second in the gene family. The many class I genes located in the Qa and Tla regions therefore might constitute a reservoir of donor sequences that can be used to alter the class I genes of the K and D loci. Such unidirectional gene conversion events affecting short DNA sequences (smaller than 50 bp) could indeed generate a large number of different class I sequences (31). It will be interesting to determine whether gene conversion is a fundamental mechanism for the diversification of other multigene families as well.

Function. Virus-specific cytotoxic T cells can be generated that recognize cells that have been infected with different viruses. These killer T cells can then be used to analyze class I restricting elements in mouse L cells transformed with various cloned class I genes and infected with the appropriate virus. With killer T cells prepared against lymphocytic choriomeningitis virus (LCMV), vesicular stomatitis virus (VSV), or influenza virus and mouse L cells trans-

formed individually with cloned class I genes, several interesting observations have been made. First, only the L^d gene product works as a restricting element in LCMV infections (32). The same is true for the VSV infection (33). In contrast, with influenza virus infection it appears that in BALB/c mice both the K^d and L^d (34) and in C57B1/10 mice both the K^b and D^b molecules (35) function as restricting elements. Second, exon shuffling experiments, in which hybrid genes were constructed between the L^d and D^d genes, have led to the conclusion that only the first or second (or both) external domains participate in the restricted recognition of antigen by the T-cell receptor. This is true for virus-specific cytotoxic T cells, directed against LCMV (36), VSV (36, 37), and influenza virus (34), and allospecific cytotoxic T lymphocytes (36, 37). In contrast, some allospecific antibodies will also recognize the third external domain (36, 38). Third, in LCMV or VSV infections the L^d molecule may have its cytoplasmic domain deleted or altered and still be capable of functioning as a restriction element in T cell–mediated cytotoxic killing (39). It appears therefore that the cytoplasmic domain does not serve as an important binding site for viral cell-surface antigens (at least in the system described above) and that it is not required for the lysis of the cell. The function of the cytoplasmic domain of the class I molecules remains uncertain.

Recombination. Truncated or partial class I genes can be introduced into mouse L cells by DNA-mediated gene transfer generating hybrid genes with the frequency of one to a few percent of that of a transfection by intact class I genes, presumably by double recombination or gene conversion (40). A series of truncated L^d genes has been constructed. From

virtually any starting combination of exons, class I antigens could be expressed containing the L^d serological determinants provided that the exon encoding the second external domain was present. The observation that truncated genes may be reconstituted in the class I gene family stands in striking contrast to the efforts to reconstitute partial genes in a variety of other examples. The question arises as to whether the ability to reconstitute truncated genes is unique to the class I gene family, is a property of most complex multigene families, or is in fact a feature of all eukaryotic genes and could be detected with appropriately sensitive assay systems. If indeed the last explanation is correct, insertion of particular genes into specific regions of the eukaryotic chromosome may be possible. Efforts are now under way to characterize the hybrid class I genes and their products to see what types of mechanisms are compatible with their generation. Recently, the reconstitution of truncated genes was confirmed with human class I genes (41).

Class II Genes

Structure. Techniques similar to those described for the class I genes have been used to isolate class II cDNA's (6). These cDNA's have been used to screen genomic libraries for the isolation of class II genes.

The DNA sequences are known for the mouse A_α^d (42), A_α^k (43), A_β^d (44, 45), A_β^k (44), A_β^b (44, 46), E_α^d (47), E_α^k (48), and E_β^d (49) genes as well as for the human DC_α (50), DC_β (51), DR_α (52), and DR_β (53) genes. Sequence comparisons demonstrate that the human DR genes are analogous to the mouse I-E genes and the human DC genes are the counterparts to the mouse I-A genes. So far the mouse homologs to the human SB genes have not been identified, although the SB_β gene appears to cross-hybridize best with the mouse $E_{\beta 2}$ gene described in the next section (54).

The mouse E_α and the human DR_α genes are split into five exons, whereas the mouse A_β and E_β genes are split into six exons (Fig. 6). As for the class I genes, there is a correlation between exon-intron organization and domain structure of the class II genes and proteins. The structural difference between the α and β genes occurs at the 3' end: α genes have only one intervening sequence in the 3' untranslated region whereas the A_β and E_β genes show two intervening sequences located in the cytoplasmic region but no intervening se-

Fig. 5. (A) Sequence diversity between mouse and human class I alleles. Amino acid sequences are compared between the H-2K^b (10) and H-2K^d (11) antigens, between the H-2D^b (63) and H-2L^d (13) antigens which are presumably encoded by alleles (6), between the HLA-A2 and HLA-A28 antigens (64), and between the HLA-B7 and HLA-B40 antigens (65). Solid lines indicate identity to the first sequence in a group of alleles; the dot indicates a deleted residue; asterisks correspond to nonassigned positions; and arrows mark the locations of introns in the K^b gene. The portion of the molecules that appears to span the membrane is indicated by vertical lines. The single-letter code has been used for amino acids: A, alanine; C, cysteine; D, aspartic acid; E, glutamic acid; F, phenylalanine; G, glycine; H, histidine; I, isoleucine; K, lysine; L, leucine; M, methionine; N, asparagine; P, proline; Q, glutamine; R, arginine; S, serine; T, threonine; V, valine; W, tryptophan; Y, tyrosine; Z, glutamic acid or glutamine. (B) Comparison of the K^b and K^{bm1} nucleotide sequences (24). The K^{bm1} sequence is identical to the K^b sequence except for seven nucleotides in the second external domain.

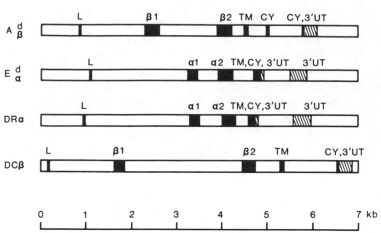

Fig. 6. Exon-intron organization of the mouse A_β^d and E_α^d and the human DR_α and DC_β genes. The mouse E_β gene has the same exon-intron organization as the A_β gene. *L*, signal or leader peptide; *α1*, *α2*, *β1*, *β2*, external domains; *TM*, transmembrane domain; *CY*, cytoplasmic domain; *3′UT*, 3′ untranslated region.

quence in the 3′ untranslated region. It is interesting that the DC_β gene—the human homolog to the mouse A_β gene—has lost exon 5 encoding part of the cytoplasmic domain probably because of a nonfunctional splice acceptor site (*51*). Mouse and human class I and class II genes show similar structural variations at their 3′ ends. It is not clear whether these changes are important for different effector functions of the molecules and for distinct interactions with cytoskeletal proteins or whether they simply reflect evolutionary variations of a nonfunctional carboxyl terminus.

Organization. The organization of the class II genes in the I region of the BALB/c mouse has been studied by chromosomal "walking" procedures (*55*). In brief, a DR_α cDNA clone was used to isolate four overlapping cosmid clones containing the homologous mouse E_α gene. Restriction fragments free of repetitive DNA sequences were then isolated from the ends of the cloned region and were used to screen the cosmid library a second time to obtain additional clones at either end of this region. This process was then carried out repeatedly and led to the isolation of about 270 kb of

DNA from the I region of the BALB/c mouse (Fig. 7). All of the serologically defined class II genes of the mouse are contained within this region—E_α and E_β as well as A_α and A_β. In addition, two more class II genes were found, $A_{\beta 2}$ and $E_{\beta 2}$. The $A_{\beta 2}$ gene appears to be a single isolated exon (*46*) and accordingly might be a pseudogene, although it has not been ruled out that the missing coding sequences are located further upstream and downstream but are only distantly related to the class II sequences cloned so far. Northern blot hybridization experiments with the DNA sequences around the $A_{\beta 2}$ gene should clarify this point. The $E_{\beta 2}$ gene appears to be a similar situation.

The α and β genes have opposite orientations to one another. This suggests that the β-β-α group was an evolutionary subunit which duplicated once in the case of the mouse to give the I-A and I-E subregion genes and perhaps twice in the case of humans to give the DR, DC, and SB sets of genes. It should be pointed out that the organization of the class II genes in a second mouse strain, the AKR mouse, from which this region has been cloned (*55*), is the same as that of the

BALB/c mouse.

The organization of the human class II α and β genes is not known to the same extent as in the mouse. It is currently believed that there are five or six genes (one DR_α, three or four DC_α-related, and one SB_α) and seven β genes (three DR_β, two DC_β, and two SB_β) (53, 56).

The I-J paradox. The I-J subregion has been mapped by serological analyses of intra-I region recombinant strains to a position between the I-A and I-E subregions (Fig. 7). The I-J subregion is of functional interest because it appears to encode I-J polypeptides which are subunits of T cell suppressor factors. However, a molecular analysis of this region suggests that the I-J polypeptides probably are not encoded here.

Comparison of the molecular map of the I region of the mouse with the genetic map has confirmed the location of A_α and A_β genes in the I-A subregion and the location of the E_α gene in the I-E subregion (Fig. 7). The E_β gene, however, is located with its 5′ end in the I-A subregion and with its 3′ end in the I-E subregion. A region of 2 kb which spans part of the long intervening sequence between exons β1 and β2 and part of the β2 exon has so far not been assigned to either the I-A or I-E subregion (57). In theory, this region could encode the antigenic determinants of the I-J polypeptide. Serological analyses of a suppressor factor secreted by suppressor T cells specific for lactate dehydrogenase B has revealed the presence of E_β and I-J determinants on the same polypeptide chain suggesting that the I-J polypeptide is encoded by a differentially spliced E_β mRNA (58). Northern blot experiments, however, carried out under highly sensitive conditions, have failed to identify RNA transcripts from the E_β gene region in a variety of I-J positive suppressor T cells (59). DNA sequence analysis of the E_β gene region in intra-I region recombinant mouse strains which encode serologically distinguishable I-J polypeptide

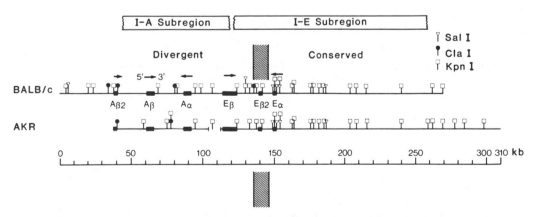

Fig. 7. Organization of the class II genes in the I region of BALB/c and AKR mice (55). The vertical bar shows the approximate location of a breakpoint between two regions of high and low restriction enzyme site variability. The gap in the AKR map indicates a region that is not represented in the isolated cosmid clones. The cloned portion of the I region has so far not been linked to the K region to the left and the S region to the right. The recombination separating the I-A from the I-E subregion has occurred in the middle of the E_β gene (see text). Note that in our previous map (55) a portion of the restriction map was inadvertently exchanged between the BALB/c and AKR mouse.

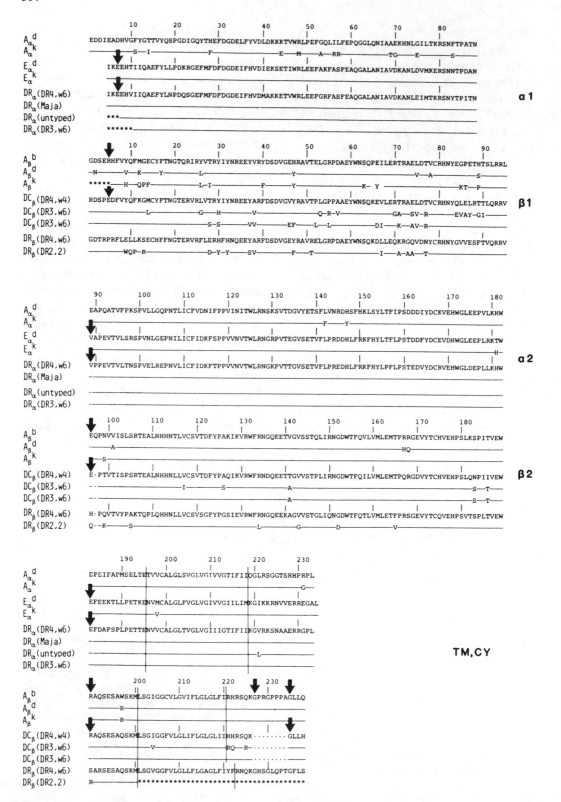

chains will help to resolve the I-J paradox. Such analyses are now under way.

Expression. Mouse and human class II genes have been introduced into mouse L cells and successfully expressed at the cytoplasmic and cell-surface levels (*60*). A third polypeptide, denoted the invariant (Ii) chain, has been found associated with class II polypeptides in the cytoplasm and has been postulated to be involved in the transport of class II polypeptides from the cytoplasm to the cell surface (*61*). It is unlikely that this hypothesis is correct because mouse L cells express very little of the invariant chain compared to B cells where class II genes are normally expressed. L cells transformed with human class II genes have been isolated which express as much human Ia antigens on the cell surface as B cells. Furthermore, co-transfer of mouse class II genes and the gene for the invariant chain into mouse L cells does not increase the relatively low cell-surface concentration of Ia antigens on the surface of some transformed cells although the Ii gene is transcribed at high levels. Recently, cell-surface expression levels in mouse L cells comparable to those seen in mouse B cells have been obtained with the transformed A_α and A_β genes (*60*). These transformed L cells also are capable of presenting antigen to T–helper cell hybridomas (*60*). The successful expression of class II genes after gene transfer will now permit dissection of the function of Ia antigens by mutagenesis in vitro.

Polymorphism. Serological, biochemical, and more recently DNA sequence analyses have shown that the mouse A_α, A_β, and E_β genes and the human DC_α, DC_β, and DR_β genes are polymorphic, whereas the mouse E_α and the human homolog, DR_α, are conserved (*7*). Sequence comparisons reveal that the alleles of polymorphic class II loci—like those for class I alleles—are very different from each other (Fig. 8). These differences are mainly found in the $\alpha1$ and $\beta1$ domains (10 to 23 percent sequence divergence at the protein level) whereas the $\alpha2$, $\beta2$, transmembrane, and cytoplasmic domains are conserved. Especially interesting is the observation that the transmembrane domain between the mouse A_α and E_α chains (*43*), the human DC_α and DR_α chains (*50*), and the DC_β and DR_β chains (*53*) are more conserved than the Ig-like $\alpha2$ and $\beta2$ domains (Fig. 8). The opposite appears to be true for class I genes (Fig. 5A) (*6*). Perhaps the transmembrane region of class II molecules is conserved because it exerts important molecular interactions, either between the α and β chains or with other transmembrane proteins (*7, 50*).

Comparison of the restriction maps of the I region from two mouse inbred strains (BALB/c and AKR) has revealed that the allelic variability of the A_α, A_β, and E_β loci correlates with restriction site differences in this region whereas the restriction map around the conserved E_α locus shows very little variation between the two strains (Fig. 7). Southern blot

Fig. 8. Sequence diversity between mouse and human class II alleles. Amino acid sequences are compared between the A_α^d (*42*) and A_α^k (*43*) alleles; between the E_α^d (*47*) and E_α^k (*48*) alleles; between four DR_α alleles from a DR4,w6 B cell line, Maja cells, an untyped individual, and a DR3,w6 B cell line (*52*); between the A_β^b (*44, 46*), A_β^d (*44, 45*), and A_β^k (*44*) alleles; between three DC_β alleles, one from a DR4,w4 homozygous individual and two from a DR3,w6 B cell line (*51*); and between two DR_β alleles from a DR4,w6 (*53*) and a DR2,2 (*66*) B cell line. Location of introns (arrows) are indicated where known. For explanations of other symbols see legend to Fig. 5.

analyses of other inbred strains confirm that the I region can be split into areas of high and low restriction site variability (55). Taken together with the variability of restriction sites around class I genes (20), it appears that the MHC can be divided into chromosomal domains that are highly divergent (K region, I-A subregion, D region) and chromosomal domains that are relatively conserved (I-E subregion, Qa, and Tla regions) (62). Increased frequencies of mutation in certain chromosomal areas therefore appear to have contributed to the exceptional diversity of the class I, K, and D alleles and the alleles of the class II A_β, A_α, and E_β loci. As discussed above, a mechanism for diversifying coding regions in class I genes appears to be gene conversion. Whether gene conversion events are also important for diversifying class II genes is not clear.

An analysis of the nine intra-I region recombinants has demonstrated that all nine recombination events have occurred within a distance of 8 kb or less at the E_β gene locus (55). This hot spot of recombination correlates approximately with the boundary between the conserved and divergent domains (Fig. 7). One wonders whether there is a connection between the propensity for recombination in this region and the transition from a conserved to a variable chromosomal domain. Perhaps certain aspects of chromosomal structure can promote or suppress the genetic mechanisms responsible for generating sequence diversity and focus recombination to a confined region on the chromosome.

Evolution of MHC Genes

The external domains closest to the cell membrane of the class I and class II molecules are homologous to one another, to β_2-microglobulin, and to the constant region domains of immunoglobulins (6). These homologies suggest that the genes encoding the class I, class II, β_2-microglobulin, and antibody gene families were derived from a common ancestor. One wonders whether additional gene families encoding cell-surface antigens will be discovered that also show homology to the genes of the MHC and the immunoglobulins. It is possible that the genes encoding the T-cell receptor molecules are also members of this supergene family.

References and Notes

1. J. Klein, *Biology of the Mouse Histocompatibility-2 Complex* (Springer-Verlag, New York, 1975); *Science* **203**, 516 (1979); G. D. Snell, J. Dausset, S. Nathenson, *Histocompatibility* (Academic Press, New York, 1976).
2. L. Flaherty, in *The Role of the Major Histocompatibility Complex in Immunology*, M. E. Dorf, Ed. (Garland, New York, 1981), p. 33; M. J. Soloski, J. W. Uhr, L. Flaherty, E. S. Vitetta, *J. Exp. Med.* **153**, 1080 (1981); J. Michaelson *et al.*, *Transplant. Proc.*, in press.
3. K. Yokoyama, E. Stockert, L. J. Old, S. Nathenson, *Proc. Natl. Acad. Sci. U.S.A.* **78**, 7078 (1981).
4. T. Cotner, H. Mashimo, P. C. Kung, G. Goldstein, J. L. Strominger, *ibid.*, p. 3858; C. Terhorst *et al.*, *Cell* **23**, 771 (1981).
5. D. A. Shackelford, J. F. Kaufman, A. J. Korman, J. L. Strominger, *Immunol. Rev.* **66**, 133 (1982); R. Tosi, N. Tanigaki, D. Centis, G. B. Ferrara, D. Pressman, *J. Exp. Med.* **148**, 1592 (1978); C. K. Hurley, S. Shaw, L. Nadler, S. Schlossman, J. D. Capra, *ibid.* **156**, 1557 (1982).
6. L. Hood, M. Steinmetz, B. Malissen, *Annu. Rev. Immunol.* **1**, 529 (1982).
7. J. F. Kaufman, C. Auffray, A. J. Korman, D. A. Shackelford, J. L. Strominger, *Cell*, in press.
8. R. M. Zinkernagel and P. C. Doherty, *Adv. Immunol.* **27**, 51 (1980).
9. Z. Nagy, C. N. Baxevanis, N. Ishii, J. Klein, *Immunol. Rev.* **60**, 59 (1981).
10. E. Weiss *et al.*, *EMBO J.* **2**, 453 (1983).
11. S. Kvist, L. Roberts, B. Dobberstein, *ibid.*, p. 245.
12. S. Kvist, personal communication.
13. K. W. Moore, B. T. Sher, Y. H. Sun, K. A. Eakle, L. Hood, *Science* **215**, 679 (1982).
14. G. A. Evans, D. H. Margulies, R. D. Camerini-Otero, K. Ozato, J. G. Seidman, *Proc. Natl. Acad. Sci. U.S.A.* **79**, 1994 (1982).
15. M. Steinmetz *et al.*, *Cell* **25**, 683 (1981).

16. M. Malissen, B. Malissen, B. R. Jordan, *Proc. Natl. Acad. Sci. U.S.A.* **79**, 893 (1982); P. A. Biro, J. Pan, A. K. Sood, R. Kole, V. B. Reddy, S. M. Weissman, *Cold Spring Harbor Symp. Quant. Biol.* **47**, 1082 (1982).
17. M. Steinmetz, A. Winoto, K. Minard, L. Hood, *Cell* **28**, 489 (1982).
18. In the original paper (*17*) 13 class I gene clusters were identified. Recently it was shown by J. Rogers and K. R. Willison [*Nature (London)* **304**, 549 (1983)] that clusters 1 and 9 overlap.
19. R. A. Flavell *et al.*, *Cold Spring Harbor Symp. Quant. Biol.* **47**, 1067 (1982).
20. A. Winoto, M. Steinmetz, L. Hood, *Proc. Natl. Acad. Sci. U.S.A.* **80**, 3425 (1983).
21. H. T. Orr and R. DeMars, *Nature (London)* **302**, 534 (1983).
22. H. M. Cann, L. Ascanio, P. Paul, A. Marcadet, J. D. Dausset, D. Cohen, *Proc. Natl. Acad. Sci. U.S.A.* **80**, 1665 (1983).
23. A. L. Mellor *et al.*, *Nature (London)* **298**, 529 (1982).
24. E. H. Weiss *et al.*, *ibid.* **301**, 671 (1983); D. H. Schulze *et al.*, *Proc. Natl. Acad. Sci. U.S.A.* **80**, 2007 (1983).
25. R. S. Goodenow, M. McMillan, M. Nicolson, B. T. Sher, K. Eakle, N. Davidson, L. Hood, *Nature (London)* **300**, 231 (1982).
26. D. H. Margulies *et al.*, *J. Immunol.* **130**, 463 (1983).
27. M. Kress, D. Cosman, G. Khoury, G. Jay, *Cell* **34**, 189 (1983).
28. J. A. Barbosa, M. E. Kamarck, P. A. Biro, S. M. Weissman, F. H. Ruddle, *Proc. Natl. Acad. Sci. U.S.A.* **79**, 6327 (1982); F. A. Lemonnier *et al.*, *Immunogenetics* **18**, 65 (1983).
29. R. Nairn, K. Yamaga, S. G. Nathenson, *Annu. Rev. Genet.* **14**, 241 (1980); L. R. Pease, D. H. Schulze, G. M. Pfaffenbach, S. G. Nathenson, *Proc. Natl. Acad. Sci. U.S.A.* **80**, 242 (1983).
30. R. A. Flavell, personal communication.
31. F. Brégère, *Biochimie* **65**, 229 (1983).
32. A. Örn *et al.*, *Nature (London)* **297**, 415 (1982).
33. J. Forman, R. S. Goodenow, L. Hood, R. Ciavarra, *J. Exp. Med.* **157**, 1261 (1983).
34. C. Reiss, G. A. Evans, D. H. Margulies, J. G. Seidman, S. J. Burakoff, *Proc. Natl. Acad. Sci. U.S.A.* **80**, 2709 (1983).
35. A. R. M. Townsend, P. M. Taylor, A. L. Mellor, B. A. Askonas, *Immunogenetics* **17**, 283 (1983).
36. I. Stroynowski *et al.*, in preparation.
37. K. Ozato, G. A. Evans, B. Shykind, D. H. Margulies, J. G. Seidman, *Proc. Natl. Acad. Sci. U.S.A.* **80**, 2040 (1983).
38. G. A. Evans, D. H. Margulies, B. Shykind, J. G. Seidman, K. Ozato, *Nature (London)* **300**, 755 (1982).
39. M. C. Zuniga, B. Malissen, M. McMillan, P. R. Brayton, S. S. Clark, J. Forman, L. Hood, *Cell*, in press.
40. R. S. Goodenow, I. Stroynowski, M. McMillan, M. Nicolson, K. Eakle, B. T. Sher, N. Davidson, L. Hood, *Nature (London)* **301**, 388 (1983).
41. S. M. Weissman and P. Lingell, personal communication.
42. M. M. Davis, D. I. Cohen, E. A. Nielsen, M. Steinmetz, W. E. Paul, L. Hood, *Proc. Natl. Acad. Sci. U.S.A.*, in press.
43. C. O. Benoist, D. J. Mathis, M. R. Kanter, V. E. Williams II, H. O. McDevitt, *ibid.* **80**, 534

(1983).
44. E. Choi, K. McIntyre, R. N. Germain, J. G. Seidman, *Science* **221**, 283 (1983).
45. M. Malissen, T. Hunkapiller, L. Hood, *ibid.*, p. 750.
46. D. Larhammar *et al.*, *Cell*, in press.
47. J. McNicholas, M. Steinmetz, T. Hunkapiller, P. Jones, L. Hood, *Science* **218**, 1229 (1982); J. J. Hyldig-Nielsen *et al.*, *Nucleic Acids Res.* **11**, 5055 (1983).
48. D. J. Mathis, C. O. Benoist, V. E. Williams II, M. R. Kanter, H. McDevitt, *Cell* **32**, 745 (1983).
49. H. Saito, R. A. Maki, L. K. Clayton, S. Tonegawa, *Proc. Natl. Acad. Sci. U.S.A.*, in press.
50. C. Auffray, A. Korman, M. Roux-Dosseto, R. Bono, J. L. Strominger, *ibid.* **79**, 6337 (1982).
51. D. Larhammar *et al.*, *ibid.*, in press; D. Larhammar *et al.*, *Hum. Immunol.*, in press; D. Larhammar *et al.*, *Proc. Natl. Acad. Sci. U.S.A.* **79**, 3687 (1982).
52. D. Larhammar *et al.*, *Cell* **30**, 153 (1982); J. S. Lee *et al.*, *Nature (London)* **299**, 750 (1983); A. J. Korman, C. Auffray, A. Schamboeck, J. L. Strominger, *Proc. Natl. Acad. Sci. U.S.A.* **79**, 6013 (1982); H. K. Das, S. K. Lawrence, S. M. Weissman, *ibid.* **80**, 3543 (1983).
53. E. O. Long, C. T. Wake, J. Gorski, B. Mach, *EMBO J.* **2**, 389 (1983).
54. B. Mach, personal communication.
55. M. Steinmetz *et al.*, *EMBO J.* **300**, 35 (1982); M. Steinmetz *et al.*, unpublished results.
56. C. Auffray, J. Kuo, R. DeMars, J. L. Strominger, *Nature (London)* **304**, 174 (1983); E. O. Long and B. Mach, personal communication.
57. J. A. Kobori, A. Winoto, E. Gibb, L. Hood, J. McNicholas, *Mol. Cell. Immunol.*, in press.
58. Z. Ikezawa *et al.*, *Proc. Natl. Acad. Sci. U.S.A.*, in press.
59. M. Kronenberg *et al.*, *ibid.*, in press.
60. B. Malissen, M. Steinmetz, M. McMillan, M. Pierres, L. Hood, *Nature (London)*, in press; C. Rabourdin-Combe and B. Mach, *ibid.* **303**, 670 (1983); B. Malissen *et al.*, in preparation.
61. S. Kvist, K. Wiman, L. Claesson, P. A. Peterson, B. Dobberstein, *Cell* **29**, 61 (1982).
62. For a discussion of the I-B and I-C subregions, see J. Klein, F. Figueroa, Z. A. Nagy, *Annu. Rev. Immunol.* **1**, 119 (1983).
63. A. A. Reyes, M. Schöld, R. B. Wallace, *Immunogenetics* **16**, 1 (1982); W. L. Maloy and J. E. Coligan, *ibid.*, p. 11.
64. J. A. Lòpez de Castro, J. L. Strominger, D. M. Strong, H. T. Orr, *Proc. Natl. Acad. Sci. U.S.A.* **79**, 3813 (1983).
65. J. A. Lòpez de Castro, R. Bragado, D. M. Strong, J. L. Strominger, *Biochemistry* **22**, 3961 (1983).
66. H. Kratzin *et al.*, *Hoppe-Seyler's Z. Physiol. Chem.* **362**, 1665 (1981).
67. We thank R. Flavell, S. Kvist, P. Lingell, E. Long, B. Mach, and S. Weissman for communication of unpublished results; J. Kaufman, D. Larhammar, J. Lòpez de Castro, R. Maki, J. Michaelson, and Z. Nagy for preprints; and G. Farmer, J. Kaufman, J. Kobori, and S. Nathenson for comments on the manuscript. This work was supported in part by grants from the National Institutes of Health. The Basel Institute for Immunology was founded and is supported by F. Hoffmann–La Roche Limited Company, Basel, Switzerland.

24. Studying Promoters and Terminators by Gene Fusion

Martin Rosenberg, Ana B. Chepelinsky, Keith McKenney

Gene fusion techniques have proved extremely useful in the study of prokaryotic gene regulation (*1–10*). These techniques have depended on the genetic fusion of an assayable, selectable gene function into the operon of interest. The fusion places the gene under the transcriptional control of that operon, thereby allowing study of the operon's regulatory information. Although genetic fusions have expanded our knowledge of operon control elements, these techniques have limitations. More recently, the concept of gene fusion has been combined with recombinant technology for the study of transcriptional regulatory elements (*11–15*). DNA fragments containing specific transcription control regions are fused in vitro to a gene function that can be readily assayed and genetically selected. This is best done in a recombinant vector system designed and constructed to circumvent the limitations inherent in the conventional genetic fusion systems so that gene regulatory elements can be studied in new ways.

We earlier described a recombinant vector system developed to isolate, compare, and characterize almost any promoter or terminator signal recognized by the *Escherichia coli* RNA polymerase (*14, 15*). In this system the *E. coli* galactokinase gene (*galK*) provides the as-

sayable, selectable function to which transcription regulatory signals are fused. There is a simple, sensitive assay for galactokinase and its expression can be made either essential or lethal to cells under the appropriate growth conditions (that is, *galK* can be selected either for or against). This dual selection system for studying gene regulatory elements utilizes plasmid, phage, and bacterial vectors, and it provides flexibility in that any construction made in the multicopy plasmid vector system can be moved to the phage vector or selectively into the bacterial chromosome. This allows regulatory signals to be studied either in single- or multicopy and in either the episomal or chromosomal state. The system is being used to study various prokaryotic regulatory signals (*16–26*). We recently expanded the application of the *galK* fusion system to study eukaryotic gene control elements in yeast (*27, 28*) and in higher cell systems (*15, 29–31*).

In this chapter, we describe several applications of our *galK* fusion vector system to the study of prokaryotic promoters and terminators. We show how the system can be used to characterize promoter signals created by mutation, to select and functionally characterize mutations that inactivate promotion, and to isolate and characterize mutations in transcription termination signals. These studies emphasize the utility of the fusion vector system for quantitative assessment of regulatory signal function both in vivo and in vitro. Other aspects of prokaryotic transcriptional regulatory signal structure and function have been reviewed (*32–35*).

Promoters Created by Mutation

The plasmid vector system, pKO, was used for isolating and studying promoters (Fig. 1A). Details of the design and construction of this vector system have been described (*14, 15, 36*). The *E. coli galK* gene is inserted into the vector in such a manner that it is not expressed (that is, not transcribed). Thus, the pKO plasmids will not complement a bacterial host cell deficient in *galK* expression (*galK⁻*). DNA fragments are inserted into the vector at any of the restriction enzyme sites (R sites) that have been engineered into the vector upstream from *galK* (Fig. 1A). Insertion of a promoter signal in proper orientation results in *galK* expression (Fig. 1B). This expression is readily seen either by selective growth in the appropriate media or in color indicator plates (Table 1). Moreover, the precise levels of expression are monitored by *galK* enzyme assay. Various natural promoter signals have been isolated, compared, and characterized with this vector system (Table 1) (*14, 15, 36*). In this section we describe the cloning and characterization of three promoter signals created by mutation from DNA sequences that previously had no promoter function.

Promoter P₄₈₂. The first such promoter was isolated from a λ transducing phage, λ482, which carries a portion of the *E. coli* galactose operon fused to phage sequences (*37*). This particular

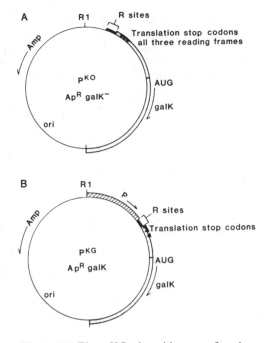

Fig. 1. (A) The pKO plasmid vector for cloning promoters. The stipled area represents the galactokinase gene (*galK*) and 168 base pairs of "leader" preceding the AUG initiation signal of *galK*. Translation stop codons were engineered into all three reading frames preventing any translation originating in the cloned insert from reaching the *galK* translation initiation signal (*14, 36*). Various restriction endonuclease sites (*R*) can be used to insert DNA fragments. There now exist at least ten pKO derivatives, which differ only in the number and types of restriction sites placed at this position. Ap^R denotes the β-lactamase gene, which provides a second selectable marker on all pKO derivatives. The replication origin (*ori*) was derived from pBR322. (B) The pKG plasmid vector for cloning terminators. This vector contains a promoter (*P*) positioned upstream from *galK*. Transcription termination sites are inserted between *P* and *galK* by means of the restriction sites (*R*) provided. All other designations are as in (A) above.

fusion was generated within the bacterial chromosome by deleting sequences between the *gal* operon and an integrated copy of the phage. The deletion [25 kilo-

Table 1. Promoters in pKO. The construction of the vectors is described in detail in the text and in (*14*), (*15*), (*36*), and (*44*). Hosts used were *E. coli* N100 (*galK⁻*; *recA⁻*) and *E. coli* S165; other appropriate *galK⁻* and *gal⁻* hosts are described in (*14*) and (*44*). Media are described in detail in (*14*) and (*45*). Activity units for *galK* are expressed as nanomoles of galactose phosphorylated per minute per milliliter of cells, with $A_{650} = 1$ (*14*). Symbols: +, growth; −, no growth; N.D., not done.

Plasmid	*galK⁻* Host in		*gal⁻* Host in LB + galactose	*galK* Activity
	Indicator	Minimal medium		
pKO	White	−	+ +	10
pKO-482	Red	+	+ −	120
pKM-1	White	−	+ +	10
pKO-*c*17	Red	+	−	350
pKM-2	White	−	+ +	10
pKO-*cin*	Red	+	−	700
pKO-*gal*	Red	+	−	650
pKO-*lac*	Red	+	−	500
pKO-*tet*	Red	+	−	550
pKO-SV40	Red	+	−	220
pKO-SV40M1	N.D.	N.D.	+	88
pKO-SV40M2	N.D.	N.D.	+	85
pKO-SV40M3	N.D.	N.D.	+	75

bases (kb)] fused sequences of the λN gene to sequences in the middle of the *gal* transferase gene (*galT*). Upon cloning DNA fragments derived from the λ482 phage into the pKO vector, we repeatedly found a small fragment (0.5 kb) that activated *galK* expression and that was derived from the fusion region. This was unexpected since no promoters were known to be located in this region. The promoter activity of this fragment, called P_{482}, was measured in vivo and compared to a variety of other pKO constructions carrying either natural or mutant promoter signals (Table 1). P_{482} is a relatively weak signal in vivo, functioning at only 20 percent of the efficiency of the more typical bacterial operon promoters such as the *lac* and *gal* promoters.

In order to position precisely the P_{482} signal on the 0.5-kb fragment, we carried out transcription studies in vitro using plasmid DNA as template. The template was cut at an appropriate restriction enzyme site positioned downstream from the P_{482} region and "run-off" transcripts labeled with ^{32}P were generated in standard transcription reactions (Fig. 2). The RNA products were resolved on polyacrylamide gels, eluted from the gel, and further analyzed by standard two-dimensional T_1-oligonucleotide analysis (not shown) (*38*). The results indicate that only a single transcription start occurs on the λ482 fragment, and this start site

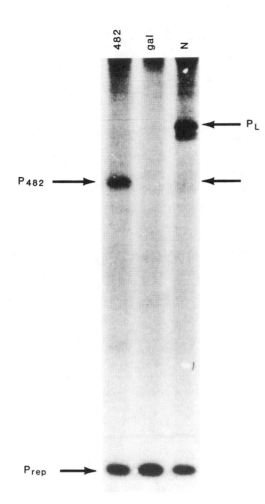

Fig. 2. Autoradiogram of a polyacrylamide gel fractionation of ^{32}P-labeled RNA synthesized in vitro from DNA templates containing the P_{482} promoter region (482), and the corresponding regions of the wild-type galT gene (gal) and the wild-type λN gene (N). Each DNA template was linearized by restriction enzyme digestion and then transcribed in vitro by standard procedures (39). The P_{482} runoff transcript is 250 bases in length and was identified by two-dimensional T_1-oligonucleotide fingerprint analysis (38). If the corresponding galT gene sequence of the λN gene sequence promoted transcription, then similarly sized RNA transcripts would have been obtained. No such RNA's were observed (←). The 110-base RNA from the P_{rep} promoter (58) serves as an internal standard and size marker. Also shown is the 320-nucleotide runoff transcript initiated from the phage λ promoter, P_L, which also occurs on the vector carrying the N gene sequence.

can be unambiguously positioned at the A residue shown in Fig. 3A. This start defines the P_{482} promoter and demonstrates that the promoter region spans the fusion junction between the λN sequence and the galT sequence. Comparison of the λ482 sequence with the corresponding regions of λ+ and the gal operon (Fig. 3A) indicates that the 25-kb deletion that generated P_{482} occurred by homologous recombination in an identical 8–base pair (bp) sequence shared by the λN gene and the galT gene. The λ482 fusion junction retains this 8-bp sequence with λN gene sequences on one side and galT sequences on the other.

The P_{482} start site occurs within the λN gene sequence adjacent to the fusion junction.

Prokaryotic promoters generally exhibit two regions of strong sequence homology, positioned 10 bp and 35 bp upstream from the transcription start site (the −10 and −35 regions, respectively) (32–34). Various tests have shown that the sequences in these regions and the conserved distance between them (17 bp) are important for promoter function (32, 33). The −10 region of P_{482} is derived from the λN gene sequence and exhibits perfect homology to the consensus sequence of the −10 region hexamer

322

Fig. 3. Promoters created by mutation. (A) DNA sequence of the P_{482} promoter region derived from the λ482 phage (see text for details). Also shown are the DNA sequences of the corresponding regions of the N gene of phage λ (λN) and the *E. coli galT* gene. The P_{482} transcription start is indicated (arrow), as is the −10 region sequence (stipled). That part of the P_{482} sequence which is in common with the N gene is overlined,

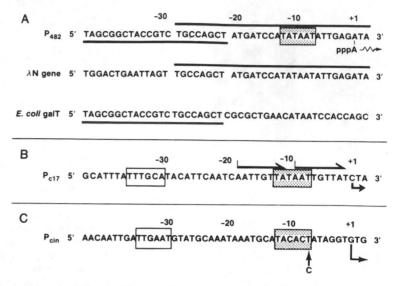

and that part which is in common with *galT* is underlined. An 8-bp homology is shared by all three sequences. The P_{482} promoter was created by a 25-kb deletion resulting from a homologous recombination event that occurred between this identical 8-bp sequence in N and *galT*. (B) DNA sequence of the P_{c17} promoter region derived from the λ*c*17 phage (*39*). The transcription start site and the −10 region and −35 region consensus sequences are indicated. Also shown is the 9-bp duplication (→) that creates the −10 region sequence at the junction of the repeat. (C) DNA sequence of the P_{cin} promoter region derived from the λ*cin* phage (*39, 40*). The base change from C to T, which creates this promoter, is indicated. All other designations are as indicated above. The symbols for the nucleic acids are A, adenine; C, cytosine; G, guanine; and T, thymine.

of *E. coli* promoters. In contrast, the −35 region of P_{482} is derived from the *galT* sequence and exhibits some—although rather poor—homology to the −35 hexamer consensus sequence. Apparently, the 25-kb deletion created the P_{482} promoter by fusing the −10 and −35 region sequences together at a distance appropriate to achieve promoter function. The rather poor efficiency of this promoter probably reflects the lack of a good −35 region recognition sequence for RNA polymerase.

We also examined the ability of the corresponding regions of the λ+ N gene and the *E. coli galT* gene, separately, to exhibit promoter function. Transcription experiments (Fig. 2) and RNA polymer-

ase filter binding assays (not shown) indicated that these regions had no promoter function. In particular, the N gene sequence (Fig. 3A) is identical with P_{482} up to position −28 of the promoter region. Thus, P_{482} and N share the same consensus −10 region sequence and the same potential start-site information. It must be the −35 region sequence of P_{482}, supplied by *galT*, which selectively allows P_{482} (and not N) to function as a promoter. Comparison of the two different −35 region sequences does not distinguish why P_{482} functions and N does not. There remain subtleties inherent in the structures of these regions that RNA polymerase can discern.

P_{c17} *and* P_{cin}. The pKO system was

used to characterize two other promoters created by mutational events. One of these, the λc17 promoter (P_{c17}) arises from an exact tandem duplication of a 9-bp sequence in a virulent mutant derivative of the phage (39). This duplication (Fig. 3B) creates a perfect −10 region hexamer consensus sequence at the junction of the repeat. Transcription studies in vitro show that RNA polymerase recognizes this region and initiates transcription 6 bp downstream from this hexamer at the indicated C residue (Fig. 3B) (39).

A small DNA fragment carrying the λc17 promoter and the corresponding fragment from λ+ was cloned into the pKO system. The resulting vectors, pKO-c17 and pKM1 respectively, are essentially identical except for the 9-bp repeat sequence. Comparison of their function in vivo (Table 1) indicates that the wild-type fragment has no promoter activity, whereas P_{c17} functions quite efficiently. Further comparisons indicate that P_{c17} functions about three times better than P_{482} and is nearly as efficient as our typical bacterial promoters (Table 1). Both P_{c17} and P_{482} contain perfect −10 region consensus sequences, yet differ dramatically in their efficiency. These functional differences probably reflect the adequacy of their respective −35 region recognition sequences. P_{c17} has a better −35 region sequence than P_{482}, although the two promoters also differ at other positions. Moreover, the −35 region of P_{c17} is part of a phage transcription termination signal, t_{R1} (39). Apparently, sequences normally used by the phage to specify termination are being used to help create the P_{c17} promoter signal. The implication of this finding is that sites of entry and exit for RNA polymerase may, in fact, share certain common features. Several other cases of overlapping promoter and terminator structures have now been reported (32).

Another promoter created by mutation was also isolated from a phage λ derivative, λcin (40). This promoter, P_{cin}, is generated by a single base substitution within an intercistronic region of the phage (Fig. 3C) (32, 39). To examine the function of this signal in vivo we cloned identical DNA fragments from the λcin derivative and the corresponding wild-type phage into the pKO vector. These two vectors, pKO-cin and pKM2, respectively, differ at only a single nucleotide position. Comparison of their activities indicates that promoter function is totally dependent on the single base pair alteration (Table 1). The point change that creates P_{cin} introduces an appropriate T · A pair at the most conserved position in the −10 region hexamer sequence (Fig. 3C). This creates a good (although not perfect) homology with the consensus sequence. In addition, P_{cin} has a good −35 region recognition sequence. The most efficient of the three mutant promoters, P_{cin} functions in vivo as well or better than many natural E. coli signals (Table 1). An interesting contradiction in P_{cin} function is the finding that P_{cin} is a rather poor promoter in vitro, notably less efficient than P_{c17} (41). This apparent discrepancy was explained by examining P_{cin} function in vitro on a supercoiled template rather than on a linear template. When superhelical DNA was used, P_{cin} function was far more efficient, analogous to the situation observed in vivo (41). Apparently, P_{cin} belongs to that class of promoters whose functional efficiency is highly dependent on the superhelical nature of the template.

We emphasize that the three promot-

324

Fig. 4. DNA sequence of the region of the SV40 genome that functions as a prokaryotic promoter, P_{SV40} (42, 44). This region also contains the polyadenylation signal for SV40 late mRNA synthesis. The region was isolated on a single-

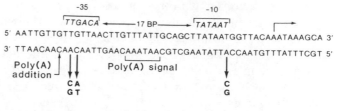

copy 237-bp Bam HI–Bcl I DNA restriction fragment (0.15 to 0.19 map units) from the SV40 genome and cloned into the pKO vector. The P_{SV40} transcription start site is indicated, as are the conserved regions of homology with prokaryotic promoters (the −10 and −35 regions). The location of the three promoter down mutations isolated by use of the pKO system is shown (see text for details). The −35 region transition of G · C to A · T was obtained independently by both hydroxylamine and *mut*D mutagenesis. The other −35 region mutation was obtained by nitrous acid mutagenesis, and the −10 region mutation was obtained with *mut*D.

ers characterized in these studies are of particular interest because their function, unlike that of most other promoters, is not regulated by any ancillary transcription factors. Thus, the efficiency with which these signals function depends solely on their ability to be recognized by RNA polymerase.

Promoter Mutations

The ability to select for or against *galK* expression suggests the potential of using the pKO vector system for isolating mutations in transcriptional regulatory elements. In particular, the negative selection should be useful for obtaining mutations that inactivate promoter function (that is, promoter down mutations). We chose for study a small DNA fragment (237 bp) that was derived from the genome of the mammalian virus SV40. This region of SV40 contains an efficient start site for transcription in vitro by *E. coli* RNA polymerase (42). The DNA sequence upstream from the start site exhibits the expected homology to naturally occurring bacterial and phage promoter signals (Fig. 4). We inserted the SV40 DNA fragment (P_{SV40}) into the

pKO vector and monitored in vivo its ability to express *galK*. The results (Table 1) indicate that P_{SV40} is a relatively weak promoter, less efficient than our standard bacterial signals. The level of expression from P_{SV40}, however, is sufficient to allow the plasmid to complement a *galK⁻* host and also to induce galactose-dependent killing in a *gal⁻* background (Table 1). This typical promoter behavior makes P_{SV40} an ideal signal to demonstrate the general utility of the pKO system for selecting and characterizing promoter mutations and accurately assessing their effects on promoter function. The study of the P_{SV40} signal serves a potential dual purpose, since this region of SV40 contains the polyadenylation regulatory signal for SV40 late messenger RNA (mRNA) synthesis (Fig. 4) (43). Thus, mutations obtained in this region not only provide information about prokaryotic promoter function, but also represent point changes in this eukaryotic regulatory region.

The procedures developed for obtaining promoter down mutations with the pKO system are outlined below and described in detail elsewhere (44). Briefly, cells containing the pKO-SV40 vector were exposed to a mutagen such as hydroxylamine or nitrous acid (*45, 46*). Mutagenized plasmid DNA was then isolated and transfected into a *gal⁻* recipient host. These cells were plated on a tryptone broth agar (TB) containing ampicillin and galactose, and survivors were selected. These survivors represent plasmid mutants that express galactokinase at reduced levels (for example, because of mutations in *galK* or promoter down mutations). In order to select out only promoter mutations, we pooled the mutants into groups and isolated the promoter fragments from the mixture of mutated plasmids. The fragments were purified by polyacrylamide gel electrophoresis, cloned into a new pKO-SV40 vector, and subjected to the same negative selection as described above. Survivors were obtained, and plasmids from individual colonies were examined by size and restriction. Those containing the appropriately sized SV40 insert were selected for sequence analysis.

Using the above procedure, we obtained three different point mutations within the P_{SV40} promoter region (Fig. 4). Two of these occurred in the −35 region and one in the −10 region. All three mutations affect promoter consensus sequences. The two −35 region mutations both reduced the efficiency of P_{SV40} in vivo by about 65 percent. Surprisingly, the −10 region mutant had a similar effect on promoter function in vivo. Alteration of this highly conserved −10 region position was expected to affect promoter function more severely. Indeed, when we examined the effects of these mutations in vitro, the −10 region mutation completely abolished P_{SV40} function, whereas the −35 region mutations resulted in low but clearly detectable levels of transcription (Fig. 5). Thus, there appears to be an inconsistency between the effects of these mutations

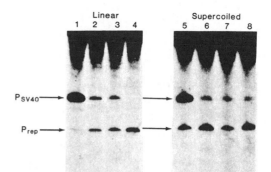

Fig. 5. Autoradiograms of polyacrylamide gel fractionation of ³²P-labeled RNA synthesized in vitro with the wild-type (lanes 1 and 5) and the mutant (−35 region mutants, lanes 2 and 3 and lanes 6 and 7; −10 region mutant, lanes 4 and 8) pKO-SV40 vectors as templates. Reactions were carried out with linearized (lanes 1, 2, 3, and 4) or supercoiled (lanes 5, 6, 7, and 8) templates as described (*39*). The 165-nucleotide-long transcript (P_{SV40}) initiates from the wild-type or mutant P_{SV40} promoters (see Fig. 4 and text for details); P_{rep} represents the 110-nucleotide RNA as in Fig. 2.

on promoter function in vivo and in vitro.

This inconsistency was resolved when the effects of these mutations were examined in vitro with supercoiled, rather than linear, templates (Fig. 5) (*44*). Supercoiling the template resulted in a marked increase in transcription from the mutant −10 region promoter (compare lanes 4 and 8 in Fig. 5). This signal now functions as well as the −35 region mutants, analogous to the results observed in vivo. Only the −10 region mutant was affected by the supercoiling. Neither the wild-type P_{SV40} nor the two −35 region mutants showed any effect. We conclude that mutation of a T · A pair to a C · G pair in this highly conserved −10 region causes promoter function to become completely dependent on supercoiling. Similarly, the function of certain natural promoters is influenced by the superhelical nature of the DNA template (47). Perhaps these promoters all contain −10 region sequences that are particularly sensitive to unwinding when the DNA is supercoiled. Local −10 region helix disruption should facilitate the entry of RNA polymerase into the site.

The pKO system can be used to obtain mutations in essentially any DNA sequence that functions as a prokaryotic promoter signal. Moreover, our data are consistent with the contention that deviation from consensus weakens promoter function. Most importantly, the pKO system allows us to quantitatively assess the functional effects of these mutations both in vivo (by galK assay; Table 1) and in vitro (by transcription assay; Fig. 5). In addition, the pKO system can be used with positive selection for galK expression, to obtain promoter up mutants (48).

Transcription Terminators

The pKO system also can be used for the isolation and characterization of transcription termination signals (14, 15).

In this case the starting vector is a pKO derivative that contains a promoter directing galK expression (for example, pKG in Fig. 1B). DNA fragments are inserted between the promoter and galK, and their ability to reduce galK expression is monitored. Insertion of almost any fragment will result in some polar effect on galK expression. However, insertion of an authentic terminator in proper orientation results in a dramatic reduction in galK levels. We have inserted various terminator signals into the pKG vector and monitored their effects on galK expression (Table 2) (15, 36). The extent to which a terminator reduces galK activity is an accurate measure of its efficiency. This was demonstrated by measuring directly the relative amounts of RNA that stop at or that read-through the termination signal in vivo (14, 49). In addition, we measured the effect of varying promoter strength on the efficiency of terminator function and found that all of the terminators tested function independently of the promoters to which they are fused (14, 36).

Table 2. Terminators in pKG. The construction of these vectors is described in detail in (14). See Table 1 for information about hosts, media, and galK activity units. Termination efficiency in vivo was calculated from galK activities using P_o and P_{gal} values without terminators as 0 percent. Termination efficiency in vitro was calculated by scanning the autoradiogram shown in Fig. 7 with a Zenieth laser densitometer and determining the relative levels of terminated (T) and read-through (RT) RNA.

pKG Vector		$galK^-$ Host in indicator	galK Activity	Termination efficiency (%)	
Promoter	Terminator			In vivo	In vitro
P_o		Red (sick)[†]	2400		
P_o	t_o	Red	50	95	85
P_{gal}		Red	650		
P_{gal}	t_o	White	15	95	85
P_{gal}	t_o1*	Red	420	35	5
P_{gal}	t_o2*	Red	170	75	50
P_{gal}	t_o3*	Red	390	40	5
P_{gal}	t_o4*	Red	250	60	30

[†]Although host is E^+T^+, this vector produces such high levels of galactokinase that it becomes galactosemic.

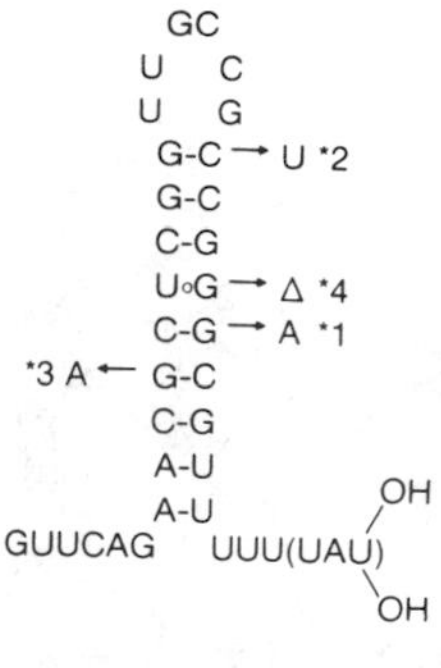

Relatively few termination signals have been studied by mutational analysis, and in most cases, there is no genetic selection for obtaining such mutations. The pKG vector system circumvents this problem and allows mutational analysis of almost any terminator. In order to demonstrate the general utility of this system, we inserted a small DNA fragment that contains the phage λ terminator, t_o, into the pKG vector. Although this terminator has been studied extensively (50–53), no mutations affecting its function have been obtained to date. There is no selection for such mutants on the phage, and moreover, t_o mutations on phage λ may be lethal. Initially, t_o was inserted into pKG downstream from its natural phage λ promoter signal, P_o. As shown in Table 2, P_o alone results in very high expression of galactokinase, whereas insertion of t_o reduces galactokinase expression by more than 95 percent. Although t_o is quite efficient, this pKG derivative still complements a $galK^-$ host (Table 2). If t_o is placed downstream from a weaker promoter (for example, P_{gal}) on a pKG derivative, again it functions with greater than 95 percent efficiency. This derivative, however, fails to complement a $galK^-$ host and grows as a white colony on the appropriate indicator plate (Table 2). We used this derivative to select mutations in the t_o signal. Cells containing this vector were mutagenized by standard procedures (45, 54). Mutagenized plasmid DNA was isolated and used to transform a $galK^-$ host. Transformants were plated out on indicator plates and $galK^+$ colonies (which are red) were obtained at frequencies varying from 1×10^{-4} to 1×10^{-5}, depending on the mutagen and the mutagenic procedure. Plasmid DNA from these colonies was characterized initially by size and restriction analysis,

Fig. 6. The primary and potential secondary structure at the 3' end of the t_o-terminated mRNA. Mutations shown were selected with the pKG vector system to affect termination function. Mutations 1*, 2*, and 3* were obtained by mutagenesis with nitrosoguanidine, whereas mutant 4* was obtained with benzopyrene (54). More than a dozen different t_o mutations have been obtained and characterized in detail with use of the pKG vector system (48); U, uracil.

and those retaining the appropriately sized t_o fragment were selected for DNA sequence analysis. The probability of obtaining only terminator mutations can be increased by isolating the insert from pooled groups of selected mutants and cloning it into the original pKG vector (analogous to the procedure used above for obtaining promoter down mutations).

Using these procedures, we obtained and characterized several mutations in the t_o signal (Fig. 6). These mutations all occurred within the potential stem and loop RNA structure (that is, the hyphenated-dyad symmetry structure in the DNA) immediately preceding the site of termination (Fig. 6). This stem and loop structure is a characteristic feature of almost all terminators, and various studies have indicated that its formation is required for terminator function (32, 55). The t_o mutations support this contention since all of them affect the stem structure and reduce its thermodynamic stability. Most importantly, the pKG vector system allows us to assess quantitatively the effects of these mutations on terminator function. Experiments carried out both in vivo (Table 2) and in vitro (Fig. 7)

328

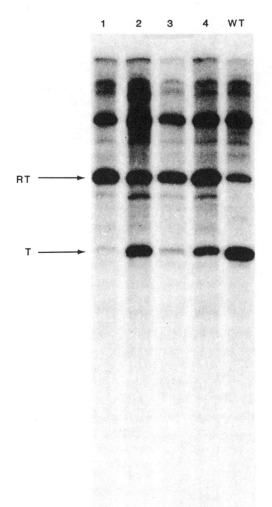

RT ⟶

T ⟶

Fig. 7. Autoradiogram of a polyacrylamide gel fractionation of ^{32}P-labeled RNA synthesized in vitro from pKG vectors carrying the wild-type (WT) and the mutant (1*, lane 1; 2*, lane 2; 3*, lane 3; 4*, lane 4) t_o terminators (see Fig. 6). The templates were linearized at a restriction site positioned 150 nucleotides beyond t_o. In each case, transcripts initiated at the P_{gal} promoter terminate either at the t_o signal (T) or read-through t_o to the end of the restriction fragment (RT). The relative levels of T and RT RNA were quantified by scanning the autoradiogram with a Zenieth laser densitometer. Termination efficiencies were calculated and are shown in Table 2.

indicate that the t_o mutations fall into three classes. Mutants 1* and 3* have the most severe effect on t_o function. This is consistent with their effect of disrupting C · G base pairings in the central region of the stem structure. In contrast, mutant 2* has the mildest effect on t_o function. Again, this is consistent with its structural effect of changing a G · C pair to a G · U pair at the top of the stem.

The fact that this relatively subtle change is readily detected shows the overall sensitivity of the selection system. The third class of t_o mutants, 4*, has an intermediate effect on t_o function. This deletion mutation disrupts a G · U pair and presumably results in the U residue being pushed out of the base-paired structure. Again, consistent with its functional effect, the unpaired residue has an intermediate effect on stem stability. Of course, it is also possible that these mutations affect important sequence features of the terminator signal in addition to their effects on the stem and loop structure.

The mutant terminators all function less efficiently in vitro than in vivo, although the relative order of their termination efficiencies are maintained (1* and 3* < 4* < 2*). The same is true for the wild-type t_o signal both on pKG (Table 2) and on phage λ (53). One possible explanation is that other transcription factors (such as rho and nus) absent in the reaction in vitro may increase the efficiency of both the normal and mutant sites in vivo. In fact, previous studies indicate that the efficiency of t_o on phage λ can be increased from 80 percent to nearly 100 percent in vitro by the addition of rho factor to the transcription reaction (53).

Conclusion

We have described several applications of the *galK* fusion vector system to the study of promoters and terminators recognized by the *E. coli* RNA polymerase. In particular, we have shown that the combination of both a positive and negative selection system and a simple assay allows the isolation, characterization, and mutational analysis of various transcriptional regulatory elements that otherwise could not be studied. The system lends itself to numerous other applications, including the study of various ancillary factors that affect transcription as well as characterization of the sequence-specific alterations induced by various mutagens and carcinogens (*54, 56*). In addition, the system has been recently adapted to the study of transcriptional regulatory elements in streptomyces (*57*), yeast (*27, 28*), and higher cell systems (*15, 29, 31*).

References and Notes

1. F. Cuzin, and F. Jacob, *C.R. Acad. Sci.* **258**, 1350 (1964).
2. F. Jacob, A. Ullmann, J. Monod, D. Kessler, E. Englesberg, *J. Mol. Biol.* **13**, 704 (1969).
3. D. Kessler and E. Englesberg, *J. Bacteriol.* **98**, 1159 (1969).
4. J. Beckwith, in *The Lactose Operon*, D. Zipser and J. Beckwith, Eds. (Cold Spring Harbor Laboratory, Cold Spring Harbor, N.Y., 1970), p. 5.
5. J. H. Miller, W. S. Reznikoff, A. E. Silverstone, K. Ippen, E. R. Singer, J. R. Beckwith, *J. Bacteriol.* **104**, 1273 (1970).
6. W. Reznikoff and K. Thornton, *ibid.* **109**, 526 (1972).
7. D. H. Mitchell, W. S. Reznikoff, J. R. Beckwith, *J. Mol. Biol.* **93**, 331 (1975).
8. M. Casadaban, *ibid.* **104**, 541 (1976).
9. P. Bassford *et al.*, in *The Operon*, J. Miller and W. Reznikoff, Eds. (Cold Spring Harbor Laboratory, Cold Spring Harbor, N.Y., 1978), p. 245.
10. M. Casadaban and S. N. Cohen, *Proc. Natl. Acad. Sci. U.S.A.* **76**, 4530 (1979).
11. E. W. West, R. L. Neve, R. L. Rodriguez, *Gene* **7**, 271 (1979).
12. G. An and J. D. Friesen, *J. Bacteriol.* **140**, 440 (1979).
13. M. Casadaban and S. Cohen, *J. Mol. Biol.* **138**, 179 (1980).
14. K. McKenney, H. Shimatake, D. Court U. Schmeissner, M. Rosenberg, in *Gene Amplification and Analysis*, J. Chirikjian and T. Papas, Eds. (Elsevier/North-Holland, New York, 1981), vol. 2, p. 383.
15. M. Rosenberg, K. McKenney, D. Schumperli, in *Promoters: Structure and Function*, M. Chamberlin and R. L. Rodriguez, Eds. (Praeger, New York, 1982), p. 387.
16. D. L. Blazey and R. O. Burns, *Proc. Natl. Acad. Sci. U.S.A.* **79**, 5011 (1982).
17. P. Youderian, S. Bouvier, M. M. Susskin, *Cell* **30**, 843 (1982).
18. G. Duester, R. M. Elford, W. M. Holmes, *ibid.*, p. 855.
19. P. Sarmientos, J. E. Sylvester, S. Contente, M. Cashel, *ibid.* **32**, 1337 (1983).
20. B. Rak, M. Lusky, M. Hable, *Nature (London)* **297**, 124 (1982).
21. H. Bedouelle, U. Schmeissner, M. Hofnung, M. Rosenberg, *J. Mol. Biol.* **161**, 519 (1982).
22. D. Drahos, G. R. Galluppi, M. Caruthers, W. Szybalski, *Gene* **18**, 343 (1982).
23. K. C. Luk and W. Szybalski, *ibid.* **17**, 247 (1982).
24. A. Miura, J. H. Krueger, S. Itoh, H. A. de Boer, M. Nomura, *Cell* **25**, 773 (1981).
25. K. C. Luk and W. Szybalski, *Virology* **125**, 403 (1983).
26. C. W. Adams and W. Hatfield, *Cell*, in press.
27. B. C. Rymond, R. S. Zitomer, D. Schumperli, M. Rosenberg, *Gene*, in press.
28. R. Zitomer, B. Rymond, D. Schumperli, M. Rosenberg, in *Gene Expression: UCLA Symposia*, D. Hamer and M. Rosenberg, Eds. (Liss, New York, in press), vol. 8.
29. D. Schumperli, B. H. Howard, M. Rosenberg, *Proc. Natl. Acad. Sci. U.S.A.* **79**, 257 (1982).
30. P. Berg *et al.*, *Mol. Cell. Biol.* **3**, 1246 (1983).
31. H. Johansen, M. Reff, M. Rosenberg, in *Gene Expression: The Translational Step and Its Control*, B. F. C. Clark, H. Peterson, J. H. Thaysen, Eds. (Munksgaard, Copenhagen, in press).
32. M. Rosenberg and D. Court, *Annu. Rev. Genet.* **13**, 319 (1979).
33. U. Sieberlist, R. B. Simpson, W. Gilbert, *Cell* **20**, 269 (1980).
34. D. Hawley and W. R. McClure, *Nucleic Acids Res.* **11**, 2237 (1983).
35. T. Platt, *Cell* **24**, 10 (1981).
36. K. McKenney, thesis, Johns Hopkins University (1982).
37. S. Adhya, M. Gottesman, D. Court, *J. Mol. Biol.* **112**, 657 (1977).
38. B. G. Barrell, in *Procedures in Nucleic Acids Research*, G. Cantoni and D. Davies, Eds. (Harper & Row, New York, 1971), vol. 2, p. 751.
39. M. Rosenberg, D. Court, D. L. Wulff, H. Shimatake, C. Brady, *Nature (London)* **272**, 414 (1978).
40. D. Wulff, *Genetics* **82**, 401 (1976).

41. M. Rosenberg, unpublished results.
42. R. Dhar, S. M. Weissman, B. S. Zain, J. Pan, A. M. Lewis, *Nucleic Acids Res.* **1**, 595 (1974).
43. M. Fitzgerald and T. Shenk, *Cell* **24**, 251 (1981).
44. A. Chepelinsky, T. Vogel, D. Court, M. Rosenberg, in preparation.
45. J. H. Miller, in *Experiments in Molecular Genetics* (Cold Spring Harbor Laboratory, Cold Spring Harbor, N.Y., 1972).
46. D. L. Wulff *et al.*, *J. Mol. Biol.* **138**, 209 (1980).
47. Y. Kano, T. Miyashita, H. Nakamura, K. Kurok, A. Nagata, F. Imamoto, *Gene* **13**, 173 (1981).
48. K. McKenney, in preparation.
49. M. Rosenberg and U. Schmeissner, in *Interaction of Translational and Transcriptional Controls in the Regulation of Gene Expression*, M. Grunberg-Manago and B. Safer, Eds. (Elsevier, New York, 1982), p. 1.
50. S. Hayes and W. Szybalski, *Mol. Gen. Genet.* **126**, 275 (1973).
51. M. Rosenberg, B. deCrombrugghe, R. Musso, *Proc. Natl. Acad. Sci. U.S.A.* **73**, 717 (1976).
52. M. Rosenberg, S. Weissman, B. deCrombrugghe, *J. Biol. Chem.* **250**, 4755 (1975).
53. B. C. Howard, B. deCrombrugghe, M. Rosenberg, *Nucleic Acids Res.* **4**, 827 (1977).
54. H. Mizusawa, C. Lee, T. Kafefuda, K. McKenney, H. Shimatake, M. Rosenberg, *Proc. Natl. Acad. Sci. U.S.A.* **78**, 6817 (1981).
55. T. Platt and R. Bean, in *Prokaryotic Gene Expression*, J. R. Beckwith *et al.*, Eds. (Cold Spring Harbor Laboratory, Cold Spring Harbor, N.Y., in press).
56. H. Mizusawa, C. Lee, T. Kakefunda, *Mutat. Res.* **82**, 47 (1981).
57. M. Brawner, M. Rosenberg, J. Auerbach, in preparation.
58. A. Levine and D. Rupp, in *Microbiology*, D. Schlessinger, Ed. (American Society for Microbiology, Washington, D.C., 1978), p. 183.
59. We thank L. Hampton and A. Venable for manuscript preparation; C. Brady and D. Sobieski for technical assistance, and M. Singer, J. Young, and J. Auerbach for helpful commentary on the manuscript.

25. Transcription of Class III Genes: Formation of Preinitiation Complexes

Andrew B. Lassar, Paul L. Martin, Robert G. Roeder

Our present understanding of the mechanisms and regulation of transcription of eukaryotic genes is limited, but the development of cell-free systems that accurately transcribe exogenous (purified) genes has begun to provide significant information about both the DNA sequences and the cellular (protein) factors involved in these processes. Although these studies [reviewed in (*1*)] have included analysis of genes transcribed by RNA polymerases I (encoding the large ribosomal RNA's), II (encoding messenger RNA's), and III (encoding small structural RNA's), this chapter is restricted to our analysis of well-characterized class III genes (those transcribed by RNA polymerase III) encoding transfer RNA (tRNA), 5S RNA, and adenovirus VA RNA (*2*).

Analysis of promoter sequences by mutagenesis of cloned genes showed that a 34-nucleotide stretch within the 5S gene is necessary and sufficient for initiation of transcription (*3, 4*), and that several tRNA genes and the adenovirus VA I gene contain internal promoter elements in addition to upstream modulatory sequences [reviewed in (*5, 6*)]. More detailed studies revealed that the tRNA promoter region contains two noncontiguous stretches of DNA, termed A and B blocks, which are also present in the VA gene promoter (*7, 8*). The 5S RNA gene also appears to contain two separable elements, one homologous to the A block of tRNA genes and the other specific to 5S genes (*6*). The promoter elements for the *Xenopus* tRNA$_1^{Met}$ and human adenovirus VA I genes (representative of genes containing A and B blocks) and the *Xenopus* 5S RNA gene are depicted in Fig. 1.

The factors that are required, along with RNA polymerase III, for transcription of purified class III genes have been analyzed by chromatographic fractionation of crude cellular extracts. Our earlier work (*9–11*) established, for both amphibian and human cells, that two factors (designated IIIB and IIIC) are necessary for transcription of the tRNA and VA RNA genes, whereas 5S genes require these same factors plus a third gene-specific factor (IIIA). Despite extensive purification (*12*), it has not yet been possible to distinguish individual IIIB and IIIC factors specific for one subgroup of class III genes. Presumably, one or more of these factors or RNA polymerase III (or a combination) interacts with the conserved sequence blocks

332

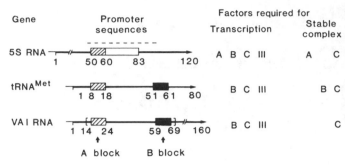

Fig. 1. Summary of transcription factor requirements, promoter regions and homologous sequences in the *Xenopus borealis* somatic 5*S* gene, the *Xenopus laevis* tRNA$_1^{Met}$ gene and the adenovirus VA I gene. Promoter regions are represented by rectangles, the A sequence block by a striped rectangle and the B sequence block by a black rectangle. Numbers indicate nucleotides downstream from the 5′ end of the mature transcript. The dashed line above the 5*S* gene indicates the region protected from deoxyribonuclease I digestion by *Xenopus laevis* factor IIIA. Brackets in the VA I gene designate the extent of the promoter as defined by deletion analysis. References to the promoter regions are: 5*S* (*3, 4, 10*); tRNA$_1^{Met}$ (*34*); VA I (*8, 35*).

in the tRNA and VA RNA gene promoters and with the common element present in the 5*S* gene. In the case of factor IIIA, a single protein of 38,000 daltons has been purified to homogeneity (from *Xenopus* oocytes) and shown to interact, in the absence of other factors, with the internal control region of both amphibian (*10*) and mammalian (*13*) 5*S* RNA genes, thus indicating its key role as an initiation factor. This factor also interacts stoichiometrically with 5*S* RNA in oocytes, apparently to stabilize the stored 5*S* RNA (*14, 15*); this interaction, plus the demonstrated potential of 5*S* RNA to inhibit factor IIIA function in vitro (*15*), suggests that, in the cell, 5*S* gene transcription in the presence of limiting amounts of this factor may be subject to autoregulation, may be restricted to previously activated genes, or both.

Before initiation of transcription, stable complexes form between purified genes and transcription factors in crude extracts, as demonstrated by Bogenhagen *et al.* (*16*) for 5*S* genes. Such complexes persist for many rounds of transcription, even in the presence of other competing templates. Evidence that

such complexes exist in vivo was provided by Parker and Roeder (*17*), who showed that chromatin isolated from immature oocytes contains (in a stable association) all the factors necessary to promote accurate transcription of endogenous oocyte-type 5*S* genes by a purified RNA polymerase III. Bogenhagen *et al.* (*16*) subsequently demonstrated that somatic cell chromatin retains, in the presence of exogenous factors and polymerase, the 5*S* gene specificity (repression of oocyte genes and expression of somatic genes) imposed in vivo. The establishment of stable complexes within an otherwise repressive chromatin structure may thus represent a key step in gene activation and may provide a means for the maintenance and propagation of a specific set of activated genes, even in the absence of other factors that may have been essential for their formation (within chromatin).

The formation of stable transcription complexes is a general feature of class III genes, and possibly of class I and class II genes as well (*18, 19*). Because of the general significance of such complexes, for understanding both mechanistic

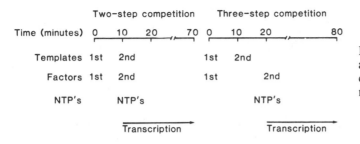

Fig. 2. Diagram of two-step and three-step incubation-competition protocols; *NTP*'s, nucleoside triphosphates.

and regulatory aspects of transcription, we examined the requirements for their formation on 5*S* RNA, tRNA, and VA RNA genes in purified DNA templates. By using separated transcription factors from human cells, we determined the minimal number and identity of the components necessary for formation of stable complexes. We also demonstrated less stable interactions as well as a promoter site interaction for a factor required by all class III genes.

Complexes on the 5*S* RNA Gene

Factors A and C are both necessary and sufficient for a stable complex. The RNA polymerase III factors from human and amphibian (*Xenopus*) cells are chromatographically similar (*9, 11*) and mediate, in homologous and heterologous combinations, accurate transcription of both amphibian and mammalian class III genes (*13*). Given this evolutionary conservation of structural and functional features of these factors, we used the more readily separated human factors to investigate the interactions of these factors with DNA (*20*). Our analysis of DNA–transcription factor complexes is based on the assay described by Bogenhagen *et al.* (*16*). This assay monitors the ability of one gene, when incubated with limiting amounts of an extract, to exclude transcription of a second (function-

ally equivalent) gene added subsequently (with remaining substrates). This assay is equivalent to the two-step protocol diagramed in Fig. 2, with all factors added in the first step. The preferential transcription of the first gene during the secondary incubation indicates the stable interaction of a limiting component or components in the first incubation.

Our initial experiments demonstrated that prior incubation of a *Xenopus* 5*S* gene with unfractionated human cell extracts (two-step protocol of Fig. 2) results in the formation of complexes that preclude transcription of a second 5*S* gene (data not shown), in agreement with the data on oocyte extracts (*16*). That this result can be reproduced in a system reconstituted with separated transcription factors (A, B, C, and RNA polymerase III) is shown in Fig. 3. As indicated, prior incubation of all factors with a 5*S* maxigene [an insertion mutant that retains a fully functional promoter (*21*)] results in preferential transcription of this gene during subsequent incubation with the wild-type 5*S* gene (lane 2 in Fig. 3); the presence of both templates during the first incubation results in equivalent levels of transcription from each (lane 1 in Fig. 3). Other control experiments indicate that prior incubation of the factors with pBR322 (containing no 5*S* sequences) does not exclude transcription of 5*S* genes added subsequently (lane 2 in Fig. 4, a and b). For convenience we refer to the partially purified fractions as factors; although further purification has failed to reveal additional multiplicity (*12*) this possibility cannot yet be excluded.

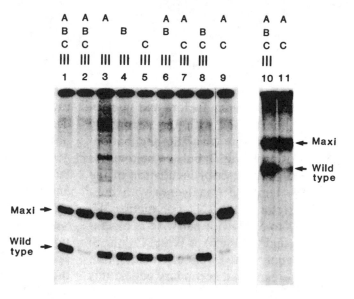

Fig. 3. Analysis of the human transcription factors that are necessary when incubated with a 5*S* RNA gene to exclude transcription from a second 5*S* gene. The autoradiograph shows the gel analysis of transcription reactions carried out in vitro with separated transcription factors. Initial incubation reactions contained the factors indicated above each lane and either 0.25 μg of the maxigene (p115/77) alone (lanes 2 to 9 and lane 11); or 0.25 μg each of the 5*S* maxigene and the wild-type 5*S* gene (pXBS1) (lanes 1 and 10). After the initial incubation, the reactions were cooled (4°C) and mixed sequentially with 0.25 μg of wild-type 5*S* RNA gene (lanes 2 to 9 and lane 11 only), any transcription factors (including RNA polymerase III) not present in the initial incubation, and nucleoside triphosphates. In this and subsequent experiments the first incubation was for 10 minutes at 30°C and transcription following nucleoside triphosphate addition was for 60 minutes at 30°C. The final reaction volume was 50 μl and contained 20 mM Hepes (pH 7.9), 70 mM KCl, 7 mM MgCl₂, 12 percent glycerol, 5 mM dithiothreitol, 600 μM each of adenosine, uridine, and cytidine triphosphates, and 25 μM [α-³²P]guanosine triphosphate (54 Ci/mmole). The initial incubation conditions were essentially those of the final incubation except for the absence of all nucleoside triphosphates. As precautionary measures the secondary incubation reactions also contained 0.02 μg of purified poly(adenosine diphosphate–ribose) polymerase to decrease random initiation by RNA polymerase III at nicks (*36*) and 10 units of placental ribonuclease inhibitor (Bolton Biologicals). After transcription was terminated the RNA's were purified (*11*) and fractionated by electrophoresis in 10 percent polyacrylamide gels containing 7M urea. The transcription factors A, B, and C were separated by chromatography of a HeLa cell extract on phosphocellulose (*9*). The 0.1M KCl phosphocellulose fraction was further purified on DEAE-cellulose (DE52) (*9*); a 0.25M KCl step was used as the standard factor A preparation. The 0.35M KCl phosphocellulose fraction was used as the standard factor B preparation. The 0.6M KCl phosphocellulose fraction was further purified by chromatography on DEAE-cellulose (*9*) and Bio-Gel A1.5M; the excluded fraction from the latter served as the standard factor C preparation. RNA polymerase III was isolated from HeLa cells (*9*). Unless otherwise noted, the experiments described in this and other figures contained 25 μg of factor A, 15 μg of factor B, 1 μg of factor C, and 50 to 100 units of RNA polymerase III (*37*). Factor B contained a substantial amount of RNA polymerase III activity, but factors A and C contained only trace amounts. Factor A contained a residual amount of factor B activity (about 2 percent of that in factor B). Otherwise the factors were not detectably cross contaminated. For the experiments in lanes 10 and 11, contaminating B activity was removed from factor A by further purification on DEAE-Sephadex (A25) and phosphocellulose (P11); the factor C used in these lanes was also further purified on DEAE-Sephadex (A25) and carboxy-methylcellulose (C25).

To determine which of the individual factors are necessary to form a stable complex on the *Xenopus* 5S RNA gene, we first incubated subsets of the chromatographically separated factors (legend to Fig. 3) with the 5S maxigene and added the remaining factors and nucleoside triphosphates with the secondary wild-type 5S gene (two-step incubation-competition in Fig. 2; but see below). As shown in Fig. 3, prior incubation of the primary template (maxigene) with individual factors (plus RNA polymerase III) (lanes 3 to 5) or with pairwise combinations A and B (lane 6) or B and C (lane 8) led to equivalent levels of transcription of the primary and secondary genes: this was the same as was observed when both templates were present during the first incubation with all factors (lane 1). However, prior incubation of the primary template with factors A and C, either with (lane 7) or without (lane 9)

RNA polymerase III diminished transcription of the secondary gene to the same extent as observed when all three factors were present in the first incubation (lane 2). Thus, factors A and C, but not RNA polymerase III or factor B, are necessary for stable complex formation. To rule out the unlikely possibility that a trace amount of B activity contaminating factors A and C might have participated in stable complex formation, we subjected these factors to further purification (legend to Fig. 3). These preparations, devoid of any detectable factor B activity, are sufficient, when incubated with a 5S gene, to reduce transcription of the secondary gene (lane 11).

The above experiments do not distinguish between the possibility that both factors A and C remain bound to the first template and the possibility that one factor catalyzes complex formation between the other factor and DNA, but

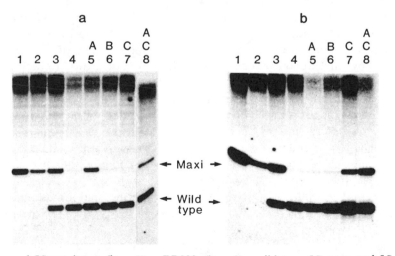

Fig. 4. Identification of components that are sequestered by the 5S gene and rendered rate-limiting for transcription of a second 5S gene. An autoradiography of transcription products separated by polyacrylamide gel electrophoresis is shown. In both (a) and (b) a mixture of factors A, B, and C was first incubated with 0.03 µg each of the following templates: pBR322 and 5S maxigene (lane 1); pBR322 (lane 2); wild-type 5S gene and 5S maxigene (lane 3); and wild-type 5S gene (lanes 4 to 8). After the initial incubation, nucleoside triphosphates and the additional transcription factors indicated above each lane were added with the following templates: none (lane 1); 5S maxigene (lane 2); none (lane 3); and 5S maxigene (lanes 4 to 8). In (a) the factor A, B, and C portions contained 3, 15, and 1 µg of protein, respectively. In (b), the factor A, B, and C portions contained 12.5, 15, and 0.08 µg of protein, respectively.

does not itself remain on the complex. If both factors remain bound to the first gene, then addition of the rate-limiting factor with the second gene should be necessary and sufficient to increase transcription of the second gene. To test this, we formed stable complexes on the wild-type 5S gene with factors A, B, and C present at varying ratios and then tested the effects of further additions of the factors on transcription of the second gene. As shown in Fig. 4a, the addition of factor A with the second gene increased second gene transcription (lane 5 versus lane 4), whereas addition of either factor B or factor C was without effect (lanes 6 and 7). In an analogous experiment, the ratio of factor A to factor C was made 50 times greater (Fig. 4b); in this case the subsequent addition of factor C enhanced second gene transcription (lane 7 versus lane 4), whereas factors A or B alone had no effect (lanes 5 and 6). The observation that factors A and C can independently be made rate-limiting for second gene transcription suggests that each is bound in the complex on the first gene and that neither functions catalytically in promoting stable complex formation by the other. However, since the transcription reactions with these separated factors yield only about one transcript per gene, we can conclude that they are bound in a stable preinitiation complex but not that they remain stably associated through many rounds of transcription.

Factor A forms a metastable complex. Although factors A and C bind to the 5S gene in a stable fashion (resistant to dissociation in the presence of a competing gene) only when both factors are present, the possibility exists that one or both may interact independently with the 5S gene to form a metastable complex. Such a metastable complex might be demonstrated if conditions could be found to rapidly convert it into a stable complex in the presence of a second gene. Therefore, we used a two-step protocol (Fig. 2) in which a previously incubated mixture (30°C) of the first gene and a limiting amount of the first factor (A or C) was added to an equilibrated mixture (30°C) containing an excess of the second stabilizing factor (C or A), factor B, RNA polymerase III, and the second gene. The success of this experiment is dependent on the rate of complex conversion by the stabilizing factor being greater than the rate of dissociation of the initial complex.

As shown in Fig. 5a, incubation of factor A with the first gene (wild type) followed by addition of the second gene (maxigene) with an excess of factor C resulted in preferential transcription of the first gene (lane 3). The reduction in the transcription of the second gene was nearly as complete as when both factors A and C were present in the first incubation with the primary gene (lane 2). This apparent interaction of factor A and the 5S gene was not observed in the experiment described above (data of Fig. 3) because (i) the ratio of factor C to factor A was eight times lower and (ii) the secondary gene and the transcription components were added to the reactions sequentially; this allowed a small but apparently sufficient amount of time for the complex to dissociate in the absence of factor C (thus establishing the equivalent of a three-step incubation-competition protocol as in the following experiment).

To further establish the metastable nature of the complex described immediately above, we used a three-step incubation-competition protocol (refer to Fig. 2) in which the secondary transcription factors were added 10 minutes after

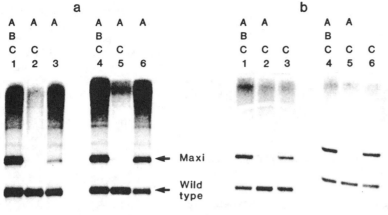

Fig. 5. Identification of the component that forms a metastable complex with the 5*S* gene. An autoradiograph of transcription products separated by polyacrylamide gel electrophoresis is shown. In lanes 1 and 4 of both (a) and (b), 0.03 μg each of the wild-type 5*S* gene and the 5*S* maxigene were first incubated with the factors indicated above each lane. In lanes 2, 3, 5, and 6, 0.03 μg of the wild-type 5*S* gene was first incubated with the factors indicated above each lane. The incubated reactions in lanes 1 to 3 were subsequently added (at 30°C) to equilibrated mixtures (at 30°C) containing nucleoside triphosphates, those transcription factors not present in the initial incubation, and either no additional DNA (lane 1) or 0.03 μg of 5*S* maxigene (lanes 2 and 3). The previously incubated reactions in lanes 4 to 6 were mixed (at 30°C) with either no additional DNA (lane 4) or 0.03 μg of 5*S* maxigene (lanes 5 and 6); after an additional 10 minutes of incubation at 30°C those transcription factors not present in the initial incubation were added along with the nucleoside triphosphates. In (a) the levels and proportions of factors A, B, and C were the same as in Fig. 4a whereas in (b) they were the same as in Fig. 4b.

the addition of the secondary (maxigene) template, thereby allowing an extended period at 30°C for dissociation. As shown in Fig. 5a, under these conditions the presence of factor A alone in the initial incubation was insufficient to exclude transcription of the second gene; this resulted in equal transcription of the two genes (lane 6), as was observed when both templates were present in the first incubation (lane 4). Thus, the complex of the primary gene and factor A, which is trapped by simultaneous exposure to an excess of factor C and a second template, is not stable when incubated with a second template in the absence of factor C.

To detect interactions of factor C with the 5*S* gene in the absence of factor A (Fig. 5b), we used a rate-limiting amount of factor C (in the first incubation) and an excess of factor A (added later) in two-step (lanes 1 to 3) and three-step (lanes 4 to 6) incubation-competition experiments. In this case, prior incubation of the primary (wild-type) gene with factor C did not exclude transcription of the second template (maxigene) when the remaining factors (including A) were added together with (lane 3), or 10 minutes after (lane 6), the secondary gene. Thus, under conditions of rate-limiting C, we were unable to detect any metastable interaction of factor C and the 5*S* gene. Under conditions of limiting factor A (lane 5 in Fig. 5a) or factor C (lane 5 in Fig. 5b), the rigorous three-step protocol again demonstrates that both factors A and C are needed for stable complex formation.

Factor C is also necessary for tRNA and VA RNA transcription. When a mix-

338

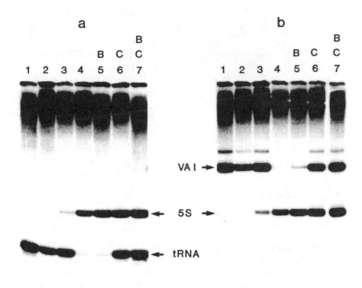

VA I →

5S →

← 5S →

← tRNA

Fig. 6. Identification of a component that is sequestered in the 5S gene stable complex and necessary for tRNA and VA I transcription. An autoradiograph of transcription products separated by gel electrophoresis is shown. In (a), a mixture of factors A, B, and C was first incubated with 0.12 μg each of the following templates: pBR322 and tRNA$_1^{Met}$ (pX1tmet1) (lane 1); pBR322 (lane 2); wild-type 5S gene and tRNA$_1^{Met}$ gene (lane 3); wild-type 5S gene (lanes 4 to 7). After the initial incubation, nucleoside triphosphates and the additional transcription factors indicated above each lane were added along with the following templates: none (lane 1); tRNA$_1^{Met}$ gene (lane 2); none (lane 3); and tRNA$_1^{Met}$ gene (lanes 4 to 7). In (b) the additions were exactly the same except that the VA I gene (pVA) was used in place of the tRNA gene. In both (a) and (b), the amounts of factors A, B, and C used were as indicated in Fig. 4b.

ture of 5S and tRNA genes or a mixture of 5S and VA RNA genes was incubated in an unfractionated extract (data not shown) or in a system reconstituted with separated factors, the tRNA gene (lane 3 in Fig. 6a) or the VA RNA gene (lane 3 in Fig. 6b) was transcribed to the exclusion of the 5S gene. These results indicate the presence of a common factor for which the tRNA or the VA RNA gene competes more effectively. To determine whether this component is one of those involved in stable complex formation on the 5S gene, we incubated the wild-type 5S gene first with a mixture of all the factors and then with the tRNA or the VA RNA gene. In this case, the 5S gene was transcribed to the near exclusion of the tRNA gene (lane 4 in Fig. 6a) or the VA gene (lane 4 in Fig. 6b). Control experiments indicated that prior incubation with pBR322 did not significantly depress transcription of the secondary

tRNA or VA I gene templates (compare lanes 1 and 2 in Fig. 6, a and b), thereby demonstrating the specificity of the competition for 5S genes and the stability of the factors during the first incubation. Thus, at least one factor that is stably bound in the 5S gene complex is also required for transcription of tRNA and VA I RNA genes.

To identify this common factor, we determined which isolated factor would relieve inhibition of tRNA or VA RNA gene transcription when added (with the tRNA or VA gene) in the competition assay. Data in Fig. 6 indicate that the inclusion of additional factor C restored tRNA or VA RNA synthesis (lanes 6 in Fig. 6, a and b), whereas additional factor B had no effect (lanes 5 in Fig. 6, a and b). Thus, a component of factor C involved in stable complex formation on 5S genes is also necessary for tRNA and VA gene transcription.

Complexes on the tRNA and
VA RNA Genes

Factors B and C are required for a stable tRNA gene complex. As discussed above, the tRNA and VA RNA genes compete for a transcription factor required for 5S gene transcription. To establish whether the tRNA gene forms a stable complex with one or more factors, we used the three-step protocol with separated factors and the VA gene as the competing template. As shown in Fig. 7b, the presence of both factors B and C in the initial incubation with the tRNA gene was sufficient to preclude transcription of the second template (lane 2). Prior incubation of the first gene with either factor alone (lanes 3 and 4 in Fig. 7b) resulted in a transcription pattern indistinguishable from that observed when both genes were initially incubated together with the required factors (lane 1).

To determine whether one of the factors interacts independently in a less stable fashion with the tRNA gene, we used the two-step incubation-competition assay (Fig. 2) and conditions analogous to those used to demonstrate a metastable interaction of the 5S gene and factor A (see above). As shown in Fig. 7a, prior incubation of the tRNA gene with factor B alone resulted—after the simultaneous addition of the remaining components and the VA RNA gene—in transcription of both genes (lane 3); the relative amounts were equivalent to those observed when both genes were present during the initial incubation (lane 1). In contrast, prior incubation with factor C alone resulted in a substantially reduced level of VA I gene transcription (lane 4), although the reduction was somewhat less than that observed when both factors B and C were present in the

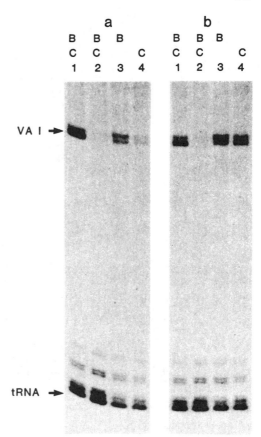

Fig. 7. Analysis of the transcription factors that are necessary, when incubated with the tRNA gene, to exclude transcription of a second template. An autoradiograph of transcription products separated by electrophoresis is shown. In both (a) and (b), the factors indicated above each lane were first incubated with the following templates: 0.5 μg of the $tRNA_I^{Met}$ gene and 0.25 μg of the VA I gene (lane 1); 0.5 μg of the $tRNA_I^{Met}$ gene (lanes 2 to 4). In (a) the previously incubated reactions were subsequently added (at 30°C) to equilibrated mixtures (at 30°C) containing nucleoside triphosphates, that transcription factor not present in the initial incubations, and either no additional DNA (lane 1) or 0.25 μg of the VA I gene (lanes 2 to 4). In (b) the previously incubated reactions were mixed (at 30°C) with either no additional DNA (lane 1) or 0.25 μg of the VA I gene (lanes 2 to 4); after an additional 10 minutes of incubation at 30°C, that transcription factor not present in the initial incubation was added along with the nucleoside triphosphates.

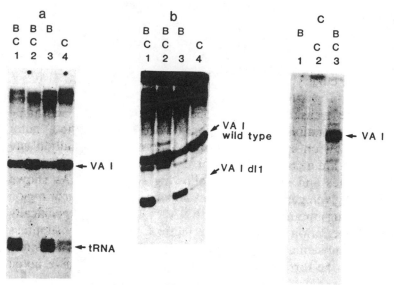

Fig. 8. Analysis of the transcription factors that are necessary when incubated with the VA I gene to exclude transcription of a second template. In (a) the factors indicated above each lane were first incubated with either 0.25 μg each of the VA I and the tRNA$_1^{Met}$ genes (lane 1) or 0.25 μg of the VA I gene alone (lanes 2 to 4). The initially incubated reactions were mixed (at 30°C) with either no additional DNA (lane 1) or with 0.25 μg of the tRNA$_1^{Met}$ gene (lanes 2 to 4); after an additional 10 minutes of incubation at 30°C, that transcription factor not present in the initial incubation was added along with the nucleoside triphosphates. In (b) the additions were identical except that 0.75 μg of the VA I deletion mutant (pVA I dl 1) was added in place of the tRNA$_1^{Met}$ gene. In (c) the VA I gene (0.25 μg) was incubated under transcription conditions in the presence of 100 units of RNA polymerase III and the factors indicated above each lane.

initial incubation (lane 2).

The above results indicate that factors B and C are both necessary to form a stable transcription complex on the tRNA$_1^{Met}$ gene in such a way that transcription of a competing VA I gene is inhibited. Although factor C can interact with the tRNA gene, it cannot by itself form a stable complex with the gene. Because RNA polymerase III was present in the factor B and factor C preparations used here, we cannot exclude the possibility that the polymerase participated in the formation of a stable complex. However, partially purified RNA polymerase III cannot substitute for either factor B or factor C preparations in supporting the formation of a stable complex (data not shown). Therefore, at least two components, distinct from RNA polymerase III, are necessary to form a stable complex on the tRNA$_1^{Met}$ gene.

Factor C alone forms a stable complex on the VA I gene. To ascertain whether the VA I gene forms a stable complex with transcription factors, we used the three-step competition protocol. This protocol can specifically detect a stable complex and unmask a transient interaction. We used the wild-type VA I gene as the primary template and either the tRNA$_1^{Met}$ gene (which uses the same factors) or a homologous VA I minigene (pVA dl 1) as the secondary competing gene. The VA I minigene contains a small deletion but retains a functional promoter (8). Prior incubation of the primary (VA I) gene with factors B and C eliminated transcription of the secondary tRNA gene or VA minigene (lane 2 in Fig. 8, a and b), whereas the presence of both the primary and the competing template in the initial incubation resulted in equal levels of transcription (lane 1 in Fig. 8, a and b). Significantly, however, prior incubation of the primary VA I gene with factor C alone (lane 4 in Fig. 8, a and b), but not with factor B alone (lane 3 in Fig. 8, a and b), significantly depressed transcription of the second template.

These experiments indicate that the wild-type VA I gene binds to factor C in such a way that transcription of a second template is greatly reduced. From an analysis of possible cross contamination of factors B and C (Fig. 8c), it is evident (lane 2) that factor C contains no detectable B activity, which might otherwise contribute to stable complex formation. Thus the VA I gene, unlike the *Xenopus* tRNA$_1^{Met}$ gene, is able to stably associate with and sequester factor C in the absence of any B activity. However, prior incubation of the VA I gene with factor C alone did not suppress second gene transcription to quite the same extent as prior incubation with both factors B and C (compare lanes 2 and 4 in Fig. 8, a and b). Thus, although factor C alone binds tightly to the VA I gene, the presence of factor B apparently increases the stability of the factor C–VA I gene complex.

Factor B association with stable complexes during transcription. Factor B is not needed to form a stable complex on the 5S gene. However, this factor stabilizes the metastable association between factor C and the tRNA gene and increases the relative stability of the factor C–VA I gene complex. Therefore, we were prompted to examine whether factor B can stably associate with a stable complex and remain bound to the template during a transcription reaction. In the first experiment the VA I gene was incubated with factor C plus decreasing amounts of factor B, and the tRNA$_1^{Met}$

gene was separately incubated only with factor C. After 10 minutes, the two reactions were combined, mixed with RNA polymerase III and substrates, and incubated for an additional hour. If factor B remained bound to the factor C–VA I gene complex under conditions of rate-limiting factor B, no tRNA transcription would be expected. In the experiment shown in lanes 2 to 6 of Fig. 9a, total transcription was proportional to the amount of added factor B, an indication that factor B was present in rate-limiting amounts. Under these conditions, transcription of the tRNA gene (incubated only with factor C) is always observed. Therefore, within the limits of our assay, factor B does not appear to remain stably bound to the factor C–VA I gene complex during the 1-hour transcription reaction.

In a similar experiment, the tRNA gene was incubated with factor C and decreasing amounts of factor B, and the VA I gene was incubated with factor C alone. The reactions were then mixed and incubated with RNA polymerase III and nucleoside triphosphates. From the experiment shown in lanes 2 to 6 of Fig. 9b, it is evident that transcription of both genes occurs at all factor B concentrations. Thus, factor B does not appear to remain stably bound to the factor C–tRNA gene complex under transcription conditions. In similar experiments with 5S genes, we were not able, in the presence of a rate-limiting amount of factor B, to find evidence for a stable interaction between factor B and the complex formed by the 5S gene and factors A and C under transcription conditions (data not shown).

Although both genes in Fig. 9 were transcribed at all concentrations of factor B, the template initially incubated with both factors B and C was in all cases

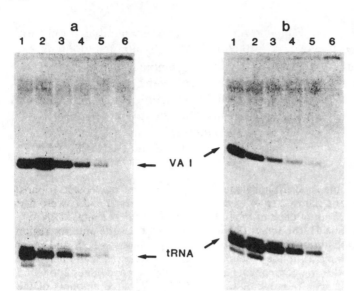

Fig. 9. Does factor B remain sequestered in a stable complex? An autoradiograph of transcription products separated by polyacrylamide gel electrophoresis is shown. (a) In one set of reactions 0.3 μg of the VA I gene was incubated for 10 minutes with a constant amount of factor C (0.4 μg) plus the following amounts of factor B: 0.75 μg (lane 1), 1.5 μg (lane 2), 0.38 μg (lane 3), 0.19 μg (lane 4), 0.09 μg (lane 5), or none (lane 6). In a second set of reactions, 0.3 μg of the $tRNA_1^{Met}$ gene was incubated for 10 minutes with 0.4 μg of factor C plus either 0.75 μg of factor B (lane 1) or with factor C alone (lanes 2 to 6). The corresponding reactions were then mixed together, supplemented with RNA polymerase III and nucleoside triphosphates, and incubated for an additional hour at 30°C. (b) The same experimental regime as described in (a) was used; however, the tRNA gene was initially incubated with factor C plus decreasing amounts of factor B, and the VA I gene was initially incubated with factors B and C (lane 1) or with factor C alone (lanes 2 to 6).

preferentially transcribed in the subsequent incubation. Therefore, it is possible that (i) factor B did bind stably to the first template but cycled onto the other template during the transcription reaction, or (ii) the assay conditions did not allow complete binding of factor B during the initial incubation.

Site of Interaction of a Common Transcription Factor

Factor C interaction with the posterior half of the tRNA gene. Both the A and B sequence blocks are necessary components of the tRNA gene promoter. Prior incubation of the intact tRNA gene with factors B and C completely eliminated subsequent VA I gene transcription (lane 2 in Fig. 10a). Prior incubation of the factors with a subclone of the anterior region of the tRNA gene (containing the A block) did not reduce VA I transcription significantly more than prior incubation with pBR322 (compare lanes 3 and 5). However, prior incubation with a subclone of the posterior region (containing the B block) reduced VA I transcription to about one-fifth that observed after prior incubation with pBR322 (compare lanes 4 and 5). [The posterior region subclone directed transcription of two novel RNA species (lane 4), which are more apparent in lane 8 of Fig. 10b. These RNA's have not been mapped in detail, but both are derived specifically from the posterior region subclone, which is transcribed at about 2 percent of the efficiency of the intact tRNA gene.]

The posterior region of the tRNA gene

Fig. 10. Competition for transcription factors by the anterior and posterior regions of the tRNA$_1^{Met}$ gene. An autoradiograph of transcription products separated by polyacrylamide gel electrophoresis is shown. (a) Factors B and C were first incubated for 10 minutes with 0.25 μg of the following templates: the intact tRNA$_1^{Met}$ gene and the VA I gene (lane 1), the intact tRNA-$_1^{Met}$ gene (lane 2), a subclone of the anterior region of the tRNA$_1^{Met}$ gene (pA-tmet) (lane 3), a subclone of the posterior region of the tRNA$_1^{Met}$ (pB-tmet) (lane 4), or pBR322 (lane

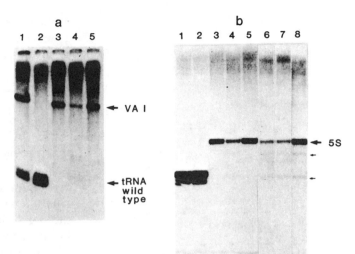

5). After the initial incubation, nucleoside triphosphates alone (lane 1) or nucleoside triphosphates and 0.25 μg of the VA I gene (lanes 2 to 5) were added. (b) factors B and C were first incubated for 10 minutes with 0.025 μg of each of the following templates: the intact tRNA$_1^{Met}$ gene and the wild-type 5S gene (lane 1), the intact tRNA$_1^{Met}$ gene (lane 2), the anterior region subclone (pA-tmet) (lane 3), the posterior region subclone (pB-tmet) (lanes 4, 6, 7, and 8), or pBR322 (lane 5). After the initial incubation the reactions were supplemented with nucleoside triphosphates, factor A, and the following components: none (lane 1), 5S gene (lanes 2 to 6), 5S gene plus factor B (lane 7), or 5S gene plus factor C (lane 8). The relative amounts of the transcription factors used in (b) were the same as in Fig. 4b (that is, the competition was performed under conditions of limiting factor C). The small arrows designate the position of RNA's derived from the posterior region subclone (pB-tmet). The anterior and posterior region subclones of the *Xenopus laevis* tRNA$_1^{Met}$ gene were constructed as described (*22*) except that the anterior (upstream from residue 30) and the posterior (downstream from residue 31) fragments were individually blunt-end ligated into the Hind III site of pBR322.

contains the B sequence block and presumably inhibits VA I transcription through an interaction with one or more transcription factors. To clarify whether this region interacts with a common factor necessary for 5S gene transcription, a competition experiment was performed with the 5S gene. Prior incubation of the intact tRNA gene with factors B and C completely inhibited subsequent 5S RNA synthesis (lane 2 in Fig. 10b). Prior incubation of the posterior region of the tRNA gene with these factors (lane 4) depressed subsequent 5S RNA transcription to one-fourth the level observed after an initial incubation with either the subclone of the anterior region (lane 3) or pBR322 (lane 5). The depression of 5S RNA synthesis was relieved by additional factor C (lane 8), but not additional factor B (lane 7). Thus, prior incubation of the factors with the posterior region of the tRNA gene depresses 5S gene transcription because of the functional depletion of factor C. A subclone containing the A sequence block of the tRNA gene does not functionally sequester this factor more than does pBR322.

Factor C interactions near the B block

344

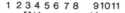

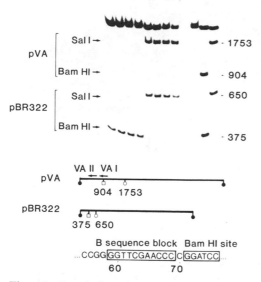

Fig. 11. Restriction site protection of a sequence adjacent to the B block in the VA I gene by factor C. An autoradiography of end-labeled DNA fragments separated by gel electrophoresis is shown. 2.5 ng each of the VA I plasmid (pVA) and pBR322, end-labeled at the Eco RI site, were mixed together with 0.3 μg of factor C. After 10 minutes of incubation at 30°C, 10 units of Bam HI (lanes 1 to 4) or 10 units of Sal I (lanes 5 to 8) were added, and the reactions were incubated at 30°C for another 2.5 minutes (lanes 1 and 5), 5 minutes (lanes 2 and 6), 10 minutes (lane 3 and 7), or 20 minutes (lanes 4 and 8). The end-labeled plasmids were incubated in the absence of factor C for 20 minutes at 30°C with no restriction enzyme (lane 9), 10 units of Bam HI (lane 10), or 10 units of Sal I (lane 11). The restriction maps of pVA and pBR322, both linearized at the Eco RI site, are shown: (●) an Eco RI site, (□) a Bam HI site; and (○) a Sal I site. The sequence of the noncoding strand of the VA I gene, adjacent to the B sequence block, is displayed; numbers below the sequence indicate the nucleotide distance downstream from the 5′ end of VA I RNA.

of the VA RNA gene. A likely factor C recognition site in the posterior half of the tRNA gene is the B sequence block. Because of the relatively greater stability

of the complex of factor C and the VA I gene, we examined whether factor C directly interacts with the B block homology in this gene. We took advantage of the presence of a single Bam HI recognition site located one nucleotide downstream from the B sequence block in the VA I gene (see Fig. 11), reasoning that a stable factor C interaction with the B sequence block might protect the adjacent Bam HI site from cleavage. For controls we monitored the protection of the Sal I site at the border of the Ad2 insert in pVA and the Bam HI and Sal I sites in pBR322 in the presence of factor C.

In the experiment shown in Fig. 11, pBR322 and pVA were mixed after they had been cleaved and end-labeled at the single Eco RI site present in each plasmid. These DNA's were incubated first with factor C for 10 minutes and then with Bam HI for an additional 2.5, 5, 10, and 20 minutes (lanes 1 to 4). Whereas the pBR322 Bam HI site was completely cleaved after 5 minutes in the presence of factor C (lane 2), 90 percent of the pVA Bam HI sites remained resistant to cleavage after 20 minutes of incubation with the enzyme (lane 4). Similarly, the labeled DNA's were incubated with factor C, followed by digestion with Sal I for 2.5, 5, 10, and 20 minutes (lanes 5 to 8). The Sal I site in both plasmids was equally accessible to this restriction enzyme in the presence of factor C. Protection of the Bam HI site within the VA I gene was not observed after incubation of the DNA with bovine serum albumin or with heat-treated factor C (80°C for 10 minutes; data not shown). Therefore, the VA I Bam HI site is specifically and stably protected by a heat-labile component present in factor C. Protection of the Bam HI site by factor C could be due either to a steric blockade of the site or to an alteration of the sequence topology (discussed below).

Conclusions and Implications

To further our understanding of basic transcription mechanisms for eukaryotic genes, and ultimately the regulation thereof, we investigated the transcription factor requirements for formation of stable (preinitiation) complexes on specific genes. These complexes are a common feature of class III genes and are inferred from the ability of a given gene, after its incubation with limiting amounts of factors, to preclude transcription of competing templates added subsequently. As summarized in Fig. 1, the formation of such complexes requires factors A and C for 5S genes, factors B and C for a tRNA gene, and only factor C for the adenovirus VA I RNA gene. These factors are presumably the key factors involved in initial promoter recognition but represent only a subset of those required overall for transcription. It should be emphasized that these experiments, because of the assay employed, do not exclude the possibility that the other factors might stably associate with these complexes. It is, in fact, likely that such complexes serve as recognition sites for these other essential components (factor B and RNA polymerase III), which could cycle during the reaction (see below).

Factor C is a pivotal component of stable complexes. Factor C, which is needed to form a stable complex on all RNA polymerase III templates tested, is itself bound in the stable complex on all of these genes and does not act simply to catalyze the formation of the complex. Whereas the VA I and tRNA$_1^{Met}$ genes directly interact with this factor, the 5S gene appears to require an additional component (factor A) to promote factor C binding. A potential recognition site for factor C on the 5S gene is discussed in the following subsection. As shown above, a subclone of the posterior region of the tRNA$_1^{Met}$ gene can specifically sequester factor C and thereby suppress either VA I or 5S RNA synthesis from a secondary template. Others have noted that the 3′ half of the tRNA$_1^{Met}$ gene, containing the B block (Fig. 1) specifically depresses transcription of the intact gene in an unfractionated oocyte extract (*22*), and the formation of a stable complex on a *Drosophila* tRNA^{Arg} gene in crude cellular extracts requires sequences in the B block (*23*). It therefore seems probable that binding of factor C to the posterior region of the tRNA$_1^{Met}$ gene is directly or indirectly dependent on interaction with the B sequence block. In support of this hypothesis, we demonstrated that factor C specifically protects from endonucleolytic cleavage the Bam HI site located just 3′ of the B sequence block in the VA I gene. The prolonged protection of this site (for at least 20 minutes) in the presence of a vast excess of the restriction enzyme strongly indicates a stable interaction of DNA and protein and is consistent with the stable interaction of the VA I gene with factor C observed in the incubation-competition assay. Protection of this site could be due either to a steric blockade or to an alteration of the topology of the DNA in this region. The B sequence block in the VA I gene has the potential to form a stem-loop structure (see below) that would include two nucleotides of the Bam HI recognition site and therefore preclude cleavage. Using deoxyribonuclease I protection experiments, we recently demonstrated that factor C interacts over the entire B sequence block of the VA I gene (12). Similarly, a yeast homogenate contains a factor that interacts with the B block of the VA I gene and several tRNA genes (24).

An interaction of human factor C with the tRNA$_1^{Met}$ gene in the absence of other factors has not yet been demonstrated directly (for example, by deoxyribonuclease I protection experiments). However, the presence of such an interaction has been inferred from two-step incubation-competition experiments (Fig. 7) in which the stabilizing B factor (added in excess with the second template) is apparently able to transform an otherwise unstable complex into a stable complex (prior to dissociation of the former). The unstable interaction of factor C with the tRNA$_1^{Met}$ gene is not simply a consequence of the use of heterologous components, since an unstable interaction of the human tRNA^{Met} gene with factor C (in the absence of factor B) has also been observed (25).

Although factor C alone binds tightly to the VA I gene, the stability of the factor C–VA I complex is apparently increased in the presence of factor B. Therefore, it seems likely that the VA I and tRNA^{Met} genes interact in a qualitatively similar manner with the transcription factors, but that they are distinguished by quantitative differences in relative affinities for factor C. If tRNA (or VA RNA) promoter function involves the factor-dependent formation of a stem-loop structure in the B block region, as suggested by Hall et al. (5), the more stable interaction of factor C with the VA gene could be due to a greater stability of the VA gene stem-loop [a stem of six GC pairs (G, guanine; C, cytosine) and a loop of six bases versus the tRNA gene stem-loop [a stem of three GC and two AT (A, adenine; T, thymine) pairs and a loop of seven bases]. Alternatively, the relative stabilities of the factor C–DNA complexes could result from sequence differences in this region (7).

The 5S gene complex involves both gene-specific and common factors. The human factor A interacts with the 5S gene in the absence of other factors, as demonstrated by the two-step incubation-competition assay and as anticipated from previous studies of the *Xenopus* factor A (10, 26, 27). However, as suggested for the *Xenopus* factor A complex (16), the human factor A–5S gene complex is unstable and readily dissociates in the presence of another 5S gene. We demonstrated that this unstable association is transformed into a stable complex in the presence of factor C, which appears to remain associated with this complex. Thus far, we have not been able to demonstrate, with the two-step incubation-competition assay, any independent interactions of factor C with the 5S gene, even though this factor forms complexes with the VA gene (tight) and the tRNA gene (weak) under the same conditions.

The foregoing observations suggest that the order of interaction of factors with the 5S gene is factor A followed by factor C. They also raise questions about the factor C recognition site and possible alterations of the factor A interactions in the presence of factor C. Apart from the fact that the factor A interaction appears to involve the entire 5S promoter sequence (Fig. 1), there is the additional observation that the factor C interaction site within the VA and tRNA gene involves a region (the B block) whose consensus sequence has not been clearly identified in the 5S promoter [(6); see below]. While an A block consensus sequence is common to the class III genes (6) and is a potential site of interaction for the common factor C, the failure to detect (in the competition assay) an interaction of factor C with a gene fragment containing this region makes it more likely that this is a recognition site for other common components, such as factor B or RNA polymerase III. These considerations raise the possibility that interaction of factor A with the promoter induces or establishes a factor C recognition site consisting either of DNA contacts or protein (factor A) contacts, or a combination of both. It may be significant that the interaction of the *Xenopus* factor A with the 5S gene induces three sites of deoxyribonuclease I hypersensitivity on the noncoding strand of the gene (*10, 27*), the most prominent of which is in a region with marked homology to the B sequence block of the tRNA promoter (*8*). It is conceivable that the factor A interaction increases the affinity of this site for factor C (as well as for deoxyribonuclease I). Deoxyribonuclease I protection studies should determine whether factor C requires a factor A "adaptor" function to recognize the promoter region of the 5S gene or whether the factor A (or factor C) interactions in binary (metastable) complexes are different from those in ternary (stable) complexes.

The transformation of a metastable complex of factor A and the 5S gene into a stable complex is reminiscent of the transition of a bacterial RNA polymerase "closed" promoter complex into a stable "open" (preinitiation) complex (*28*). Although it is unclear whether factors A and C induce the equivalent of an open complex on the 5S gene, there are several relevant observations. (i) The *Xenopus* factor A alone effects a small change in helix rotation (equivalent to an unwinding of 2 to 4 base pairs) (*29*). (ii) The *Xenopus* factor A makes contacts with phosphate and guanine residues primarily on the noncoding strand of the 5S gene promoter (*27*); this leads to the suggestion that factor A might transiently shift to the noncoding strand during transcription. (iii) Preliminary studies (*30*) indicate that the *Xenopus* factor A, in the presence of other factors from an oocyte extract, can bind specifically to a single-stranded M13 clone containing the noncoding strand of the 5S gene. It is tempting to speculate, therefore, that factor C may enhance the interaction of factor A with the noncoding strand of the 5S gene and thereby induce a stable "open" complex on the gene.

Sequence of factor interactions. On the basis of our analyses of factor requirements for formation of metastable as opposed to stable complexes, it appears that the order of factor interactions for the 5S gene is factor A, factor C, and factor B or RNA polymerase III, whereas that for tRNA and VA RNA genes is factor C, factor B, and RNA polymerase III.

Although we have no information on the role of factor B in 5S gene transcription, it appears to stabilize the factor C–tRNA gene complex and, to a much lesser extent, the factor C–VA gene complex. We have attempted to determine whether factor B simply catalyzes the stable association of factor C or is itself bound into a stable complex on these templates. Under our conditions of analysis, factor B does not appear to remain stably bound to the VA I and tRNA genes in the presence of factor C or to the 5S gene in the presence of factors A and C, respectively. Although it seems, from the assay employed, that factor B exchanges between templates during transcription in vitro, we cannot rule out the possibility that our incubation conditions do not permit the assembly of factor B into a stable complex that might otherwise exist in vivo (but see note added in proof). In fact, the first study suggesting the presence of stable complexes within natural templates (*17*) indicated that isolated chromatin is associated with all the components (presumably including factors A, B, and C) necessary to promote transcription of the endogenous 5S genes by purified RNA polymerase III. We have also found that recombinant SV40 minichromosomes containing tRNA genes can be isolated in association with transcription factors B and C, but not RNA polymerase III (*25*). Thus, it is conceivable that factor B associates with the other factors in a preinitiation complex, which can be isolated with cellular and viral chromatin but which cycles during the transcription reaction. These chromatin studies, along with our demonstration that stable complexes can form on class III genes in the absence of RNA polymerase III, suggest that the final recognition event before transcription involves the RNA polymerase and protein-DNA contacts in the preinitiation complex.

Implications for gene regulation. Since the class III genes thus far tested share at least three common transcription factors (factors B, C, and RNA polymerase III), their relative activities during physiological transitions in which one or more factors become rate-limiting may be in part determined by their relative affinities for individual factors. The remarkable stability of the stable complexes also provides a means for maintaining the transcription potential of one set of genes to the exclusion of another, potentially competing, set (*16*) and emphasizes the special role of those factors involved in complex formation. One ex-

ample of a situation in which these considerations may be relevant is the lytic infection of human cells by adenovirus 2. This process occurs with a high level of replication (many thousandfold) and transcription of the viral VA RNA genes (which account for the vast majority of class III transcripts). Although it is not yet established that any of the factors (particularly factor C) actually becomes rate-limiting during infection, the level of 5S synthesis remains unaltered, while that of tRNA synthesis is dramatically reduced (*31*). Apart from the fact that cellular factors might be modified during infection to accommodate the establishment of viral transcription complexes, it is also possible that the VA I gene may have evolved to bind factor C more tightly in the absence of other factors so as to compete more effectively for limiting amounts of this factor (free or bound) within the cell.

A second example concerns the differentially expressed classes of 5S RNA genes in *Xenopus* (*16*); these present a somewhat special case since they are subject to regulation by both common and gene-specific (factor A) components. Exactly how these genes are differentially regulated is unclear, but Brown and his colleagues (*16, 32*) have demonstrated that this reflects the selective establishment and maintenance of stable complexes on one class of genes in somatic cells that contain limiting amounts of factor A (*14*). These investigators have also described the general implication of stable complexes for the maintenance and propagation of the activated state of a gene.

A key issue is how these complexes are established in the cell within the context of the natural chromatin structures and, in particular, whether they can be established on a "static" structure (under the influence of other factors) or whether stable complex formation might be linked to other general events (such as DNA replication), which make this structure more flexible (accessible) (*32, 33*). Thus, while the present studies represent an important step in defining how these complexes are established on purified genes, they must ultimately be extended to chromatin templates and to the analysis of other regulatory factors.

Note added in proof: Recent kinetic analyses (*30*) suggest that the rate of association of factor B with the 5*S* gene is considerably slower than that for factors A and C. In experiments, performed as in Fig. 9, preferential transcription of one gene has now been shown to be directly proportional to the length of time this gene was initially incubated with factor B. This observation suggests that factor B is sequestered in a stable complex on class III genes only after an extended incubation (40 minutes).

References and Notes

1. N. Heintz and R. G. Roeder, in *Genetic Engineering*, J. K. Setlow and A. Hollaender, Eds. (Plenum, New York, 1982), vol. 4, p. 57.
2. The term "encoding" is used in a broad sense to indicate the DNA sequences whose transcription generates the RNA species indicated.
3. S. Sakonju, D. F. Bogenhagen, D. D. Brown, *Cell* **19**, 13 (1980).
4. D. F. Bogenhagen, S. Sakonju, D. D. Brown, *ibid*., p. 27.
5. B. D. Hall, S. G. Clarkson, G. Tocchini-Valentini, *ibid*. **29**, 33 (1982).
6. G. Ciliberto, G. Raugei, F. Costanzo, L. Dente, R. Cortese, *ibid*. **32**, 725 (1983).
7. G. Galli, H. Hofstetter, M. L. Birnstiel, *Nature (London)* **294**, 626 (1981).
8. D. M. Fowlkes and T. Shenk, *Cell* **22**, 405 (1980).
9. J. Segall, T. Matsui, R. G. Roeder, *J. Biol. Chem.* **255**, 11986 (1980).
10. D. R. Engelke, S. Y. Ng, B. S. Shastry, R. G. Roeder, *Cell* **19**, 717 (1980).
11. B. S. Shastry, S. Y. Ng, R. G. Roeder, *J. Biol. Chem.* **257**, 12979 (1982).
12. P. L. Martin, unpublished observations.
13. B. Emerson and R. G. Roeder, in preparation.
14. B. M. Honda and R. G. Roeder, *Cell* **22**, 119 (1980).
15. H. R. B. Pelham and D. D. Brown, *Proc. Natl. Acad. Sci. U.S.A.* **77**, 4170 (1980).
16. D. F. Bogenhagen, W. M. Wormington, D. D. Brown, *Cell* **28**, 413 (1982).
17. C. S. Parker and R. G. Roeder, *Proc. Natl. Acad. Sci. U.S.A.* **74**, 44 (1977).
18. C. Wandelt and I. Grummt, *Nucleic Acids Res.* **11**, 3795 (1983).
19. B. L. Davison, J. M. Egly, E. R. Mulvihill, P. Chambon, *Nature (London)* **301**, 680 (1983).
20. Throughout this study we have used human transcription factors in conjunction with heterologous genes (the *Xenopus* 5*S* RNA and tRNA$_1^{Met}$ genes), as well as the homologous VA I gene in human adenovirus 2. The conclusions based on the studies with amphibian genes are justified on the basis of the following: (i) the sequences of the human and amphibian tRNA$_1^{Met}$ species, and therefore the internal control sequences, are identical; (ii) the human 5*S* RNA and the *Xenopus* somatic 5*S* RNA species are 94 percent homologous overall and differ by only one base pair in the internal control region consisting of about 50 base pairs.
21. The recombinant DNA plasmids containing the *Xenopus borealis* somatic type 5*S* gene (pXBS1) and the 5*S* maxigene (p115/77) were obtained from D. Brown and his colleagues [R. C. Peterson, J. L. Doering, D. D. Brown, *Cell* **20**, 131 (1980); D. F. Bogenhagen and D. D. Brown, *ibid*. **24**, 261 (1981)]. The plasmids containing the adenovirus 2 wild-type VA I gene (pVA) and minigene (pVA dl 1) were obtained from T. Shenk (*8*). The construction of the plasmid containing the *Xenopus laevis* tRNA$_1^{Met}$ gene (pX1tmet1) is outlined in (*10*). B. Shastry of our laboratory provided us with plasmids containing the anterior (pA-tmet) and posterior (pB-tmet) regions of the tRNA$_1^{Met}$ gene.
22. A. Kressman *et al.*, *Nucleic Acids Res.* **7**, 1749 (1979).
23. J. Schaack, S. Sharp, T. Dingermann, D. Soll, *J. Biol. Chem.* **258**, 2447 (1983).
24. R. Klemenz, D. J. Stillman, E. P. Geiduschek, *Proc. Natl. Acad. Sci. U.S.A.* **79**, 6191 (1982).
25. A. B. Lassar, unpublished observations.
26. S. Sakonju, D. D. Brown, D. Engelke, S. Y. Ng, B. S. Shastry, R. G. Roeder, *Cell* **23**, 665 (1981).
27. S. Sakonju and D. D. Brown, *ibid*. **31**, 395 (1982).
28. M. J. Chamberlin, in *RNA Polymerase*, R. Losick and M. Chamberlin, Eds. (Cold Spring Harbor Laboratory, Cold Spring Harbor, N.Y., 1976), p. 159.
29. W. F. Reynolds and J. M. Gottesfeld, *Proc. Natl. Acad. Sci. U.S.A.* **80**, 1862 (1983).
30. J. J. Bieker and R. G. Roeder, unpublished observations.
31. H. Soderlund, U. Pettersson, B. Vennstrom, L. Philipson, *Cell* **7**, 585 (1976).

32. W. M. Wormington, M. Schlissel, D. D. Brown, *Cold Spring Harbor Symp. Quant. Biol.* **47**, 879 (1982).
33. J. Gottesfeld and L. S. Bloomer, *Cell* **28**, 781 (1982).
34. H. Hofstetter, A. Kressmann, M. L. Birnstiel, *ibid.* **24**, 573 (1981).
35. R. Guilfoyle and R. Weinmann, *Proc. Natl. Acad. Sci. U.S.A.* **78**, 3378 (1981).
36. E. Slattery, J. D. Dignam, T. Matsui, R. G. Roeder, *J. Biol. Chem.* **258**, 5955 (1983).
37. P. A. Weil, J. Segall, B. Harris, S. Y. Ng, R. G. Roeder, *ibid.* **254**, 6163 (1979).

38. We thank M. Birnstiel, D. Brown, T. Shenk, B. Shastry, and M. Zasloff for recombinant DNA plasmids, and M. Sawadogo, J. Segall, and E. Slattery for preparations of factor C, RNA polymerase III, and poly(ADP-ribose) polymerase, respectively. A.B.L. thanks H. Sive and N. Heintz for advice and encouragement during the course of this work. Supported by research grants CA 24223 and CA 24891 from the National Cancer Institute and by grant NP-284 from the American Cancer Society. P.L.M. was supported by Medical Scientist training grant GM07200 from the National Institutes of Health.

26. BK Viral Enhancer Element and a Human Cellular Homolog

Nadia Rosenthal, Michel Kress, Peter Gruss, George Khoury

Identification of elements that control the initiation of transcription is a crucial step in understanding the regulation of eukaryotic gene expression. Approaches to the problem of transcriptional control with animal viruses as a model system have recently uncovered transcriptional regulatory elements, called enhancers. The prototype enhancer was originally identified in the DNA virus SV40 as a set of cis-essential sequences required for efficient expression of early viral genes (1). These elements increase the level of transcription of an adjacent gene from its promoter in a fashion that is relatively independent of position and orientation (2). Subsequent studies uncovered similar elements in a number of DNA viruses including polyoma virus (3), papilloma virus (4), and adenovirus (5, 6). Retroviruses also contain enhancer elements in their long terminal repeats (7–10).

Although there is no extended sequence homology among these elements, a 7- to 10-bp (base pair) consensus or "core" sequence has been identified in a number of enhancers. Deletions or mutations in the core sequence of SV40 obliterate enhancer activity (2, 11), suggesting that it is an important component of the enhancer. Apart from the core, viral enhancer elements show very little sequence similarity even in closely related viruses.

The limited coding capacity of certain viruses makes them dependent on host cell regulatory molecules that are normally directed toward the expression of cellular genes. In some cases these cellular factors, as yet undefined, appear to mediate the activity of viral enhancers in a host-specific way. For example, when compared to the 72-bp repeats of SV40, the enhancer associated with the long terminal repeat (LTR) of Moloney murine sarcoma virus is more active in murine cells than it is in primate cells (8, 10). The host cell preference of several viral enhancers (8, 10, 12, 13) suggests that similar transcriptional regulatory elements associated with host genes may interact with a limited set of cellular factors, contributing to the cell specificity of gene expression. The recent description of tissue-specific enhancer elements in mouse immunoglobulin gene introns (14–16) strongly supports this supposition, and suggests that enhancers may be a general feature of cellular gene regulation.

We have used the human papovavirus BKV as a viral model of eukaryotic transcriptional control. This virus was first isolated from the urine of an immunosuppressed patient (17) and is suspected of causing an inapparent childhood infection (18). The virus grows optimally in human tissue culture and undergoes an abortive cycle in nonprimate cells, transforming rodent cells in vitro and inducing tumors in hamsters (*19*). Papovaviruses BKV (BK virus) and SV40 are remarkably similar, sharing more than 80 percent of their nucleotide sequences (*20, 21*). They differ substantially in only a small stretch of tandem repeated nucleotides to the "late" side of the replication origin (*19–22*). In SV40, these sequences include the 72-bp enhancer element. The dissimilarity of the SV40 and BKV repeated sequences suggests that they may not have evolved from a common viral ancestor (*20*), but may have derived from the host cell genome. Our study was undertaken to assign an enhancer function to the BKV repeats, to demonstrate the presence of homologous human genomic sequences, and to assess their ability to function as an enhancer element.

Construction of BKV-CAT
Expression Plasmids

Comparison of the BKV and SV40 genomes reveals a region of extensive sequence heterology situated to the late side of the replication origins (*19–22*). For both viruses, this region begins with an AT-rich (A, adenine; T, thymine) stretch that includes the Goldberg-Hogness or TATA box for the early (T antigen) transcriptional units. In SV40 the TATA box is preceded by three GC-rich 21-bp repeats (G, guanine; C, cytosine), each containing two copies of the sequence CCGCCC. The role of these repeats is not clear, but they may be involved in RNA polymerase binding and viral DNA replication (*2, 23*). Adjacent to the 21-bp repeats are two tandem 72-bp repeats, which have been characterized as enhancer elements for early SV40 gene expression (*1, 2*) (Fig. 1).

The Dunlop strain of BKV contains a 68-bp triplication (the central copy of which is missing 18 nucleotides) preceding the AT-rich region (*20*). This set of nucleotides bears some similarity to both the 21-bp and the 72-bp SV40 tandem repeats. In each of the BKV units, there is one copy of a GC-rich hexanucleotide (CCTCCC) analogous to those in the SV40 21-bp repeats. In addition, each of the BKV units contains the sequence GGTCATGGTTTG, similar to the proposed SV40 enhancer core sequence (GGTGTGGAAAG).

To test the triplicated BKV sequence for enhancer activity, we isolated a 216-bp fragment, containing all three repeats without a TATA box or replication origin, by Hae III restriction enzyme cleavage of the BKV genome (Fig. 1). We used the chloramphenicol acetyltransferase (CAT) assay to evaluate enhancer activity (*24*). In this assay, a bacterial gene encoding the enzyme CAT is linked to several eukaryotic regulatory signals from the early transcription unit of SV40. The resulting plasmid (pA$_{10}$ cat$_2$) includes a portion of the "early" SV40 promoter (the 21-bp repeats and TATA box) from which the enhancer sequence has been deleted, an intron, and a polyadenylation signal (*8, 24*). The addition of enhancer elements to pA$_{10}$ cat$_2$ results in efficient CAT gene expression when introduced into eukaryotic cells. The amount of gene product (CAT) is measured by its in vitro conversion of chloramphenicol to an acetylated form. Since eukaryotic cells do not contain a gene for the CAT enzyme, there is no background. The assay therefore provides a sensitive, quantitative, and reproducible estimate of gene activity induced by added enhancer sequences.

Since the prototypic enhancer se-

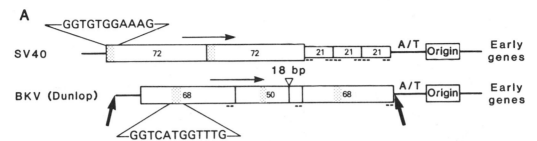

Fig. 1. Analysis of the BKV tandem triplication. (A) A comparison of the tandem repeated regions of SV40 (*19*) and BKV (Dunlop strain) (*20*). The diagram presents the control regions adjacent to the papovaviral replication origins. The three BKV 68 tandem repeats (the central copy has an 18-bp deletion) are located upstream from the early TATA box, as are both sets of SV40 repeats. The stippled region marks the putative enhancer core sequence in SV40 (GGTGTGGAAAG) and an analogous sequence in BKV (GGTCATGGTTTG); dashes underline the GC-rich 21-bp repeats in SV40 (CCGCCC) and similar GC-rich hexanucleotide sequences in BKV (CCTCCC). Arrows indicate Hae III sites used to excise a 216-bp fragment containing the BKV tandem repeats. (B) Structure of the BKV repeat-containing expression plasmids pBKs5′cat, pBKa5′cat, and pBKs3′cat. Bam HI linkers were ligated to the Hae III blunt ends of the 216-bp BKV subfragment containing the tandem repeats. Plasmid pA₁₀cat₂ was cleaved with either Bgl II or Bam HI generating cohesive termini. Linear vectors were ligated with the BKV 216-bp fragment (*46*) and recombinant plasmids were transfected into *Escherichia coli* HB101 by the calcium phosphate method (*25*). Alternative orientations of the repeats (with respect to their position in the BKV early transcription unit) were selected in 5′ position, and the sense orientation was in the 3′ position. pBKs5′cat, BKV repeats in the sense orientation relative to the CAT gene, inserted at the Bgl II site (5′ position). pBKa5′cat, BKV repeats in the antisense orientation at the Bgl II site (5′ position). pBKs3′cat, BKV repeats in the sense orientation at the Bam HI site (3′ position).

quences appear to function in a position and orientation independent fashion (*2*), the 216-bp BKV fragment described above was placed in both sense (s) and antisense (a) orientations (relative to its position in the BKV genome) at the 5′ end of the gene (pBKs5′cat and pBKa5′cat, respectively), and in the s orientation at the 3′ end of the gene (pBKs3′cat). In the latter construction, the BKV sequences are 3 kb upstream or 2 kb downstream from the SV40 promoter elements in the circular molecule (Fig. 1).

Enhancer Activity of the BKV Repeats

Each plasmid containing the BKV triplication was separately transfected

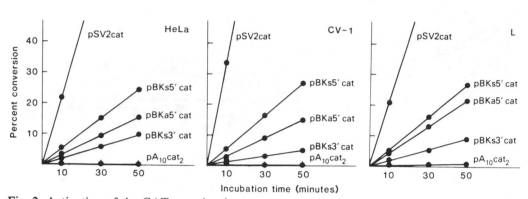

Fig. 2. Activation of the CAT gene by the repeat sequences from BKV and SV40. Equivalent amounts (25 μg) of the CAT plasmids containing the BKV repeats (pBKs5'cat, pBKa5'cat, and pBKs3'cat), the SV40 repeats (pSV2cat), or no enhancer element (pA$_{10}$cat$_2$) were introduced into human HeLa cells, monkey CV-1 cells, or mouse L cells (10^6 cells in 100-mm dishes) by calcium precipitation (8, 24). Cultures were harvested 48 hours after transfection, and protein extracts were prepared and analyzed for CAT activity (24). Conversion of chloramphenicol (percent) to an acetylated form was calculated by thin-layer chromatography and radioactive scintillation counting of the spots cut from the plate. Values are an average of three separate experiments, each performed on duplicate plates.

into semiconfluent HeLa (human), CV-1 (monkey), or L (mouse) cells by the calcium phosphate method (25). After 48 hours, the cells were harvested, and total protein was extracted and assayed for CAT activity (8, 24). Enzyme assays for each set of transfected cells are shown as time course in Fig. 2. The effect of the BKV repeats on CAT expression is compared to the SV40 72-bp repeats (pSV2cat) and to the plasmid with no enhancer (pA$_{10}$cat$_2$). Kinetic analyses of the CAT activity of the BKV constructs normalized against pSV2cat levels in each cell type are presented in Table 1.

These data show that the BKV fragment enhances CAT expression from the heterologous SV40 promoter in both orientations and at a distal 3' location in all three cell types. The construct containing the SV40 enhancer, pSV2cat, induces CAT expression in HeLa and L cells to levels four times as high and in CV-1 cells six times as high as pBKs5'cat, the analogous construct con-

taining the BKV repeats. This difference may reflect properties of the individual constructions; for example, in the BKV plasmids the 68-bp triplication, each of which contains its own GC-rich sequence, is separated from the TATA box by the SV40 GC-rich 21-bp repeats. Alternatively, the relative strengths of the BKV and SV40 enhancers measured in this assay may reflect a true difference of enhancer activity in vivo. This difference is consistent with the biological properties of the two viruses, since it has been shown that BKV grows more slowly in primate cells than does SV40 (26). The induction of CAT activity by plasmids with the BKV sequences in the 5' location were reproducibly higher than induction by the plasmid in which they were positioned 3' to the CAT gene, although the 3' antisense orientation was not tested. We have obtained similar results in the analysis of enhancer sequences from murine sarcoma virus (9). Whether the differences in activity reflect the increased distance between enhancer and promoter elements, cryptic plasmid promoters which compete for activity (27), or a contribution from promoter sequences within the BK repeats, remains unclear.

In summary, the 68-bp BKV triplication functions as an enhancer element for gene expression in a number of cell types without a pronounced host cell preference. Like other enhancer elements, it has the properties of position and orientation independence although the level of gene enhancement appears to depend on the location of the BKV sequence in any particular construct.

Homologous Sequences in the Human Genome

To investigate the possibility that viral enhancers may have cellular homologs, we screened a human genomic λ library (28) for sequences related to the BKV tandem triplication with the 216-bp BKV Hae III fragment as a probe. One genomic clone (Hbk9) that hybridized strongly with the probe after repeated plaque purifications was selected for further analysis. Restriction enzyme mapping and Southern blot analysis (29) generated a map of the clone (Fig. 3). All of the BKV-homologous sequences are located within a 1.8-kb Eco RI fragment at one end of the 14.6-kb human sequence inserted in Hbk9. The possibility that Hbk9 contained sequences homologous to regions of BKV other than the enhancer segment was tested by hybridizing a ^{32}P-labeled nick-translated probe of the BKV genome minus the enhancer to a Southern blot of Eco RI–cleaved Hbk9 DNA. The absence of a signal indicates that the human BKV-homologous segments are not associated with an integrated virus (data not presented).

To determine whether the BKV-homologous sequences in clone Hbk9 were represented elsewhere in the human genome, we used the 1.45-kb Eco RI–Pst I fragment from this clone to probe a Southern blot of human genomic DNA cleaved with Eco RI or Hinf I. The probe hybridizes to only one band in each digest (Fig. 4), suggesting that the region homologous to the BKV enhancer represented in clone Hbk9 is present at a single chromosomal site. The size of the fragment (2.7 kb) in the Eco RI digests (Fig. 4, lanes 1 and 3) is larger than 1.8 kb, reflecting the fact that construction of the library generated artificial Eco RI sites at the ends of the clones. Therefore, the 2.7-kb fragment observed in the genomic DNA's is only partially represented in Hbk9. The single 1.45-kb fragment detected by hybridization of the enhancer probe to the Hinf I digest of human genomic DNA (lanes 2 and 4) is entirely included in clone Hbk9. No additional bands were detected in identical blots hybridized under less stringent conditions (data not presented). These results suggest that there are no other significant stretches of sequences homologous to the BKV repeats in the human genome either adjacent to those included in Hbk9, or at other locations.

A similar analysis was performed on DNA from two different monkey cell sources (AGMK and CV-1) and a mouse cell line (NIH 3T3) cleaved with Eco RI or Hinf I and hybridized under the same conditions. The BKV-related sequence is present in the monkey genome (Fig. 4, lanes 5 to 8), but absent from the mouse genome (lanes 9 and 10). The size of the internal Hinf I fragment is slightly smaller in the monkey genome (1.3 kb; Fig. 4, lanes 6 and 8) than in the human genome (1.45 kb), perhaps reflecting a deletion or

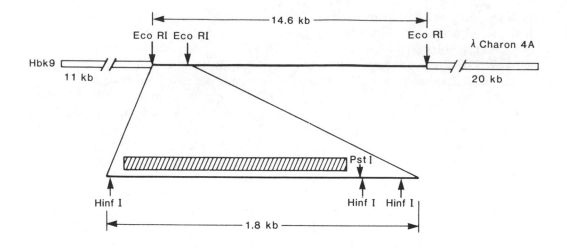

M 1 2 3 4 5 6 7 8 9 10

kb
23.1
9.4
6.6

4.3

2.3
2.0

0.56

Fig. 3 (above). Map of clone Hbk9. A human genomic library, constructed by cloning a Hae III–Alu I partial digest of human DNA into λ vector Charon 4A by way of Eco RI linkers (28), was screened with the 216-bp BKV Hae III fragment (see Fig. 1) as a ^{32}P-labeled probe. Under stringent conditions [6× SSC (0.9M NaCl, 0.09M sodium citrate), 50 percent formamide at 37°C], 12 clones from a genomic library equivalent (800,000 clones) hybridized to the probe. After repeated plaque purifications only one clone, Hbk9, annealed strongly and was selected for further study. A detailed map was generated from restriction enzyme analysis and Southern blotting with the BKV repeat probe (data not shown). The entire sequence homologous to BKV (hatched bar) is contained within the 1.8-kb Eco RI fragment at one end of clone Hbk9. Fig. 4 (left). Hybridization of human, monkey, and mouse genomic DNA with the human BKV-homologous repeats. Genomic DNA's (10 μg) were digested with either Eco RI or Hinf I and subjected to electrophoresis on a 1 percent agarose gel. After transfer to nitrocellulose paper (29), the digested DNA was hybridized with a ^{32}P-labeled nick-translated probe representing the 1.45-kb Eco RI–Pst I fragment from Hbk9. This fragment contains all the BKV-homologous sequences in the clone. Hybridization conditions were 3× SSC at 60°C. Lane M, ^{32}P end-labeled λ-Hind III marker; lanes 1 and 2, adult human leukocyte DNA, sample A; lanes 3 and 4, adult human leukocyte DNA, sample B; lanes 5 and 6, CV-1 cell monkey DNA; lanes 7 and 8, AGMK cell monkey DNA; lanes 9 and 10, NIH 3T3 mouse DNA. For each pair of DNA's, the left lane is an Eco RI digest, and the right lane is a Hinf I digest.

Eco RI linker
     Hinf I
└─►TTCT<u>GAGTC</u>AATTAAAACTCTTTTCTTTATAAAATTACCCAGTCTCATGTATTTCTTCATAGCAGCATCGAGAATGAAGGAATA

CACCTTCCTTAGTTCGTGACTATCACCTCTCTGGTTGTGGCTATCACATACTTGGTTGTGATTATCAACCTCCCTGGTTATGGTGA

CATCTTCCCTGACTGTGGCTATCACCTCCCTGGTTGTGGTTATTACCTCCCTGGTTGTGATCATCATCTCCTTCCGTTGTGGTTAT

CACCTTCCCTTGGTTGTGGATAT — — — ~1 kb — — CACCTCCCTCATTGTGGTTATCACTTCCCTGGTCGTGTTAT

CACCTCCCTGGTTGTGGTCATCACCTCCCTCATTGTGGTCATCATTCCCCTGGTTGTGGTTATCACTTCCTTTGTTGTGGATCTCA

CTTCCCTCGTTGTGGTTCTCACCTCCCTCTGTGGTGGTGATTACTTTTCTCACTGTGATTTCCTGCTTCTTTATTGCCCACTCACT

  Pst I   **Hinf I**
ACA<u>CTGCAG</u>ATCATTGAGGAGACA<u>GACTC</u>AGCCTTTTATCTTTTATGCCTGACCAAATACATGTATCTTAATATCAACTTTTTCTC

ATAATTTAATGAGCATCTACATTGTTGGGTTGAGCAAATACACACCGCTCCTTCCCTCCTGGAGCTTGCAGCACACAGCCAATAAG

                                         Hinf I
AGGCATGCAATGACCCAGTTCATTGCCACTAAGTCAGCAGAGCATTGGGTCACCATGACAACAGG<u>GAATC</u>ATGGGGTTAAATGGTAG

                                       Eco RI
GAAAAGCAGGCTTCACGAAGGAAGTGAAATAAATGCATGCTGTTTTCTGAATTTTGCCTTTTTAGTCAGCAT<u>GAATTC</u>

Fig. 5. Sequence of the BKV enhancer-homologous human locus and flanking DNA. Sequence analysis was performed on subclones of the 1.8-kb Eco RI fragment in an M13 vector (*30*), by the primer extension method in the presence of 2′,3′-dideoxy nucleoside triphosphates, and buffer gradient gels (*31*). Arrows above the sequences show the repeat periodicity beginning and ending within the sequenced fragment. The central 1-kb segment containing analogous repeats has been omitted for simplicity.

polymorphism in the number of repeat units. The 2.7-kb Eco RI fragment present in human DNA appears as a 7.0-kb band in monkey DNA (lanes 5 and 7), presumably due to the loss of an Eco RI site.

Tandem Repeats in the Human Sequence

The nucleotide sequence of the 1.8-kb Eco RI fragment was determined after subcloning into M13 (*30*) by the dideoxy primer extension method (*31*). A portion of the region homologous to the BKV enhancer is shown in Fig. 5. A series of 20- to 21-bp repeats begins about 100 bp inside the terminal Eco RI site and extends for 1.4 kb, ending about 60 bp before the single Pst I site (Fig. 3). A representative group of 12 repeats is shown in Fig. 6, with the sequence of the BKV tandem repeat for comparison. Adjacent human genomic repeats are non-

Human
Cellular repeats

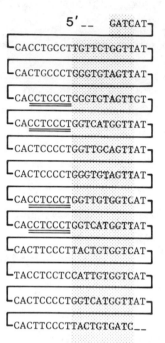

Fig. 6. A representative subclone from the human locus generated by digestion of the 1.8-kb Eco RI fragment with Sau 3A I. The sequence is arranged to show the tandem 21-bp repeated structure. The sequence of the BKV repeats is presented below for comparison. Single underlines mark the putative BKV enhancer core sequence. Stippling defines the BKV core sequence and homologous sequences in the human clone. Double underlines mark a GC-rich hexanucleotide in BKV (the apparent counterpart of the GC-rich element in the SV40 21-bp repeats) which occurs frequently in the human tandem repeats. The sequence shown is part of the 1-kb tandem repeated region marked by dashes in Fig. 5.

BKV repeats

5'__GTCATGCACTTTCCTTCCTGAGGTCATGGTTTGGCTGCATTCCATGGGTAAGCAGCTCCTCCCTGTGA

⌐GTCATGCACTTTCCTTCCTGAGGTCATGGTTTGGCTGCATTCCCCTGTGA

⌐GTCATGCACTTTCCTTCCTGAGGTCATGGTTTGGCTGCATTCCATGGGTAAGCAGCTCCTCCCTGTGG__

identical but are > 70 percent homologous to one other. Like the BKV enhancer, the human tandem repeats are not especially GC-rich (this subclone is 53 percent GC). A 10-bp oligonucleotide represented in several repeats (GGTCATGGTT) matches the putative core sequence found in the BKV enhancer. Each repeat has a sequence that is homologous, but not always identical, to this core sequence. Further, the hexanucleotide CCTCCC present in the BKV triplication and similar to the hexanucleotide present in SV40 21-bp repeats (CCGCCC) appears frequently in the human subclone (double underline). We cannot exclude the possibility that a few copies of these repeats exist in an isolated form elsewhere in the human genome. On the basis of the Southern blot analysis (Fig. 4), however, it is unlikely that extensive tandem repeats such as those found in clone Hbk9 are present at another locus.

Enhancer Activity of the Human Repeats

Although the sequence length and arrangement of the human genomic tandem repeats is different from that of the BKV enhancer, certain similarities such as the core region and the GC-rich hexanucleotides are impressive. To examine the possibility that these structural similarities underlie an analogous function, we tested the human tandem repeats for cellular enhancer activity. The entire 1.8-kb Eco RI fragment containing all of the repeat units was cloned in both orientations at the 5' end of the CAT gene (the Bgl II site) in $pA_{10}cat_2$, the vector used to test the BKV repeats (see Fig. 1) or at the 3' end of the CAT gene (the Bam HI site) in the same vector. In the latter constructions, the human sequence is separated from the CAT gene promoter elements by 2 to 3 kb in the circular plasmid. Alternate orientations were designated s (sense), and a (antisense)

with respect to their homology to the BKV repeats.

The recombinant plasmids p1.8s5'cat, p1.8a5'cat, p1.8s3'cat and p1.8a3'cat were introduced into HeLa, CV-1, or L cells under the same conditions that were used previously for plasmids containing the BKV enhancer. The CAT assays were performed on the cellular extracts prepared 48 hours after transfection.

Figure 7 shows representative time courses of CAT assays for the four plasmids as well as pBKs5'cat in each cell type. These data are shown in Table 1 as kinetic analyses normalized to the CAT activity of pBKs5'cat. In both HeLa and L cells the human tandem repeats enhance the expression of CAT in all positions and orientations. In these cells lines, they are generally five times less active than the BKV enhancer in analogous constructs but are 5 to 20 times more active than the control plasmid

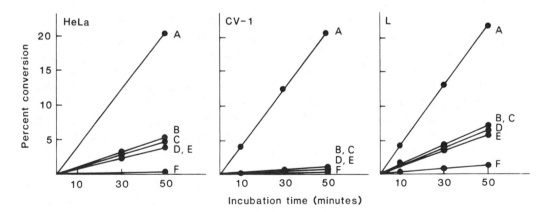

Fig. 7. Activation of the CAT gene activity by the human genomic repeat locus. The human genomic 1.8-kb Eco RI fragment (see Fig. 3) was subcloned via Bam HI linkers into either the 5' or 3' positions of $pA_{10}cat_2$ (Fig. 1). Plasmids containing this fragment in both orientations (sense and antisense) at each position (5' and 3') were selected. CAT assays were performed as described in Fig. 2 on cells transfected by the four recombinant plasmids p1.8s5'cat (B), p1.8a5'cat (C), p1.8s3'cat (D), p1.8a3'cat (E); and by pBKs5'cat (A) and $pA_{10}cat_2$ (F), the positive and negative controls, respectively. Values represent an average of three separate experiments, each performed on duplicate plates.

Table 1. Enhancer activity (relative) of the BKV repeats and a homologous human genomic segment. In the upper portion of the table is a kinetic analysis of CAT activity of the BKV constructs relative to pSV2cat in each cell type (Fig. 2). The lower portion of the table shows the kinetic analysis of the CAT activity of the human tandem repeat constructs relative to pBKs5'cat in each cell type (Fig. 7).

Plasmid	HeLa	CV-1	L
BKV constructs			
pSV2cat	100	100	100
pBKs5'cat	25	18.5	25
pBKa5'cat	15.5	9.6	23.3
pBKs3'cat	9.8	3.5	8.8
$pA_{10}cat_2$	0.2	0.1	1.2
Human constructs			
pBKs5'cat	100	100	100
p1.8s5'cat	25	5	33
p1.8a5'cat	23	5	33
p1.8s3'cat	19	4	30.8
p1.8a3'cat	19	4	27.2
$pA_{10}cat_2$	1	1	5.0

$pA_{10}cat_2$, which contains no enhancer element. Unlike the BKV enhancer, none of these constructs enhanced CAT gene expression significantly over background levels in CV-1 cells (Table 1).

Several subfragments of the 1.8-kb segment containing 4 or 12 human tandem repeat units were also subcloned into the $pA_{10}cat_2$ vector and tested for enhancer activity in all three cell types. Each of the smaller inserts induced approximately the same levels of CAT gene expression as the complete 1.8-kb fragment in HeLa and L cells, and were also inactive in CV-1 cells (data not presented).

Evidence for Cellular Enhancers

The experiments presented above describe the characterization of the BKV enhancer element and the isolation of a human tandem repeated sequence homologous to it. When linked to a test gene and introduced into mammalian tissue culture cells, this human locus exhibits several characteristics ascribed to viral enhancers (2). First, the human sequence elevates the expression of the linked CAT gene from a heterologous SV40 promoter. Second, the expression of the CAT gene is increased by the human tandem repeats in both proximal and distal positions from the promoter. Finally, the orientation of the repeats relative to the CAT transcription unit, and the number of repeat units included in the constructs, do not qualitatively affect their enhancing capacity.

These host cellular sequences enhance CAT expression to levels between 5 and 20 times the baseline expression seen in the absence of enhancers. Compared to the levels of CAT expression in cells transfected with the BKV enhancer constructs, however, the homologous human sequences are only about 20 percent as active in HeLa and L cells and are essentially inactive in CV-1 cells. Several possible explanations can be advanced for the lower level of enhancer activity of the human tandem repeats compared to the viral enhancer element. It seems reasonable to suggest that many host genes, expressed at low levels in a particular cell, are not associated with a strong enhancing element. Viruses have evolved to compete with cellular transcriptional units in the cells they infect. As a result, the affinity of viral enhancers for cellular factors may exceed the affinity of homologous cellular regulatory sequences for these factors. The comparatively low enhancing ability of the human tandem repeated element may be typical of certain cellular enhancers. In support of this model, similar enhancing ability has recently been reported for a random fragment of mouse DNA, isolated by its ability to restore the transformation potential of a polyoma virus, whose enhancer had been deleted. The sequence responsible for activating polyoma virus early gene expression has been mapped to a 58-bp segment of mouse DNA with no obvious homology to known viral enhancer sequences. Transformation of rat cells by the recombinant virus was 20 to 40 percent as efficient as that of wild-type virus (32).

Alternatively, the locus we have isolated may function at considerably higher levels in a tissue that we have not yet tested. Our observation that the human tandem repeated sequences act as enhancers in HeLa and L cells but not in CV-1 cells (even though the monkey genome contains homologous counterparts) may indicate that their activity is not host-specific but rather cell-specific. The possibility that enhancers may affect the expression of associated genes in a tissue-specific way is supported by studies with several viral enhancers (8–12) as well as by experiments involving polyoma viruses with mutations in their enhancer elements. These mutant viruses exhibit an altered phenotype that allows them to grow on undifferentiated teratocarcinoma stem cells, whereas wild-type polyoma virus cannot (33). Also, a naturally occurring variant of BKV with a single small deletion in the tandem repeated region can transform hamster and rat cells more efficiently than wild-type BKV but grows more slowly in human cells (34). This same variant induces an unusually high number of insulinomas when injected into hamsters (35).

The tissue-specific expression of some cellular genes may be controlled in the same way. The sea urchin histone H2a gene (36), and the human α-globin gene (37), are examples of cellular coding sequences that may be regulated by enhancer-like elements. Several groups of investigators have identified a region in introns of the mouse immunoglobulin heavy chain (14, 15) and light chain (16) genes which acts as an enhancer for the immunoglobulin gene expression. A short, repeated sequence, present in the heavy chain gene intron (14, 15), closely resembles the enhancer core sequence defined in SV40 (2, 8, 11). An interesting aspect of this discovery is that the immunoglobulin enhancers activate adjacent genes at high levels only in lymphoid cells (14–16). These studies suggest that differences in the sequences of either viral or cellular enhancer elements may dictate the tissue-specific transcription of adjacent genes through interaction with factors which are specifically present in those cells.

Other examples of short tandem repeated sequences have been found to be associated with several human structural genes. These include the polymorphic 14- to 15-bp repeats upstream of the insulin gene which appear to be unique in the genome (38), a block of 14-bp repeats in the intron of the zeta-globin gene (39), and an 800- to 900-bp stretch of 28-bp repeats in the 3' flanking region of the proto-oncogene c-Ha-ras-1 (40). These sequences do not share extended homology with the BKV-like repeats, and their role in regulating the expression of linked genes remains to be determined.

The potential association of the BKV-homologous human tandem repeats with a functional gene will first require the identification of an adjacent sequence coding for a specific transcript. Although there are no open reading frames in the repeats or flanking DNA sequence so far examined, a potential TATA box and an appropriately spaced initiation codon near the internal Eco RI site at the end of the 1.8-kb fragment may signal the beginning of a coding region just beyond the end of the sequenced subclone.

Structure of Enhancer Elements

It seems clear that two different tandem repeated sequences fulfill an analogous role in the two closely related papovaviruses SV40 and BKV. Enhancer equivalents in cellular DNA might be expected to retain a structural similarity to the tandem repeated sequences of viral enhancers, reflecting a related function. Several previous studies were designed to test this possibility by isolating cellular sequences homologous to viral control elements. Sequences from both monkey (41) and human (42) genomes have been obtained by hybridization to the SV40 Hind III C fragment, which contains the origin of DNA replication as well as the transcriptional regulatory sequences. Both the monkey and human sequences isolated with this probe were homologous to the region surrounding the viral origin of replication, containing multiple copies of the GC-rich hexanucleotide (CCGCCC) found in the SV40 21-bp repeats. The monkey sequences are present in the genome in about 100 copies and can promote bidirectional transcription without a TATA box in CV-1 cells (43), although no enhancer activity is observed (44). The human sequences related to SV40 have been shown to enhance the frequency of thymidine kinase positive (tk$^+$) colony selection when a linked herpes simplex virus tk gene is introduced into LTK$^-$ cells (42). These sequences are present in multiple copies in the human genome.

In contrast, the human locus isolated with the BKV repeat probe appears to be unique in the genome. It does not hybridize with any other portion of the BK viral DNA besides the tandem triplication. Although no clear structural relationship exists between the BKV 68-bp triplication and the human 20- to 21-bp repeats, short stretches of homology, such as the enhancer core element (GGTCATGGTTAT) and the GC-rich hexanucleotide (CCTCCC), appear in many of the repeat units, and are probably responsible for the strong hydridization of the BKV probe to the human locus. Further, limited areas of homology to the human tandem repeats can be identified in other viral enhancer elements. For example, sequences in both the BKV tandem triplication (ATGCACTTTCCT) and several human cellular repeat elements (TATCACTTCCCT), are similar to a repeated element located in the adenovirus type 5 E1A enhancer region [TTTCACTTCCT, antisense strand (6)].

The varied arrangement of these homologous oligonucleotides in viral and cellular enhancers suggests that if certain essential elements are retained, enhancer structure may be flexible without loss of function. For example, the two major variants of BKV (Dunlop and MM) differ significantly in the arrangement of their repeated segments (20, 21). Other viable strains of BKV have been isolated which display a wider variation of sequence arrangements in the tandem repeat region (34, 45). A common ancestral sequence may have been acquired by the BKV prototype and evolved in different ways to produce a series of effective viral transcriptional control elements.

Clearly, the BKV enhancer did not derive directly from a transduced portion of the cellular repeats described above; the viral repeats contain stretches of sequence, absent from the human locus, which presumably contribute to the ability of viral enhancer to function both efficiently and independently of cell type. Yet, the persistence in the human genome of tandem repeats with both structural and functional analogies to the BKV enhancer implies a degree of evolutionary relatedness between viral control elements and host cell sequences. Whether the unique locus of cellular repeats represents a functional element for adjacent genes in the human genome remains to be determined.

References and Notes

1. C. Benoist and P. Chambon, *Nature (London)* **290**, 304 (1981); P. Gruss, R. Dhar, G. Khoury, *Proc. Natl. Acad. Sci. U.S.A.* **78**, 943 (1981).
2. P. Moreau, R. Hen, B. Wasylyk, R. Everett, M. P. Gaub, P. Chambon, *Nucleic Acids Res.* **9**, 6047 (1981); J. Banerji, S. Rusconi, W. Schaffner, *Cell* **27**, 299 (1981); M. Fromm and P. Berg, *J. Mol. Appl. Gen.* **1**, 457 (1982); *Mol. Cell. Biol.* **3**, 991 (1983).
3. J. de Villiers and W. Schaffner, *Nucleic Acids Res.* **9**, 6251 (1981); C. Tyndall, G. La Mantia, C. M. Thacker, J. Favaloro, R. Kamen, *ibid.*, p. 6231.
4. M. Lusky, L. Berg, H. Weiher, M. Botchan, *Mol. Cell. Biol.* **3**, 1108 (1983); Y.-C. Yang *et al.*, personal communication.
5. D. L. Weeks and N. C. Jones, *Mol. Cell. Biol.* **3**, 1222 (1983); J. Nevins *et al.*, personal communication; P. Chambon *et al.*, personal communication.
6. P. Hearing and T. Shenk, *Cell* **33**, 695 (1983).
7. B. Levinson, G. Khoury, G. Vande Woude, P. Gruss, *Nature (London)* **295**, 568 (1982); C. M. Gorman, G. T. Merlino, M. C. Willingham, I. Pastan, B. H. Howard, *Proc. Natl. Acad. Sci. U.S.A.* **79**, 6777 (1982); D. J. Jolly, A. C. Esty, S. Subramani, T. Friedmann, I. M. Verma, *Nucleic Acids Res.* **11**, 1855 (1983); P. A. Luciw, J. M. Bishop, H. E. Varmus, M. A. Capecchi, *Cell* **33**, 705 (1983).
8. L. A. Laimins, G. Khoury, C. Gorman, B. Howard, P. Gruss, *Proc. Natl. Acad. Sci. U.S.A.* **79**, 6453 (1982).
9. L. A. Laimins, P. Gruss, R. Pozzati, G. Khoury, *J. Virol.*, in press.
10. M. Kriegler and M. Botchan, *Mol. Cell. Biol.* **3**, 325 (1983).
11. H. Weiher, M. König, P. Gruss, *Science* **219**, 626 (1983); M. Kessel, personal communication.
12. B. J. Byrne, M. S. Davis, J. Yamaguchi, D. Bergsma, K. N. Subramanian, *Proc. Natl. Acad. Sci. U.S.A.* **80**, 721 (1983).
13. J. de Villiers, L. Olson, C. Tyndall, W. Schaffner, *Nucleic Acids Res.* **10**, 7965 (1982);
    P. E. Berg *et al.*, *Mol. Cell. Biol.* **3**, 1246 (1983).
14. S. D. Gillies, S. L. Morrison, V. T. Oi, S. Tonegawa, *Cell* **33**, 717 (1983).
15. J. Banerji, L. Olson, W. Schaffner, *ibid.*, p. 729.
16. C. Queen and D. Baltimore, *ibid.*, p. 741.
17. S. D. Gardner, A. M. Field, D. V. Coleman, B. Holme, *Lancet* **1971-I**, 1253 (1971).
18. S. D. Gardner, *Br. Med. J.* **1**, 77 (1973); K. V. Shah, R. N. Daniel, R. Warszawski, *J. Infect. Dis.* **128**, 784 (1973); P. Brown, T. Tsai, D. C. Gajdusek, *Am. J. Epidemiol.* **102**, 331 (1975).
19. For a review see J. Tooze, Ed., *Molecular Biology of Tumor Viruses. DNA Tumor Viruses*, (Cold Spring Harbor Press, Cold Spring Harbor, N.Y., rev. ed. 2, 1981).
20. I. Seif, G. Khoury, R. Dhar, *Cell* **18**, 963 (1979).
21. R. C. A. Yang and R. Wu, *Science* **206**, 456 (1979).
22. P. M. Howley, M. F. Mullarkey, K. K. Takemoto, M. A. Martin, *J. Virol.* **15**, 173 (1975); G. Khoury, P. M. Howley, J. Garon, M. F. Mullarkey, K. K. Takemoto, M. A. Martin, *Proc. Natl. Acad. Sci. U.S.A.* **72**, 2563 (1975); J. E. Osborn, S. M. Robertson, B. L. Padgett, D. L. Walker, B. Weisblum, *J. Virol.* **19**, 675 (1976).
23. R. D. Everett, D. Baty, P. Chambon, *Nucleic Acids Res.* **11**, 2447 (1983).
24. C. M. Gorman, L. F. Moffat, B. H. Howard, *Mol. Cell. Biol.* **2**, 1044 (1982).
25. M. Mandel and A. Higa, *J. Mol. Biol.* **53**, 154 (1970).
26. N. M. Maraldi, G. Barbanti-Brodano, M. Portolani, M. LaPlaca, *J. Gen. Virol.* **27**, 71 (1975).
27. B. Wasylyk, C. Wasylyk, P. Augereau, P. Chambon, *Cell* **32**, 503 (1983).
28. R. M. Lawn, E. F. Fritsch, R. C. Parker, G. Blake, T. Maniatis, *ibid.* **15**, 1157 (1978).
29. E. M. Southern, *J. Mol. Biol.* **98**, 503 (1975).
30. J. Messing and J. Vieira, *Gene* **19**, 269 (1982).
31. F. Sanger, S. Nicklen, A. R. Coulson, *Proc. Natl. Acad. Sci. U.S.A.* **74**, 5463 (1977); M. D. Biggin, T. J. Gibson, G. F. Hong, *ibid.* **80**, 3963 (1983).
32. M. Fried, M. Griffiths, B. Davies, G. Bjursell, G. La Mantia, L. Lania, *ibid.*, p. 2117.
33. M. Katinka, M. Yaniv, M. Vasseur, D. Blangy, *Cell* **20**, 393 (1980); F. K. Fujimura, P. L. Deininger, T. Friedmann, E. Linney, *ibid.* **23**, 809 (1981); M. Katinka, M. Vasseur, N. Montreau, M. Yaniv, D. Blangy, *Nature (London)* **290**, 720 (1981); K. Sekikawa and A. J. Levine, *Proc. Natl. Acad. Sci. U.S.A.* **78**, 1100 (1981); F. K. Fujimura and E. Linney, *ibid.* **79**, 1479 (1982).
34. S. Watanabe and K. Yoshiike, *J. Virol.* **42**, 978 (1982).
35. ———, A. Nozawa, Y. Yuasa, S. Uchida, *ibid.* **32**, 934 (1979).
36. R. Grosschedl and M. L. Birnstiel, *Proc. Natl. Acad. Sci. U.S.A.* **77**, 1432 (1980).
37. P. Mellon, V. Parker, Y. Gluzman, T. Maniatis, *Cell* **27**, 279 (1981); R. K. Humphries *et al.*, *ibid.* **30**, 173 (1982).
38. G. I. Bell, M. J. Selby, W. J. Rutter, *Nature (London)* **295**, 31 (1982); P. S. Rotwein *et al.*, *N. Engl. J. Med.* **308**, 65 (1983).
39. N. J. Proudfoot, A. Gil, T. Maniatis, *Cell* **31**, 553 (1982).
40. D. J. Capon, E. Y. Chen, A. D. Levinson, P. H. Seeburg, D. V. Goeddel, *Nature (London)* **302**, 33 (1983).

364

41. C. Queen, S. T. Lord, T. F. McCutchan, M. F. Singer, *Mol. Cell. Biol.* **1**, 1061 (1981).
42. S. E. Conrad and M. R. Botchan, *ibid.* **2**, 949 (1982).
43. J. Saffer and M. Singer, in press.
44. S. Subramani and J. Saffer, personal communication.
45. J. van der Noordaa, personal communication.
46. P. Gruss and G. Khoury, *Proc. Natl. Acad. Sci. U.S.A.* **78**, 133 (1981).

47. We thank Y. Barra, J. Brady, R. Brent, D. Cosman, P. Howley, G. Jay, M. Kessel, L. Laimins, M. Martin, R. Muschel, R. Pozzatti, J. Savarese, and M. Singer for helpful discussions and editing; A. B. Rabson and R. Koller for gifts of AGMK and human DNA's; J. Duvall, M. Chang, M. Priest, and D. Hawkins for technical assistance. N.R. was supported by a Damon Runyon–Walter Winchell Cancer Fund fellowship.

27. Duplication of an Insertion Sequence During Transpositional Recombination

Ted A. Weinert, Nancy A. Schaus, Nigel D. F. Grindley

The genomes of a wide variety of eukaryotic and prokaryotic organisms contain segments of DNA that can move from one location to another and can mediate other genetic rearrangements. Indeed, these transposable elements (transposons) provide the molecular basis for the genetic instability that has puzzled and intrigued geneticists for several decades (*1*).

Many different transposons have been identified in Gram-negative bacteria and extensively characterized. Most of them fall into one of two groups (*2*): the rather homogeneous Tn*3* family of transposons, and the more heterogeneous collection of insertion sequences (IS) (together with the composite transposons that contain a segment of DNA flanked by two copies of an IS). Attempts to understand the mechanisms of transpositional recombination have focused on genetic and structural characterization of the transposons themselves and of the products formed during recombination. One of the primary questions has been whether a transposon is duplicated during transpositional recombination.

In the case of Tn*3* and related transposons there is a strong evidence that transposition is a replicative process (*3*).

During the first stage of transposition, donor and target replicons are fused to form a cointegrate. This intermediate contains two copies of Tn*3*, one at each junction between donor and target DNA sequences (*4*). From this cointegrate, simple insertions can then be generated by a site-specific recombination between the two transposon copies. For the second group of transposons, the IS elements, the evidence for replicative transposition is much weaker. Although IS elements do promote the fusion of replicons, this occurs only infrequently (at about 1 percent of the frequency of simple insertions) (*5–7*), and once formed the resultant cointegrates are generally stable in a RecA⁻ host strain. Simple insertions of an IS are therefore thought to be generated not by breakdown of a cointegrate intermediate but rather by a one-step process that results directly in the integration of a single IS copy at a target site. From the strong dependence of cointegrate formation on *recA* activity that is found with the IS*50* composite transposon, Tn*5* (*7*), it has been argued that the cointegrates observed may result from simple insertions from dimers of the donor replicon rather than from true replicon fusion between the target

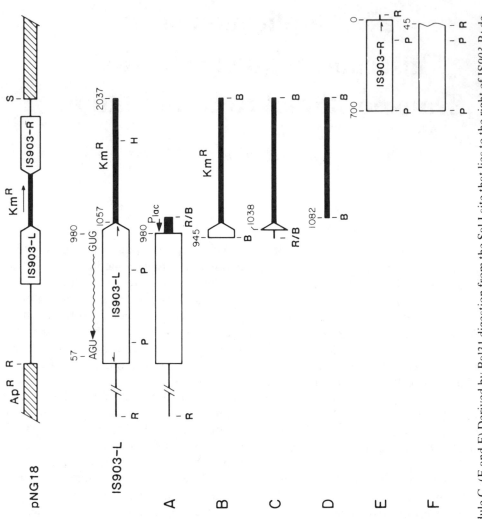

Fig. 1. Tn903 and modules for construction of IS903 derivatives. Restriction endonuclease cleavage sites are: B, Bam HI; H, Hind III; P, Pvu II; R, Eco RI; S, Sal I. The plasmid pNG18, a derivative of pBR322 that carries Tn903, has been described (13); pBR322 sequences are shown as shaded blocks. IS903-L and IS903-R are defined relative to the direction of transcription of the kanamycin resistance gene (Km^R) and to the Eco RI and Sal I sites. IS903 contains a single long coding frame that starts with a GUG at position 980 and ends with the UGA at position 59; the translation product of this reading frame is absolutely required for transpositional recombination. The short half-arrows at each end of IS903 indicate the 18-bp terminal inverted repeats. (A) The right end of IS903-L has been removed and replaced with a 100-bp Eco RI–Pvu II fragment from pGL101 (33) that carries the lacUV5 promoter. The fusion abuts the flush end of the Pvu II site to position 980 of IS903 (the translational start site). Module A has either an Eco RI or a Bam HI site at the promoter-proximal end. (B to D) Three Km^R modules. They share a common right end that was constructed by insertion of a Bam HI linker into the Fnu4H I site that lies across the junction between Km^R and IS903-R. The left end of module B is a Bam HI linker at the Ava II site of IS903 (position 945) (13). Module C contains exactly 20 bp from the right end of IS903-L; it is separated from the terminal Eco RI or Bam HI sites by 40 bp of non-IS903 sequences. Module D contains a Bam HI linker at position 1082 of Tn903; it was derived by Bal31 digestion into the left end of module C. (E and F) Derived by Bal31 digestion from the Sal I site that lies to the right of IS903-R; deletions were terminated with Eco RI linkers, and end points were determined by restriction endonuclease and DNA sequence analyses. The deletion in module E stops 10 bp short of the right (outer) end of IS903-R while that in module F removes the terminal 45 bp of IS903-R (but leaves the coding frame intact).

and a monomer of the donor (8). Apart from cointegrate formation, the only other overtly replicative transpositional process is "inversion-insertion" (also called "duplicative inversion") (2): the inversion of a DNA segment adjacent to a transposon, coupled to an insertion of the element in the opposing orientation at the other end of the inverted DNA segment (see Fig. 5B). However, only three examples of such IS-mediated inversion-insertions have been documented (two with IS1 and one with IS10) and all were detected in RecA$^+$ hosts (9, 10). Thus the possibility remains that these rearrangements took place in two unlinked steps: an intermolecular insertion of the IS in inverted orientation, followed by recA-mediated recombination between the two IS copies to invert the intervening DNA segment.

With evidence for the apparently replicative IS transpositional processes of replicon fusion and inversion-insertion in some doubt, it is not surprising that evidence for a replicative process in the formation of simple insertions or a fourth IS-promoted genetic rearrangement, adjacent deletions, is essentially nonexistent. Interestingly, bacteriophage Mu, representative of a third group of bacterial transposons (2), provides the first direct evidence that simple insertions may occur by a conservative, nonreplicative mechanism (11). Yet it is clear in the case of Mu that the major transpositional pathway is a replicative process since it is only by transposition that the Mu genome is replicated during the phage lytic cycle (12).

Analysis of IS903-Mediated

Intramolecular Events

In an effort to gain more insight into the mechanism of IS transpositional re-

combination we have begun a systematic study of intramolecular rearrangements mediated by IS903 in a host strain that is deficient in homologous recombination.

IS903 is the component of the composite transposon Tn903 that provides the functions and sites for transpositional recombination (13). The IS is 1057 base pairs (bp) in length, has a long open reading frame (307 codons) that encodes a transposase, and has perfect terminal inverted repeats of 18 bp (13, 14) (Fig. 1). Transposition of IS903 or of Tn903 results in duplication of a 9-bp target sequence with one copy at each end of the integrated element (15). Tn903 transposes at a low frequency as a result of inefficient expression of the transposase gene. To increase the frequency of transpositional recombination and to ensure that expression of the transposase was not influenced by the presence of the IS903 end adjacent to the start of the gene, we have constructed a derivative in which the transposase gene is transcribed from the lacUV5 promoter (Fig. 1A). When incorporated into a complete Tn903, this promoter fusion increased transposition by a factor of about 100 (16).

So that we can select for IS-mediated intramolecular rearrangements we have cloned a conditionally lethal gene close to IS903 derivatives on a multicopy plasmid. The gene we have used is galK; expression of galK in a galE$^-$T$^-$ strain of Escherichia coli is lethal in the presence of galactose because toxic levels of galactose-1-phosphate accumulate. The plasmids pTW75 and pTW76 were constructed (see Fig. 2) and were introduced into the host strain NG135 (K12 galΔS165 recA56 strA) by transformation. Individual transformants were grown in Luria broth overnight to allow formation and segregation of rearrangements of the plasmids. Cells (10^7) from

368

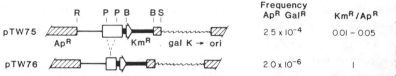

	Frequency Ap^R Gal^R	Km^R/Ap^R
pTW75	2.5 x 10^{-4}	0.01 – 0.05
pTW76	2.0 x 10^{-6}	1

Fig. 2. IS*903* mediates deletions. The structures of pTW75 and pTW76 are as shown. pTW75 is a derivative of pBR322 that contains the Tn*903* modules A and B (see Fig. 1) inserted between the Eco RI and Bam HI sites (pBR322 sequences are shown as shaded blocks). The *galK* segment (wavy line) is the entire 2.5-kb segment of pKG1900 (*34*) that runs from the Eco RI site to the *gal*-pBR322 fusion point (the Pvu II site of pBR322); this region contains the *galK* gene of *E. coli* under control of the *gal* promoter. pTW76 is identical to pTW75 except that the 520-bp Pvu II fragment from within IS*903* has been deleted to inactivate the transposase. Plasmids were introduced into the host strain NG135 (K12 *gal*ΔS165 *recA56 strA*) by transformation. Rearrangements that inactivated the *galK* gene were selected by plating about 10^7 cells from a series of independent overnight cultures onto LB-agar plates containing 1 percent galactose and carbenicillin (40 μg/ml); plates were incubated at 42°C. The frequencies of Ap^R Gal^R indicate the proportion of cells that survive, averaged from four to six independent cultures. Km^R/Ap^R indicates the proportion of Ap^R Gal^R clones that retained resistance to kanamycin.

each overnight culture were plated on LB agar plates supplemented with 1 percent galactose (to select for events that inactivate *galK*) and carbenicillin (50 μg/ml) (to ensure retention of the plasmid). About 100 times as many survivors were obtained from cultures of cells harboring pTW75, the plasmid with an active IS*903*, as from those with pTW76, which contains a deleted transposase gene (Fig. 2). More than 95 percent of the galactose-resistant (Gal^R) cells that initially contained pTW75 simultaneously became sensitive to kanamycin. This suggested that a single deletion event was responsible for loss of both kanamycin resistance (Km^R) and *galK* expression. Extraction of plasmid DNA and analysis with restriction endonucleases showed that the pTW75 plasmids suffered deletions that spanned the region between the IS*903* and *galK* (Fig. 3). However, as expected from results obtained with other IS elements (*17*), the IS*903* itself was retained; a Taq I site 18 bp inside the deletion-proximal end was retained in every event analyzed. DNA sequence analysis confirmed that the

IS*903* terminal inverted repeat was joined to new target DNA from the *galK* region of the plasmid (data not shown). As can be seen from Fig. 3 the deletions extended to various end points. This is consistent with the view that IS*903* does not have any marked specificity for its target site (*13, 15*).

Analysis of plasmid DNA isolated from Gal^R survivors from cells containing the transposase-defective control plasmid pTW76 showed that the background level of survivors was due in part to insertions of IS*1* and IS*2* into the *galK* region. Some plasmids gave the same restriction map as the parental pTW76 and proved to retain an active *galK* gene; we suspect that a chromosomal mutation rendered their hosts resistant to galactose.

Several replicative models for transposition predict that both deletions and inversion-insertions are the result of an intramolecular cointegrate process (*18–20*). Whether the outcome is deletion or inversion-insertion is determined only by the orientation of the target site when it interacts with the transposon. By demanding retention of kanamycin resistance along with acquisition of galactose resistance we can select for IS903-mediated events that inactivate *galK* without deleting the intervening DNA. We have analyzed 20 Km^R Gal^R clones from strains with pTW75 or with the structurally similar plasmid pTW90 (see Fig. 4). None of these contained inversion-insertions, although five did contain a second insertion of IS903; the rest were not IS903-mediated events.

Deletion Formation Requires

Both Ends of IS903

Formally, the result of an IS-mediated deletion is a new junction between one end of the IS and the target DNA; the other IS end remains at its original location. We have constructed plasmids to test whether the deletion-distal end of IS903 plays a role in formation of deletions adjacent to the other end. Deletion formation from the left end of IS903-L was tested with the plasmids pTW105 and pTW106. Plasmid pTW106 differs from pTW105 only in that it contains an IS903 terminus at its right end (Fig. 4A). Rearrangements resulting in galactose resistance occur in pTW106 at normal frequency (similar to pTW75), but are reduced to background levels in pTW105 (Fig. 4A). Restriction analysis of plasmid DNA from Gal^R clones showed, as expected, that pTW106 was yielding a high frequency of IS903-mediated deletions, but that loss of the deletion-distal IS end prevented formation of similar deletions in pTW105.

Analogous experiments with a second pair of plasmids, pTW90 and pTW88, gave similar results (Fig. 4B), showing that the left end of IS903-L is required for the normal high frequency of deletion formation from the right end. In the case of pTW88, however, restriction analysis of plasmid DNA from Gal^R clones showed that a few deletions joining the right end of IS903 to *galK* had occurred. Since both ends of IS903 are clearly required for a high frequency of deletion formation, we suspect that an alternative sequence is fulfilling the role of the deletion-distal terminus in the low frequency formation of IS903-mediated deletions in pTW88. One potential sequence with partial homology to the IS903 end resides within IS903 itself at position 931 to 939 (13); this 9-bp sequence is identical to position 2 to 10 in the terminal inverted repeat and in pTW88 has the correct (inverted) orientation relative to the deletion-proximal end. Machida *et al.* (21) showed that IS102, a transposon highly homologous to IS903 (22), can occasionally use sequences with partial homology to the terminal inverted repeat as alternative ends in transposition.

For both pTW105 and pTW88 we investigated whether replacing an IS903 end restored deletion formation to its normal high frequency. Using the module that contains just 20 bp from the right end of IS903-L, we constructed the plasmids pTW107 and pTW110 (see Fig. 4). In both cases the recombinogenic activity of IS903 was completely regained. We analyzed plasmid DNA from more than 100 Gal^R clones derived from pTW106 and pTW107; all contained deletions adjacent to IS903; none contained an inversion-insertion.

It is noteworthy that deletion formation in pTW90 is consistently between one-third and one-sixth as efficient as that in either pTW75 or pTW110, even though the IS903 sequences in the two are identical; the only difference between pTW90 and pTW75 is the DNA sequence between the left end of IS903-

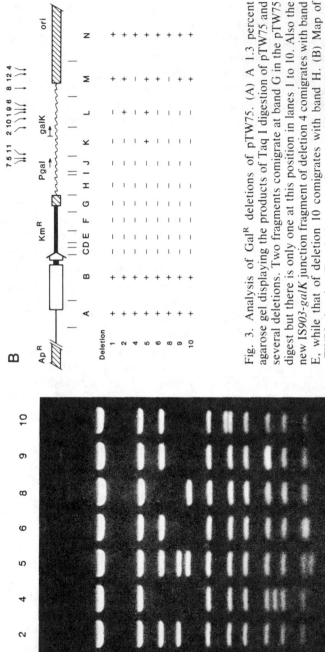

Fig. 3. Analysis of Gal^R deletions of pTW75. (A) A 1.3 percent agarose gel displaying the products of Taq I digestion of pTW75 and several deletions. Two fragments comigrate at band G in the pTW75 digest but there is only one at this position in lanes 1 to 10. Also the new IS903-galK junction fragment of deletion 4 comigrates with band E, while that of deletion 10 comigrates with band H. (B) Map of pTW75 showing Taq I cleavage sites and deletion end points. For each of the deletions analyzed in (A) the presence (+) or absence (−) of specific restriction fragments is indicated below the map.

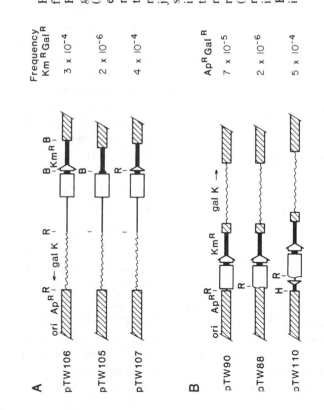

Fig. 4. Deletion formation requires both ends of an IS. (A) Deletions from the left end of IS903-L. pTW106 contains modules A and B (see Fig. 1) inserted between the Eco RI and Bam HI sites of pBR322. The galK segment is the 2.6-kb Eco RI–Tth111 I fragment from pKG1800 (34) and is inserted into the Eco RI site with the direction of galK expression as shown. pTW105 is like pTW106 but contains the Km^R module D (Fig. 1) and hence has no IS903 terminal inverted repeat at the IS-Km^R junction. pTW107 is like pTW106 but contains the Km^R module C; it has 20 bp from the right end of IS903-L at the IS-Km^R junction. Frequencies of Gal^R derivatives were determined as described in Fig. 2. (B) Deletions from the right end of IS903-L. pTW90 is like pTW75 (Fig. 2) except that the left portion of the IS903 and all the DNA adjacent to the Eco RI site of pTW75 has been replaced with module E; the translational reading frame and both ends of the IS are retained. pTW88 is like pTW90 but contains module F in place of E (Fig. 1); pTW88 therefore does not have an intact terminal inverted repeat at the IS-Ap^R junction. pTW110 was derived from pTW88 by inserting the 720-bp Eco RI–Hind III segment from module C into the Eco RI site, in the orientation shown, to provide the left-terminal inverted repeat.

Frequency
$Km^R Gal^R$

pTW106 3×10^{-4}

pTW105 2×10^{-6}

pTW107 4×10^{-4}

$Ap^R Gal^R$

pTW90 7×10^{-5}

pTW88 2×10^{-6}

pTW110 5×10^{-4}

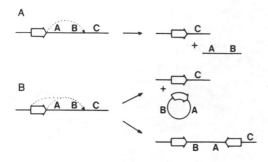

Fig. 5. Deletion formation by an IS. (A) Transpositional recombination involving just one IS end. The actual mechanism could be conservative, involving double-strand cuts at the IS end and the target (32), or it could be replicative, involving transfer of a single strand of the IS to the cut target site (19, 31). (B) Transpositional recombination involving both IS ends. For a deletion to be obtained, this must be a replicative process (otherwise the left IS junction will be broken). This is the intramolecular cointegrate pathway [for details see (18) and (19)] and, depending only on the orientation of the target relative to the IS ends, will result in a deletion (top) or an inversion-insertion.

L and the Eco RI site of pBR322. Previous analyses of the behavior of IS903-R (from which the left IS end of pTW90 was derived; see Figs. 1 and 4) also suggest that the right end of this IS has reduced transpositional activity (13, 16). We conclude that the sequence immediately adjacent to an IS end can have a strong influence on its transpositional activity.

Both Products of an IS903-Mediated Deletion Can Be Recovered

That IS-mediated deletion formation requires both IS ends can be explained in two ways. Initiation of all transpositional activity may require the formation of a complex of two IS ends and the transposase, even though only one of the ends may subsequently be joined to the target (see Fig. 5A). Alternatively, both IS ends may actually take part in the recombinational process and be joined to target sequences (Fig. 5B). The second explanation is an alternative way of saying that deletions occur by an intramolecular cointegrate process, rather than by a direct simple insertion process.

A prediction arising from the second hypothesis is that deletions should be replicative and reciprocal, releasing the deleted DNA as a circle with a copy of the IS joining the two ends of the deleted segment. Testing this prediction requires the construction of a DNA substrate that contains a replication origin between the IS end and the target DNA. We have achieved this through the simple expedient of isolating IS903-mediated cointegrates between pTW75 and the conjugative plasmid pOX38, a derivative of the E. coli F factor that lacks transposons (23). Cointegrates are readily isolated by selecting for the conjugative transfer of pTW75 from a host strain containing pOX38 into an F⁻ recipient. Since pTW75 is not normally mobilizable, the only way it can be transferred is through formation of a recombinant with pOX38. As diagrammed in Fig. 6, we have shown that such recombinants are cointegrates with two copies of IS903 (5).

In attempting to determine whether a single deletion event generates two recoverable products, let us consider the process shown in Fig. 6. A deletion into galK mediated by the IS903 proximal to the ampicillin resistance (Ap^R) gene [but not one mediated by the IS proximal to the kanamycin resistance (Km^R) gene] will generate two products, each with a separate origin of replication. However, since distinguishable plasmids with the same replication system are incompatible, each product will be incompatible

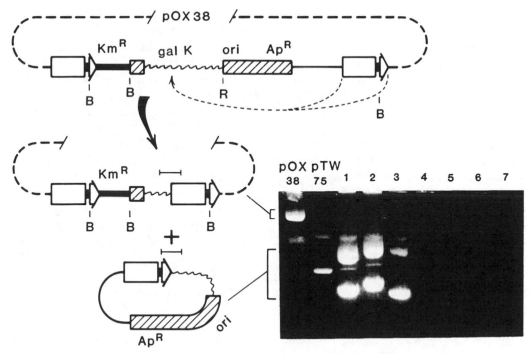

Fig. 6. Structure of a pOX38::pTW75 cointegrate and predicted deletion products. The cointegrate (top) is a fusion of pOX38 (dashed lines) and pTW75 that contains one copy of IS*903* at each junction between the parent replicons. Deletion from the right, Ap^R-proximal IS*903* into *galK* (but not from the Km^R-proximal IS*903*) is predicted to create the two replicons pOX38-Km^R and pBR322-Ap^R shown below if deletion occurs by a replicative cointegrate pathway. Displayed on the right are plasmid DNA's from seven independent Gal^R Km^R clones analyzed by electrophoresis on a 0.7 percent agarose gel. The two left lanes show pOX38 and pTW75; lanes 1 to 3 show DNA of three clones that contained both high- and low-copy plasmids (reciprocal products of a deletion event); lanes 4 to 7 show DNA from four clones that contain only a low-copy plasmid. The bars (⊢—⊣) indicate the regions of the pOX38-Km^R and pBR322-Ap^R replicons that were sequenced (see Fig. 7).

with the parent double-origin cointegrate. A cell in which a deletion has just been formed will contain several copies of the parent cointegrate (*24*) and one copy of each product replicon. How can we maximize the chances of recovering those cells in which both products have survived? We reasoned that because of its low potential copy number, the pOX38-Km^R product would stand the least chance of survival. In fact, since the copy number of the parent plasmid already exceeds that normally allowed

by the F replication control system, pOX38-Km^R will rarely replicate or segregate away from its parent replicon. Therefore, to recover those rare cells that have retained the pOX38-Km^R product replicon requires selecting for retention of kanamycin resistance at the same time as selecting for acquisition of galactose resistance (*25*). What of the other (potential) reciprocal product, the pBR322-Ap^R replicon? Although the pBR322 replication system increases the copy number of the pOX38::pTW75 parent plasmid above that of pOX38, it remains considerably lower than the copy number of pBR322 itself (or of derivatives such as pTW75). Since the total number of pBR322 replication origins in the parental strain will be less than the number in a strain that contained only pTW75, it seemed likely that a pBR322-Ap^R replicon formed in a deletion would stand a good chance of being replicated and, therefore, of being segregated into any cell that had captured a pOX38-Km^R product. Events that inactivate galK other than IS903-mediated deletions will not remove the pBR322 origin of pOX38::pTW75. Such plasmids will be likely to compete with the parent replicon on an approximately equal basis and might therefore predominate in the Gal^R Km^R progeny. To detect possible reciprocal deletions among the selected clones we therefore screened plasmid DNA from individual colonies for the presence of a small multicopy plasmid.

Gal^R Km^R clones from NG135 carrying pOX38::pTW75 cointegrates were selected as before. Such clones arose at a frequency of about 2×10^{-4} for 12 different cointegrates tested. Electrophoretic analysis of plasmid DNA showed that some Gal^R Km^R colonies contained both a small high-copy plasmid and a large low-copy plasmid (lanes 1 to 3 in Fig. 6). A total of 145 colonies were analyzed from 12 different cointegrates, and in six colonies we detected two plasmids of the size and copy number expected for a reciprocal deletion.

All six pairs of plasmids have been extensively analyzed to determine whether, in fact, each pair was derived from a single event. The six large low-copy plasmids had the following properties. They could transfer Km^R at high frequency in bacterial matings but had lost Ap^R and galK activity. Molecular

analyses demonstrated that each retained two copies of IS903. For five of the six, this was shown by first subcloning into pNG16 (13) an Eco RI fragment that contained the entire pTW75-derived DNA segment (the single Eco RI site of pTW75 is lost from the parental pOX38::pTW75 in the deletion formation). In digests of the subclones with Taq I and with Pvu II the internal IS903 fragments (Pvu II, 520 bp or Taq I, 950 bp) were present in twice the molar amount of the other fragments. Digestion of the parental cointegrates with Bam HI releases a 1.1-kilobase (kb) and a 7.5-kb fragment from the pTW75 region of each plasmid. Bam HI digestion of the Km^R deletion products released the expected 1.1-kb fragment (diagnostic of the Km^R region) and a new fragment of 2 to 3 kb that contained the new IS-galK junction. The size of this new fragment is indicative of the deletion end point within galK and therefore differs among the six plasmids analyzed.

The six corresponding low molecular weight, high-copy plasmids had the following properties. They conferred resistance to ampicillin, but not to kanamycin, and had lost galK activity. Each contained a single copy of IS903, since Taq I digests produced the diagnostic 950-bp fragment in amounts equimolar to the other fragments. The Taq I digests showed that the general structure of the multicopy plasmids was the same as that of the Km^S deletion products of pTW75 (Fig. 3) and the deletion end points could be precisely determined in the same manner. In all cases the extent of the galK region carried by a multicopy plasmid was complementary to that carried by the corresponding pOX38-Km^R deletion product, so that together each pair of plasmids contained one complete set of galK sequences.

Fig. 7. DNA sequences of reciprocal products of IS903 deletions. The sequences of one DNA strand across the IS903-galK junction of the two products from three separate deletion events (Δ33, Δ21, and Δ15) are shown. The IS903 terminal sequences are shown in large type

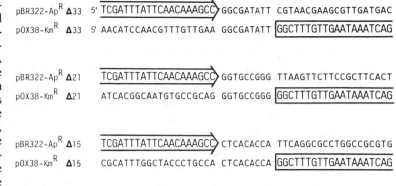

and are boxed; the arrowhead indicates the right (Km^R-proximal) end of IS903-L and corresponds to the arrowhead in Fig. 6. The galK coding strand is shown in smaller type. The sequences are aligned to show the 9-bp galK target sequence that occurs at each junction. Sequences were determined by the dideoxy chain termination method of Sanger et al. (35), with restriction fragments cloned into the single-strand M13 vectors mp8 or mp9 (36).

The true test of reciprocity in formation of these deletions is to show by DNA sequence analysis that the new IS903-galK junctions of both products occur at the same site. For three pairs of deletion products we have sequenced these junctions (the regions indicated by the bars in Fig. 6) and the results are shown in Fig. 7. Each pair of plasmids shares a common 9-bp target sequence at the IS903-galK junction. The remaining galK sequences are mutually exclusive, with the low-copy plasmid containing the beginning of the galK gene and the multicopy plasmid the end. The shared 9 bp was expected since Tn903 causes duplication of a 9-bp target sequence during intermolecular transposition (15).

It is clear from these results that deletion formation by IS903 is a reciprocal recombination event involving both ends of the IS. Since the parental cointegrate contains two copies of the IS, and the two replicons resulting from the deletion together contain a total of three (two on the pOX38-Km^R replicon, one on the pBR322-Ap^R replicon), it also clearly

involves replication of the IS element that mediates the event.

As mentioned above, only six of 145 Km^R Gal^R colonies screened yielded two separate replicons. We have carried out a preliminary analysis of the events that do not result in the production of two replicons. Analysis of 12 clones that contained only a large low-copy plasmid showed that all retained both the Km^R selected marker and the unselected Ap^R locus. All 12 transferred both Ap^R and Km^R at high frequency with 100 percent linkage but had lost galK activity. This proves that these 12 Gal^R clones did not arise by a deletion adjacent to IS903. A preliminary analysis by restriction digestion of plasmid DNA isolated from some of the Ap^R Km^R Gal^R colonies suggest that most of these colonies arose by mutations in galK that are unrelated to IS903. As discussed above, one reasonable explanation for the relatively low yield of IS903-mediated adjacent deletions in this system (relative to the high yield in pTW75 where more than 95 percent of all events were deletions) lies in the incompatibility of the pOX38-Km^R deletion product with the parental cointegrate.

An important question is whether all IS903 deletions occur by a reciprocal process. Unfortunately, the problems associated with plasmid incompatibility make the system that we have used to demonstrate reciprocity a poor one for addressing this question quantitatively. Incompatibility between the parent and product replicons could influence the results in three ways. First, it may reduce the frequency of deletion events recovered (as we argue above); second, it may result in the loss of one product from a reciprocal event, suggesting possible nonreciprocity; and third, it may result in stronger selection against recovery of nonreciprocal deletions than against reciprocal deletions (26). With these limitations in mind we have looked among Gal^R Km^R clones for possible nonreciprocal deletion products. Deletions into galK that retain Km^R must have originated from the Ap^R-proximal IS903 and, if nonreciprocal, should lose Ap^R. We have screened 50 Gal^R Km^R clones and found just one that had lost Ap^R.

Conclusions and Discussion

It has proved difficult to obtain conclusive evidence that any genetic rearrangements mediated by transpositional recombination of an IS element involve duplication of the IS. This is partly because of the very low frequency of those rearrangements in which both donor and target are recovered intact (as in replicon fusion or inversion-insertion), and the resultant concern that such processes may depend on additional events such as the dimerization of a plasmid donor (which can occur even in RecA$^-$ cells at a detectable frequency) (27).

Using a selective procedure to obtain intramolecular events promoted by IS903 in a RecA$^-$ host, we have shown that the most frequent event is the formation of adjacent deletions. These deletions occur at normal frequencies only if both IS ends are intact, suggesting that the deletion-distal IS end also participates in the recombination. Interestingly, the only other case in which deletion formation has been shown to require both transposon ends is for phage Mu (28), a transposon that clearly has a high frequency of replicative cointegrate formation (29). We were able to recover two products from a single deletion event by giving the deleted segment a replication origin of its own. Each product was a separate replicon with a copy of the mediating IS and the 9-bp target sequence. While these results do not prove that all IS903 recombinational events are replicative, they do indicate that a replicative mechanism is a major pathway of transpositional recombination. Determining whether simple insertion of an IS is a replicative process will probably have to await a biochemical characterization of the recombination.

Our findings provide strong support for the idea that IS-mediated deletions are formed by an intramolecular cointegrate process as was first suggested by Shapiro (18). However, these findings do not distinguish between molecular models that propose simultaneous ligation of both transposon ends to the target (18, 30), and those that propose that these ligations are separated in time, with transposon replication interposed (19, 20, 31). If the most frequent intramolecular rearrangement mediated by an isolated IS element occurs by a cointegrate process, then our results raise two paradoxes. First, in plasmids such as pTW75, why do we not observe inversion-insertions at about the same frequency as adjacent deletions, since both are predicted to be alternative products of the same process (see Fig. 5B)? Perhaps in our assay, in which the target is separated from the IS by only about 3 kb, its orientation relative to the IS ends is determined by topological considerations or by other plasmid properties (such as direction of replication). Second, in intermolecular transposition of IS*903*, simple insertions appear to be favored over cointegrates by a factor of about 20, the reverse of the intramolecular results (*5, 16*). Perhaps simple insertion is normally a conservative process involving excision of the IS and consequent loss of its parent replicon (*32*), so that intramolecular simple insertions would be suicidal.

References and Notes

1. *Cold Spring Harbor Symp. Quant. Biol.* **45** (1981); J. A. Shapiro, *Mobile Genetic Elements* (Academic Press, New York, 1983).
2. N. Kleckner, *Annu. Rev. Genet.* **15**, 341 (1981).
3. N. D. F. Grindley, *Cell* **32**, 3 (1983).
4. R. Gill, F. Heffron, G. Dougan, S. Falkow, *J. Bacteriol.* **136**, 742 (1978).
5. N. D. F. Grindley and C. M. Joyce, *Cold Spring Harbor Symp. Quant. Biol.* **45**, 125 (1981).
6. D. J. Galas and M. Chandler, *J. Mol. Biol.* **154**, 245 (1982).
7. B. J. Hirschel, D. J. Galas, M. Chandler, *Proc. Natl. Acad. Sci. U.S.A.* **79**, 4530 (1982).
8. D. E. Berg, *ibid.* **80**, 792 (1983).
9. G. Cornelis and H. Saedler, *Mol. Gen. Genet.* **178**, 367 (1980); N. Kleckner and D. G. Ross, *J. Mol. Biol.* **144**, 215 (1980).
10. H. Saedler, G. Cornelis, J. Cullum, B. Schumacher, H. Sommer, *Cold Spring Harbor Symp. Quant. Biol.* **45**, 93 (1981).
11. J. C. Liebart, P. Ghelardini, L. Paolozzi, *Proc. Natl. Acad. Sci. U.S.A.* **79**, 4362 (1982).
12. E. Ljunquist and A. I. Bukhari, *ibid.* **74**, 3143 (1977).
13. N. D. F. Grindley and C. M. Joyce, *ibid.* **77**, 7176 (1980).
14. A. Oka, H. Sugisaki, M. Takanami, *J. Mol. Biol.* **147**, 217 (1981).
15. A. Oka, N. Nomura, K. Sugimoto, H. Sugisaki, M. Takanami, *Nature (London)* **276**, 845 (1978).
16. T. A. Weinert, N. A. Schaus, N. D. F. Grindley, unpublished results.
17. H. Ohtsubo and E. Ohtsubo, *Proc. Natl. Acad. Sci. U.S.A.* **75**, 615 (1978); A. Bernardi and F. Bernardi, *Gene* **13**, 103 (1981).
18. J. A. Shapiro, *Proc. Natl. Acad. Sci. U.S.A.* **76**, 1933 (1979).
19. R. M. Harshey and A. I. Bukhari, *ibid.* **78**, 1090 (1981).
20. D. J. Galas and M. Chandler, *ibid.*, p. 4858.
21. Y. Machida, C. Machida, E. Ohtsubo, *Cell* **30**, 29 (1982).
22. A. Bernardi and F. Bernardi, *Nucleic Acids Res.* **9**, 2905 (1981).
23. M. S. Guyer *et al.*, *Cold Spring Harbor Symp. Quant. Biol.* **45**, 135 (1981).
24. Since the parent cointegrate contains the replication system of the multicopy plasmid pBR322, its copy number is intermediate; it is higher than that of pOX38 which, like the F factor, is one to two copies per cell, but is lower than that of pBR322 because of its larger size (about 60 kilobases).
25. The selection for Km^R also prevents us from recovering deletions from the Km^R-proximal IS*903* into *galK* since all of these would lose kanamycin resistance (and none could give two recoverable products whether deletions were reciprocal or not).
26. This is because the pBR322-Ap^R replicon resulting from a reciprocal deletion may moderate replication of the parent molecule and therefore improve the chances of survival of the pOX38-Km^R deletion product.
27. R. A. Fishel, A. A. James, R. Kolodner, *Nature (London)* **294**, 184 (1981).
28. M. Faelen and A. Toussaint, *J. Bacteriol.* **136**, 447 (1978); a similar claim has been made for IS*1* (*10*), however, it seems likely that the IS*2* insertion into the IS*1* end has actually disrupted transposase expression and may well have left the terminal sequence intact.
29. R. M. Harshey, *Proc. Natl. Acad. Sci. U.S.A.* **80**, 2012 (1983).
30. A. Arthur and D. Sherratt, *Mol. Gen. Genet.* **175**, 267 (1979).
31. N. D. F. Grindley and D. J. Sherratt, *Cold Spring Harbor Symp. Quant. Biol.* **43**, 1257 (1979).
32. D. E. Berg, in *DNA Insertion Elements, Plasmids, and Episomes*, A. I. Bukhari, J. A. Shapiro, S. L. Adhya, Eds. (Cold Spring Harbor Laboratory, Cold Spring Harbor, N.Y., 1977), p. 205.
33. L. Guarente, G. Lauer, T. M. Roberts, M. Ptashne, *Cell* **20**, 543 (1980).
34. K. McKenney, H. Shimatake, D. Court, U. Schmeissner, C. Brady, M. Rosenberg, in *Gene Amplification and Analysis*, J. C. Chirikjian and T. S. Papas, Eds. (Elsevier-North Holland, Amsterdam 1981), vol. 2, p. 383.
35. F. Sanger, S. Nicklen, A. R. Coulson, *Proc. Natl. Acad. Sci. U.S.A.* **74**, 5463 (1977).
36. J. Messing and J. Vieira, *Gene* **19**, 269 (1982).
37. We thank G. Hatfull and C. Joyce for discussions; A. Weiner, C. Joyce, and T. Platt for critically reading the manuscript and B. Newman for some plasmid constructions. This work was supported by NIH grant GM28470.

28. Translocations Among Antibody Genes in Human Cancer

Philip Leder, Jim Battey, Gilbert Lenoir
Christopher Moulding, William Murphy, Huntington Potter
Timothy Stewart, Rebecca Taub

Geneticists have become increasingly aware of the fact that genes move, that they change position within and between chromosomes, and that they thus alter their relationships to one another with important regulatory and structural consequences. One dramatic example of this occurs as part of the process by which the immunoglobulin (Ig) genes are normally formed by joining subgenomic segments of DNA in various combinations to create the enormous diversity reflected by the immune system (*1*). Another example, by no means normal and with an apparently more sinister outcome, is represented by the somatic translocations that consistently accompany certain human neoplasms (*2*). In recent months, these two phenomena have been physically linked by studies showing that the human cellular oncogene c-*myc* is joined to one of the Ig loci by a translocation that characteristically accompanies a human malignancy called Burkitt lymphoma (*3–7*). Similar results have been obtained in mouse plasmacytomas (*8–13*).

The juxtaposition of these two rather well characterized genetic systems allows us to address two important—if poorly understood—questions: First, what are the molecular genetic consequences of these translocations and how do they alter the normal function and control of these genes? And second, how does their interaction contribute to the process of malignant transformation? While work in a number of laboratories is still in its earliest stages, certain observations already allow us to evaluate the most obvious models and to advance others. Our purpose here will be to consider briefly the normal Ig and *myc* genes before turning to specific molecular aspects of certain Burkitt lymphoma translocations and the early answers they bring to the questions we have posed.

Associations Between Chromosomal Translocations and Neoplasia

The close association between specific chromosomal translocations and certain human neoplasms is well established (*2*). Such translocations are of two types: constitutional, that is, those carried by each of the individual's cells; and somatic, those that arise in a particular cell and are carried by its neoplastic progeny. It is generally held that such constitutional translocations (and other chromosomal abnormalities) predispose an organism to the development of a malignancy, but require a second event, presumably another mutation, to consummate the malignant transformation (14). For example, in hereditary renal cell carcinoma there is a constitutional translocation involving chromosomes 3 and 8 [t(3;8)] that is associated with the development of renal cell carcinoma during the fourth decade of life (15). Somatic translocations, in contrast, presumably arise in a single somatic cell and contribute to the transformation of that cell and its progeny alone. It is not likely that either translocation is sufficient to accomplish the malignant transformation; it is quite likely that other critical events have occurred or will occur (16). Nevertheless, the tight association between particular malignancies and specific translocations [t(9;22) in chronic myelogenous leukemia and t(2;8), t(8;14), and t(8;22) in Burkitt lymphoma] makes a very strong, if circumstantial, argument that these translocations are causally related to the development of the neoplasm.

The discovery of oncogenes, originally noted as transforming genes carried or activated by retroviruses [see review (16)], combined with a growing understanding of transcriptional control mechanisms, provided the basis for two molecular models that could explain how a translocation might induce malignancy (17). A translocation could disturb the regulation of an oncogene, for example, by providing a new promoter region or some other control element that would activate the oncogene (18). Alternatively, it might alter the coding sequence of a gene, changing its protein product from a benign to a malignant form (19).

The Burkitt Lymphoma Model

The matter of how a translocation might affect an oncogene was put in perspective by Ohno et al. (20), who noticed that there was a correlation between the chromosomes involved in the translocations in human Burkitt lymphomas and murine plasmacytomas and the chromosomes that carry the antibody heavy and light chain genes. Since these translocations occurred in antibody producing cells, Klein (21) suggested that such translocations might introduce an oncogene into a position close to one of the Ig transcriptional promoters. The association between Ig genes and the observed translocations was strengthened by mapping data that placed the Ig heavy chain genes on chromosome band 14q32, the κ light chain gene on chromosome band 2p11, and the λ light chain gene on chromosome band 22q11 (22), precisely the chromosomal bands representing the breakpoints seen in the Burkitt translocations (albeit that these "bands" extend over 10^7 base pairs of chromosomal DNA). Furthermore, when one of the light chain chromosomes (2 or 22) was involved in the translocation, the affected chromosome usually carried a light chain gene of the type expressed in that particular cell line (23). For example, Burkitt cells that contain translocations involving chromosome 2 usually make κ rather than λ light chains. This further suggested that the translocations might involve an actively transcribed locus.

It is also important to recognize that the translocations noted in the Burkitt lymphoma are reciprocal, that is, they represent grossly conservative exchanges of large chromosomal segments (Fig. 1). Moreover, the chromosome common to each of the translocations is

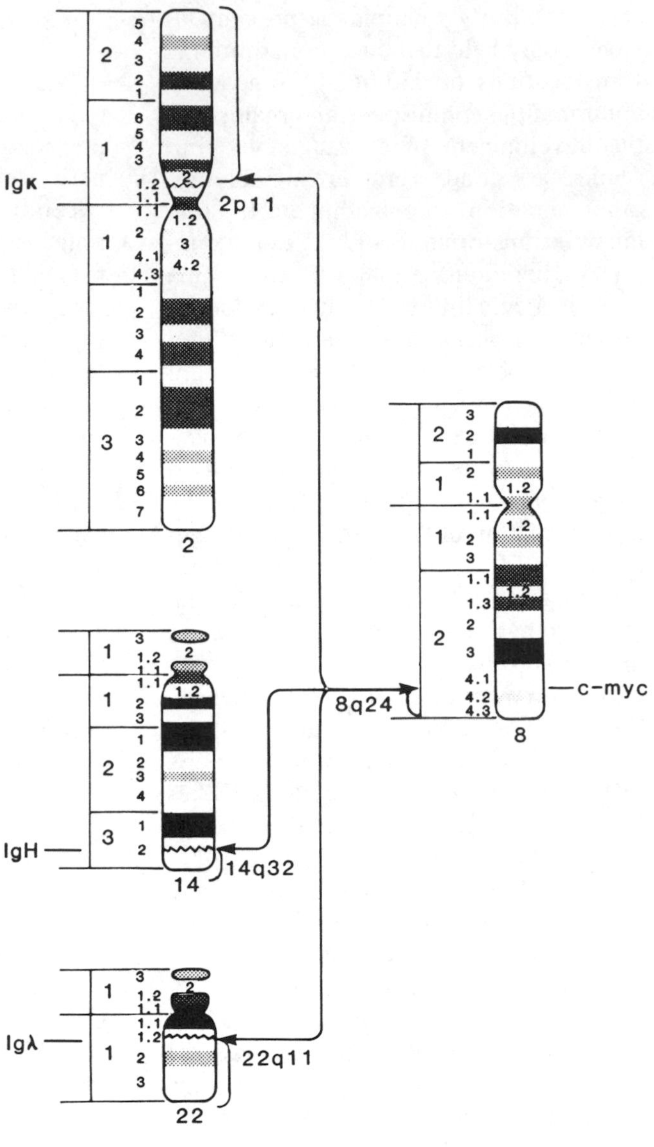

Fig. 1. Diagrammatic representation of the human chromosomes involved in the specific translocations of Burkitt lymphoma. Chromosomes 2, 14, 22, and 8 are shown with their characteristic Giemsa-banding patterns. The positions of the Igκ, IgH, and Igλ (22) chains are indicated, as is the position of the c-*myc* gene. The arrows point to breakpoints at which chromosomes 2, 14, or 22 reciprocally exchange chromosomal segments with chromosome 8. Approximately 75 percent of the translocations involve chromosomes 8 and 14 (*44*).

chromosome 8 which, according to the model. (*21*), should encode the critical oncogene.

The Combinatorial Nature of Immunoglobulin Loci

The Ig loci involved in these translocations have a very special property: they undergo site- or region-specific recombination that is critical for the development of antibody diversity (*1*). As shown in Fig. 2, one such recombination joins widely separated segments of DNA called V, D, and J regions to form active variable (V) regions in heavy (H) and light (L) chain loci. The other, switch (S) recombination, operates only in the heavy chain locus and moves or "switches" the finished heavy chain V-region gene from one heavy chain constant region to another. Both of these types of recombination are a required part of immunocyte development. The physical maps of all three human loci are shown in Fig. 2, together with a diagrammatic representation of the recombinational events.

The signal sequences thought to be involved in VDJ and VJ recombination, pairs of hepta- and nonanucleotides, occur on the edges of the V, D, and J segments that are joined to form the

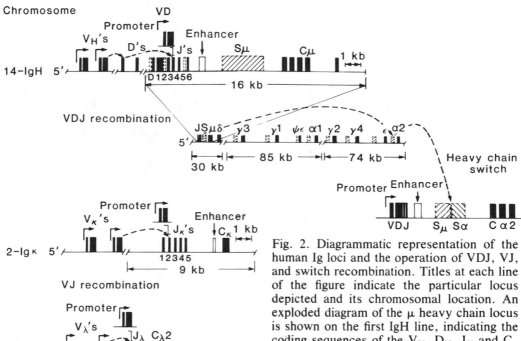

Fig. 2. Diagrammatic representation of the human Ig loci and the operation of VDJ, VJ, and switch recombination. Titles at each line of the figure indicate the particular locus depicted and its chromosomal location. An exploded diagram of the μ heavy chain locus is shown on the first IgH line, indicating the coding sequences of the V_H, D_H, J_H and C_μ domains as filled bars. Note that there are multiple V, D, and J regions. Breaks in the solid underline of each map indicate where gene segments have not been physically linked. The dashed boxes represent pseudo J regions, the open box is the putative human μ enhancer sequence, and the hatched box is the μ switch recombination signal. Arrows indicate the position of the putative V-region promoters and above the line is a recombined VD sequence at the position where it will join a J region to form a complete and active VDJ sequence (VDJ recombination). The second line shows the physical map of the entire heavy chain locus. The dashed arrows indicate segments joined by a sample switch reaction which draws a complete VDJ sequence from its initial position adjacent a μ constant region domain to a switch signal near the α2 heavy chain gene. An exploded diagram of the "switched" gene is shown in the last line with the retained enhancer indicated. The second diagram (Igκ) similarly shows the human κ locus with a dashed arrow indicating the path of VJ recombination. The putative enhancer region is shown. The first line of the third diagram (Igλ) shows an exploded diagram of VJ recombination occurring in one of the six human λ constant region genes. Note there are multiple V regions, but presumably only one J region associated with each of the six λ constant region sequences (lower line).

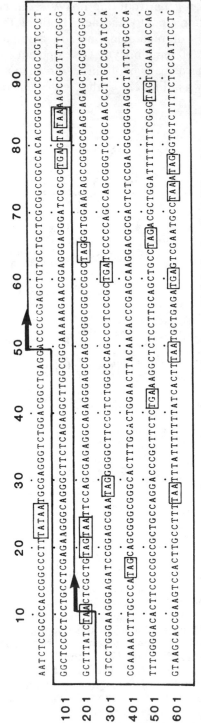

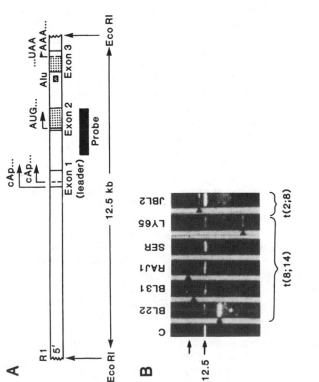

A

B

Fig. 3. Physical map of the human *c-myc* gene and demonstration of rearranged *c-myc*-containing fragments in Burkitt lymphoma cells. (A) The diagram shows a 12.5-kb Eco R1 fragment encoding the *c-myc* gene. The boxes within the segment represent the three *c-myc* exons. The first exon encodes two transcription initiation points, indicated as arrows with the "cAp..." symbols. The position of the translational initiation and termination codons are shown, as is the polyadenylate addition site (AAA...). A small hatched box in the second intervening sequence indicates the position of a highly repeated "Alu" sequence. (B) Each lane represents an in situ hybridization analysis (Southern blot) of DNA derived from normal and Burkitt lymphoma cell lines that have been digested with Eco R1 and probed with the *c-myc* DNA fragment [indicated by the solid bar in (A)]. The designation of each Burkitt cell line is indicated above each lane and the translocation found in each line is indicated below each lane. These rearrangements have been described previously (3). Lane C, the control, contains DNA derived from normal human white blood cells. The normal 12.5-kb Eco R1 fragment is indicated by an arrow and the rearranged *c-myc* fragments are indicated by triangles.

Fig. 4. Sequence of the untranslatable leader exon of the *c-myc* gene. The sequence of the leader exon (29) is shown with small boxes around its two TATAA boxes and each of the termination codons that occur within its transcribed sequence. The transcribed sequence is also boxed with heavy arrows indicating the positions of the two transcription initiation points.

intact V-region sequence. The switch region signals, on the other hand, consist of 1- to 2-kilobase segments of DNA largely made up of recurring pentanucleotide sequences (24). One such segment is encoded on the 5' side of each of the heavy chain constant region genes (except the delta gene). During the switch reaction, the completed V region, initially adjacent to the μ constant region gene, is joined to one of the other switch signals transferring the V region with its encoded specificity and transcriptional control signals to one of the successively encoded heavy chain genes. In this way, each of the γ, ε, and α heavy chains can be expressed in the descendents of a precursor cell that originally expressed only the μ heavy chain. Delta gene expression and the choice between membrane and secreted Ig's seem to depend on alternative messenger RNA processing pathways (25).

The Regulatory Consequences of Immunoglobulin Gene Recombination

Both recombinational events occurring during immunocyte maturation have important implications with regard to the regulated expression of the Ig genes. The heavy chain V region is formed by selecting one of several hundred V-region subgenes and joining it to one of several dozen D segments (D segments occur in the heavy chain locus only) and then to one of five or six J segments (see Fig. 2). Since each of the V-region subgenes has a promoter region encoded close to its 5' end, VDJ recombination brings this promoter close to the constant region sequence, thereby forming a complete Ig coding sequence with its appropriate transcriptional initiation site.

The paradox of why the many potential promoter regions are inactive in their germ line (unrearranged) configuration (26) and active when drawn close to the constant region subgene was partially resolved by the recent discovery that a small segment of DNA between the J and switch regions in the heavy chain and between the J and constant regions in the κ chain gene is actually a B-cell specific enhancer sequence (27). The enhancer is apparently necessary for the activation of the V-region associated promoters in B cells. (The enhancer sequences are indicated diagrammatically in the heavy chain and κ loci shown in Fig. 2.) Enhancer sequences have yet to be identified in the λ locus or in species other than the mouse, but since sequences homologous to known mouse enhancer sequences are conserved in man (28), it is reasonable to postulate that they will be found in other species as well. Thus, at least two elements occur within the Ig loci that could influence gene expression in a B-cell specific manner, the V-region associated promoters and the constant region enhancer sequences.

The Normal Human *myc* Gene

While little is known about the actual function of the c-*myc* protein, the structure of its gene is known in detail (29). The gene is encoded in three discontinuous exons separated by two large intervening sequences as shown diagrammatically in Fig. 3A. The first exon has several interesting features (Figs. 3A and 4), including the fact that it forms the major portion of a segment of DNA that is tightly conserved between man and mouse (30). Given that this tight evolutionary conservation suggests functional selection, it was surprising to discover that the 550-base-long segment contained no translational initiation codons (eight would have been expected in a random sequence of this length). Furthermore, the sequence contains multiple termination codons in all three reading frames and is, therefore, an untranslated messenger RNA (mRNA) leader sequence. In addition, this region encodes at least two active promoters with transcription initiation sites located about 150 base pairs from one another within the leader sequence (*30*). Curiously, the 5′ ends of transcripts from each of the promoters can be drawn as short stem and loop structures, although many alternative configurations are also possible (*30*).

The remaining portion of the c-*myc* gene contains two coding exons that direct the synthesis of a protein 439 amino acids in length that is particularly rich in amino acids carrying acidic, basic, and hydroxyl groups (*29*). The function of the normal protein is not known. However, when the avian c-*myc* gene is taken up by a retrovirus, it forms a fusion protein with the viral gag (group specific antigen) gene product and, in this form, participates in the transformation of several avian cell types [for a review see (*31*)]. The product of the fused gene is a nuclear protein that binds without apparent specificity to double-stranded DNA (*32*).

Structure of c-*myc* Rearrangements in Burkitt Lymphoma Cell Lines

The search for the crossover point of the translocation that joins chromosomes 8 and 14 in Burkitt lymphoma was facilitated by studies in the mouse that had detected a series of aberrantly rearranged fragments of DNA that were joined to the α Ig switch signal in a large number of murine plasmacytomas (*33*). By taking advantage of the fact that the

avian leukosis virus frequently integrates near and activates a c-*myc* gene in avian B-cell lymphoma, we and others were able to show that the murine c-*myc* and the Ig α constant region genes were physically linked in a single fragment of genomic DNA (*8–13*). By using appropriate probes it was further shown that the c-*myc* and the human Ig μ genes were joined in several Burkitt lymphoma cell lines and that c-*myc* had undergone some form of rearrangement in the majority of Burkitt cell lines (*3–7*). An example of such an experiment is shown in Fig. 3B, in which a probe corresponding to the midportion of the human c-*myc* gene detects c-*myc* encoding Eco RI fragments of DNA derived from several Burkitt cell lines. As shown in the figure, the presence of rearranged and nonrearranged c-*myc* fragments suggests that only one of the two c-*myc* alleles has undergone rearrangement in these cell lines and that this rearrangement has occurred within a few thousand bases of the c-*myc* gene. Note, however, that the cell line SER displays only a germ line band implying that the translocation has occurred at a distance greater than can be assessed by using Eco RI restriction sites.

The exact nature of several of these c-*myc* rearrangements has been determined by cloning the relevant genes and determining their structure by direct sequence analysis (*30, 34*). Two examples of rearranged c-*myc* genes derived from Burkitt cell lines are diagrammed in Fig. 5. In both cases the c-*myc* gene is joined to a switch region sequence located 5′ to the μ heavy chain constant region gene, the region normally involved in switch-type recombination. In both cases the orientation of the c-*myc* and Ig μ genes are in opposite transcriptional directions. In the case of cell line A (Fig. 5A),

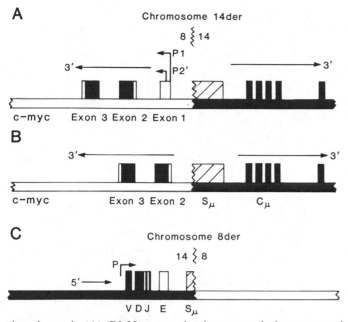

A Chromosome 14der

8 ⟩ 14

P1
P2'
3' ←
→ 3'

c-myc   Exon 3 Exon 2 Exon 1

B

3' ←
→ 3'

c-myc   Exon 3 Exon 2 S$_\mu$ C$_\mu$

C Chromosome 8der

14 ⟩ 8

P
5' →

V D J E   S$_\mu$

Fig. 5. Diagrammatic representation of DNA fragments formed by translocations between chromosomes 8 and 14. (A) Map of the c-*myc* (open bar) and Ig μ (filled bar) genes as they are rearranged in the Burkitt line BL22 (*30*). The coding sequences are indicated by boxes on the chromosomal DNA segment. The filled boxes have amino acid–coding function. The hatched box is the μ switch signal. The transcriptional direction of each segment is given by the arrow above it. (B) Map of the genes as they rearranged in the Burkitt line Ly 65 (*46*). Symbols are as in (A). (C) Hypothetical representation of the reciprocal product that one would expect in the translocation shown in (A) (BL22), assuming it were entirely conservative and assuming the Ig gene had undergone VDJ recombination. The symbols have the same value as above, but the VDJ segment refers to completed IgH V-region gene (see Fig. 2) and the E segment refers to the position of the suspected human IgH enhancer sequence (*26*).

the c-*myc* promoter or leader sequence has been retained, but in line B (Fig. 5B), this exon has been lost as a consequence of recombination. Since the observed translocations are reciprocal, the reciprocal product should also be present within the Burkitt cells (*35*). Though these reciprocal products have not been characterized in detail, their expected structure is shown diagrammatically in order to indicate that the enhancer sequence normally associated with the heavy chain μ region would not be retained by the chromosome that carries the rearranged c-*myc* gene (compare to Fig. 2). Thus, these rearranged c-*myc* genes can neither use a promoter region normally used by Ig heavy chain genes, nor can they be influenced by its known enhancer. In addition, the complete sequence of the amino acid coding exons of

the translocated c-*myc* gene shown in Fig. 5A (BL22) has been determined and is identical to that of the normal gene, suggesting that their protein products are also qualitatively identical (*30*).

Consequences of c-*myc* Translocation at the Level of Expression

The activity of the c-*myc* gene as measured by the steady-state level of c-*myc* mRNA is elevated in a number of human non-Burkitt tumors (*36*). The situation in Burkitt lymphoma is less clear and the analysis is made difficult because little is known about the expression of c-*myc* in normal tissue (*5, 7, 37*). Nevertheless, our own experience indicates that the level of c-*myc* transcript in Burkitt lines is usually, but not always, elevated when

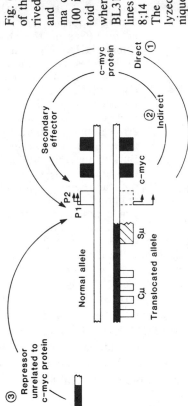

Fig. 6 (left). Analysis of the transcripts derived from normal and Burkitt lymphoma cell lines. IARC 100 is a lymphoblastoid control cell line, whereas BL16 and BL31 are Burkitt cell lines that carry the 8;14 translocation. The mRNA was analyzed by the technique of Berk and Sharp (45) as modi-

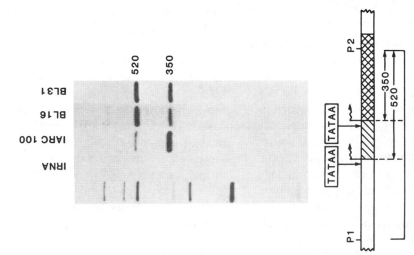

fied (30, 46) to obtain uniformly labeled, single-stranded probes that were synthesized by cloning the Pst (P) fragment indicated in the figure in the MP9 vector system. The first lane represents size control standards (an Eco R1/Hind III digest of the plasmid pBR322) of the following lengths: 1630 bp, 1000 bp, 630 bp, 507 bp, 396 bp, 344 bp, 298 bp, 220 bp, and 150 bp. The bottom diagram shows the map of the probe derived from the first *c-myc* exon. The position of each of the two TATAA boxes is shown as are the expected lengths of the protected fragments that would arise from the two *c-myc* promoters.   Fig. 7 (right). A model for the trans negative control of normal *c-myc* expression. The diagram of the normal (upper) and translocated *c-myc* (lower) genes are as described in Fig. 4. The two *c-myc* promoters are indicated by arrows and the symbols P1 (5' most) and P2. The arrows indicate the direction of transcription. The model is described in the text but indicates three potential models of trans-mediated repression of the normal *c-myc* gene: (i) direct autorepression by the *c-myc* protein, (ii) indirect autoregulation by a repressor that responds to the level of *c-myc* protein, or (iii) regulation by a repressor unrelated to the *c-myc* protein. The target of this repression is suggested to be the conserved dual promoter-leader sequence of the *c-myc* gene. In some Burkitt translocations this target is damaged or lost, thus releasing the translocated *c-myc* gene from this trans control, altering its expression or promoter choice (P1 or P2) in the Burkitt cell (see Fig. 5B). The negative control element is referred to as a repressor but could also serve to destabilize *c-myc* mRNA.

compared to EBV-immortalized, nonmalignant lymphoblastoid cells (*38*). Hence, there is variation in c-*myc* expression among Burkitt lines. Similarly, certain mouse plasmacytomas seem to have increased levels of c-*myc* transcript while others do not (*10, 11, 13, 39*).

In the absence of consistent findings, we have turned to a more revealing analysis of the c-*myc* mRNA transcript in Burkitt cells. By using S1-nuclease analysis, we are able to detect and quantitate the steady-state levels of the mRNA transcripts derived from each of c-*myc*'s two promoters. As shown in Fig. 6, the normal gene in the lymphoblastoid cell line, IARC 100, uses both promoter regions with the steady-state level of transcripts favoring the promoter producing the shorter transcript, P2. However, in the two Burkitt lines the longer transcript increases relative to the shorter.

Obviously, this relation between c-*myc* promoters will not prevail in every Burkitt cell line (see, for example, the c-*myc* gene illustrated in Fig. 5B which has lost its promoter or leader exon entirely). Indeed, most of the c-*myc* genes analyzed in murine plasmacytomas have lost their promoter-leader exons (*8–13*). Nevertheless, the conserved nature of the sequence, the presence of dual promoters, the inversion of transcript ratios, and the frequent loss of the promoter-leader sequence in oncogenic translocations point to the importance of this region in regulating the expression of the c-*myc* gene. Furthermore, a number of studies in the mouse system have indicated that expression of the normal (unrearranged) allele is often profoundly reduced in plasmacytomas carrying a rearranged c-*myc* allele (*6, 13*). Indeed, in each case in which we have been able to distinguish the products of the normal and translocated alleles in Burkitt cell lines, we have found that the transcript of the normal allele is either undetectable or profoundly reduced by comparison to that of the product of the translocated allele (*38*). Very recent experiments involving the expression of normal and translocated Burkitt chromosomes in mouse myeloma–human Burkitt lymphoma cell lines are also consistent with this conclusion (*40*).

The Deregulation of c-*myc*: A Model

In view of the variety of crossover points that occur in c-*myc* translocations, we are likely to find that there are a number of mechanisms by which the regulation of the c-*myc* can be altered. Indeed, the collection of translocations represented in the Burkitt lymphomas provides an array of mutations that will help us to understand the controls that operate upon both the c-*myc* and Ig genes. To this end, any regulatory scheme should allow us to explain at least three observations: the fact that the normal c-*myc* allele is often inactive or less active in the presence of the rearranged allele, the significance of the conserved dual promoter-leader exon of the c-*myc* gene and its P1/P2 transcript ratio, and the fact that the Ig loci are so consistently involved in these B-cell translocations.

Granting that little is known, let us nevertheless consider the regulatory model shown diagrammatically in Fig. 7. The model holds that that c-*myc* is normally regulated by a trans-acting repressor. More complex models, including those that involve positive control elements, are possible; but negative regulation requires fewer assumptions. It is also attractive to suppose that this repression is medicated directly or indirectly by the cellular level of the c-*myc* protein, although repression unrelated to the c-*myc* protein cannot be ruled out. Thus, an elevated level of c-*myc* protein produced from the deregulated, translocated allele in a Burkitt cell could bring about the repression of the normal c-*myc* allele. Let us further assume that the target of this trans regulation is the dual promoter-leader segment conserved at the 5′ region of the c-*myc* gene. Since some of the translocations we observe damage this region (*38*), they can be thought of as operator-promoter constitutive mutations that defeat this control. This could be accomplished by deleting the first exon or subtly altering its structure. Such alterations occur even at a great distance from the site of chromosomal recombination (*39*). Alternatively, deregulation could also occur by substituting an overriding positive control element for a flanking region of c-*myc* DNA or by changing the structure of the c-*myc* or succeeding regulatory proteins (a repressor constitutive mutation).

The control function could also operate either to influence the level of mRNA, the promoter used, or both. The fact that the two promoter regions generate mRNA's that differ in their untranslated leader sequences and are differentially expressed in lymphoblastoid and Burkitt cells allows us to suggest that deregulation, in certain cases, shifts transcription to the first promoter region generating mRNA's with longer leader sequences which, in turn, might affect their ability to direct the synthesis of c-*myc* protein. It is also possible that the regular control element acts as a destabilizer of c-*myc* mRNA rather than a conventional repressor that would prevent its transcription.

One virtue of this trans-negative control model is that it is consistent with the behavior of the normal c-*myc* allele in Burkitt cells and it allows us to focus on an evolutionarily conserved segment of the c-*myc* gene as a potential cis-acting control site. The other virtue, in view of the availability of DNA-mediated B-cell transforming protocols (*19*) and the relevant cloned genes, is that it is not difficult to design tests for the model. Obviously, it would be useful to have an assay for the level of the c-*myc* protein in control and transformed cells. Progress in this regard has been reported recently in the form of an antibody directed against the avian c-*myc* protein (*41*). It is also possible to link the putative c-*myc* control region to a more easily assayed protein and view its function in cells producing greater and lesser amounts of the c-*myc* transcript. In particular, the possibility that c-*myc* is subject to tight temporal regulation, especially with respect to the cell cycle, deserves consideration.

The Role of the Immunoglobulin Locus

We have alluded to a possible function of the Ig locus in affecting the expression of the c-*myc* gene, by contributing either a powerful positive control element or a region-wide configuration of chromatin that is more conducive to c-*myc* expression in B cells. It is still tempting to consider the role that the recombination systems of the Ig genes might have played in generating these translocations. While it is clear that not all the translocated c-*myc* genes will break into an Ig locus at a switch signal, most of the t(8;14) translocations do involve this region. Thus, although it is now established that the c-*myc* gene does not encode an extensive switchlike sequence (*42*), a convincing evaluation of this possibility awaits the analysis of variant translocations (*23*) in which the c-*myc* gene translocates to one of the light chain loci that do not employ switching functions.

The Role of the c-*myc* Gene in Transformation

The specific role that the c-*myc* protein plays in normal cells is still obscure. Its presence in the nucleus (*41*) and the ability of c-*myc*-related proteins to bind to double-stranded DNA (*32*) lead one to consider any of the cardinal reactions of mitosis, DNA replication, and transcription that might profoundly affect cell growth and division. Once again, answers to this question must await the development of techniques that allow the isolation of the c-*myc* protein and its further biochemical analysis. Specific antisera should greatly facilitate this process, as should the availability of artificial mutations that alter the gene's ability to transform normal cells. In the accompanying chapter by Weinberg (*16*), it is shown that in certain cell systems c-*myc* cannot transform cells by itself but requires a complementary oncogene. Indeed, an additional transforming gene, B*lym*, has been isolated from Burkitt cells (*43*). Complementation assays, coupled with detailed knowledge of the c-*myc* gene and the Ig region into which it falls, provide an experimental framework in which to seek answers to this important question.

References and Notes

1. P. Leder, *Sci. Am.* **246**, 102 (1982); S. Tonegawa, *Nature* **302**, 575 (1983).
2. J. J. Yunis, *Science* **221**, 227 (1983); J. D. Rowley, *Cancer Invest.* **1**, 267 (1983).
3. R. Taub *et al.*, *Proc. Natl. Acad. Sci. U.S.A.* **79**, 7837 (1982).
4. R. Dalla-Favera, S. Martinotti, R. C. Gallo, J. Erikson, C. M. Croce, *Science* **219**, 963 (1983).
5. J. Erikson, A. Ar-Rushdi, H. L. Drwinga, P. C. Nowell, C. M. Croce, *Proc. Natl. Acad. Sci. U.S.A.* **80**, 820 (1983).
6. J. M. Adams, S. Gerondakis, E. Webb, L. M. Corcoran, S. Cory, *ibid.*, p. 1982.
7. P. H. Hamlyn and T. H. Rabbits, *Nature (London)* **304**, 135 (1983).
8. G. L. Shen-Ong, E. J. Keath, S. P. Piccoli, M. D. Cole, *Cell* **31**, 443 (1982).
9. R. Taub *et al.*, *Proc. Natl. Acad. Sci. U.S.A.* **79**, 7837 (1982).
10. J. M. Adams, S. Gerondakis, E. Webb, L. M. Corcoran, S. Cory, *ibid.* **80**, 1982 (1983).
11. K. B. Marcu *et al.*, *ibid.*, p. 519.
12. S. Crews, R. Barth, L. Hood, J. Prehn, K. Calame, *Science* **218**, 1319 (1982).
13. L. W. Stanton, R. Watt, K. B. Marcu, *Nature (London)* **303**, 401 (1983).
14. A. G. Knudson, *Semin. Oncol.* **5**, 57 (1978).
15. A. J. Cohen *et al.*, *N. Engl. J. Med.* **11**, 592 (1979).
16. H. Land, L. F. Parada, R. A. Weinberg, *Science* **222**, 771 (1983).
17. J. Cairns, *Cancer: Science and Society* (Freeman, San Francisco, 1960), pp. 134–135.
18. W. S. Hayward, B. G. Neel, S. M. Astrin, *Nature (London)* **290**, 475 (1981).
19. C. J. Tabin *et al.*, *ibid.* **300**, 143 (1982); E. Taparowsky *et al.*, *ibid.*, p. 762.
20. S. Ohno *et al.*, *Cell* **18**, 1001 (1979).
21. G. Klein, *Nature (London)* **294**, 313 (1981).
22. I. R. Kirsch, C. C. Morton, K. Nakahara, P. Leder, *Science* **216**, 301 (1982); S. Malcolm *et al.*, *Proc. Natl. Acad. Sci. U.S.A.* **79**, 4957 (1982); O. W. McBride, D. Swan, P. Hieter, G. Hollis, *Cytogenet. Cell Genet.* **32**, 297 (1982); I. R. Kirsch *et al.*, unpublished observations.
23. G. M. Lenoir, J. L. Preud'homme, A. Bernheim, R. Berger, *Nature (London)* **298**, 474 (1982).
24. M. M. Davis, S. K. Kim, L. E. Hood, *Science* **209**, 1360 (1980); T. Nikaido, Y. Yamawaki-Kataoka, T. Honjo, *J. Biol. Chem.* **257**, 7322 (1982); L. W. Stanton and K. B. Marcu, *Nucleic Acids Res.* **10**, 5993 (1982).
25. M. Kehry *et al.*, *Cell* **21**, 393 (1980); P. W. Tucker *et al.*, *Ann. N.Y. Acad. Sci.* **399**, 26 (1982).
26. R. P. Perry, *Cell* **33**, 647 (1983).
27. M. Mercola, X.-F. Wang, J. Olsen, K. Calame, *Science* **221**, 663 (1983); J. Banerji, L. Olson, W. Schaffner, *Cell* **33**, 729 (1983); S. D. Gillies, S. L. Morrison, V. T. Oi, S. Tonegawa, *ibid.*, p. 717; C. Queen and D. Baltimore, *ibid.*, p. 741.
28. L. Emorine, M. Kuehl, L. Weir, P. Leder, E. Max, *Nature (London)* **304**, 447 (1983).
29. W. W. Colby, E. Y. Chen, D. H. Smith, A. D. Levinson, *ibid.* **301**, 722 (1983); R. Watt *et al.*, *ibid.* **303**, 725 (1983).
30. J. Battey *et al.*, *Cell* **34**, 779 (1983).
31. R. Weiss, *Nature (London)* **279**, 9 (1982).
32. P. Donner, I. Greiser-Wilke, K. Moelling, *Nature (London)* **296**, 262 (1982).
33. I. R. Kirsch *et al.*, *Nature (London)* **293**, 585 (1981); J. Adams *et al.*, *Proc. Natl. Acad. Sci. U.S.A.* **79**, 6966 (1982); L. J. Harris, R. B. Lang, K. Marcu, *ibid.*, p. 4175.
34. W. Murphy, J. Battey, R. Taub, P. Leder, unpublished results.
35. S. Cory, S. Gerondakis, J. M. Adams, *EMBO J.* **2**, 697 (1983).

390

36. R. Dalla-Favera, F. Wong-Staal, R. C. Gallo, *Nature (London)* **299**, 61 (1982); S. Collins and M. Groudine, *ibid.* **298**, 679 (1982); K. Alitalo, M. Schwab, C. C. Lin, H. E. Varmus, J. M. Bishop, *Proc. Natl. Acad. Sci. U.S.A.* **80**, 1707 (1983).
37. R. T. Maguire, T. S. Robsin, S. S. Thorgiersson, C. A. Hielman, *Proc. Natl. Acad. Sci. U.S.A.* **80**, 1947 (1983); R. Taub *et al.*, in preparation.
38. R. Taub, J. Battey, G. Lenoir, P. Leder, in preparation.
39. G. L. C. Shen-Ong, E. J. Keath, S. P. Piccoli, M. D. Cole, *Cell* **31**, 443 (1982); J. F. Mushinski, S. R. Bauer, M. Potter, E. P. Reddy, *Proc. Natl. Acad. Sci. U.S.A.* **80**, 1073 (1983).
40. N. Kazuko *et al.*, *Proc. Natl. Acad. Sci. U.S.A.* **80**, 4822 (1983).
41. S. R. Hann, H. D. Adams, L. R. Rohrschneider, R. N. Eisenman, *Cell*, in press.
42. K. Calame *et al.*, *Proc. Natl. Acad. Sci. U.S.A.* **79**, 6994 (1982); J. Battey *et al.*, *Cell*, in press.
43. A. Diamond, G. M. Cooper, S. Ritz, M.-A. Lane, *Nature (London)* **305**, 112 (1983).
44. G. Lenoir, unpublished results.
45. A. J. Berk and P. A. Sharp, *Cell* **12**, 721 (1977).
46. T. J. Ley, N. P. Anagnou, G. Pepe, A. W. Nienhuis, *Proc. Natl. Acad. Sci. U.S.A.* **79**, 4775 (1982).
47. We thank T. Broderick for assistance in the preparation of this manuscript. We also thank E. I. duPont de Nemours and Company, Inc. and the American Business Cancer Research Foundation for grant support. J.B. was supported by the American Cancer Society, H.P. by the Anna Fuller Foundation, and R.T. by Aid for Cancer Research.

29. Cellular Oncogenes and Multistep Carcinogenesis

Hartmut Land, Luis F. Parada, Robert A. Weinberg

Two independent lines of work, each pursuing cellular oncogenes, have converged over the last several years. Initially, the two research areas confronted problems that were ostensibly unconnected. The first focused on the mechanisms by which a variety of animal retroviruses are able to transform infected cells and induce tumors in their own host species. The other, using procedures of gene transfer, investigated the molecular mechanisms responsible for tumors of nonviral origin, such as those human tumors traceable to chemical causes. We now realize that common molecular determinants may be responsible for tumors of both classes. These determinants, the cellular oncogenes, constitute a functionally heterogeneous group of genes, members of which may cooperate with one another in order to achieve the transformation of cells.

Retrovirus-Associated Oncogenes

An initial insight into cellular oncogenes came from study of Rous sarcoma virus (RSV). Retroviruses such as RSV have been studied intensively for the past decade, in part because of their unusual molecular biology involving reverse transcription and the high-efficiency integration of their genomes into the cellular chromosome. Another of their traits, still poorly understood, opened up study of cellular oncogenes: retroviruses are able to pick up and transduce cellular genetic information.

Upon dissecting the genome of RSV, Stehelin, Varmus, Bishop, and Vogt found two distinct portions (*1*). The first portion includes the genes responsible for viral replication, which involves the complex processes of reverse transcription, integration, and progeny virus particle formation. The other portion contains the *src* gene, which enables the virus to induce sarcomas in vivo and to transform chicken fibroblasts in monolayer culture. This *src* gene is now known to encode the structure of the tyrosine kinase termed pp60*src* (*2*). As these workers showed (*1*), the *src* oncogene is not a bona fide viral gene at all, but rather stems from a closely related gene residing in the genome of the chicken. This antecedent gene, sometimes termed a proto-oncogene, is a normal cellular gene and an integral part of the chicken genome (*3*).

This work proved that the cellular genome contains a gene that can exhibit strong transforming properties when properly activated. RSV served as a paradigm for more than 30 other animal retroviruses, each of which was also shown to have acquired a cellular oncogene during its brief evolution. Retroviruses thus represent useful devices to scan the cellular genome for the presence of proto-oncogenes. It seems that these hybrid transforming retroviruses usually exist ephemerally, picking up and activating a host proto-oncogene, inducing a tumor, and dying together with the afflicted host. Timely isolation of the virus from a tumor-bearing host can save the virus and its associated oncogene from oblivion.

A current listing of the various retrovirus-associated cellular oncogenes is shown in Table 1. As new transforming retroviruses are isolated and characterized, the list grows, but only in small increments. Characterization of many of the recent viral isolates has led to the rediscovery of proto-oncogenes already known from the study of other viruses. For example, the *myc* proto-oncogene is known to us from its association with no fewer than four distinct avian retrovirus strains (5). A recently characterized feline sarcoma was found to harbor the *sis* oncogene, known from earlier work with simian sarcoma virus, while another feline sarcoma virus carries the *abl* gene, originally described as part of the genome of Abelson murine leukemia virus (6). Therefore, we may be exhausting the repertoire of proto-oncogenes that can be retrieved from the cellular genome by retroviruses.

Transfected Tumor Oncogenes

A more recent body of work, begun 5 years ago, revealed a second group of cell-associated oncogenes. The initial experiments in this area were designed to demonstrate the molecular determinants that are responsible for transformation of cells exposed to chemical carcinogens. The design of these experiments was simple. Samples of DNA were extracted from chemically transformed cells and introduced into appropriate, untransformed recipients. The monolayer cultures of these transfected recipient cells were then scanned for foci of transformants. Induction of such foci would indicate the presence of dominantly acting, transforming information in the donor cell DNA.

The gene transfer experiments soon showed that certain types of chemically transformed cells carry oncogenic sequences in their DNA (7). The existence of such transforming sequences has subsequently been demonstrated in the DNA of a large number of different human tumor cell lines and tumor biopsies (8, 9). For example, the DNA of a human bladder carcinoma cell line could be used to induce a number of foci on mouse fibroblast monolayers (10, 11). Cells of the foci grew out into fibrosarcomas when inoculated into young mice. Such foci were not observed when DNA of nontumor origin was tested in the transfection-focus assay.

The calcium phosphate transfection technique of Graham and van der Eb (12) has been used in these experiments. The recipient cells have generally been cells of the NIH 3T3 mouse fibroblast line. These cells were originally chosen because they were found to be particularly efficient at taking up and fixing exogenous, transfected DNA (13). As we discuss below, other properties of these cells have assumed increasing importance.

Many types of tumor cells develop transforming sequences in their DNA during their progression from the normal to the cancerous state. A list of these tumors includes carcinomas of the bowel, lung, bladder, pancreas, skin, and breast; fibro- and rhabdomyosarcomas; glioblastomas; a neuroblastoma; and a variety of hematopoietic neoplasms (7–11; 14–18). The oncogenes associated with these tumors are presumed to be important in inducing the transformed phenotypes of the tumor cells, but that role remains unproved. The existing experiments only demonstrate that these oncogenes can transform foreign cells into which they have been introduced by gene transfer.

The donor tumor cell yielding the transforming DNA may differ substantially from the cell used as recipient in a transfection. For example, an oncogene derived from a human bladder carcinoma can transform an NIH 3T3 mouse fibroblast (10, 11). This suggests that this particular oncogene can transform cells from a variety of tissues, but it also points out a weakness in the existing experiments: another oncogene, able to transform only bladder epithelial cells, would never have been detected in these experiments. This may help to explain the fact that only 20 percent or so of the tumor cell lines tested have yielded active oncogenes in NIH 3T3 transfection assays. Perhaps the remaining 80 percent of the tumors harbor oncogenes that require specialized recipient cells in order to register in a transfection focus assay. In work published to date, only rodent fibroblasts have been used, and these may not be responsive to such specialized oncogenes. Other explanations could be entertained for the negative results. For example, certain oncogenes may act as recessive or weakly transforming alleles and totally escape detection in the currently used transfection-focus assay.

Several of the active tumor oncogenes have been isolated by molecular cloning. These include the oncogene of the T24/EJ human bladder carcinoma cell line (19–21), the B*lym* oncogenes of a chicken lymphoma and a Burkitt's lymphoma (22), an oncogene of a human lung carcinoma (23), and one from a human neuroblastoma (23) that has been found as well in leukemias and sarcomas (23–25). In each case, a simple and fundamental truth has emerged. Each oncogene is closely related to a counterpart DNA sequence present in the normal cellular genome. Once again, one speaks of oncogenes and antecedent proto-oncogenes, although in this case the mechanism of activation does not involve intervention by a retrovirus.

Relationships Between the Two Groups of Proto-Oncogenes

The study of retroviruses and the use of transfection has allowed delineation of two groups of cellular proto-oncogenes. The two groups are, however, not separate and distinct. Instead, we now realize that they have some members in common. As first shown last year, the Ki-*ras* oncogene carried by Kirsten murine sarcoma virus is homologous to oncogenes detected by transfection in the DNA of human lung and colon carcinomas (26). The Ha-*ras* oncogene of Harvey murine sarcoma virus is the homolog of the well-studied oncogene of the human EJ/T24 bladder carcinoma cell line (26, 27). These relationships made it clear that certain cellular proto-oncogenes can become activated in two alternative ways. They may become associated with retroviruses, or they may become altered via mutational events that depend on nonvi-

Table 1. Cellular oncogenes. The retrovirus-associated oncogenes are grouped into three gene families (*src* to *raf*; Ha- to N-*ras*; *myc* to *ski*) and a group of genes having no known homology to one another or to any other oncogene. The *mam* (30) and *neu* (29) genes have not yet been isolated by molecular cloning. Each gene is presumably found in one or more copies in the genomes of all vertebrates, although this is not yet documented for many genes in this table. A group of other genes that may function as oncogenes has been discovered but is still incompletely characterized: the genes *erbA* and *ets* are found together with *erbB* and *myb* oncogenes in the genomes of avian erythroblastosis and E26 virus, respectively; *int 1* and *int 2* are altered by mouse mammary tumor virus provirus insertion; *MLVI 1* and *MLVI 2* are altered by murine leukemia virus provirus insertion. These last four genes may therefore be activated in a fashion similar to the avian leukosis virus-mediated activation of *myc* (33–35). Two other sequences, human Ha-*ras* 2 and Ki-*ras* 1, are closely related to two genes listed in this table; it remains unclear whether they are complete genes or pseudogenes.

Acro-nym	Origin	Species of isolation	Chromosomal location		Subcellular location (69, 73) of virally encoded protein	Activity of virally encoded protein (74)
			Human (24, 40, 71)	Mouse (72)		
src	Rous sarcoma virus	Chicken	20	2	Plasma membrane	Tyrosine kinase
yes	Y73 sarcoma virus	Chicken				Tyrosine kinase
fps(=fes)	Fujinami (ST feline) sarcoma virus	Chicken (cat)	15	7	Cytoplasm	Tyrosine kinase
abl	Abelson murine leukemia virus	Mouse	9	2	Plasma membrane	Tyrosine kinase
ros	UR II avian sarcoma virus	Chicken			Cytoplasmic membranes	Tyrosine kinase
fgr	Gardner-Rasheed feline sarcoma virus	Cat				Tyrosine kinase
erbB	Avian erythroblastosis virus	Chicken	7		Plasma membrane	Related to EGF receptor gene
fms	McDonough feline sarcoma virus	Cat	5		Cytoplasmic membranes	
mos	Moloney murine sarcoma virus	Mouse	8	4	Cytoplasm	
raf (=mil)	3611 murine sarcoma virus	Mouse	3	6		

Acro- nym	Origin	Species of isolation	Chromosomal location		Subcellular location (69, 73) of virally encoded protein	Activity of virally encoded protein (74)
			Human (24, 40, 71)	Mouse (72)		
Ha-*ras*1	Harvey murine sarcoma virus	Rat	11	7	Plasma mem- brane	Guanosine diphosphate or guanosine triphos- phate binding
Ki-*ras*2	Kirsten murine sarcoma virus	Rat	12	6	Plasma mem- brane	Guanosine diphosphate or guanosine triphos- phate binding
N-*ras*	Neuroblastoma, leukemias, sarcomas (*by transfection*)	Human	2			
myc	Avian MC29 myelocytomatosis virus	Chicken	8	15	Nuclear matrix	
N-*myc*	Neuroblastomas (*by sequence hybridization*)	Human	2			
myb	Avian myeloblastosis virus	Chicken	6	10	Nuclear matrix	
ski	Avian SKV770 virus	Chicken	1			
fos	FBJ osteosarcoma virus	Mouse	2		Nucleus	
rel	Reticuloendotheliosis virus	Turkey				
sis	Simian sarcoma virus	Woolly monkey	22	15	Cytoplasm	Related to PDGF gene
	Unrelated oncogenes known only from transfection					
Blym	Bursal lymphomas	Chicken	1			
mam	Mammary carcinomas	Mice, human				
neu	Neuroblastomas, glioblastomas	Rat				

ral mechanisms.

Examination of Table 1 reveals at least 18 different cellular genes that have been activated into oncogenes by various retroviruses. Curiously, only two of these, the Ha- and Ki-*ras* genes, have also been detected by transfection of tumor DNA's. This might suggest that the remaining 16 cellular genes are not readily activated by the mutational mechanisms that occur during nonviral carcinogenesis; or this might indicate a weakness in the existing transfection-focus assay, which may not register the presence of various oncogenes in tumor DNA.

Fortunately, other techniques are available for detecting the presence of active oncogenes in tumor DNA. Thus, examination of gene structure by the Southern technique has revealed altered (and probably activated) versions of the cellular *myc, myb,* and *abl* genes in several types of human and mouse tumors of nonviral etiology. These oncogenes, originally known from their association with the avian myelocytomatosis and myeloblastosis viruses and Abelson murine leukemia virus, are not readily detected in a transfection test involving NIH 3T3 cells. Other procedures will undoubtedly reveal more genes of this retrovirus-associated group that are active as well in spontaneous or chemically induced tumors.

As shown in Table 1, other oncogenes have been detected by transfection, but these genes have no counterparts among the oncogenes carried by known transforming retroviruses. These include oncogenes from chicken and Burkitt's lymphomas (*22, 28*), rat neuro- and glioblastomas (*11, 29*), and a group of mammary carcinomas (*30*). Perhaps these cellular genes have a structure or physiology that is incompatible with their mobilization by retroviruses.

Mechanisms of Activation of Proto-Oncogenes

The proto-oncogenes and the proteins that they specify form a structurally and functionally heterogeneous group. It is therefore not surprising that various molecular mechanisms are involved in activation of these genes. In fact, five separate mechanisms of proto-oncogene activation have been found to date.

The first mechanism to be documented involves over-expression of a proto-oncogene following acquisition of a novel transcriptional promoter. As Vande Woude and his colleagues showed, the *mos* proto-oncogene of mice, which is biologically inactive after molecular cloning, can be converted experimentally into a potent oncogene by addition of a strong transcriptional promoter (*31*). Another example of this mechanism comes from analogous activation of the Ha-*ras* proto-oncogene of rats (*32*). These oncogenes, created by ligation of cloned DNA segments, acquire activity because their transcripts are produced at much higher levels than those afforded by the promoters associated with the related normal proto-oncogenes.

This theme is repeated in oncogenes created by more natural processes. Thus, the *myc* and *erb*B proto-oncogenes present in several avian hematopoietic neoplasias have become activated after adjacent integration of an avian leukosis proviral DNA segment. This viral segment provides strong transcriptional promoter which, once again, replaces the indigenous promoters of these genes (*33–35*). Many retroviruses may activate acquired cellular genes by forcing overexpression via the viral transcriptional promoter.

A second mechanism of activation involves overexpression due to amplification of the proto-oncogene or oncogene. The *myc* proto-oncogene is amplified 30 to 50 times in the human promyelocytic leukemia cell line HL-60 (*36, 37*), and is present in comparable amounts in a neuroendocrinal tumor of the colon (*38*). A Ki-*ras* gene is amplified three to five times in a human colon carcinoma cell line (*15*) and as much as 60-fold in an adrenocortical tumor of mice (*39*). Recently, 30 to 100 copies of a newly discovered relative of the *myc* gene, termed N-*myc*, were found in a number of human neuroblastomas (*40*) and a human chronic myelogenous leukemia cell line has been found to carry extra copies of the cellular *abl* gene (*41*). In these cases, the increased gene copy number is presumed to cause corresponding increases in transcript and gene product.

A third mechanism influences levels of transcription and, in turn, the amounts of gene product. This mechanism depends on the poorly understood mechanism of action of "enhancer" sequences, which can increase utilization of transcriptional promoters to which they become linked. The linked promoter may be as far as several kilobases away, and the enhancer may be positioned upstream or downstream of the promoter (*42, 43*). One example of this is the presence of retrovirus genome fragments downstream from the *myc* gene in avian lymphomas (*34*). Here the retrovirus elements appear to act by contributing not a promoter but an enhancer sequence.

Yet another mechanism involves the *myc* oncogene: recent work on mouse plasmacytomas and human Burkitt's lymphomas has demonstrated the juxtaposition of *myc* and immunoglobulin domains following chromosomal translocation. This appears to result in deregulation of the *myc* gene, which loses regulatory sequences of its own and acquires instead normally unlinked sequences involved in immunoglobulin production. This mechanism is explored by Leder in chapter 28 (*44*). Rearranged *myb* sequences have been found in certain mouse plasmacytomas (*45*), but their detailed structure and mechanism of activation remain to be elucidated.

The fifth mechanism depends on alteration in the structure of the oncogene protein. This mechanism is most well documented in the case of the oncogene proteins encoded by the *ras* genes. In the case of the human bladder carcinoma oncogene of the T24/EJ cell line, it is clear that a simple point mutation converted the Ha-*ras* proto-oncogene into a potent oncogene. This G to T transversion caused the glycine, normally present as the 12th residue of the encoded 21,000-dalton protein, to be replaced by a valine (*46*). Another activated version of this gene encodes an aspartate residue at this position (*47*). Recent work on related oncogenes of the Ki-*ras* group also shows that alterations of the 12th residue of the encoded p21 protein lead to oncogenic activation (*48*). A slightly different result stems from study of a human lung carcinoma Ha-*ras* oncogene which carries a mutation affecting amino acid 61 of the p21 protein (*49*). It appears that these changes do not affect the levels of expression of these genes, only the structure of the encoded proteins.

These published results, along with as yet unpublished work of others, suggest that the codons specifying residues 12 and 61 represent critical sites which, when mutated, will often create oncogenic alleles. It seems that point mutations elsewhere in the proto-oncogenes may only serve to inactivate these genes instead of converting them into potent oncogenes.

Although the structures of these various activated oncogenes have been explored in great detail, the precise mechanisms responsible for their creation in spontaneously arising tumors remain obscure. It is widely assumed that these oncogenes are formed by somatic mutation. However, we have little direct proof of this. For example, there is no published comparison of an activated *ras* tumor oncogene with the homologous sequences prepared from the DNA of adjacent normal tissue.

Tissue Specificity of Oncogene Activation

One explanation for the existence of many different oncogenes might be related to the variety of tumors that arise in the body. Each oncogene might become activated only in certain tissue compartments and be specialized in transforming cells of that tissue. The existing results on the *ras* genes and the *myc* gene are not compatible with such a scheme. For example, the N-*ras* oncogene has been detected via transfection in DNA of sarcomas, lymphomas, leukemias of the myeloid lineage, a neuroblastoma, and a colon carcinoma (*14, 16, 23–25*). And the cellular *myc* oncogene has been implicated in the transformation of various hematopoietic cells as well as a neuroendocrinal tumor of the colon (*33, 34, 36–38*). This means that the N-*ras* and *myc* proto-oncogenes are susceptible to activation in a variety of tissues. Moreover, each of the resulting activated oncogenes seems able to affect the behavior of a variety of cell types. This suggests that by studying the effects of *myc* and *ras* on one type of cell (for example, fibroblasts), one may obtain data that are applicable to the transformation of a variety of cell types.

The lack of tissue specificity of these *myc* and *ras* oncogenes does not set the pattern for all oncogenes. Other, less well-characterized oncogenes have been found to date only in association with specific types of tumors. These include an oncogene of chicken lymphomas (*28*), one of rat neuro- and glioblastomas (*29*), one associated with various mammary carcinomas (*30*), and a group of oncogenes, each member of which is associated with tumors representing a specific stage of lymphoid differentiation (*50*).

Limited Powers of a Single Oncogene

The study of cellular oncogenes has generated a long list of these important agents of cellular transformation. But this list reveals little about the complex processes of tumorigenesis in vivo. The creation of a tumor cell within a tissue would seem to require far more than the activation of one of these oncogenes within the cell. Spontaneous or chemically induced tumorigenesis is known to be a multistep process, while the activation of an oncogene such as Ha-*ras* seems to occur as a single, discrete event.

This discrepancy has led to a suspicion that activation of an oncogene such as Ha-*ras* may represent only one component of a multistep process. Furthermore, questions can be raised about the NIH 3T3 cells which are forced into the tumor state after acquisition of only one oncogene (*7–10*). Investigators in several laboratories have pursued this issue by monitoring the activities of an Ha-*ras* oncogene in cells other than NIH 3T3. Their work provides direct demonstration of the limited powers of a single oncogene, acting alone, and of the necessity for cooperative interaction between different oncogenes (*51, 52, 53*).

In our own laboratory we used secondary rat embryo fibroblasts (REF's) as recipients of transfected oncogenes (*51*). Such cells are only several cell generations removed from those present within the rat embryo, and probably deviate only minimally from fully "normal" cells. When the Ha-*ras* oncogene was applied to REF's in monolayer culture, no foci of transformed cells grew out in the following weeks. Cultures of established cells of the rat-1 or NIH 3T3 lines responded to transfection of the oncogene by producing hundreds of foci under comparable conditions. These results were not due to an inability of the transfected gene to establish itself within the REF's. Rather, it was clear that the REF's could not respond to the acquired gene and encoded gene product by yielding detectable foci of transformants.

The *ras* oncogene was not totally silent in these REF's. If the transfected REF cultures were dispersed and suspended in soft agar, colonies of transformants grew out. This indicated that one transformation phenotype, that of anchorage independence, could indeed be produced by the *ras* oncogene. The presence of the *ras* oncogene could also be revealed in another way. The *ras* oncogene was transfected together with the Ecogpt gene that confers resistance to the cytostatic effects of mycophenolic acid (*54*). The co-transfection protocol ensures that the small number of cells that acquired the Ecogpt gene also took up the *ras* oncogene (*55*). A small number of mycophenolic acid–resistant colonies grew out, and as many as 80 percent of these colonies contained morphologically transformed cells. Therefore, if the growth of the surrounding, untransfected cells was suppressed, then the change in cellular morphology due to the *ras* oncogene could be observed.

Transformants could be isolated from the colonies growing in soft agar and foci growing in the mycophenolic acid–treated monolayers. However, attempts to expand these various transfected cells into larger cell populations failed almost without exception. The *ras*-carrying REF's usually grew for several more cell-doublings and entered a crisis leading to death of all the cells. Attempts at seeding tumors with these cells invariably failed.

The powers of this Ha-*ras* oncogene were thus very limited when the gene was expressed within REF's. However, if recipient cells used for transfection had been previously established and immortalized in culture, as was the case with the rat-1 (or NIH 3T3) cells, a subsequently introduced oncogene was able to force the cells into a fully transformed, tumorigenic state in a single step. Stated differently, it appeared that one consequence of establishing or immortalizing cells in culture was the activation of cellular functions that could cooperate with the *ras* gene to create the full transformation phenotype. The established cells thus appeared to possess all of the traits required for tumorigenicity save those few that the acquired oncogene would specify. A similar conclusion has been reached independently by others (*52*).

These results bore on the issue of multistep carcinogenesis. They showed that a single genetic alteration, such as one leading to creation of a *ras* oncogene, was insufficient to achieve tumorigenic conversion of a normal fibroblast. By implication, other cooperating alterations of the cell were required, the precise nature of which was unclear.

Cooperation Between *ras* and Viral Oncogenes

Work on several DNA tumor viruses, notably polyoma and adenovirus, had demonstrated viral genes that could induce a cell to grow continuously in culture (*56, 57*). Thus, the poorly understood changes that are achieved when a cell line becomes established in culture can be mimicked by specific, well-defined viral genes. These oncogenes, unlike those associated with retroviruses, are truly viral, having evolved in association with the viral genomes over extended periods of time.

In the case of polyoma virus, three separate proteins, the small, middle, and large T antigens, are encoded by the "early" replicative region of the genome that is also active in virus-transformed cells. Dissection of these genes from one another had been hindered by the fact that they overlap within the viral genome. Kamen and his colleagues circumvented this problem by constructing clones that were, in effect, reverse transcripts of each of the three early viral messenger RNA's (mRNA's) (*58*). When the biological activity of these clones was tested by Rassoulzadegan, Cuzin, and their colleagues, distinct biological properties could be assigned to the middle T and large T antigen clones (*56*).

The middle T antigen was found to induce morphological alteration and anchorage independence, while the large T antigen altered serum dependence and life-span in culture. These and other results (*57*) were of great importance, since they showed that some of the critical traits associated with transformation could be assigned to distinct, separable viral genes. Perhaps the phenotypes of establishment and immortalization which rendered cells reactive to the *ras* oncogene could be elicited as well by one or another of these viral oncogenes.

When the middle T and *ras* oncogene clones were co-transfected into REF's, no new phenotypes were observed beyond those induced by *ras* alone. But the large T antigen clone and *ras* together achieved dramatic results. Rapidly expanding foci of transformed cells were induced in the co-transfected cultures. These foci, containing morphologically altered cells, were easily developed into mass cultures and seeded rapidly growing tumors upon inoculation into nude mice (*51*). While the *ras* gene alone behaved like an incomplete oncogene, it was clear that the two oncogenes together achieved complete conversion to tumorigenicity.

While this work was under way, analogous experiments were performed by H. E. Ruley of Cold Spring Harbor Laboratory, in which he examined the cooperation of the *ras* oncogene with the Ela early gene of adenovirus (*53*). Further experiments in our laboratory soon confirmed Ruley's finding that this adenovirus gene could replace the polyoma large antigen gene in a co-transfection with the *ras* oncogene. In both cases, the conversion of a normal cell into a tumor cell could be achieved by the cooperation of two distinct genes, one cellular and one viral.

Cooperation Between *ras* and a Second Cellular Oncogene

These experiments proved that *ras* could induce tumorigenicity when aided by a viral oncogene, and suggested mechanisms whereby DNA tumor viruses might contribute to tumorigenesis by providing one or more of the oncogenes required for this process. However, these data shed little light on those types of carcinogenesis that have no apparent viral involvement. Were there cellular genes which, like large T or Ela, could cooperate with *ras* in creating the tumorigenic state?

An obvious candidate was suggested by earlier work on the cellular *myc* oncogene. Cooper and Neiman had found that chicken lymphomas carried an oncogene capable of fibroblast transformation (termed B*lym*) in addition to the leukosis virus-activated *myc* oncogene (*59*). In our own laboratory, an active *ras* oncogene [called N-*ras* (*23*)] had been found to coexist with altered versions of the *myc* in both a promyelocytic leukemia and in an American Burkitt's lymphoma (*25*). In all these instances, an apparently activated *myc* gene was found together with an oncogene that was capable, like Ha-*ras*, of transforming NIH 3T3 fibroblasts. Perhaps the coexistence of these active oncogenes within each tumor reflected essential roles that they played together during the tumorigenic process.

This suggested that we try to aid the *ras* gene by introducing it together with an active *myc* oncogene into the REF's. A molecular clone of the provirus of avian MC29 myelocytomatosis virus (*60*), provided by J. M. Bishop, was used as a source of an activated *myc* oncogene. When this *myc* clone was applied to rat-1 cells or REF's, no apparent effect on cellular phenotype was observed. However, when the Ha-*ras* and *myc* oncogene clones were applied together to the REF cultures, dense foci of morphologically transformed cells were found. Acting together, *myc* and *ras* were able to do what neither could do on its own. These co-transfected cells expanded into vigorously growing cultures and seeded rapidly growing tumors in nude mice. This provided some of the

first experimental evidence for explaining why multiple cellular oncogenes were found activated in certain tumors—each must perform a distinct function which is required for successful tumorigenesis. Moreover, such experiments provide some explanation at the molecular level of the multistep process of carcinogenesis: each step may reflect a requirement for the activation of a distinct cellular gene, such as an oncogene.

Further Implications of the *ras-myc* Synergism

These results showed that cellular oncogenes, like their counterparts in the genomes of DNA tumor viruses, are functionally heterogeneous. Different oncogenes appear to exert qualitatively distinct effects on the cell. This requires a rethinking of the term oncogene, which cannot simply imply a gene that evokes morphological alteration and focus-formation. Instead, as is obvious from the earlier work with the DNA tumor viruses (*56*, *57*) and the presently described experiments (*51*, *53*), oncogenes may contribute in a variety of ways to the conversion of a normal cell into a tumor cell.

This raises the question of how many different oncogene functions must cooperate in order to convert a normal cell into one that is tumorigenic. The present results might be taken to indicate that two cellular genes, *ras* and *myc*, are able in concert to achieve this end point. But we are reluctant to conclude this after detailed examination of the tumors induced by *ras* plus *myc*. Initial observations showed that these tumors grew to a substantial size (2 centimeters in diameter) and then stopped growing; in contrast, the *ras* plus large T antigen tumors grew until they killed the host animal.

Perhaps the large T antigen contributes multiple functions that are required for full transformation, only one of which corresponds to a function provided by *myc*.

A tumor cell may thus require additional functions beyond those several provided by the *ras* and *myc* genes. The search for a third type of oncogene function may require new biological assays. Most encouraging is the prospect that the number of separate cellular genes involved in the entire process is limited to as few as three. Activation of each of these genes may define an essential step in the carcinogenic process.

Categorization of Viral and Cellular Oncogenes

As mentioned earlier, the number of distinct cellular proto-oncogenes and associated oncogenes now exceeds 20, scattered throughout the cellular genome (Table 1). At least ten different oncogenes have been reported as parts of the genomes of various DNA tumor viruses (*61*). Does this imply the existence of 30 separate physiological functions, or can the number of distinct oncogene functions be very small?

One measure of simplification comes from comparison of structures of the various genes and their encoded proteins. Structural homology often implies functional analogy. In the case of three *ras* genes, Ha-*ras*, Ki-*ras*, and N-*ras*, this principle seems to be on firm footing: although the three genes are widely diverged in overall sequence, the encoded proteins are almost 90 percent identical in amino acid sequence (*23, 62*).

A second group of cellular genes includes those that have demonstrable tyrosine kinase activity and several struc-turally related genes whose products have not yet been associated with an enzymatic activity. This is the gene group that includes *src, yes, fes/fps, abl, ros, fgr, erbB, fms, mos,* and *raf*. While these genes may exhibit structural homologies, conclusions concerning functional analogy are problematical: the homologies are only vestigial (*63*); the encoded gene products are associated with different cellular sites (Table 1) (*64*); and these oncogenes are all distantly related to the gene encoding the catalytic subunit of the cyclic AMP (adenosine $3',5'$-monophosphate)–dependent protein kinase (*65*), whose functioning appears to be quite unrelated to cellular transformation. Evolution may have conferred distinct functions on the diverse members of this group, and attempts at associating all these genes with one type of transforming function are unjustified at present.

Further complexity is encountered when attempting to categorize the oncogenes of the DNA tumor viruses, and to relate these genes and encoded functions to those oncogenes of cellular origin. These viral oncogenes have not been acquired from a cellular genome within the past decades, as is the case with the retrovirus-associated genes. Instead, they are truly viral, having been evolved independently by these viruses, probably over many millions of years. Within a family of such viruses (for example, adenoviruses), clear and obvious homologies and analogies can be discerned. But between the families of DNA tumor viruses (that is, adeno-, herpes-, and papovaviruses) and the cellular genome no obvious homologies have been defined. One important and intriguing exception to this has been recently reported—a vestigial homology between the Ela antigen of adenovirus and the cellular *myc* and *myb* genes (*66*).

One resolution of these complexities may come from *functional* assays of these disparate genes. An example of such an assay is provided by the co-transfection test described above in which genes can be defined by their ability to help *ras* or *myc* to transform REF's. Using such criteria, we have placed Ha-*ras*, N-*ras*, and polyoma middle T in one functional group, each member of which is able to cooperate with *myc* in transformation. Conversely, we have assigned *myc*, large T, Ela, and the ill-defined cellular "establishment/immortalization genes" to a second group, since each member of this group helps *ras* to transform REF's (*51, 53*). This categorization is being extended by way of co-transfection tests with a variety of cloned viral or cellular oncogenes.

Other types of functional tests could be envisioned as well. For example, one assay might depend on the ability of cloned viral or cellular oncogenes to complement mutant viral genes required for a full cycle of viral replication. One test of this type has already been performed. An immediate early gene of pseudorabies virus is able to provide functions lacking in an Ela mutant of adenovirus (*67*). Perhaps this gene will eventually be placed in the functional classes including Ela, *myc*, and large T.

A third strategy has also yielded important insights into the functional relations among oncogenes (*68*). Revertants of virally transformed cells have been isolated which resist attempted retransformation by viruses carrying Ha-*ras*, Ki-*ras*, *fes*, or *src* oncogenes. However, these cells can be retransformed by viruses carrying the *sis, mos*, or *fms* oncogenes. This suggests that the activities of the first four oncogenes converge on a common target that is bypassed by the last three. Taken in concert, the results of these tests may allow one to allocate the large number of oncogenes to a small number of groups, each group containing the genes whose functions impinge on a common regulatory pathway.

One aspect of the already established groupings is most intriguing. This concerns the cellular localization of the gene products encoded by the oncogenes that have been categorized by the co-transfection tests. The proteins made by one group—*myc*, large T, and Ela—are all associated with nuclear structures, perhaps the nuclear matrix (*69*). In contrast, the *ras* proteins and the middle T antigen are attached to the inner surface of the plasma membrane (*70*). This is compatible with the presence of one vital cellular target of oncogene action in the nucleus and another near the plasma membrane. Perhaps both targets must be acted on by oncogene proteins in order to achieve full transformation of the cell.

Prospects

The procedures of gene transfer and molecular cloning have made it possible to dissect out some of the centrally important determinants of the cancer process. These determinants—the oncogenes—act pleiotropically, since their gene products clearly affect complex regulatory cascades within the cell. Many of these cascades will be understood over the next decade, and with this will come insight into the molecular bases of some of the well-known idiosyncracies of the cancer cell, including its altered shape, substrate interaction, growth factor dependence, and energy metabolism.

It also appears that other peculiarities of the carcinogenic process may be explained in terms of the sequential activation of certain oncogenes. The experimental induction of cancer involving initiators and promoters may reflect requirements for activation of specific genes. For example, recent work in Great Britain demonstrated that tumor cells could be created in a two-step process involving initial immortalization by a chemical carcinogen followed by introduction of a cloned oncogene (52). The progression of tumors from precancerous growths, such as papillomas and adenomas, into autonomously growing cancers may also have an underlying molecular basis involving oncogenes.

This is not to say that all aspects of the cancer process will be readily understood in terms of the oncogenes with which we are now familiar. Cancer cells can modulate their antigenicity to evade the immune defenses. They can also acquire an ability to break off from a primary tumor and seed secondary growths at distant sites. Such cancer phenotypes do not represent initial derangements in growth control, but rather secondary adaptations that favor survival and clonal expansion. The precedent of the oncogenes leads us to the belief that even these complex biological phenomena will also be traced back to alteration of specific genes.

The eventual development of novel therapeutics against cancer cells will require discovery of agents that recognize targets that are present only in the cancer cell and are at the same time essential for the continued growth of this cell. Oncogenes and their proteins represent good candidates for targets of this sort. These deviant forms of the proto-oncogenes may be specific to cancer cells. And unlike a variety of other cancer cell traits, such as certain surface antigens, oncogenes may be indispensable for the ongoing growth of the tumor cell. By learning how the oncogene-encoded proteins work, we may learn how to antagonize their functioning and one day know how to reverse the engines that drive cancer cells forward.

References and Notes

1. D. Stehelin, H. E. Varmus, J. M. Bishop, P. K. Vogt, *Nature (London)* **260**, 170 (1976).
2. J. S. Brugge and R. L. Erikson, *ibid.* **269**, 346 (1977); T. Hunter and B. M. Sefton, *Proc. Natl. Acad. Sci. U.S.A.* **77**, 1311 (1980).
3. S. H. Hughes *et al.*, *Proc. Natl. Acad. Sci. U.S.A.* **76**, 1348 (1979).
4. A. Frankel and P. Fischinger, *ibid.* **73**, 3705 (1976).
5. J. Coffin *et al.*, *J. Virol.* **40**, 953 (1981).
6. P. Besmer, H. W. Snyder, J. E. Murphy, W. D. Hedy, A. Parodi, *ibid.* **46**, 606 (1983); P. Besmer *et al.*, *Nature (London)* **303**, 825 (1983).
7. C. Shih, B. Shilo, M. Goldfarb, A. Dannenberg, R. A. Weinberg *Proc. Natl. Acad. Sci. U.S.A.* **76**, 5714 (1979).
8. G. M. Cooper, *Science* **217**, 801 (1982).
9. R. A. Weinberg, *Adv. Cancer Res.* **36**, 149 (1982).
10. T. G. Krontiris and G. M. Cooper, *Proc. Natl. Acad. Sci. U.S.A.* **78**, 1181 (1981).
11. C. Shih, L. C. Padhy, M. Murray, R. A. Weinberg, *Nature (London)* **290**, 261 (1981).
12. F. L. Graham and A. van der Eb, *Virology* **52**, 456 (1973).
13. D. Smotkin, A. M. Gianni, S. Rozenblatt, R. A. Weinberg, *Proc. Natl. Acad. Sci. U.S.A.* **72**, 4910 (1975).
14. C. J. Marshall, A. Hall, R. A. Weiss, *Nature (London)* **299**, 171 (1982).
15. M. McCoy *et al.*, *ibid.* **302**, 79 (1983).
16. M. J. Murray, B-Z. Shilo, C. Shih, R. A. Weinberg, *Cell* **25**, 355 (1981).
17. M. Perucho *et al.*, *ibid.* **27**, 467 (1981).
18. S. Pulciani *et al.*, *Nature (London)* **300**, 539 (1982).
19. M. Goldfarb, K. Shimizu, M. Perucho, M. Wigler, *ibid.* **296**, 404 (1982).
20. S. Pulciani *et al.*, *Proc. Natl. Acad. Sci. U.S.A.* **79**, 2845 (1982).
21. C. Shih and R. A. Weinberg, *Cell* **29**, 161 (1982).
22. G. Goubin, D. S. Goldman, J. Luce, P. E. Neiman, G. M. Cooper, *Nature (London)* **302**, 114 (1983); A. Diamond, G. M. Cooper, J. Ritz, M. Lane, *ibid.* **305**, 112 (1983).
23. K. Shimizu *et al.*, *Proc. Natl. Acad. Sci. U.S.A.* **80**, 2112 (1983); K. Shimizu, M. Goldfarb, M. Perucho, M. Wigler, *ibid.*, p. 383; K. Shimizu *et al.*, *Nature (London)* **304**, 497 (1983).
24. C. J. Marshall, A. Hall, R. A. Weiss, *Nature (London)* **299**, 171 (1982); A. Hall, C. J. Marshall, N. K. Spurr, R. A. Weiss, *ibid.* **303**, 396 (1983).
25. M. J. Murray *et al.*, *Cell* **33**, 149 (1983).
26. C. J. Der, T. G. Krontiris, G. M. Cooper, *Proc. Natl. Acad. Sci. U.S.A.* **79**, 3637 (1982).

27. L. F. Parada, C. J. Tabin, C. Shih, R. A. Weinberg, *Nature (London)* **297**, 474 (1982); E. Santos, S. Tronick, S. A. Aaronson, S. Pulciani, M. Barbacid, *ibid.* **298**, 343 (1982).
28. G. M. Cooper and P. E. Neiman, *ibid.* **287**, 656 (1980).
29. L. C. Padhy, C. Shih, D. Cowing, R. Finkelstein, R. A. Weinberg, *Cell* **28**, 865 (1982).
30. M. A. Lane, A. Sainten, G. M. Cooper, *Proc. Natl. Acad. Sci. U.S.A.* **78**, 5185 (1981).
31. D. G. Blair *et al.*, *Science* **212**, 941 (1981).
32. D. DeFeo *et al.*, *Proc. Natl. Acad. Sci. U.S.A.* **78**, 3328 (1981).
33. W. S. Hayward, B. G. Neel, S. M. Astrin, *Nature (London)* **290**, 475 (1981).
34. G. S. Payne, J. M. Bishop, H. E. Varmus, *ibid.* **295**, 209 (1982).
35. Y-K. Fung, W. G. Lewis, L. B. Crittenden, H-J. Kung, *Cell* **33**, 357 (1983).
36. S. J. Collins and M. Groudine, *Nature (London)* **298**, 679 (1982).
37. R. Dalla-Favera, *ibid.* **299**, 61 (1982).
38. K. Alitalo, M. Schwab, C. C. Lin, H. E. Varmus, J. M. Bishop, *Proc. Natl. Acad. Sci. U.S.A.* **80**, 1707 (1983).
39. M. Schwab, K. Alitalo, H. E. Varmus, J. M. Bishop, D. George, *Nature (London)* **303**, 497 (1983).
40. M. Schwab *et al.*, *ibid.* **304**, 245 (1983); F. Alt, personal communication.
41. S. J. Collins and M. Groudine, *Proc. Natl. Acad. Sci. U.S.A.* **80**, 4813 (1983).
42. P. Gruss, R. Dhar, G. Khoury, *ibid.* **78**, 943 (1981).
43. S. E. Conrad and M. Botchan, *Mol. Cell. Biol.* **2**, 969 (1982); J. Banerji, S. Rusconi, W. Schaffner, *Cell* **27**, 299 (1981); B. Levinson, G. Khoury, G. Vande Woude, P. Gruss, *Nature (London)* **295**, 568 (1982).
44. P. Leder, *Science* **222**, 765 (1983).
45. J. F. Mushinski, M. Potter, S. R. Bauer, E. P. Reddy, *ibid.* **220**, 795 (1983).
46. C. J. Tabin *et al.*, *Nature (London)* **300**, 143 (1982); E. P. Reddy, R. K. Reynolds, E. Santos, M. Barbacid, *ibid.*, p. 149; E. Taparowsky *et al.*, *ibid.*, p. 762; D. J. Capon, E. Y. Chen, A. D. Levinson, P. H. Seeburg, D. V. Goeddel, *ibid.* **302**, 33 (1983).
47. E. Santos *et al.*, *Proc. Natl. Acad. Sci. U.S.A.* **80**, 4679 (1983).
48. D. J. Capon *et al.*, *Nature (London)* **304**, 507 (1983).
49. Y. Yuasa *et al.*, *ibid.* **303**, 775 (1983).
50. M. A. Lane, A. Sainten, G. M. Cooper, *Cell* **28**, 873 (1982).
51. H. Land, L. F. Parada, R. A. Weinberg, *Nature (London)* **304**, 596 (1983).
52. R. F. Newbold and R. W. Overell, *ibid.* **304**, 648 (1983).
53. H. E. Ruley, *ibid.*, p. 602.
54. R. Mulligan and P. Berg, *Proc. Natl. Acad. Sci. U.S.A.* **78**, 2072 (1981).
55. M. Perucho, D. Hanahan, M. Wigler, *Cell* **22**, 309 (1980).
56. M. Rassoulzadegan, A. Cowie, A. Carr, N. Glaichenhaus, R. Kamen, F. Cuzin, *Nature (London)* **300**, 713 (1982); M. Rassoulzadegan *et al.*, *Proc. Natl. Acad. Sci. U.S.A.* **80**, 4354 (1983).
57. A. Houweling, P. J. van den Elsen, A. J. van der Eb, *Virology* **105**, 537 (1980); P. J. van den Elsen, S. de Pater, A. Houweling, J. van der Veer, A. van der Eb, *Gene* **18**, 175 (1982).
58. R. Treisman, U. Novak, J. Favaloro, R. Kamen, *Nature (London)* **292**, 595 (1981); C. Tyndall, G. LaMantia, C. M. Thacker, J. Favaloro, R. Kamen, *Nucleic Acids Res.* **9**, 6231 (1981).
59. G. M. Cooper and P. E. Neiman, *ibid.* **292**, 857 (1981).
60. B. Vennstrom, C. Moscovici, H. Goodman, J. M. Bishop, *J. Virol.* **39**, 625 (1981).
61. G. Klein, Ed., *Viral Oncology* (Raven, New York, 1980); G. Klein, Ed., *Advances in Viral Oncology* (Raven, New York, 1983), vol. 3.
62. J. M. Cunningham and R. A. Weinberg, in preparation; R. Dhar *et al.*, *Science* **217**, 934 (1982); N. Tsuchida, T. Ryder, E. Ohtsubo, *ibid.*, p. 937.
63. C. van Beveren *et al.*, *Nature (London)* **289**, 258 (1981); J. Groffen, N. Heisterkamp, F. J. Reynolds, Jr., J. R. Stephenson, *ibid.* **304**, 167 (1983); N. Kitamura, A. Kitamura, K. Toyoshima, Y. Hirayama, *ibid.* **297**, 205 (1982); M. Shibuya and H. Hanafusa, *Cell* **30**, 787 (1982); A. Hampe, I. Laprevotte, F. Galibert, L. A. Fedele, C. Sherr, *ibid.* **30**, 775 (1982); personal communication; T. Yamamoto and M. Yoshida, in press; G. Mark and U. Rapp, personal communication.
64. M. Privalsky and J. M. Bishop, personal communication.
65. W. C. Barker and M. O. Dayhoff, *Proc. Natl. Acad. Sci. U.S.A.* **79**, 2836 (1982).
66. R. Ralston and J. M. Bishop, in preparation.
67. L. T. Feldman, M. J. Imperiale, J. R. Nevins, *Proc. Natl. Acad. Sci. U.S.A.* **79**, 4952 (1982).
68. M. Noda, Z. Selinger, E. M. Scolnick, R. Bassin, *ibid.* **80**, 5602 (1983).
69. P. Donner, J. Greiser-Wilke, K. Moelling, *Nature (London)* **296**, 262 (1982); H. D. Abrams, L. R. Rohrschneider, R. M. Eisenman, *Cell* **29**, 427 (1982); Y. Ito, N. Spurr, R. Dulbecco, *Proc. Natl. Acad. Sci. U.S.A.* **74**, 1259 (1977); L. T. Feldman and J. R. Nevins, *Mol. Cell. Biol.* **3**, 829 (1983).
70. M. C. Willingham, I. Pastan, T. Y. Shih, E. M. Scolnick, *Cell* **19**, 1005 (1981); Y. Ito, *Virology* **98**, 261 (1979); B. S. Schaffhausen, J. Dorai, G. Arakere, T. L. Benjamin, *Mol. Cell. Biol.* **2**, 1187 (1982).
71. J. D. Rowley, *Nature (London)* **301**, 290 (1983); P. E. Barker, G. Mark, E. Stavnezer, personal communication; C. C. Morton, R. A. Taub, A. Diamond, M. A. Lane, G. M. Cooper, *Science*, in press; J. Groffen *et al.*, *Nucleic Acids Res.* **11**, 6331 (1983); N. K. Spurr *et al.*, *EMBO J.* **3**, 159 (1984).
72. C. Kozak, M. A. Gunnell, L. R. Rapp, *J. Virol.*, in press; S. Crews *et al.*, *Science* **218**, 1319 (1982); S. P. Goff *et al.*, *ibid.* p. 1317; C. A. Kozak, J. F. Sears, M. D. Hoggan, *ibid.*, in press; C. A. Kozak, J. F. Sears, M. D. Hoggan, *Science* **221**, 867 (1983); D. M. Swan *et al.*, *J. Virol.* **44**, 752 (1982); B. G. Neel *et al.*, *Proc. Natl. Acad. Sci. U.S.A.* **79**, 7842 (1982); T. Bonner, S. O'Brien, W. Nash, U. Rapp, in preparation; A. Y. Sakaguchi, P. A. Lalley, B. V. Zabel, R. W. Ellis, E. M. Scolnick, S. L. Naylor, *Proc. Natl. Acad. Sci. U.S.A.* **81**, 525 (1984).
73. S. A. Courtneidge, A. D. Levinson, J. M. Bishop, *Proc. Natl. Acad. Sci. U.S.A.* **77**, 3783 (1980); R. Feldman, E. Wang, H. Hanafusa, *J.*

406

Virol. **45**, 782 (1983); M. A. Boss, G. Dreyfuss, D. Baltimore, *ibid.* **40**, 472 (1981); J. M. Bishop, personal communication; S. J. Anderson, M. Furth, L. Wolff, S. K. Ruscetti, C. J. Sherr, *J. Virol.* **44**, 696 (1982); J. Papkoff, E. A. Nigg, T. Hunter, *Cell* **33**, 161 (1983); M. C. Willingham, I. Pastan, T. Y. Shih, E. M. Scolnick, *ibid.* **19**, 1005 (1981); K. H. Klempnauer and J. M. Bishop, personal communication; I. M. Verma, personal communication; K. Robbins and S. Aaronson, personal communication; H. Beng and M. Hayman, *Cell* **36**, 963 (1984).

74. J. M. Bishop and H. E. Varmus, *RNA Tumor Viruses*, R. Weiss, N. Teich, H. E. Varmus, J. Coffin, Eds. (Cold Spring Harbor Laboratory, Cold Spring Harbor, N.Y., 1982), p. 999; S. R. Tronick, S. Rasheed, M. B. Gardner, S. Aaronson, K. Robbins, *J. Virol.*, in press; E. M. Scolnick, A. Papageorge, T. Y. Shih, *Proc. Natl. Acad. Sci. U.S.A.* **76**, 5355 (1979); J. Downward *et al.*, *Nature (London)* **307**, 521 (1984); R. F. Doolittle *et al.*, *Science* **221**, 275 (1983); M. D. Waterfield *et al.*, *Nature (London)* **304**, 35 (1983).

75. P. Barker, G. Mark, C. Kozak, C. Sherr, G. Cooper, S. Rasheed, J. M. Bishop, P. Leder, and U. Francke are thanked for permission to quote their unpublished results. S. Vazakas, D. Stern, and G. Foulkes are thanked for their help in preparing the manuscript. H.L. is supported by the Deutsche Forschungsgemeinschaft. This work was supported by NCI grants CA26717 and CA14051.

30. Yeast RNA Polymerase II Genes: Isolation with Antibody Probes

Richard A. Young and Ronald W. Davis

Three distinct classes of RNA polymerase are responsible for the transcription of DNA into RNA in eukaryotes (*1, 2*). RNA polymerase I synthesizes ribosomal RNA; RNA polymerase II is responsible for the transcription of messenger RNA (mRNA); and RNA polymerase III synthesizes small RNA's such as transfer RNA and 5*S* ribosomal RNA. The RNA polymerase within each class is composed of 8 to 12 subunits, some of which belong only to that class and some of which are shared by polymerase from the other classes (*3*). Attempts to confirm and extend these observations have been hampered by the structural and functional complexities of these enzymes, by the limitations of current in vitro biochemical assays, and by the paucity of RNA polymerase mutants and difficulties in their isolation.

A thorough understanding of the processes controlling transcription and thus gene expression requires a detailed understanding of the components of the transcription apparatus. RNA polymerase subunits have been defined empirically as the smallest number of protein components that copurify and retain DNA-dependent RNA synthesis activity in vitro. However, this approach does not distinguish between proteins that are required for activity and those that simply copurify. Moreover, the assays used to define RNA polymerase subunits have not been useful in identifying proteins required for transcription initiation and termination activities, nor do they reveal other possible functions in which RNA polymerases might participate (for example, RNA processing).

Several factors make a systematic investigation of RNA polymerase subunit structure and function compelling in yeast. Yeast RNA polymerases have undergone careful biochemical scrutiny at the subunit level (*4, 5*). In addition, yeast RNA polymerases appear structurally and functionally very similar to those of higher eukaryotes; by immunological criteria, the two large RNA polymerase II subunits (220,000 and 150,000 daltons in yeast) are particularly well conserved (*6*). Finally, yeasts are amenable to study with a combination of biochemical and genetic tools. Thus, the isolation of genes encoding yeast RNA polymerase subunits should facilitate a genetic and biochemical definition of the enzyme's structure and function in eukaryotes.

As a means of cloning gene sequences efficiently when antibodies are used as probes of their polypeptide products, a method has been developed that permits

408

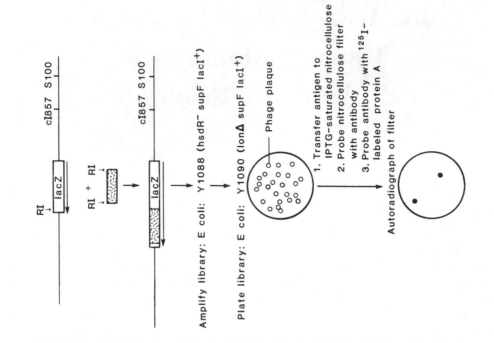

Fig. 1. Screening λgt11 phage plaques for specific antigens. This cartoon depicts construction of the recombinant library and the screening procedure: foreign DNA (genomic DNA or cDNA) is inserted into the unique Eco RI restriction site of λgt11 to produce a library of recombinant phage. The library is amplified by producing plate stocks at 42°C on *E. coli* Y1088 [*supE supF metB trpR hsdR⁻ hsdM⁺ tonA21 proC*::Tn5 *proC*::Tn5 *lacU169 proC*::Tn5 (pMC9)](15). Important features of this strain include *supF* (required for suppression of the phage amber mutation in the S gene), *hsdR⁻ hsdM⁺* (necessary to prevent restriction of foreign DNA prior to host modification), *lacU169* (a deletion of the lac operon reduces host-phage recombination and is necessary to distinguish between λgt11 recombinants (generally little or no β-galactosidase activity) from nonrecombinants (β-galactosidase activity), and pMC9 (16) (a pBR322 plasmid carrying *lacI* to repress expression of foreign genes that might be detrimental to host cell and phage growth). To screen the library for specific antigen-producing clones, λgt11 recombinant phage are plated on a lawn of *E. coli* Y1090 [Δ*lacU169 proA⁺* Δ*lon araD139 strA supF* [*trpC22*::Tn10] (pMC9)] (15) and incubated at 42°C for 3 to 4 hours. This host is deficient in the *lon* protease, thereby reducing the degradation of expressed antigens (7). A dry nitrocellulose filter, previously saturated with 10 m*M* isopropyl thio-β-D-galactopyranoside (IPTG), is overlaid; the plates are then removed to 37°C for 2 to 8 hours. IPTG is a gratuitous inducer of *lacZ* transcription that in turn directs the expression of foreign DNA inserts in λgt11. The position of the filter is marked with a needle, the filter is removed, washed in TBS buffer (50 m*M* tris, *p*H 8.0, and 150 m*M* NaCl), and incubated in TBS plus fetal calf serum (20 percent) for 10 minutes at room temperature. The filter is then incubated in TBS plus 20 percent fetal calf serum and antibody [serum or IgG (10 mg/ml) is diluted approximately 1:100] for 1 hour at room temperature. This solution can be reused several times. The filter is subjected to three 5-minute washings in TBS, then incubated with ¹²⁵I-labeled protein A (10⁶ count/min per 90-mm filter; specific activity, 30 μCi/μg) in TBS plus 20 percent fetal calf serum. Finally, the filter is washed for 5 minutes in TBS, 5 minutes in TBS plus 0.1 percent NP-40, and 5 minutes in TBS before drying and autoradiography. Good signals are obtained after 4 to 8 hours of exposure at −70°C when Kodak X-Omat AR film is used with a Cronex Lightning Plus intensifying screen.

rapid screening of large libraries of recombinant DNA in the phage expression vector λgt11 (7). This method was used with two modifications to isolate RNA polymerase II subunit genes (Fig. 1). Antigen produced in λ phage plaques rather than in λ lysogen colonies was immobilized on nitrocellulose filters. Host cells carrying multiple copies of the lac repressor gene, lacI, were used to conditionally regulate the potentially deleterious expression of the foreign genes controlled by the lacZ promoter. Only after taking this latter precaution was it possible to isolate some of the genes of interest.

Genes for Yeast RNA Polymerase II

Rabbit antiserum directed against purified yeast RNA polymerase II was used to probe a λgt11 library of yeast genomic DNA containing 2×10^6 recombinant phage (Fig. 2). In a screen of 10^6 recombinants, 60 independent clones that produced strong signals were isolated. Thirty of these recombinant DNA clones were further screened for their ability to produce antigens in common with each of the two large yeast RNA polymerase II subunits (220,000 and 150,000 daltons). Arrays of phage plaques were probed with rabbit immunoglobulin G (IgG) directed against each of the two subunits, which had been purified by sodium dodecyl sulfate (SDS)–polyacrylamide gel electrophoresis (Fig. 3). Four of the clones (Y3001, Y3002, Y3007, and Y3023) produced strong signals with the antibody to the 220,000-dalton subunit, and two others (Y3015 and Y3024) gave strong signals with the antibody to the 150,000-dalton subunit. Twenty-four of the recombinant clones produced no signals with the respective antibodies to the two subunits; among these were clones

that contain DNA for other RNA polymerase II subunits (8).

Recombinant DNA λgt11 clones that produced strong signals with the two subunit antibodies were examined in more detail by mapping their insert DNA's with restriction enzymes. Of the recombinant DNA phage that produced signals with the antibody to the 220,000-dalton subunit, two appeared identical (Y3002 and Y3023), and these shared DNA sequences with the other two (Y3001 and Y3007) (Fig. 4A). In each case, the inserted DNA was in the same orientation with respect to the λgt11 lacZ transcription unit. Recombinant DNA clones that were identified with the antibody to the 150,000 subunit likewise shared some DNA which, in both cases, was inserted in the same orientation with respect to lacZ (Fig. 4B).

Confirmation of gene identity. It is possible to misidentify a gene with this procedure, either because the protein it encodes shares an epitope with the protein of interest, or because some component of the antibody probe is directed against a contaminant in the original antigen preparation (the RNA polymerase). Thus, it was necessary to confirm the identity of these recombinant clones with an additional experiment. A radioimmune assay was designed to measure the ability of antigen expressed from different recombinant clones to prevent binding of native RNA polymerase II to multivalent subunit IgG. Antibodies to the subunits were bound to microtiter wells; crude *Escherichia coli* lysate from cells induced for recombinant antigen production was bound to the antibody; and the remaining available antigen-binding sites were assayed by adding ^{125}I-labeled yeast RNA polymerase II. Figure 5A shows the results of this assay, in which the antibody to the 220,000-dalton subunit was used to ex-

410

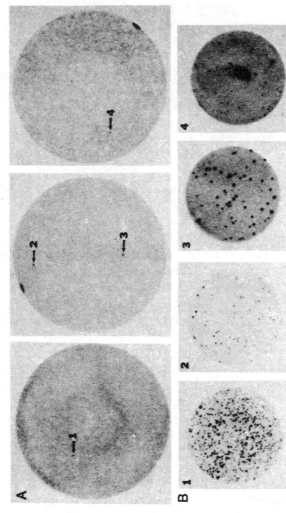

Fig. 2. Screening a λgt11 recombinant yeast genomic DNA library for RNA polymerase II subunit clones. A library containing 2×10^6 individual recombinants was constructed by Snyder (17) as follows. *Saccharomyces cerevisiae* X2180 DNA was mechanically sheared to an average length of approximately 5 kilobases (kb); this DNA was treated with T4 DNA polymerase and Eco RI methylase before ligation with synthetic Eco RI linkers and digestion with Eco RI. The DNA fragments were subjected to electrophoresis in an agarose gel, and fragments of 2.5 to 10 kb were eluted and inserted into Eco RI–cleaved and phosphatase-treated λgt11 DNA with T4 DNA ligase. Phage were packaged and amplified on *E. coli* Y1088. (A) Plaques (5×10^4) on 150-mm plates were screened as described in the legend to Fig. 1 with the use of a 1:100 dilution of rabbit serum produced against purified yeast RNA polymerase II. This serum and the IgG directed against individual subunits required removal of significant levels of antibody reactive to *E. coli* antigens. Removing the antibodies to the *E. coli* was accomplished most efficiently by mixing 2 ml of serum with 5 ml of Sepharose 4B resin to which was bound approximately 3 mg of a BNN 97 [C600 (λgt11)] (7) lysate, incubating the mixture overnight at 4°C, and loading it onto a column from which serum was eluted with an equal volume of fetal calf serum. The *E. coli* affinity column was constructed with CNBr-activated Sepharose 4B according to the manufacturer's (Pharmacia Fine Chemicals AB) protocol. (B) A 4-mm-diameter agar plug at the position of each of the signals in (A) was removed from the plates and incubated in 10 m*M* tris-HCl, p*H* 7.5, and 10 m*M* MgSO$_4$ for at least 1 hour. Phage in this solution were replated for plaques on 90-mm plates at a density of approximately 10^3 plaque-forming units (PFU) and rescreened. This replating and screening process was repeated until all plaques on the plate produced a signal.

Fig. 3. Probing candidates for RNA polymerase II recombinant DNA clones for 220,000- and 150,000-dalton subunit antigens. Thirty λgt11 recombinant DNA clones were plated in drops of 10^2 PFU on *E. coli* Y1090. The arrays were probed as described in Fig. 1

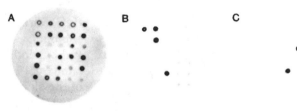

for antigen contained in the two largest yeast RNA polymerase II subunits, using purified IgG directed against the proteins purified by SDS–polyacrylamide gel electrophoresis (5, 6). Signals produced when the array was probed with serum directed against whole purified RNA polymerase II, those obtained with the antibody to the 220,000-dalton subunit, and those obtained with the antibody to the 150,000-dalton subunit are shown in (A), (B), and (C), respectively. Nonrecombinant λgt11 phage produced the plaque signal in the extreme lower right of each array.

amine antigens expressed by clones Y3001, Y3002, and Y3007 in *E. coli*. Antigen in Y3002 and Y3007 lysates was nearly as proficient in binding RNA polymerase II combining sites in the multivalent subunit antibody as was pure yeast RNA polymerase II itself. The lysate produced by Y3001 was able to remove approximately 50 percent of the binding sites available to the labeled yeast enzyme. In contrast, a lysate of λgt11 in the same host was unable to compete for any RNA polymerase combining sites in the subunit antibody. Therefore, Y3002 and Y3007 appear to contain most of the RNA polymerase II epitopes recognized by the antibody to the 220,000-dalton subunit. The Y3001 lysate probably expresses fewer epitopes since the insertion breakpoint of the genomic DNA in the Y3001 clone is transcriptionally downstream from those in Y3002 and Y3007 (Fig. 4A). A similar experiment was performed with IgG directed against the 150,000-dalton subunit (Fig. 5B). *Escherichia coli* lysates containing antigen produced by Y3015 and Y3024 were both able to titrate more than 50 percent of the available RNA polymerase II combining sites. These results establish that the isolated clones

encode most of the epitopes recognized by the two multivalent IgG preparations and thus provide compelling evidence that these recombinants specify at least a portion of the two large RNA polymerase II subunits.

Gene copy number. To ascertain whether the cloned DNA sequences are unique in the haploid genome, we examined the copy number of yeast genomic DNA sequences homologous to Y3002 and Y3015 insert DNA by quantitative hybridization analysis (*9, 10*). Known quantities of yeast genomic DNA were digested with restriction endonucleases; DNA fragments were separated electrophoretically on an agarose gel from which they were transferred to nitrocellulose, immobilized, and then hybridized with labeled insert DNA from recombinant clones. Various known amounts of cloned DNA, cleaved with the same restriction enzyme, were included as titration standards. The results indicated that DNA for the 220,000-dalton subunit of RNA polymerase II exists in single copy in the haploid yeast genome (Fig. 6). A similar experiment with cloned DNA encoding the 150,000-dalton subunit indicated that this subunit gene also occurs in single copy in the yeast genome. Thus,

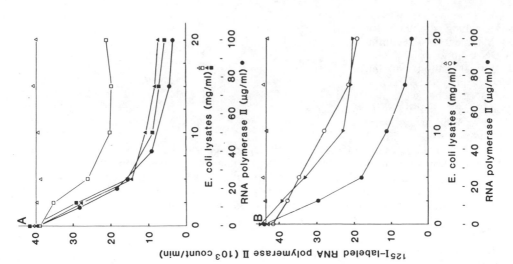

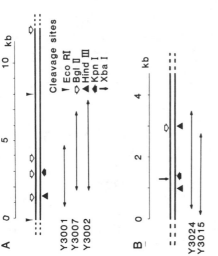

Fig. 4 (left). DNA restriction maps of cloned genomic loci were deduced by restriction analysis of the yeast DNA inserts in λgt11 clones Y3001, Y3002, Y3007, Y3015, and Y3024 and confirmed by direct mapping of those sites in the genome (9). (A) The RPO1 locus; (B) the RPO2 locus. Horizontal arrows indicate the extent of each clone's DNA insert. LacZ promoter–directed transcription of the DNA inserts in λgt11 occurs from right to left. RPO1 DNA is transcribed in the same direction (from right to left) in yeast (8). Fig. 5 (right). Ability of antigens specified by specific λgt11 clones to exclude native yeast RNA polymerase II from combining sites for the antibody to the 220,000-dalton subunit. Purified polyvalent IgG directed against (A) the 220,000-dalton subunit or (B) the 150,000-dalton subunit (5) was bound to microtiter wells at saturating concentrations (0.07 mg/ml) for 1 hour in TBS (50 mM tris, pH 8.0, and 150 mM NaCl). Excess antibody was removed and the wells were washed twice with TBS plus 10 percent fetal calf serum (5 minutes each time). Escherichia coli lysates at various concentrations in TBS were incubated for 30 minutes with the bound antibody. The lysate was removed, the wells were washed twice with TBS (5 minutes each time), and saturating amounts of ^{125}I-labeled yeast RNA polymerase II [labeled to a specific activity 10^7 cpm/µg with chloramine T (18)] were added. After incubation for 30 minutes, the unbound ^{125}I-labeled RNA polymerase was removed, wells were washed three times (5 minutes each time) with TBS, and finally the ^{125}I count was determined. Pure unlabeled RNA polymerase II, rather than E. coli lysate, was used as a control. Lysates were produced as follows: E. coli Y1089 (ΔlacU169 proA$^+$ Δlon araD139 strA hflA150 [chr::Tn10] (pMC9) (15) cells were lysogenized with Y3001, Y3002, Y3007, Y3015, Y3024, and λgt11. A 50-ml culture of lysogen was grown at 32°C to an absorbance of 0.5 at 550 nm and induced for phage production by temperature shift to 44°C for 20 minutes. IPTG was added to 5 mM to induce antigen production, and the temperature was reduced to 37°C for 1 hour. Cells were harvested by centrifugation, and the pellet was suspended in 1.25 ml of TBS plus 0.2 mM phenylmethylsulfenyl fluoride at 0°C. Cells were disrupted by freezing in liquid nitrogen, thawing, then freezing once again. (●) Purified yeast RNA polymerase II; (□) Y3001 lysate; (▲) Y3002 lysate; (■) Y3007 lysate; (○) Y3015 lysate; (▼) Y3024 lysate; and (△) λgt11 lysate.

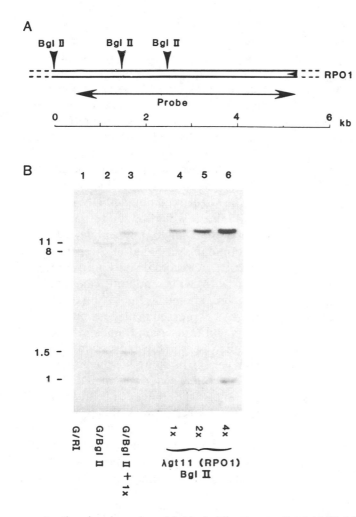

Fig. 6. Quantitation of genomic DNA sequences homologous to RPO1 DNA. RPO1 sequences were titrated by immobilizing yeast strain 2180 genomic DNA restriction fragments on a nitrocellulose filter (9) and hybridizing with the ^{32}P-labeled 5.5-kb insert of Y3002 [shown in (A)]. (B) Yeast genomic (G) DNA (2.2 µg) was digested to completion with Eco RI (lane 1) or Bgl II (lanes 2 and 3). Lanes 3, 4, 5, and 6 contain 8, 8, 16, and 32 ng of Y3002 phage DNA digested with BglII, representing one (1X), one, two, and four gene equivalents of DNA, respectively [assuming 13,800 kb per haploid genome (19)]. Before digestion, 2.2 µg of carrier DNA (*Bacillus amyloliquefaciens*) was added to Y3002 DNA destined for lanes 3 to 6. Hybridization (20) was carried out in probe excess (2 µg). The signal obtained with a known amount of genomic DNA could be compared to that obtained with known amounts of the cloned DNA restriction fragments. Since signal strengths can be accurately compared only between identically sized DNA fragments, the signal produced by hybridization to the 1-kb Bgl II DNA fragment shared by both Y3002 and the yeast genome is compared. A densitometer scan of the autoradiograph indicates that the amount of probe hybridized to the 1-kb band is equivalent in lanes 2 and 4, consistent with the presence of a single genomic copy of the probe sequences. Moreover, the densitometer scan of this band in lane 3, where one gene equivalent of Y3002 DNA has been added to the genomic DNA, confirms the expected result for a single-copy sequence; that is, twice as much label is hybridized to this position than in lanes 2 and 4. All other signals (the 1.5-kb and 8-kb Bgl II fragments of genomic DNA and the 17.8-kb Bgl II fragment containing λ DNA from Y3002) correspond to those expected with this particular probe. Finally, since Y3002 insert DNA contains no internal Eco RI cleavage sites, the presence of a single 8-kb Eco RI genomic fragment is consistent with the interpretation of a single-copy sequence.

the cloned DNA sequences represent the genes that are expressed by the cell. The single-copy genes for the 220,000- and 150,000-dalton subunits of yeast RNA polymerase II have been designated RPO1 and RPO2, respectively.

Future prospects for RNA polymerase. The isolation of genes for the two large subunits of yeast RNA polymerase II and their presence in single copy in the

414

genome will facilitate the construction of mutants at these loci. Conditionally lethal mutations with readily identifiable defects in transcription will help to identify the putative subunits as authentic components of the RNA polymerase. Moreover, the analysis of second-site suppressors (*11*) of these conditionally lethal mutations may reveal previously uncharacterized gene products with important roles in transcription (*12*).

Gene Isolation with Antibody Probes: Other Applications

The power of the gene isolation technique described here lies in the ability to screen large numbers ($> 10^6$) of antigen-producing recombinant DNA's efficiently. Thus, it provides an effective strategy for the isolation of genes whose protein products are easily purified and makes feasible new approaches to complex antigenic problems that are amenable to a systematic clonal analysis. For example, one application involves identifying the protein components of human pathogens that are targets of the immune system: malarial blood-stage antigens that are candidates for protective vaccines have been isolated from a λgt11 complementary DNA library of *Plasmodium falciparum* with the use of human serum antibodies (*13*).

Further considerations for expression libraries. The factors that influence the successful use of antibody probes to isolate and identify clones from recombinant DNA expression libraries merit further comment. As with most cloning techniques, success usually depends on the kind and quality of the probe. Polyvalent serum antibodies from which components active against *E. coli* have

been removed have proved to be satisfactory probes. Monoclonal antibodies can also be used to isolate antigen-producing clones (*14*). Monoclonal antibodies alone, however, may recognize more than the unique DNA expression products of interest since single epitopes can be shared by different proteins in the same cell or organism. Hence, a single monoclonal antibody cannot be used to identify definitively the cloned gene.

The ideal recombinant DNA expression library would have the potential to produce all single polypeptide antigenic determinants encoded in the genome of interest. A recombinant library of genomic DNA with randomly generated insert breakpoints is most suitable since DNA is expressed in all possible orientations and translation frames irrespective of differences in the expression of particular genes. In contrast, the representation of coding sequences in cDNA libraries reflects differences in cellular mRNA levels. Thus, expression libraries containing genomic DNA rather than complementary DNA may be more suitable for a thorough examination of coding capacity of eukaryotes with small genome sizes.

References and Notes

1. P. Chambon, *Annu. Rev. of Biochem.* **44**, 613 (1975).
2. R. G. Roeder, in *RNA Polymerase*, R. Losick and M. Chamberlin, Eds. (Cold Spring Harbor Laboratory, Cold Spring Harbor, N.Y., 1976), p. 285.
3. M. R. Paule, *Trends Biochem. Sci.* **6**, 128 (1981).
4. A. Sentenac and B. Hall, in *The Molecular Biology of the Yeast Saccharomyces*, J. N. Strathern, E. W. Jones, J. R. Broach, Eds. (Cold Spring Harbor Laboratory, Cold Spring Harbor, N.Y., 1982), p. 561.
5. J.-M. Buhler, J. Huet, K. E. Davies, A. Sentenac, P. Fromageot, *J. Biol. Chem.* **255**, 9949 (1980).
6. J. Huet, A. Sentenac, P. Fromageot, *ibid.* **257**, 2613 (1982).

7. R. A. Young and R. W. Davis, *Proc. Natl. Acad. Sci. U.S.A.* **80**, 1194 (1983).
8. R. A. Young, unpublished data.
9. E. M. Southern, *J. Mol. Biol.* **98**, 503 (1975).
10. R. A. Young, O. Hagenbuchle, U. Schibler, *Cell* **23**, 451 (1981).
11. P. W. Hartman and J. R. Roth, *Adv. Genet.* **17**, 1 (1973).
12. This chapter describes the isolation of genes for two of the approximately ten subunits of RNA polymerase II. Genes for the other subunits of this enzyme are being cloned in our laboratory and those for yeast RNA polymerases I and III are being isolated by J.-M. Buhler and A. Sentenac. The study of a complete set of genes for the classically defined RNA polymerase proteins should play an important role in defining the eukaryotic transcription apparatus.
13. D. J. Kemp, R. L. Coppel, A. F. Cowman, R. B. Saint, G. V. Brown, R. F. Anders, *Proc. Natl. Acad. Sci. U.S.A.* **80**, 3787 (1983).
14. T. St. John, personal communication.
15. Y1088 was derived from KM392 (itself a derivative of LE392) by transformation with plasmid pMC9, a pBR322 plasmid carrying *lac*I (*16*). Y1089 was derived from BNN103 (*7*) by transformation with pMC9. Y1090 was constructed by phage P1 tranduction of *sup*F from BNN99 (*7*) into BNN96 (*7*), followed by transformation with pMC9. The λgt11 lysogen BNN97 (*7*) and the strains Y1088, Y1089, and Y1090 are available through the American Type Culture Collection, Rockville, Md. 20852.
16. M. P. Calos, T. S. Lebkowski, M. R. Botchan, *Proc. Natl. Acad. Sci. U.S.A.* **80**, 3015 (1983).
17. M. Snyder, unpublished data.
18. W. H. Hunter and F. C. Greenwood, *Nature (London)* **194**, 495 (1962).
19. R. K. Mortimer and D. Schild, in *The Molecular Biology of the Yeast Saccharomyces*, J. N. Strathern, E. W. Jones, J. R. Broach, Eds. (Cold Spring Harbor Laboratory, Cold Spring Harbor, N.Y., 1982), p. 11.
20. R. W. Davis, D. Botstein, J. R. Roth, in *Advanced Bacterial Genetics* (Cold Spring Harbor Laboratory, Cold Spring Harbor, N.Y., 1980), p. 174.
21. We thank D. Ruden and C. Parker for the essential contributions of purified yeast RNA polymerase II; J. Huet, J.-M. Buhler, and A. Sentenac for subunit antibodies; M. Snyder for the λgt11 yeast genomic DNA library; D. Manoli for technical assistance; M. Calos for pMC9; K. Moore for KM392; and A. Buchman, J.-M. Buhler, C. Mann, B. J. Meyer, C. Parker, A. Sentenac, S. Scherer, and T. St. John for enlightening discussions.

31. Directed Mutagenesis of Dihydrofolate Reductase

Jesus E. Villafranca, Elizabeth E. Howell, Donald H. Voet
Marjorie S. Strobel, Richard C. Ogden
John N. Abelson, Joseph Kraut

The enzyme dihydrofolate reductase (DHFR; E.C. 1.5.1.3) (*1*), is found in every kind of organism, from bacteria to mammals, and in large amounts in rapidly dividing cell lines. It catalyzes the NADPH-dependent (NADPH, reduced form of nicotinamide adenine dinucleotide phosphate) reduction of 7,8-dihydrofolate to 5,6,7,8-tetrahydrofolate, which in turn plays a central metabolic role as a carrier of one-carbon units in the biosynthesis of thymidylate, purines, and some amino acids (*2*). An unusual feature of thymidylate biosynthesis in particular is that tetrahydrofolate is oxidized to dihydrofolate in the course of a one-carbon transfer to uridylate. Thus blockade of the DHFR-catalyzed reduction of dihydrofolate back to tetrahydrofolate in a rapidly proliferating cell results in the depletion of its tetrahydrofolate pool, with consequent cessation of DNA synthesis and, ultimately, stasis and cell death.

Furthermore, DHFR is especially susceptible to inhibition by synthetic folate analogs (the antifolates), some of which show a high degree of species selectivity. These peculiarities of DHFR enzymology have assumed practical importance in the clinical treatment of a number of diseases, notably the leukemias and other cancers, and certain bacterial and protozoal infections, against which chemotherapy with antifolates such as methotrexate, trimethoprim, and pyrimethamine proves to be effective (*3*). Not surprisingly, therefore, DHFR has become an enzyme of considerable interest to pharmaceutical chemists and drug designers.

Being the smallest of the well-characterized nicotinamide-dependent oxidoreductases, DHFR is also of interest to the structural biochemist. For example, the *Escherichia coli* enzyme consists of just a single 159-residue polypeptide chain. Thus DHFR presents an opportunity to study the stereochemistry of nicotinamide activation by high-resolution x-ray diffraction methods.

Motivated by these considerations, Matthews and Kraut and their co-workers (*4, 5*) have during the past few years determined the x-ray crystal structures of DHFR's derived from three species—*E. coli*, *Lactobacillus casei*, and chicken (the last being representative of all vertebrate DHFR's, which are highly homologous—at the maximum practical resolution and degree of refinement. Examination of these structures reveals a characteristic, highly conserved backbone chain fold, even though their amino acid sequences are only about 25 percent homologous, and provides a catalog of enzyme-substrate interactions, about half of which are also conserved. One can guess how some of these interactions might contribute to the catalytic mechanism, but reasons for the evolutionary conservation of others remain obscure. In addition, a few residues that do not interact directly with the substrate or cofactor are also conserved in the known DHFR sequences. Thus, many new questions are raised by the x-ray structures; but what is of overriding importance is that these questions are specific and highly focused.

It has been somewhat easier to ask incisive questions about the function of some part of an enzyme, given its three-dimensional structure, than it has been to devise equally incisive experiments to answer them. In recent years, however, a powerful new experimental tool has been developed by molecular biologists. The contemporary techniques for manipulating DNA make it possible to alter a cloned gene in vitro so as to change any specific base in the sequence to any other base, to delete a given segment of the gene, or to insert a new segment wherever one wishes (6, 7). This technique, sometimes known as site-directed mutagenesis, has been increasingly used to investigate the function of genes themselves and of their RNA transcripts (8). But only recently has the realization begun to spread among those preoccupied with relations between structure and function in protein molecules—the gene products—that site-directed mutagenesis is prospectively a powerful experimental tool with which to answer their questions as well (9).

In this chapter, we describe the beginning of a series of in vitro site-directed mutagenesis experiments, the purpose of which is to increase our understanding of the DHFR molecule in particular, and of enzyme-protein structure in general. For several reasons the DHFR of E. coli is especially well suited as a subject for such experiments. It is a relatively simple, unprocessed water-soluble protein, so that expression from an E. coli compatible vector in an E. coli host should be straightforward. The gene has already been cloned and sequenced (10). A convenient in vivo selection for mutants with DHFR activity can be devised with the use of trimethoprim as an antibiotic. And finally, the three-dimensional structure of E. coli DHFR has been thoroughly characterized by high-resolution x-ray crystallography, and a number of mechanistic hypotheses have been proposed (4, 5). It is important to recognize that our ability to formulate precise questions about the DHFR molecule and to design relevant mutagenesis experiments depends entirely on the availability of precise geometrical information provided by the x-ray structure of the molecule.

Certainly the most practical and efficient procedure for in vitro generation of specific mutations at a given locus is that which uses synthetic oligodeoxyribonucleotides as mutagens, as outlined by Itakura and Riggs (11). We report here on the application of this method to the construction of three mutant E. coli DHFR genes and on our preliminary investigation into the properties of the resulting mutant enzymes. The three mutations targeted the residues of aspartic acid at position 27, proline at position 39, and glycine at position 95, which are approximately located as shown by the lower, upper, and middle circles, respectively, in Fig. 1. They were designed to illuminate both the enzymic mechanism

418

and certain aspects of chain folding and dynamics. In the following sections we describe the rationale underlying the design of these particular mutations.

Design of Mutations

The puzzle of Asp-27 is typical of many encountered in structural enzy-

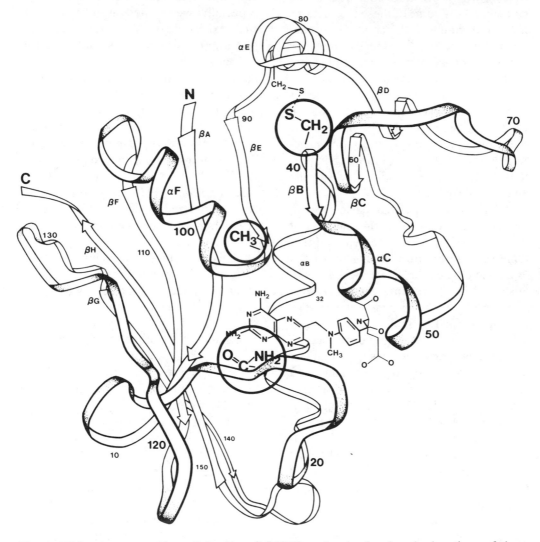

Fig. 1. Ribbon representation of the *E. coli* DHFR molecule showing the locations of three mutations made by oligonucleotide-directed mutagenesis. The upper circle shows the residue 39 mutation of proline to cysteine, the middle circle the residue 95 mutation of glycine to alanine, and the lower circle the residue 27 mutation of aspartic acid to asparagine. Beta strands (represented by arrows) and alpha helices are labeled. The approximate position of every tenth residue is indicated. A bound methotrexate molecule is depicted in the enzyme active site, but the cofactor NADPH is not.

mology. A crucial question in this field is how an enzyme stabilizes the activated transition state complex for the reaction being catalyzed. In the molecular structures of DHFR we find Asp-27 buried below the enzyme surface, sequestered from external solvent, and poised, we believe, to form a hydrogen-bonded salt linkage with the pteridine ring of the substrate. In any event, the x-ray results clearly establish that Asp-27 does interact in this way with 2,4-diaminohetero-cyclic inhibitors and that the pteridine ring of a substrate would occupy the same site, but turned upside down. Because the DHFR-catalyzed reaction involves hydride ion transfer between the nicotinamide's C-4 and the substrate's pteridine ring at C-6, one can assume that the transition state must have some degree of carbonium ion character at C-6, presumably induced by protonation at N-5. Thus the role of Asp-27 may well be to serve as the ultimate proton donor and to stabilize the transition state by providing a negatively charged carboxylate counterion to hydrogen bond with the resulting positively charged pteridine ring.

The difficulty with this simple picture, however, is that although protonation ought to occur at N-5, the x-ray structure clearly shows that the Asp-27 side chain would instead be hydrogen-bonded to N-3 and the 2-amino group. But whether or not its function has been correctly surmised, an aspartic acid residue is conserved at this position in all of the bacterial DHFR's of known sequence, and it is replaced by a glutamic acid residue at a structurally equivalent position in the vertebrate DHFR's.

The first mutagenesis experiment described here was designed to explore this paradox. By mutating Asp-27 to an asparagine, we expect to leave the catalytic-site geometry essentially undisturbed while simultaneously removing the side chain as a potential proton source and negatively charged counterion. Several kinds of questions come to mind. Will the mutant enzyme still function? Will it still bind 2,4-diaminoheterocyclic inhibitors upside down? Will it even fold up in the native configuration?

The second mutagenesis experiment is designed primarily to shed light on chain folding and molecular dynamics and only indirectly on mechanism. In this experiment, we attempt to introduce a new disulfide bridge into the DHFR molecule. We know of no report of a species of naturally occurring DHFR that contains even a single intrachain disulfide bridge.

The basis for deciding where to insert the new disulfide bridge was quite straightforward. Focusing on Pro-39, we find that this amino acid residue lies at the beginning of the extended strand beta B, opposite Cys-85 in another chain segment. If Pro-39 could be mutated to a cysteine, the latter might form a disulfide bridge with Cys-85 upon oxidation. Both residues are sufficiently far removed from the substrate or cofactor binding areas that minor chemical modifications would not be expected to interfere with the activity of the enzyme, and indeed reaction of Cys-85 with 5,5'-dithiobis(2-nitrobenzoic acid) does not (12). Neither residue is conserved in other species.

Simple modeling experiments show that Pro-39 and Cys-85 are relatively positioned so that the distance between their alpha carbons is 6.0 angstroms, about right for a disulfide bridge (12). Either a left-handed or right-handed bridge should be possible geometrically, and no other groups are close enough to interfere with its formation.

In an attempt to see if there is any indication that disulfide bridges tend to occur between backbone chain segments with certain favorable geometries or relative orientations, we briefly examined a sample of 11 disulfide bridges in four highly refined protein structures deposited in the Brookhaven Protein Data Bank. All were different, and none of them resembled our proposed bridge at Cys-85.

What questions can we ask with this mutagenesis experiment? First, can a disulfide bridge actually be formed at a site chosen by us? Do we know enough about the geometrical requirements for disulfide formation to select a suitable site? Will such a bridge stabilize the molecule with respect to thermal denaturation? Will it alter the activity of the enzyme? One might conceive that the activity would increase because certain ineffective equilibrium conformations are now eliminated. On the other hand, the activity might decrease because increased molecular rigidity interferes with some motion required by the mechanism. Conceivably, both changes could occur but with different temperature dependencies.

To explain the rationale behind our third mutagenesis experiment we must first present some background information. It is known from the x-ray structures that all three DHFR molecules contain the same Gly-Gly pair linked by an unusual *cis* peptide bond (Gly-95–Gly-96 in the *E. coli* enzyme) and that an equivalent pair of glycine residues also occurs in all the other known DHFR sequences. Thus it is probable that this bit of topography plays some role in the working of the molecule, possibly as a conformational switch of some kind. That such a switch might be involved in initiating hydride transfer is suggested by the following observations. The Gly-Gly pair lies at the NH_2-terminus of the strand beta E, constituting a very short loop connecting beta E with alpha F. However, Ile-94, the residue preceding Gly-95, is included as part of beta E; its carbonyl oxygen is twisted out of the ordinary parallel beta sheet hydrogen-bonding pattern (a structural feature sometimes called a beta bulge) and is pointing instead toward the C-4 atom of the cofactor's nicotinamide ring. Arguments have been presented that this carbonyl oxygen is part of an array of oxygen atoms surrounding the nicotinamide ring which helps to activate it with respect to hydride transfer [see Filman *et al.* (5)]. Our idea was that if there is any validity to this notion, disrupting this peculiar bit of local geometry might prevent the molecule from functioning.

A minimal change that should nevertheless alter the geometry of this chain segment would be the mutation of the first glycine, Gly-95, to an alanine. Inspection of the structure shows that the beta carbon of an alanine at position 95 would be about 2.4 angstroms from the carbonyl oxygen of Ile-94, 2.8 angstroms from the alpha carbon of Gly-96, and 2.6 angstroms from C-5 of the cofactor's nicotinamide ring, contacts that are all at least 1 angstroms too close to be accommodated by the unperturbed structure. Exactly what would happen to the structure as a result of this substitution is unpredictable, but some change is almost certain to result.

Mutagenesis

Oligonucleotide-directed mutagenesis of the gene encoding *E. coli* DHFR was achieved with techniques similar to those described by Zoller and Smith (7). Restriction fragments (1.0 and 1.6 kilobases) from the plasmid pCV29 (13) containing the wild-type *E. coli* DHFR gene (*fol*) were cloned into bacteriophage M13mp8. Oligonucleotides designed to produce the desired mutations were then used as primers on the single-stranded phage DNA. Following extension and ligation by the large fragment of *E. coli* polymerase I and T4 DNA ligase, the resulting covalently closed heteroduplex DNA was isolated from agarose gels run in the presence of ethidium bromide. After transfection of *E. coli* strain JM103, plaques were picked and mutants identified by dot-blot hybridization (oligonucleotide hybridization with nitrocellulose-bound phage DNA) (6, 7, 14) with the corresponding ^{32}P-labeled mutagenic oligonucleotides, dissociation temperature differences being used to distinguish wild-type from mutant phage (see Fig. 2). Since at this stage a single plaque may contain a mixture of wild-type and mutant phage, dot-blot positives were plaque-purified to obtain homogeneous mutants. These were initially verified by detection of restriction site changes resulting from mutagenesis. The entire gene for each mutant DHFR was subsequently sequenced by the Sanger method (15) to ascertain that no changes other than those intended had been introduced.

Figure 3 shows the oligonucleotides used for DHFR mutagenesis with the corresponding region of the gene to which they anneal. In designing the oligonucleotides, we considered the following. (i) The primer should be sufficiently long that spurious priming is minimal under mutagenesis reaction conditions. (ii) The amino acid codon change should give a reasonable temperature difference (5 to 10 degrees) for dissociation of the

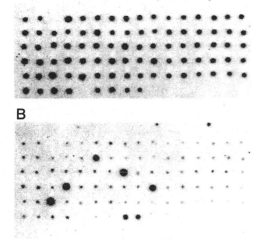

Fig. 2. Detection of residue 39 proline-to-cysteine mutants. (A) An autoradiogram resulting from hybridization of ^{32}P-labeled mutagenic oligonucleotide with single-stranded phage DNA blotted on a nitrocellulose filter at 20°C. (B) Autoradiogram after the filter was washed at 58°C for 10 minutes (6, 7, 14).

mutagenic oligonucleotide from the wild-type and the mutant template (14). (iii) Since we anticipated cloning into plasmid vectors for enzyme overproduction, changes in restriction sites that could facilitate identification of mutants during subcloning should also be included. The restriction site changes did indeed prove to be quite helpful with respect to the foregoing, but predictions of the extent of spurious priming were not always reliable. In the mutagenesis of Gly-95 to alanine, for example, the mutagenic oligonucleotide was calculated to produce insignificant secondary priming. However, of three mutants that were positive by dot-blot hybridization, only one contained the desired sequence change. The other positives were mutations located, in one case, outside the DHFR gene, and in the other case at the correct position but resulting in a 186-base deletion of the

```
                          94                      Asp
Asp/Asn 27   Gene      5'-CTG   CCT   GCC  ¹GAT   CTC   GCC   TGG-3'              ¹Sau 3A I present
                          | | |  | | |  | | |   * | *  | | |  | | |  | | |
             Oligo        GAC   GGA   CGG   TTG   GAG   CGG   ACC                 Sau 3A I removed
                                            Asn

                          295               Ile   Gly
Gly/Ala 95   Gene         ATC   ATG   GTG   ATT   GGC   GGC   GGT   CG            Alu I not present
                          | | |  | | |  | | |  | | *  | * *  | | |  | | |  | |
             Oligo        TAG   TAC   CAC   TAT   C₂GA  CCG   CCA   GC            ²Alu I created
                                            Ile   Ala

                          113         Pro                     Gly
Pro/Cys 39   Gene         AAT   AAA   CCC   GTG   ATT   ATG   GG³C  CGC   CAT   ³Hae III removed
                          | | |  | | |  * * |  | | |  | | |  | | |  | | *  | | |  | | |
             Oligo        TTA   TTT   ACG   CAC   TAA   TAC   CCC₄  GCG   GTA   ⁴Hha I created
                                      Cys                     Gly
```

Fig. 3. Mutagenic oligonucleotides and their complementary *E. coli* DHFR gene sequences. Asterisks denote mismatches between the gene and the oligonucleotide. Superscripts and subscript numbers mark sites of cleavage by restriction enzymes indicated at the right of the sequence. Gene sequence numbering is as indicated in (*13*). The oligonucleotides were synthesized by the phosphotriester method (*26*).

3′ end of the structural gene. Similar problems were observed with a 17-base oligonucleotide that was used initially for mutagenesis of Asp-27 to asparagine but was later discarded in favor of the 21-base oligonucleotide shown in Fig. 3. We found that testing a candidate oligonucleotide as a primer for dideoxy sequencing provided a good prediction of its usefulness for mutagenesis. Oligonucleotides that gave a mixed pattern on a sequencing gel, indicating multiple priming sites, were less likely to produce the desired mutation.

With the exception of the mutation of Asp-27 to asparagine, mutagenesis of DHFR achieved efficiencies between 5 and 30 percent, comparable to those reported by others (*6, 7*). The low frequency of 0.3 percent observed for the Asp-27 mutation is consistent with the notion that DNA repair of M13 in *E. coli* occurs at or near asymmetrically A-methylated GATC sites (G, guanine; A, adenine; T, thymine; C, cytosine) (*16*). It has been shown that this repair results in marker recoveries having a strong bias in favor of the methylated strand, which is the wild-type strand in our case. In Fig. 3, the oligonucleotide mismatch for the Asp-27 mutation occurs precisely at a GATC sequence. The low frequency of this mutation suggests that repair occurs right at GATC sites and that even mismatched GATC sites are recognized.

Since we planned to study structure-function correlations in the mutant DHFR's in detail, we believed it was necessary to sequence the entire DHFR gene for each mutant to verify that only the intended mutation was present (Fig. 4). This precaution seemed to be especially prudent when we discovered that our first mutation of Pro-39 to cysteine did, in fact, contain an additional unintended point mutation changing Trp-30 to a serine. The Trp-30 mutation was already present in the single-stranded template originally used for in vitro extension.

DHFR Gene Expression

In addition to the DHFR gene, the plasmid pCV29 was shown by sequence analysis to contain a point mutation in the DHFR promoter that results in overproduction of the enzyme (*13*). The presence of this mutant promoter can be monitored by the loss of a Sal I restriction site. However, even with the mutant promoter, we observed a low level (less than 1 percent of the total protein) of DHFR production in cells persistently infected with M13mp8 containing *fol*. This contrasts with the high level of expression of the *Bacillus stearothermophilus* tyrosyl transfer RNA synthetase gene cloned into M13, where the synthetase protein level approaches 50 percent of total soluble protein (*9*). The reasons for this difference are not yet known.

Increased production of the wild-type DHFR, as well as the Asn-27 and Cys-39 mutant proteins, was achieved by cloning a Bam HI fragment containing the DHFR gene from M13mp8 into the plasmid pUC8 (*17*) maintained in *E. coli* strain SK383. However, we observed that plasmids that contained the mutant promoter and that were purified from cultures not kept under the selective pressure of trimethoprim (TMP) gave a restriction pattern indicating that partial reversion to the wild-type *fol* gene had occurred, presumably as a result of recombination between the plasmid and the chromosomal genes. This reversion seems to be related to the presence of the mutant promoter in *fol*, since it is not observed when the wild-type promoter is present. The problem was circumvented by growing starter cultures in the presence of TMP and then washing the pelleted cells before inoculating the large-scale growth media. The procedure was monitored by restriction analysis of plasmid DNA.

Since resistance to TMP is necessary to prevent reversion by recombination, genes coding for inactive mutant DHFR's cannot be expressed in the plasmid pUC8 as outlined above. Such is the case for the Ala-95 mutant. Fortunately, no reversion has been observed for the wild-type or any of the mutant genes

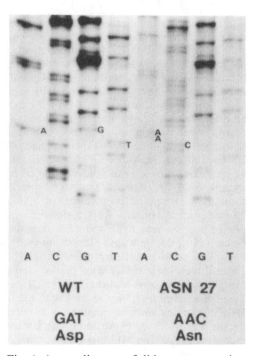

Fig. 4. Autoradiogram of dideoxy sequencing gel comparing the wt *E. coli* DHFR gene sequence with the Asn-27 mutant gene sequence. The codon change (reading from top to bottom) is GAT (wt, Asp) to AAC (Asn).

when in M13, and expression of the Ala-95 mutant protein was obtained, albeit at much lower levels, in the mutant phage.

From the foregoing, it is evident that the degree of TMP resistance of cells carrying a given mutant DHFR gene provides a useful, preliminary in vivo assay for mutant enzyme activity. For example, at TMP concentrations of 10 μg/ml, we noticed that the growth rate of cells containing the Asn-27 plasmid was markedly decreased with respect to the growth rate of cells containing the wild-type plasmid or Cys-39 plasmid. This observation suggested that the Asn-27 mutant enzyme had reduced activity. Further, our inability to maintain the Ala-95 mutation in pUC8 suggested that the Ala-95 protein is inactive.

Fig. 5. Asn-27 mutant protein overproduction and purification visualized by Coomassie blue staining of SDS-PAGE. Overproduction of the mutant protein can be seen by comparing the lysates of *E. coli* containing pUC8 with (lane B) and without (lane A) the DHFR gene insert. In the purification of DHFR, 1 to 3 liters of cells in early stationary phase are lysed, either by sonication or Brij treatment (*27*). The lysate (lane B) was then applied to a 2.5 by 200 cm Sephadex G-75 column. The major peak following the void volume corresponds to DHFR (lane C). This step typically resulted in an initial purification of 50-fold ($\geq$ 90 percent pure). Application of the pooled protein peak to an aminohexylagarose column (1 by 18.5 cm) and elution with a 0 to 0.6M KCl gradient futher purified the DHFR about threefold (lane D) (*25*). The last step in the purification was elution from a DEAE-

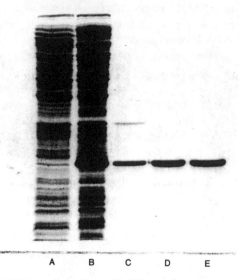

Sephadex column (1.5 by 38 cm) with a 0 to 0.7M KCl gradient (lane E). The various mutant DHFR proteins were homogeneous as determined by PAGE. A typical yield when the pUC8 vector was used for expression was 8 mg of protein per liter, whereas purification of Ala-95 mutant expressed in M13mp8 resulted in < 0.3 mg of protein per liter. The bottom of the gel is the anode end.

Protein Purification and
Initial Characterization

Mutant protein production was detected by comparison of cellular lysates by sodium dodecyl sulfate (SDS)–reducing polyacrylamide gel electrophoresis (PAGE). The control lysate was obtained from cells containing the plasmid or phage without the DHFR gene insert. A prominent new protein band in the lysate from cells containing the mutant DHFR gene was presumed to be the mutant protein (see lanes A and B in Fig. 5).

Since our mutagenesis experiments are expected to generate some totally inactive DHFR's, we developed a purification procedure that is not dependent on enzyme binding of inhibitors or substrates but rather on general physical properties of the protein. The purification process was monitored by PAGE

rather than by activity assays; this again allows the purification of inactive proteins. Details of the purification procedure are described in Fig. 5.

As a preliminary characterization, purified proteins were examined by nondenaturing PAGE, in which mobility depends on the shape and charge of the proteins. In addition, the nondenaturing gel system allows in situ enzyme assays by staining for activity (*18*). Thus we were able to observe, at least qualitatively, any gross differences in physical properties and catalytic activities resulting from the various mutations.

For mutants with very low enzyme activity, contamination with wild-type DHFR of chromosomal or recombined plasmid origin (or both) was a serious concern, and additional separation methods were used to further purify these mutant enzymes. In addition, in the case of the Asn-27 protein, the possibility of posttranslational deamidation (to aspartic acid) had to be considered. The degree of contamination with wild-type DHFR was monitored by activity stains on nondenaturing gels.

Asn-27 mutant protein. Nondenaturing gel electrophoresis of the Asn-27 protein shows that the mutant protein did not migrate as fast as the wild-type DHFR (lane D in Fig. 6). The lower electrophoretic mobility of the Asn-27 protein is consistent with the anticipated alteration in charge (Asp-27 → asparagine). Activity stains of the Asn-27 protein on a nondenaturing gel showed bands in both the wild-type and the mutant positions. This observation of distinct and separate bands on an activity-stained electrophoretic gel clearly shows that the mutant protein has its own intrinsic enzymic activity, although at a much lower level than the wild-type DHFR. In the isolated Asn-27 mutant protein preparation we found that, although wild-type contamination was less than 1 percent of the total protein, it accounted for more than 90 percent of the total activity.

Affinity chromatography with immobilized methotrexate (MTX) was used initially in an attempt to separate the wild-type and Asn-27 proteins. The Asn-27 protein bound to immobilized MTX, but did not elute under high salt–high pH conditions (1M KCl, pH 9.0) (19). After addition of folic acid, the wild-type and Asn-27 proteins eluted together. Although these elution conditions may not allow separation of proteins with MTX affinity differences of as much as 1000-fold, the results indicate that the mutant Asn-27 protein still has significant affinity for MTX.

The isoelectric points (pI's) of the wild-type and Asn-27 proteins, as determined by marker analysis (20) in analytical scale polyacrylamide tube isoelectric focusing gels, were found to be 4.5 and 4.8, respectively. This large a difference in pI values makes the wild-type and Asn-27 proteins easily separable on a preparative scale by granulated bed isoelectric focusing when a pH gradient of short range (4 to 6) is used. A peak in the enzyme activity profile corresponds to the pI value of the mutant Asn-27 protein; no activity was detected at the pI value corresponding to the wild-type DHFR. This experiment again shows that the Asn-27 protein has its own intrinsic activity. The observation that the pI of the mutant Asn-27 protein is slightly higher than that of the wild type is in accord with the mutation of Asp-27 to asparagine. These pI values are comparable to the value of 4.6 previously reported for the RT500 form 1 of the *E. coli* DHFR (21).

Cys-39 mutant protein. As expected, the purified Cys-39 mutant protein was

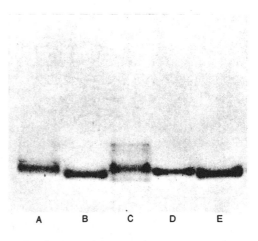

Fig. 6. A nondenaturing reducing electrophoretic gel of wt and mutant DHFR proteins visualized by Coomassie Blue Staining. Lanes B and E are wt protein, lane A is the Cys-39 protein, lane C is the Ala-95 protein and lane D is the Asn-27 protein. The bottom of the gel is the anode end.

found to contain a total of three sulfhydryls (versus two in the wild type) by both Ellman's titration of the fully reduced protein (22) and by cysteic acid determination (23).

Nondenaturing gel electrophoresis of the Cys-39 protein in the absence of reducing agents showed that the mutant DHFR was present in several forms. After reduction with either dithiothreitol (10 mM) or 2-mercaptoethanol (100 mM), only one form remained; this indicates that the multiplicity of forms is probably due to various inter- and intramolecular disulfide bridgings and other oxidation states of the cysteine residues. Since the Cys-39 protein was purified under nonreducing conditions to prevent reduction of the anticipated Cys-39–Cys-85 disulfide, it is likely that the protein underwent cysteine oxidation to the sulfenic and disulfide states, both of which are readily reduced by thiols.

Ellman's titrations of the nonreduced protein showed that fewer than one free sulfhydryl was present. This result indicates that most of the cysteines have been oxidized and, although it seemed likely that one form would have the desired Cys-39–Cys-85 intrachain disulfide, we have not yet shown definitively that it has actually been formed.

Activity staining of the Cys-39 protein in nondenaturing gels revealed that all the DHFR species were active, with the fully reduced form showing the highest activity. Indeed, a comparison of the activities of nonreduced versus reduced Cys-39 mutants showed that activity almost doubled on complete reduction of the protein.

Ala-95 mutant protein. Nondenaturing gel electrophoresis of the Ala-95 DHFR shows that the mutant protein does not migrate as fast as the wild-type protein (lane D in Fig. 6). Since an alteration in charge is not anticipated for the Ala-95 DHFR (glycine → alanine), the different band position may be due to a conformational change. Activity staining of the Ala-95 protein in a nondenaturing gel shows a band in the wild-type position only. This suggests that the residual activity associated with the Ala-95 preparation is due to copurifying wild-type DHFR.

Specific activities. Specific activities of the various mutant DHFR proteins and of the wild-type protein were determined at pH 7.0 and room temperature by the procedure of Baccanari and Joyner (24). The specific activities are 50 units per milligram of protein for both the wild-type and fully reduced Cys-39 and 0.05 unit per milligram of protein for the Asn-27. For these specific activity measurements, copurifying wild-type DHFR was removed from the Asn-27 protein only and not from the Cys-39 preparation, since the latter has full activity and the wild type constitutes less than 1 percent of the total protein. As a check on our activity measurement procedure, we found that the specific activity for the wild-type DHFR is comparable to the specific activity for the RT500 form 1 *E. coli* enzyme reported by Baccanari *et al.* (21).

Discussion

Using oligonucleotide-directed mutagenesis, we generated three different mutant DHFR proteins. Initial characterization of these mutant proteins indicates that substantial changes in protein character are associated with each modification.

For the Asn-27 protein, a low specific activity (0.1 percent of that of the wild type) was seen. This observation strongly supports the postulated role of the Asp-27 side chain in catalysis. Nevertheless, that there remains some residual activity suggests that the Asp-27 residue (wild type) is not the sole factor involved in stabilizing the protonated transition state.

The Cys-39 mutant shows that a cysteine at position 39 does not seem to affect enzymic activity of DHFR, since the mutant is fully active in the reduced form. Our preliminary data suggest, however, that activity is significantly diminished on oxidation of the protein, and although we have not unequivocally established the formation of the Cys-39–Cys-85 intrachain disulfide, its existence seems likely since oxidation of wild-type Cys-85 and Cys-152 with Ellman's reagent has no effect on enzymic activity (12). The diminished activity of the oxidized Cys-39 protein could result, then, from a loss of some dynamic flexibility in the molecule when the alpha E helix is tethered by a disulfide to the beta B strand, but a structural explanation for this hypothesis is not readily apparent from inspection of the DHFR structure.

Our preliminary tests indicate that substitition of an alanine for Gly-95 causes complete inactivation of DHFR. Also the lower mobility of the Ala-95 protein on nondenaturing gels suggests that a change in conformation has occurred. These two results are consistent with our expectation that an alanine at position 95 would disturb the conformation of the Gly-95–Gly-96 *cis* peptide and thereby affect the activation of the nicotinamide ring of NADPH. Extensive changes in structure have probably not occurred since the behavior of the Ala-95 protein on an aminohexylagarose column (25) during purification was identical to that of the wild-type DHFR, an indication that the general DHFR protein fold has been retained in the Ala-95 protein.

The above experiments establish that the technique of directed mutagenesis, in conjunction with accurate three-dimensional x-ray crystal structure determinations, constitutes a powerful tool for investigating relations between structure and function in enzymes. This approach might be of value in inducing useful functional changes in enzyme molecules.

References and Notes

1. The abbreviations utilized are dihydrofolate reductase, DHFR; trimethoprim, TMP; sodium dodecyl sulfate–reducing polyacrylamide gel electrophoresis, SDS-PAGE; methotrexate, MTX; aspartic acid, Asp; asparagine, Asn; proline, Pro; cysteine, Cys; glycine, Gly; alanine, Ala; Ile, isoleucine; and Trp, tryptophan.
2. R. L. Blakley, *The Biochemistry of Folic Acid and Related Pteridines* (North-Holland, Amsterdam, 1969); M. Friedkin, *Adv. Enzymol.* **38**, 37 (1973); J. E. Gready, *Adv. Pharmacol. Chemother.* **17**, 37 (1980).
3. F. M. Huennekens, K. S. Vitols, J. M. Whitely, V. G. Neef, *Methods Cancer Res.* **13**, 199 (1976); J. J. McCormack, *Med. Res. Rev.* **1**, 303 (1980); B. Roth and C. C. Cheng, *Prog. Med. Chem.* **19**, 269 (1982).
4. D. A. Matthews *et al.*, *Science* **197**, 452 (1977); D. A. Matthews *et al.*, *J. Biol. Chem.* **253**, 6946 (1978); D. A. Matthews, R. A. Alden, S. T. Freer, N. Xuong, J. Kraut, *ibid.* **254**, 4144 (1979); K. W. Volz *et al.*, *ibid.* **257**, 2528 (1982); J. T. Bolin, D. J. Filman, D. A. Matthews, R. C. Hamlin, J. Kraut, *ibid.*, p. 13650.
5. D. J. Filman, J. T. Bolin, D. A. Matthews, J. Kraut, *J. Biol. Chem.* **257**, 13663 (1982).
6. D. Shortel, D. DiMaio, D. Nathans, *Annu. Rev. Genet.* **15**, 265 (1981).
7. M. J. Zoller and M. Smith, *Nucleic Acids Res.* **10**, 6487 (1982); M. Smith, *Trends Biochem. Sci.* (December 1982), p. 440.
8. R. B. Wallace, P. F. Johnson, S. Tanaka, M. Schold, K. Itakura, J. Abelson, *Science* **209**, 1396 (1980).
9. R. B. Wallace, M. Schold, M. J. Johnson, P. Dembek, K. Itakura, *Nucleic Acids Res.* **9**, 3647 (1981); G. F. M. Simons, G. H. Veeneman, R. N. H. Konings, J. H. Van Boom, J. G. G. Schoenmakers, *ibid.* **10**, 821 (1982); S. Inouye, X. Soberon, T. Franceschini, K. Nakamura, K. Itakura, M. Inouye, *Proc. Natl. Acad. Sci. U.S.A.* **79**, 3438 (1982); G. Dalbadie-McFarland, L. W. Cohen, A. D. Riggs, C. Morin, K. Itakura, J. H. Richards, *ibid.*, p. 6409; G. Winter, A. R. Fersht, A. J. Wilkinson, M. Zoller, M. Smith, *Nature (London)* **299**, 756 (1982).
10. D. R. Smith and J. M. Calvo, *Nucleic Acids Res.* **8**, 2255 (1980).

428

11. K. Itakura and A. D. Riggs, *Science* **209**, 1401 (1980).
12. M. N. Williams and C. D. Bennett, *J. Biol. Chem.* **252**, 6871 (1977).
13. D. R. Smith and J. M. Calvo, *Mol. Gen. Genet.* **187**, 72 (1982).
14. R. B. Wallace, M. J. Johnson, T. Hirose, T. Miyake, E. H. Kawashima, K. Itakura, *Nucleic Acids Res.* **9**, 879 (1981).
15. F. Sanger, S. Nicklen, A. R. Coulson, *Proc. Natl. Acad. Sci. U.S.A.* **74**, 5463 (1977); F. Sanger, A. R. Coulson, B. G. Barrell, A. J. H. Smith, B. A. Roe, *J. Mol. Biol.* **143**, 161 (1980).
16. R. Wagner and M. Meselson, *Proc. Natl. Acad. Sci. U.S.A.* **73**, 4135 (1976); W. Kramer, K. Schughart, H. J. Fritz, *Nucleic Acids Res.* **10**, 6475 (1982); A. L. Lu, S. Clark, P. Modrich, *Proc. Natl. Acad. Sci. U.S.A.* **80**, 4639 (1983).
17. J. Messing and J. Vierra, *Gene* **19**, 259 (1982).
18. M. Hiebert, J. Gauldie, B. L. Hillcoat, *Anal. Biochem.* **46**, 433 (1972).
19. D. P. Baccanari, D. Stone, L. Kuyper, *J. Biol. Chem.* **256**, 1738 (1981).
20. T. Laas, I. Olsson, L. Soderberg, *Anal. Bio-*

chem. **101**, 449 (1980).
21. D. P. Baccanari, D. Averett, C. Briggs, J. Burchall, *Biochemistry* **16**, 3566 (1979).
22. G. L. Ellman, *Arch. Biochem. Biophys.* **82**, 70 (1959).
23. S. Moore, *J. Biol. Chem.* **238**, 235 (1963).
24. D. P. Baccanari and S. S. Joyner, *Biochemistry* **20**, 1710 (1981).
25. S. S. Joyner and D. P. Baccanari, *Fed. Proc. Fed. Am. Soc. Exp. Biol.* **41**, 1283 (1982).
26. K. Miyoshi, T. Huang, K. Itakura, *Nucleic Acids Res.* **8**, 5491 (1980).
27. D. Baccanari, A. Phillips, S. Smith, D. Sinski, J. Burchall, *Biochemistry* **14**, 5267 (1975).
28. We thank R. Matthews for providing the *E. coli* strain CV634, which contained the plasmid pCV29; P. Price for the cysteic acid determinations; and R. Aust, E. Dyke, F. Lopez, and M. E. Ford for technical assistance. Supported in part by contract N00014-88-C-1482 (to J.K.) from the Office of Naval Research, Public Health Service fellowship F32 GM09375 (to E.E.H.), and NIH grants GM10928 and CA17374 (to J.K.).

32. Surface Molecules Identify Groups of Growing Axons

R. D. G. McKay, S. Hockfield, J. Johansen
I. Thompson, K. Frederiksen

In contrast to those of vertebrates, the nervous systems of many invertebrates contain relatively few neurons. In the leech, for example, the central nervous system is made up of a total of 10^4 neurons, but these are arranged in repeating similar ganglia, each composed of only 400 neurons. Within a ganglion many of the neurons are bilaterally symmetrical so the basic unit of the leech nervous system is a 200 cell half ganglion. This anatomical simplicity of the organization of neuronal cell bodies in the leech offers a great advantage as an experimental system (*1*). We made use of this anatomical simplicity to screen a large number of monoclonal antibodies, raised against the dissected nerve cord, for the ability to recognize antigens present in subsets of neurons (*2*). The initial fusions generated several hundred hybridoma cell lines.

Using a whole mount preparation of the leech ganglion as our immunohistochemical assay, we found that approximately 10 percent of these lines secreted antibody that bound to subsets of neurons. These monoclonal antibodies, which bound to subsets of neurons, often bound to overlapping subsets; but in no cases in our initial studies did we find two antibodies which recognized the same subset of neurons. As we saw more

than 30 different staining patterns without a repeat, there is a high statistical probability that there are more than 200 differentially distributed antigens in the leech nerve cord. These data suggest that the nervous system is made up of a complex series of chemically differentiated cell types; they are consistent with measurements of a high degree of neuronal complexity obtained by different methods in vertebrate nervous systems (*3, 4*). These data are also consistent with models where synaptic networks and other differentiated physiological functions and anatomical features of the nervous system result from molecular differences between neurons.

Another important consequence of the production of antibodies to antigens in subsets of neurons is that these antibodies have allowed us to see surprising new features in the cellular organization of the leech nervous system and that of vertebrate (*5–7*). In the leech, we have made use of the simple anatomy of its central nerve cord to show that axons are organized into stereotyped groups (*5*). The leech central nervous system consists of a chain of segmental ganglia. Large bundles of axons, the connectives, run between each pair of ganglia, allowing for the integration of neuronal signals and behavior over the length of the animal. Each connective contains approximately 5000 axons that form two large lateral bundles and one smaller medial bundle. These bundles are subdivided into smaller groups, axon fascicles, by the process of two glial cells. Some of the axons in the connective arise from ganglionic neurons, others arise from peripheral neurons. We have shown with our panel of monoclonal antibodies that the positions of antibody-identified subsets of axons in the leech connective occupy highly stereotyped positions and are often grouped into axon fascicles (5). These results and the results of experiments in which we have located the axons of physiologically identified neurons (8) suggest that functionally related neurons can be identified by the location of their central axons. The developmental events that place axons next to particular neighbors is likely to be an important part of the mechanism that establishes specific synaptic relations between neurons.

Because of the possible importance of the observation that axons maintain precise anatomical relations as they travel through the connective, we have extended our analysis of the organization of axons. In this chapter we describe the use of two monoclonal antibodies to obtain a more detailed understanding of the anatomy of adult and embryonic axons. We also show that the antigenic differences associated with the surface of subsets of axons in the leech connective are carried on glycosylated, protease sensitive molecules. Developmental studies show that this family of protease sensitive, glycosylated antigens are differentially expressed on some axons from early stages of axon outgrowth.

Surface Antigens on Axon Subsets

Each of the two monoclonal antibodies we have used in this study, Lan 3-2 and Lan 4-2, recognize a subset of mechanosensory neurons. Each standard segmental ganglion of the leech nerve cord contains seven pairs of large, bilaterally symmetrical, mechanosensory neurons. Included in these are two pairs (one medial and one lateral pair) of neurons that respond to noxious stimulation of the skin, the N cells (9). Monoclonal antibody Lan 3-2 recognizes both the medial and lateral pair of N cells; antibody Lan 4-2 recognizes only the lateral pair in each standard segmental ganglion (Fig. 1). In addition to staining cell bodies, Lan 3-2 and Lan 4-2 stain symmetrically disposed groups of axons in the ventrolateral quadrants of the connective (Fig. 2, A and D). The positions of these stained axons is consistent over the rostrocaudal axis of each animal and among animals of the same species. Both antibodies stain subsets of the axons in the lateral axon bundles.

Electron microscopy of connectives stained with each of these antibodies shows that antibody-positive axons travel together in fascicles. Most antibody-positive bundles of axons are bound by the processes of the connective glial cells. Figure 2C illustrates a fascicle of Lan 3-2 positive axons delimited by glial cell processes and surrounded by fascicles of antibody-negative axons. While the staining patterns of Lan 3-2 and Lan 4-2 are similar by light microscopy, electron microscopy shows that Lan 4-2 and Lan 3-2 recognize overlapping sets of axons; Lan 3-2 predominantly stains small-diameter axons (0.1 to 0.5 μm),

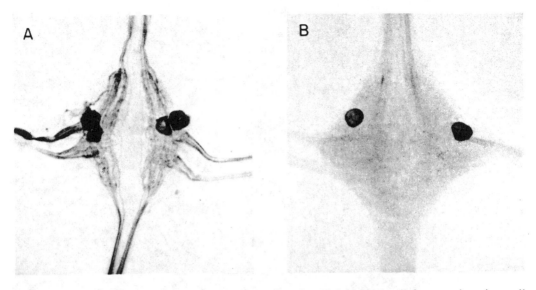

Fig. 1. Antibody binding to subsets of cell bodies. Lan 3-2 binds to all four nociceptive cell bodies (A) and Lan 4-2 binds only to the lateral nociceptive cell bodies (B) of *Hemopis marmorata* midbody ganglia (*21*). The derivation of the monoclonal antibodies Lan 3-2 and Lan 4-2 has been described previously (*2, 5, 9*). Immunohistochemistry at the light microscope level. Fixed whole mounts of adult leech ganglia were processed as described previously (*2*). The immunohistochemical analysis of the developing nervous system was performed as in the adult; the dissection of 4 percent formalin fixed leech embryos was carried out by fine tungsten mounted wires.

and Lan 4-2 stains both small and large diameter (greater than 0.5 μm) axons (Fig. 2, C and F).

Lan 3-2 and Lan 4-2 bind to surface antigens by two criteria. First, in high magnification electron micrographs of axons (Fig. 2, C and F) antibody staining is associated with the perimeter of stained axons while the axoplasm is free of stain. Second, Lan 3-2 stains the four N cells in unfixed, living preparations of leech ganglia where the connective tissue capsule of the ganglion has been opened to allow the monoclonal antibody access to the surface of neuronal cell bodies. When these preparations were fixed after antibody staining and

processed for electron microscopy, the antigen was clearly present on the outer surface of labeled neurons (*9*).

Symmetrical Organization of Axon Fascicles

The symmetrical organization of antibody-labeled axons is shown in the light micrographs in Fig. 2, A and D. Further analyses by electron microscopy revealed the features of axon symmetry in greater detail. The symmetry in the organization of antigenically identified bundles of axons (Fig. 3) was diagramed by

432

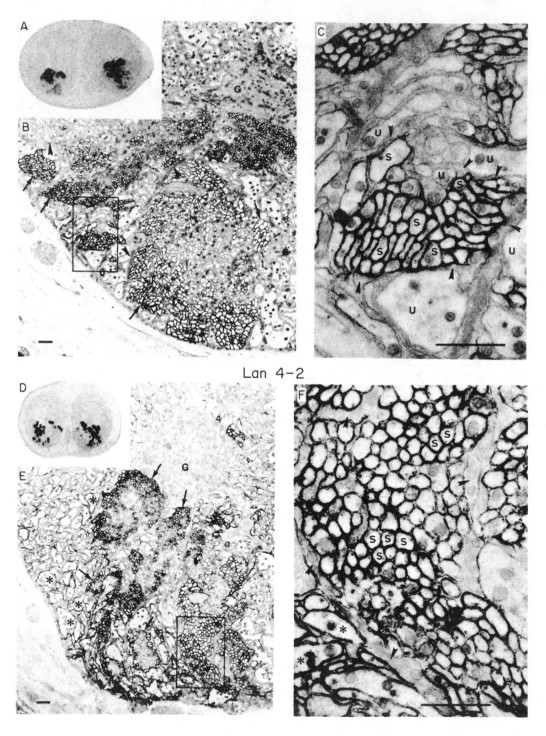

Lan 4-2

tracing antibody-identified bundles of axons in a montage of low magnification electron micrographs from a single cross section of the connective. Serial sections adjacent to the one illustrated were examined to ensure that antibody penetration was uniform. This confirmed that the selective staining of axons was not a result of uneven antibody accessibility. Using a new technique which improved antibody penetration (*10*), we could accurately compare the positions and organization of bundles of axons on both sides of the connective and increase the resolution of stained profiles to the level of single axons. High magnification electron micrographs of corresponding symmetrical bundles of axons from the diagramed cross section of the connective show more precisely the organization of stained axons (Fig. 3, inset). These micrographs show that while the symmetry of axon organization is clear, it is not geometrically perfect. The lack of perfect symmetry is reflected not only

in the position of particular bundles, but also in the number of stained profiles in any given bundle. For example, the largest symmetrical bundles (Fig. 3, inset) have 16 and 21 stained profiles, respectively.

The data presented in Fig. 3 confirm our previous observation that Lan 3-2 and Lan 4-2 bind to symmetrically arranged groups of axons. The single axon resolution we have now obtained allows us to extend our previous observations in two ways. First, where previously it was unclear whether the antigen was present on all the axons in a bundle or only on the most peripheral axons, we now have shown that all the axons throughout many fascicles share a surface antigenic determinant. Second, because we can now count the number of axons recognized by an antibody we have shown that while the symmetrical organization of axons is clear the precise features of fasciculation are not perfectly conserved.

Fig. 2. Antibody binding to subsets of axons. Cross sections of the connective shown at the light level (A and D), at low power (B and E) and at high power (C and F) electron microscopy. The symmetrical organization of axon subsets is shown in the light micrographs. More details of the organization of antibody identified axon fascicles can be seen in the electron micrographs. The glial cell is marked *G* and the processes of the glial cell are indicated by arrowheads. Fascicles of labeled axons are marked by arrows. Stained and unstained axon profiles are marked *S* and *U* respectively. Lan 4-2 recognizes a set of larger axons; examples of these are marked with an asterisk. Following the protocol of Eldred *et al.* (*10*), adult nerve cord or whole leech embryos were fixed in 4 percent paraformaldehyde at *p*H 7.4 (30 minutes, room temperature) followed by 4 percent paraformaldehyde at *p*H 1.0 (2 to 12 hours, 4°C). Small pieces of tissue were immersed in 1 percent sodium borohydride (30 minutes), washed in buffer and then run through graded alcohols (10, 20, 40, 20, and 10 percent) back to buffer. Tissue was incubated in first antibody overnight, washed in buffer and second antibody [horseradish peroxidase conjugated rabbit antibody to mouse antiserum (Cappel)] for 2 hours. Peroxidase was visualized with 3,3'-diaminobenzidine; the tissue was postfixed in 2 percent OsO_4 and embedded in Epon-Araldite. Sections from the first 5 to 10 μm of the tissue surface were examined unstained in the electron microscope.

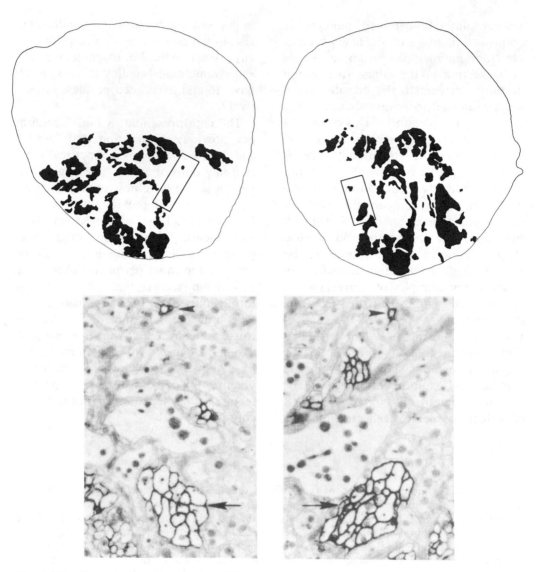

Fig. 3. Diagram showing the distribution Lan 3-2 identified axon bundles. The boxes marked in the diagram are shown in the inset electron micrographs.

Embryological Distribution of

Lan 3-2 Antigen

We have examined the developmental appearance of the Lan 3-2 antigen in two species of leech, *Hemopis marmorata* and *Helobdella triserialis*. The central nervous system (CNS) of *Helobdella* does not contain Lan 3-2–positive cell bodies but does contain the symmetrically disposed groups of Lan 3-2–positive axons which are also stained in *Hemopis marmorata* (5). In early embryos of both these species Lan 3-2–positive axons and cell bodies are first seen in the peripheral skin. Axons carrying these specific antigens grow from the cell bodies in the periphery into the CNS.

The development of Lan 3-2–positive axons in *Helobdella triserialis* is shown in Fig. 4. The antigen is first seen in groups of peripheral cells aligned along the central annulus of each segment on the dorsal body wall. In Fig. 4A, a section of the body wall of an early stage 11 embryo is shown stained in whole mount; several groups of peripheral neurons already express the Lan 3-2 antigen in their cell bodies and processes. Each more central group of cells (marked *C*) is progressively less differentiated, but the cell bodies and processes are already antigenically positive. At high magnification (Fig. 4B) the cell bodies and processes of one of the group of cells marked *P* in Fig. 4A. We can see that, in addition to the major processes, a network of fine antigenically positive processes are present. These fine processes, which are close to the limit of resolution of the light microscope, are detectable because of the deposition of horseradish peroxidase reaction product. The size and morphology of these fine processes suggest that they are the filopodia of the growing processes of axons.

The processes of the peripheral cell groups elongate toward the CNS forming distinct fiber bundles with the processes of more centrally located groups of neurons. When these processes reach the CNS they arborize within the ganglia (Fig. 4D). Here again, immunocytochemistry shows by light microscopy that the arbors formed by these peripheral neurons carry the Lan 3-2 antigens (Fig. 4C). As the processes grow further in the CNS, they send branches rostrally and caudally to form symmetrically arranged rows of axons in the midbody ganglia (marked *G* in Fig. 4D). Figure 4D shows the relation between the peripheral neurons and the antigenically positive central axons. As we are able to stain transient structures, filopodia, and central arbors, we are able to conclude that the antigens are part of the growing tip of the axon.

The disposition of Lan 3-2–positive axons in the isolated CNS of the late stage 11 embryo is shown in Fig. 4E. In this case, the CNS was dissected and stained in whole mount. In the rostral body segments, a well-developed fiber pattern is apparent; in more caudal segments the fiber tracts are less well developed. This observation is consistent with the general rule of a rostral-caudal gradient of differentiation. An exception is seen in the most caudal seven ganglia which later form the tail ganglion. In the tail ganglia, the Lan 3-2–positive fibers grow into the ganglia and arborize extensively at early stage 11, a time when the head ganglia are the only other antigenically positive central structures. In spite of their early appearance in the tail ganglia, antigenically positive fibers do not cross into the most caudal of the midbody ganglia even though these ganglia are directly adjacent to one another.

In embryonic as well as adult *Helobdella*, Lan 3-2–positive cell bodies have only been observed in the periphery; the adult central nervous system contains Lan 3-2–positive axons but not cell bodies. Our embryological studies indicate that many of these central axons are derived from peripheral neurons (Fig. 4). The distribution of axons in the adult nerve cords of *Hemopis marmorata* and *Hirudo medicinalis* is similar to that seen in *Helobdella*. We have obtained *Hemopis* embryos from leeches captured from the wild. The general pattern of development is similar to that seen in *Helobdella*; that is, segmentally arranged rows of peripheral groups of Lan 3-2–positive

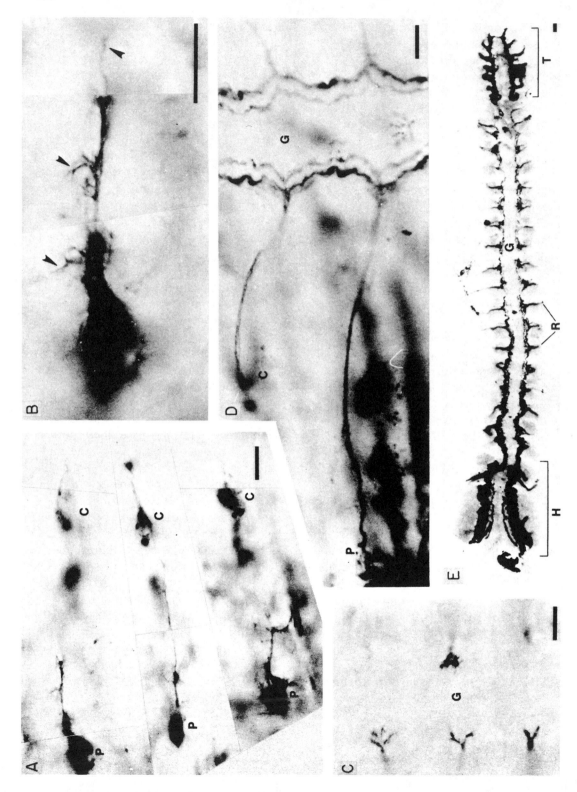

cell bodies send their processes into the CNS. These fibers arborize to give symmetrically disposed groups of axons. This is shown in Fig. 5A where symmetrically arranged axons travel through a ganglion (the neuronal cell bodies are marked *N*). Immunoelectron microscopy shows that in the connective and neuropil of the *Hemopis* embryo the Lan 3-2 antigen is present on the surface of developing processes (Fig. 5B). These antigenically positive processes run in bundles before the processes of glial cells have separated them from unstained neighboring axons. Similarly, electron microscopy of *Helobdella* embryos shows that the Lan 3-2 antigen is present on the surface of axons that form fascicles early in development.

Our developmental data shows that Lan 3-2 recognizes surface antigens expressed by neurons from the earliest stages of axon outgrowth and that antigenically positive bundles of axons occupy symmetrical locations in the connective at early stages in development (Figs. 4 and 5).

Biochemical Characterization of Lan 3-2 and Lan 4-2 Antigens

One of the technical advantages in using monoclonal antibodies to study complex tissues is that the same reagents can be used for both immunohistochemical and biochemical analysis.

Our histochemical studies described here show that the antigens recognized by Lan 3-2 and Lan 4-2 have an anatomical distribution in the adult and embryonic nervous system which shows that the surfaces of different groups of growing axons can be chemically distinct. Here we describe experiments designed to determine the biochemical nature of the molecules carrying these surface antigenic determinants.

On immunoblots of proteins extracted from the leech central nervous system, Lan 3-2 binds to a series of high molecular weight antigens. Figure 6 shows that Lan 3-2, in contrast to other immunoglobulin Gl (IgGl) monoclonal antibodies, specifically recognizes three major bands between 90,000 and 130,000 daltons in the species *Hemopis marmorata*. All three of these bands are sensitive to treatment with protease K (Fig. 6, lane 4).

The anatomical data suggest the possibility that Lan 3-2 and Lan 4-2 recognize related antigens. This possibility is strengthened by the biochemical results shown in Fig. 6B. Proteins extracted from the nerve cord of *Hemopis marmorata* were analyzed with the immunoblot procedure (Lan 4-2, Fig. 6B, lane 1; Lan 3-2, Fig. 6B, lane 2). Lan 4-2 binds strongly to a 130,000-dalton band which comigrates with the band of antigens of high molecular size recognized by Lan 3-2. Like the antigens recognized by Lan 3-2, the Lan 4-2 130,000-dalton

Fig. 4. Expression of Lan 3-2 antigens on neuronal processes during development in *Helobdella triserialis*. In the middle annulus of each segment a group of cutaneous neurons express antigens which bind the monoclonal antibody Lan 3-2 from early stages of neurite growth (A). These cell bodies and processes at higher magnification are shown in (B). These processes arborize as they grow into the central ganglia (marked *G*) as shown in (C) where they form a symmetrically organized fiber array (D and E). In (D) the processes extending from the cutaneous cells (marked *P* and *C*) can be seen extending into the central ganglia. In (E), a stage 11 nervous system is shown in whole mount after staining with Lan 3-2. All the preparations shown here were obtained from stage 11 embryos (*22*). All scale bars represent 10 μm.

438

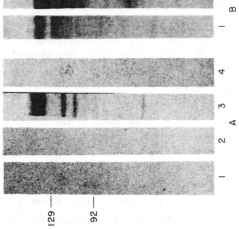

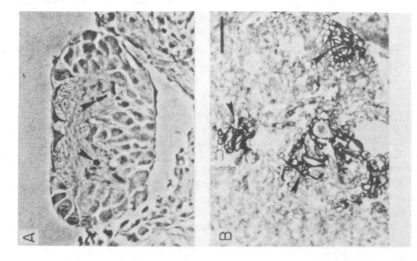

Fig. 5 (left). Symmetrically organized antigenically distinct axon fascicles in the developing cord of *Hemopis marmorata*. By light microscopy, symmetrically organized groups of antigenically positive processes can be seen in this cross section through a ganglion. Neuronal cell bodies are marked N and labeled processes indicated by arrowheads. By electron microscopy, these processes are seen to carry antigen on their surface and run in bundles (B). The scale bar represents 1.75 μm. Fig. 6 (right). (A) Lan 3-2 binds to specific antigens on Western blots. Leech neural antigens were extracted from the dissected nerve cord by homogenization in Laemmli loading buffer and boiling. The solubilized material was placed on polyacrylamide gels (10 percent) and electro-transferred to nitrocellulose. The lanes carrying material from five ganglia were challenged with control monoclonal antibodies of the same subclass as Lan 3-2 in lanes 1 and 2 and Lan 3-2 in lane 3. The bound monoclonal antibodies were visualized with second mouse antibody conjugated to peroxidase. Exposing the solubilized antigen to protease K before gel electrophoresis abolished antibody binding (lane 4). (B) Lan 4-2 binds to a major high molecular weight antigen (lane 1) which comigrates with the Lan 3-2 high molecular weight antigen (lane 2). Leech antigens were extracted from the nerve cord in Laemmli buffer (23). After electrophoresis on 10 percent polyacrylamide gels, the antigens were electroblotted onto nitrocellulose paper and challenged with antibodies (24). Peroxidase conjugated second antibody (1:200, Miles-Yeda) was used as a tracer and chloronaphthol was used as a substrate. In lane 4, the sodium dodecyl sulfate and mercaptoethanol-solubilized leech antigens were treated with 5 μg of protease K (Boehringer-Mannheim) per milliliter for 20 minutes before electrophoresis.

antigen is protease sensitive.

The Lan 3-2–positive antigens can be extracted from the leech central nervous system in high yield by 1 percent Triton X-100. The solubilized antigens were selectively bound by lectins covalently linked to agarose beads. The Lan 3-2 antigens from *Hirudo medicinalis* bind to concanavalin A (Con A) beads and lentil lectin beads but not to beads carrying wheat germ agglutinin (WGA) (Fig. 7). These antigens can be specifically eluted with sugar and no additional antigen is subsequently eluted by sodium dodecyl sulfate and mercaptoethanol. Lectin binding experiments also show that the antigen bound by Lan 4-2 is glycosylated. It will be interesting to determine in more detail the chemical relation between these antigenically reactive bands. Our biochemical data are consistent with our immunohistochemical observations, as we might expect to find glycosylated proteins on the surface of cells. Since these antigens can be easily extracted from leech nerve cord and are glycosylated and protease sensitive, we suggest that they form a family of related surface glycoproteins. Whether there are additional members of this family of antigens present on the surface of different axon subsets remains to be determined.

The fact that the Lan 3-2 antigens are glycosylated raises the possibility that the antigenic determinant recognized by Lan 3-2 is itself a carbohydrate structure. Accordingly, nitrocellulose strips carrying the leech antigens were incubated with increasing dilutions of Lan 3-2 in the presence and absence of various sugars. The binding of Lan 3-2 to the nitrocellulose bound antigen was specifically inhibited by methylmannoside and not by other sugars (Fig. 8). This observation suggests that the antigenic determinant recognized by Lan 3-2 is composed, at least in part, of carbohydrate. The

antigens recognized by Lan 4-2 are also glycosylated since they can be specifically bound to and eluted from lectin beads, but no sugar we have tested blocks the binding of Lan 4-2 in this assay (9).

Significance of Stereotyped
Axon Organization

We show here that two antibodies against surface determinants bind to physiologically related cell bodies, anatomically related axons and similar protease sensitive, glycosylated antigens. These antigens are expressed from early stages of neurite outgrowth. Therefore during process outgrowth, axon surfaces can carry specific surface markers (glycosylated proteins) that distinguish the axons in a given fascicle from axons in neighboring groups.

The general organization of axon fascicles is symmetrical and stereotyped. A conclusion we have confirmed using the tracer enzyme horseradish peroxidase to locate the axons of physiologically identified individual neurons in the connective. For example, the axons of the mechanosensory cells were shown to run together (9). This observation that axons of physiologically similar cells run together is consistent with the observation of Stretton and Kravitz (11) who showed that functionally similar groups of axons run in stereotyped fascicles in the neuropil of the lobster.

In simpler invertebrates with fewer axons a stereotyped organization of the nerve cord is also found. The anatomy of the nematode nerve cord is known in detail (12, 13) and identified axons are found in symmetrical and stereotyped locations. In nematodes most axons do not branch and have fixed lengths; it follows from these facts that the position of the axon plays an important role in determining the possible synapses a neuron can make.

These observations and observations on other invertebrate species (*14–19*) show that axon location in the central nerve cord is determined, that physiologically distinct axons occupy specific locations and suggest that this organization

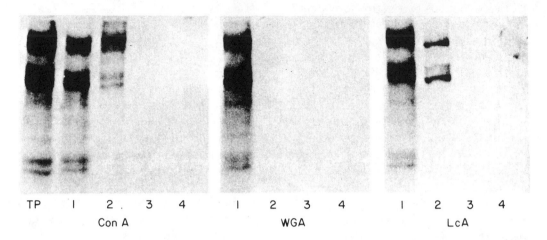

TP 1 2 3 4   1 2 3 4   1 2 3 4

Con A   WGA   LcA

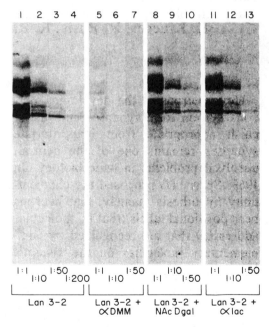

1 2 3 4 5 6 7 8 9 10 11 12 13

1:1   1:50   1:1 1:50 1:10   1:1   1:50
1:10 1:200   1:10   1:1 1:50   1:10

Lan 3-2   Lan 3-2 +   Lan 3-2 +   Lan 3-2 +
             αDMM   NAc Dgal   αlac

Fig. 7 (top). The Lan 3-2 antigens were glycosylated. Leech antigens were extracted from the dissected nerve cord by homogenizing in buffer A (10 percent Triton X-100, 150 mmole NaCl, 10 mmole tris-HCl, *p*H 8.0, 2 mmole EDTA, 1 mmole PMSF). Triton X-100 solubilized leech neural antigens were incubated with agarose beads covalently linked to the lectins Con A, WGA, LcA (LKB) for 1 hour on ice. The beads were then washed three times with buffer A (lane 1 shows unbound antigens) and eluted with 0.5 mmole sugar solutions (lanes 2 and 3, methylmannoside for Con A; *N*-acetyl-D-glucosamine for WGA; D-glucose for LcA). The sugar eluted beads were then boiled in a small sample of Laemmli buffer and samples of this elution were also run on a 10 percent polyacrylamide gel (lane 4). A sample of the total Triton-solubilized material is shown in the lane TP. These samples were transferred to nitrocellulose after electrophoresis and analyzed by immunoblotting with Lan 3-2 antibody. The major antigens recognized by Lan 3-2 bind to Con A and LcA agarose beads and are specifically eluted with sugar.

Fig. 8 (right). Lan 3-2 binding is blocked by methylmannoside. Increasing dilutions of Lan 3-2 as marked gave a progressively weaker signal on Western blots (lanes 1, 2, 3, and 4). This binding of Lan 3-2 is markedly reduced in the presence of 500 m*M* methylmannoside (lanes 5, 6, and 7) but is unaltered by 500 m*M* *N*-acetyl-D-galactosamine or α-lactose (lanes 8 to 13). The conditions for the extraction and immunoblotting of leech antigens were as in Fig. 6.

plays an important role in establishing specific synaptic contacts between neurons.

In invertebrates, cellular studies on the axonal development of identified cells in many different species shows that specific neurons recognize specific central axon tracts and regions of the neuropil. These studies suggest that a process of selective fasciculation mediated by cell contact is responsible for the specific arrangement of neuronal processes. In recent work, it has been shown that the filopodia of individual neurons can correctly distinguish certain axon fascicles (20).

Our data provide direct evidence for the presence of chemical differences on the surfaces of axon fascicles in the adult and in the embryo. These antigenic differences are present on the filopodia and are carried on a family of protease-sensitive, high molecular weight glycoconjugates. We do not yet know whether the particular antigens we have described are themselves directly involved in the mechanisms that guide selective axon fasciculation, but the fact that these molecular differences are present from early embryonic stages is consistent with the possibility that molecular differences between axon fascicles are responsible for the elaborate and precise geometry of axon outgrowth.

References and Notes

1. K. J. Muller, J. G. Nicholls, G. S. Stent, *Neurobiology of the Leech* (Cold Spring Harbor Laboratory, Cold Spring Harbor, N.Y., 1982).
2. B. Zipser and R. McKay, *Nature (London)* 289, 549 (1981).
3. W. Hahn, N. Chaudhari, L. Beck, D. Peffley Wilberk, *Cold Spring Harbor Symp. Quant. Biol.*, in press.
4. D. M. Chikaraishi, M. H. Brilliant, E. J. Lewis, *ibid.*, in press.
5. S. Hockfield and R. McKay, *J. Neurosci.* 3, 369 (1983).
6. R. McKay and S. Hockfield, *Proc. Natl. Acad. Sci. U.S.A.* 79, 6747 (1983).
7. S. Hockfield, R. McKay, S. Hendry, E. G. Jones, *Cold Spring Harbor Symp. Quant. Biol.*, in press.
8. R. D. G. McKay, S. Hockfield, J. Johansen, K. Fredericksen, *ibid.*, in press.
9. D. A. Baylor and J. G. Nicholls, *J. Physiol. (London)* 203, 571 (1969).
10. W. D. Eldred, C. Zucker, H. J. Karten, S. Yazulla, *J. Histochem. Cytochem.* 31, 285 (1983).
11. A. O. W. Stretton and E. A. Kravitz, in *Intracellular Staining in Neurobiology*, S. B. Kater and C. Nicholson, Eds. (Springer-Verlag, New York, 1973).
12. C. D. Johnson and A. O. W. Stretton, in *Nematodes as Biological Models* (Academic Press, New York, 1980), vol. 1, pp. 159–195.
13. J. G. White, E. Southgate, J. N. Thomson, S. Brenner, *Cold Spring Harbor Symp. Quant. Biol.*, in press.
14. C. A. G. Wiersma, *J. Comp. Neurol.* 110, 421 (1958).
15. J. A. Raper, M. Bastiani, C. S. Goodman, *J. Neurosci.* 3, 31 (1983).
16. H. Anderson, *J. Embryol. Exp. Morphol.* 46, 147 (1978).
17. A. Ghysen, *Nature (London)* 274, 869 (1978).
18. R. K. Murphey, S. E. Johnson, D. S. Sakaguchi, *J. Neurosci.* 3, 312 (1983).
19. C. S. Goodman, J. A. Raper, R. K. Ho, S. Chang, *Symp. Soc. Dev. Biol.* 40, 275 (1982).
20. J. A. Raper *et al.*, *Cold Spring Harbor Symp. Quant. Biol.*, in press.
21. *Hemopis marmorata* was obtained from the Wholesale Bait Co., Ohio. *Hirudo medicinalis* was obtained from Blutegel Import und Versand, West Germany. *Helobdella triserialis* was obtained from Dr. David Weisblat, University of California, Berkeley. Embryos from *Helobdella triserialis* were readily obtained from our laboratory breeding stocks. *Hemopis* embryos were obtained by culturing leeches obtained gravid from the wild.
22. D. A. Weisblat, G. Harper, G. S. Stent, R. T. Sawyer, *Dev. Biol.* 76, 56 (1983).
23. U. K. Laemmli, *Nature (London)* 227, 680 (1970).
24. H. Towbin, T. Staehlin, J. Gordon, *Proc. Natl. Acad. Sci. U.S.A.* 76, 4350 (1979).
25. We thank J. Watson for support and encouragement and J. Nicholls for comments on the manuscript. Supported by grants from the NIH (NS 17556 and NS 18040), from the Danish Science Research Council, and from the British Medical Research Council. We thank Lynn Kleiner and Elizabeth Waldvogel for their technical assistance.

33. Modulation of Synapse Formation by Cyclic Adenosine Monophosphate

M. Nirenberg, S. Wilson, H. Higashida, A. Rotter
K. Krueger, N. Busis, R. Ray, J. G. Kenimer, M. Adler

How neurons in the developing nervous system form synapses and distinguish appropriate from inappropriate synapses remains one of the central, unsolved problems in neurobiology. In 1963, Sperry (1) proposed the chemoaffinity hypothesis; namely, that neurons bear positional labels (that is, molecular addresses) that are recognized by complementary molecules on the synaptic target cells and thereby determine the specificity of neuronal connections. He also suggested that two gradients of molecules on retina neurons at right angles to one another, which interact with complementary molecules on the target neurons in the tectum, might be a mechanism for matching synaptic connections and reproducing a point-to-point map of the retina in the tectum. If synapse recognition molecules exist, monoclonal antibody technology should be a powerful tool for their detection. Many investigators are now using this approach.

Other mechanisms such as regulation of gene expression by environmental factors such as hormones, neuromodulators, transynaptic communication, or molecules secreted by neighboring or other cells surely play important roles in the assembly of synaptic circuits. For example, Le Douarin (2) and Patterson (3) and their colleagues have shown that during development neurons from the neural crest can express either the gene for tyrosine hydroxylase, which catalyzes the first step in the pathway for norepinephrine synthesis, or the gene for choline acetyltransferase, which catalyzes the synthesis of acetylcholine, depending on the presence of an extracellular macromolecule, purified by Weber (4), which is secreted by other cells, or the extent of depolarization of the neuron. In addition, Mudge (5) has shown that the expression of somatostatin, a peptide transmitter or neuromodulator, by dorsal root ganglia sensory neurons is dependent on molecules secreted by nonneural cells. Raff *et al.* (6) also have shown that fetal calf serum markedly influences the differentiation pathway expressed by glial cells in the central nervous system.

Edelman and his colleagues (7) discovered a neuronal glycoprotein rich in sialic acid residues, termed N-CAM (neural cell adhesion molecule), that mediates intercellular adhesion in the absence of Ca^{2+} and probably plays an important role in the development of the nervous system by conserving the topographic relationships between individual neurons or axons (or both) in a set of neurons, even though axons may migrate long distances before synapsing. Molecules that mediate Ca^{2+}-dependent intercellular adhesion (8) and factors that promote retina cell adhesion, such as cognin (9), and ligand and agglutinin (10), also have been described, but little is known about their function in the nervous system. Other mechanisms such as contact guidance, chemotaxis, cell survival factors, guidance of neurites by glia (11), and selection for synchronous or sequential transmission across two or more synapses that innervate a neuron may also play important roles in synaptogenesis.

We have used monoclonal antibodies and cultured cell systems to study synapse formation and plasticity. Some studies with retina cells are discussed first, and then studies on the plasticity of synapses formed by clonal neuroblastoma-hybrid cells with striated muscle cells are reviewed.

A dorsal-ventral gradient of protein in retina. Trisler *et al.* (*12*) obtained a monoclonal antibody that recognizes a cell membrane protein distributed in a large dorsal-ventral topographic gradient in chick retina (Fig. 1). The concentration of antigen detected at the dorsal margin was at least 35-fold higher than that found at the ventral margin of the

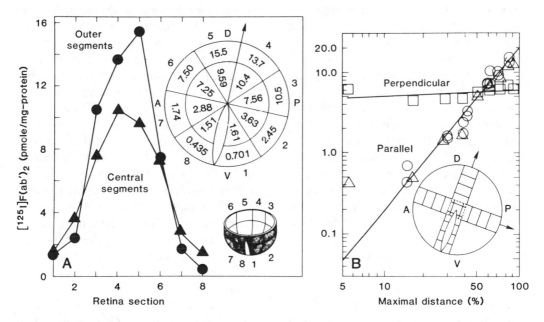

Fig. 1. Geometry of the TOP gradient in 14-day chicken embryo retina (*12*). (A) Specifically bound ^{125}I-labeled $F(ab')_2$ (pmole per milligram of protein) is shown on the ordinates in (A) and (B) and within the appropriate segment of retina tested. (B) The circumference of the retina is 14.5 mm which corresponds to 100 percent on the abscissa. (△) Strips of retina from ventroanterior (0 percent) to dorsoposterior (100 percent) retina margins were removed, and each was cut into nine segments and assayed for TOP. (□) Strips of retina from anterior (0 percent) to posterior (100 percent) margins of the retina perpendicular to the choroid fissure were prepared and assayed as above; (○) data from panel A.

retina, and the concentration of antigen detected varied continuously and logarithmically with the logarithm of distance along the circumference of the retina from ventral to dorsal poles of the gradient. Thus, the protein defines a bilaterally symmetrical, dorsal-ventral axis of the retina and can be used as a marker of cell position in the retina with respect to the dorsal-ventral axis. The antigen, termed TOP (toponimic), was detected on all cells examined in dorsal and middle retina, but more TOP was detected on cells from dorsal retina than on cells from middle retina.

The TOP antigen was solubilized and purified by antibody-agarose column chromatography and sodium dodecyl sulfate (SDS)–polyacrylamide gel electrophoresis. A single band of protein was obtained with a molecular weight (M_r) of approximately 47,000 (13). TOP was detected in optic cups of 48-hour chick embryos (14), and evidence for a gradient of TOP was found in 4-day embryo retinas. A gradient therefore is generated as neurons are generated in the retina and the gradient is maintained throughout embryonic development and in the adult. Neurons first appear in the central portion of retina and then are added in concentric, ever widening rings. Thus, central retina is the oldest portion of the retina and peripheral retina is the youngest. How a dorsal-ventral gradient is generated as the retina forms and is perpetuated is not known.

TOP was detected, in order of decreasing concentration, in retina, cerebrum, and thalamus; little or no antigen was found in other parts of the nervous system or in other tissues. Gradients of TOP were found in chicken, turkey, duck, and quail retina, but the antigen was not detected in rat, *Xenopus laevis*, *Rana pipiens*, or goldfish retina.

The antigenicity of TOP is destroyed by trypsin; however, cells dissociated with trypsin from dorsal, middle, or ventral retina, cultured separately or combined in various proportions, continue to synthesize the antigen and accumulate the amount of TOP that would be expected with cells from the corresponding region in the intact retina in ovo. Thus, the number of antigen molecules detected on retina cells after 10 days in culture depends on the prior position of the cells in the intact retina.

These results suggest that the retina is composed of a gradient of cells that express different amounts of TOP, depending on the position of the cells in retina along the dorsal-ventral axis of the retina. The function of TOP is not known. Monoclonal antibodies that recognize an anterior-posterior gradient of molecules in retina were looked for, but were not found (15). However, the demonstration that TOP is a cell membrane protein and is expressed on the basis of cell position in the retina, rather than cell type, suggests that TOP may play a role in the specification of positional information in the retina. We are trying to clone complementary DNA (cDNA) corresponding to TOP messenger RNA (mRNA) to use to define the amino acid sequence of TOP and to explore the mechanism of regulating TOP expression.

Other monoclonal antibodies to retina. Grunwald *et al.* (16) showed that antibody 13H9 recognizes cell membrane protein detected on most or all cells in retina; however, antigen was not detected on neurons or glia in other parts of the nervous system. It is of interest to determine whether the protein specifies a compartment of cells; that is, functions as a cell adhesion molecule that enables retina cells to adhere preferentially to one another rather than to other cells. Three monoclonal antibodies recognize antigens that are restricted to the outer synaptic layer of retina (113F4, 92A2, and 18B8); another antibody (16G6) recognizes antigen in both the inner and outer synaptic layers of retina. Antibody 18B8 binds to glycoproteins and unidentified species of gangliosides (17). Other monoclonal antibodies are specific for a single class of cells in retina such as photoreceptors, horizontal neurons, Müller cells, or ganglion neurons, or for a family of cells such as those in the inner nuclear layer of retina. Another monoclonal antibody, A_2B_5 (18), recognizes unidentified gangliosides with sialic acid residues and glycoproteins (17) that are markers of neurons and some glia (6, 18).

Cultured retina cells. Chick retina contains abundant nicotinic and muscarinic acetylcholine receptors that mostly are distributed in layers within the inner synaptic layer of retina (19). Cultured neurons dissociated from chick embryo retina also express choline acetyltransferase and acetylcholine receptors, and the neurons form approximately as many synapses in vitro (1.5×10^9 synapses per milligram of protein) as they do in ovo, as judged by electron microscopy (20).

The specificity of synapse formation by retina neurons was examined by coculturing dissociated chick embryo or rat retina neurons with inappropriate synaptic partner cells such as striated muscle cells that possess many nicotinic acetylcholine receptors. Retina neurons form functional synapses with most striated muscle cells in 90 minutes, but these synapses are transient and slowly disappear over a period of 5 to 10 days (21–23). Cholinergic neurons that are able to synapse with myotubes first appear in chick retina on day 6 of embryonic development, are most abundant on day 8 and comprise approximately 8 percent of the retina cell population, and lose the ability to form synapses with myotubes by day 16 of embryonic development (23). However, synapses between retina neurons increase during the culture period and remain abundant after all synapses between retina neurons and muscle cells terminate.

Two processes contribute to the turnover of retina neuron synapses with myotubes. First, retina neurons are able to form synapses with striated muscle cells only for a short time during development (23); and second, synapses between retina neurons and myotubes terminate because retina neurons preferentially adhere to other retina cells rather than to myotubes (21).

Preparations of neurons from chick embryo spinal cord, which presumably contain motor neurons that normally innervate striated muscle cells, also form synapses with cultured muscle cells, but the number of synapses remains constant during subsequent culture (22). Therefore, spinal cord neurons either form stable, long-lived synapses with muscle cells or attain a steady state wherein the rate of synapse formation is equal to the rate of synapse termination. These results show that inappropriate synapses between retina neurons and myotubes form rapidly and are terminated slowly, that synapses formed by cholinergic neurons from retina and spinal

446

cord turn over at different rates, and that differences in synapse turnover rates of two populations of synapses can result in the selective retention of one population and the loss of the other.

Clonal Neuroblastoma Cell Lines

Adult neurons do not divide; however, the establishment of clonal lines of neuroblastoma cells from a transplantable mouse neuroblastoma tumor (C-1300) of spontaneous origin provided a source of relatively homogeneous populations of dividing cells of neural origin (24). Characterization of these (24) and other (25) clonal lines of C-1300 neuroblastoma showed that the cells have excitable membranes (26) and other neural properties, and that the expression of genes for neural properties is inherited and thus can be perpetuated. Clonally inherited differences in phenotype also were found; for example, some neuroblastoma cell lines synthesize acetylcholine (25), others catecholamines; but most do not synthesize these compounds.

Cells from neuroblastoma lines that synthesize acetylcholine were cocultured with striated muscle cells, which possess abundant nicotinic acetylcholine receptors, or with cardiac muscle cells that have muscarinic acetylcholine receptors. However, for several years we, and others, failed to detect synapses. We thought that these cell lines might not express all genes for proteins that might be required for synaptic communication, and therefore we fused neuroblastoma cells with other cells and generated many somatic hybrid cell lines (26). Hybrid cell lines were found that express new neural properties not detected with parental cells (27, 28); with other hybrid cell lines some neural properties were extin-

guished. Eventually five cell lines were found that synthesize acetylcholine and form many synapses with cultured myotubes (32, 33). The early attempts to form synapses with neuroblastoma cells failed for two reasons. (i) The extent of neural maturation and ability of cells to form synapses are regulated and are highly sensitive to environmental conditions, making it necessary to find conditions that yield populations of "differentiated" cells. (ii) Most, but not all, of the cholinergic neuroblastoma cell lines that were tested do, indeed, lack reactions that are required for synapse formation. Empirically, we found that populations of neuroblastoma or hybrid cells can be shifted from a poorly differentiated, synapse incompetent state, to a well-differentiated, synapse competent state, by increasing intracellular levels of cyclic adenosine monophosphate (AMP) for days. Selection for nondividing cells also yields well-differentiated populations of cells.

In Fig. 2 are shown photomicrographs of cells from four of the five cell lines that form many synapses with striated muscle cells. The NBr10-A and NBr20-A cells originated by fusion of mouse neuroblastoma N18TG-2 (26) with clonal BRL30-E rat liver cells, NCB-20 cells (29) resulted from fusion of N18TG-2 cells with fetal Chinese hamster brain cells, and NG108-15 (30) resulted from fusion of N18TG-2 with C6BU-1 (28) rat glioma cells. Few neurites or synapses were found when cells were in the logarithmic phase of growth. However, exposure of cells for 7 days to 1 mM dibutyryl cyclic AMP, which promotes neurite extension, and to 1 percent (rather than 5 percent) fetal bovine serum, which reduces neurite retraction, yields cells with neurites that can be more than 2 mm in length (31).

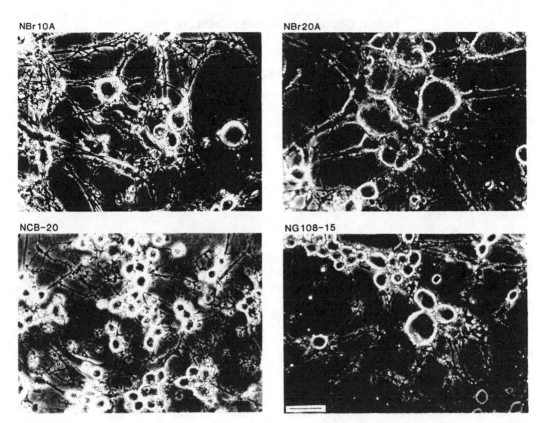

Fig. 2. Neuroblastoma hybrid cells from lines that form many synapses with cultured myotubes were treated for 7 days with 1 m*M* dibutyryl cyclic AMP and the concentration of fetal bovine serum was reduced from 5 to 1 percent between day 5 and day 7. The bar in the lower right hand panel corresponds to 50 μm in each panel. [Data from (*32*)]

Other cell lines have high concentrations of acetylcholine, adhere well to myotubes, but do not form synapses (*32*). A summary of phenotypes of cell lines with or without synaptic defects is shown in Table 1. The NBr10-A, NBr20-A, NCB-20, NG108-15, and NS-26 neuroblastoma cells (*25*) form many synapses with cultured myotubes (*32, 33*), synthesize acetylcholine (*32*), have functional voltage-sensitive Ca^{2+} channels (*34*), have small clear vesicles approximately 60 nm in diameter and large dense-core vesicles 180 nm in diameter (*41*), and release acetylcholine into the medium and a protein that stimulates the aggrega-

tion of nicotinic acetylcholine receptors on myotube plasma membranes (*35*). Cells from three lines take up Ca^{2+} ions slowly (*34*) and secrete little acetylcholine when depolarized by 80 m*M* K^+ ions, and form few synapses with muscle cells. Cells from two lines lack functional voltage-sensitive Ca^{2+} channels (*34*) and do not form synapses. Cells from five lines take up Ca^{2+} when depolarized by K^+ ions but do not respond by secreting more acetylcholine (*32*), and few or no synapses were found. These cells lack a Ca^{2+}-dependent acetylcholine secretion reaction (or reactions); however, acetylcholine is secreted into the medium in

Table 1. Cell line phenotypes [see (32, 34, 35)].

Cell lines (No.)	ACh* formation	K$^+$-Dependent		Vesicles		ACh receptor aggregation protein	Synapse
		^{45}Ca^{2+} uptake	[^{3}H]ACh release	Small clear	Large dense core		
5	+	+++	+++	+	+	+	+++
3	+	+	+	+	+	+	+
2	+	−	−	+	+	+	−
5	+	++	−	+	+	+	− or +
3	+	++	±	+	−	−	− or +
9	−		−				−

*Acetylcholine (ACh).

the basal, unstimulated state. Cells from three lines have small clear vesicles but lack large dense-core vesicles and functional protein that induces nicotinic acetylcholine receptor aggregation on myotube membranes (35), and form few or no synapses. Nine additional cell lines have little or no choline acetyltransferase activity, and therefore they synthesize little or no acetylcholine (32) and do not form functional synapses with striated muscle cells.

Regulation of synaptogenesis. Thus far, we have identified 12 species of receptors that are expressed by NG108-15 cells, including receptors for prostaglandin E$_1$ (PGE$_1$) (36, 37), prostaglandin F$_2$ (PGF$_2$) (36), adenosine (38), Met-enkephalin (36), alpha-2-adrenergic receptors (39), depolarizing muscarinic acetylcholine receptors (40), serotonin and LSD receptors (29), and receptors for bradykinin, neurotensin, angiotensin II, and somatastatin (32), and have defined cell responses to the ligands for these receptors. Some receptors, such as those for PGE$_1$, mediate activation of adenylate cyclase; other receptors such as Met-enkephalin receptors, muscarinic depolarizing acetylcholine receptors, and alpha-2-adrenergic receptors mediate inhibition of adenylate cyclase.

Increase of cyclic AMP in neuroblastoma or hybrid cells for 5 to 7 days, obtained either by treating cells with PGE$_1$ to increase the endogenous rate of cyclic AMP synthesis or by inhibition of cyclic nucleotide phosphodiesterase with dibutyryl cyclic AMP, or theophylline, resulted in increases in the percentage of myotubes tested that were innervated and the rate of spontaneous secretion of acetylcholine from NG108-15 cells at synapses (32) (Table 2). Presumably, each depolarizing response of a myotube to acetylcholine is due to the spontaneous secretion of acetylcholine from a single NG108-15 vesicle. NG108-15 cells and myotubes were cocultured and treated for 5 to 7 days with the compounds shown; then myotubes were assayed for synapses by intracellular microelectrode recording. Treatment of cells with 1 mM dibutyryl cyclic AMP, 1 mM theophylline, or 10 μM PGE$_1$ increased the percentage of muscle cells tested that were innervated from 15 to approximately 60 percent and increased 14- to 20-fold the frequency of spontaneous synaptic responses of myotubes (the miniature end-plate potential frequency). Treatment of cells with 10 μM PGE$_1$ and 1 mM theophylline resulted in innervation of 98 percent of the myotubes tested and increased the frequency of synaptic responses of myotubes 45-fold. No immediate effect of these compounds on the cell membrane potential or rate of acetylcholine secretion was detected. Half-maximal increases in synapses and rate of spontaneous acetylcholine secretion at synapses were observed when cellular cyclic AMP levels were increased for 1 to 2 days; maximal increases were obtained when cells were treated for 3 to 5 days (32).

In other experiments, NG108-15 cells were incubated with PGE_1, theophylline, dibutyryl cyclic AMP, or PGE_1 and theophylline for 5 to 7 days; then the compounds were withdrawn and cells were incubated for an additional 4 to 14 days to determine whether the effects on synapses and acetylcholine secretion were reversible. On withdrawal of the compounds, synapses and acetylcholine secretion gradually returned to control values in 7 to 11 days (32). Thus, the effects of the compounds on synapses are expressed slowly and are long-lived.

Cyclic AMP levels of NG108-15 cells increase markedly in the presence of 10 μM PGE_1 and 1 mM theophylline and remain higher than those of control cells for seven or more days. Intracellular acetylcholine in NG108-15 cells also increases eight- and threefold when cells are treated for 3 days with PGE_1 and theophylline or dibutyryl cyclic AMP, respectively (32). NG108-15 cells treated with dibutyryl cyclic AMP (41) or PGE_1 and theophylline (32) for five or more days contain many large dense-core vesicles and small clear vesicles, whereas control cells contain few vesicles. The cyclic AMP-dependent increase in intracellular acetylcholine is due, at least in part, to an increase in the number of acetylcholine storage vesicles in cells.

Depolarization of NG108-15 or NBr10-A cells with 80 mM K^+ ions, in place of

Table 2. Effect of culture conditions on synaptogenesis and acetylcholine secretion by NG108-15 cells. Each value is the mean of values obtained from more than 75 myotubes. [Data from (32)]

Culture conditions	Myotubes with synapses (%)	Synaptic response frequency*
Control	15	0.7
1 mM dibutyryl cyclic AMP	55	14
1 mM theophylline	64	10
10 μM PGE_1	63	11
10 μM PGE_1 + 1 mM theophylline	98	32

*The number per minute per myotube.

80 mM Na^+ ions, has no effect on the rate of acetylcholine secretion by untreated NG108-15 or NBr10-A cells. However, cells gradually are shifted from an unresponsive to a responsive state with respect to depolarization-dependent secretion of acetylcholine when treated for 5 to 7 days with 1 mM dibutyryl cyclic AMP or 10 μM PGE_1 and 1 mM theophylline. Half-maximal and maximal increases in acetylcholine secretion due to cell depolarization were obtained when NG108-15 cells were treated with 1 mM dibutyryl cyclic AMP for 2 and 5 days, respectively (42).

Depolarization of nerve terminals is known to activate voltage-sensitive Ca^{2+} channels; Ca^{2+} ions then flow into the cytoplasm of axon terminals and increase the rate of secretion of transmitter at the synapse. We therefore examined the effect of prolonged elevation of cyclic AMP levels of NBr10-A or NG108-15 cells on voltage-sensitive Ca^{2+} channel activity. Four kinds of assays were used (34). $^{45}Ca^{2+}$ flux, net uptake of Ca^{2+} by cells was measured with a Ca^{2+}

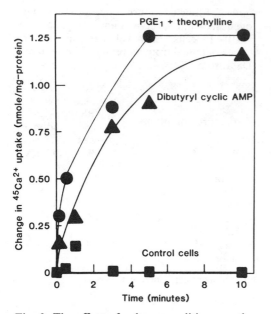

Fig. 3. The effect of culture conditions on the expression of functional voltage-sensitive Ca^{2+} channels of NBr10-A cells. Uptake of $^{45}Ca^{2+}$ due to activation of voltage-sensitive Ca^{2+} channels of untreated logarithmically dividing control NBr10-A cells, cells cultured for 6 days with 1 mM dibutyryl cyclic AMP, or 10 μM PGE$_1$ and 1 mM theophylline. The cells were depolarized with 80 mM K$^+$ (in place of 80 mM Na$^+$). Values for $^{45}Ca^{2+}$ binding to cells or uptake at 5.4 mM K$^+$, which were not inhibited by 100 μM D-600 and were not mediated by voltage-sensitive Ca^{2+} channels, were subtracted from the values shown. Uptake of Ca^{2+} dependent on cell depolarization was completely inhibited by 100 μM D-600. [Data from (34)]

specific electrode, Ca^{2+} fluxes were determined in the presence of murexide by a spectrophotometric assay with a stopped-flow apparatus, and Ca^{2+} action potentials of cells were assayed by intracellular microelectrode recording. We found by each method of assay that logarithmically dividing control cells have little or no voltage-sensitive Ca^{2+} channel activity; however, prolonged elevation of cellular cyclic AMP activation

of adenylate cyclase of cells with PGE$_1$, or by inhibition of cyclic nucleotide phosphodiesterase with dibutyryl cyclic AMP or theophylline, gradually results in the acquisition of functional voltage-sensitive Ca^{2+} channels by cells. Assay of Ca^{2+} action potentials elicited by electrical stimulation of single cells with intracellular microelectric recording showed that most untreated NG108-15 or NBr10-A cells lack functional voltage-sensitive Ca^{2+} channels. However, Ca^{2+} action potentials were found in 100 percent of the cells tested that had been treated for four more days with dibutyryl cyclic AMP.

As shown in Fig. 3, $^{45}Ca^{2+}$ uptake by logarithmically dividing, control NBr10-A cells is not affected by depolarization of cells with 80 mM K$^+$. However, cells that had been treated for 7 days with 10 μM PGE$_1$ and 1 mM theophylline or with 1 mM dibutyryl cyclic AMP respond to depolarization by 80 mM K$^+$ with a rapid influx of $^{45}Ca^{2+}$ via voltage-sensitive Ca^{2+} channels (34). Depolarization-dependent $^{45}Ca^{2+}$ uptake is inhibited completely by $1 \times 10^{-4}M$ D-600 (half-maximal inhibition was obtained with $9 \times 10^{-7}M$ D-600), an alkaloid known to inhibit voltage-sensitive Ca^{2+} channels and slow Na$^+$ channels. $^{45}Ca^{2+}$ uptake also is inhibited by La^{3+}, Co^{2+}, and Ni^{2+} ions.

Exposure of NG108-15 cells to PGE$_1$ increases cellular cyclic AMP levels within seconds; however, no immediate effects of PGE$_1$, PGE$_1$ and theophylline, or dibutyryl cyclic AMP on voltage-sensitive Ca^{2+} channel activity were detected. Half-maximal and maximal voltage-sensitive Ca^{2+} channel activity were expressed by cells that had been treated with PGE$_1$ and theophylline or dibutyryl cyclic AMP for 2 and 4 days, respectively.

Relatively weak voltage-sensitive Ca^{2+} channel activity appears in untreated NBr10-A cells when cells form confluent monolayers. Thus, cell concentration or adhesive interactions between cells also regulates the expression of voltage-sensitive Ca^{2+} to some extent.

Nitrendipine and other dihydropyridine derivatives inhibit voltage-sensitive Ca^{2+} channels of smooth muscle (43), striated muscle (44), and cardiac muscle (45), and specific binding sites for ^{3}H-labeled nitrendipine have been found in these tissues and in brain (46). The nitrendipine receptors are thought to be part of the voltage-sensitive Ca^{2+} channel complex, perhaps functioning as regulators of channel activity.

Kongsamut and Müller have shown that $^{45}Ca^{2+}$ uptake by NG108-15 cells mediated by voltage-sensitive Ca^{2+} channels is inhibited by nitrendipine (47). We have confirmed this and find that NBr10-A cells are inhibited half-maximally by 3 nM nitrendipine. A single class of specific binding sites for ^{3}H-labeled nitrendipine was found in membranes from NBr10-A cells that had been treated with PGE$_1$ and theophylline with a dissociation constant, estimated by Scatchard analysis, of $2 \times 10^{-10} M$, which is similar to values reported for other tissues (43, 45–46). The maximum number of specific nitrendipine binding sites was estimated to be 61 fmole per milligram of NBr10-A membrane protein, which is equivalent to approximately 16,000 specific sites for nitrendipine per cell. In contrast, few or no specific binding sites for ^{3}H-labeled nitrendipine were detected in membranes from untreated, logarithmically dividing NBr10-A cells. These results show that cyclic AMP regulates the number of specific nitrendipine receptors per cell. Specific binding sites for ^{3}H-labeled nitrendipine

also were not detected in membranes prepared from two lines of hybrid cells (SB21B-1 and SB37-B) that lack functional voltage-sensitive Ca^{2+} channels and do not synapse with muscle cells.

Cyclic AMP increases the probability of opening Ca^{2+} channels of cardiac muscle cells (48); however, responses to cyclic AMP are rapid and thus differ from the slow effects found with NBr10-A cells.

The molecular weights of nitrendipine receptors in intact membranes of smooth muscle (49), transverse tubule membranes of skeletal muscle, and cerebral cortex synaptic membranes (44) were estimated by radiation inactivation target analysis to be 278,000, 210,000, and 210,000, respectively. Available information suggests that the nitrendipine receptor complex is a glycoprotein with N-acetylglucosamine or sialic acid residues (or both) (50). Nitrendipine receptors of smooth and cardiac muscle were reported to be covalently labeled with a radioactive affinity label analog of nitrendipine, ^{3}H-labeled 2,6-dimethyl-3,5-dicarbomethoxy - 4 - (2 - isothiocyanatophenyl)-1,4-dihydropyridine; labeled protein then was solubilized and fractionated. A peak of labeled protein with a molecular weight of 45,000 was identified (49). These results suggest that the molecular weight of voltage-sensitive Ca^{2+} channel in membranes is 210,000 to 278,000, that each channel is composed of two or more subunits, and that one subunit is a protein with a molecular weight of 45,000, which binds nitrendipine.

NG108-15 cells that had been grown with or without 10 μM PGE$_1$ were incubated with [^{35}S]methionine to label the protein; the ^{35}S-labeled glycoproteins then were solubilized and fractionated by wheat germ agglutinin-, ricin-, or len-

452

til-lectin column chromatography and by two-dimensional gel electrophoresis (*51*). Elevation of cellular cyclic AMP levels resulted in the disappearance of some ^{35}S-labeled glycoproteins, the appearance of new ^{35}S-labeled glycoproteins with different molecular weights, changes in the apparent abundance of some ^{35}S-labeled glycoproteins, as well as changes in the isoelectric points of other ^{35}S-labeled glycoproteins. A ^{35}S-labeled glycoprotein with a molecular weight of approximately 45,000 was eluted from wheat germ agglutinin–Sepharose with N-acetylglucosamine was obtained from cells with high cyclic AMP levels, but was not detected in untreated cells. Twelve ^{35}S-glycoproteins were detected that were expressed by NG108-15 cells with high cyclic AMP levels but not by control cells, and many other ^{35}S-labeled glycoproteins were obtained from PGE$_1$-treated cells with radioactivities 2.5- to 10-fold higher than those of control cells. These results extend previous reports of differentiation-specific changes in neuroblastoma proteins (*52*).

Exposure of neuroblastoma or hybrid cells to dibutyryl cyclic AMP alters the levels of some species of polysomal mRNA (*53*). Polysomal polyadenylated (poly A$^+$) RNA from "undifferentiated" and "differentiated" neuroblastoma cells were compared; many species of polysomal poly A$^+$ RNA were found in RNA from undifferentiated cells, but not differentiated cells (*54, 55*), and conversely, many species of poly A$^+$ RNA were expressed by differentiated neuroblastoma cells that were not expressed by undifferentiated cells (*55*).

In prokaryotic cells (cyclic AMP · catabolite activator protein) complexes bind to certain sites on DNA and thereby regulate the initiation of transcription of certain genes. Cyclic AMP also regulates the levels of some species of mRNA and protein in eukaryotic cells (*56*), but relatively little is known about the mechanisms of regulation. Cyclic AMP markedly increases the expression of many neural properties in neuroblastoma or hybrid cells, such as voltage-sensitive channels for Ca^{2+}, Na$^+$, and K$^+$, and also Ca^{2+}-dependent K$^+$ channels, neurite extension, vesicles, synapses, acetylcholinesterase, and with some cell lines, choline acetyltransferase, or tyrosine hydroxylase activities. We find that cyclic AMP regulates synaptogenesis, at least in part, by regulating the expression of voltage-sensitive Ca^{2+} channels, which are required for stimulus-dependent secretion of transmitter at synapses. The results suggest that cyclic AMP affects posttranslational modifications of some species of glycoprotein. Appropriate cloned cDNA probes are needed to determine whether cyclic AMP affects the levels of some species of mRNA and to define further the cyclic AMP–dependent mechanisms that affect synapse formation and plasticity.

References and Notes

1. R. W. Sperry, *Proc. Natl. Acad. Sci. U.S.A.* **50**, 703 (1963).
2. N. M. Le Douarin and M. A. Teillet, *Dev. Biol.* **41**, 162 (1974).
3. P. H. Patterson, *Annu. Rev. Neurosci.* **1**, 1 (1978).
4. M. J. Weber, *J. Biol. Chem.* **256**, 3447 (1981).
5. A. W. Mudge, *Nature (London)* **292**, 764 (1981).
6. M. C. Raff, R. H. Miller, M. Noble, *Nature (London)* **303**, 390 (1983).
7. S. Hoffman and G. M. Edelman, *Proc. Natl. Acad. Sci. U.S.A.* **80**, 5762 (1983).
8. M. Takeichi, H. S. Ozaki, K. Tokunaga, T. S. Okada, *Dev. Biol.* **70**, 195 (1979); H. Urushihara, H. S. Ozaki, M. Takeichi, *ibid.*, p. 206; G. B. Grunwald, R. L. Geller, J. Lilien, *J. Cell Biol.* **85**, 766 (1980).
9. R. E. Hausman and A. A. Moscona, *Exp. Cell Res.* **119**, 191 (1979).
10. R. Rutz and J. Lilien, *J. Cell Sci.* **36**, 323 (1979).
11. J. Silver and R. L. Sidman, *J. Comp. Neurol.* **189**, 101 (1980).
12. G. D. Trisler, M. D. Schneider, M. Nirenberg,

Proc. Natl. Acad. Sci. U.S.A. **78**, 2145 (1981).

13. J. R. Moskal, G. D. Trisler, M. Nirenberg, in preparation.

14. G. D. Trisler, M. D. Schneider, J. R. Moskal, M. Nirenberg, in *Monoclonal Antibodies To Neural Antigens*, R. McKay, M. C. Raff, L. F. Reichardt, Eds. [*Cold Spring Harbor Rep. Neurosci.* **2**, 231 (1981)].

15. G. D. Trisler, unpublished.

16. G. B. Grunwald, G. D. Trisler, M. Nirenberg, in preparation.

17. P. Fredman, G. B. Grunwald, G. D. Trisler, M. Nirenberg, V. Ginsburg, in preparation.

18. G. S. Eisenbarth, F. S. Walsh, M. Nirenberg, *Proc. Natl. Acad. Sci. U.S.A.* **76**, 4913 (1979); J. Schnitzer and M. Schachner, *Cell Tissue Res.* **224**, 625 (1982).

19. Z. Vogel and M. Nirenberg, *Proc. Natl. Acad. Sci. U.S.A.* **73**, 1806 (1976); H. Sugiyama, M. P. Daniels, M. Nirenberg, *ibid.* **74**, 5524 (1977).

20. Z. Vogel, M. P. Daniels, M. Nirenberg, *ibid.* **73**, 2370 (1976).

21. D. G. Puro, F. G. De Mello, M. Nirenberg, *ibid.* **74**, 4977 (1977).

22. J. M. Thompson, G. S. Eisenbarth, R. R. Ruffolo, Jr., M. Nirenberg, *Int. J. Dev. Neurosci.* **1**, 25 (1983).

23. R. R. Ruffolo, Jr., G. S. Eisenbarth, J. M. Thompson, M. Nirenberg, *Proc. Natl. Acad. Sci. U.S.A.* **75**, 2281 (1978).

24. G. Augusti-Tocco and G. Sato, *ibid.* **64**, 311 (1969).

25. T. Amano, E. Richelson, M. Nirenberg, *ibid.* **69**, 258 (1972).

26. P. Nelson, W. Ruffner, M. Nirenberg, *ibid.* **64**, 1004 (1969); J. Minna, D. Glazer, M. Nirenberg, *Nature (London) New Biol.* **235**, 225 (1972).

27. L. A. Greene *et al.*, *Proc. Natl. Acad. Sci. U.S.A.* **72**, 4923 (1975).

28. T. Amano, B. Hamprecht, and W. Kemper, *Exp. Cell Res.* **85**, 399 (1974).

29. J. MacDermot, H. Higashida, S. P. Wilson, H. Matsuzawa, J. Minna, M. Nirenberg, *Proc. Natl. Acad. Sci. U.S.A.* **76**, 1135 (1979).

30. W. A. Klee and M. Nirenberg, *ibid.* **71**, 3474 (1974).

31. N. W. Seeds, A. G. Gilman, T. Amano, M. W. Nirenberg, *ibid.* **66**, 160 (1970).

32. H. Higashida, S. P. Wilson, M. Nirenberg, in preparation; S. P. Wilson, H. Higashida, M. Nirenberg, in preparation.

33. P. Nelson, C. Christian, M. Nirenberg, *Proc. Natl. Acad. Sci. U.S.A.* **73**, 123 (1976).

34. A. Rotter, R. Ray, M. Nirenberg, *Fed. Proc. Fed. Am. Soc. Exp. Biol.* **38**, 476 (1979); A. Rotter, R. Ray, M. Adler, M. Nirenberg, in preparation; P. Darveneza and M. Nirenberg, in preparation.

35. H. C. Bauer, M. P. Daniels, P. A. Pudimat, J. Jacques, H. Sugayama, C. N. Christian, *Brain Res.* **209**, 395 (1981); N. A. Busis, M. P. Daniels, H. C. Bauer, P. A. Pudimat, P. Sonderegger, A. E. Schaffner, M. Nirenberg, in preparation.

36. H. Matsuzawa and M. Nirenberg, *Proc. Natl. Acad. Sci. U.S.A.* **72**, 3472 (1975).

37. S. K. Sharma, W. A. Klee, M. Nirenberg, *ibid.* **74**, 3365 (1977).

38. J. G. Kenimer and M. Nirenberg, *Mol. Pharmacol.* **20**, 585 (1981).

39. S. L. Sabol and M. Nirenberg, *J. Biol. Chem.* **254**, 1913 (1979).

40. N. M. Nathanson, W. L. Klein, M. Nirenberg, *Proc. Natl. Acad. Sci. U.S.A.* **75**, 1788 (1978).

41. M. P. Daniels and B. Hamprecht, *J. Cell Biol.* **63**, 691 (1974).

42. R. McGee, P. Simpson, C. Christian, M. Mata, P. Nelson, M. Nirenberg, *Proc. Natl. Acad. Sci. U.S.A.* **75**, 1314 (1978).

43. G. T. Bolger, P. J. Gengo, E. M. Luchowski, H. Siegel, D. J. Triggle, R. A. Janis, *Biochem. Biophys. Res. Commun.* **104**, 1604 (1982).

44. R. I. Norman, M. Borsotto, M. Fosset, M. Lazdunski, J. C. Ellory, *ibid.* **111**, 878 (1983).

45. F. J. Ehlert, E. Itoga, W. R. Roeske, H. I. Yamamura, *ibid.* **104**, 937 (1982).

46. K. M. M. Murphy and S. H. Snyder, *Eur. J. Pharmacol.* **77**, 201 (1982).

47. S. Kongsamut, personal communication.

48. H. Reuter, *Nature (London)* **301**, 569 (1983).

49. J. C. Venter, C. M. Fraser, J. S. Schaber, C. Y. Jung, G. Bolger, D. J. Triggle, *J. Biol. Chem.* **258**, 9344 (1983).

50. B. M. Curtis and W. A. Catterall, *ibid.*, p. 7280 (1983).

51. K. E. Krueger, M. J. Miller, M. Nirenberg, in preparation.

52. R. Truding, M. L. Shelanski, M. P. Daniels, P. Morell, *J. Biol. Chem.* **249**, 3973 (1974); N. Prashad, B. Wischmeyer, C. Evetts, F. Baskin, R. Rosenberg, *Cell Diff.* **6**, 147 (1977); N. Prashad and R. N. Rosenberg, *Biochim. Biophys. Acta* **539**, 459 (1978); F. C. Charalampous, *Arch. Biochem. Biophys.* **181**, 103 (1977); J. H. Garvican and G. L. Brown, *Eur. J. Biochem.* **76**, 251 (1977); R. N. Rosenberg, C. K. Vance, M. Morrison, N. Prashad, J. Meyne, F. Baskin, *J. Neurochem.* **30**, 1343 (1978); N. Zisapel and U. Z. Littauer, *Eur. J. Biochem.* **95**, 51 (1979); U. Z. Littauer, M. Y. Giovanni, M. C. Glick, *J. Biol. Chem.* **255**, 5448 (1980).

53. M. R. Morrison, S. Pardue, N. Prashad, D. E. Croall, R. Brodeur, *Eur. J. Biochem.* **106**, 463 (1980).

54. A. Felsani, F. Berthelot, F. Gros, B. Croizat, *ibid.* **92**, 569 (1978).

55. L. D. Grouse, B. K. Schrier, C. H. Letendre, M. Y. Zubairi, P. G. Nelson, *J. Biol. Chem.* **255**, 3871 (1980).

56. D. F. Derda, M. F. Miles, J. S. Schweppe, R. A. Jungmann, *ibid.*, p. 11112; M. F. Miles, P. Hung, R. A. Jungmann, *ibid.* **256**, 12545 (1981); R. A. Maurer, *Nature (London)* **294**, 94 (1981); W. H. Lamers, R. W. Hanson, H. M. Meisner, *Proc. Natl. Acad. Sci. U.S.A.* **79**, 5137 (1982); S. M. Landfear, P. Lefevre, S. Chung, H. F. Lodish, *Mol. Cell. Biol.* **2**, 1417 (1982); J. R. Wu and L. F. Johnson, *J. Cell Physiol.* **110**, 183 (1982); G. Mangiarotti, A. Ceccarelli, H. F. Lodish, *Nature (London)* **301**, 616 (1983).

34. In situ Hybridization to Study the Origin and Fate of Identified Neurons

Linda B. McAllister, Richard H. Scheller
Eric R. Kandel, Richard Axel

The nervous system consists of a vast network of cells, many of which are anatomically and functionally unique. An extreme example of neuronal diversity is seen in the nematode worm *Caenorhabditis elegans*, in which each of the 273 cells in its nervous system differ from each (*1, 2*). But even in the complex nervous systems of vertebrates where there are 10^{12} nerve cells, many cell groups can be distinguished from one another (*3–5*). This diversity suggests that characteristic nerve cells or cell groups express distinct sets of genes not expressed in other nerve cells.

How does one begin to characterize the pattern of gene expression of individual neurons within nervous systems composed of from 10^2 to 10^{12} cells? It is now possible to isolate genes expressed in individual neurons and to relate the activities of specific genes to the particular functions of individual neurons. The expression of these genes can then be explored in both the developing and adult nervous system by hybridization in situ to messenger RNA (mRNA) in tissue sections. We have isolated a gene family encoding the peptides mediating egg-laying behavior in the marine snail, *Aplysia*. In the study described here we have used in situ hybridization to mRNA to trace the developmental origin and ultimate fate of the neurons expressing these genes.

The simple nervous system of the marine mollusc *Aplysia* is particularly suitable for analyzing neuron-specific gene expression because it contains only about 20,000 central nerve cells which are collected into four pairs of symmetric ganglia and a single asymmetric abdominal ganglion. Moreover, many neurons in these ganglia may be recognized by highly reproducible characteristics such as size, shape, position, pigmentation, and function (*6*). These properties have made it possible to relate the function of particular cells to specific patterns of behavior and may permit us to attribute neuronal function to the expression of specific genes. In addition to being few in number, neurons in *Aplysia* can be large, up to 1 millimeter in diameter. Most of these large cells are highly polyploid and contain as much as 2 micrograms of DNA, more than 10^5 times the content of the haploid genome (*7, 8*). Furthermore, our data indicate that the mRNA content is also proportional to cell size, such that the largest of cells contains up to 5 nanograms of mRNA.

Our studies on the relation between the expression of specific genes and the generation of specific behavioral patterns initially focused on egg laying. In *Aplysia*, egg laying consists of a stereotypic fixed action pattern consisting of several behavioral components, aspects of which are understood at both the cellular and molecular level. As the fertilized egg string is extruded, the animal stops walking and feeding, catches the string in its mouth, and waves its head back and forth, depositing the eggs in a folded mass on the ocean floor. The expression of the behavioral sequence is thought to involve the actions of a combination of peptides synthesized and released by the bag cells, two symmetrical clusters of neurons located at the rostral margins of the abdominal ganglion (*9–12*). The bag cells release a 36–amino acid peptide, the egg-laying hormone (ELH), along with other peptides that directly mediate the behavioral components associated with egg laying (*10, 11, 13–15*). Excitation of the bag cells can be elicited in vitro by either one or two related peptides, A or B peptide, released from the atrial gland, an exocrine organ within the large reproductive tract (*16–18*).

Earlier, we isolated and sequenced the three genes that encode the A, B, and ELH peptides (*19, 20*). The three genes are 90 percent homologous in sequence and are representatives of a small multigene family. The genes encode a protein precursor, in which the active peptides are flanked by internal cleavage sites, providing the potential to generate multiple small peptides. Although each of the three genes share significant nucleotide sequence homology, they have diverged so that different member genes express functionally related but nonoverlapping sets of neuroactive peptides in different tissues.

We have investigated the expression of this gene family in the nervous system and peripheral organs of adult and developing *Aplysia*, by means of in situ hybridization to mRNA and application of immunocytochemical techniques of the peptide products of the ELH gene family. As would be expected from the homology shared by the three genes, we detected the mRNA for egg laying in the bag cells and atrial gland. However, we also encountered in the adult an extensive network of additional neurons that express the gene family. Further, we found that the gene family is expressed surprisingly early in development in cells of premetamorphic animals. We have therefore used these genes as developmental markers to explore the origin of the cells that express ELH. We found that the ELH-producing nerve cells do not originate in the nervous system but in a proliferative, ectodermal zone of the body wall. They then appear to migrate into the central ganglia along connective tissue fiber tracts that connect the body wall with the nervous system.

Genes Encoding Egg-Laying Peptides

During the egg-laying season, more than half of the protein synthetic machinery of the bag cells is devoted to the production of polypeptide precursors of ELH neuroactive peptide ELH. The bag cells also release several other peptides, and this collection of peptides presumably results in the characteristic and stereotypic behavioral repertoire associated with egg laying. We have determined the nucleotide sequence of the ELH gene as well as the genes encoding

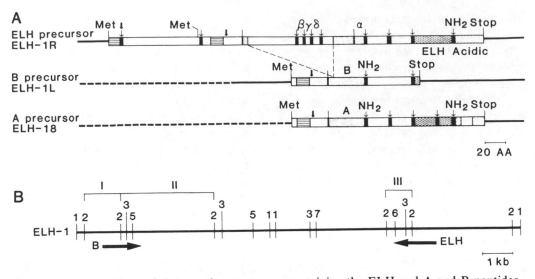

Fig. 1. (A) Comparison of the protein precursors containing the ELH and A and B peptides. Coding regions are derived from the only in-phase amino acid reading frames that match in vitro translation molecular weights. Each of the three proteins is initiated by a methionine followed by a hydrophobic region (horizontal bars). Thick arrows represent the putative site of cleavage of the signal sequence. A line above the sequence represents potential cleavages at single arginine residues (vertical line), while thin arrows represent potential or known cleavages at dibasic, tribasic, or tetrabasic residues. If carboxyl terminal amidation is believed to occur, an NH$_2$ appears above the arrow. The A or B peptide homology is represented by stippled boxes (dots). The ELH homology is represented by crosshatched boxes (grids). The acidic peptide homology is respresented by parallel lines enclosed in boxes (diagonal bars). Solid lines symbolize sequences noncoding regions, and dotted lines depict regions not sequences. (B) DNA probes for in situ hybridization. The restriction enzyme map of the recombinant phage ELH-l containing linked genes encoding ELH and B peptide (20), 1, Eco RI, 2, Pst I, 3, Xho I, 5, Pvu II, 6, Hind III, 7, Bgl II. Arrows indicate the position of mRNA's and point in the direction of transcription. Three Pst I fragments were used as probes in this study. Fragments I and II span the 5' and 3' ends of a gene encoding B peptide. Probe III includes the 3' portion of an ELH gene.

the A and B peptides (19, 20). The ELH and the A and B peptide genes (Fig. 1) are all members of a small multigene family in which at least one member encodes a number of different peptides. The sequences of these genes suggests several possible mechanisms whereby nerve cells can utilize polyproteins and give families to generate diverse sets of neuroactive peptides.

First, the gene for ELH encodes a protein consisting of 271 amino acid residues while the ELH peptide itself con-

sists of only 36 amino acids. Thus, ELH is synthesized as part of a larger precursor molecule, and its release requires cleavage at pairs of basic residues that flank the ELH sequence. The precursor, however, contains eight additional pairs of basic residues that may serve as cleavage sites flanking putative neuroactive peptides (Fig. 1). Are these potential sites in fact recognized and cleaved? Are the precursors actually a polyprotein? Three peptides, alpha and beta bag cell factor, as well as the acidic peptide, have been isolated from extracts of bag cells and appear to be coordinately released with ELH (21). We have found that each of these peptides is encoded in the ELH precursor and is bounded by cleavage sites. A role for at least two of these peptides, alpha and beta bag cell factor as neurotransmitters altering the activity of specific neurons within the abdominal ganglion, has been demonstrated (21).

Furthermore, the ELH gene is only one member of a small multigene family. We have identified two genes expressed in the atrial gland which are 90 percent homologous to the ELH gene but have diverged at essential loci to generate individual, nonoverlapping sets of peptides (Fig. 1). These two genes encode the A and B peptide, which in vitro are capable of initiating the excitation of the bag cells and the release of ELH. Thus these three members of a multigene family are expressed in a tissue-specific manner. The A and B peptide precursors are synthesized in the atrial gland but not the bag cells, while the ELH precursor is expressed in the bag cells but not the atrial gland. These conclusions derive from three sets of observations: (i) Antibody to A peptide does not cross-react with the bag cells; (ii) under stringent conditions of hybridization (20), complementary DNA (cDNA) probes from the bag cells do not anneal with the A or B peptide genes and conversely cDNA probes from the atrial gland fail to hybridize with the ELH precursor gene; and (iii) extensive screening of an abdominal ganglion cDNA library has failed to reveal a single cDNA clone encoding A or B peptide under conditions that identify about 100 clones encoding ELH (22).

These observations illustrate two important points concerning the evolution of neuropeptides and the generation of diversity in the nervous system. First, the ELH family consists of a minimum of three genes. At least three of the genes diverge in coding regions to generate distinct sets of peptides expressed in different tissues. Each gene encodes a precursor protein consisting of three regions of homology: A or B, ELH, and acidic peptide. Each gene has diverged, presumably satisfying the functional requirements of the tissue in which they are expressed. The homologies among the genes encoding the A, B, and ELH suggest that these genes have arisen from a common ancestor. Although the genes share significant nucleotide homology they have diverged not only by single base changes but also by larger insertions, deletions, and transpositions, so that different member genes express functionally related but not nonoverlapping sets of neuroactive peptides.

Second, the number of possible combinations of egg-laying peptides is made even greater by the fact that these peptides are encoded by a small family of genes in which each member has diverged to generate new peptides. Further, these genes encode polyproteins with the ability to generate a large number of additional combinations of peptides merely by altering the pathway of processing in different cell types or in the same cell in response to different stimuli. This multiplicity suggests combinatorial mechanisms that may be important in generating some of the morphologic and functional diversity characteristic of the nervous system; for example, the expression of different combinations of ion channels, or the expression of different combinations of recognition molecules. In the specific case of the ELH polyproteins, this diversity may reflect the release of different combinations of peptide transmitters.

458

A System of ELH-containing Neurons in the Adult

We have demonstrated that different members of the gene family encoding the egg-laying peptides are expressed in the bag cells and atrial gland. To explore systematically the expression of the egg-laying peptides throughout the nervous system, we have examined by in situ hybridization and immunocytochemical methods, sections through ganglia of large mature animals, as well as whole mounts of the entire central nervous system of small animals. The application of these two procedures to serial tissue sections made it possible to determine the site of synthesis of the RNA encoding the egg-laying peptides as well as to demonstrate that this RNA is indeed translated to generate immunologically cross-reactive peptides. These two complementing procedures are important in analyzing gene expression in the nervous system, since the presence of specific proteins in a particular neuron or cluster of neurons need not indicate synthesis at that site but could reflect uptake by the neuron from distant sites of synthesis (23).

Individual probes consisting of defined sequences from the 3' or 5' regions of the genes encoding B peptide or ELH were chosen for hybridization in situ. The regions encompassed by these probes are shown in Fig. 1. Probes 2 and 3 both derive from the 3' region of the genes encoding B peptide and ELH and include ELH coding sequences. Probe 1 derives from the 5' portion of the gene encoding B peptide and includes the sequence for this hormone. Under the hybridization conditions used in our experiments, however, each of the individual probes cross-hybridize to mRNA's encoding the precursors for each of the three peptides, A, B, or ELH. Thus, the in situ hybridizations do not permit us to distinguish between mRNA's derived from the different members of the ELH gene family. (For simplicity we use the term ELH-positive cells to describe cells expressing any member of the ELH gene family.) In situ hybridization experiments were complemented by immunocytochemical methods, with affinity-purified antibodies (24), directed against either A peptide or ELH.

The bag cells, an electrically interconnected cluster of cells, are the primary site of ELH synthesis. Activation of a single cell within the cluster causes all of the cells to fire in synchrony, leading to the coordinated release of ELH and its companion peptides. In situ hybridization to sections through the bag cells (Plate II, A to C) indicates that all of the bag cells contain mRNA transcribed by at least one member of the ELH gene family. It is somewhat surprising that we find mRNA in the axons as well as the cell bodies, since axons are thought to be devoid of ribosomes.

The specificity of hybridization to ELH mRNA is supported by control experiments, which reveal no hybridization when pBR322 plasmid sequences are used as a hybridization probe. Furthermore, hybridization with specific ELH probes is eliminated by treating tissue sections with ribonuclease either before or after the hybridization reaction. Finally, grains are clearly localized to the cytoplasm rather than to the nucleus, an indication that hybridization occurs with mRNA rather than with DNA.

The bag cells and their processes also react with antibody directed against ELH (Plate II D). We have previously shown that the precursor protein synthesized in vitro with bag cell mRNA reacts with antibodies to ELH and antibodies to A peptide. However, the bag cells themselves do not react with antibody to A peptide, suggesting that the cross-reactive peptide sequences are rapidly degraded in vivo after cleavage of the precursor protein. The specificity of the ELH antibody was shown by previous in vitro translation experiments in which the antibody immunoprecipitated only the precursors to ELH, A peptides, or B peptides in the midst of a host of other proteins (20). Moreover, no staining occurred with serums from nonimmune animals. These observations confirm previous studies demonstrating that the bag cells are a primary site of synthesis of ELH mRNA and peptide (19, 25, 26).

The immunofluorescent studies of Chiu and Strumwasser based on serial sections have shown that occasional unidentified neurons located outside the bag cell cluster express ELH-related peptides (26, 27). To identify all the cells that constitute the network of neurons expressing members of the ELH gene family, we exposed whole mounts of the total central nervous system taken from young animals as well as tissue sections to DNA and antibody probes. These in situ hybridization and immunofluorescence experiments reveal a network of cells producing both ELH-related RNA and cross-reactive protein in all of the major ganglia of the central nervous system, with the exception of the pedal ganglia (Plate III).

Several conclusions may be drawn from examining these ganglia with both in situ hybridization and immunofluorescence (Plates III and IV). First, there exists a network of at least 20 other cells in the central nervous system of *Aplysia* expressing the egg-laying genes in addition to the primary cluster of bag cell neurons (27). Second, in the buccal, abdominal, and cerebral ganglia, the individual cells or cell clusters expressing the ELH genes maintain invariant positions (Plate III). In contrast, in the pleural ganglion, positive cells appear to vary both in position and number (Plate II, E and F). Third, the combination of immunofluorescence and in situ hybridization demonstrates that these cells are the site of both transcription and translation of the egg-laying genes. Fourth, the neurons of the bag cells, as well as the other cells producing ELH or related peptides, send off a complex array of processes readily discernible with antibody to ELH. This network of processes presumably (Plate III) allows the egg-laying peptides to be released throughout the central nervous system. The release of ELH-like peptides therefore may not be restricted to the bag cells. Thus, as has been suggested (27), ELH may serve a significant role as neurotransmitter in other ganglia.

The Atrial Gland Expresses Egg-Laying Genes

We have also examined nonneural tissue for the expression of egg-laying genes. As noted previously, the atrial gland is the site of synthesis and release of the A and B peptides, which are thought to initiate egg laying. As expected, we detected both the egg-laying peptide and its mRNA in the cells of this gland.

The luminal surface of the common hermaphroditic duct of *Aplysia* is formed by a continuous epithelium composed of three functionally and anatomically discrete segments including the atrial gland, the red hemiduct, and the white hemiduct (Plate IV, A and B) (28). On in situ hybridization, an intense accumulation of grains is observed only in the columnar cells of the atrial gland (Plate IV B).

Immunofluorescence with either anti-body to A peptide or antibody to ELH similarly identified the egg-laying peptides only within the atrial gland of the duct (Plate IV A). The same staining occurs with antibody against A peptide to ELH, since the A peptide precursor encodes a peptide that shares significant homology with ELH. Further, the pattern of antibody staining clearly defines the transitional epithelium demarcating the border of the atrial gland and the red hermaphroditic duct.

Development of the Bag Cells and Other Neurons That Express ELH

When are the ELH genes first expressed during development, and where do the bag cells and other neurons of the ELH system originate? Do they develop in situ within the ganglia, or do the ELH-producing cells develop in a neuronal proliferative zone and then migrate into the ganglia? The use of ELH gene probes for in situ hybridization along with antibodies to ELH permits us to address these questions by analyzing the expression of ELH during the development of the nervous system in *Aplysia*.

Aplysia is an annual organism that undergoes five developmental stages before reaching sexual maturity. The reproductive animal lays long egg strands containing approximately 10^6 fertilized ova packaged in egg cases, each composed of approximately ten eggs (29). Egg laying initiates the first, or embryonic, phase of development, which lasts about 10 days. The second, or veliger larval, phase begins when the egg case ruptures, releasing ciliated veliger larvae that feed on unicellular phytoplankton. After 34 days, the veliger larvae stop swimming and enter the third, or metamorphic, phase. The organism settles on specific species of seaweeds and metamorphoses within 2 to 3 days into a benthic juvenile that crawls and eats microalgae. In the 60 to 90 days of the fourth, juvenile, phase of development, the animal gradually grows into a fifth phase, a much larger, sexually mature adult (30, 31).

Substantial anlage of all of the ganglia of the mature central nervous system are present at the beginning of the second, or veliger, larval stage, and these ganglia are quite well developed at metamorphosis. This is consistent with the animal's behavioral repertoire, which, except for reproductive capabilities, is essentially complete at metamorphosis. The bag cells appear rostral to the abdominal ganglion early in juvenile development but do not attain full size until much later (30, 31).

We have performed in situ hybridization experiments together with immunocytochemical experiments on sections of the developing organism from the formation of the veliger larvae, through metamorphosis, to the adult. The central ganglia are already present in primitive form in the veliger larvae, although no bag cells are apparent. At this early stage, we detected cells producing ELH or related peptides in a proliferative zone of epidermal cells lining the body wall long before the bag cells were present. In situ hybridization to sections of the veliger larvae 25 days after hatching and 10 days before metamorphosis reveals an array of hybridizing cells distributed throughout the entire length of the inner surface of the body wall, with one particularly dense cluster of cells expressing ELH-related mRNA along the body cavity close to the head ganglia (Plate V, A to C). During this early stage in development, this proliferative ectoderm of the body wall is the major site of cells expressing the ELH genes, although occasional positive cells are observed within the central nervous system as well.

ELH-positive cells continue to accumulate in this proliferative zone throughout development. After metamorphosis, small clusters of these cells can be seen extending into the body cavity along what appear to be fibrous connective tissue strands. These strands connect the inner surface of the body wall with the central ganglia and appear to serve as pathways for neurons migrating from the proliferative ectoderm to the central nervous system (Plate V, D and E). One particularly clear example is shown in Plate V F, in which two strongly hybridizing cells are observed on a connective tissue fiber that has attached to the pleural-abdominal connective. The cells then leave the fiber tracts and appear to migrate along neural connectives to their appropriate location within the central nervous system.

We have focused primarily on the development of the bag cell cluster because it represents a large and clearly delineated neuronal cell group in the adult. The bag cells first appear on the pleuroabdominal connective at about 10 to 20 days after metamorphosis when in situ hybridization reveals a primitive cluster of ten cells some distance from the abdominal ganglion (Plate VI, A and B). The cluster gradually increases in size over the next 50 days, accumulating about 200 cells, each slightly larger than 20 micrometers. This cluster has now moved much closer to the ganglion and bulges from the connective (Plate VI, C to F). As the animal, now sexually mature and reproductively capable, continues to grow during the next 100 days, the bag cells increase in size and number until the full complement of 400 cells is reached with each cell more than 50 μm

in diameter (32). The increase in cell number could be accounted for by continued proliferation of precursors within the ectoderm of the body wall and subsequent migration. We cannot, however, exclude the possibility that cell division is occurring within the primitive bag cell cluster itself.

The proliferative zone of the body wall extends throughout the length of the organism, suggesting that these cells are also precursors of the network of neurons expressing ELH or related peptides in other ganglia as well. Although we have not traced the origins of specific ELH-positive cells within other ganglia, we observe cells migrating along fibers connecting the body wall with other individual ganglia. Plate VI D illustrates a pair of ELH-positive cells positioned along a fiber connecting the body wall to the cerebral ganglia.

The migratory step that is present in the development of ELH-positive cells in the central nervous system sharply contrasts with the development of the cells expressing this gene family in the atrial gland. In the adult, the atrial gland comprises a segment of the luminal surface of the hermaphroditic duct. Hybridization in situ on sections of the hermaphroditic duct in animals ranging from 20 days after metamorphosis to young adults first reveals positive cells only at 40 days after metamorphosis (Plate IV, C and D). The distribution of ELH-positive cells, present in the thickened proliferative epithelium of the duct, suggests that these cells originate from the epithelial cells of the hermaphroditic duct itself. No positive cells have ever been observed in surrounding tissue migrating to the duct. We presume, then, that ELH-positive cells of the atrial gland develop in situ rather than migrate from distant zones of proliferation.

Neuroactive Peptides and the Generation of Behavior

Peptides can mediate behavior in invertebrates and vertebrates. We can now begin to ask what makes peptides suited to the task. Behavior is produced by the interaction of nerve cells that are interconnected in specific ways. Thus, the behavioral potential of an organism is in part encoded by the specificity of the wiring within its nervous system. By releasing neurotransmitter substances at their synapses, neurons are able to communicate rapidly through point-to-point contact. Like the conventional transmitter substances, neuroactive peptides can act locally as neurotransmitters on neighboring neurons. However, when they are secreted into the circulation, these peptides can also act as neurohormones at distant sites. Both of these functions are carried out by ELH, for example, which serves as a neurotransmitter by specifically altering the properties of individual neurons in the abdominal ganglion (14, 15), as well as a neurohormone by acting distantly to cause contraction of the smooth muscle follicles of the ovotestis (33, 34). The ability of ELH to exert its different effects on a diverse family of target cells—different central neurons and effector organs—illustrates an important property of neuropeptides—namely, that they are capable of coordinating changes in the nervous system with effector events in order to achieve a common behavioral end.

Coordinate control, but on the molecular level, is also evident in the way in which polyproteins are synthesized. A single promoter element and a single translational initiator can control the simultaneous expression of several different peptides. Moreover, this coordination may extend beyond protein synthe-sis to the packaging of a set of peptides into single vesicles. Small peptides cleaved from a single precursor may be contained together in the same vesicle and therefore released at the same time by an action potential. In this way, coordinate synthesis may be coupled with coordinate release of companion peptides, on the one hand, and with coordinate control over neural and effector events on the other.

A third property that makes peptides especially good candidates for coordinating functions derives from the nature of their polyprotein precursors. Merely by altering the pathway of processing, many different combinations of peptides can be produced from one precursor. Such alternative processing is illustrated by the precursor of pro-opiomelanocortin (POMC), which undergoes differential processing in the anterior and intermediate lobes of the pituitary and, as a result, generates different peptides in different structures (35–37). The purpose of this diversity might be to activate different patterns of behavior by modulating the activity of various combinations of neurons or target organs. The egg-laying peptides have even greater potential for achieving diversity, since the EHL precursor contains ten potential cleavage sites and its constituent peptides are encoded by a small family of genes in which each member has diverged to generate new peptides.

The fact that active peptide sequences are interspersed in the midst of nonfunctional protein sequences enhances the potential for evolutionary change in peptides and therefore in behavior. The functionally inert amino acids that intervene between two peptide sequences offer a natural repository for evolutionary changes in which additional active peptides may be created without interrupting the preexisting set. In this manner, base changes within this intervening protein sequence may create new processing sites. Alternatively, sequences with their own preexisting cleavage sites may be inserted in this region. For example, the ELH precursor contains a 240–base pair (bp) stretch not present in the homologous precursor expressed in the atrial gland. This small insertion encodes three candidate peptides, one of which appears to have arisen from a small internal duplication. Thus, internal duplications within a precursor also provide a mechanism to test new peptide possibilities without destroying the old. This is also apparent in the family of genes encoding the opioid peptides of vertebrates (38). In this manner, the number of peptides expressed by the ELH precursor has expanded without altering the ability of the polypeptide to express active ELH.

Finally, the individual behaviors may now be ascribed to individual peptides or groups of peptides. Different combinations of overlapping peptides could then give rise to different behavioral patterns with overlapping elements. Both egg-laying and feeding behavior in *Aplysia* involves head waving. Common peptides may elicit this activity in both feeding and egg laying in association with other peptides to generate these two distinct fixed action patterns. In this manner, more complex behaviors may be assembled by combining simple units of behavior, each mediated by one or a small number of neuropeptides.

Studying Gene Expression in Nerve Cells by in situ Hybridization

The analysis of specific gene expression in the nervous system poses prob-

lems analogous to those encountered in the study of early development. In each case, individual cells or groups of cells are thought to express distinct combinations of genes. Using in situ hybridization to mRNA in tissue sections together with indirect immunocytochemistry, we have traced the ELH-positive cells from their origins in the embryo to their definitive location in the mature nervous system. We have identified three classes of cells in the developing and adult organism that express genes of the ELH family: nerve cells, atrial gland cells, and progenitor cells in the body wall. These techniques are useful for identifying one or a small number of cells in a large population expressing a particular combination of genes and gene products. For example, against a background of 2000 cells in the abdominal ganglion, we have been able to detect the three invariant cells that express members of the ELH gene family. Both in situ hybridizations and immunofluorescence define the bag cells as the major site of synthesis of ELH. Earlier immunocytochemical studies (26, 27) first revealed a variable number of ELH-positive cells outside the bag cell clusters. Using whole mounts of the central nervous system taken from young animals, we detected a system of widely ramifying cells that express ELH, with some large and invariant members distributed throughout the CNS. Thus, our data and those of Chiu and Strumwasser (26) suggest that ELH may be used extensively as a neurotransmitter throughout the entire central nervous system.

The finding of this extensive system of ELH neurons raises questions as to its function. Do these cells participate with the bag cells to generate the egg-laying repertoire of behaviors? We do not know at present which of the egg-laying peptides are expressed by the individual cells outside of the bag cell cluster. Perhaps these cells release A and B peptides and initiate the discharge of the bag cells. Alternatively, the cells could mediate one or another of the individual behaviors associated with egg laying (such as head waving, grasping the egg strand by the mouth, and inhibition of feeding and walking). Unlike the bag cell processes, which traverse the sheath and release their product diffusely into the hemolymph, the processes of the ELH-containing neurons located in the cerebral, buccal, and pleural ganglia are restricted to the central nervous system and send their processes into the neuropil. In some instances these processes contact the cell bodies of neurons forming a halo of what appear to be axosomatic contacts (Plate III C). The secretory product of the ELH-positive neurons in the central nervous system may act therefore more like a conventional transmitter than a neurohormone released into the bloodstream.

Finally, the ELH genes expressed in neurons other than the bag cells may not be involved in egg laying at all but may express different sets of peptide neurotransmitters required for other behavioral processes.

Development of Central Neurons in

Aplysia

In all animals the brain develops as a specialization of the skin, the ectoderm of the body surface. Depending on the organism and the particular neurons, neurogenesis may proceed by proliferation in situ and subsequent differentiation or by proliferation followed by migration over long distances (39–41). In certain invertebrates—including nematode worms, annelid worms, and insects—the ectodermal cells in the body wall give rise to a neural epithelium. Within this neural epithelium primitive neuroblasts lose their contact with the inner and outer surface of the ectoderm, round up, and frequently proliferate in situ giving rise to clones of progeny neurons, a development that typically does not involve migration over any significant distance [for review (40); for occasional exceptions (2)]. Other neurons, common in the nervous system of vertebrates, develop from the columnar ectodermal cells that withdraw from the mitotic cycle to migrate over varying distances to their definitive locations.

By labeling fertilized eggs with thymidine, Jacob et al. (42) found that the central neurons in Aplysia derive from a proliferative ectodermal zone in the body wall where almost all mitosis occurs. Postmitotic neurons then leave the body wall and migrate to form the central ganglia by crawling along connective tissue strands. We have here provided independent and direct evidence for this mode of development by studying a specific population of neurons that can be identified and marked by its characteristic pattern of gene expression. We have found that, before metamorphosis and through much of juvenile development, ELH-producing cells are present in the body wall and in the body cavity. Some of the cells in the body cavity are directly apposed to ganglia or are located on connective tissue strands that join these ganglia or their connectives to the body wall. Thus, the neurons use what appear to be nonneural connective tissue cells as a migratory path to the nervous system, a mechanism analogous to that of the nerve cells of the cerebral cortex which use radial glial fibers as guides for migration (*43*).

Our data, and those of Jacob, thus suggest an interesting similarity in the development of certain invertebrate neurons and those of vertebrates, particularly the cells of the neural crest (*44, 45*). The occurrence of a migratory step in *Aplysia* makes it likely that migration may also prove a more significant feature in the development of other invertebrate animals than has previously been appreciated.

Consequences of a Migratory Step in the Differentiation of Neurons

Given two modes of neurogenesis, what are the anatomic and functional consequences of each? Our study suggests that cell division followed by migration allows one proliferative zone to seed diverse segments of the nervous system (the bag cells as well as the rest of the central ganglia) with ELH-producing cells. The function of the ELH-producing neurons outside of the bag cell cluster is unknown. It is possible that the pattern of gene expression in these various ELH-producing cells may be different. A clone of identical ELH-producing cells arising in a single proliferative zone may therefore diversify during the migration process itself or in response to different environments in which the cells ultimately reside.

We would suggest that in situ neurogenesis optimizes the development of a more precisely and more rigorously preprogrammed nervous system by minimizing extraneous influences and assuring that neurons will undergo the later steps of differentiation in the same microenvironment in which they undergo

their final mitotic division. This is consistent with the findings in *C. elegans*, which indicate that much of a nerve cell's fate is programmed and is determined by its lineage (*1, 2*), except when the cell migrates (*46*). Neurogenesis followed by migration may permit the development of a less rigidly determined nervous system (*44, 46*). Migration provides a population of neurons with the additional opportunity to encounter multiple spheres of influences along the course of migration and, more important, with the opportunity to end up in a new microenvironment at their final destination. This is most clearly evident in certain neurons of the neural crest that migrate over considerable distances and whose ultimate choice of transmitter is determined by the local environment of the definitive target (*47*). Nevertheless, mechanisms exist whereby cells can be determined prior to migration and be relatively little influenced by their journey (*48*).

Precocious Expression of ELH

A striking feature of our findings is that the presumptive bag cells express the genes for ELH very early in development. Animals do not begin to release eggs until 60 days after metamorphosis. Yet a full 70 days earlier (10 days before metamorphosis) and well before the cells begin their apparent migration into the nervous system, they express genes encoding ELH. Qualitatively similar findings have been made in certain other migrating vertebrate neurons. Neural crest cells that migrate from the neural tube to form the ganglia of the autonomic nervous system synthesize acetylcholine (or norepinephrine) before they reach

466

their final destination (*44*). On the other hand, cells in the CNS of the grasshopper that differentiate in situ and do not migrate express octopamine and proctolin only after their mature morphology is largely established and just before they begin to form synapses (*49, 50*).

Thus, early in development the bag cell precursors express in abundance a gene product whose function is thought to be required only in the sexually mature adult. Perhaps migrating cells require specific gene products encoded with the ELH polyprotein for pathfinding and other developmental purposes. In this manner specific neurotransmitters or neurohormones may play different roles in different stages of development: an early role in guiding developmental processes and a later role in dictating the program of specific behaviors in the adult.

References and Notes

1. S. Brenner, *Genetics* **77**, 71 (1974).
2. J. E. Sulston and H. R. Horvitz, *Dev. Bio.* **56**, 110 (1977).
3. G. D. Trisler, M. D. Schneider and M. Nirenberg, *Proc. Natl. Acad. Sci. U.S.A.* **78**, 2145 (1981).
4. D. G. Attardi and R. W. Sperry, *Exp. Neurol.* **7**, 46 (1963).
5. S. Hockfield and R. McKay, *J. Neurosci.* **3**, 369 (1983).
6. E. R. Kandel, *Behavioral Biology of Aplysia* (Freeman, San Francisco, 1979).
7. R. E. Coggeshall, B. A. Yaksta, F. J. Swartz, *Chromosoma* **32**, 205 (1971).
8. R. J. Lasek and W. J. Dower, *Science* **172**, 278 (1971).
9. E. R. Kandel, in *The Interneuron*, A. Scheibel, Ed. (UCLA Press, Los Angeles, 1970), p. 71.
10. F. Strumwasser, L. K. Kaczmarek, A. Y. Chiu, E. Heller, K. R. Jennings, D. P. Viele, in *Peptides: Integrators of Cell and Tissue Function*, F. E. Bloom, Ed. (Raven, New York, 1980), pp. 197–218.
11. J. E. Blankenship, in *The Role of Peptides in Neuronal Function*, J. L. Barker and T. G. Smith, Jr., Eds. (Dekker, New York, 1980), pp. 160–187.
12. E. Mayeri and B. Rothman, in *Neurosecretion—Molecules, Cells and Systems*, D. S. Farner and K. Lederis, Eds. (Plenum, New York, 1982), pp. 307–318.
13. I. Kupfermann, *Am. Zool* **12**, 513 (1972).
14. E. Mayeri, P. Brownell, W. D. Branton, *J. Neurophysiol.* **42**, 1165 (1979).
15. E. Mayeri, P. Brownell, W. D. Branton, *ibid.*, p. 1185 (1979).
16. S. Arch, T. Smock, R. Gurvis, C. McCarthy, *J. Comp. Physiol.* **128**, 67 (1978).
17. E. Heller, L. K. Kaczmarek, M. W. Hunkapiller, L. E. Hood, F. Strumwasser, *Proc. Natl. Acad. Sci. U.S.A.* **77**, 2328 (1980).
18. D. H. Schlesinger, S. P. Babirak, J. E. Blankenship, in *Symposium on Neurohypophyseal Peptide Hormones and Other Biologically Active Peptides*, D. H. Schlesinger, Ed. (Elsevier/North-Holland, New York, 1981), pp. 137–150.
19. R. H. Scheller, J. F. Jackson, L. B. McAllister, J. H. Schwartz, E. R. Kandel, R. Axel, *Cell* **28**, 707 (1982).
20. R. H. Scheller, J. F. Jackson, L. B. McAllister, B. S. Rothman, E. Mayeri, R. Axel, *ibid.* **32**, 7 (1983).
21. B. S. Rothman and E. Mayeri, unpublished observations.
22. R. H. Scheller, unpublished observations.
23. S. J. Watson and H. Akil, *Neuroscience Commentaries* **1**, 10 (1981).
24. Provided by E. Mayeri and B. Rothman of the University of California, San Francisco.
25. S. Arch, *J. Gen. Physiol.* **60**, 102 (1972b).
26. A. Y. Chiu and F. Strumwasser, *J. Neurosci.* **1**, 812 (1981).
27. A. Y. Chiu, thesis, California Institute of Technology (1981).
28. M. Beard, L. Milleatia, C. Masouka, S. Arch, *Tissue Cell* **14**, 297 (1982).
29. P. Kandel and T. Capo, *The Veliger* **22**, 194 (1979).
30. A. Kriegstein, V. Castellucci, E. R. Kandel, *Proc. Natl. Acad. Sci. U.S.A.* **71**, 3654 (1974).
31. A. R. Kriegstein, *ibid.* **74**, 375 (1977).
32. W. T. Frazier, E. R. Kandel, I. Kupfermann, R. Waziri, R. E. Coggeshall, *J. Neurophysiol.* **30**, 1288 (1967).
33. F. E. Dudek and S. S. Tobe, *Gen. Comp. Endocrinol.* **36**, 618 (1979).
34. B. S. Rothman, G. Weir, F. E. Dudek, *Science* **197**, 490 (1982).
35. R. E. Mains, B. A. Eipper and N. Ling, *Proc. Natl. Acad. Sci. U.S.A.* **74**, 3014 (1977).
36. J. L. Roberts and E. Herbert, *ibid.*, p. 4826.
37. _____, *ibid.*, p. 530.
38. E. Herbert, *Cold Spring Harbor Symp. Quant. Biol.*, in press.
39. P. H. Patterson and D. Purves, *Readings in Developmental Neurobiology* (Cold Spring Harbor Laboratory, Cold Spring Harbor, N.Y., 1982).
40. C. S. Goodman and K. G. Pearson, *Neurol. Res. Prog. Bull.* **20** (6), 773 (1982).
41. C. M. Bate, *J. Embryol. Exp. Morphol.* **35**, 107 (1976).
42. M. Jacob, S. Schacher, V. Castelucci, *Soc. Neurosci. Abstr.* **5**, 164 (1979); M. Jacob, *J. Neurosci.*, in press.
43. P. Rakic, *Comp. Neurol.* **141**, 283 (1971).

44. N. M. Le Douarin, *Nature (London)* **286**, 663 (1980).
45. J. H. Weston, *Adv. Morphogenesis* **8**, 41 (1970).
46. M. Chalfie, J. N. Thompson, J. E. Sulston, *Science*, in press.
47. P. H. Patterson *et al.*, *Cold Spring Harbor Symp. Quant. Biol.* **40**, 389 (1975).
48. C. S. Lelieve, G. G. Schweizer, C. M. Ziller, N. M. Le Douarin, *Dev. Biol.* **177**, 362 (1980).
49. C. S. Goodman and N. C. Spitzer, *Nature (London)* **280**, 208 (1979).
50. M. Taghert and W. Goodman, in preparation.
51. The protocol for tissue preparation and in situ hybridization involves modification of procedures previously published by L. Angerer and R. Angerer [*Nucleic Acids Res.* **9**, 2819 (1981)] and R. Venezky, L. Angerer, and R. Angerer [*Cell* **24**, 385 (1981)]. Ganglia were dissected and tissues were placed directly into Bouin's fixative. Optimal fixation times were empirically determined; ganglia from a 250-g animal required 6 to 8 hours and the hermaphroditic duct required 10 to 12 hours at room temperature. The tissue was cleared of fixative in several changes of $0.2M$ phosphate buffer and 30 percent sucrose at 4°C and dehydrated with an ethanol series (50, 70, 85, 95, 99, and 100 percent) at room temperature (3 changes, >1.5 hours of each). The tissue was placed in xylenes until translucent (5 to 10 minutes for adult tissues), transferred to a xylene-paraffin mixture (1:1) for 1 hour at 58°C, placed in paraffin for 1 hour at 58°C, and finally embedded in fresh paraffin. Microscope slides frosted on one side were washed in mild detergent, rinsed in water, rinsed in 100 percent ethanol, and then immersed in 5 percent gelatin, 0.1 percent $CrK(SO_4)_2$ for 10 minutes, and air-dried. Serial sections (5 μm) were collected on gelatin-coated slides and fixed to slides (2 days at 55°C). Paraffin was removed from slides with xylenes (two changes in 15 minutes) and hydrated. In the hydration series, the 70 percent ethanol is saturated with $LiCO_4$ in order to remove the picric acid. Appropriate sections were selected for hybridization. Every 20th section was stained for 2 minutes in 0.125 percent methylene blue, dehydrated into xylenes, and mounted on a coverslip (Permount). Experimental slides were treated with proteinase K (Boehringer Mannheim, 1 μg/ml in $0.1M$ tris, pH 7.5, $.05M$ EDTA, pH 7.5) at 37°C for 1/2 hour, washed several times in distilled water, dehydrated to 100 percent ethanol, and used immediately or stored in a desiccator (for a maximum of 24 hours). The control slides, after proteinase K treatment and washing, were treated with ribonuclease (BRL; 100 μg/ml in $0.1M$ tris, pH 7.5), for 1 hour at room temperature.
52. Proteinase K–treated, dehydrated slides for in situ hybridization were placed in moist chambers which were equilibrated with the hybridization solution excluding the nucleic acid. ^{125}I-labeled DNA probes were prepared with ^{125}I-labeled CTP as described [Robins *et al.*, *Cell* **23**, 29 (1981)]. The DNA probes were diluted to 400 ng/ml, denatured by boiling at 100°C for 5 minutes, then quenched on ice. The probe was brought to $0.3M$ NaCl, 30 percent formamide, $0.1M$ tris, pH 7.5, 4 mM EDTA, pH 7.5, $2\times$ Denhardts solution, 2 percent dextran sulfate, and pipetted directly onto tissue sections at a concentration of 200 ng/ml. Each section was covered with the smallest possible volume; 30 to 50 μl was necessary to cover a cross section through an adult hermaphroditic duct while only 2 μl was necessary for the ganglia of a very young animal. The slide chambers were wrapped in Parafilm and foil and placed in an oven at 48°C for 12 hours. The hybridized slides were washed twice for 1 hour in $4\times$ SSC, $2\times$ SSC, $1\times$ SSC, $0.5\times$ SSC, and $0.2\times$ SSC + 0.5 percent P_i or PP_i. The $4\times$ SSC rinses the formamide and was conducted at room temperature while the subsequent washes were done at 37°C. Potassium iodide was added to $0.1M$ in the $4\times$, $2\times$, and $1\times$ washing solutions. Washed slides were dehydrated, dipped in photographic emulsion, and exposed at 4°C for 1 week.
53. Tissue for immunocytochemistry was processed as described for in situ hybridization with the exception of the protease treatment. The primary antibodies, rabbit antibody to ELH or rabbit IgG to A peptide were kindly provided by E. Mayeri and B. Rothman (*24*). The specificity of these antibodies was established by radioimmune assays with purified ELH and A or B peptides. Immunocytochemistry with peroxidase-conjugated goat antibody to rabbit IgG was performed as described by R. Mesa-Tejada [*J. Histochem. Cytochem.* **26**, 532 (1978)].
54. Indirect immunofluorescence was performed on whole CNS's from 10- to 35-day postmetamorphic animals and on whole premetamorphic animals by a modification of procedures of R. Goldstein, J. Kistler and J. Schwartz (submitted to *Neuroscience*). The whole CNS's from juvenile animals and the whole premetamorphic animals were processed as described above, but for this assay the tissue was rehydrated after fixation, clearing, and dehydration, then blocked 6 to 12 hours in 50 percent normal goat serum, 0.25 percent saponin at 4°C. The tissue was incubated with the primary antibody at 100 μg/ml in 1 percent normal goat serum, 0.25 percent saponin for 3.5 days, washed 6 hours in $0.1M$ phosphate buffer, pH 7.4, incubated 3 hours with a rhodamine-conjugated goat antiserum to rabbit IgG at a dilution of 0.1000 in 1 percent normal goat serum and treated with 0.25 percent saponin, washed for 3 hours in phosphate buffer; a coverslip in 66 percent glycerol in phosphate buffer was put in place, and the preparation was visualized and photographed with a Leitz immunofluorescence microscope.
55. We thank the members of the Center for Neurobiology and Behavior for their continued assistance and especially wish to thank Drs. Hank Kistler, Tom Capo, and James Schwartz. We also thank E. Mayeri and B. Rothman for providing the antibodies used in this study. This work was supported by NIH grants NCl-5RO1 CA-16346 and 5 PO1 CA-23767 to R.A., by NIH grants GM-32099 and MH-18558 and a grant from the Klingenstein Foundation to E.R.K. and by the Office of Naval Research (N0014-83-K-0166).

35. Metallothionein-Human GH Fusion Genes Stimulate Growth of Mice

Richard D. Palmiter, Gunnar Norstedt, Richard E. Gelinas
Robert E. Hammer, Ralph L. Brinster

Growth of vertebrates is mediated in part by the cascade of polypeptide hormones depicted in Fig. 1. This pathway emanates from the hypothalamus which responds to neurotransmitters by liberating either somatostatin or growth hormone–releasing factor into the portal circulation; these polypeptide hormones impinge on the pituitary to either inhibit or stimulate, respectively, the synthesis and secretion of growth hormone (GH) (*1*). Growth hormone is released periodically from the pituitary. The amplitude of the cycles of release is more striking in males than in females (*2*); the significance of this difference in secretory patterns on sexual differentiation is only beginning to be appreciated (*3*). Nevertheless, in both sexes GH is thought to stimulate the liver to produce insulin-like growth factor I (IGF-I) (*4*), a polypeptide hormone, also called somatomedin C, which shows homology to proinsulin (*5*). IGF-I is thought to mediate growth by activating receptors on peripheral tissues (*6*).

In a previous study we showed that it was possible to manipulate this pathway by introducing rat GH (rGH) genes into fertilized mouse eggs (*7*). Most of the mice that incorporated the gene into their chromosomes, called transgenic mice, grew larger than normal. The success of this approach depended on the fusion of the rGH structural gene to the mouse metallothionein-I (MT-I) gene promoter, a technique used previously to obtain expression of microinjected thymidine kinase genes (*8*). This promoter is from a "housekeeping" gene which is expressed in most cells and is regulated by a variety of environmental stimuli (*9*). One class of stimuli includes certain heavy metals, such as cadmium and zinc, which are postulated to bind to regulatory proteins that interact with promoter sequences located in the region 40 to 180 base pairs (bp) upstream of the transcription start site (*10*). The consequence of using this particular fusion gene was that rGH was produced in the same tissues as MT-I, instead of the pituitary, with the result that circulating rGH reached levels several hundred times higher than normally achieved (*7*). This extrapituitary production of GH is depicted as the GH shunt in Fig. 1. Some of the transgenic mice grew to almost twice the size of their normal littermates.

We have extended these studies, as

Fig. 1. Growth hormone (GH) cascade. GH participates in the regulation of growth as depicted in this diagram. The hypothalamic neuropeptides somatostatin and GH-releasing factor act on the pituitary to inhibit or stimulate, respectively, the release of GH. GH stimulates the hepatic production of insulin-like growth factor I (IGF-I) which in turn acts on peripheral tissues to stimulate their growth. This endocrine system is regulated at several different levels; possible points of feedback regulation by GH or IGF-I are indicated. The rGH or hGH shunt refers to the extrapituitary production of rGH or hGH as achieved by gene transfer. These foreign GH genes are insensitive to normal feedback mechanisms.

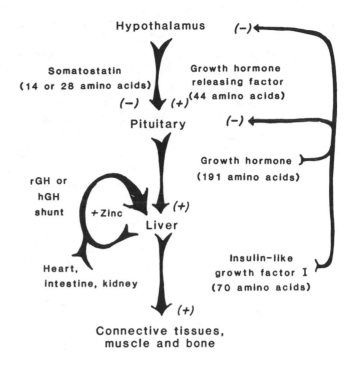

reported here, by showing that the more distantly related human GH gene (hGH) is also capable of promoting accelerated growth of mice. This gene and its products are more easily distinguished from the endogenous mouse counterparts allowing certain technical advantages over our initial constructions with the rGH gene. The genetic engineering of mice with a hGH shunt and the regulation of this modified GH cascade are described below.

Growth of Mice-Bearing
MThGH Fusion Genes

Two different constructions were prepared in which the mouse MT-I promoter was fused to the hGH$_N$ structural gene that was isolated from one of a pair of cosmids that include the entire GH gene family (11). These fusion genes are desig-

nated MThGH; our previous constructions with rGH are hereafter designated MTrGH. In both cases, the unique Bam HI site that is located just upstream of the initiation codon of hGH was utilized (12); in one construction (plasmid 111, Fig. 2) it was fused to a Bam HI linker sequence inserted at the +6 position of the MT-I gene (13), in the other (plasmid 112, Fig. 2) we utilized the existing Bgl II site located at +64 of the MT-I gene. The latter construction also includes a piece of phage λ DNA on the 3′ side of the hGH gene, a remnant from a previous construction that is presumably inconsequential. In both cases, the linear fragments indicated by the interior arrows were isolated and about a thousand copies were injected into the male pronucleus of fertilized mouse eggs. In one set of experiments the eggs and sperm were from the inbred C57 mouse line, in a second set the eggs and sperm were from

470

C57 × SJL hybrids. A total of 101 mice developed from these eggs: 6.3 percent of the C57 eggs surviving injection developed into mice compared to 10.4 percent of the hybrid eggs. Retention of the hGH gene sequences in these mice was scored by "tail blots" (*14*) in which tail DNA was denatured, spotted onto nitrocellulose, and hybridized with a 1-kb Pvu II probe that spans most of the hGH structural gene (see Fig. 2). A total of 33 out of 101 of the animals were positive for hGH DNA. To quantitate the number of hGH sequences, we determined the DNA content of the samples, spotted samples in duplicate along with normal human DNA as standard, hybridized as above, and determined the radioactivity. In Table 1, the transgenic animals are listed according to MThGH gene copy number, which varied from 0.9 to 455 copies of the MThGH gene per cell, because we are not sure that there is a meaningful difference in the expression of the two fusion gene constructs in either inbred or hybrid mice.

Table 1 also summarizes the growth ratio of these transgenic animals compared to sex-matched littermates. A majority (23 out of 33) of the transgenic

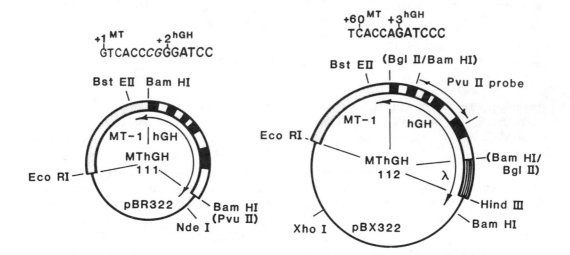

Fig. 2. Construction of metallothionein-human growth hormone (MThGH) plasmids. For MThGH 111, a Bam HI linker sequence (CGGGATCCCG) was inserted between the +6 position of mouse MT-I gene and the Pvu II site of pBR322. Then a 2.15-kb Bam HI fragment including the hGH structural gene was excised from a 2.65-kb Eco RI subclone of hGH$_N$ in the polylinker of pUC12 and inserted into the Bam HI site of the MT-I vector to give a 6.3-kb plasmid. The sequence at the MT-I/hGH junction is shown [see (*12*) and (*13*) for more sequence information]; the seventh and eighth nucleotides are derived from the Bam HI linker. For MThGH 112, a MT-I vector was used in which the Bgl II site of MT-I (at position +64) was followed by a 0.7-kb BgI II-Hind III fragment of phage lambda in a pBR322 derivative called pBX322 because of the Xho I linker in the copy control region. The same 2.15-kb hGH Bam HI fragment was inserted into this vector to generate an 8.9-kb plasmid. The sequence at the MT-I/hGH junction is shown. The stippled region represents 5′ flanking sequences of MT-I; solid boxes represent hGH exons; open boxes represent hGH introns and 3′ flanking sequences; striped box represents phage lambda sequences; and the solid line represent pBR322. The inner arrows indicate the DNA fragments that were isolated and microinjected into mouse eggs. The location of the Pvu II probe used to detect transgenic mice is indicated by the outer arrows.

Table 1. Expression of MThGH genes in transgenic mice. All mice that were positive for hGH gene sequences are listed. Animals were either inbred (C57-) or hybrids (Hyb-) developing from C57 × SJL eggs fertilized by C57 × SJL sperm.

Animal	Plas- mid*	Gene copy num- ber/ cell†	Liver hGH mRNA (molecules/cell)‡			Serum hGH (ng/ml)§			Relative growth (ratio)¶
			Con- trol	+Zn	+Cd	Con- trol	+Zn	+Cd	
C57-173-2♀	111	455	902	2,730		9,600	130,000		1.82
C57-173-3♂	111	405				120			1.43
C57-168-5♂	112	91	15	210		90	4,000		1.26
Hyb-194-2♀	112	47.3				< l.d.			0.96
Hyb-182-3♂	111	45				3,700	14,600		1.67
Hyb-182-2♀	111	44				64,000			1.30
C57-168-6♀	112	38.5			818	3,500		27,800	[1.74]
Hyb-185-2♂	111	34				80			1.24
C57-167-2♀	112	18.5			1,242	4,600		18,900	(1.55)
Hyb-186-4♀	111	18				8,200	143,000		2.14
Hyb-197-3♀	112	12.2				25			0.96
C57-168-2♀	112	11.7				100			1.30
Hyb-184-5♂	111	10.4				520	18,000		1.70
Hyb-186-3♀	111	10.2	2	345		80	6,400		1.34
C57-167-5♂	112	6.8				10			1.18
Hyb-180-1♂	111	6.3				3,000			1.55
C57-168-4♀	112	6.1				45			1.20
Hyb-198-3♀	112	6.1				190			1.02
Hyb-186-5♂	111	4.1			990	6,500		19,800	(1.95)
Hyb-186-1♂	111	3.5			657	2,900		4,500	(1.84)
Hyb-198-2♀	112	2.6				100			(2.16)
Hyb-182-4♀	111	2.3				1,200			0.97
Hyb-184-1♀	111	2.0				250	11,900		2.37
Hyb-184-7♀	111	2.0				30			0.96
C57-161-1♀	112	1.6				40			1.29
Hyb-194-3♀	112	1.4				< l.d.			0.93
Hyb-194-6♂	112	1.4				< l.d.			0.99
Hyb-194-8♀	112	1.3				80			1.03
C57-168-3♀	112	1.2				75			1.52
Hyb-184-2♂	111	1.1				275			2.03
C57-170-1♂	111	0.9				< l.d.			0.87
Hyb-194-4♂	112	0.9				60			1.01
Hyb-197-5♀	112	0.9	1	12		20	35		1.77

*About 1000 copies of linear DNA fragments isolated from MThGH plasmids 111 or 112 (see Fig. 2) were microinjected into the male pronucleus (8). †Tail DNA (3 μg) was denatured in base, spotted onto nitrocellulose, baked, hybridized with the nick-translated Pvu II probe (see Fig. 2) as described (14), and washed. The radioactivity was then measured by scintillation counting. For quantitation we assumed that human DNA has five homologous sequences (11) per haploid genome of 3.2 pg. ‡MThGH mRNA was measured by solution hybridization (19) with a ^{32}P-labeled cDNA derived from a 272-bp Taq I fragment that covers parts of exons 4 and 5 of human placental lactogen (20). A partial hepatectomy was performed on four of the mice (control values) before we supplemented the water with 25 mM ZnSO$_4$ for 2 weeks, at which time a second partial hepatectomy was performed (+Zn). Four other animals were injected twice with CdSO$_4$ (1 mg/kg) 18 and 4 hours before they were killed (+Cd); see Table 3. Experiments were performed when the animals were 7 to 21 weeks old. §Human GH was measured in triplicate by radioimmunoassay on serum samples (up to 10 μl) drawn before (control) or after treatment with ZnSO$_4$ or CdSO$_4$. < l.d., less than lower than limit of detection (~ 10 ng/ml) with standard assay. ¶The relative weights of transgenic mice compared with sex-matched littermates at 16 weeks of age are shown. Weights in parentheses were taken at 10 weeks, weights in brackets were taken at 6 weeks.

animals grew more than 18 percent larger than their littermates; several were twice as large. There is no correlation between growth rate and MThGH gene copy number as some of the largest animals had only a few copies, but most (seven out of ten) of the transgenic animals that did not grow larger had less than three copies.

To explore the basis of enhanced growth of these transgenic animals, we measured the amount of hGH in the serum by radioimmunoassay (Table 1). The circulating hGH levels ranged from undetectable to 64 μg/ml compared to normal values of 10 to 100 ng of mouse GH per milliliter (15). All of the transgenic mice that grew larger than controls had immunoreactive hGH in their serum, but the relations between growth rate and circulating hGH levels are crude. It appears that less than 100 ng of hGH per milliliter is sufficient to stimulate nearly maximal growth, but it is perplexing that some animals with intermediate or high levels of circulating hGH do not grow as well as others. A most interesting case is Hyb-182-4♀; this animal apparently expresses the gene, since substantial amounts of immunoreactive hGH are present in the serum, but it still fails to grow more than normal.

The growth rate of the largest transgenic mouse, which had integrated two copies of MThGH gene per cell and had a moderate level of circulating hGH (250 ng/ml), is shown in Fig. 3A together with a typical normal littermate of the same sex. These two animals are shown on the cover at 24 weeks of age. Mice expressing MThGH genes are already larger than littermates at weaning (~ 5 weeks) and they grow rapidly until 11 to 13 weeks; during this time the growth rate is typically two to three times that of normal mice of this strain. To establish more accurately when GH first begins to be

effective, we bred mouse C57-173-3♂ and compared the growth rates of offspring that did and did not receive the MThGH genes from their father. Figure 3B shows that accelerated growth begins between 16 and 22 days after birth. We have not yet systematically examined MThGH gene expression during fetal development, but we do know that these genes are expressed before birth. Thus, we suspect that the mice became sensitive to GH 2 to 3 weeks after birth. This experiment also documents that the enhanced growth rate is heritable, a point that has also been established with the transgenic mice expressing MTrGH fusion genes (16).

Consequences of High Levels of Circulating hGH

Because the hGH is produced in these transgenic animals from fetal stages onward, their immune system presumably recognizes hGH as self. Thus, long-term stimulation by hGH delivered in this manner may be more effective than delivery based on injection or continuous infusion into newborn or adult animals. Since GH is thought to mediate growth indirectly via the stimulation of IGF-I (4), we anticipated that animals growing rapidly in response to hGH would have elevated IGF-I levels in their serum. Table 2 summarizes the results from four transgenic animals from which we obtained blood samples successively over a period of a month after supplementing their water with 25 mM ZnSO$_4$. The hGH concentrations of individual animals were relatively constant over this period but varied from animal to animal. IGF-I levels were elevated about two- to threefold and were inversely correlated with the high-circulating hGH concentrations. This inverse relationship might

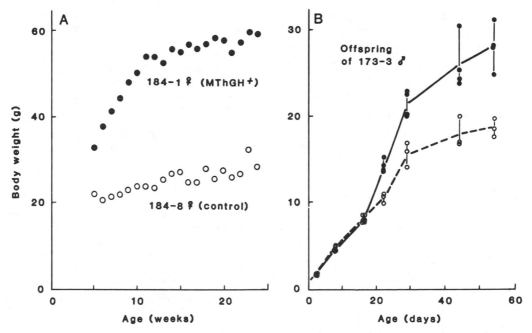

Fig. 3. Comparative growth of transgenic mice expressing MThGH genes and controls. (A) Body weights of a transgenic female (Hyb-184-1, solid circles) and a control female littermate (Hyb-184-8, open circles) were recorded weekly after weaning. The water was supplemented with 25 mM ZnSO₄ at 17 weeks. (B) A transgenic male (C57-173-3) was outbred producing seven pups in the first litter. The mice were marked and their weights were recorded periodically; subsequently hybridization of tail DNA with the Pvu II probe revealed that four offspring inherited the MThGH genes (solid circles) and three did not (open circles). Individual body weights are indicated; significant ($P < 0.05$) differences in weights of mice with and without MThGH genes were evident at 22 days and older (Student's t-test). A second litter was similarly analyzed and showed the same growth relationships.

help explain the lack of correlation between hGH concentrations and growth.

Because of the long-term exposure to elevated concentrations of hGH, we were curious to know whether histological examination of the pituitaries of these transgenic animals would reveal abnormalities. Pituitaries of three transgenic mice were examined after applying Slidders' strain (17) which differentiates many of the pituitary cell types. Two of the mice (Hyb-197-5♀ and Hyb-184-5♂) had few (less than 1 percent) acidophilic cells representing somatotrophs and lactotrophs which synthesize GH and pro-

lactin, respectively, while the third transgenic mouse (C57-173-2♀) had only 25 percent of the normal number of acidophilic cells. (Plate VII, A and B). The transgenic pituitaries resembled those of *lit/lit* mice (Plate VII C) which have a genetic deficiency in GH production (18).

Regulation of hGH Synthesis by Heavy Metals

Because these fusion genes carry the mouse MT-I gene promoter, we were interested to know whether MThGH messenger RNA (mRNA) would be inducible by heavy metals such as cadmium or zinc. To quantitate MThGH mRNA levels we used a solution hybridization protocol which is sensitive enough to detect less than one molecule of mRNA per cell (*19*). As a probe we used a Taq 1 fragment (272 bp corresponding to parts of exons 4 and 5) isolated from a homologous, human placental lactogen complementary DNA (cDNA) clone (*20*). This fragment was nick-translated and the cDNA strand was purified as described previously (*19*). Control experiments revealed that it hybridized equally well to human placenta and human pituitary RNA under standard hybridization conditions. To measure induction by heavy metals, we subjected the mice to a partial hepatectomy and then switched them to a water supply containing 25 mM ZnSO$_4$. Two weeks later we subjected the mice to another partial hepatectomy. Table 1 shows that in four transgenic mice treated in this way, Zn treatment increased the amount of MThGH mRNA between 3- and 170-fold. Thus, the foreign genes seem to be regulated in a manner similar to the endogenous MT-I genes (*21*). The induction in MThGH mRNA also resulted in an increase in circulating hGH (Table 1). Hepatectomy alone stimulates MT gene expression (*9*), but controls have shown that this stimulation subsides within 2 weeks (*14*).

Tissue Specific Expression of MThGH Genes

Given that foreign genes can be expressed in transgenic animals, one of the salient questions is whether these genes are regulated properly. The mouse MT-I gene can be considered a "housekeep-

Table 2. Effects of high hGH concentrations on mouse IGF-I levels. Serial blood samples were collected four times between 17 and 21 weeks of growth on a diet supplemented with 25 mM ZnSO$_4$ in the drinking water. Serum was prepared and hGH was measured by radioimmunoassay (RIA) with a kit obtained from the NIAMDD. The RIA procedures were adapted for use with small-volume samples but otherwise were performed essentially as recommended by the NIAMDD. [^{125}I]-labeled tracers were prepared by means of Iodogen (Pierce Chemical Company). No measurable immunoreactivity of hGH could be found in the serum of control mice. IGF-I was determined by human placental membrane radioreceptor assay with pure human IGF-I being used as standard (*28*). Serum samples were extracted with acid-ethanol to enable us to assay the total IGF-I. Four serum samples were individually assayed for total IGF-I; transgenic mice had significantly ($P < 0.05$) higher levels of IGF-I than controls.

Animal	hGH (μg/ml)	IGF-I (μg/ml)
Hyb-182-3♂	14.6 ± 1.4*	1.48 ± 0.13
Hyb-184-1♀	11.9 ± 0.7	1.73 ± 0.06
Hyb-184-5♂	18.0 ± 1.5	1.21 ± 0.08
Hyb-186-4♀	143.0 ± 6.5	1.04 ± 0.12
Controls	0	0.55 ± 0.04

*Standard error of the mean, $N = 4$ (samples per animal collected about 1 week apart).

ing" gene in that it is expressed in nearly all tissues (with the exception of thymus) and it is inducible by heavy metals in most of these tissues, although the extent of induction varies considerably from tissue to tissue (*21*). A reasonable model is that the MT-I gene is regulated by a metal-binding protein that interacts with the promoter. Thus, in the simplest case, we expected that proper regulation would be reflected in a constant ratio of MThGH mRNA to the endogenous mouse MT-I mRNA when comparing one tissue to another.

Table 3 shows the results of MThGH

and MT-I mRNA determinations from eight tissues of four transgenic animals that were stimulated with CdSO$_4$. When one compares the MThGH to MT-I mRNA ratios in different tissues of the same transgenic animal, it is apparent that they are far from constant, varying from 32- to 187-fold. The extreme exam-

Table 3. Tissue specific expression of MThGH fusion genes. Total nucleic acids (TNA) were prepared from the indicated tissues derived from transgenic mice (7 to 13 weeks old) stimulated with CdSO$_4$ (1 mg/kg; 18 and 4 hours before they were killed). Samples were digested with proteinase K in sodium dodecyl sulfate and then extracted with phenol and chloroform (14). The TNA samples were used to determine mRNA levels (MT-I and MThGH) by solution hybridization to ^{32}P-labeled cDNA probes as described (19). The number of molecules per cell were calculated by assuming that there are 6.4 pg of DNA per cell and that MT-I mRNA and hGH mRNA are 391 and 1000 bases long, respectively. The DNA concentration was determined by a fluorescence method (29).

Tissue	Animal	Molecules of MT-I mRNA per cell	Molecules of MThGH mRNA per cell	Ratio of MThGH to MT-I
Liver	C57-168-6♀	2560	818	.32
	C57-167-2♀	2230	1240	.56
	Hyb-186-1♂	2490	657	.26
	Hyb-186-5♂	2310	990	.43
Kidney	C57-168-6♀	680	4.6	.007
	C57-167-2♀	283	0.9	.003
	Hyb-186-1♂	139	93	.67*
	Hyb-186-5♂	203	5	.024
Intestine	C57-168-6♀	681	33	.05
	C57-167-2♀	381	28	.07
	Hyb-186-1♂	378	5	.01
	Hyb-186-5♂	377	22	.06
Heart	C57-168-6♀	211	22	.10
	C57-167-2♀	210	33	.16
	Hyb-186-1♂	191	110	.58*
	Hyb-186-5♂	200	166	.83*
Brain	C57-168-6♀	162	2.2	.01
	C57-167-2♀	135	2.6	.02
	Hyb-186-1♂	126	37	.29*
	Hyb-186-5♂	91	1	.01
Spleen	C57-168-6♀	33	1.6	.05
	C57-167-2♀	24	1.4	.06
	Hyb-186-1♂	5	0.2	.04
	Hyb-186-5♂	10	6	.60*
Lung	C57-168-6♀	31	1.3	.04
	C57-167-2♀	40	1	.03
	Hyb-186-1♂	12	1	.08
	Hyb-186-5♂	13	1	.08
Testis	Hyb-186-1♂	166	56	.34
	Hyb-186-5♂	169	113	.67

*Marked deviation of ratio from average.

ple is animal C57-167-2♀, which expresses the MThGH gene well in the liver but hardly at all in the kidney. Since both mRNA's are measured in triplicate from the same total nucleic acid preparation and the endogenous MT-I mRNA levels are relatively constant from animal to animal, these different ratios are unlikely to be due to mRNA quantitation errors. In these comparisons, the differences in mRNA ratios could be due either to tissue specific differences in transcriptional response of the endogenous MT-I genes and the foreign MThGH genes or to differences in the relative stability of the two mRNA's from tissue to tissue. If the latter were true, then one might expect the ratios in the same tissue of different animals to be constant. When these comparisons are made (Table 3) we observe that the ratios are similar within a given tissue for most, but not all, of the animals.

Our interpretation of these results is that there is a systematic hierarchy of MThGH mRNA production in different tissues relative to the endogenous MT-I mRNA: liver > testis > heart > (lung, spleen, intestine) > (kidney, brain). This hierarchy is the product of differential transcription and stability of MThGH mRNA relative to MT-I mRNA. Superimposed on this hierarchy are some strong position effects that are tissue specific. These position effects show up as extraordinarily high or low MThGH to MT-I mRNA ratios; for example, the kidney, brain, and heart of animal Hyb-186-1♂ express MThGH genes extraordinarily well, and the intestine expresses them poorly. Likewise, the heart, testis, and spleen of animal Hyb-186-5♂ express MThGH genes well. These results might be the consequence of chromosomal integration near a gene that is expressed in a comparable tissue specific manner.

Implications and Conclusions

This chapter complements and extends our previous work on the expression of MTrGH fusion genes in mice. It shows that enhanced growth does not depend on a highly homologous peptide because rat and human GH differ in 67 out of 191 amino acids (22). The maximum size (about twice normal) achieved with expression of MThGH genes is similar to that achieved with MTrGH genes. This growth is obtained in some transgenic mice with less than 100 ng of hGH per milliliter (Table 1) which is somewhat higher than the average circulating level of mice GH (mGH) (15). Thus, it appears that both mGH and hGH are of similar potency when binding to mGH receptors.

Growth is thought to result from activation of hepatic GH receptors which in turn stimulate the synthesis and secretion of IGF-I, a 70–amino acid peptide hormone that circulates to peripheral tissues to stimulate their growth (4). We have shown that IGF-I concentrations are elevated about two- to threefold, consistent with the hypothesis that IGF-I plays an important role in the GH cascade. The mice appear to be normally proportioned, rather than acromegalic, presumably because of the continuous exposure to increased hGH; but how this apparent allometric growth is coordinated is not clear. We do not know, for example, whether all tissues contain receptors for IGF-I or whether some of the tissues respond to yet other growth factors released in response to elevated IGF-I.

We have noted that transgenic mice do not commence greater than normal growth until about 3 weeks of age despite the presence of excess hGH prior to that time. This observation suggests that some later step in the GH cascade is rate-limiting in newborn mice; for example, production or responsiveness to IGF-I. These results are consistent with the notion that fetal and newborn growth is controlled by other hormones (23). One intriguing hypothesis (24) is that another member of the GH gene family, namely placental lactogen (also known as chorionic somatomammotropin), stimulates fetal growth acting via IGF-II. Thus, in this view two homologous gene families have diverged so that one member of each controls fetal growth and another member of each controls adult growth. The data also show that mice become insensitive to the growth stimulating properties of hGH when they are about 3 months old.

Histological examination revealed that the number of acidophilic pituitary cells was severely reduced, presumably due to feedback inhibition by the increased concentrations of hGH or IGF-I as depicted in Fig. 1. It is not yet clear whether the somatotrophs are present but do not appear acidophilic or whether they fail to develop. The histology of the pituitary, coupled with the high levels of hGH lead us to conclude that expression of the foreign MThGH genes is responsible for the accelerated growth of the transgenic mice.

The overall efficiency of achieving transgenic animals that grow significantly larger than their littermates averaged 70 percent in these experiments, a value lower than that reported for MTrGH (7) but more meaningful since it is based on 33 rather than 7 animals. This level of expression is similar to that achieved with MT-thymidine kinase fusion genes (14). But this high frequency of expression is not universally true of MT fusion genes because MT-human α-globin and MT-β-galactosidase constructs have not worked well (25). Despite this high ratio of expressors, we have little control on the level of expression of the foreign

genes. In the 23 animals described here, the circulating level of hGH in serum ranged from 10 to 64,000 ng/ml in the absence of exogenous heavy metals (Table 1). Some of this variability might result from the number of integrated genes, but the site of integration probably has the most profound effect. These results are similar to those observed with integrated viral genomes (26), but they contrast with the relative uniformity of expression of genes introduced into *Drosophila* by P element vectors (27). These differences might relate to either the different mechanisms of gene commitment in flies and mice (for example, DNA methylation) or to an important role of the P element itself in promoting gene expression in a uniform manner (perhaps by preventing encroachment of neighboring chromatin influences). Development of a comparable vector for mammalian gene transfer would clearly be advantageous. Nevertheless, the current methods allow some insight into the role of chromatin position on gene expression because in each animal the insertion site is different.

The high level of expression of MThGH genes in some animals allows quantitation of mRNA concentrations in various tissues of transgenic animals. Transgenic mice expressing herpesvirus thymidine kinase have been unsatisfactory for these studies because the concentration of thymidine kinase mRNA is too low to quantitate in most tissues (8). For this study, we deliberately chose four animals with high levels of circulating hGH. These four animals showed similar high levels of MThGH mRNA in the liver, but lower, variable levels of MThGH mRNA in other tissues. Considering the mass of these tissues relative to the pituitary, it is not surprising that the circulating hGH was high, averaging 4400 ng/ml prior to treatment with cadmium. The data in Table 3 show that expression of the MThGH genes is particularly favored in the liver, testis, and heart, since the ratios of MThGH mRNA to the endogenous MT-I reference mRNA are highest in these tissues. This might be due to a higher percentage of responsive cells, establishment of more efficient chromatin structure, higher levels of proteins that enhance transcription, or greater stability of the fusion mRNA in these tissues. Superimposed on a hierarchy of expression in different tissues, there are some striking departures which are attributed to tissue specific position effects. For example, if the foreign genes were integrated near a locus that was normally activated only in the kidney, then we might expect an unusually high level of MThGH expression in the kidney.

One particularly bothersome aspect of our results is that there is a poor relation between gene dosage and the level of expression. A simple explanation (that is unfortunately hard to prove) is that only one or a few genes in the tandem arrays (8, 14) are actually expressed. If these favored genes were at the ends of the arrays then they would be subject to neighboring chromatin influences. If, on the other hand, all genes within the array were expressed equally, it would be harder to explain the position effects because some of these arrays are hundreds of kilobases long and the genes in the middle of these arrays would be expected to have an identical environment. These considerations suggest that the use of longer DNA fragments, rather than the minimal fragments employed here which have only 400 bp of MT-I gene sequence, might effectively isolate the individual genes in the tandem arrays and thereby result in better gene dosage relationships and less influence of neigh-boring chromatin.

Another feature of MThGH fusion genes that is documented here is that in all animals tested the level of hepatic MThGH mRNA or serum hGH increased in response to $CdSO_4$ or $ZnSO_4$ administration (Table 1). In similar studies we have shown that $CdSO_4$ increases the rate of transcription from MTrGH genes (16). Thus, it appears that these MT fusion genes respond to heavy metals like their endogenous MT-I gene counterparts and proves that this transcriptional response does not depend on MT structural gene sequences or chromosomal location.

Figure 3 shows that rapid growth of transgenic mice is heritable. This is not surprising in view of our parallel studies in which we have shown that MTrGH fusion genes are transmitted in a Mendelian manner to half of the offspring during two generations and that all of the mice that inherit the MTrGH fusion gene grow two to three times faster than their normal littermates (16).

It is clear that transgenic animals generated by microinjection of foreign genes into fertilized eggs provide access to a number of important developmental, genetic, and endocrine questions. We are in the process of generating a homozygous line of giant mice on the C57 background. These mice should provide a valuable resource for analysis of gene inheritance and expression as well as the consequences of excess GH production on various physiological processes.

References and Notes

1. P. Brazeau *et al.*, *Science* **179**, 77 (1973); J. Rivier, J. Spiess, M. Thorner, W. Vale, *Nature (London)* **300**, 276 (1982).
2. L. C. Terry *et al.*, *Clin. Endocrinol.* **6**, 195 (1977); S. Eden, *Endocrinology* **105**, 555 (1979).

3. J. A. Gustafssen, A. Mode, G. Norstedt, P. Skett, *Annu. Rev. Physiol.* **44**, 51 (1983).
4. W. H. Daughaday, K. Hall, M. S. Raben, W. D. Salmon, Jr., J. L. Van den Brande, J. J. Van Wyk, *Nature (London)* **235**, 107 (1972).
5. E. Schoenle, J. Zapf, R. E. Humbel, E. R. Froesch, *ibid.* **296**, 252 (1982); D. G. Klapper, M. E. Svoboda, J. J. Van Wyk, *Endocrinology* **112**, 2215 (1983).
6. J. J. Van Wyk *et al.*, *Recent Prog. Horm. Res.* **30**, 259 (1974); J. Zapf, E. R. Froesch, R. E. Humbel, *Curr. Top. Cell Res.* **19**, 257 (1981).
7. R. D. Palmiter *et al.*, *Nature (London)* **300**, 611 (1982).
8. R. L. Brinster *et al.*, *Cell* **27**, 223 (1981).
9. J. H. R. Kägi and M. Nordberg, *Metallothionein* (Birhäuser Verlag, Basel, 1979).
10. R. L. Brinster, H. Y. Chen, R. Warren, A. Sarthy, R. D. Palmiter, *Nature (London)* **296**, 39 (1982).
11. G. Barsh, P. Seeburg, R. Gelinas, *Nucleic Acids Res.* **11**, 3939 (1983).
12. P. H. Seeburg, *DNA* **1**, 239 (1982).
13. N. Glanville, D. M. Durnam, R. D. Palmiter, *Nature (London)* **292**, 267 (1981).
14. R. D. Palmiter, H. Y. Chen, R. L. Brinster, *Cell* **29**, 701 (1982).
15. Y. N. Sinha, F. W. Selby, U. J. Lewis, W. P. Vanderlaan, *Endocrinology* **91**, 784 (1972); A. C. Herrington, D. Harrison, J. Graystone, *ibid.* **112**, 2032 (1983).
16. N. C. Birnberg *et al.*, in preparation.
17. W. Slidders, *J. Pathol. Bacteriol.* **82**, 532 (1961).
18. W. G. Beamer and E. M. Eicher, *J. Endocrinol.* **71**, 37 (1976).
19. D. M. Durnam and R. D. Palmiter, *Anal. Biochem.* **131**, 385 (1983).
20. P. H. Seeburg *et al.*, *Cell* **12**, 157 (1977).
21. D. M. Durnam and R. D. Palmiter, *J. Biol. Chem.* **256**, 5712 (1981).
22. P. H. Seeburg, J. Shine, J. A. Martial, J. D. Baxter, H. M. Goodman, *Nature (London)* **270**, 486 (1977).
23. A. Jost, *Contrib. Gynec. Obstet.* **5**, 1 (1979); A. T. Holder, M. Wallis, P. Biggs, M. A. Preece, *J. Endocrinol.* **85**, 35 (1980).
24. T. W. Hurley, A. J. D'Ercole, S. Handwerger, L. E. Underwood, R. W. Furlanto, R. E. Fellows, *Endocrinology* **101**, 1635 (1977); S. O. Adams, S. P. Nissley, S. Handwerger, M. M. Rechler, *Nature (London)* **302**, 150 (1983).
25. C. Lau, Y. W. Kan, R. L. Brinster, R. D. Palmiter, unpublished observations.
26. S. C. Feinstein, S. R. Ross, K. R. Yamamoto, *J. Mol. Biol.* **156**, 549 (1982).
27. A. C. Spradling and G. M. Rubin, *Cell* **34**, 47 (1983); S. B. Scholnick, B. A. Morgan, J. Hirsh, *ibid.*, p. 37; D. A. Goldberg, J. W. Posakony, T. Maniatis, *ibid.*, p. 39.
28. E. M. Spencer, *J. Clin. Endocrinol. Metab.* **50**, 182 (1980).
29. C. Labarca and K. Paigen, *Anal. Biochem.* **102**, 322 (1980).
30. G. L. Humason, *Animal Tissue Techniques* (Freeman, San Francisco, ed. 3, 1972), p. 16.
31. We thank M. Trumbauer and M. Yagle for technical assistance, A. Dudley for secretarial help, and G. Barsh, G. Stuart, and T. Roush for preparing various DNA subclones used for these studies. We also thank E. M. Spencer (Children's Hospital, San Francisco) for performing the radioreceptor assays of IGF-I and C. Quaife and M. Wilhyde for help with histology. G.N. was supported by the Swedish Medical Research Council. The research was funded in part by grants from the National Institutes of Health (HD-07155, HD-09172, HD-17321, and AM-31322), the National Science Foundation (PCM-81-07172), and the American Heart Association (80-728).

36. Introduction of Genetic Material into Plant Cells

A. Caplan, L. Herrera-Estrella, D. Inzé, E. Van Haute
M. Van Montagu, J. Schell, P. Zambryski

Many techniques have been proposed for the transfer of DNA to plants such as direct DNA uptake, microinjection of pure DNA, and the use of viral vectors. To date, the simplest and most successful method has made use of the natural gene vector system of *Agrobacterium tumefaciens*.

Agrobacterium tumefaciens is a soil microorganism that is capable of infecting a broad assortment of dicotyledonous plants after they have been wounded (*1*). As a result of this infection, the wound tissue begins to proliferate as a neoplastic growth commonly referred to as a crown gall tumor. Once induced, the tumors no longer require the presence of bacteria to continue growing (*2*). Among the most important of the new properties of these transformed cells are first, that they can grow axenically in vitro without the hormone supplements normally required by plant cell cultures, and second, that they can synthesize a variety of compounds unique to tumors. The latter compounds, which are termed opines, can be metabolized specifically by the bacteria responsible for inciting the tumor (*3*).

The genes responsible for hormone-independent growth, for the ability to induce opine biosynthesis, and for the ability to metabolize opines are all encoded by the tumor-inducing (Ti) plasmid of *A. tumefaciens* (*4–6*). A specific portion of the Ti plasmid, the T-DNA, is transferred from the plasmid to the nucleus of a susceptible plant host (*7*). There the DNA is integrated into plant chromosomes as a unit with discrete end points (*8, 9*), which contains the genes responsible for opine biosynthesis and for tumor growth (*5, 6, 10–12*).

We discuss here some of the recent experiments that indicate (i) how DNA might be transferred from the bacterium to the plant, (ii) which sequences are involved in the integration of plasmid DNA into the plant chromosome, and (iii) how the integrated DNA appears to influence the growth properties of the infected cell. On the basis of data from these experiments it has been possible to transform the Ti plasmid into a simple and reliable gene-transfer vector and to use this vector to investigate tumorigenesis and to introduce prototypes of genes that may be used to investigate the genetic control of plant development. These techniques may form the basis for new developments in research on agriculturally important plant species.

Ti Plasmid Sequences

Essential for Tumor Formation

Agrobacteria that have been cured of their Ti plasmid no longer induce tumors (*13*); thus the first attempts to determine the identity and location of the genes responsible for tumorigenesis concentrated on the Ti plasmid. By means of transposon mutagenesis (*5, 6, 10*) and, more recently, by analysis of the effects of substantial deletion mutations (*14, 15*), it has been possible to demonstrate that the Ti plasmid contains two distinct and separate regions that are essential to produce transformed cells (Fig. 1).

The first region, the T-DNA, contains all of the Ti plasmid sequences found in most established tumor lines. In some plasmids, for example pTiA6NC, pTiAch5, and pTiB6S3, this region is divided into two adjacent independently acting DNA segments (*9*), one of 13.6 kilobases (left T-DNA) and one of approximately 7 kb (right T-DNA). A characteristic of this type of plasmid is that one of the genes of the left T-DNA encodes the synthase for one of the opines, octopine (*16*). Other plasmids, for example, pTiT37 or pTiC58, transfer a single T-DNA of 23 kb (*8*) which carries the gene encoding the synthase for nopaline, another opine (*5, 17*). Both T-DNA's have been studied extensively to identify the functions responsible for tumor formation and for transfer to plants.

The T-DNA's from both classes of Ti plasmids encode a variety of polyadenylated transcripts (*18*), six of which map in a common 9-kb DNA segment (*19*). These six transcripts are arranged in the order 5, 2, 1, 4, 6a, 6b across the T-DNA region (Fig. 2). Throughout this chapter, T-DNA genes will be referred to by the

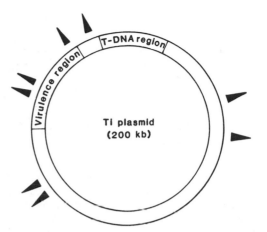

Fig. 1. Schematic diagram of the Ti plasmid. The relative locations of the two portions of the nopaline Ti plasmid that govern tumor formation are indicated as the virulence and T-DNA regions. The triangles surrounding the plasmid show the approximate locations of oncogenes that have been inserted in a plasmid that lacks the oncogenes of the normal T-DNA region (*38*).

number given to their transcript, for example, gene *1* encodes transcript 1. Mutations in the nonhomologous regions of the two types of T-DNA, and in the genes for transcripts 5, 6a, and 6b, have either no or limited influence on tumor formation (*11, 12, 20*).

Three of the genes of the common DNA appear to be directly responsible for tumor formation. Normal crown gall tumors are unorganized, whereas tumors obtained from mutants containing insertions in gene *4* (the Roi locus) allow root formation on most of the plants on which they are tested (*11, 20, 21*). Tumors induced by mutants of genes *1* or *2* (the Shi locus) grow as green calli that sprout both normal and malformed shoots (*11, 12, 20, 21*). In analogy to what is known about plant growth regulators, the effect

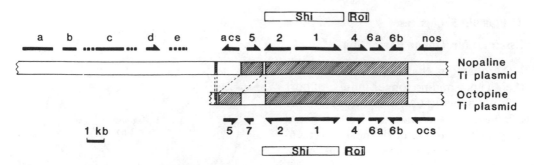

Fig. 2. The genetic organization of the T-DNA's of nopaline and octopine Ti plasmids. The nomenclature and locations of the polyadenylated transcripts are shown as either bars or arrows according to whether the direction of transcription is known (*18*). The upper T-DNA is characteristic of the pTiC58 T-DNA which contains the genes for nopaline synthase (*nos*) and the synthase for an opine, agrocinopine (*acs*). The lower T-DNA is characteristic of pTiB6S3 which encodes octopine synthase or *ocs*. The hatched areas mark the regions of homology (common DNA) between the two T-DNA's (*19*). The box with the abbreviation *Shi* indicates which transcripts control shoot inhibition; *Roi* indicates the transcript that controls root inhibition. The ends of the T-DNA that are used in integration into plant genomes are presented as jagged lines.

of gene *4* can be thought of as "cytokinin-like," so that inactivating it might result in a low cytokinin to auxin ratio, and hence, to root formation. Similarly, the combined effects of genes *1* and *2* can be thought of as "auxin-like," since mutations in either gene appear to increase the cytokinin to auxin ratio of tumors, and this might in turn lead to shoot formation (*21, 22*). Therefore, the undifferentiated appearance of a crown gall tumor and its ability to grow without exogenous hormones must reflect the combined activities of the products of genes *1*, *2*, and *4*. Some support for this model comes from studies on growth of Shi⁻ or Roi⁻ tumors (Fig. 2) in vitro. It has been found that tobacco tumors induced by T-DNA mutants in gene *4* require cytokinin in vitro for optimal growth (*20, 23*). Similarly, tobacco tumors induced by T-DNA mutants in the Shi locus are auxin-dependent in tissue culture unless they can form sufficient shootlike structures to manufacture the necessary auxin (*24*).

The second portion of the Ti plasmid containing sequences essential for tumor formation has been termed the virulence or *vir* region (Fig. 1) in order to distinguish the genes encoded there from the oncogenes of the T-DNA. The DNA sequences of the *vir* region have not been found in established tumor lines, and therefore are not essential for tumor maintenance (*8, 9, 25*).

These functions were studied in greater detail by transposon insertion mutagenesis of the *vir* region of an octopine Ti plasmid (*26, 27*). Each avirulent mutation in the *vir*-region was tested for its ability to be complemented *in trans* in the bacterium by overlapping cosmid clones carrying other *vir* insertion mutations. These results demonstrated that the *vir* functions are organized into at least ten independent complementation groups.

It is not clear how the *vir* functions contribute to the formation of crown gall tumors. A number of mutations have been identified that markedly reduce the specific affinity of *Agrobacterium* cells for plant cells, but all of these map to the bacterial chromosome (*28*), and it is possible that the Ti plasmid does not play a major role in the formation of these sorts of contacts (*28, 29*). Furthermore, *vir* mutants cannot complement each other when coinfected on the same wound (*27*). This indicates that none of the products of the *vir* functions is readily diffusible between bacteria.

Recent experiments have indicated that the T and *vir* regions act as physically self-contained units. For these studies, the genes of each region were cloned on independent replicons. It was found that neither region was oncogenic by itself, but that the two together complemented each other to stimulate tumor formation (*30*). Moreover, plasmids containing the T region of a nopaline plasmid (pTiT37 or pTiC58) complements the *vir* region of an octopine plasmid (pTiAch5 or pTiB6S3) and vice versa, demonstrating that neither set of genes contains oncogenic functions specific to one class of plasmid (*14*).

Transfer of the T-DNA from *Agrobacterium* to Plant Cells

The interaction between *Agrobacterium* and plant cells sets in motion a chain of events that ultimately transfers the T-DNA from the Ti plasmid into the plant nuclear DNA. To discuss how this transfer occurs, one must first point out which portions of the Ti plasmid are associated with the integrated DNA and which portions may be essential for transfer to the plant.

There is little variation in the ends of the T-DNA from different tumor cell lines analyzed to date. In all cases, the homology between sequences present in the Ti plasmid and those in the tumor DNA ends within, or proximal to, a 25-base pair "terminal sequence" (Fig. 3) that flanks the T region of the plasmid as direct (albeit, imperfect) repeats (*31–34*). The T-DNA borders occur one base before or at the first base pair of the right copy of this sequence in at least three different tumor lines (*31, 34*). The left border of the integrated T-DNA seems to be more variable than the right, but nonetheless occurs within 100 bp of the left 25-bp sequence (*31, 33*).

Extensive deletions have been made at each of the ends of the T region in order to determine whether each end is functionally equivalent to the other. A deletion of the right end makes the T region virtually avirulent on most plant species (*5, 20, 35*). By contrast, deletions of the left end have no apparent effect on the tumor-forming ability of the T region

G C T G G	T G G C A G G A T A T A T T G	T G	G T G T A A A C	A A A T T	Nopaline L
G T G T T	T G A C A G G A T A T A T T G	G C	G G G T A A A C	C T A A G	Nopaline R
A G C G G	C G G C A G G A T A T A T T C	A A	T T G T A A A T	G G C T T	Octopine L
C T G A C	T G G C A G G A T A T A T A C	C G	T T G T A A T T	T G A G C	Octopine R

Fig. 3. Comparison of the 25-bp terminal sequence at the T-DNA borders of the nopaline and octopine Ti plasmids. The box indicates the homology between the terminal sequences flanking the (*L*, left; *R*, right) T-DNA regions of nopaline pTiC58 (or pTiT37) and octopine pTiB6S3 Ti plasmids (*31–34*). The two bases at positions 16 and 17 that are not conserved among the four sequences are also enclosed.

(20). In fact, recent experiments show that a clone containing only the nopaline synthase (*nos*) gene and the right border is fully capable of transferring the *nos* gene to the plant when it is inserted in the *vir* region of a Ti plasmid or when it is part of a free replicon that is complemented by a Ti plasmid in *Agrobacterium* (36). Since a "terminal sequence" is closely associated with normal T-DNA ends and also with the end of an unusually short T-DNA (37), it is thought important for T-DNA integration. It is likely that there are related sequences elsewhere on the plasmid that can substitute for the end that is missing in these mutated T regions.

The observations on the differences between the ends of the T region can be interpreted in at least two ways. One is to assume that the requirements for integration are more stringent for the right end of the T-DNA than for the left. The other is to propose that the requirements for integration are similar but that the right end contains another function, such as a transit sequence that directs the transfer of adjacent DNA to plants.

There are also two hypotheses concerning the actual process of T-DNA transfer. One possibility is that the T region separates at the borders from the remainder of the plasmid during the normal course of infection and enters the plant cell alone. Alternatively, the whole Ti plasmid might enter the plant cell and be lost later, after the T-DNA has entered a host chromosome. The latter proposition has been tested by use of a unique set of plasmids (38). These are derived from a nononcogenic mutant (pGV3850) of the plasmid pTiC58 which lacks the *onc* genes present in the central core of the T-DNA (Fig. 4). This plasmid still contains both ends of the T-DNA region required for transfer and integration of DNA into plants as well as the gene for the synthesis of the opine nopaline (39). Next, a clone containing the oncogenes but lacking the left and right ends of the T-DNA region was inserted into eight different sites (Fig. 1) around the map of this nononcogenic Ti plasmid. Five of the eight aberrantly reconstituted plasmids (those that do not have insertions that inactivate *vir* genes) induce tumors, although not as efficiently as normal plasmids (38). In contrast, when the oncogenes and the nononcogenic Ti plasmid are maintained as separate replicons, no tumors can be produced.

The interpretation of these observations is that the genes of the central core of the T-region can induce tumors but cannot promote their own transfer or stabilization in plant cells. Consequently, these genes enter the plant only when linked to a plasmid containing transfer or integration sequences, or both. The new location of the oncogenes appears to be unimportant, suggesting that most, if not all, of the Ti plasmid might be able to enter cells of the plant host. It is possible, however, that transfer of sequences outside of the normal T region borders represents errors in discrimination by the transfer apparatus. Such rare events would be amplified by the very nature of tumorous growth to the point where they can be seen. These results are notable, but further tests are warranted to determine whether the whole of the Ti plasmid enters the plant cell during the course of normal infection.

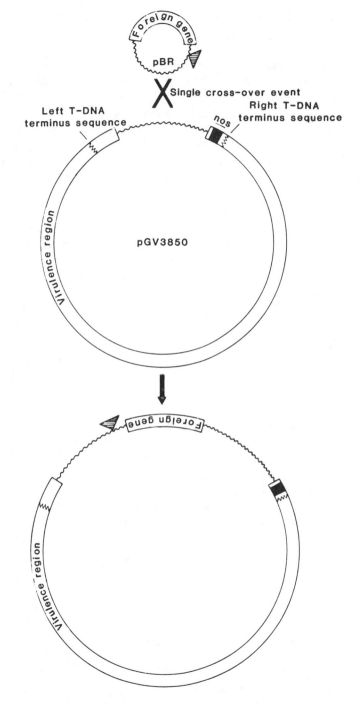

Fig. 4. Ti plasmid vector pGV3850, an acceptor for foreign genes whose expression is to be monitored in whole plants. The structure of Ti plasmid vector pGV3850 (*39*) is diagramed. It contains all Ti plasmid sequences (shown in white) except for the internal oncogenes of the T-DNA. The oncogenes have been replaced by pBR322 (shown as a wavy line). Only the *nos* gene (indicated in black) as well as the T-DNA border terminal sequences (indicated by jagged lines) of the T-DNA region remain. A foreign gene of interest cloned in a pBR-type plasmid can be inserted into pGV3850 by a single recombination event through the homologous pBR sequences. The hatched triangle indicates an additional antibiotic resistance marker gene other than ampicillin resistance in order to select for the recombination event. Recombination between homologous pBR regions results in the relative reversal of the foreign gene in the cointegrate structure seen below.

Design of a Vector for Foreign DNA Transfer

Although the exact role of the T region terminal sequences requires further study, there is no doubt that the T-DNA can transfer to the plant genome in a predictable and rather precise manner. Furthermore, it has been possible to increase the size of the T-DNA by at least 14 kb through the insertion of foreign DNA without affecting transfer (40), and it is likely that even larger DNA inserts can be transferred equally well. Current research is focused on the design of modified Ti plasmid derivatives that will be useful for genetic engineering of plants. There are two major characteristics that need to be incorporated into these new Ti vectors: (i) they must allow efficient DNA transfer to plant cells without interfering with normal plant growth and development, and (ii) they must allow foreign DNA to be inserted easily in between the terminal sequences flanking the T-region.

Recently, such a Ti plasmid vector was constructed (39). pGV3850 is a non-oncogenic derivative of the nopaline Ti plasmid C58. This vector utilizes the natural transfer properties of the Ti plasmids and has the following characteristics: (i) the T-DNA border regions and all the contiguous Ti plasmid sequences outside the T-DNA-region; (ii) the DNA near the right T-DNA border encoding nopaline synthase as a marker for transformed cells; and (iii) the internal T-DNA genes that determine the undifferentiated crown gall phenotype have been deleted and are replaced by the commonly used cloning vehicle, pBR322. The pBR322 sequence contained between the T-DNA border regions serves as a region of homology for recombination to introduce foreign DNA's cloned in pBR322

derivatives. The structure of pGV3850 as well as its use as an acceptor plasmid are shown in Fig. 4.

The use of this system involves straightforward genetic techniques: a single cross-over event between the pBR322 region of pGV3850 and the pBR region of the plasmid carrying the gene of interest produces a cointegrated plasmid that can be used to transform plants. The direct mobilization of plasmids containing pBR sequences from *Escherichia coli* to *Agrobacterium* is possible because of the recent progress in the use of helper plasmids able to mobilize and transfer pBR (41). As pBR itself cannot replicate in *Agrobacterium*, the only way in which it can be maintained is by recombination with the homologous region in the Ti plasmid. As shown in Fig. 4, the cointegrated structure contains a duplication of the pBR sequences; however, this apparently does not lead to instability. The cointegrate can be maintained in *Agrobacterium* by including and selecting for a drug resistance marker other than ampicillin in the pBR vehicle containing the foreign gene. It is unlikely that the cointegrate will be unstable in the plant cell as the plant genome is composed of much repeated DNA, including, at times, the T-DNA itself which can be present in tandem copies (8, 34).

We have studied the transformation of plant cells with pGV3850 and have demonstrated that the shortened T-DNA can be efficiently transferred to several plant species including tobacco, petunia, carrot, and potato. Furthermore, in vitro cocultivation of tobacco protoplasts with *Agrobacterium* containing either wild-type Ti plasmid or pGV3850 yields transformed cells at the same frequency (42). Using infected tobacco as a model system, we were able to regenerate plants containing the T-DNA of pGV3850 and to confirm the structure of this T-DNA by Southern hybridization. These results are the first demonstration that the T-DNA borders alone are sufficient to allow transfer and stably integrate the DNA contained between the borders.

The presence of the nopaline synthase (nos) gene in this vector makes it easy to monitor the efficiency of transformation using pGV3850. For example, several independent tobacco plantlets were inoculated with pGV3850. The tissue at the site of inoculation was removed, propagated as callus in tissue culture, and then tested for the presence of nopaline; 25 percent of the calli were nos positive. These calli, which contained a mixture of transformed and untransformed cells, were then transferred to a medium that induces plant regeneration. Between 9 and 78 percent of the regenerated plants derived from different nos-positive calli contained nopaline, indicating that transformation was remarkably efficient.

Use of pGV3850 to Study the Genes Involved in Tumorigenesis

The following experiments demonstrate the usefulness of the plasmid vector pGV3850 and prove that genes can be transferred and stably maintained in the plant cell genome by means of this system. The genes chosen were those of the T-DNA region itself that encode functions that induce tumors. In the first experiment the entire region of the T-DNA that is responsible for the wild-type tumor phenotype was cloned in a pBR-derived plasmid, and recombined into the pBR322-region of pGV3850 (39). Agrobacteria containing this cointegrate have been used to infect plants and have produced wild-type tumors. This tissue

is stable in vitro, contains nopaline synthase activity, and has been growing as a tumor for over 10 months.

In a second series of experiments, pBR-derived clones of each of the individual T-DNA oncogenes have been recombined with pGV3850 (43). These experiments were designed to analyze the contribution of each onc gene to the development of a tumor and have fulfilled two purposes. First, they have demonstrated that the T-DNA genes 1, 2, and 4 can be expressed independently of all other genes, and second, that only gene 4 can induce tumors by itself. In order to do this, specific T-DNA fragments in a pBR vehicle were introduced into the T region of pGV3850. Strains carrying each construction were coinfected on the same wound with a strain carrying a T-region insertion mutation. These experiments demonstrated that Ti plasmids that could transfer only gene 1 to plants could complement the Shi⁻ phenotype of a strain with a mutation in gene 1. Similarly, plasmids that could transfer only gene 2 could complement a strain with a mutation in gene 2. Neither gene 1 nor gene 2 could induce tumors by themselves, but coinfections of a strain carrying only gene 1 with another strain carrying only gene 2 produce small tumors on tobacco. Strains carrying gene 4 produced tumors without the aid of other T-DNA genes; in vitro these tumors produce shoots.

These experiments together with those discussed earlier indicate that there are two separate pathways of tumorigenesis: one is a shoot-suppressing and root-stimulating (auxin-like) pathway encoded by genes 1 and 2, and the other is a root-suppressing, shoot-stimulating (cytokinin-like) pathway encoded by gene 4. As techniques are developed to modulate the levels of expression of these genes, for example, by putting them under the control of inducible promoters, it is hoped that further insight about the mechanism of action of T-DNA genes can be gained.

Development of Systems to Express Genes in Plants

One of the major goals in the use of *Agrobacterium* is to take advantage of its natural properties in order to introduce and express new genes in plants. The first successful attempts to introduce foreign DNA into plant cells were done with bacterial transposons. Tn7 (*40*) and Tn5 (*11*) were inserted in vivo into the T-DNA of Ti plasmids pTiT37 and pTiA6NC, respectively, and were found to be efficiently cotransferred with the T-DNA. The genes encoded by these transposons failed to be expressed, presumably because the eukaryotic transcriptional machinery of the plant did not recognize the promoter sequences of these prokaryotic genes. Further attempts to express heterologous eukaryotic genes, such as the yeast alcohol dehydrogenase gene (*23*) or genes from mammalian cells, such as β-globin (*44*), interferon (*45*), and genes under control of the SV40 early promoter (*46*), showed that none of these genes was transcribed in plant cells. This suggests that specific transcription factors or signals that are required for their expression are present only in the cells or specific tissues of their original hosts.

It became obvious that the first step for the expression of heterologous genes in plants would require the use of transcriptional signals from a gene that is known to be functional in plants. So far, only a few sets of genes have been isolated, and most of these are highly regulated or specific for only a particular stage of the plant. For example, the leghemoglobin (*47*) or zein (*48*) and phaseolin (*49*) gene families are expressed only in either *Rhizobium*-induced nodules or in plant seeds, respectively. One of the best candidates to be used as a donor of transcriptional signals was the *nos* gene. It is known that this gene is normally expressed both in callus tissue and in most of the plant tissues regenerated from calli containing the opine gene (*50*).

The nucleotide sequence of *nos* (*51*) reveals that its controlling signals share most of the characteristics of other plant genes in particular (*52*), and of other eukaryotic genes in general (*53*). At the 5′ end, the *nos* gene contains sequences homologous to the TATA or Hogness box, 35 bp upstream of the start of transcription, and a sequence similar to the AGGA box consensus sequence for plant genes 60 to 80 bp upstream of the 5′ end of the transcript. At the 3′ end, it has the sequences AATAAA and AATAAT, approximately 135 and 50 bp from the polyadenylation site, which strongly resemble the consensus sequence similarly placed in animal genes (*53*). It is worth mentioning that most of the T-DNA genes seem to lack introns (*37, 51, 54*). This, however, is not exceptional since there are other plant genes that lack introns, such as the maize zein gene family (*48*).

A series of expression vectors has been constructed containing the promoter and terminator signals for transcription of the *nos* gene; in between these signals are unique restriction sites for the insertion of any desired coding sequence (*55, 56*). One of these vectors was first used to express a homologous gene, the T-DNA–encoded octopine synthase gene, and a heterologous gene, the bacterial chloramphenicol acetyltransferase gene from the plasmid vector pBR325 (55, 57). In both cases the *nos* promoter and termination signals are enough to produce a transcript that is recognized by the translation machinery of the plant cells to produce an active protein. This constitutes the first example of the expression of a foreign protein in plant cells.

As demonstrated for bacterial and mammalian cells, one of the first steps to the development of efficient transformation systems is the construction of dominant selectable markers. These allow cells that have acquired new genes via transformation to be selected and identified easily. For this reason, vectors based on the *nos* regulatory signal were tested for their ability to express bacterial genes that encode resistance to antibiotics, such as G418, kanamycin, or methotrexate, which are highly toxic to plant cells. By means of these chimeric genes it was demonstrated that the proteins encoded by the aminoglycoside phosphotransferase II (APH II) from Tn5 (56, 58, 59), aminoglycoside phosphotransferase I (APH I) from Tn903 (59), or the dihydrofolate reductase that is methotrexate-insensitive from R67 (56) can be used to confer to plant cells resistance to kanamycin, G418, or methotrexate, respectively. In each case, the chimeric genes were transferred via the Ti plasmid to plant cells by an in vitro transformation technique. In this protocol, protoplasts that are undergoing cell wall regeneration are incubated with *A. tumefaciens* for 14 to 30 hours and then treated with antibiotics to kill the bacteria. After 1 to 2 weeks, small fast-growing plant cell colonies can be exposed to selective medium containing 50 to 100 μg of kanamycin per milliliter (56, 58, 59).

These experiments have shown that four different bacterial coding sequences are properly expressed and translated into active proteins in plant cells. Thus, the codon usage for the plant translation machinery may allow expression of any other bacterial, fungal, or mammalian gene, including those which could confer a useful trait to plant cells. At the same time, it is important to consider that there are not enough data to know whether all foreign proteins will be stable in plant cells once they are synthesized, especially if they are to be produced on a large scale.

These results demonstrate that the Ti plasmid can be used to transfer and express genes in plants. Now more sophisticated studies of gene regulation can be attempted. For example, one of the most exciting areas in plant biology is the study of how factors such as light regulate genes. Several members of the gene families involved with photosynthesis have been isolated, notably the families encoding the small subunit (ss) of the ribulose bisphosphate carboxylase (60, 61) and the chlorophyll-binding protein (62). The *ss* gene product participates in CO_2 fixation and the conversion of CO_2 into carbohydrates by using the energy obtained during photosynthesis with the aid of the chlorophyll-binding protein.

The expression of these two gene families has been shown to be light-induced at the transcriptional level in green tissue (60, 61). It is interesting to determine whether this type of light-regulated gene is controlled by the sequences 5' to the promoter or by sequences in another part of this gene. Recently, a chimeric gene was constructed containing 900 bp of the promoter region of a small subunit gene isolated from pea (61), coupled to the CAT coding sequence from Tn9 and the 3' end sequence of the *nos* gene (63). This chimeric gene was introduced into tobacco cells by using the Ti plasmid as a vector, and the light regulation of the CAT activity was assayed in green tissues. The 900 bp of the 5' upstream region of the *ss* gene are sufficient to confer light-inducible expression of the CAT coding sequence (*63*). This finding constitutes the first evidence that the regulation of a plant gene is determined by sequences upstream of its promoter and, additionally, that a promoter from one plant species (pea) can function in the cells of another plant (tobacco).

One of the ultimate aims in the use of the Ti plasmids of *Agrobacterium* as a tool for studying gene expression in plants is to obtain fully differentiated plants that express sequences introduced by means of the Ti plasmid. This has recently been achieved (*64*) by inserting the NOS-APH(II) chimeric gene into the vector pGV3850 via homologous recombination through pBR322. Kanamycin-resistant colonies were obtained after in vitro transformation of tobacco protoplasts with *Agrobacterium* containing pGV3850::NOS-APH(II). The calli were grown in vitro until the tissue was axenic and were then transferred to medium containing a ratio of plant phytohormones that promotes plant regeneration. In contrast to calli induced with the wild-type Ti plasmids that are unable to differentiate in this medium, the kanamycin-resistant tissue transformed with pGV3850::NOS-APH(II) is able to produce shoots that later also form normal roots. In order to demonstrate that the regenerates retain the introduced marker functions, the top shoots of these plants were transferred to medium containing 100 μg of kanamycin per milliliter. They were able to form roots and maintain normal growth. In contrast, the top shoots of normal tobacco plants are not capable of root formation, and eventually die on kanamycin-containing medium.

Prospectives

The experiments presented here not only emphasize the effectiveness of the Ti plasmid as a vector for transfer of foreign genes to plants but also its potential to study the expression and regulation of the transferred genes. Future experiments will lead to a better understanding of how the T-DNA is transferred as well as how it carries out its biological effects. These studies will undoubtedly allow the design of improved Ti plasmid vectors.

For example, there is much interest in a binary system consisting of a modified T-DNA on one plasmid and the Ti-specific functions of the *vir* region on another. Initial experiments have shown that this system can transfer the oncogenic functions of the T-DNA region to plants (*30*). It is now necessary to show that a nononcogenic T-DNA derivative containing only the border regions can also be transferred efficiently to plant cells. The drawback of this system is that a wide host range replicon must be used in order to maintain the T-DNA as a separate plasmid in both *E. coli* (where cloning can be done easily) and *Agrobacterium*. Such replicons are often large and contain multiple restriction sites; a functional T-DNA–replicon vehicle should be as small as possible to provide unique restriction sites suitable for cloning DNA.

Although we have limited our discussion of DNA vectors to use of the Ti plasmid system, there are other possible candidates. Cauliflower mosaic virus (*65*) has been studied extensively since it can infect leaves in situ and later move systematically throughout the entire plant. This system is surely limited both in its host range and in its ability to transfer more than 500 bp of foreign DNA (66), but it may be of more practical value as a source of DNA regulatory sequences in constructions to be transferred and expressed in plants. Geminiviruses (67) have recently attracted attention since they are pathogens of a wide variety of plants including legumes and cereals and thus are potential candidates to introduce genes into monocotyledonous plants. However, the basic biology of geminiviruses is still being investigated; the genome of such a virus was cloned recently in *E. coli* and its sequence is being determined.

Another possible vector system is modeled on the recent successful use of transposable elements containing foreign DNA as carriers to introduce DNA into *Drosophila* (68). P-elements containing DNA inserts can be injected into *Drosophila* embryos where they integrate at random and are expressed in a tissue-specific developmentally regulated manner. Analogous types of experiments may be possible in plants. There is extensive biological information available on the "behavior" of plant movable elements (69). The Ac/Ds "controlling elements" of corn in particular look promising for adaptation as gene vectors and some of these elements have recently been cloned (70).

It is clear that DNA transfer to plants can be achieved by using existing techniques, and the number of possible vectors will probably increase in the future. We have demonstrated that the Ti plasmid can be used as an effective acceptor plasmid for any foreign DNA sequence, and that plant cells transformed with such a vector are fully capable of growth and differentiation. Thus we can now begin to study aspects of plant biology that are necessary both for basic knowledge and for more applied research. The totipotency of plant cells, in addition to their ability to grow under various environmental conditions, makes them particularly interesting subjects. The successful use of DNA transfer vectors for plants is dependent on advances in two major areas of plant research, namely (i) the isolation of particularly interesting genes and an analysis of their control; and (ii) the improvement of plant tissue culture techniques that will make it possible to study more agronomically important species.

Major efforts will be directed toward the isolation of plant genes that provide fundamental information. For example, an analysis of genes regulated by light is necessary to answer questions basic to the physiology of plants; our experiments indicate that the control regions of such genes are readily amenable to analysis. Additional studies of isolated genes will help define what is required for the transport of gene products to different organelles or for conferring resistance to pathogens or environmental stress.

To date, the major hosts for Ti-mediated DNA transfer experiments have been various species of *Nicotiana* (for example, tobacco). Potatoes (71), carrots (72), and flax (73) have been used to a lesser extent. *Agrobacterium* is known to infect many species throughout the whole spectrum of dicotyledonous plants, although few are amenable to tissue culture techniques. There has been significant progress in the culture of several of the *Brassica* (for example, rapeseed) (74) and *Solanum* (for example, eggplant) (75); however, many other important

492

crop plants, such as the legumes, alfalfa, and soybean cannot yet be propagated easily in tissue culture.

There is no DNA transfer system available for monocotyledonous plants, which include the important cereal food crops. Thus far, the monocotyledons have been resistant to infection by the Ti system of *Agrobacterium*. The barrier to infection may be either the transfer of DNA or the inability of the infected cells to respond in a tumorous fashion. The use of nononcogenic Ti plasmid vectors in combination with new selectable marker genes may eventually help to solve this problem.

In conclusion, the availability of recombinant DNA techniques and the discovery of the Ti plasmid system have opened the plant kingdom to gene transfer experiments. We expect that the techniques outlined here will help to elucidate interesting biological pathways that are unique to plants.

References and Notes

1. A. C. Braun, in *Molecular Biology of Plant Tumors*, G. Kahl and J. Schell, Eds. (Academic Press, New York, 1982), pp. 155–210.
2. A. C. Braun, *Am. J. Bot.* **30**, 674 (1943).
3. A. Goldmann-Ménagé, *Ann. Sci. Nat. Bot.* (12° Sér.) **11**, 233 (1970); B. Lejeune, thesis, CNRS, N° A08029 Paris (1973); A. Petit, thesis, CNRS, Paris (1977); J. Tempé and A. Petit, in *Molecular Biology of Plant Tumors*, G. Kahl and J. Schell, Eds. (Academic Press, New York, 1982), pp. 451–459.
4. I. Zaenen, N. Van Larebeke, H. Teuchy, M. Van Montagu, J. Schell, *J. Mol. Biol.* **86**, 109 (1974); N. Van Larebeke, G. Engler, M. Holsters, S. Van den Elsacker, I. Zaenen, R. A. Schilperoort, J. Schell, *Nature (London)* **252**, 169 (1974); N. Van Larebeke, C. Genetello, J. P. Hernalsteens, A. Depicker, I. Zaenen, E. Messens, M. Van Montagu, J. Schell, *Mol. Gen. Genet.* **152**, 119 (1975); B. Watson, T. C. Currier, M. P. Gordon, M.-D. Chilton, E. W. Nester, *J. Bacteriol.* **123**, 255 (1975).
5. M. Holsters *et al.*, *Plasmid* **3**, 212 (1980).
6. H. De Greve, H. Scraemer, J. Seurinck, M. Van Montagu, J. Schell, *Plasmid* **6**, 235 (1981).
7. M.-D. Chilton, R. K. Saiki, N. Yadav, M. P. Gordon, F. Quetier, *Proc. Natl. Acad. Sci. U.S.A.* **77**, 4060 (1980); L. Willmitzer, M. De Beuckeleer, M. Lemmers, M. Van Montagu, J. Schell, *Nature (London)* **287**, 359 (1980).
8. M. Lemmers *et al.*, *J. Mol. Biol.* **144**, 353 (1980); P. Zambryski *et al.*, *Science* **209**, 1385 (1980).
9. M. F. Thomashow, R. Nutter, A. L. Montoya, M. P. Gordon, E. W. Nester, *Cell* **19**, 729 (1980); M. De Beuckeleer *et al.*, *Mol. Gen. Genet.* **183**, 283 (1981).
10. D. J. Garfinkel and E. W. Nester, *J. Bacteriol.* **144**, 732 (1980).
11. D. J. Garfinkel *et al.*, *Cell* **27**, 143 (1981).
12. J. Leemans *et al.*, *EMBO J.* **1**, 147 (1982).
13. R. H. Hamilton and M. Z. Fall, *Experientia* **27**, 229 (1971); G. Engler *et al.*, *Mol. Gen. Genet.* **138**, 345 (1975).
14. E. Van Haute, unpublished results.
15. J. Hille, I. Klasen, R. A. Schilperoort, *Plasmid* **7**, 107 (1982).
16. J. Schröder, A. Hillebrandt, W. Klipp, A. Pühler, *Nucleic Acids Res.* **9**, 5187 (1981); N. Murai and J. D. Kemp, *Proc. Natl. Acad. Sci. U.S.A.* **79**, 86 (1982).
17. D. W. Sutton, J. D. Kemp, E. Hack, *Plant Physiol.* **62**, 363 (1978).
18. L. Willmitzer, G. Simons, J. Schell, *EMBO J.* **1**, 139 (1982); M. Bevan and M.-D. Chilton, *J. Mol. Appl. Genet.* **1**, 539 (1982); L. Willmitzer *et al.*, *Cell* **32**, 1045 (1983).
19. M.-D. Chilton, M. H. Drummond, D. J. Merlo, D. Sciaky, *Nature (London)* **275**, 147 (1978); A. Depicker, M. Van Montagu, J. Schell, *ibid.*, p. 150; G. Engler, A. Depicker, R. Maenhaut, R. Villarroel-Mandiola, M. Van Montagu, J. Schell, *J. Mol. Biol.* **152**, 183 (1981).
20. H. Joos, D. Inzé, A. Caplan, M. Sormann, M. Van Montagu, J. Schell, *Cell* **32**, 1057 (1983).
21. G. Ooms, P. J. Hooykaas, G. Moleman, R. A. Schilperoort, *Gene* **14**, 33 (1981).
22. R. M. Amasino and C. O. Miller, *Plant Physiol.* **69**, 389 (1982); R. O. Morris *et al.*, in *Plant Growth Substances 1982*, P. F. Wareing, Ed. (Academic Press, London, 1982), pp. 175–183.
23. K. A. Barton, A. N. Binns, A. J. M. Matzke, M.-D. Chilton, *Cell* **32**, 1033 (1983).
24. A. N. Binns, D. Sciaky, H. N. Wood, *ibid.* **31**, 605 (1982).
25. G. Ooms, T. J. G. Regensburg-Tuink, M. H. Hofker, P. J. J. Hooykaas, R. A. Schilperoort, *Plant Mol. Biol.* **1**, 265 (1982).
26. H. J. Klee, M. P. Gordon, E. W. Nester, *J. Bacteriol.* **150**, 327 (1982); H. J. Klee, F. F. White, V. N. Iyer, M. P. Gordon, E. W. Nester, *ibid.*, p. 878.
27. V. N. Iyer, H. J. Klee, E. W. Nester, *Mol. Gen. Genet.* **188**, 418 (1982).
28. C. J. Douglas, W. Halperin, E. W. Nester, *J. Bacteriol.* **152**, 1265 (1982).
29. A. Matthysse, K. V. Holmes, R. H. G. Gurlitz, *ibid.* **145**, 583 (1981).
30. A. J. de Framond, K. A. Barton, M.-D. Chilton, *Bio/Technology* **1**, 262 (1983); A. Hoekema, P. R. Hirsch, P. J. J. Hooykaas, R. A. Schilperoort, *Nature (London)* **303**, 179 (1983).
31. P. Zambryski, A. Depicker, K. Kruger, H. M. Goodman, *J. Mol. Appl. Genet.* **1**, 361 (1982).
32. R. B. Simpson *et al.*, *Cell* **29**, 1005 (1982).
33. N. S. Yadav, J. Vanderleyden, D. R. Bennett, W. M. Barnes, M.-D. Chilton, *Proc. Natl.*

Acad. Sci. U.S.A. **79**, 6322 (1982).
34. M. Holsters *et al.*, *Mol. Gen. Genet.* **190**, 35 (1983).
35. G. Ooms *et al.*, *Plasmid* **7**, 15 (1982).
36. A. Caplan, unpublished results.
37. J. Gielen *et al.*, *EMBO J.* **3**, 835 (1984).
38. H. Joos, B. Timmerman, M. Van Montagu, J. Schell. *EMBO J.* **2**, 2151 (1983).
39. P. Zambryski, H. Joos, C. Genetello, J. Leemans, M. Van Montagu, J. Schell, *ibid.*, p. 2143 (1983).
40. J. P. Hernalsteens *et al.*, *Nature (London)* **287**, 654 (1980); M. Holsters, R. Villarroel, M. Van Montagu, J. Schell, *Mol. Gen. Genet.* **185**, 283 (1982).
41. E. Van Haute *et al.*, *EMBO J.* **2**, 411 (1983).
42. M. De Block, unpublished results.
43. D. Inzé *et al.*, *Mol. Gen. Genet.* **194**, 265 (1984).
44. C. H. Shaw, J. Leemans, C. H. Shaw, M. Van Montagu, J. Schell, *Gene* **23**, 315 (1983).
45. J. Leemans, unpublished results.
46. D. Llewellyn, C. Koncz, L. Willmitzer, L. Herrera-Estrella, J. Schell, in preparation.
47. N. Brisson and D. P. Verma, *Proc. Natl. Acad. Sci. U.S.A.* **79**, 4055 (1982); O. Wiborg, J. Hyldig-Nielsen, E. Jensen, K. Paludan, K. Marcker, *Nucleic Acids Res.* **10**, 3487 (1982).
48. D. Geraghty, M. A. Peifer, I. Rubenstein, J. Messing, *Nucleic Acids Res.* **9**, 5163 (1981); K. Pedersen, J. Devereux, R. D. Wilson, E. Sheldom, B. A. Larkins, *Cell* **29**, 1015 (1982).
49. S. M. Sun, J. L. Slightom, T. C. Hall, *Nature (London)* **289**, 37 (1981).
50. L. Otten *et al.*, *Mol. Gen. Genet.* **183**, 209 (1981); H. De Greve *et al.*, *Nature (London)* **300**, 752 (1982); A. Wöstemeyer *et al.*, in *Genetic Engineering in Eukaryotes*, P. Lurquin and A. Kleinhofs Eds. (Plenum, New York, 1983), pp. 137–151.
51. A. Depicker, S. Stachel, P. Dhaese, P. Zambryski, H. M. Goodman, *J. Mol. Appl. Genet.* **1**, 561 (1982); W. M. Barnes, M. Bevan, M.-D. Chilton, *Nucleic Acids Res.* **11**, 369 (1983).
52. J. Messing, D. Geraghty, G. Heidecker, N.-T. Hu, J. Kridl, I. Rubenstein, in *Genetic Engineering of Plants, An Agricultural Perspective*, T. Kosuge, C. P. Meredith, A. Hollaender, Eds. (Plenum, New York, 1983), pp. 211–227.
53. R. Breathnach and P. Chambon, *Annu. Rev. Biochem.* **50**, 349 (1981).
54. H. De Greve *et al.*, *J. Mol. Appl. Genet.* **1**, 449 (1982); P. Dhaese, H. De Greve, J. Gielen, J. Seurinck, M. Van Montagu, J. Schell, *EMBO J.* **2**, 419 (1983).
55. L. Herrera-Estrella, A. Depicker, M. Van Montagu, J. Schell, *Nature (London)* **303**, 209 (1983).
56. L. Herrera-Estrella *et al.*, *EMBO J.* **2**, 987 (1983).
57. F. Bolivar, *Gene* **4**, 121 (1978).
58. M. W. Bevan, R. B. Flavell, M.-D. Chilton,

Nature (London) **304**, 184 (1983).
59. R. T. Fraley *et al.*, *Proc. Natl. Acad. Sci. U.S.A.* **80**, 4803 (1983).
60. S. L. Berry-Lowe, T. D. McKnight, D. M. Shah, R. B. Meagher, *J. Mol. Appl. Genet.* **1**, 483 (1982); R. Broglie, G. Coruzzi, G. Lamppa, B. Keith, N.-H. Chua, *Bio/Technology* **1**, 55 (1983); P. Dunsmuir, S. Smith, J. Bedbrook, *Nucleic Acids Res.* **11**, 4177 (1983).
61. A. Cashmore, in *Genetic Engineering of Plants, An Agricultural Perspective*, T. Kosuge, C. P. Meredith, A. Hollaender, Eds. (Plenum, New York, 1983), pp. 29–38.
62. G. Coruzzi, R. Broglie, A. Cashmore, N. H. Chua, *J. Biol. Chem.* **258**, 1399 (1983).
63. L. Herrera-Estrella *et al.*, *Nature (London)*, submitted.
64. M. De Block, L. Herrera-Estrella, M. Van Montagu, J. Schell, P. Zambryski, *EMBO J.*, submitted.
65. B. Hohn and T. Hohn, in *Molecular Biology of Plant Tumors*, G. Kahl and J. Schell, Eds. (Academic Press, New York, 1982), pp. 549–560.
66. B. Gronenborn, R. C. Gardner, S. Schaefer, R. J. Sheperd, *Nature (London)* **294**, 773 (1981).
67. D. M. Bisaro, W. D. O. Hamilton, R. H. A. Coutts, K. W. Buck, *Nucleic Acids Res.* **10**, 4913 (1982).
68. A. Spradling and G. M. Rubin, *Science* **218**, 341 (1982); G. M. Rubin and A. Spradling, *ibid.*, p. 348.
69. B. McClintock, *Dev. Biol. Suppl.* **1**, 84 (1967); N. Federoff, in *Mobile Genetic Elements*, J. A. Shapiro, Ed. (Academic Press, New York, 1983), pp. 1–63.
70. M. Geiser *et al.*, *EMBO J.* **1**, 455 (1982); N. Federoff, J. Maurais, D. Chaleff, *J. Mol. Appl. Genet.* **2**, 11 (1983); W. J. Peacock, Fifteenth Miami Winter Symposium on Advances in Gene Technology: Molecular Genetics of Plants and Animals (1983), Abstr. 28; P. Starlinger *et al.*, *J. Cell Biochem. Suppl.* **7B**, 246 (1983).
71. A. Wöstemeyer, thesis, Universität Köln (1982); G. Ooms, A. Korp, J. Roberts, *Theor. Appl. Genet.* **66**, 169 (1983).
72. M.-D. Chilton *et al.*, *Nature (London)* **295**, 432 (1982).
73. A. G. Hepburn, L. E. Clarke, K. S. Bundy, J. White, *J. Mol. Appl. Genet.* **2**, 211 (1983).
74. M. D. Sacristan, *Theor. Appl. Genet.* **61**, 193 (1982).
75. S. Gleddie, W. Keller, G. Setterfield, *Can. J. Bot.* **61**, 656 (1983).
76. We thank all the members of the Laboratory of Genetics at the State University of Gent for their helpful discussions. We also thank M. De Cock for assembling the manuscript, A. Verstraete and K. Spruyt for the art work, and M. Rykowski for critically reading the paper.

About the Authors

John N. Abelson is a member of the Agouron Institute, La Jolla, and professor of biology at the California Institute of Technology, Pasadena, California.

Philip H. Abelson is the editor of *Science*.

M. Adler is a member of the Laboratory of Biochemical Genetics, National Heart, Lung, and Blood Institute, National Institutes of Health, Bethesda, Maryland.

Richard Axel is on the staff of the Institute of Cancer Research and Center for Neurobiology and Behavior, College of Physicians and Surgeons, Columbia University, New York, New York.

Tina Barsby is a research scientist at Allelix, Inc., Mississauga, Ontario.

Kenneth A. Barton is a molecular geneticist at Cetus Madison Corporation, Middleton, Wisconsin.

Jim Battey is associated with the Department of Genetics, Harvard Medical School, Boston, Massachusetts.

Dennis Bidney is a research scientist with Advanced Genetic Sciences, Manhattan, Kansas.

Frederick R. Blattner is a professor in the Department of Genetics at the University of Wisconsin, Madison, Wisconsin.

Norman E. Borlaug is a former director of the Wheat Program, International Maize and Wheat Improvement Center (CIMMYT), Mexico City, Mexico, and now serves CIMMYT as a consultant.

Winston J. Brill is director of research at Cetus Madison Corporation, Middleton, Wisconsin.

Ralph L. Brinster is Richard King Mellon Professor of Reproductive Physiology at the School of Veterinary Medicine, University of Pennsylvania, Philadelphia, Pennsylvania.

Lee A. Bulla, Jr. is a professor in the Department of Bacteriology and Biochemistry, associate dean of the College of Agriculture, and associate director of the Agricultural Experiment Station at the University of Idaho, Moscow, Idaho.

R. M. Busche is a planning consultant in the Central Research and Development Department, E. I. du Pont de Nemours and Company, Wilmington, Delaware.

N. Busis is a member of the Laboratory of Biochemical Genetics, National Heart, Lung, and Blood Institute, National Institutes of Health, Bethesda, Maryland.

A. Caplan is a member of the Laboratorium voor Genetica, Rijksuniversiteit Gent, Gent, Belgium.

R. S. Chaleff is staff scientist at the Central Research and Development Department, E. I. Du Pont de Nemours and Company, Wilmington, Delaware.

Ana B. Chepelinsky, formerly at the Laboratory of Biochemistry, National Cancer Institute, is in the Department of Molecular and Developmental Biology, the National Eye Institute, National Institutes of Health, Bethesda, Maryland.

Charles L. Cooney is a professor in the Department of Chemical Engineering, Massachusetts Institute of Technology, Cambridge, Massachusetts.

Lawrence Corey is professor of microbiology, laboratory medicine, and immunology at the University of Washington School of Medicine, Seattle, Washington.

William Cushley is an assistant professor in the Department of Biochemistry, University of Glasgow, Glasgow, Scotland, United Kingdom.

Ronald W. Davis is on the staff of the Department of Biochemistry, Stanford University School of Medicine, Stanford, California.

Arnold L. Demain is professor of industrial microbiology in the Department of Nutrition and Food Science, Massachusetts Institute of Technology, Cambridge, Massachusetts.

Catherine Desaymard is a member of the Department of Cell Biology at Albert Einstein College of Medicine, Bronx, New York.

Richard P. Elander is vice president of Biotechnology, Fermentation Research and Development, Industrial Division, Bristol-Myers Company, Syracuse, New York.

Peter Farnum is a senior scientist at Weyerhaeuser Company, Tacoma, Washington.

K. Frederiksen is at the Cold Spring Harbor Laboratory, Cold Spring Harbor, New York.

Richard E. Gelinas is an associate member of the Fred Hutchinson Cancer Research Center, Seattle, Washington.

Angela M. Giusti is a member of the Department of Cell Biology at Albert Einstein College of Medicine, Bronx, New York.

David V. Goeddel is a staff scientist in the Department of Molecular Biology, Genentech, Inc., South San Francisco, California.

Lynn C. Goldstein is a staff member of Genetic Systems Corporation, Seattle, Washington.

Nicola Green is a member of the Department of Molecular Biology, Research Institute of Scripps Clinic, La Jolla, California.

Nigel D. F. Grindley is an associate professor in the Department of Molecular Biophysics and Biochemistry, Yale University, New Haven, Connecticut.

Peter Gruss is at the Center for Molecular Biology, University of Heidelberg, Heidelberg, West Germany.

Robert E. Hammer is a research associate at the School of Veterinary Medicine, University of Pennsylvania, Philadelphia, Pennsylvania.

H. Hunter Handsfield is director of the Sexually Transmitted Disease Control Program of Seattle-King County Department of Public Health and an associate professor of medicine in the Department of Medicine at the University of Washington, Seattle, Washington.

R. W. F. Hardy is director of life sciences in the Central Research and Development Department, E. I. du Pont de Nemours and Company, Wilmington, Delaware.

Barbara Haseltine is a member of the Department of Cell Biology at Albert Einstein College of Medicine, Bronx, New York.

L. Herrera-Estrella is a member of the Laboratorium voor Genetica, Rijksuniversiteit Gent, Gent, Belgium.

H. Higashida is a member of the Laboratory of Biochemical Genetics, National Heart, Lung, and Blood Institute, National Institutes of Health, Bethesda, Maryland.

Ronald A. Hitzeman is a senior scientist in the Department of Molecular Biology, Genentech, Inc., South San Francisco, California.

S. Hockfield is at the Cold Spring Harbor Laboratory, Cold Spring Harbor, New York.

King K. Holmes is chief of medicine at Harborview Medical Center, and professor and vice chairman of the Department of Medicine, University of Washington, Seattle, Washington.

Leroy E. Hood is Bowles Professor of Biology and chairman of the Division of Biology, California Institute of Technology, Pasadena, California.

Elizabeth E. Howell is a member of the Agouron Institute, La Jolla, California.

Michael W. Hunkapiller is a senior research fellow at the Division of Biology, California Institute of Technology, Pasadena, California.

D. Inzé is a member of the Laboratorium voor Genetica, Rijksuniversiteit Gent, Gent, Belgium.

J. Johansen is at the Cold Spring Harbor Laboratory, Cold Spring Harbor, New York.

Irving S. Johnson is vice president of research, Lilly Research Laboratories, a division of Eli Lilly and Company, Indianapolis, Indiana.

Eric R. Kandel is on the staff of the Institute of Cancer Research and Center for Neurobiology and Behavior, College of Physicians and Surgeons, Columbia University, New York, New York.

Roger Kemble is a research scientist at Allelix, Inc., Mississauga, Ontario.

J. G. Kenimer is a member of the Laboratory of Biochemical Genetics, National Heart, Lung, and Blood Institute, National Institutes of Health, Bethesda, Maryland.

George Khoury is a staff member of the Laboratory of Molecular Virology, National Cancer Institute, Bethesda, Maryland.

Alexander M. Klibanov is associate professor of applied biochemistry and Henry L. Doherty Professor in the Department of Nutrition and Food Science, Massachusetts Institute of Technology, Cambridge, Massachusetts.

Joan S. Knapp is a research assistant professor in the Department of Medicine at the University of Washington School of Medicine, Seattle, Washington.

William J. Kohr is a research associate in the Department of Protein Biochemistry, Genentech, Inc., South San Francisco, California.

Monika König is a microbiologist at the Laboratory of Molecular Virology, National Cancer Institute, National Institutes of Health, Bethesda, Maryland.

Joseph Kraut is a professor of chemistry at the University of California, San Diego, and a member of the Agouron Institute, La Jolla, California.

Michael Kress is a staff member of the Laboratory of Molecular Virology, National Cancer Institute, National Institutes of Health, Bethesda, Maryland.

Keith A. Krolick is an assistant professor in the Department of Microbiology at the University of Texas Health Science Center, San Antonio, Texas.

K. Krueger is a member of the Laboratory of Biochemical Genetics, National Heart, Lung, and Blood Institute, National Institutes of Health, Bethesda, Maryland.

J. Laurence Kulp is vice president for research and development at Weyerhaeuser Company, Tacoma, Washington.

Cho-Chou Kuo is in the Department of Pathobiology, School of Public Health at the University of Washington School of Medicine, Seattle, Washington.

Hartmut Land is a postdoctoral associate with the Whitehead Institute for Biomedical Research and the Massachusetts Institute of Technology, Cambridge, Massachusetts.

Andrew B. Lassar is at the Laboratory of Biochemistry and Molecular Biology, The Rockefeller University, New York, New York.

Philip Leder is associated with the Department of Genetics, Harvard Medical School, Boston, Massachusetts.

Gilbert Lenoir is at the International Agency for Research on Cancer, World Health Organization, Lyon, France.

Richard A. Lerner is a member of the Department of Molecular Biology, Research Institute of Scripps Clinic, La Jolla, California.

David W. Leung is a scientist in the Department of Molecular Biology, Genentech, Inc., South San Francisco, California.

Howard L. Levine is a senior scientist at Applied Molecular Genetics, Inc., Newbury Park, California.

A. J. Lingg is a professor in the Department of Bacteriology and Biochemistry, University of Idaho, Moscow, Idaho.

John H. Litchfield is a research leader at Battelle Memorial Institute, Columbus Laboratories, Columbus, Ohio.

Paul L. Martin is at the Laboratory of Biochemistry and Molecular Biology, The Rockefeller University, New York, New York.

Linda B. McAllister, formerly on the staff of the Institute of Cancer Research and Center for Neurobiology and Behavior, College of Physicians and Surgeons, Columbia University, is now at the School of Medicine, Stanford University, Stanford, California.

C. C. McDonald is a research manager in the Central Research and Development Department, E. I. du Pont de Nemours and Company, Wilmington, Delaware.

R. D. G. McKay is at the Cold Spring Harbor Laboratory, Cold Spring Harbor, New York.

Keith McKenney, formerly at the Laboratory of Biochemistry, National Cancer Institute, National Institutes of Health, is now at the Laboratory of Molecular Biology, Medical Research Council Centre, University Medical School, Cambridge, England.

Lois K. Miller is associate professor in the Department of Bacteriology and Biochemistry, University of Idaho, Moscow, Idaho.

Muneo Miyama-Inaba is a postdoctoral fellow in the Department of Microbiology, University of Texas Southwestern Medical School, Dallas, Texas.

Christopher Moulding is associated with the Department of Genetics, Harvard Medical School, Boston, Massachusetts.

William Murphy is associated with the Department of Genetics, Harvard Medical School, Boston, Massachusetts.

T. K. Ng is a research biologist in the Central Research and Development Department, E. I. du Pont de Nemours and Company, Wilmington, Delaware.

M. Nirenberg is a member of the Laboratory of Biochemical Genetics, National Heart, Lung, and Blood Institute, National Institutes of Health, Bethesda, Maryland.

Gunnar Norstedt is a visiting scientist at the Howard Hughes Medical Institute, University of Washington, Seattle, Washington, from the Karolinska Institute, Stockholm, Sweden.

Shirley Norton is a staff member in the Departments of Molecular Biology and Vaccine Development, Genentech, Inc., South San Francisco, California.

Robert C. Nowinski is a staff member of Genetic Systems Corporation and also affiliate professor in the Department of Microbiology at the University of Washington School of Medicine, Seattle, Washington.

John F. Obijeski is a staff member in the Departments of Molecular Biology and Vaccine Development, Genentech, Inc., South San Francisco, California.

Richard C. Ogden is a member of the Agouron Institute, La Jolla, California.

Richard D. Palmiter is professor of biochemistry at the Howard Hughes Medical Institute, Department of Biochemistry, University of Washington, Seattle, Washington.

Luis F. Parada is a research assistant at the Whitehead Institute for Biomedical Research and the Massachusetts Institute of Technology, Cambridge, Massachusetts.

L. Jeanne Perry is a research associate in the Department of Protein Biochemistry, Genentech, Inc., South San Francisco, California.

Roberta R. Pollock is a member of the Department of Cell Biology at Albert Einstein College of Medicine, Bronx, New York.

Huntington Potter is associated with the Department of Genetics, Harvard Medical School, Boston, Massachusetts.

R. Ray is a member of the Laboratory of Biochemical Genetics, National Heart, Lung, and Blood Institute, National Institutes of Health, Bethesda, Maryland.

Robert G. Roeder is at the Laboratory of Biochemistry and Molecular Biology, The Rockefeller University, New York, New York.

Martin Rosenberg is on the staff of the Laboratory of Biochemistry, National Cancer Institute, National Institutes of Health, Bethesda, Maryland, and is currently the director of the Department of Molecular Genetics, Smith Kline & French Laboratories, Philadelphia, Pennsylvania.

Nadia Rosenthal is a staff member of the Laboratory of Molecular Virology, National Cancer Institute, National Institutes of Health, Bethesda, Maryland.

A. Rotter is a member of the Laboratory of Biochemical Genetics, National Heart, Lung, and Blood Institute, National Institutes of Health, Bethesda, Maryland.

Matthew D. Scharff is a member of the Department of Cell Biology at Albert Einstein College of Medicine, Bronx, New York.

Nancy A. Schaus is a senior biologist in the Molecular Genetics Department, Lilly Research Laboratories, a division of Eli Lilly and Company, Indianapolis, Indiana.

J. Schell is a member of the Laboratorium voor Genetica, Rijksuniversiteit Gent, Gent, Belgium.

Richard H. Scheller, formerly on the staff of the Institute of Cancer Research and Center for Neurobiology and Behavior, College of Physicians and Surgeons, Columbia University, is now with the Department of Biological Sciences, Stanford University, Stanford, California.

James F. Shepard is director of plant biology at Allelix, Inc., Mississauga, Ontario.

Thomas M. Shinnick is a member of the Department of Molecular Biology, Research Institute of Scripps Clinic, La Jolla, California.

Walter E. Stamm is head of the Division of Infectious Diseases at Harborview Medical Center, Seattle, Washington, and associate professor of medicine in the Department of Medicine at the University of Washington School of Medicine

Michael Steinmetz is at the Basel Institute for Immunology, Basel, Switzerland.

Timothy Stewart is associated with the Department of Genetics, Harvard Medical School, Boston, Massachusetts.

Linda Stong is a staff member of Genetic Systems Corporation, Seattle, Washington.

Marjorie S. Strobel is a member of the Agouron Institute, La Jolla, California.

J. Gregor Sutcliffe is a member of the Department of Molecular Biology, Research Institute of Scripps Clinic, La Jolla, California.

Milton R. Tam is a staff member of Genetic Systems Corporation, Seattle, Washington.

Rebecca Taub is associated with the Department of Genetics, Harvard Medical School, Boston, Massachusetts.

Jean-Luc Teillaud is a member of the Department of Cell Biology at Albert Einstein College of Medicine, Bronx, New York.

I. Thompson is at the Cold Spring Harbor Laboratory, Cold Spring Harbor, New York.

Roger Timmis is a senior scientist at Weyerhaeuser Company, Tacoma, Washington.

Jonathan W. Uhr is professor and chairman of the Department of Microbiology, professor of internal medicine, and Mary Nell and Ralph B. Rogers Professor of Immunology at the University of Texas Southwestern Medical School, Dallas, Texas.

Kevin M. Ulmer is director of exploratory research at Genex Corporation, Gaithersburg, Maryland.

E. Van Haute is a member of the Laboratorium voor Genetica, Rijksuniversiteit Gent, Gent, Belgium.

M. Van Montagu is a member of the Laboratorium voor Genetica, Rijksuniversiteit Gent, Gent, Belgium.

Jesus E. Villafranca is a member of the Agouron Institute, La Jolla, and also a postgraduate research chemist at the University of California, San Diego, California.

Ellen S. Vitetta is professor of microbiology in the University of Texas Southwestern Medical School, Dallas, Texas.

Donald H. Voet is professor of chemistry at the University of Pennsylvania, Philadelphia, Pennsylvania.

John N. Vournakis is a professor in the Department of Biology at Syracuse University, Syracuse, New York.

Hans Weiher is a postdoctoral fellow at the Heinrich Pette Institute, Hamburg, West Germany.

Robert A. Weinberg is a professor in the Department of Biology, Massachusetts Institute of Technology and the Whitehead Institute for Biomedical Research, Cambridge, Massachusetts.

Ted A. Weinert is a graduate student in the Department of Molecular Biophysics and Biochemistry, Yale University, New Haven, Connecticut.

S. Wilson is a member of the Laboratory of Biochemical Genetics, National Heart, Lung, and Blood Institute, National Institutes of Health, Bethesda, Maryland.

Dale E. Yelton is a member of the Department of Cell Biology at Albert Einstein College of Medicine, Bronx, New York.

Elizabeth Yelverton is a staff member in the Departments of Molecular Biology and Vaccine Development, Genentech, Inc., South San Francisco, California.

Richard A. Young is on the staff of the Department of Biochemistry, Stanford University School of Medicine, Stanford, California.

Donald J. Zack is a member of the Department of Cell Biology at Albert Einstein College of Medicine, Bronx, New York.

P. Zambryski is a member of the Laboratorium voor Genetica, Rijksuniversiteit Gent, Gent, Belgium.

Index

Biotechnology & Biological Frontiers

Covering the most important topics at the forefront of biological research and development, this book consists of 36 outstanding papers by 136 scientists representing industrial, university, and governmental laboratories worldwide. Of interest to researchers and students in all fields of biology, agriculture, and the health sciences, this volume contains both fundamental research techniques and practical applications.

Topics covered:
Antibody diversity
Bioreactors
Biosynthesis
Cell mutations
Cellular oncogenes
Directed mutagenesis
Enzyme catalysts
Feedstock chemicals
Forest yields
Gene fusion
Gene transcription
Genetic engineering
Genetic transfer
Growth stimulation
Histocompatibility
Immunotoxins
Insecticides
In situ hybridization
Interferon
Microbial products
Modulation synapses
Monoclonal antibodies
Plant breeding
Plant genetic materials
Protein engineering
Protein sequencing
Protein sites
Recombinant DNA
RNA polymerase
Sequence duplication
Single-cell proteins
Surface molecules
Translocation
Viral enhancers
Viral mutations